2013

SHANGHAI

上海统计年鉴

STATISTICAL YEARBOOK

上 海 市 统 计 局
国家统计局上海调查总队

SHANGHAI MUNICIPAL STATISTICS BUREAU
SURVEY OFFICE OF THE NATIONAL BUREAU
OF STATISTICS IN SHANGHAI

中国统计出版社
China Statistics Press

《上海统计年鉴—2013》编辑委员会

EDITORIAL BOARD

编者说明

一、《上海统计年鉴——2013》是一本信息高度密集的资料工具书。本书收录了2012年上海的经济和社会等各方面的统计数据，以及重要年份和改革开放以来的主要统计数据。

二、全书内容分为24个篇目，即：1. 综合；2. 人口；3. 从业人员和职工工资；4. 国民经济核算；5. 财政收支；6. 能源与环境；7. 固定资产投资；8. 对外经济贸易和旅游；9. 价格水平；10. 人民生活；11. 城市建设；12. 农业；13. 工业；14. 建筑业；15. 交通运输、邮政和信息传输；16. 批发和零售；17. 金融业；18. 房地产业；19. 科学技术；20. 教育；21. 卫生、社会保障和社会福利业；22. 文化和体育；23. 法律、公证和其他；24. 企业景气指数与消费者信心指数。为便于读者正确地使用资料，各篇目还附有简要说明和主要统计指标解释。

三、本年鉴数据不作特别说明以外，是由上海市统计局和国家统计局上海调查总队通过年报调查收集。

四、资料中所使用的度量衡单位均采用国际统一标准计量单位。

五、本年鉴总量指标计算所采用的价格均为现行价格。

六、本年鉴部分数据合计数或相对数由于单位取舍不同产生的计算误差均未作机械调整。

七、本年鉴表中的符号使用说明：

“…”表示数据不足本表最小计量单位数；

“空格”表示该项统计数据不详或无该项数据；

“#”表示其中的主要项。

八、《上海统计年鉴》公开出版以来，受到了国内外广大读者的关心和支持，对本年鉴的内容和编辑工作提出了许多宝贵的意见，对此我们深表谢意。限于我们的水平，欢迎读者继续对年鉴的不足之处给予批评和指正，帮助我们进一步改进年鉴的编辑工作，以期更好地为广大读者服务。

EDITOR'S NOTE

Ⅰ. Shanghai Statistical Yearbook 2013 contains comprehensive statistics of Shanghai's social and economic development in 2012 and selected data of some important years and of the period since China adopted the policy of reform and opening to the outside world.

Ⅱ. The book is composed of 24 parts viz. 1. General Survey; 2. Population; 3. Employment and Wages; 4. National Economic Accounting; 5. Fiscal Revenue and Expenditure; 6. Energy and Environment Protection; 7. Investment in Fixed Assets; 8. Foreign Economic Relations, Trade and Tourism; 9. Prices; 10. Living Standards; 11. Urban Construction; 12. Agriculture; 13. Industry; 14. Construction; 15. Transportation, Posts and Information Transmission; 16. Wholesale and Retail; 17. Finance; 18. Real Estate; 19. Science and Technology; 20. Education; 21. Health, Social Security and Social Welfare; 22. Culture and Sports; 23. Laws, Notary and others; 24. Prosperity Index on Enterprises and Consumer Confidence Index. In order to make readers using materials correctly, brief introduction and explanations of major statistical indicators are attached before and after every chapter.

Ⅲ. Main part of the data in this yearbook are investigated and collected by Shanghai Municipal Statistical Bureau and Survey Office of the National Bureau of Statistics in Shanghai, we haven't mentioned especially.

Ⅳ. The international standard unit of measurement is applied in this book.

Ⅴ. The prices used for gross indicators' calculating in this yearbook are current prices.

Ⅵ. Statistical discrepancies in this book due to rounding are not adjusted.

Ⅶ. Marks in this book: … means not large enough to be rounded into the least unit of measurement; Blank space means data are not available; # indicates major item in a category.

Ⅸ. Previous editions of Shanghai Statistical Yearbook have won wide acclaim among the readers. In order to excel, we welcome all candid comments and criticism from our readers.

目录 CONTENTS

第一篇 CHAPTER 1 综 合 GENERAL SURVEY

简要说明 …… 2
BRIEF INTRODUCTION

表 1.1 行政区划（2012） …… 3
ADMINISTRATIVE DIVISION

表 1.2 主要气象指标（2012） …… 4
MAIN CLIMATE INDICATORS

表 1.3 各月主要气象指标(2012) …… 4
MAIN CLIMATE INDICATORS OF EVERY MONTH

表 1.4 主要年份社会经济主要指标 …… 5
MAJOR SOCIAL AND ECONOMIC INDICATORS IN MAIN YEARS

表 1.5 主要年份社会经济主要指标发展速度 …… 10
GROWTH RATE OF MAJOR SOCIAL AND ECONOMIC INDICATORS IN MAIN YEARS

表 1.6 主要年份社会经济发展结构指标 …… 12
STRUCTURAL INDICATORS OF SOCIAL AND ECONOMIC DEVELOPMENT IN MAIN YEARS

表 1.7 各时期社会经济主要指标 …… 14
MAJOR SOCIAL AND ECONOMIC INDICATORS OF EACH PERIOD

表 1.8 各时期社会经济主要指标平均增长率 …… 15
GROWTH RATE OF MAJOR SOCIAL AND ECONOMIC INDICATORS OF EACH PERIOD

表 1.9 国民经济主要指标比上年增长(1978~2012) …… 16
GROWTH RATE OF MAJOR NATIONAL ECONOMIC INDICATORS OVER PRECEDING YEAR

表 1.10 上海社会经济主要指标占全国比重(2012) …… 18
PERCENTAGE OF THE NATIONAL TOTAL OF SHANGHAI'S MAJOR SOCIAL AND ECONOMIC INDICATORS

表 1.11 主要年份人大情况 …… 19
BASIC STATISTICS OF SHANGHAI MUNICIPAL PEOPLE'S CONGRESS IN MAIN YEAES

表 1.12 主要年份政协情况 …… 19
BASIC STATISTICS ON SHANGHAI MUNICIPAL PEOPLE'S POLITICAL CONSULTATIVE CONFERENCE IN MAIN YEARS

主要统计指标解释 …… 20
EXPLANATORY NOTES TO MAJOR STATISTICAL INDICATORS

第二篇 CHAPTER 2 人 口 POPULATION

简要说明 …… 26
BRIEF INTRODUCTION

目录
CONTENTS

表 2.1 户数、人口、人口密度和户籍人口期望寿命(1978 ~ 2012) …… 28
TOTAL HOUSEHOLDS,POPULATION,DENSITY OF REGISTERED POPULATION AND LIFE EXPECTANCY

表 2.2 各区、县土地面积、常住人口及人口密度(2012) …… 30
LAND AREA, POPULATION AND DENSITY OF POPULATION IN DISTRICTS AND COUNTIES

表 2.3 主要年份户籍人口出生率、死亡率、自然增长率 …… 31
BIRTH RATE,DEATH RATE AND NATURAL GROWTH RATE OF POPULATION IN MAIN YEARS

表 2.4 主要年份户籍人口迁移 …… 31
MIGRATION IN MAIN YEARS

表 2.5 各区、县户籍人口迁移(2012) …… 32
MIGRATION IN DISTRICTS AND COUNTIES

表 2.6 各区、县户籍人口年龄构成(2012) …… 33
AGE STRUCTURE OF REGISTERED POPULATION IN DISTRICTS AND COUNTIES

表 2.7 各区、县户籍老年人口年龄构成(2012) …… 34
AGE STRUCTURE OF REGISTERED AGING POPULATION IN DISTRICTS AND COUNTIES

表 2.8 各区、县计划生育基本情况(2012) …… 35
FAMILY PLANNING IN DISTRICTS AND COUNTIES

表 2.9 主要年份婚姻情况 …… 36
MARRIAGE STATISTICS IN MAIN YEARS

表 2.10 主要年份涉外婚姻情况 …… 36
CHINESE-FOREIGN MARRIAGE IN MAIN YEARS

表 2.11 主要年份在沪外国常住人口 …… 37
RESIDENT FOREIGNERS IN SHANGHAI IN MAIN YEARS

主要统计指标解释 …… 38
EXPLANATORY NOTES TO MAJOR STATISTICAL INDICATORS

第三篇 CHAPTER 3 从业人员和职工工资 EMPLOYMENT AND WAGES

简要说明 …… 42
BRIEF INTRODUCTION

表 3.1 全社会各行业从业人员(2010~2012) …… 44
QUANTITY OF WHOLE SOCIAL EMPLOYEES IN DIFFERENT SECTORS

表 3.2 各行业职工人数(2012) …… 45
QUANTITY OF STAFF AND WORKERS IN DIFFERENT SECTORS

表 3.3 主要年份城镇登记失业人数和城镇登记失业率 …… 46
QUANTITY OF URBAN REGISTERED UNEMPLOYED AND URBAN REGISTERED UNEMPLOYMENT RATE IN MAIN YEARS

表 3.4 主要年份新增就业岗位 …… 46
NEWLY ADDED WORKING POST IN MAIN YEARS

表 3.5　主要年份离休、退休及退职职工人数 …… 46
QUANTITY OF RETIRED AND RESIGNED PERSONS IN MAIN YEARS

表 3.6　从业人员工资总额(1978~2012) …… 47
TOTAL WAGES OF EMPLOYEES

表 3.7　从业人员平均工资(2012) …… 48
AVERAGE WAGES OF EMPLOYEES

表 3.8　职工工资总额和平均工资(1978~2012) …… 49
TOTAL WAGES AND AVERAGE ANNUAL WAGES OF STAFF AND WORKERS

表 3.9　职工工资总额(2012) …… 50
TOTAL WAGES OF STAFF AND WORKERS

表 3.10　职工平均工资(2012) …… 51
AVERAGE ANNUAL WAGES OF STAFF AND WORKERS

表 3.11　主要年份离退休、退职人员养老金 …… 52
PENSION FOR STAFF IN MAIN YEARS

表 3.12　离退休、退职人员养老金(2012) …… 52
PENSION FOR NONWORKING STAFF AND WORKERS

主要统计指标解释 …… 53
EXPLANATORY NOTES TO MAJOR STATISTICAL INDICATORS

第四篇 CHAPTER 4　国民经济核算　NATIONAL ECONOMIC ACCOUNTING

简要说明 …… 58
BRIEF INTRODUCTION

表 4.1　上海市生产总值(1978~2012) …… 60
GROSS DOMESTIC PRODUCT

表 4.2　上海市生产总值比上年增长(1978~2012) …… 61
GROWTH RATE OF GROSS DOMESTIC PRODUCT RAISED PRECEDING YEAR

表 4.3　上海市生产总值指数(以 1978 年为 100,1978~2012) …… 62
INDEX OF GROSS DOMESTIC PRODUCT (1978=100)

表 4.4　上海市生产总值构成(1978~2012) …… 63
STRUCTURE OF GROSS DOMESTIC PRODUCT

表 4.5　上海市人均生产总值(1978~2012) …… 64
PER CAPITA GROSS DOMESTIC PRODUCT

表 4.6　主要年份上海市生产总值(按三次产业分) …… 65
GROSS DOMESTIC PRODUCT (CLASSIFIED BY THREE INDUSTRIES) IN MAIN YEARS

表 4.7　主要年份上海市生产总值比上年增长(按三次产业分) …… 66
GROWTH RATE OF GROSS DOMESTIC PRODUCT IN MAIN YEARS (CLASSIFIED BY THREE INDUSTRIES)

目录
CONTENTS

表 4.8　上海市生产总值收入法项目(1978~2012) …… 67
GROSS DOMESTIC PRODUCT(BY INCOME ITEM)
表 4.9　上海市生产总值收入法项目构成(1978~2012) …… 68
STRUCTURE OF GROSS DOMESTIC PRODUCT(BY INCOME ITEM)
表 4.10　主要年份上海市生产总值(按所有制分) …… 69
GROSS DOMESTIC PRODUCT (BY OWNERSHIP) IN MAIN YEARS
表 4.11　主要年份非公有制经济增加值(按产业分) …… 70
ADDED VALUE OF NON-PUBLIC-OWNED (GROUPED BY INDUSTRY) IN MAIN YEARS
表 4.12　上海市生产总值(支出法)(1978~2012) …… 71
GROSS DOMESTIC PRODUCT (BY EXPENDITURE APPROACH)
表 4.13　最终消费支出及构成(1978~2012) …… 72
FINAL CONSUMPTION AND COMPOSITION
表 4.14　居民消费水平及指数(1978~2012) …… 73
HOUSEHOLD CONSUMPTION LEVEL AND INDEX
表 4.15　资本形成总额和指数(1978~2012) …… 74
GROSS CAPITAL FORMATION AND INDEX
表 4.16　主要年份旅游产业增加值 …… 75
VALUE ADDED OF TOURISM INDUSTRY IN MAIN YEARS
表 4.17　主要年份信息产业增加值 …… 75
VALUE ADDED OF INFORMATION INDUSTRY IN MAIN YEARS
表 4.18　全员劳动生产率(1978~2012) …… 76
OVERALL LABOUR PRODUCTIVITY
主要统计指标解释 …… 77
EXPLANATORY NOTES TO MAJOR STATISTICAL INDICATORS

第五篇 CHAPTER 5 财政收支 FISCAL REVENUE AND EXPENDITURE

简要说明 …… 84
BRIEF INTRODUCTION
表 5.1　地方财政收支(1978~2012) …… 85
LOCAL FISCAL REVENUES AND EXPENDITURES
表 5.2　主要年份地方财政收入 …… 86
LOCAL FISCAL REVENUE IN MAIN YEARS
表 5.3　主要年份区县级财政收支 …… 87
FISICAL REVENUE AND EXPENDITURES OF DISTRICTS AND COUNTIES IN MAIN YEARS
表 5.4　地方财政支出(2010~2012) …… 88
LOCAL FISCAL EXPENDITURES

表 5.5 主要年份全市税收总收入 …… 88
TAXATION(TAX SCOPE)IN MAIN YEARS
主要统计指标解释 …… 89
EXPLANATORY NOTES TO MAJOR STATISTICAL INDICATORS

第六篇 CHAPTER 6 能源与环境 ENERGY AND ENVIRONMENT PROTECTION

简要说明 …… 92
BRIEF INTRODUCTION
表 6.1 主要年份能源消耗基本情况 …… 94
ENERGY CONSUMPTION IN MAIN YEARS
表 6.2 能源消费弹性系数 (1978~2012) …… 95
ELASTICITY OF ENERGY CONSUMPTION
表 6.3 主要年份能源消费总量 …… 96
FINAL CONSUMPTION OF ENERGY IN MAIN YEARS
表 6.4 主要年份平均每人生活用能源 …… 96
ANNUAL RESIDENT ENERGY CONSUMPTION PER CAPITA IN MAIN YEARS
表 6.5 平均每天各种能源消费量(2009~2012) …… 96
AVERAGE DAILY ENERGY CONSUMPTION BY VARIETY
表 6.6 主要年份能源终端消费量 …… 97
FINAL CONSUMPTION OF ENERGY IN MAIN YEARS
表 6.7 主要年份工业能源终端消费量 …… 97
FINAL CONSUMPTION OF ENERGY INDUSTRY IN MAIN YEARS
表 6.8 主要年份能源平衡表(标准量) …… 98
BALANCE SHEET OF ENERGY IN MAIN YEARS (STANDARD EQUIVALENT)
表 6.9 能源终端消费量(2012) …… 99
FINAL CONSUMPTION OF ENERGY (QUANTITY IN KIND)
表 6.10 煤炭、石油、电力平衡表 (2012) …… 100
COAL,PETROLEUM,ELECTRICITY BALANCE SHEEET
表 6.11 电力建设情况(2009~2012) …… 101
STATISTICS OF ELECTRIC POWER COUSTRUCTION
表 6.12 主要年份环保投入 …… 102
INVESTMENT ON ENVIRONMENT PROTECTION IN MAIN YEARS
表 6.13 主要年份工业固体废弃物防治 …… 102
PREVENTION AND CURE OF INDUSTRIAL SOLID WASTES IN MAIN YEARS
表 6.14 水环境保护(1995~2012) …… 103
WATER ENVIRONMENT PROTECTION

目录
CONTENTS

表 6.15 大气环境保护（1995~2012）…… 103
ATMOSPHERE ENVIRONMENT PROTECTION

表 6.16 主要年份环境空气状况 …… 104
AMBIENT AIR CONDITION IN MAIN YEARS

表 6.17 主要年份声环境及治理 …… 104
NOISE ENVIRONMENT AND TREATMENT IN MAIN YEARS

表 6.18 城市环境卫生情况 (1978~2012) …… 105
URBAN ENVIRONMENTAL SITUATION

表 6.19 环境卫生设施 (1978~2012) …… 106
URBAN ENVIRONMENTAL SANITATION

主要统计指标解释 …… 107
EXPLANATORY NOTES TO MAJOR STATISTICAL INDICATORS

第七篇 CHAPTER 7 固定资产投资 INVESTMENT IN FIXED ASSETS

简要说明 …… 114
BRIEF INTRODUCTION

表 7.1 全社会固定资产投资总额(按投资类别分)(1978~2012) …… 116
TOTAL INVESTMENT IN FIXED ASSETS(GROUPED BY TYPE OF INVESTMENT)

表 7.2 全社会固定资产投资总额(按经济类型分)(1978~2012) …… 117
TOTAL INVESTMENT IN FIXED ASSETS (GROUPED BY ECONOMIC TYPES)

表 7.3 主要年份全社会固定资产投资主要指标 …… 118
MAJOR INDICATORS OF TOTAL INVESTMENT IN FIXED ASSETS IN MAIN YEARS

表 7.4 地方固定资产投资主要指标（2011~2012） …… 119
MAJOR INDICATORS OF LOCAL INVESTMENT IN FIXED ASSETS

表 7.5 建设项目固定资产投资主要指标(2012) …… 120
MAJOR INDICATORS OF INVESTMENT IN FIXED ASSETS OF THE CONSTRUCTION PROJECT

表 7.6 工业各行业固定资产投资主要指标（2012） …… 121
MAIN INDICATORS OF INVESTMENT IN FIXED ASSETS OF VARIOUS INDUSTRIES

表 7.7 六大重点发展工业行业固定资产投资额(2011~2012) …… 122
FIXED ASSETS INVESTMENT IN SIX KEY INDUSTRIES

表 7.8 主要年份新增固定资产 …… 122
NEWLY INCREASED FIXED ASSETS IN MAIN YEARS

表 7.9 主要年份固定资产投资资金来源 …… 122
CAPITAL SOURCES OF FIXED ASSETS INVESTMENT IN MAIN YEARS

表 7.10 全社会房屋施工面积、竣工面积(1985~2012) …… 123
TOTAL FLOOR SPACE OF CONSTRUCTION AND COMPLETED BUILDINGS

表 7.11 住宅投资和竣工建筑面积(1978 ~ 2012) …… 124

INVESTMENT IN RESIDENTIAL HOUSING AND FLOOR SPACE OF BUILDINGS COMPLETED
主要统计指标解释 …… 125
EXPLANATORY NOTES TO MAJOR STATISTICAL INDICATORS

第八篇 CHAPTER 8 对外经济贸易和旅游 FOREIGN ECONOMIC RELATIONS, TRADE AND TOURISM

简要说明 …… 134
BRIEF INTRODUCTION
表 8.1 主要年份上海关区出口总额 …… 138
TOTAL EXPORT TRADE VOLUME THROUGH CUSTOMES IN MAIN YEARS
表 8.2 主要年份上海关区进口总额 …… 138
TOTAL IMPORT TRADE VOLUME THROUGH CUSTOMES IN MAIN YEARS
表 8.3 主要年份按国别(地区)分的上海关区出口总额 …… 139
TOTAL EXPORT TRADE VOLUME THROUGH CUSTOMES BY COUNTRIES AND REGIONS IN MAIN YEARS
表 8.4 主要年份按国别(地区)分的上海关区进口总额 …… 140
TOTAL IMPORT TRADE VOLUME THROUGH CUSTOMES BY COUNTRIES AND REGIONS IN MAIN YEARS
表 8.5 主要年份上海市进出口总额 …… 141
TOTAL VALUE OF FOREIGN TRADE IMPORTS AND EXPORTS IN MAIN YEARS
表 8.6 主要年份上海市出口总额 …… 141
TOTAL VALUE OF FOREIGN TRADE EXPORTS IN MAIN YEARS
表 8.7 主要年份按国别(地区)分的上海市出口总额 …… 142
TOTAL VALUE OF FOREIGN TRADE EXPORTS BY COUNTRIES AND REGIONS IN MAIN YEARS
表 8.8 主要年份按国别(地区)分的上海市进口总额 …… 143
TOTAL VALUE OF FOREIGN TRADE IMPORTS BY COUNTRIES AND REGIONS IN MAIN YEARS
表 8.9 主要年份进出口商品检验情况 …… 144
IMPORTS AND EXPORTS INSPECTION IN MAIN YEARS
表 8.10 主要年份直接吸收外资情况 …… 144
FOREIGN DIRECT INVESTMENT IN MAIN YEARS
表 8.11 外商直接投资合同项目和金额（2012） …… 145
NUMBER OF CONTRACTS SINGNED AND VALUES OF FOREIGN DIRECT INVESTMENT PROJECTS
表 8.12 主要年份引进技术设备实际到货金额 …… 146
ARRIVED CAPITAL THROUGH IMPORTED TECHNOLOGY AND EQUIPMENT IN MAIN YEARS
表 8.13 对外承包工程和劳务合作(2011~2012) …… 146
OVERSEAS CONTRACTED PROJECTS AND LABOR SERVICES COOPERATION
表 8.14 海外企业情况（2011 ~ 2012） …… 147
ENTERPRISES ABROAD
表 8.15 国际会展(2010~2012) …… 147
INTERNATIONAL CONFERENCE AND EXHIBITION

目录
CONTENTS

表 8.16 主要年份旅行社接待经营情况 …… 147
TOURISTS RECEIVED BY TOUR AGENCIES IN MAIN YEARS
表 8.17 主要年份旅游景点基本情况 …… 148
BASIC STATISTICS OF SCENIC SPOTS IN MAIN YEARS
表 8.18 主要年份国内旅游者来沪人数和人均消费支出 …… 148
NUMBER OF DOMESTIC TOURISTS VISITING SHANGHAI AND PER CAPITA CONSUMPTION EXPENDITURES IN MAIN YEARS
表 8.19 旅游星级饭店基本情况（2012）…… 149
BASIC STATISTICS OF STAR-RATED TOURISM HOTELS
表 8.20 主要年份国际旅游入境人数 …… 149
NUMBER OF OVERSEAS TOURISTS THROUGH SHANGHAI CUSTOM IN MAIN YEARS
主要统计指标解释 …… 150
EXPLANATORY NOTES TO MAJOR STATISTICAL INDICATORS

第九篇 CHAPTER 9 价格水平 PRICES

简要说明 …… 154
BRIEF INTRODUCTION
表 9.1 居民消费价格和商品零售价格指数(1978~2012）…… 160
OVERALL RESIDENTS CONSUMER PRICE INDEX AND RETAIL PRICE INDEX
表 9.2 居民消费价格指数(1991~2012,以 1990 年价格为 100）…… 161
OVERALL RESIDENTS CONSUMER PRICE INDEX (1990=100)
表 9.3 居民消费价格指数(1991~2012,以上年价格为 100）…… 162
OVERALL RESIDENTS CONSUMER PRICE INDEX (PRECEDING YEAR=100)
表 9.4 主要年份居民消费价格指数（以上年价格为 100）…… 163
CLASSIFIED RESIDENTS CONSUMER PRICE INDEX IN MAIN YEARS(PRECEDING YEAR=100)
表 9.5 主要年份商品零售价格指数（以上年价格为 100）…… 165
CLASSIFIED RETAIL PRICE INDEX IN MAIN YEARS (PRECEDING YEAR =100)
表 9.6 工业生产者出厂价格指数（2005~2012,以 2000 年价格为 100）…… 166
PRODUCER PRICE INDEX FOR INDUSTRIAL PRODUCTS (2000=100)
表 9.7 工业生产者出厂价格指数（2005~2012,以 2000 年价格为 100)(按国民经济行业分）…… 167
PRODUCER PRICE INDEX FOR INDUSTRIAL PRODUCTS(GROUPED BY NATIONAL INDUSTRIES,2000=100)
表 9.8 工业生产者出厂价格指数（2005~2012,以上年价格为 100）…… 169
PRODUCER PRICE INDEX FOR INDUSTRIAL PRODUCTS(PRECEDING YEAR =100)
表 9.9 工业生产者出厂价格指数（2005~2012,以上年价格为 100)(按国民经济行业分）…… 170
PRODUCER PRICE INDEX FOR INDUSTRIAL PRODUCTS(GROUPED BY NATIONAL INDUSTRIES,PRECEDING YEAR=100)

表 9.10 工业生产者购进价格指数（2005~2012,以 2000 年价格为 100）…… 172
PRODUCER PURCHASING PRCIE INDEX (2000=100)
表 9.11 工业生产者购进价格指数（2005~2012,以上年价格为 100）…… 173
PRODUCER PURCHASING PRICE INDEX(PRECEDING YEAR =100)
表 9.12 固定资产投资价格指数（2001~2012，以 2000 年价格为 100）…… 174
PRICE INDEX OF INVESTMENT IN FIXED ASSETS (2000= 100)
表 9.13 固定资产投资价格指数（1995~2012，以上年价格为 100）…… 174
PRICE INDEX OF INVESTMENT IN FIXED ASSETS (PRECEDING YEAR =100)
表 9.14 房屋租赁和土地交易价格指数（2005~2012，以 2000 年价格为 100）…… 175
PRICE INDEX OF HOUSE AND RESIDENCE(2000=100)
表 9.15 房屋租赁和土地交易价格指数（2005~2012，以上年价格为 100）…… 175
PRICE INDEX OF HOUSE AND RESIDENCE(PRECEDING YEAR=100
主要统计指标解释 …… 176
EXPLANATORY NOTES TO MAJOR STATISTICAL INDICATORS

第十篇 CHAPTER 10 人民生活 LIVING STANDARDS

简要说明 …… 180
BRIEF INTRODUCTION
表 10.1 主要年份城乡居民家庭人均收入及恩格尔系数 …… 184
PER CAPITA ANNUAL INCOME AND ENGEL'S COEFFICIENT OF URBAN AND RURAL HOUSEHOLDS
表 10.2 储蓄存款年末余额（1997~2012）…… 184
SAVINGS DEPOSITS AT YEAR-END
表 10.3 城市居民家庭生活基本情况（1980~2012）…… 185
BASIC STATISTICS OF URBAN HOUSEHOLDS
表 10.4 城市居民家庭生活基本情况（2012，按收入水平分组）…… 187
BASIC STATISTICS OF URBAN HOUSEHOLD INCOME AND EXPENDITURES (2012, GROUPED BY INCOME LEVEL)
表 10.5 主要年份城市居民家庭人均可支配收入 …… 189
PER CAPITA DISPOSABLE INCOME OF URBAN HOUSEHOLDS IN MAIN YEARS
表 10.6 主要年份城市居民家庭人均可支配收入与消费支出 …… 189
PER CAPITA ANNUAL DISPOSABLE INCOME AND CONSUMPTION EXPENDITURES OF URBAN HOUSEHOLDS IN MAIN YEARS
表 10.7 主要年份城市居民家庭人均消费支出 …… 190
PER CAPITA CONSUMPTION EXPENDITURES OF URBAN HOUSEHOLDS IN MAIN YEARS
表 10.8 主要年份城市居民家庭人均消费支出构成 …… 190
COMPOSITION OF PER CAPITA CONSUMTION EXPENDITURES OF URBAN HOUSEHOLDS IN MAIN YEARS

目录
CONTENTS

表 10.9 主要年份城市居民家庭人均消费支出 …… 191
PER CAPITA CONSUMPTION EXPENDITURES OF URBAN HOUSEHOLD IN MAIN YEARS

表 10.10 城市居民家庭人均消费支出（2012,按收入水平分组）…… 192
PER CAPITA CONSUMPTION EXPENDITURES OF URBAN HOUSEHOLD (2012,GROUPED BY INCOME LEVEL)

表 10.11 城市居民家庭平均每人主要消费品消费量(2009~2012）…… 194
PER CAPITA CONSUMPTION OF MAJOR CONSUMER GOODS OF URBAN HOUSEHOLDS

表 10.12 主要年份平均每百户城市居民家庭年末耐用消费品拥有量 …… 194
PER 100 URBAN HOUSEHOLDS YEAR-END POSSESSION OF DURABLE CONSUMER GOODS IN MAIN YEARS

表 10.13 农村居民家庭生活基本情况（1990 ~ 2012）…… 195
BASIC STATISTICS OF RURAL HOUSEHOLDS

表 10.14 主要年份农村居民家庭人均可支配收入 …… 197
PER CAPITA DISPOSABLE INCOME OF RURAL HOUSEHOLDS IN MAIN YEARS

表 10.15 农村居民家庭人均可支配收入和人均生活消费支出(2000~2012）…… 197
PER CAPITA DISPOSABLE INCOME AND LIVING EXPENDITURES FOR CONSUMPTION OF RURAL HOUSEHOLDS

表 10.16 主要年份农村居民家庭人均生活消费支出 …… 198
PER CAPITA CONSUMPTION EXPENDITURES OF RURAL HOUSEHOLDS IN MAIN YEARS

表 10.17 主要年份农村居民家庭人均生活消费支出构成 …… 198
COMPOSITION OF PER CAPITA CONSUMER EXPENDITURES OF RURAL HOUSEHOLDS IN MAIN YEARS

表 10.18 农村居民家庭人均可支配收入(2012,按收入水平分组）…… 199
AVERAGE PER CAPITA DISPOSABLE INCOME OF RURAL HOUSEHOLDS(GROUPED BY INCOME LEVEL)

表 10.19 农村居民家庭人均生活消费支出（2012,按收入水平分组）…… 200
PER CAPITA EXPENDITURES OF RURAL HOUSEHOLDS (2012,GROUPED BY INCOME LEVEL)

表 10.20 主要年份农村居民家庭平均每人主要消费品消费量 …… 201
PER CAPITA CONSUMPTION OF MAJOR CONSUMER GOODS OF RURAL HOUSEHOLDS IN MAIN YEARS

表 10.21 主要年份平均每百户农村居民家庭年末耐用消费品拥有量 …… 201
PER 100 RURAL HOUSEHOLD YEAR-END POSSESSION OF DURABLE CONSUMER GOODS IN MAIN YEARS

主要统计指标解释 …… 202
EXPLANATORY NOTES TO MAJOR STATISTICAL INDICATORS

第十一篇 CHAPTER 18 城市建设 URBAN CONSTRUCTION

简要说明 …… 206
BRIEF INTRODUCTION

表 11.1 主要年份城市基础设施投资额 …… 208
URBAN INFRASTRUCTURE INVESTMENT IN MAIN YEARS

表 11.2 用于公用事业和市政建设的投资额（1985~2012）…… 209
INVESTMENT IN PUBLIC UTILITIES AND CIVIL CONSTRUCTION

表 11.3　主要年份各类房屋构成情况 …… 210
COMPOSITION OF BUILDING IN MAIN YEARS
表 11.4　主要年份八层以上房屋情况 …… 210
BUILDINGS OVER EIGHT STOREYS IN MAIN YEARS
表 11.5　各区、县房屋建筑分布情况（2012） …… 211
DISTRIBUTION OF BUILDINGS IN DIFFERENT DISTRICTS AND COUNTIES
表 11.6　各区、县各类房屋分布情况（2012） …… 212
DISTRIBUTION OF VARIOUS BUILDINGS IN DIFFERENT DISTRICTS AND COUNTIES
表 11.7　各区、县八层以上房屋分布（2012） …… 216
DISTRIBUTION OF BUILDINGS OVER EIGHT STOREYS BY DISTRICTS AND COUNTIES
表 11.8　主要年份市政工程设施情况 …… 218
CIVIL FACILITIES IN MAIN YEARS
表 11.9　主要年份自来水情况 …… 218
TAP WATER SUPPLY IN MAIN YEARS
表 11.10　主要年份用电量 …… 219
ELECTRICITY POWER CONSUMPTION IN MAIN YEARS
表 11.11　主要年份电力建设情况 …… 219
ELECTRICITY POWER CONSTRUCTION IN MAIN YEARS
表 11.12　主要年份煤气、液化石油气、天然气情况 …… 220
GAS,LIQUEFIED PETROLEUM GAS AND NATURAL GAS
表 11.13　主要年份公共交通和轮渡情况 …… 220
PUBLIC TRANSPORTATION AND FERRY IN MAIN YEARS
表 11.14　轨道交通、城市快速路、黄浦江大桥和隧道基本情况（2009～2012） …… 221
BASIC FACTS OF RAILWAY COMMUNICATION, URBAN EXPRESSWAYS, BRIDGES ACROSS HUANGPU RIVER AND TUNNELS
表 11.15　主要年份城市设施水平 …… 221
LEVEL OF URBAN FACILITIES IN MAIN YEARS
表 11.16　主要年份城市绿地情况 …… 222
URBAN GREEN SPACE IN MAIN YEARS
表 11.17　各区、县绿化面积（2012） …… 223
URBAN GREEN AREA IN DIFFERENT DISTRICTS AND COUNTIES
主要统计指标解释 …… 224
EXPLANATORY NOTES TO MAJOR STATISTICAL INDICATORS

第十二篇 CHAPTER 12 农　业 AGRICULTURE

简要说明 …… 228
BRIEF INTRODUCTION

目录
CONTENTS

表 12.1　农业总产值 (1978~2012) ………… 232
GROSS OUTPUT VALUE OF AGRICULTURE
表 12.2　农业总产值指数 (以 1978 年为 100,1978~2012) ………… 233
GROSS OUTPUT VALUE INDEX OF AGRICULTURE (1978 =100)
表 12.3　耕地面积(1978~2012) ………… 234
AREAS UNDER CULTIVATION
表 12.4　主要年份农村户数、人口和从业人员 ………… 235
RURAL HOUSEHOLDS,POPULATION AND EMPLOYEES IN MAIN YEARS
表 12.5　主要年份农作物总播种面积 ………… 235
TOTAL SOWN AREA OF PLANTING IN MAIN YEARS
表 12.6　主要年份农副产品产量 ………… 236
OUTPUT OF MAJOR FARM AND SIDELINE PRODUCTS IN MAIN YEARS
表 12.7　农牧业特色种养产品产量 (2011~2012) ………… 236
OUTPUT OF SPECIAL PRODUCTS IN FARMING AND ANIMAL HUSBANDRY
表 12.8　主要农副产品产量与建国以来最高年产量的比较 (2012) ………… 237
OUTPUT OF MAJOR FARM AND SIDELINE PRODUCTS IN COMPARISON WITH THE PEAK YEAR SINCE 1949
表 12.9　主要年份农业商品产值和商品率 ………… 238
OUTPUT VALUE OF AGRICULTURAL COMMODITY AND COMMODITY RATE IN MAIN YEARS
表 12.10　主要年份农产品出口情况 ………… 238
EXPORTS OF AGRICULTURAL PRODUCTS IN MAIN YEARS
表 12.11　主要年份农田水利投资 ………… 239
INVESTMENT IN FARM WATER CONSERVANCY IN MAIN YEARS
表 12.12　主要年份农村用电量 ………… 240
RURAL ELECTRICITY POWER CONSUMPTION IN MAIN YEARS
表 12.13　主要年份农业机械拥有量 ………… 241
POSSESSION OF AGRICULTURAL MACHINERY IN MAIN YEARS
表 12.14　主要年份农业技术应用和综合开发情况 ………… 242
TECHNOLOGY APPLICATIONS AND INTEGRATIVE EXPLOITATION IN AGRICULTURE IN MAIN YEARS
表 12.15　市级农业园区基本情况(2012) ………… 243
MAJOR INDICATORS OF MUNICIPAL AGRICULTURAL ZONE
表 12.16　域外市属农场农业生产情况(2011~2012) ………… 244
AGRICULTURAL PRODUCTION OF EXTERNAL MUNICIPAL FARM
主要统计指标解释 ………… 245
EXPLANATORY NOTES TO MAJOR STATISTICAL INDICATORS

第十三篇 CHAPTER 13 工业 INDUSTRY

简要说明 ………… 250
BRIEF INTRODUCTION

表 13.1 工业总产值及指数（1978~2012） …… 252
GROSS OUTPUT VALUE OF INDUSTRY AND INDEX
表 13.2 各区、县工业企业主要指标（2012） …… 253
MAJOR INDICATIORS OF INDUSTRIAL ENTERPRISES IN DISTRICTS AND COUNTIES
表 13.3 规模以上工业企业主要指标（2012） …… 254
MAJOR INDICATORS OF THE CITY'S INDUSTRIAL ENTERPRISES ABOVE THE SET SCALE
表 13.4 工业企业销售产值(2012） …… 262
SALES VALUE OF INDUSTRIAL ENTERPRISES
表 13.5 工业企业经济效益指标（2012） …… 264
ECONOMIC EFFICIENCY INDICATORS OF INDUSTRIAL ENTERPRISES
表 13.6 国有控股企业主要指标占全市比重（2012） …… 265
PROPORTION OF THE MAJOR INDICATORS OF ENTERPRISES WITH THE STATE HOLDING MAJOR SHARES
表 13.7 六个重点发展工业行业主要指标（2012） …… 266
MAJOR INDICATORS OF SIX KEY INDUSTRIES ABOVE THE SET SCALE
表 13.8 信息产品制造业主要指标（2012） …… 267
MAJOR INDICATORS OF INFORMATION PRODUCTS MANUFACTURERING INDUSTRY
表 13.9 高技术产业主要指标（2011~2012） …… 268
MAIN FACT ABOUT HIGH TECHNOLOGY INDUSTRY
表 13.10 都市型工业主要指标（2011~2012） …… 270
MAIN INDICATORS OF URBAN INDUSTRIES
表 13.11 主要年份工业产品产量 …… 273
OUTPUT OF INDUSTRIAL PRODUCTS IN MAIN YEARS
表 13.12 主要工业产品生产、销售总量（2012） …… 276
OUTPUT AND SALES OF MAIN INDUSTRIAL PRODUCTS
表 13.13 大型工业企业主要指标（2012） …… 278
MAJOR INDICATORS OF LARGE SIZED INDUSTRIAL ENTERPRISES
表 13.14 中型工业企业主要指标（2012） …… 282
MAJOR INDICATORS OF MEDIUM SIZED INDUSTRIAL ENTERPRISES
表 13.15 小型工业企业主要指标（2012） …… 286
MAJOR INDICATORS OF SMALL SIZED INDUSTRIAL ENTERPRISES
表 13.16 国家级、市级工业园区主要经济指标（2012） …… 290
MAJOR ECONOMIC INDICATORS OF MUNICIPAL AND NATIONAL INDUSTRIAL ZONE
主要统计指标解释 …… 298
EXPLANATORY NOTES TO MAJOR STATISTICAL INDICATORS

第十四篇 CHAPTER 14 建筑业 CONSTRUCTION

简要说明 …… 306
BRIEF INTRODUCTION

目录 CONTENTS

表 14.1 建筑业主要指标(1978~2012) …… 308
MAJOR INDICATORS OF CONSTRUCTION INDUSTRY
表 14.2 建筑业主要指标(2012) …… 309
MAJOR INDICATORS OF CONSTRUCTION INDUSTRY
表 14.3 各区、县建筑业主要指标(2012) …… 312
MAIN CONSTRUCTION INDICATORS OF DISTRICTS AND COUNTIES
表 14.4 建筑业主要财务指标(2012) …… 314
MAJOR ACCOUNTING INDICATORS OF CONSTRUCTION ENTERPRISES
表 14.5 建筑业签订合同情况(2012) …… 317
SITUATION OF CONSTRUCTION CONTRACTS
表 14.6 建筑业承包工程完成情况(2012) …… 318
COMPLETION OF CONTRACTED PROJECTS BY CONSTRUCTION ENTERPRISES
主要统计指标解释 …… 319
EXPLANATORY NOTES TO MAJOR STATISTICAL INDICATORS

第十五篇 CHAPTER 15 交通运输、邮政和信息传输 TRANSPORTATION, POSTS AND INFORMATION TRANSMISSION

简要说明 …… 322
BRIEF INTRODUCTION
表 15.1 主要年份运输线路长度 …… 324
LENGTHS OF TRAFFIC LINES IN MAIN YEARS
表 15.2 主要年份交通运输主要指标 …… 324
MAJOR INDICATORS OF TRANSPORTATION IN MAIN YEARS
表 15.3 主要年份旅客发送量 …… 325
PASSENGER DEPARTING IN MAIN YEARS
表 15.4 主要年份旅客周转量 …… 325
TURNOVER VOLUME OF PASSENGER TRAFFIC IN MAIN YEARS
表 15.5 主要年份货物运输量 …… 326
FREIGHT TRAFFIC VOLUME IN MAIN YEARS
表 15.6 主要年份货物周转量 …… 326
TURNOVER VOLUME OF FREIGHT TRAFFIC IN MAIN YEARS
表 15.7 主要年份港口码头情况 …… 327
PORTS IN MAIN YEARS
表 15.8 主要年份港口货物吞吐量 …… 327
PORT FREIGHT THROUGHPUT IN MAIN YEARS
表 15.9 主要年份国际集装箱吞吐量(按进出港分) …… 328
INTERNATIONAL CONTAINERS AND CARGO THROUGHPUT OF FOREIGN TRADE IN MAIN YEARS

表 15.10 邮轮经济发展情况(2011~2012) …… 328
CRUISE ECONOMIC DEVELOPMENT

表 15.11 经营性停车场(库)营运情况(2010 ~ 2012) …… 329
STATISTICS OF PARKING LOTS (GARAGES) OPERATION

表 15.12 民用车辆拥有量(2010 ~ 2012) …… 329
CIVIL MOTOR VEHICLES

表 15.13 个人民用车量拥有量(2010 ~ 2012) …… 329
INDIVIDUAL CIVIL MOTOR VEHICLES

表 15.14 邮政电信主要指标(2010~2012) …… 330
POST AND TELECOMMUNICATION IN MAIN YEARS

表 15.15 主要年份邮政业务主要指标 …… 330
MAJOR INDICATORS OF POSTAL BUSINESS IN MAIN YEARS

表 15.16 主要年份电信业务主要指标 …… 331
MAJOR INDICATORS OF TELECOM BUSINESS IN MAIN YEARS

表 15.17 主要年份邮电通信水平 …… 332
POSTAL AND TELECOM LEVEL IN MAIN YEARS

表 15.18 主要年份信息化基础设施情况 …… 332
INFRASTRUCTURE OF INFORMATIZATION IN MAIN YEARS

表 15.19 主要年份信息服务业经营情况 …… 333
OPERATION OF INFORMATION SERVICE INDUSTRY IN MAIN YEARS

表 15.20 信息技术应用(2009~2012) …… 333
APPLICATION OF INFORMATION TECHNOLOGY

主要统计指标解释 …… 334
EXPLANATORY NOTES TO MAJOR STATISTICAL INDICATORS

第十六篇 CHAPTER 16 批发和零售 WHOLESALE AND RETAIL

简要说明 …… 340
BRIEF INTRODUCTION

表 16.1 批发零售贸易业、餐饮业从业人员(1978~2012) …… 342
EMPLOYEES OF WHOLESALES, RETAILERS AND CATERING

表 16.2 限额以上批发贸易业产业活动单位和从业人员(2012) …… 343
QUANTITY OF BUSINESS UNITS AND EMPLOYEES OF WHOLESALE TRADE ABOVE THE SET SCALE

表 16.3 限额以上零售贸易业产业活动单位和从业人员(2012) …… 344
QUANTITY OF BUSINESS UNITS AND EMPLOYEES OF RETAIL TRADE ABOVE THE SET SCALE

表 16.4 社会消费品零售总额(1978~2012) …… 345
TOTAL RETAIL SALES OF CONSUMER GOODS

目录
CONTENTS

表 16.5 主要年份批发零售贸易业销售、库存总额 …… 348
PURCHASE, SALES AND INVENTORY OF WHOLESALE AND RETAIL TRADE IN MAIN YEARS

表 16.6 批发零售贸易业商品销售、库存总额(2012) …… 348
PURCHASE, SALES AND INVENTORY OF WHOLESALE AND RETAIL TRADE

表 16.7 汽车交易情况(2010~2012) …… 348
DISTRIBUTION OF AUTOMOBILE

表 16.8 限额以上批发贸易业商品购、销、存总额(2012) …… 349
PURCHASE, SALES AND INVENTORY OF WHOLESALE TRADE ABOVE THE SET SCALE

表 16.9 限额以上零售贸易业商品购、销、存总额(2012) …… 351
PURCHASE, SALES AND INVENTORY OF RETAIL TRADE ABOVE THE SET SCALE

表 16.10 主要年份限额以上批发零售贸易业主要生产资料销售量 …… 351
SALES OF MAJOR MEANS OF PRODUCT MATERIAL OF WHOLESALE AND RETAIL SALES TRADE ABOVE THE SET SCALE IN MAIN YEARS

表 16.11 限额以上批发零售贸易业主要商品分类销售额(2012) …… 352
TOTAL SALES OF ENTERPRISES ABOVE THE SET SCALE IN WHOLESALE AND RETAIL TRADE BY CATEGORY OF MAIN COMMODITIES

表 16.12 商品交易市场成交情况(2012) …… 353
DEALS IN MERCHANDISE EXCHANGE MARKET

表 16.13 主要年份限额以上批发零售贸易业主要财务指标 …… 354
MAIN FINANCIAL INDICATORS OF WHOLESALE AND RETAIL SALES ABOVE THE SET SCALE IN MAIN YEARS

表 16.14 主要年份限额以上餐饮业主要财务指标 …… 355
MAIN FINANCIAL INDICATORS OF CATERING SECTOR ABOVE THE SET SCALE IN MAIN YEARS

表 16.15 主要年份限额以上连锁零售业、住宿和餐饮业经营情况 …… 355
BASIC STATISTICS OF CHAIN RETAIL, ACCOMMODATION AND CATERING ABOVE THE SET SCALE IN MAIN YEARS

表 16.16 限额以上批发零售贸易业主要财务指标(2012) …… 356
MAIN FINANCIAL INDICATORS OF WHOLESALE AND RETAIL ENTERPRISES ABOVE THE SET SCALE

表 16.17 限额以上住宿餐饮业主要财务指标(2012) …… 360
MAIN FINANCIAL INDICATORS OF ACCOMMODATION AND CATERING ENTERPRISES ABOVE THE SET SCALE

主要统计指标解释 …… 362
EXPLANATORY NOTES TO MAJOR STATISTICAL INDICATORS

第十七篇 CHAPTER 17 金融业 FINANCE

简要说明 …… 366
BRIEF INTRODUCTION

表 17.1 原保险保费收入和赔付支出(1978 ~ 2012) …… 367
PREMIUM OF PRIMARY INSURANCE AND PAYMENT

表 17.2 金融机构存贷款年末余额(2010～2012) …… 368
SAVING DEPOSIT AND LOAN BALANCE OF FINANCIAL INSTITUTIONS AT YEAR-END

表 17.3 中资金融机构人民币存款年末余额(2012) …… 368
RMB SAVING DEPOSIT OF CHINESE FINANCIAL INSTITUTIONS AT YEAR-END

表 17.4 中资金融机构人民币贷款年末余额(2012) …… 369
RMB LOAN BALANCE OF CHINESE FINANCIAL INSTITUTIONS AT YEAR-END

表 17.5 个人消费贷款及公积金贷款(2010～2012) …… 369
PERSONAL CONSUMPTION LOAN AND ACCUMULATION FUND LOAN

表 17.6 年末金融业单位数(2011～2012) …… 370
QUANTITY OF FINANCIAL INSTITUTIONS

表 17.7 主要金融市场成交概况(2010～2012) …… 370
DEAL STATISTICS OF MAIN FANANCIAL MARKET

表 17.8 金融机构人民币存款基准利率(1990～2012) …… 371
BENCHMARK INTEREST RATE OF RMB DEPOSIT FOR FINANCIAL INSTITUTIONS

表 17.9 金融机构人民币贷款基准利率 (1991～2012) …… 372
BENCHMARK INTEREST RATE OF RMB LOAN FOR FINANCIAL INSTITUTIONS

表 17.10 上海证券交易所上市公司股本结构(2010～2012) …… 373
CAPITAL STOCK STRUCTURE OF PUBLIC COMPANIES IN SHANGHAI STOCK EXCHANGE

表 17.11 上海证券交易所市场概况(2010～2012) …… 373
SHANGHAI STOCK EXCHANGE MARKET

表 17.12 主要年份上证综合指数 …… 374
THE SHANGHAI COMPOSITE INDEX IN MAIN YEARS

表 17.13 上证各类指数概况(2012) …… 374
ALL KINDS OF INDEX OF SHANGHAI

表 17.14 上海证券交易所有价证券成交总额(2009～2012) …… 375
TOTAL VOLUME OF PRICED SECURITIES TRADING IN SHANGHAI STOCK EXCHANGE

表 17.15 主要年份上海证券交易所股票账户开户情况 …… 375
ACCOUNT-OPENING BY INVESTORS IN SHANGHAI STOCK EXCHANGE IN MAIN YEARS

主要统计指标解释 …… 376
EXPLANATORY NOTES TO MAJOR STATISTICAL INDICATORS

第十八篇 CHAPTER 18 房地产业 REAL ESTATE

简要说明 …… 380
BRIEF INTRODUCTION

表 18.1 主要年份房地产开发投资和经营情况 …… 382
INVESTMENT AND OPERATION IN REAL ESTATE DEVELOPMENT IN MAIN YEARS

目录
CONTENTS

表 18.2 主要年份房地产开发企业房屋建筑面积和造价 …… 383
CONSTRUCTION AREA AND COST OF PROPERTY DEVELOPED BY REAL ESTATE COMPANIES IN MAIN YEARS
表 18.3 主要年份商品房销售和出租情况 …… 384
COMMODITY HOUSING SOLD AND LEASED IN MAIN YEARS
表 18.4 每百户城市居民家庭房屋产权构成(2009 ~ 2012) …… 384
PROPERTY RIGHT STRUCTURE OF TOWNSMAN TENEMENT PER HUNDRED HOUSEHOLDS
表 18.5 房屋征收(拆迁)情况(1995 ~ 2012) …… 385
BUILDINGS EXPROPRIATION (RESETTLEMENT)
表 18.6 各区房屋征收(拆迁)情况(2012) …… 385
BUILDINGS EXPROPRIATION (RESETTLEMENT) IN DIFFERENT DISTRICTS
表 18.7 土地使用权出让情况(2012) …… 386
LEASE OF LAND PLOT TENURE
表 18.8 存量房交易情况(1994 ~ 2012) …… 386
EXCHANGE OF SECOND-HAND HOUSES
主要统计指标解释 …… 387
EXPLANATORY NOTES TO MAJOR STATISTICAL INDICATORS

第十九篇 CHAPTER 19 科学技术 SCIENCE AND TECHNOLOGY

简要说明 …… 390
BRIEF INTRODUCTION
表 19.1 主要年份科技活动主要指标 …… 392
MAIN INDICATORS OF SCIENTIFIC AND TECHOLOGICAL ACTIVITIES IN MAIN YEARS
表 19.2 主要年份研究与试验发展(R&D)经费按执行部门分类 …… 392
EXPENDITURES ON R&D GROUPED BY EXECUTIVE DEPARTMENT IN MAIN YEARS
表 19.3 主要年份研究与试验发展(R&D)活动情况 …… 393
BASIC STATISTICS OF SCIENTIFIC AND TECHNOLOGICAL ACTIVITIES IN MAIN YEARS
表 19.4 国有企事业单位专业技术人员基本情况(2012) …… 394
PROFESSIONAL AND TECHNICAL PERSONNEL IN STATE-OWNED ENTERPRISES AND INSTITUTIONS
表 19.5 主要年份各类技术合同项目 …… 395
VARIOUS TECHNOLOGICAL CONTRACTS IN MAIN YEARS
表 19.6 主要年份各类技术合同成交金额 …… 395
TOTAL CONTRACTED VALUE IN VARIOUS TECHNOLOGICAL CONTRACTS IN MAIN YEARS
表 19.7 科技成果 (2000 ~ 2012) …… 396
ACHIEVEMENTS IN SCIENTIFIC AND TECHNICAL RESEARCH
表 19.8 主要年份科研机构研究与试验发展(R&D)活动情况 …… 397
RESEARCH AND DEVELOPMENT(R&D) ACTIVITIES OF SCIENTIFIC RESEARCH INSTITUTIONS

表 19.9 主要年份获得科技成果奖励情况 …… 398
ACHIEVEMENTS AWARDED IN SCIENTIFIC AND TECHNOLOGICAL RESEARCH IN MAIN YEARS
表 19.10 主要年份自然科学研究与技术开发机构课题情况 …… 398
PROJECTS OF NATURAL SCIENCE RESEARCH AND TECHNOLOGICAL DEVELOPMENT INSTITUTIONS IN MAIN YEARS
表 19.11 自然科学研究与技术开发机构课题情况(2012) …… 399
STATISTICS OF PROJECTS OF NATURAL SCIENCE RESEARCH AND DEVELOPMENT INSTITUTIONS
表 19.12 自然科学研究与技术开发机构论文与著作情况 (2012) …… 399
PAPERS AND WORKS OF NATURAL SCIENCE RESEARCH AND TECHNOLOGICAL DEVELOPMENT INSTITUTIONS
表 19.13 区县级以上国有单位独立研究与开发机构人员(2012) …… 400
PERSONNEL OF STATE-OWNED INDEPENDENT RESEARCH AND DEVELOPMENT INSTITUTIONS ABOVE DISTRICT AND COUNTY LEVEL
表 19.14 主要年份区县级属研究与开发机构状况 …… 400
RESEARCH AND DEVELOPMENT INSTITUTIONS AT DISTRICT AND COUNTY LEVEL IN MAIN YEARS
表 19.15 主要年份高等学校研究与试验发展(R&D)活动情况 …… 401
RESERCH AND DEVELOPMENT(R&D) ACTIVITIES OF HIGHER EDUCATION IN MAIN YEARS
表 19.16 高等学校科技活动人员 (2012) …… 402
SCIENTIFIC AND TECHNOLOGICAL PERSONNEL OF INSTITUTIONS OF HIGHER EDUCATION
表 19.17 高等学校研究机构和课题情况 (2012) …… 402
RESEARCH INSTITUTIONS AND PROJECT OF HIGHER EDUCATION
表 19.18 主要年份专利申请量和授权量 …… 403
PATENT APPLICATIONS AND CERTIFIED IN MAIN YEARS
表 19.19 科协系统出版物和科技服务情况 (2012) …… 403
PUBLICATIONS AND CONSULATIVE ACTIVITIES OF SCIENCE AND TECHNOLOGY ASSOCIATIONS
表 19.20 科协系统科普活动和科技培训情况 (2012) …… 404
PROMOTING SCIENCE ACTIVITIES AND TRAINING PROGRAM ORGANIZED BY SCIENCE AND TECHNOLOGY ASSOCIATIONS
表 19.21 各级科协机构和人员 (2012) …… 404
INSTITUTIONS AND PERSONNEL OF SCIENCE AND TECHNOLOGY ASSOCIATIONS AT VARIOUS LEVELS
表 19.22 科协系统学术交流情况 (2012) …… 405
ACADEMIC EXCHANGES OF SCIENCE AND TECHNOLOGY ASSOCIATIONS
表 19.23 主要年份民营科技企业状况 …… 406
SCIENTIFIC AND TECHNOLOGICAL RESEARCH INSTITUTIONS RUN BY LOCAL PEOPLE IN MAIN YEARS
表 19.24 主要年份规模以上工业企业研究与试验发展(R&D)活动情况 …… 407
BASIC STATISTICS OF SCIENTIFIC AND TECHNOLOGICAL ACTIVITIES IN MAIN YEARS
表 19.25 规模以上工业企业科技活动人员情况 (2012) …… 408
PERSONNEL FOR SCIENCE AND TECHNIC ACTIVITY IN INDUSTRIAL ENTERPRISES ABOVE THE SET SCALE
表 19.26 规模以上工业企业科技项目数与科技经费支出情况 (2012) …… 409
SCIENCE AND TECHNIC PROJECTS AND EXPENDITURES OF INDUSTRIAL ENTERPRISES ABOVE THE SET SCALE

目录 CONTENTS

表 19.27 规模以上工业企业 R&D 经费内部支出来源构成 (2012) ………… 410
STRUCTURE OF R&D INNER EXPENDITURE SOURCE IN INDUSTRIAL ENTERPRISES ABOVE THE SET SCALE

表 19.28 规模以上工业企业办科技机构情况 (2012) ………… 411
SCIENCE AND TECHNIC RESEARCH INSTITUTIONS FUNDED BY INDUSTRIAL ENTERPRISES ABOVE THE SET SCALE

表 19.29 规模以上工业企业其他技术活动费用支出情况 (2012) ………… 412
SPECIAL TECHNICAL PROJECT FUNDS OF INDUSTRIAL ENTERPRISES ABOVE THE SET SCALE

表 19.30 规模以上工业企业新产品产出情况 (2012) ………… 413
OUTPUT OF NEW PRODUCTS OF INDUSTRIAL ENTERPRISES ABOVE THE SET SCALE

表 19.31 主要年份大中型工业企业科技活动情况 ………… 414
SCIENCE AND TECHNIC ACTIVITIES OF LARGE AND MEDIUM INDUSTRIAL ENTERPRISES IN MAIN YEARS

主要统计指标解释 ………… 415
EXPLANATORY NOTES TO MAJOR STATISTICAL INDICATORS

第二十篇 CHAPTER 20 教育 EDUCATION

简要说明 ………… 420
BRIEF INTRODUCTION

表 20.1 主要年份教育事业基本情况 ………… 421
BASIC STATISTICS OF EDUCATION IN MAIN YEARS

表 20.2 每万人口在校学生数、每个教师负担学生数(1978~2012) ………… 423
STUDENTS ENROLLMENT PER 10 000 PERSONS AND STUDENTS TAUGHT

表 20.3 各级各类学校在校学生数(1978 ~ 2012) ………… 424
STUDENTS ENROLLMENT BY VARIOUS SCHOOLS

表 20.4 主要年份各阶段教育实施情况 ………… 425
BASIC STATISTICS OF VARIOUS PHASES EDUCATION IN MAIN YEARS

表 20.5 主要年份各级民办学校基本情况 ………… 425
BASIC STATISTICS OF CIVIL SCHOOLS IN MAIN YEARS

表 20.6 民办学校(园)基本情况(2012) ………… 426
BASIC STATISTICS OF CIVIL SCHOOLS

表 20.7 主要年份外国留学生情况 ………… 426
STATISTICS OF FOREIGN STUDENT IN MAIN YEARS

表 20.8 主要年份研究生人数 ………… 427
QUANTITY OF GRADUATE STUDENTS IN MAIN YEARS

表 20.9 普通高等学校基本情况 (2012) ………… 428
BASIC STATISTICS OF INSTITUTIONS OF HIGHER EDUCATION

表 20.10 普通高等学校分科专任教师数 (2012) ………… 428
FULL-TIME TEACHERS IN INSTITUTIONS OF HIGHER EDUCATION BY SUBJECTS

表 20.11 普通高等学校本科分科学生数（2012）…… 429
UNDERGRADUATE STUDENTS IN INSTITUTIONS OF HIGHER EDUCATION BY SUBJECTS
表 20.12 中等专业学校基本情况（2012）…… 429
BASIC STATISTICS OF SPECIALIZED SECONDARY SCHOOLS
表 20.13 各区、县普通中学基本情况（2012）…… 430
BASIC STATISTICS OF REGULAR SECONDARY SCHOOLS BY DISTRICT
表 20.14 各区、县普通中学初、高中学生基本情况（2012）…… 431
BASIC STATISTICS OF REGULAR JUNIOR AND SENIOR SCHOOLS' STUDENTS BY DISTRICT
表 20.15 各区、县普通小学基本情况（2012）…… 432
BASIC STATISTICS OF REGULAR PRIMARY SCHOOLS BY DISTRICT
表 20.16 主要年份实验性示范性中学基本情况 …… 433
BASIC STATISTICS OF SECONDARY CAMPUS SCHOOL IN MAIN YEARS
表 20.17 主要年份幼儿园基本情况 …… 433
BASIC STATISTICS OF KINDERGARTENS IN MAIN YEARS
表 20.18 主要年份特殊教育基本情况 …… 433
BASIC STATISTICS OF SPECIAL EDUCATION IN MAIN YEARS
表 20.19 网络教育本科学生情况（2012）…… 434
BASIC STATISTICS OF UNDERGRADUATE STUDENTS OF NETWORK EDUCATION BY SUBJECT
表 20.20 各级各类成人学校基本情况（2012）…… 434
BASIC STATISTICS OF ADULT SCHOOLS AT VARIOUS LEVELS
主要统计指标解释 …… 435
EXPLANATORY NOTES TO MAJOR STATISTICAL INDICATORS

第二十一篇 CHAPTER 21 卫生、社会保障和社会福利业 HEALTH,SOCIAL SECURITY AND SOCIAL WELFARE

简要说明 …… 440
BRIEF INTRODUCTION
表 21.1 卫生事业基本情况（1978~2012）…… 442
BASIC STATISTICS OF PUBLIC HEALTH
表 21.2 各类卫生机构、床位及人员数（2012）…… 443
VARIOUS HEALTH CARE INSTITUTIONS, BEDS AND PERSONNEL
表 21.3 各区、县卫生机构基本情况（2012）…… 445
STATISTICS OF HEALTH CARE INSTITUTIONS BY DISTRICT AND COUNTIES
表 21.4 医疗机构病床使用情况（2012）…… 446
STATISTICS OF HOSPITAL BED USAGE IN MEDICAL TREATMENT INSTITUTION
表 21.5 医疗机构诊疗人次和入院人数（2012）…… 446
PATIENTS TREATED AND IN-PATIENTS IN MEDICAL TREATMENT INSTITUTION

目录
CONTENTS

表 21.6　前十位疾病死亡原因和构成（2012）…… 447
THE TOP 10 DEATH-CAUSING DISEASES AND COMPOSITION

表 21.7　婴儿前五位疾病死亡原因和构成（2012）…… 447
THE TOP 5 INFANT DEATH-CAUSING DISEASES AND COMPOSITON

表 21.8　婴儿死亡率、新生儿死亡率、孕产妇死亡率(2009 ~ 2012）…… 447
DEATH RATE OF INFANT,NEW BORN,PREGNANT AND LYING-IN WOMAN

表 21.9　主要年份防病工作情况 …… 448
BASIC STATISTICS OF DISEASE PREVENTION IN MAIN YEARS

表 21.10　家庭病床情况（2012）…… 448
FAMILY SICKBEDS

表 21.11　主要年份妇幼卫生工作情况 …… 449
BASIC STATISTICS OF GYNAECOLOGY AND PAEDIATRICS IN MAIN YEARS

表 21.12　主要年份公民献血、用血情况 …… 449
BLOOD OFFER AND USE OF CITIZENS IN MAIN YEARS

表 21.13　主要年份社会保险参保人数 …… 450
QUANTITY OF PARTICIPANTS IN SOCIAL INSURANCE IN MAIN YEARS

表 21.14　主要年份社会保障标准 …… 450
SOCIAL SECURITY STANDARD IN MAIN YEARS

表 21.15　社会福利院、儿童福利院、社会福利医院和收养性老年福利机构情况(1980 ~ 2012）…… 451
INSTITUTIONS OF SOCIAL WELFARE, CHILDREN WELFARE, SOCIAL WELFARE HOSPITALS AND ADOPTIVE SENIORS WELFARE INSTITUTIONS

表 21.16　主要年份社会福利事业机构数和职工人数 …… 453
QUANTITY OF SOCIAL WELFARE INSTITUTIONS AND STAFF AND WORKERS IN MAIN YEARS

表 21.17　主要年份民间组织情况 …… 453
STATISTICS OF CIVIL ORGANIZATIONS AND CHARITY IN MAIN YEARS

表 21.18　主要年份养老服务 …… 454
ENDOWMENT SERVICE IN MAIN YEARS

表 21.19　主要年份老年医疗服务 …… 454
MEDICARE SERVICE FOR AGED PEOPLE IN MAIN YEARS

表 21.20　主要年份红十字会基本情况 …… 455
BASIC STATISICS ON RED CROSS SOCIETY OF CHINA SHANGHAI MUNICIPAL BRANCH IN MAIN YEARS

表 21.21　全市残疾人各残疾类别人数情况(2012）…… 456
THE NUMBER OF CASES OF EACH TYPE OF DISABILITY

主要统计指标解释 …… 457
EXPLANATORY NOTES TO MAJOR STATISTICAL INDICATORS

第二十二篇 CHAPTER 22 文化和体育 CULTURE AND SPORTS

简要说明 …… 464
BRIEF INTRODUCTION

表 22.1 主要年份文化机构数 …… 465
QUANTITY OF CULTURAL INSTITUTIONS IN MAIN YEARS

表 22.2 影剧院、艺术表演场所、艺术表演团体数(1978～2012) …… 466
QUANTITY OF CINEMAS AND THEATRES AND ART PERFORMANCE TROUPES

表 22.3 主要年份主要文化机构从业人员数 …… 467
QUANTITY OF EMPLOYEES IN MAJOR CULTURAL INSTITUTIONSS IN MAIN YAERS

表 22.4 主要文化机构和人员数(2012) …… 467
MAJOR CULTURAL INSTITUTIONS AND PERSONNEL

表 22.5 群众艺术馆和文化馆(站)情况(2012) …… 468
MASS ART AND CULTURAL CENTERS

表 22.6 艺术表演团体情况(2012) …… 468
BASIC STATISTICS OF ART TROUPES

表 22.7 艺术表演场馆基本情况(2012) …… 469
ART PERFORMANCE PLACES

表 22.8 博物馆、纪念馆情况(2012) …… 470
STATISTICS OF MUSEUMS AND MEMORIALS

表 22.9 主要年份文物保护维修情况 …… 470
PRESERVATION AND MAINTAIN OF HISTORICAL RELICS IN MAIN YEARS

表 22.10 主要年份广播电台、电视台情况 …… 471
TELEVISION STATIONS AND BROADCASTING STATIONS

表 22.11 电视和广播公共节目播出时间(2012) …… 471
PLAYING HOURS OF TELEVISION AND BROADCASTING PUBLIC PROGRAMS

表 22.12 主要年份有线电视基本情况 …… 471
BASIC STATISTICS ON CABLE TELEVISION IN MAIN YEARS

表 22.13 电影摄制、译制和放映情况(1978～2012) …… 472
PRODUCTION, DUBBING AND SHOWING OF FILMS

表 22.14 主要年份电影发行放映情况 …… 473
BASIC STATISTICS OF FILM DISTRIBUTION AND PROJECTION IN MAIN YEARS

表 22.15 电影公益场放映情况(2009～2012) …… 473
FILM PROJECTION FOR PUBLIC GOOD

表 22.16 文化娱乐机构基本情况(2012) …… 474
BASIC STATISTICS OF CULTURE AND ENTERTAINMENT INSTITUTIONS

目录
CONTENTS

表 22.17 公共图书馆情况（2012） ······ 474
PUBLIC LIBRARIES
表 22.18 图书出版数量(1978～2012) ······ 475
BOOKS PUBLISHED
表 22.19 期刊出版数量(1978～2012) ······ 476
PERIODICALS PUBLISHED
表 22.20 报纸出版数量(1978～2012) ······ 477
NEWSPAPER PUBLISHED
表 22.21 主要年份新闻出版机构和人员数 ······ 478
NUMBER OF INSTITUTIONS AND PERSONS ENGAGED IN NEWS AND PUBLISHING
表 22.22 图书出版数量（2012） ······ 478
BOOKS PUBLISHED
表 22.23 期刊出版数量（2012） ······ 479
PERIODICALS PUBLISHED
表 22.24 报纸出版数量（2012） ······ 479
NEWSPAPER PUBLISHED
表 22.25 音像电子出版数量（2012） ······ 479
AUDIO, VIDEO AND ELECTRON PUBLISHED
表 22.26 档案机构基本情况(2012) ······ 480
BASIC STATISTICS OF ARCHIVE INSTITUTIONS
表 22.27 主要年份优秀运动员、教练员情况 ······ 481
BASIC STATISTICS ON EXCELLENT ATHLETES AND COACHES
表 22.28 体育系统职工人数(2012) ······ 481
STAFF AND WORKERS IN SPORTS SECTORS
表 22.29 群众体育健身活动场所情况(2009～2012) ······ 481
MASS PHYSICAL ACTIVITIES IN MAIN YEARS
主要统计指标解释 ······ 482
EXPLANATORY NOTES TO MAJOR STATISTICAL INDICATORS

第二十三篇 CHAPTER 23 法律、公证和其他 LAWS,NOTARY AND OTHERS

简要说明 ······ 486
BRIEF INTRODUCTION
表 23.1 主要年份律师、公证及调解工作基本情况 ······ 487
BASIC STATISTICS OF LAWYERS, NOTARIZATIONS AND MEDIATIONS IN MAIN YEARS
表 23.2 主要年份国内和涉外公证文书分类情况 ······ 488
DOMESTIC AND FOREIGN NOTARIAL DOCUMENTS BY TYPE IN MAIN YEARS
表 23.3 主要年份公安机关立案的刑事案件情况 ······ 489
CRIMINAL CASES REGISTERED IN PUBLIC SECURITY ORGANS IN MAIN YEARS

表 23.4 主要年份公安机关查处治安案件情况 …… 489
OFFENSE CASES AGAINST PUBLIC ORDER HANDLED BY PUBLIC SECURITY ORGANS IN MAIN YEARS
表 23.5 交通事故和火灾情况（1980～2012）…… 490
BASIC STATISTICS OF TRAFFIC ACCIDENTS AND FIRES
表 23.6 交通事故情况（2012）…… 491
BASIC STATISTICS ON TRAFFIC ACCIDENTS
表 23.7 火灾事故情况（2012）…… 491
BASIC STATISTICS ON FIRES
表 23.8 检察院直接立案侦查案件情况（2012）…… 492
CASES UNDER DIRECT INVESTIGATION BY PROCURATOR'S OFFICES
表 23.9 检察院民事、行政案件办理情况（2012）…… 492
CIVIL CASES AND ADMINISTRATIVE CASES HANDLED BY PROCURATOR'S OFFICES
表 23.10 检察院申诉案件处理情况（2012）…… 493
APPEALS HANDLED BY PROCURATOR'S OFFICES
表 23.11 法院各类案件办理情况（2012）…… 494
CASES HANDLED BY COURTS
表 23.12 法院执行案件情况（2012）…… 495
CASES EXECUTED BY COURTS
表 23.13 主要年份法院各类案件结案情况 …… 495
CASES ENDED BY COURTS IN MAIN YEARS
主要统计指标解释 …… 496
EXPLANATORY NOTES TO MAJOR STATISTICAL INDICATORS

第二十四篇 CHAPTER 24 企业景气指数与消费者信心指数 PROSPERITY INDEX ON ENTERPRISES AND CONSUMER CONFIDENCE INDEX

简要说明 …… 500
BRIEF INTRODUCTION
表 24.1 消费者信心指数（2012）…… 502
CONSUMER CONFIDENCE INDEX
表 24.2 企业景气指数、企业家信心指数（1999~2012）…… 502
PROSPERITY INDEX ON ENTERPRISES AND INDEXS OF CONFIDENCE ON MACRO ECONOMY BY ENTERPRISERS
表 24.3 企业景气指数（2012）…… 503
PROSPERITY INDEX ON ENTERPRISES
表 24.4 企业家信心指数（2012）…… 504
INDEX OF CONFIDENCE ON MACRO ECONOMY BY ENTERPRISERS
主要统计指标解释 …… 505
EXPLANATORY NOTES TO MAJOR STATISTICAL INDICATORS

第一篇

CHAPTER 1

综　合

GENERAL SURVEY

简要说明

本篇章主要内容和资料来源

一、综合资料主要包括上海市行政区划、国民经济和社会发展综合资料两部分。分别由上海市民政局、上海市统计局和国家统计局上海调查总队编辑整理。

二、"行政区划"资料，由上海市民政局根据上海市政府批准的、截止到上一年末上海市区划变更情况汇总整理并提供。

三、国民经济和社会发展综合资料是抽取全书的精华，通过对各篇章主要统计指标及其速度、结构、比例和效益等的加工计算，来反映国民经济和社会发展的总体情况。

BRIEF INTRODUCTION

Main Contents and Sources of Data

1. This chapter consists of two parts: divisions of Shanghai administrative areas and summary data on the national economy and social development, which are compiled by the Shanghai Municipal Civil Affairs Bureau, Shanghai Municipal Statistics Bureau and the Survey Office of the National Bureau of Statistics in Shanghai.

2. Data on divisions of administrative areas in Shanghai, are prepared and provided by the Shanghai Municipal Civil Affairs Bureau on the basis of the changes in the divisions of administrative areas as approved by the Shanghai municipal government at the end of the previous year.

3. The summary data on the national economy and social development reflect on the overall situation of the economy and social development by presenting further processed statistics including growth, structure, ratio, and efficiency data derived from other chapters.

表 1.1 行政区划（2012）
ADMINISTRATIVE DIVISION

单位：个（unit）

地 区	District	镇 Towns	乡 Township	街道办事处 Urban Sub-district Office	居民委员会 Neighbourhood Committees	村民委员会 Village Committees
全 市	**Total**	**108**	**2**	**98**	**3 914**	**1 613**
浦东新区	Pudong New Area	24		12	795	372
黄 浦 区	Huangpu			10	189	
徐 汇 区	Xuhui	1		12	306	
长 宁 区	Changning	1		9	182	
静 安 区	Jing'an			5	73	
普 陀 区	Putuo	3		6	233	7
闸 北 区	Zhabei	1		8	208	1
虹 口 区	Hongkou			8	229	
杨 浦 区	Yangpu	1		11	305	
闵 行 区	Minhang	9		3	387	136
宝 山 区	Baoshan	9		3	347	108
嘉 定 区	Jiading	7		3	137	147
金 山 区	Jinshan	9		1	87	124
松 江 区	Songjiang	11		4	182	87
青 浦 区	Qingpu	8		3	88	184
奉 贤 区	Fengxian	8			100	177
崇 明 县	Chongming	16	2		66	270

注：本表数据由上海市民政局提供。
Note: Data in this table are provided by Shanghai Civil Affairs Bureau.

表 1.2 主要气象指标（2012）
MAIN CLIMATE INDICATORS

指 标	Indicators	2012	指 标	Indicators	2012
平均气温(℃)	Annual Average Temperature	17.1	蒸发量(毫米)	Evaporation (mm)	713.6
极端最高气温(℃)	Utmost Highest Air Temperature	38.0	降水量(毫米)	Precipitation(mm)	1 435.8
极端最低气温(℃)	Utmost Lowest Air Temperature	-2.5	降雨日(天)	Annual Rainy Days(day)	151
日照时间 (小时)	Annual Sunshine Time(h)	1 420.1	无霜期(天)	Frost-free Period(day)	324

表 1.3 各月主要气象指标(2012)
MAIN CLIMATE INDICATORS OF EVERY MONTH

月 份	Month	平均气温(℃) Annual Average Temperature (℃)	极端最高气温(℃) Utmost Highest Air Temperature(℃)	极端最低气温(℃) Utmost Lowest Air Temperature(℃)	平均最高(℃) Average Maximum temperature(℃)	平均最低(℃) Average Minimum temperature(℃)
1 月	Jan.	5.1	10.4	-2.3	7.4	3.3
2 月	Feb.	4.8	12.1	-2.5	7.3	2.8
3 月	Mar.	9.8	26.1	0.8	13.9	7.0
4 月	Apr.	17.6	28.0	8.8	22.5	14.3
5 月	May.	21.6	33.7	14.9	26.2	18.3
6 月	Jun.	24.7	36.1	19.0	28.1	22.5
7 月	Jul.	29.9	38.0	22.6	34.2	26.9
8 月	Aug.	29.0	36.4	23.5	32.8	26.7
9 月	Sep.	23.9	32.1	17.1	27.8	21.5
10 月	Oct.	20.1	26.5	11.2	23.7	17.4
11 月	Nov.	12.6	19.6	4.8	15.7	10.1
12 月	Dec.	6.6	17.5	-2.5	9.3	4.3

表 1.3 续表 continued

月 份	Month	日照时间 (小时) Annual Sunshine Time(h)	降水量(毫米) Precipitation (mm)	降雨日(天) Annual Rainy Days (day)	蒸发量(毫米) Evaporation (mm)
1 月	Jan.	23.4	68.4	12	27.3
2 月	Feb.	38.8	88.3	17	26.8
3 月	Mar.	124.8	132.8	18	43.6
4 月	Apr.	162.7	98.9	12	72.6
5 月	May.	163.4	124.5	12	84.6
6 月	Jun.	99.9	170.7	14	56.8
7 月	Jul.	214.5	149.9	12	121.9
8 月	Aug.	199.2	253.2	12	94.5
9 月	Sep.	159.5	107.3	9	65.8
10 月	Oct.	151.5	18.9	7	62.9
11 月	Nov.	65.0	132.8	12	31.9
12 月	Dec.	17.4	90.1	14	24.9

注：本页资料由上海市气象局提供。
Note: Data on this page are provided by Shanghai Meteorological Bureau.

表 1.4　主要年份社会经济主要指标
MAJOR SOCIAL AND ECONOMIC INDICATORS IN MAIN YEARS

指　标	Indicators	1990	2000	2010	2011	2012
人口与就业	**Population and Employment**					
人　口	**Population**					
年末常住人口(万人)	Year-end Resident Population (10 000 persons)	1 334.00	1 608.60	2 302.66	2 347.46	2 380.43
年末户籍人口(万人)	Year-end Registered Population(10 000 persons)	1 283.35	1 321.63	1 412.32	1 419.36	1 426.93
#非农业人口	Non-agricultural Population	864.46	986.16	1 254.95	1 267.76	1 280.82
就　业	**Employment**					
职工人数(万人)	Staff and Workers(10 000 persons)	508.10	390.14	648.49	868.42	944.47
城镇登记失业率(%)	Registered Unemployment Rate in Urban Areas (%)	1.5	3.5	4.2	4.2	4.2
宏观经济	**Macro Economy**					
国民经济核算	**Domestic Economic Accounts**					
上海市生产总值(亿元)	Gross Domestic Product(100 million yuan)	781.66	4 771.17	17 165.98	19 195.69	20 181.72
第一产业	Primary Industry	34.24	76.68	114.15	124.94	127.80
第二产业	Secondary Industry	505.70	2 207.63	7 218.32	7 927.89	7 854.77
#工　业	Industry	469.83	1 998.96	6 536.21	7 208.59	7 097.76
第三产业	Tertiary Industry	241.82	2 486.86	9 833.51	11 142.86	12 199.15
人均生产总值(元)(按常住人口计算)	Per Capita Gross Domestic Product(yuan) (Calculated by Resident Population)	5 911	30 047	76 074	82 560	85 373
经济增长贡献率(%)	Contribution Rate of Economic Growth (%)					
第一产业	Primary Industry	2.5	0.6	-0.4	-0.1	…
第二产业	Secondary Industry	62.6	55.7	69.2	32.7	17.3
#工　业	Industry	74.6	54.7	66.6	34.4	14.4
第三产业	Tertiary Industry	37.2	43.7	31.2	67.4	82.7
固定资产投资	**Investment in Fixed Assets**					
全社会固定资产投资总额(亿元)	Total Investment in Fixed Assets(100 million yuan)	227.08	1 869.67	5 317.67	5 067.09	5 254.38
#房地产投资	Investment in Real Estate	8.16	566.17	1 980.68	2 170.31	2 381.36

表 1.4 续表 1 continued

	指　标 Indicators	1990	2000	2010	2011	2012
财　政	**Public Finance**					
地方财政收入(亿元)	**Local Fiscal Revenue(100 million yuan)**	**166.99**	**497.96**	**2 873.58**	**3 429.83**	**3 743.71**
地方财政支出(亿元)	Local Fiscal Expenditure(100 million yuan)	75.56	622.84	3 302.89	3 914.88	4 184.02
价　格	**Price**					
居民消费价格指数(上年=100)	Consumer Price Index(preceding =100)	106.3	102.5	103.1	105.2	102.8
商品零售价格指数(上年=100)	Retail Price Index(preceding =100)	104.8	96.4	101.7	104.1	101.2
外商直接投资	**Foreign Direct Investment**					
签订合同项目（个）	Number of Contracts (unit)	203	1 814	3 906	4 329	4 043
签订合同金额（亿美元）	Contractual Foreign Investment(100 million USD)	2.14	63.90	153.07	201.03	223.38
实际到位金额（亿美元）	**Foreign Investment Actually Absorbed (100 million USD)**	**1.77**	**31.60**	**111.21**	**126.01**	**151.85**
产　业	**Industries**					
农　业	**Agriculture**					
农业总产值（亿元）	Gross Output Value of Agriculture (100 million yuan)	68.16	216.50	287.03	314.58	321.73
工　业	**Industry**					
工业总产值（亿元）	Gross Output Value of Industry (100 million yuan)	1 642.75	7 022.98	31 038.57	33 834.44	33 186.41
轻工业	Light Industry	846.63	2 903.40	6 692.35	7 420.92	7 507.02
重工业	Heavy Industry	796.12	4 119.59	24 346.22	26 413.52	25 679.39
建筑业	**Construction**					
总产值（亿元）	Gross Output Value (100 million yuan)	75.62	631.64	4 300.19	4 586.28	4 843.44
交通运输、邮政业和信息传输	**Transportation,Post and Information Transmission**					
货物运输量（万吨）	Freight Transportation Volume (10 000 tons)	22 848	47 954	81 024	93 318	94 376
旅客发送量（万人次）	Passenger Departures (10 000 person-times)	3 835	6 893	13 432	13 519	14 547
港口货物吞吐量（万吨）	Port Cargo throughput (10 000 tons)	13 959	20 440	65 339	72 758	73 559
国际标准集装箱吞吐量(万 TEU)	**International Container Throughput Capacity (10 000TEU)**	**45.60**	**561.20**	**2 906.90**	**3 173.93**	**3 252.94**
邮电业务总量(亿元)	Revenue from Post and Telecommunications Services (100 million yuan)	10.23	171.70	1 016.44	465.45	638.18
年末固定电话用户（万户）	Year-end Installed Telephone Subscribers (10 000 households)	45.69	549.00	935.91	926.43	902.90

表 1.4 续表2 continued

指　标	Indicators	1990	2000	2010	2011	2012
批发和零售	**Wholesale and Retail**					
社会消费品零售总额（亿元）	Retail Sales of Consumer Goods (100 million yuan)	333.86	1 865.28	6 070.50	6 814.80	7 412.30
批发零售业商品销售总额（亿元）	Total Sales of Wholesale and Retail (100 million yuan)	1 305.41	7 474.81	37 383.25	46 075.87	53 795.10
对外经济贸易	**Foreign Trade**					
上海关区进出口总额（亿美元）	Total Trade Value Through Customs (100 million USD)	172.89	1 093.11	6 846.45	8 123.14	8 013.10
进口额	Imports	86.27	477.39	2 613.05	3 123.50	3 101.54
出口额	Exports	86.62	615.72	4 233.40	4 999.64	4 911.56
上海进出口总额（亿美元）	Total Value of Imports and Exports (100 million USD)	74.31	547.10	3 688.69	4 374.36	4 367.58
进口额	Imports	21.10	293.56	1 880.85	2 276.47	2 299.51
出口额	Exports	53.21	253.54	1 807.84	2 097.89	2 068.07
国际旅游	**International Tourism**					
上海入境境外旅游者人数（万人次）	Number of Foreign Tourists Through Shanghai Custom (10 000 persons-times)	89.30	181.40	851.12	817.57	800.40
国际旅游（外汇）收入（亿美元）	Foreign Exchange Earnings from International Tourism (100 million USD)	2.31	16.13	64.05	58.35	55.82
金融保险	**Finance and Insurance**					
金融机构存款余额（亿元）	Total Saving Deposits of Financial Institutions (100 million yuan)	851.51	9 349.83	52 190.04	58 186.48	63 555.25
金融机构贷款余额（亿元）	Total Loan Balance of Financial Institutions (100 million yuan)	1 106.80	7 254.26	34 154.17	37 196.79	40 982.48
有价证券成交总额（亿元）	Total Volume of Priced Security Trade (100 million)		49 901	398 396	454 652	547 535
#股　票	Stocks		31 374	304 312	237 560	164 545
原保险保费收入（亿元）	Premium of Primary Income (100 million yuan)	8.99	127.23	883.86	753.11	820.64
原保险赔付支出（亿元）	Payment of Primary Insurance (100 million yuan)	2.22	36.44	194.54	260.71	255.79
教育、科技、文化	**Education, Science&Technology and Culture**					
教　育	**Education**					
在校学生数（万人）	Students Enrollment (10 000 persons)					
高等学校	Institutions of Higher Education	12.13	22.68	51.57	51.13	50.66
普通中学	Regular Secondary Schools	48.31	79.54	59.44	59.17	59.04
小　学	Primary Schools	110.19	78.86	70.16	73.11	76.04
每万人拥有大学生（人）	Number of College and University Students Per 10 000 Persons (person)	90	141	224	218	213

表 1.4 续表 3 continued

	指 标 Indicators	1990	2000	2010	2011	2012
科 技	**Science and Technology**					
科技成果（项）	Achievements in Science and Technology（item）	2 092	1 102	2 318	2 388	2 415
研究与试验发展经费支出（亿元）	Research and Development Expenditures（100 million yuan）	10.13	76.73	481.70	597.62	679.46
研究与试验发展经费支出相当于上海市生产总值比例(%)	**R&D Expenditure as Percentage of Gross Domestic Product（%）**	**1.30**	**1.61**	**2.81**	**3.11**	**3.37**
文 化	**Culture**					
出版数量	Number of Publications					
图 书（亿册、张）	Books（100 million copies）	2.98	2.54	2.89	2.89	3.35
期 刊（亿册）	Periodicals（100 million copies）	1.73	1.85	1.78	1.82	1.76
报 纸（亿份）	Newspapers（100 million copies）	16.16	16.77	15.90	15.61	14.54
故事影片产量（部）	Feature Films Produced(film)	16	10	19	25	22
家庭、生活、环境	**Family, Living and Environment**					
家 庭	**Household**					
家庭总户数（万户）	Total Households（10 000 households）	415.28	475.73	519.27	522.01	524.31
平均每户家庭人口（人）	**Average Persons per Household（person）**	**3.1**	**2.8**	**2.7**	**2.7**	**2.7**
婚 姻	**Marriages and Divorces**					
准予登记结婚（万对）	Marriage Registration Permitted（10 000 couples）	10.77	9.31	13.03	14.89	14.42
离婚人数（万人）	Divorce（10 000 persons）	3.27	6.36	9.34	9.57	10.57
住 宅	**Housing**					
城镇居民人均住房居住面积（平方米）	Per Capita Net Floor Space of Urban Residents(sq. m)	6.6	11.8	16.7	17.0	17.3
农村居民家庭人均居住面积（平方米）	Per Capita Net Floor Space of Rural Residents(sq. m)	37.08	53.58	59.68	58.90	60.42
生 活	**Living**					
城市居民家庭人均可支配收入（元）	**Per Capita Annual Disposable Income of Urban Households(yuan)**	**2 182**	**11 718**	**31 838**	**36 230**	**40 188**
城市居民家庭人均消费支出（元）	Per Capita Annual Consumption Expenditures of Urban Households(yuan)	1 937	8 868	23 200	25 102	26 253
农村居民家庭人均可支配收入（元）	Per Capita Annual Disposable Income of Rural Households(yuan)	1 665	5 565	13 746	15 644	17 401
农村居民家庭人均生活消费支出（元）	Per Capita Annual Consumption Expenditure of Rural Households(yuan)	1 262	4 138	10 225	11 272	12 096
储蓄存款余额（亿元）	Saving Deposits(100 million yuan)	252.16	2 627.07	16 249.29	17 958.22	20 247.24

表 1.4 续表 4　continued

	指　标 Indicators	1990	2000	2010	2011	2012
工　资	**Wages**					
职工工资总额(亿元)	Total Wages of Staff and Workers (100 million yuan)	146.78	614.53	3 018.55	4 505.57	5 347.99
职工平均工资(元)	Average Wages of Staff and Workers (yuan)	2 917	15 420	46 757	51 968	56 300
卫　生	**Health Care**					
医　院(个)	Quantity of Hospitals (unit)	462	459	306	308	317
医　生(万人)	Doctors (10 000 persons)	5.82	4.99	5.13	5.21	5.42
医院床位数(万张)	Quantity of Hospital Beds (10 000 beds)	6.21	7.31	8.48	8.75	9.00
每万人拥有医生(人)	Quantity of Doctors Per 10 000 Persons (person)	44	31	22	22	23
城市建设	**Urban Construction**					
城市基础设施投资额(亿元)	Investment in Urban Infrastructure (100 million yuan)	47.22	449.90	1 497.46	1 157.34	1 038.61
自来水售水量(亿立方米)	Sales Volume of Tap Water (100 million cu. m)	12.25	19.75	24.44	24.41	24.35
用电量(亿千瓦时)	Electric Power Consumption (100 million kwh)	264.74	559.51	1 295.87	1 339.63	1 353.45
天然气销售总量(亿立方米)	Total Sales Volume of Natural Gas (100 million cu. m)		2.16	42.66	51.47	60.01
年末出租车运营总数(辆)	Year-end Operating Taxi Vehicles (vehicle)	11 298	42 943	50 007	50 438	50 683
运营公交车辆数(辆)	Total Number of Public Buses (vehicle)	6 264	17 939	17 455	16 589	16 695
道路长度(公里)	Length of Roads (km)	1 631	6 641	16 687	16 792	17 316
城市人均公园绿地面积(平方米)	Public Green Areas Per Capita (sq. m)	1.02	4.60	13.00	13.10	13.29
城市绿化覆盖率(%)	Coverage Rate of Urban Green Areas (%)	12.4	22.2	38.2	38.2	38.3
森林覆盖率(%)	Coverage Rate of Forest (%)	5.5	9.2	12.6	12.6	12.6
环境保护投资相当于上海市生产总值比例(%)	Environment Protection Investment as Percentage of Gross Domestic Product (%)		3.10	2.96	2.91	2.83
环境空气质量优良率(%)	Rate of Good Ambient Air Quality (%)		80.8	92.1	92.3	93.7
火灾、交通事故	**Fires and Traffic Accidents**					
火灾发生数(起)	Quantity of Fires (unit)	2 146	5 164	5 703	5 813	4 469
火灾损失额(万元)	Loss of Fires (10 000 yuan)	1 868	1 919	22 949	11 000	6 924
交通事故发生数(万起)	Quantity of Traffic Accidents (10 000 unit)	0.76	4.13	0.22	0.21	0.23
交通事故损失额(万元)	Loss of Traffic Accidents (10 000 yuan)	1 345	20 391	967	1 349	1 488

注：本表总量指标中的价值量指标均按当年价格计算。
Note: The data in value terms in the table are calculated at current prices.

表 1.5 主要年份社会经济主要指标发展速度
GROWTH RATE OF MAJOR SOCIAL AND ECONOMIC INDICATORS IN MAIN YEARS

单位:%

指 标	Indicators	2012 年比下列各年增长 Indicator's Growth Rate Between 2012 and Year Below			
		1990	2000	2010	2011
年末常住人口	Year-end Residnet Population	78.4	48.0	3.4	1.4
上海市生产总值	Gross Domestic Product	10.1 倍	2.5 倍	16.3	7.5
第一产业	Primary Industry	12.7	-11.1	-0.2	0.5
第二产业	Secondary Industry	9 倍	2.3 倍	9.6	3.1
第三产业	Tertiary Industry	12.9 倍	2.7 倍	21.2	10.6
全社会固定资产投资总额	Total Investment in Fixed Assets	23.5 倍	1.9 倍	4.0	3.7
地方财政收入	Local Fiscal Revenue	21.4 倍	6.5 倍	30.3	9.2
地方财政支出	Local Fiscal Expenditure	54.4 倍	5.7 倍	26.7	6.9
农业总产值	Gross Output Value of Agriculture	42.1	-10.3	-0.1	0.5
工业总产值	Gross Output Value of Industry	17.9 倍	3.6 倍	6.3	-0.3
轻工业	Light Industry	8.2 倍	1.8 倍	9.7	1.3
重工业	Heavy Industry	27.2 倍	4.7 倍	5.4	-0.7
货物运输量	Freight Transportation Volume	3.1 倍	96.8	16.5	1.1
旅客发送量	Passenger Departures	2.8 倍	1.1 倍	8.3	7.6
港口货物吞吐量	Port Cargo Throughput	4.3 倍	2.6 倍	12.6	1.1
社会消费品零售总额	Retail Sales of Consumer Goods	21.2 倍	3 倍	22.1	8.8
上海关区进出口总额	Total Trade Value Through Customs	45.3 倍	6.3 倍	17.0	-1.4
进口额	Imports	35 倍	5.5 倍	18.7	-0.7
出口额	Exports	55.7 倍	7 倍	16	-1.8
上海进出口总额	Total Value of Imports and Exports	57.8 倍	7 倍	18.4	-0.2
进口额	Imports	108 倍	6.8 倍	22.3	1.0
出口额	Exports	37.9 倍	7.2 倍	14.4	-1.4
直接吸收外资	Foreign Direct Investment				
签订合同项目	Number of Contracts	18.9 倍	1.2 倍	3.5	-6.6
签订合同金额	Contractual Foreign Investment	103.4 倍	2.5 倍	45.9	11.1
实际到位金额	Foreign Investment Actually Absorbed	84.8 倍	3.8 倍	36.5	20.5
城市居民家庭人均可支配收入	Per Capita Annual Disposable Income of Urban Households	19 倍	2.7 倍	26.2	10.9
城市居民家庭人均消费支出	Per Capita Annual Consumption Expenditures of Urban Households	12.5 倍	1.9 倍	13.2	4.6
农村居民家庭人均可支配收入	Per Capita Annual Disposable Income of Rural Households	9.5 倍	2.1 倍	26.6	11.2
农村居民家庭人均生活消费支出	Per Capita Annual Consumption Expenditures of Rural Households	8.6 倍	1.9 倍	18.3	7.3
城市基础设施投资额	Investment in Urban Infrastructure	22.3 倍	1.3 倍	-25.5	-9.8
医 生	Doctors	-6.9	8.6	5.7	4.0
高等学校在校学生	Student Enrollment of Institutions of Higher Education	3.2 倍	1.2 倍	-1.8	-0.9

注：本表速度指标中，上海市生产总值及三次产业、工业总产值、农业总产值均按可比价格计算。

Note: The growth rates of the following indicators are calculated by comparable prices: Gross Domestic Product and three industries, gross output value of agriculture and Industry.

表 1.5 续表 continued

单位:%

指 标	Indicators	平均每年增长 Indicators' Average Annual Growth Rate 1991~2012	2001~2012	2011~2012
年末常住人口	Year-end Resident Population	2.7	3.3	1.7
上海市生产总值	Gross Domestic Product	11.6	10.9	7.8
第一产业	Primary Industry	0.5	-1.0	-0.1
第二产业	Secondary Industry	11.1	10.4	4.7
第三产业	Tertiary Industry	12.7	11.5	10.1
全社会固定资产投资总额	Total Investment in Fixed Assets	19.0	11.3	1.4
地方财政收入	Local Fiscal Revenue	15.2	18.3	14.1
地方财政支出	Local Fiscal Expenditure	20.0	17.2	12.6
农业总产值	Gross Output Value of Agriculture	1.6	-0.9	-0.1
工业总产值	Gross Output Value of Industry	14.3	13.6	3.1
轻工业	Light Industry	10.6	9.1	4.7
重工业	Heavy Industry	16.4	15.6	2.6
货物运输量	Freight Transportation Volume	6.7	5.8	7.9
旅客发送量	Passenger Departures	6.2	6.4	4.1
港口货物吞吐量	Port Cargo Throughput	7.8	11.3	6.1
社会消费品零售总额	Retail Sales of Consumer Goods	15.1	12.2	10.5
上海关区进出口总额	Total Trade Value Through Customs	19.0	18.1	8.2
进口额	Imports	17.7	16.9	8.9
出口额	Exports	20.1	18.9	7.7
上海市进出口总额	Total Value of Imports and Exports	20.3	18.9	8.8
进口额	Imports	23.8	18.7	10.6
出口额	Exports	18.1	19.1	7.0
城市居民家庭人均可支配收入	Per Capita Annual Disposable Income of Urban Households	14.6	11.6	12.4
城市居民家庭人均消费支出	Per Capita Annual Consumption Expenditures of Urban Households	12.6	9.4	6.4
农村居民家庭人均可支配收入	Per Capita Annual Disposable Income of Rural Households	11.3	10.0	12.5
农村居民家庭人均生活消费支出	Per Capita Consumption Expenditure of Rural Households	10.8	9.4	8.8
医 生	Doctors	-0.3	0.7	2.8
高等学校在校学生	Student Enrollment of Institutions of Higher Education	6.7	6.9	-0.9
城市基础设施投资额	Investment in Urban Infrastructure	20.7	13.2	-15.0

表 1.6　主要年份社会经济发展结构指标
STRUCTURAL INDICATORS OF SOCIAL AND ECONOMIC DEVELOPMENT IN MAIN YEARS

单位:%

指标	Indicators	1990	2000	2010	2011	2012
农业非农业人口结构	Structure of Agriculture and Non-agriculture	100	100	100	100	100
农　业	Agriculture	32.6	25.4	11.1	10.7	10.2
非农业	Non-agriculture	67.4	74.6	88.9	89.3	89.8
人口性别结构	Structure of Sex	100	100	100	100	100
男	Male	50.4	50.4	49.8	49.8	49.7
女	Female	49.6	49.6	50.2	50.2	50.3
上海市生产总值产业结构	Industrial Structure of GDP	100	100	100	100	100
第一产业	Primary Industry	4.4	1.6	0.7	0.7	0.6
第二产业	Secondary Industry	64.7	46.3	42.0	41.3	39.0
第三产业	Tertiary Industry	30.9	52.1	57.3	58.0	60.4
上海市生产总值所有制结构	Ownership Structure of GDP	100	100	100	100	100
公有制经济	Public State-owned	95.4	71.4	50.5	49.9	49.3
国有经济	State-owned	71.2	55.0	45.2	45.1	44.6
集体经济	Collective-owned	24.2	16.4	5.3	4.8	4.7
非公有制经济	Non-state-owned	4.6	28.6	49.5	50.1	50.7
全社会固定资产投资所有制结构	Ownership Structure of Total Investment	100	100	100	100	100
国有经济	State-owned	84.7	44.4	42.0	37.0	35.3
非国有经济	Non-State-owned	15.3	55.6	58.0	63.0	64.7
地方财政收入结构	Structure of Local Fiscal Revenue	100	100	100	100	100
# 增值税	Value-added Tax		18.8	13.5	12.1	17.8
营业税	Business Tax		30.9	32.5	30.4	24.0
企业所得税	Enterprise Income Tax		20.7	21.1	21.3	21.6
个人所得税	Personal Income Tax		12.1	9.1	9.2	8.5
外商直接投资实际吸收外资结构	Foreign Direct Investment Structure of Foreign Investment Actually Absorbed	100	100	100	100	100
# 合资企业	Joint Ventures	61.0	40.9	16.0	15.8	17.9
合作企业	Coopratïve Enterprises	37.9	9.5	1.5	2.0	3.8
独资企业	Sole-foreign Enterprises	1.1	49.6	81.6	81.0	77.9
农业总产值结构	Structure of Gross Output Value of Agriculture	100	100	100.0	100.0	100.0
# 种植业	Planting	42.7	41.5	54.1	52.5	53.3
牧　业	Animal Husbandry	44.4	40.3	21.9	24.6	22.6
渔　业	Fishery	11.8	17.5	18.3	17.4	17.9
工业总产值结构	Structure of Gross Output Value of Industry	100	100	100	100	100
轻工业	Light Industry	51.5	41.3	21.6	21.9	22.6
重工业	Heavy Industry	48.5	58.7	78.4	78.1	77.4

表 1.6 续表 continued

单位:%

	指 标 Indicators	1990	2000	2010	2011	2012
货物运输总量结构	Structure of Freight Transportation	100	100	100	100	100
铁 路	Railways	5.5	2.2	1.2	1.0	0.9
公 路	Roadways	38.2	59.1	50.5	45.7	45.5
水 运	Waterways	56.3	38.5	47.9	52.9	53.3
民用航空	Civil Aviation	…	0.2	0.5	0.4	0.4
社会消费品零售总额结构	Structure of Retail Sales of Consumer Goods	100	100	100	100	100
吃	Food	42.6	39.8	30.1	29.9	28.4
穿	Clothing	15.7	13.4	11.3	11.1	11.6
用	Articles	41.1	46.0	52.7	52.7	53.8
烧	Fuels	0.6	0.8	5.9	6.3	6.1
上海市出口总额结构	Structure of Exports		100	100	100	100
#一般贸易	General Trade		40.1	35.0	36.8	38.2
加工贸易	Processing Trade		58.3	55.5	52.0	49.1
中资金融机构人民币存款结构	Structure of RMB Saving Deposit in Chinese Financial Instituation	100	100	100	100	100
#单位存款	Unit Deposets	43.1	56.9	45.0	57.4	56.2
储蓄存款	Saving Deposits	41.1	32.5	33.2	32.6	33.9
中资金融机构人民币贷款结构	Structure of RMB Loans in Chinese Financial Instituation	100	100	100	100	100
#短期贷款	Short Term Loans	75.2	72.9	24.0	25.7	26.7
中长期贷款	Medium and Long Term Loans	14.8	18.0	68.2	67.0	63.1
在校学生结构	Structure of Students Enrollment	100	100	100	100	100
大学生	University and College Students	7.1	12.5	28.5	27.9	27.3
中学生	Secondary Students	28.3	43.9	32.8	32.2	31.8
小学生	Primary Students	64.6	43.6	38.7	39.9	40.9
城市居民消费支出结构	Consumption Structure of Urban Households	100	100	100	100	100
#食 品	Food	56.5	44.5	33.5	35.5	36.8
衣 着	Clothing	10.7	6.4	7.7	8.2	8.0
家庭设备、用品及服务	Household Facilities, Articles and Services	10.1	7.7	7.8	7.3	7.3
交通和通信	Transportation and Communications	3.0	8.6	17.6	15.2	17.4
教育文化娱乐服务	Cultural, Education and Recreation Services	11.9	14.5	14.5	14.9	14.2
居 住	Residence	4.7	9.0	9.3	8.9	6.8
农村居民消费支出结构	Consumption Structure of Rural Households	100	100	100	100	100
#食 品	Food	46.4	44.0	37.2	40.1	40.0
衣 着	Clothing	8.5	4.9	5.4	5.7	5.8
家庭设备、用品及服务	Household Facilities, Articles and Services	10.2	5.4	5.2	5.8	5.3
交通和通信	Transportation and Communications	0.5	6.7	14.3	11.6	14.1
文教娱乐用品及服务	Culture, Education, Recreation Articles and Services	4.7	13.5	9.9	10.1	9.0
居 住	Residence	21.6	17.5	20.2	16.0	15.2
卫生机构数结构	Structure of Health Care Institutions	100	100	100	100	100
#医 院	Hospitals	6.0	10.4	9.4	9.2	9.1
卫生技术人员结构	Structure of Medical Professionals	100	100	100	100	100
#医 生	Doctors	49.2	46.6	37.9	37.5	37.1
护师、护士	Senior and Junior Nurses	27.6	34.4	41.3	42.3	43.3

注：2011 年起单位存款口径进行了调整，故与往年数据不可比。
Note: The statistic caliber of unit deposits has been adjusted since 2011, so the data are not comparable with the previous years.

表 1.7 各时期社会经济主要指标
MAJOR SOCIAL AND ECONOMIC INDICATORS OF EACH PERIOD

时期 Period		上海市生产总值（亿元）Gross Domestic Product (100 million yuan)	其中 of which 第一产业 Primary Industry	第二产业 Secondary Industry	第三产业 Tertiary Industry	地方财政收入（亿元）Local Fiscal Revenue (100 million yuan)
"一五"时期	"First Five-year Plan" Period	293.26	12.56	163.89	116.81	14.93
"二五"时期	"Second Five-year Plan" Period	568.99	21.03	412.70	135.26	304.28
1963～1965		304.94	17.28	220.81	66.85	172.51
"三五"时期	"Third Five-year Plan" Period	657.06	37.64	487.88	131.54	374.19
"四五"时期	"Fourth Five-year Plan" Period	918.76	42.75	708.84	167.17	633.79
"五五"时期	"Fifth Five-year Plan" Period	1 309.61	49.26	1 004.23	256.12	797.56
"六五"时期	"Sixth Five-year Plan" Period	1 871.24	74.20	1 349.98	447.06	846.92
"七五"时期	"Seventh Five-year Plan" Period	3 162.79	132.52	2 105.23	925.04	846.96
"八五"时期	"Eighth Five-year Plan" Period	8 017.61	213.47	4 698.27	3 105.87	1 006.06
"九五"时期	"Ninth Five-year Plan" Period	19 157.33	365.76	9 434.90	9 356.67	1 962.85
"十五"时期	"Tenth Five-year Plan" Period	34 965.87	412.41	16 507.97	18 045.49	4 792.94
"十一五"时期	"Eleventh Five-year Program" Period	69 348.55	535.42	29 846.95	38 966.18	11 499.22

表 1.7 续表 continued

时期 Period		地方财政支出（亿元）Local Fiscal Expenditure (100 million yuan)	工业总产值（亿元）Gross Output Value of Industry (100 million yuan)	全社会固定资产投资总额（亿元）Total Investment in Fixed Assets (100 million yuan)	上海市出口总额（亿美元）Total Exports Value (100 million USD)	社会消费品零售总额（亿元）Retail Sales of Consumer Goods (100 million yuan)
"一五"时期	"First Five-year Plan" Period	12.25	512.03	19.29	17.46	121.02
"二五"时期	"Second Five-year Plan" Period	60.79	1 069.50	55.60	31.00	145.82
1963～1965		19.28	596.63	20.29	20.12	79.50
"三五"时期	"Third Five-year Plan" Period	39.41	1 334.94	34.77	43.08	153.86
"四五"时期	"Fourth Five-year Plan" Period	86.78	1 894.01	95.79	92.86	200.62
"五五"时期	"Fifth Five-year Plan" Period	111.30	2 550.91	151.44	150.33	302.07
"六五"时期	"Sixth Five-year Plan" Period	138.52	3 509.15	412.74	180.08	576.32
"七五"时期	"Seventh Five-year Plan" Period	327.68	6 498.13	1 020.34	226.96	1 383.16
"八五"时期	"Eighth Five-year Plan" Period	775.11	17 308.90	3 994.67	403.31	3 408.52
"九五"时期	"Ninth Five-year Plan" Period	2 421.50	29 776.04	9 620.86	880.57	7 874.26
"十五"时期	"Tenth Five-year Plan" Period	5 762.87	59 716.74	13 261.11	2 724.27	12 261.12
"十一五"时期	"Eleventh Five-year Program" Period	12 925.94	124 634.89	23 804.15	7 495.49	23 069.47

表 1.8 各时期社会经济主要指标平均增长率
GROWTH RATE OF MAJOR SOCIAL AND ECONOMIC INDICATORS OF EACH PERIOD

单位:%

时 期	Period	上海市生产总值 Gross Domestic Product	其中 of which 第一产业 Primary Industry	第二产业 Secondary Industry	第三产业 Tertiary Industry	地 方 财政收入 Local Fiscal Revenue
"一五"时期	"First Five-year Plan" Period	13.8	3.3	18.4	8.3	12.6
"二五"时期	"Second Five-year Plan" Period	1.6	1.3	4.1	-3.1	57.2
1963~1965		17.0	11.6	21.8	5.6	12.3
"三五"时期	"Third Five-year Plan" Period	8.7	3.3	9.7	5.7	9.7
"四五"时期	"Fourth Five-year Plan" Period	6.6	-1.6	7.1	6.2	6.4
"五五"时期	"Fifth Five-year Plan" Period	8.4	0.9	8.6	8.6	5.1
"六五"时期	"Sixth Five-year Plan" Period	9.1	4.3	8.3	12.3	1.1
"七五"时期	"Seventh Five-year Plan" Period	5.7	1.2	5.0	8.0	-1.6
"八五"时期	"Eighth Five-year Plan" Period	13.1	1.4	13.9	12.8	6.0
"九五"时期	"Ninth Five-year Plan" Period	11.5	3.4	9.7	15.5	17.0
"十五"时期	"Tenth Five-year Plan" Period	11.9	-1.4	13.1	11.2	23.6
"十一五"时期	"Eleventh Five-year Program" Period	11.2	-0.9	10.2	12.3	14.9

表 1.8 续表 continued

单位:%

时 期	Period	地 方 财政支出 Local Fiscal Expenditure	工 业 总产值 Gross Output Value of Industry	全社会固定资产投资总额 Total Investment in Fixed Assets	上海市出口总额 Total Exports Value	社会消费品零售总额 Retail Sales of Consumer Goods
"一五"时期	"First Five-year Plan" Period	12.3	14.5	23.1	30.6	5.6
"二五"时期	"Second Five-year Plan" Period	0.6	4.9	26.5	4.2	1.2
1963~1965		25.2	18.8	31.4	11.4	-0.1
"三五"时期	"Third Five-year Plan" Period	11.2	10.2	-3.6	2.5	3.3
"四五"时期	"Fourth Five-year Plan" Period	15.5	7.5	19.4	20.7	8.4
"五五"时期	"Fifth Five-year Plan" Period	-6.3	7.6	-2.4	14.0	11.0
"六五"时期	"Sixth Five-year Plan" Period	19.2	7.7	20.6	-4.7	16.6
"七五"时期	"Seventh Five-year Plan" Period	10.4	5.9	18.7	9.6	14.0
"八五"时期	"Eighth Five-year Plan" Period	28.8	18.0	45.4	16.8	25.8
"九五"时期	"Ninth Five-year Plan" Period	18.4	12.3	6.2	17.0	12.2
"十五"时期	"Tenth Five-year Plan" Period	21.7	19.2	11.9	29.0	9.8
"十一五"时期	"Eleventh Five-year Program" Period	14.7	12.6	10.0	14.8	15.3

表 1.9 国民经济主要指标比上年增长(1978～2012)
GROWTH RATE OF MAJOR NATIONAL ECONOMIC INDICATORS OVER PRECEDING YEAR

单位:%

年 份 Year	上海市 生产总值 Gross Domestic Product	地 方 财政收入 Local Fiscal Revenue	地 方 财政支出 Local Fiscal Expenditure	工 业 总产值 Gross Output Value of Industry	全社会固定资产 投资总额 Total Investment in Fixed Assets
1978	15.8	14.6	51.4	12.1	55.1
1979	7.4	2.1	4.0	8.6	27.5
1980	8.4	1.2	-29.1	6.5	27.7
1981	5.6	-0.2	-0.6	3.7	20.2
1982	7.2	-3.6	8.5	4.7	30.7
1983	7.8	-6.9	8.3	7.0	6.5
1984	11.6	4.8	35.4	9.9	21.5
1985	13.4	12.4	51.9	13.5	28.5
1986	4.4	-2.6	28.2	5.5	23.9
1987	7.5	-5.8	-8.9	6.7	26.8
1988	10.1	-4.3	22.3	10.5	31.7
1989	3.0	3.3	11.3	3.0	-12.4
1990	3.5	0.1	3.1	4.0	5.7
1991	7.1	5.1	13.9	14.1	13.7
1992	14.8	5.7	10.4	20.2	38.4
1993	15.1	30.6	36.1	20.0	83.0
1994	14.5	-27.7	52.3	18.2	71.8
1995	14.3	29.6	36.0	17.4	42.6
1996	13.1	26.9	27.9	15.5	21.9
1997	12.8	22.1	25.2	14.5	1.3
1998	10.3	11.3	12.1	7.8	-0.6
1999	10.4	10.1	13.7	10.5	-5.5
2000	11.0	15.3	14.0	13.5	0.7
2001	10.5	24.6	16.6	16.4	6.7
2002	11.3	16.1	20.9	14.6	9.6
2003	12.3	24.9	25.6	31.4	12.1
2004	14.2	24.5	26.6	20.3	25.8
2005	11.4	28.7	19.0	13.9	14.8
2006	12.7	11.6	9.2	13.9	10.8
2007	15.2	31.4	21.4	15.7	13.6
2008	9.7	13.3	18.9	8.1	8.3
2009	8.2	7.7	15.3	3.2	9.2
2010	10.3	13.1	10.5	22.9	0.8
2011	8.2	19.4	18.5	6.6	0.3
2012	7.5	9.2	6.9	-0.3	3.7

表 1.9 续表 continued

单位:%

年　份 Year	上海市 进出口总额 Total Value of Import and Export	#出口总额 Export	社会消费品 零售总额 Retail Sales of Consumer Goods	直接吸收 外资合同金额 Contracted Foreign Direct Investment	直接吸收 外资实际 到位金额 Actually Absorbed Foreign Direct Investment	港口货物 吞吐量 Cargo Handled at Ports	城市居民家庭 人均可支配收入 Per Capita Annual Disposable Income of Urban Households
1978	30.4	30.3	9.8			30.6	
1979	28.2	27.0	26.2			5.0	
1980	16.2	16.1	17.8			1.6	
1981	-7.9	-10.8	10.3	1.0 倍	…	-1.7	平
1982	-6.2	-5.3	1.2	1.8 倍	…	7.7	3.5
1983	6.3	1.2	12.1	1.8 倍	2.7 倍	2.4	4.0
1984	6.3	-1.7	22.9	3.1 倍	1.5 倍	9.5	21.6
1985	17.6	-6.3	40.1	56.4	1.2 倍	12.2	28.9
1986	0.6	6.6	13.5	-68.9	58.1	11.6	20.3
1987	15.2	16.1	14.4	35.8	1.2 倍	1.8	11.1
1988	20.8	10.7	31.3	28.7	71.7	3.8	19.9
1989	8.3	9.3	12.0	6.6	15.9	9.6	14.6
1990	-5.3	5.7	0.7	20.9	-58.1	-4.4	10.5
1991	8.2	7.9	14.4	30.4	-1.1	5.2	13.9
1992	21.3	14.2	21.7	5.7 倍	6.2 倍	11.0	21.1
1993	30.5	12.6	45.4	1.0 倍	84.1	8.0	42.2
1994	24.6	23.0	23.5	42.3	39.4	-5.8	37.2
1995	19.9	27.5	25.9	0.2	0.6	-0.1	22.2
1996	17.0	14.3	19.7	8.4	45.1	-1.0	13.8
1997	11.2	11.2	14.1	-8.4	2.0	…	3.4
1998	26.6	8.4	11.0	9.9	-24.3	-0.1	4.0
1999	23.2	17.7	8.1	-29.8	-16.2	13.7	24.6
2000	41.7	35.0	8.3	55.7	3.7	9.7	7.2
2001	11.3	9.0	8.1	15.4	39.0	8.1	9.9
2002	19.3	16.0	9.3	43.4	14.5	19.4	11.5
2003	54.7	51.2	9.1	23.5	30.1	19.8	12.2
2004	42.4	51.6	10.5	12.6	11.8	19.8	12.2
2005	16.5	23.4	12.1	18.3	4.7	16.9	11.8
2006	22.1	25.2	13.3	5.4	3.8	21.3	10.8
2007	24.4	26.7	14.8	2.0	11.4	4.5	14.3
2008	13.8	17.7	18.2	15.1	27.3	3.6	12.9
2009	-13.8	-16.2	13.0	-22.3	4.5	1.8	8.1
2010	32.8	27.4	17.3	15.1	5.5	10.4	10.4
2011	18.6	16.0	12.3	31.3	13.3	11.4	13.8
2012	-0.2	-1.4	8.8	11.1	20.5	1.1	10.9

表 1.10 上海社会经济主要指标占全国比重(2012)
PERCENTAGE OF THE NATIONAL TOTAL OF SHANGHAI'S MAJOR SOCIAL AND ECONOMIC INDICATORS

指 标	Indicators	全 国 Country	上 海 Shanghai	上海占全国比重(%) Percentage of the National Total(%)
生产总值(亿元)	Gross Domestic Product (100 million yuan)	519 322.1	20 181.72	3.9
第一产业	Primary Industry	52 377.0	127.80	0.2
第二产业	Secondary Industry	235 318.6	7 854.77	3.3
#工 业	Industry	199 859.6	7 097.76	3.6
第三产业	Tertiary Industry	231 626.5	12 199.15	5.3
港口货物吞吐量(亿吨)	Port Cargo Handled at Seaports (100 millions tons)	107.76	7.36	6.8
邮电业务总量(亿元)	Revenue of Post and Telecommunication (100 million yuan)	15 021.5	190.83	1.3
全社会固定资产投资总额(亿元)	Total Investment in Fixed Assets (100 million yuan)	374 675.7	5 254.38	1.4
社会消费品零售总额(亿元)	Retail Sales of Consumer Goods (100 million yuan)	210 307	7 412.30	3.5
上海关区进出口总额(亿美元)	Total Trade Value Through Customs (100 million USD)	38 667.61	8 013.10	20.7
进口额	Imports	18 178.26	3 101.54	17.1
出口额	Exports	20 489.35	4 911.56	24.0
外商直接投资实际到位金额(亿美元)	Foreign Direct Investment Actually Absorbed (100 million USD)	1 117.16	151.85	13.6
国际旅游入境人数(万人次)	Number of International Tourists (10 000 person-times)	13 240.5	800.40	6.0
研究与试验发展经费支出(亿元)	Research and Development Expenditure (100 million yuan)	10 240.00	679.46	6.6
图书出版量(亿册/张)	Books Published (100 million copies/signatures)	81	3.35	4.1
期 刊(亿册)	Periodicals (100 million copies)	34	1.76	5.2
报纸出版量(亿份)	Newspapers Published (100 million copies)	476	14.54	3.1
医 生(万人)	Doctors (10 000 persons)	261.6	5.42	2.1
医院床位数(万张)	Beds in Hospitals (10 000 beds)	416.1	9.00	2.2

注:全国港口货物吞吐量统计口径为沿海规模以上港口货物吞吐量。
Note: The statistical range of national port cargo handled at seaports is port cargo handled at coastal seaports above the set scale.

表 1.11 主要年份人大情况
BASIC STATISTICS OF SHANGHAI MUNICIPAL PEOPLE'S CONGRESS IN MAIN YEARS

类 别	Types	2000	2010	2011	2012
全国人大代表人数(人)	Quantity of National Congress(person)	68	66	66	65
#女 性	Female	17	17	17	17
全国人大代表提出议案(件)	Proposals Offered by National Congress Representations (case)		21	21	21
市人大代表人数(人)	Quantity of Municipal Congress Representatives (person)	865	864	864	864
#女 性	Female	203	244	244	243
市人大常委会组成人员数(人)	Quantity of Municipal Standing Committee (person)	65	64	65	65
#女 性	Female	13	9	11	10
市人大代表提出议案(件)	Proposals Offered by Municipal Congress Representatives(case)		78	20	65
区县人大代表人数(人)	Quantity of District Level Congress Representatives(person)	4 944	4 667	4 542	4 640
#女 性	Female	1 451	1 454	1 442	1 555
区县人大常委人数(人)	Quantity of District Level Standing Committee (person)	432	414	435	463
#女 性	Female	67	94	95	124

注：本表数据由市人大代表工作委员会提供。
Note: Data in this Table are provided by Shanghai Committee of People's Congress.

表 1.12 主要年份政协情况
BASIC STATISTICS ON SHANGHAI MUNICIPAL PEOPLE'S POLITICAL CONSULTATIVE CONFERENCE IN MAIN YEARS

类 别	Types	2000	2010	2011	2012
全国政协委员人数(人)	Quantity of National Commissary (person)	104	109	108	108
#女 性	Female	20	18	18	18
全国政协委员提出提案(件)	Proposals Offered by National Commissary (case)		30	241	241
市政协委员人数(人)	Quantity of Municipal Commissary(person)	729	817	826	815
#女 性	Female	120	168	170	185
市政协常委人数(人)	Quantity of Municipal Standing Committee(person)	121	132	145	141
#女 性	Female	20	24	25	23
市政协委员提出提案(件)	Proposals Offered by Municipal Commissary (case)	1 197	944	964	978
区县政协委员人数(人)	Quantity of District Level Commissary(person)	4 802	5 280	5 166	5 084
#女 性	Female	1 230	1 459	1 467	1 537
区县政协常委人数(人)	Quantity of District Level Standing Committee(person)	707	709	700	740
#女 性	Female	174	154	147	200

注：本表数据由市政协提供。
Note: Data in this table are provided by Shanghai Municipal People's Political Consultative Conference

上 / 海 / 统 / 计 / 年 / 鉴

主要统计指标解释

■ 行政区划

指国家对行政区域的划分。根据宪法规定，我国的行政区域划分如下：(1)全国分为省、自治区、直辖市；(2)省、自治区分为自治州、县、自治县、市；(3)自治州分为县、自治县、市；(4)县、自治县分为乡、民族乡、镇；(5)直辖市和较大的市分为区、县；(6)国家在必要时设立的特别行政区。

■ 气　候

指地球与大气之间长期能量交换与质量交换所形成的一种自然环境状态，它是多种因素综合作用的结果。气候既是人类生活和生产的环境要素之一，又是供给人类生活和生产的重要资源。气温、降水、湿度等气象要素的多年平均值是用来描述一个地区气候状况的主要参数，而各种气象要素某年、某月的平均值(或总量)则可以反映出该时期天气气候状况的重要特征。

■ 气　温

指空气的温度，一般以摄氏度(℃)为单位表示。气象观测的温度表是放在离地面约 1.5 米处通风良好的百叶箱里测量的，因此，通常说的气温指的是离地面 1.5 米处百叶箱中的温度。其统计计算方法为：

月平均气温是将全月各日的平均气温相加，除以该月的天数而得。

年平均气温是将 12 个月的月平均气温累加后除以 12 而得。

■ 降水量

指从天空降落到地面的液态或固态(经融化后)水，未经蒸发、渗透、流失而在地面上积聚的深度。其统计计算方法为：

月降水量是将全月各日的降水量累加而得。

年降水量是将 12 个月的月降水量累加而得。

■ 日照时间

指太阳实际照射地面的时间。其统计方法与降水量相同。

■ 国民经济行业分类

《国民经济行业分类》国家标准于 1984 年首次发布，1994 年对其进行了第一次修订，2002 年为第二次修订，2011 年为第三次修订。

本年鉴的行业分类除特别说明外均使用 2011 年修订的行业分类标准。

2011 年新行业分类标准立足我国社会经济发展的实际情况，确保国家经济结构和产业结构的完整性、科学性和可观察性；确保国家统计、核算真实的反映我国的经济结构和产业结构。此次修订不仅坚持行业分类的修订原则和国际惯例，同时顺应《国务院关于加快培育和发展战略性新兴产业的决定》要求，准确反映一定时期内国民经济行业的构成状况。

此次修订主要调整如下：

1. 调整部门门类名称和顺序。如将“信息传输、计算机服务和软件业”更名为“信息传输、软件业和信息技术服务业”，将“科学研究、技术服务和地址勘查业”更名为“科学研究和技术服务业”，将“居民服务和其他服务业”更名为“居民服务、修理和其他服务业”，将“卫生、社会保障和社会福利业”更名为“卫生和社会工作”。但整体行业门类的数目保持不变，保证了行业分类的延续性。

2. 为与联合国分类相对应以及反映我国产业的状况，行业大类由 95 个调整为 96 个，新增了“开采辅助活动”、“汽车制造业”、“金属制造、机械和设备修理业”、“房屋建筑业”、“互联网和相关服务”、“机动车、电子产品和日用品修理业”等 6 大类，减少了“建筑装修业”、“城市公共交通业”、“其他金融活动”、“地址勘查业”等 4 大类，合并“橡胶制品业”和“塑料制品业”为一个大类。

3. 为反映我国日益发展的互联网、信息技术、金融、影视娱乐等产业，行业中类新增了“互联网接入及相关服务”、“信息系统集成服务”、“化纤织造及印染精加工”等中类，取消了“猪的饲养”、“纺织制成品制造”等中类。

4. 为与联合国 ISIC Rev.4 的小类进行转换同时反映我国新兴产业，行业小类增加了“稻谷种植”、“食用菌种植”“葡萄的种植”等小类，取消了“常用有色金属压延加工”、“制帽”、“车辆、飞机及工程机械轮胎制造”等小类。

■ 各个计划时期

表内所用各个“时期”代表的年分如下：恢复时期为 1950 到 1952 年；第一个五年计划时期(简称“一五”时期)为 1953 到 1957 年；第二个五年计划时期(简称“二五”时期)为 1958 到 1962 年；第三个五年计划时期(简称“三五”时期)为

主要统计指标解释

1966 到 1970 年；第四个五年计划时期（简称“四五”时期）为 1971 到 1975 年；第五个五年计划时期（简称“五五”时期）为 1976 到 1980 年；第六个五年计划时期（简称“六五”时期）为 1981 到 1985 年；第七个五年计划时期（简称“七五”时期）为 1986 到 1990 年；第八个五年计划时期（简称“八五”时期）为 1991 到 1995 年；第九个五年计划时期（简称“九五”时期）为 1996 到 2000 年；第十个五年计划时期（简称“十五”时期）为 2001 到 2005 年；第十一个五年规划时期（简称“十一五”时期）为 2006 到 2010 年。

■ 指　数

指数是一种表明社会经济现象动态的相对数。运用指数可以测定不能直接相加和直接对比的社会经济现象的总动态；可以分析社会经济现象总变动中各因素变动的影响程度；可以研究总平均指标变动中各组标志水平和总体结构变动的作用。它是在把各个年份的产值换算成可比价格的基础上，根据定基数等于相应各个环比指数的连乘积这个换算关系计算出来的。

本年鉴所列的上海市生产总值、工业总产值、农业总产值等指标增长速度，就是分别使用上海市生产总值指数、工业总产值指数、农业总产值指数直接计算的。

■ 平均每年增长速度

在我国计算平均增长速度有两种方法。一种是习惯上经常使用的“水平法”，又称几何平均法，是以间隔期最后一年的水平同基期水平对比来计算平均每年增长（或下降）速度；另一种是“累计法”，又称代数平均法或方程法，是以间隔期内各年水平的总和同基期水平对比来计算平均每年增长（或下降）速度。

在一般正常情况下，两种方法计算的平均每年增长速度比较接近。但在经济发展不平衡，出现大起大落时，两种方法计算的结果差别较大。

本年鉴内所列的平均每年增长速度，除固定资产投资、直接吸收外资是用“累计法”计算以外，其余均用“水平法”计算。从某年到某年平均增长速度的年份，均不包括基期年在内。如 1991-2009 年平均增长速度是以 1990 年为基期计算的，余类推。

SHANGHAI STATISTICAL YEARBOOK

EXPLANATORY NOTES TO MAJOR STATISTICAL INDICATORS

□ Administrative Division

Administrative Division refers to the division of administrative areas by the state. The Constitution of the People's Republic of China stipulates that the administrative areas in China are divided as: 1) The whole country is divided into provinces, autonomous regions and municipalities directly under the central government; 2)Provinces and autonomous regions are divided into autonomous prefectures, counties, autonomous counties and cities; 3) Autonomous prefectures are divided into counties, autonomous counties and cities; 4) Counties and autonomous counties are divided into townships, nationality townships and towns; 5) Municipalities and large cities are divided into districts and counties, 6) The state shall, when necessary, establish special administrative regions.

□ Climate

Climate refers to the natural environmental status formed by the long-term exchange of energy and mass between the earth and the air, and is the results of interaction of many factors. Climate is both one of the environment factors and the important resources for the living and production activities of the human being. The average values across several years of meteorological factors such as temperature, rainfall and humidity are used as important parameters to describe the climate of a region, while the average values (or total values) of a given year or month of meteorological factors reflect the key characteristics of climate for that period of time.

□ Temperature

Temperature refers to the air temperature. It often uses centigrade as the unit. The thermometry used for weather observation is put in a breezy shutter, which is 1.5 meters high from the ground. Therefore, the commonly used temperature refers to the temperature in the breezy shutter 1.5 meters away from the ground. The calculation method is as follows:

Monthly average temperature is the summation of average daily temperature of one month divided by the actual days of that particular month. Annual average temperature is the summation of monthly average of a year divided by 12 months.

□ Volume of Precipitation

Volume of Precipitation refers to the deepness of liquid state or solid state (thawed) water falling from the sky to the ground that has not been evaporated, infiltrated or run off. The calculation method is as follows:

Monthly precipitation is the summation of daily precipitation of a month.

Annual precipitation is the summation of 12 months precipitation of a year.

□ Sunshine Hours

Sunshine Hours refer to the actual hours of sun irradiating the earth. The calculation method is the same as that of the precipitation.

□ Classification of the Sectors of the National Economy

The national standard of <Classification of the Sectors of the National Economy> was first released in 1984, and was revised for the first time in 1994, for the second revision in 2002, and for the third revision in 2011.

Unless otherwise started, the industry classification used in this yearbook was based on Industrial Classification Standard revised in 2011.

The new industrial classification standard was based on China's social and economic development, to ensure that the national economic structure and industrial structure is integrity, scientific, and observability; to ensure national statistics and accounting reflecting the economic structure and industrial structure integrity. This revision was not only adhere to revision principle of industry classification and international practice, and conformed to the requirement in <State Council on accelerating the cultivation and development of emerging industries of strategic decision>, accurately reflect the composition of national economy industry in a given period.

The revision was mainly adjusted as follows:

1. Adjusting sector category name and order. For example, "information transmission, computer service and software industry" was renamed to "information transmission, software industry and information technology service", "scientific research, techni-

EXPLANATORY NOTES TO MAJOR STATISTICAL INDICATORS

cal service and geological prospecting" was renamed to "scientific research and technical service", "resident service and other services" was renamed to "resident service, repairs and other services", "health, social security and social welfare" was renamed to "health and social work". But the overall number of industry categories remain unchanged, ensuring the continuity of industry classification.

2. In order to correspond with the classification of the United Nations, and reflect the situation of our industry, number of industry categories was adjusted from 95 to 96, six new categories, "mining support activities", "the automotive manufacturing", "metal products, machinery and equipment repair industry", "housing construction", "internet and related services", "motor vehicles, electronics and daily necessities repair industry" were added, and four categories, "building decoration industry", "urban public transport industry", "other financial activities", "geological prospecting" were reduced. "Rubber products manufacturing" and "plastic products manufacturing" were combined into one category.

3. In order to reflect our growing internet, information technology, finance, entertainment and other industries, new medium categories, "internet and related services", "information integration system services", "fiber weaving and dyeing and finishing" were added, "pig breeding", "textile manufactured goods manufacturing" were reduced.

4. In order to convert with ISIC Rev.4 and reflect our emerging industries, new minimal categories, "rice planting", "mushroom cultivation", "grape cultivation" were added, "common non-ferrous metal rolling processing", "hat manufacturing", "vehicles, aircraft and construction machinery tire manufacturing" were reduced.

□ Various Planning Periods

The conventional division of time period in this statistical yearbook is as follows: Rehabilitation Period, 1950–1952; The First Five-Year Plan period (cited as first-five period), 1953–1957; The Second Five-Year Plan period (cited as second-five period), 1958–1962; The Third Five-Year Plan period (cited as third-five period), 1966–1970; The Fourth Five-Year Plan period (cited as fourth-five period), 1971–1975; The Fifth Five-Year Plan period (cited as fifth-five period), 1976–1980; The Sixth Five-Year Plan period (cited as sixth-five period), 1981–1985; The Seventh Five-Year Plan period (cited as seventh-five period) 1986–1990; The Eight Five-Year Plan period (cited as eighth-five period), 1991–1995; The Ninth Five-Year Plan period (cited as ninth-five period),1996–2000;The Tenth Five-Year Plan period (cited as tenth-five period),2001–2005; The eleventh Five-Year Plan period (cited as eleventh-five period),2006–2010.

□ Index

Index refers to the relative figures indicating social and economic phenomena and developments. Index is used to evaluate the overall development of social and economic phenomena which can not be determined by simple addition or direct comparison. It is also used to analyze the outcome of various changes in the general phenomenon movement of social and economic development, and to study the level of each sub-index in the changes of general average index and the role of the changes of the overall structure. It is calculated at the comparable prices conversed from the output value of each year, using the formula of index number with fixed base period equal to the continuous product of its relative chain index .

The increases of Shanghai Gross Domestic Product, industrial output value and agricultural output value compared with the previous year, which are listed in this yearbook, are calculated according to Shanghai GDP index, industrial output value index and agricultural output value index.

□ Average Annual Growth Rate

Two methods for calculating Average Annual Growth Rate are applied in China, one is often called "level approach" or geometry average, which is derived by comparing the growth rate for the last year of the interval with that of the beginning year; the other is called "accumulating approach" or algebraic average or equation method, which is calculated by comparing the total growth rate of each year for the interval with that of base year .

Usually the results calculated by the two methods are fairly close, but they differ sharply when imbalance occurred in economic development with striking fluctuations in growth.

The Average Annual Growth Rates listed in this statistical yearbook are calculated by "level approach" except for the growth rate of investment in fixed assets and foreign capital absorbed. The base years are not listed when the years are listed for average annual growth rates for instance, the average annual growth rate of 1991–2009 is calculated with the base year 1990, and the analogy of this is also for the rest.

第二篇

CHAPTER 2

人　口

POPULATION

简要说明

一、本篇资料的主要内容

本篇资料反映上海市 1978~2012 年人口方面的基本情况，包括全市及各区县的主要人口统计数据，如：1978~2012 年全市常住人口数和户籍人口数；2012 年各区县常住人口数和外省市来沪常住人口数；1990~2012 年户籍人口自然增长和机械增长变动；2012 年各区县户籍人口年龄构成、计划生育情况；主要年份外籍常住人口数等。

二、本篇的资料来源

本篇资料由上海市统计局人口和就业统计处整理。1982、1990、2000、2010 年年末常住人口数据为当年普查数据推算数，其余年份数据为年度人口抽样调查推算数据，部分年份数据根据人口普查数据进行了修订。表 2-1 中除常住人口数据外，其余数据统计范围均为户籍人口，由市公安局提供。表 2-2 中土地面积由市民政局提供，各区县常住人口数和外省市来沪常住人口数根据 2012 年全国人口变动情况抽样调查数据推算。表 2-3 至表 2-7 数据统计范围均为户籍人口，由市公安局提供。表 2-8 数据统计范围为户籍人口，由市卫生和计划生育委员会提供。表 2-11 由市公安局出入境管理局提供。

三、本篇的统计调查方法

目前由上海市统计局人口和就业统计处实施的人口统计调查有：

在逢“0”的年份进行全国人口普查；在逢”5”的年份进行全国 1%人口抽样调查；其余年份进行全国人口变动情况抽样调查，其样本量约占全市总人口的 1.3‰左右。人口抽样调查是以全国为总体，省级单位为次总体，采用分层、多阶段、整群概率比例抽样方法抽取样本。

BRIEF INTRODUCTION

I. Main Contents

Data in this chapter reflect the basic conditions of Shanghai's population between 1978 and 2012, including data of the city as well as districts and counties under it. For example: there are data of the city's permanent residents and registered population between 1978 and 2012; permanent residents and residents from other provinces and cities in districts and counties in 2012; changes of registered population's natural growth and mechanical growth between 1990 and 2012; registered population age structure in districts and counties in 2012 and their conditions of family planning; population of foreign residents in main years.

II. Sources of Data

Data in this chapter are collected, prepared, and provided by the Department of Population and Employment Statistics of the Shanghai Statistics Bureau. Data of permanent residents by the year end for 1982, 1990, 2000 and 2010 are the census year estimates; the rest of the data are estimates from the annual national sample survey on population changes and data for selected years have been revised according to the census results. Data in table 2–1, provided by the Shanghai Public Security Bureau, refer to registered population, with permanent residents in exception. Land area data in table 2–2 are provided by the Shanghai Civil Affairs Bureau, and the data on permanent residents in districts and counties, and residents from other provinces and cities are estimates based on national sample survey on population changes in 2012. Data in table 2–3 to table 2–7, provided by the Shanghai Public Security Bureau, all refer to registered population. Data in table 2–8, provided by the Shanghai Municipal Health and Family Planning Commission, refer to registered population. Data in table 2–11 are provided by the Shanghai Public Security Bureau Exit–Entry Administration.

III. Survey Methodology

The statistical surveys on population which are conducted by the Department of Population and Employment Statistics of the Shanghai Statistics Bureau are as follows:

The national population census is conducted in the year ending with 0; the national 1 percent population sample survey is conducted in the year ending with 5; sample surveys on population changes are conducted in the rest of the years which cover about 1.3 per thousand of the total population of the city. The sample survey on population change takes the whole nation as the population sample with each province, autonomous region or municipality as sub–populations, and the stratified multi–stage systematic PPS cluster sampling scheme is used.

表 2.1 户数、人口、人口密度和户籍人口期望寿命(1978～2012)

TOTAL HOUSEHOLDS, POPULATION, DENSITY OF REGISTERED POPULATION AND LIFE EXPECTANCY

年 份 Year	总户数 (万户) Total Households (10 000 households)	平均每户人口 (人) Average Persons Per Household (person)	常住人口 (万人) Year-end Resident Population (10 000 persons)	人口密度 (人/平方公里) Density of Population (person/sq. km)	年末户籍人口 (万人) Year-end Registered Population (10 000 persons)	按性别分 Grouped by Sex	
						男 性 Male	女 性 Female
1978	291.69	3.8	1 104.00	1 785	1 098.28	542.70	555.58
1979	296.71	3.8	1 137.00	1 838	1 132.14	560.40	571.74
1980	303.87	3.8	1 152.00	1 862	1 146.52	569.30	577.22
1981	314.56	3.7	1 168.00	1 888	1 162.84	578.76	584.08
1982	321.71	3.7	1 186.00	1 917	1 180.51	588.82	591.69
1983	330.60	3.6	1 201.00	1 942	1 194.01	596.67	597.34
1984	340.78	3.5	1 217.00	1 968	1 204.78	602.59	602.19
1985	351.72	3.5	1 233.00	1 993	1 216.69	609.70	606.99
1986	364.92	3.4	1 249.00	1 970	1 232.33	618.88	613.45
1987	380.19	3.3	1 265.00	1 995	1 249.51	628.78	620.73
1988	394.95	3.2	1 288.00	2 031	1 262.42	635.82	626.60
1989	406.82	3.1	1 311.00	2 067	1 276.45	643.51	632.94
1990	415.28	3.1	1 334.00	2 104	1 283.35	647.13	636.22
1991	425.84	3.0	1 350.00	2 128	1 287.20	649.03	638.17
1992	431.67	3.0	1 365.00	2 154	1 289.37	649.97	639.40
1993	438.69	3.0	1 381.00	2 179	1 294.74	652.92	641.82
1994	444.38	2.9	1 398.00	2 204	1 298.81	655.14	643.67
1995	450.76	2.9	1 414.00	2 230	1 301.37	656.48	644.89
1996	457.49	2.9	1 451.00	2 288	1 304.43	657.86	646.57
1997	461.40	2.8	1 489.00	2 348	1 305.46	657.93	647.53
1998	465.72	2.8	1 527.00	2 409	1 306.58	658.22	648.36
1999	470.11	2.8	1 567.00	2 472	1 313.12	661.19	651.93
2000	475.73	2.8	1 608.60	2 537	1 321.63	665.51	656.12
2001	478.92	2.8	1 668.33	2 631	1 327.14	668.32	658.82
2002	481.77	2.8	1 712.97	2 702	1 334.23	672.05	662.18
2003	486.06	2.8	1 765.84	2 785	1 341.77	675.47	666.30
2004	490.58	2.8	1 834.98	2 894	1 352.39	680.38	672.01
2005	496.69	2.7	1 890.26	2 981	1 360.26	683.51	676.75
2006	499.54	2.7	1 964.11	3 098	1 368.08	686.66	681.42
2007	503.29	2.7	2 063.58	3 255	1 378.86	691.08	687.78
2008	506.64	2.7	2 140.65	3 376	1 391.04	695.57	695.47
2009	509.79	2.7	2 210.28	3 486	1 400.70	699.25	701.45
2010	519.27	2.7	2 302.66	3 632	1 412.32	703.57	708.75
2011	522.01	2.7	2 347.46	3 702	1 419.36	706.37	712.99
2012	524.31	2.7	2 380.43	3 754	1 426.93	709.62	717.31

注：户数和年末户籍人口由市公安局提供，户籍人口期望寿命由市卫生和计划生育委员会提供。

Note: The figures of household and year-end registered population are provided by Shanghai Municipal Public Security Bureau, and the figures of life expendency are provided by Shanghai Municipal Health and Family Planning Commission.

表 2.1 续表 continued

年　份 Year	按农业非农业分 Grouped by Agriculture and Non-agriculture		非农业人口占总人口比重（%） Percentage of Non-agriculture Population in Total（%）	户籍人口期望寿命（岁） Life Expectancy of Registered Population（year）	其　中 of which	
	农　业 Agriculture	非农业 Non-agriculture			男　性 Male	女　性 Female
1978	453.05	645.23	58.7	73.35	70.69	74.78
1979	444.76	687.38	60.7	73.14	70.64	75.48
1980	444.09	702.43	61.3	73.33	71.25	75.36
1981	447.76	715.08	61.5	73.38	71.28	75.47
1982	449.20	731.31	61.9	74.04	71.77	76.25
1983	448.15	745.86	62.5	73.23	71.15	75.26
1984	444.03	760.75	63.1	73.90	71.73	76.17
1985	440.32	776.37	63.8	74.27	72.14	76.37
1986	429.77	802.56	65.1	74.71	72.54	76.85
1987	427.20	822.31	65.8	74.46	72.32	76.60
1988	423.49	838.93	66.5	74.63	72.50	76.77
1989	420.61	855.84	67.0	74.98	72.85	77.12
1990	418.89	864.46	67.4	75.46	73.16	77.74
1991	417.32	869.88	67.6	75.79	73.58	77.95
1992	413.82	875.55	67.9	75.97	74.04	77.91
1993	401.28	893.46	69.0	75.97	74.04	77.91
1994	388.32	910.49	70.1	76.26	74.29	78.23
1995	379.67	921.70	70.8	76.03	74.11	77.97
1996	372.29	932.14	71.5	76.11	74.07	78.21
1997	362.43	943.03	72.2	77.20	75.18	79.21
1998	352.93	953.65	73.0	77.03	75.06	79.02
1999	343.49	969.63	73.8	78.44	76.38	80.53
2000	335.47	986.16	74.6	78.77	76.71	80.81
2001	328.07	999.07	75.3	79.66	77.47	81.83
2002	315.42	1 018.81	76.4	79.52	77.36	81.63
2003	300.38	1 041.39	77.6	79.80	77.78	81.81
2004	254.79	1 097.60	81.2	80.29	78.08	82.48
2005	211.32	1 148.94	84.5	80.13	77.89	82.36
2006	194.78	1 173.30	85.8	80.97	78.64	83.29
2007	181.92	1 196.94	86.8	81.08	78.87	83.29
2008	174.48	1 216.56	87.5	81.28	79.06	83.50
2009	164.54	1 236.16	88.3	81.73	79.42	84.06
2010	157.37	1 254.95	88.9	82.13	79.82	84.44
2011	151.60	1 267.76	89.3	82.51	80.23	84.80
2012	146.11	1 280.82	89.8	82.41	80.18	84.67

表2.2 各区、县土地面积、常住人口及人口密度（2012）
LAND AREA, POPULATION AND DENSITY OF POPULATION IN DISTRICTS AND COUNTIES

地 区	District	土地面积（平方公里）Land Area (sq. km)	年末常住人口（万人）Year-end Resident Population (10 000 persons)	其中 of which 外来人口 Floating People	人口密度（人/平方公里）Density of Population (person/sq·km)
全 市	**Total**	**6 340.50**	**2 380.43**	**960.24**	**3 754**
浦东新区	Pudong New Area	1 210.41	526.39	222.84	4 349
黄 浦 区	Huangpu	20.46	70.48	18.20	34 448
徐 汇 区	Xuhui	54.76	111.12	29.41	20 292
长 宁 区	Changning	38.30	69.73	17.85	18 206
静 安 区	Jing'an	7.62	25.58	6.07	33 570
普 陀 区	Putuo	54.83	129.20	34.66	23 564
闸 北 区	Zhabei	29.26	84.61	20.52	28 917
虹 口 区	Hongkou	23.48	84.56	18.65	36 014
杨 浦 区	Yangpu	60.73	132.07	26.56	21 747
闵 行 区	Minhang	370.75	250.80	126.02	6 765
宝 山 区	Baoshan	270.99	197.19	81.53	7 277
嘉 定 区	Jiading	464.20	152.77	88.08	3 291
金 山 区	Jinshan	586.05	76.16	23.64	1 300
松 江 区	Songjiang	605.64	169.84	104.83	2 804
青 浦 区	Qingpu	670.14	116.98	69.25	1 746
奉 贤 区	Fengxian	687.39	112.99	57.15	1 644
崇 明 县	Chongming	1 185.49	69.96	14.98	590

表 2.3 主要年份户籍人口出生率、死亡率、自然增长率
BIRTH RATE, DEATH RATE AND NATURAL GROWTH RATE OF POPULATION IN MAIN YEARS

年 份 Year	出 生 Birth		死 亡 Death		自然增长 Natural Growth	
	人 数 (万人) Population (10 000 persons)	出生率 (‰) Birth Rate (‰)	人 数 (万人) Population (10 000 persons)	死亡率 (‰) Death Rate (‰)	人 数 (万人) Population (10 000 persons)	自然增长率 (‰) Natural Growth Rate(‰)
1990	13.12	10.25	8.63	6.74	4.49	3.51
1995	7.11	5.47	9.79	7.53	-2.68	-2.06
1996	6.79	5.21	9.77	7.50	-2.98	-2.29
1997	6.42	4.92	9.57	7.33	-3.15	-2.41
1998	6.17	4.73	10.13	7.75	-3.96	-3.03
1999	6.56	5.01	9.54	7.28	-2.98	-2.27
2000	6.95	5.27	9.45	7.17	-2.50	-1.90
2001	5.76	4.34	9.34	7.05	-3.58	-2.71
2002	6.20	4.66	9.67	7.27	-3.47	-2.61
2003	5.73	4.28	10.07	7.52	-4.34	-3.24
2004	8.09	6.00	9.65	7.16	-1.56	-1.16
2005	8.25	6.08	10.23	7.54	-1.98	-1.46
2006	8.12	5.95	9.80	7.19	-1.68	-1.24
2007	10.08	7.34	10.22	7.44	-0.14	-0.10
2008	9.67	6.98	10.70	7.73	-1.03	-0.75
2009	9.23	6.62	10.67	7.64	-1.44	-1.02
2010	10.02	7.13	10.87	7.73	-0.84	-0.60
2011	10.15	7.17	11.11	7.85	-0.96	-0.68
2012	12.11	8.51	11.74	8.25	0.37	0.26

表 2.4 主要年份户籍人口迁移
MIGRATION IN MAIN YEARS

年 份 Year	迁 入 Inflows		迁 出 Outflows		机械增长 Mechanical Increase	
	人 口 (万人) Population (10 000 persons)	迁入率 (‰) Rate of Inflows (‰)	人 口 (万人) Population (10 000 persons)	迁出率 (‰) Rate of Outflows (‰)	人 口 (万人) Population (10 000 persons)	增长率 (‰) Growth Rate (‰)
1990	12.18	9.52	10.72	8.38	1.46	1.14
1995	13.12	10.09	6.47	4.98	6.65	5.11
1996	13.01	9.99	6.41	4.92	6.60	5.07
1997	11.47	8.79	5.72	4.38	5.75	4.41
1998	11.73	8.98	5.04	3.86	6.69	5.12
1999	14.06	10.73	5.08	3.88	8.98	6.85
2000	15.16	11.51	5.32	4.04	9.84	7.47
2001	14.63	11.05	5.56	4.20	9.07	6.85
2002	15.41	11.58	4.38	3.29	11.03	8.29
2003	14.92	11.15	3.69	2.76	11.23	8.39
2004	13.93	10.34	2.74	2.03	11.19	8.31
2005	12.96	9.55	3.46	2.55	9.50	7.00
2006	12.86	9.43	3.50	2.57	9.36	6.86
2007	14.69	10.70	3.95	2.88	10.74	7.82
2008	17.28	12.48	4.29	3.10	12.99	9.38
2009	15.72	11.26	4.77	3.42	10.95	7.84
2010	17.22	12.24	4.97	3.53	12.25	8.71
2011	13.15	9.29	5.33	3.76	7.82	5.53
2012	12.96	8.11	5.89	4.14	7.07	3.97

表2.5 各区、县户籍人口迁移(2012)
MIGRATION IN DISTRICTS AND COUNTIES

地　区	District	迁　入(人) Inflows(person)		迁　出(人) Outflows(person)	
		市内迁入 From Inside of the City	市外迁入 From Outside of the City	迁往市内 To the Inside of the City	迁往市外 To the Outside of the City
全　市	**Total**	**7 468**	**129 620**	**7 638**	**58 944**
浦东新区	Pudong New Area	587	24 666	592	10 646
黄 浦 区	Huangpu	78	5 435	74	1 031
徐 汇 区	Xuhui	148	13 338	125	7 914
长 宁 区	Changning	61	7 957	70	2 245
静 安 区	Jing'an	21	1 239	18	392
普 陀 区	Putuo	178	5 159	184	1 730
闸 北 区	Zhabei	238	4 798	215	1 534
虹 口 区	Hongkou	184	4 292	170	2 000
杨 浦 区	Yangpu	310	18 401	373	12 428
闵 行 区	Minhang	435	13 227	282	5 893
宝 山 区	Baoshan	1 644	8 551	1 273	2 988
嘉 定 区	Jiading	86	3 456	40	1 565
金 山 区	Jinshan	20	1 111	39	319
松 江 区	Songjiang	86	12 570	39	6 311
青 浦 区	Qingpu	19	1 928	16	620
奉 贤 区	Fengxian	21	1 782	21	978
崇 明 县	Chongming	3 352	1 710	4 107	350

表2.6 各区、县户籍人口年龄构成(2012)
AGE STRUCTURE OF REGISTERED POPULATION IN DISTRICTS AND COUNTIES

单位:万人(10 000 persons)

地区	District	合计 Total	17岁及以下 17 and below	18~34岁 18~34	35~59岁 35~59	60岁及以上 60 and above
全 市	**Total**	**1 426.93**	**150.72**	**323.63**	**585.26**	**367.32**
浦东新区	Pudong New Area	281.12	32.87	63.93	115.70	68.63
黄浦区	Huangpu	90.36	8.18	20.81	36.54	24.82
徐汇区	Xuhui	91.69	10.10	21.96	35.23	24.40
长宁区	Changning	62.65	5.76	17.38	23.72	15.78
静安区	Jing'an	30.10	3.04	6.49	11.78	8.80
普陀区	Putuo	88.38	8.35	19.21	36.70	24.12
闸北区	Zhabei	68.69	6.36	15.42	28.56	18.36
虹口区	Hongkou	79.00	7.16	17.45	32.29	22.10
杨浦区	Yangpu	109.32	9.48	27.98	43.53	28.32
闵行区	Minhang	100.12	12.87	22.87	40.16	24.22
宝山区	Baoshan	90.65	9.85	19.74	38.14	22.91
嘉定区	Jiading	56.71	6.32	11.84	23.36	15.19
金山区	Jinshan	51.70	5.68	10.47	22.95	12.60
松江区	Songjiang	58.88	7.23	14.44	23.86	13.35
青浦区	Qingpu	46.50	5.22	9.71	20.35	11.23
奉贤区	Fengxian	52.53	6.01	10.73	22.83	12.96
崇明县	Chongming	68.54	6.23	13.21	29.57	19.53

表2.7 各区、县户籍老年人口年龄构成(2012)
AGE STRUCTURE OF REGISTERED AGING POPULATION IN DISTRICTS AND COUNTIES

单位:万人(10 000 persons)

地区	District	合计 Total	60～64岁 60～64	65～79岁 65～79	80岁及以上 80 and above
全市	**Total**	**367.32**	**122.05**	**178.24**	**67.03**
浦东新区	Pudong New Area	68.63	23.32	33.53	11.78
黄浦区	Huangpu	24.82	8.52	10.79	5.51
徐汇区	Xuhui	24.40	7.45	12.02	4.93
长宁区	Changning	15.78	4.85	7.66	3.27
静安区	Jing'an	8.80	2.81	4.05	1.94
普陀区	Putuo	24.12	8.48	10.89	4.75
闸北区	Zhabei	18.36	6.50	8.29	3.58
虹口区	Hongkou	22.10	7.53	10.07	4.49
杨浦区	Yangpu	28.32	9.71	13.01	5.60
闵行区	Minhang	24.22	7.94	12.29	4.00
宝山区	Baoshan	22.91	8.16	10.93	3.82
嘉定区	Jiading	15.19	4.94	7.69	2.56
金山区	Jinshan	12.60	4.08	6.73	1.79
松江区	Songjiang	13.35	4.25	7.01	2.09
青浦区	Qingpu	11.23	3.44	5.98	1.80
奉贤区	Fengxian	12.96	4.24	6.79	1.92
崇明县	Chongming	19.53	5.85	10.50	3.19

表2.8 各区、县计划生育基本情况(2012)
FAMILY PLANNING IN DISTRICTS AND COUNTIES

地 区	District	出生人数（万人）Birth (10 000 persons)	已婚育龄妇女人数（万人）Married Women at Childbearing Age (10 000 persons)	采取避孕措施人数（万人）Married People Adopting Contraception (10 000 persons)	计 划 生育率（%）Family Planning Rate (%)	避孕率（%）Comprehensive Contraception Rate (%)
全 市	**Total**	**12.11**	**214.48**	**168.08**	**99.2**	**78.4**
浦东新区	Pudong New Area	2.66	45.79	37.21	99.9	81.3
黄 浦 区	Huangpu	0.80	11.21	7.50	99.0	66.9
徐 汇 区	Xuhui	0.76	12.14	9.05	99.2	74.5
长 宁 区	Changning	0.61	8.62	6.13	99.1	71.1
静 安 区	Jing'an	0.25	3.74	2.78	99.6	74.5
普 陀 区	Putuo	0.75	10.68	7.77	99.3	72.8
闸 北 区	Zhabei	0.59	8.66	6.22	98.9	71.8
虹 口 区	Hongkou	0.65	10.20	7.22	98.7	70.8
杨 浦 区	Yangpu	0.86	13.21	10.24	99.1	77.5
闵 行 区	Minhang	1.05	15.69	12.22	99.5	77.9
宝 山 区	Baoshan	0.77	13.15	10.71	98.9	81.5
嘉 定 区	Jiading	0.42	9.41	7.94	99.4	84.3
金 山 区	Jinshan	0.34	9.85	7.98	98.6	81.1
松 江 区	Songjiang	0.52	10.51	8.93	98.2	85.0
青 浦 区	Qingpu	0.32	9.30	7.36	98.1	79.2
奉 贤 区	Fengxian	0.37	9.58	8.10	98.3	84.6
崇 明 县	Chongming	0.39	12.75	10.73	98.6	84.1

表 2.9 主要年份婚姻情况
MARRIAGE STATISTICS IN MAIN YEARS

年 份 Year	准予登记结婚（万对） Marriage Registration Permitted (10 000 couples)	初 婚（万人） First Marriage (10 000 persons)	再 婚（万人） Remarriage (10 000 persons)	其 中 of which 女 性 Female	离婚人数（万人） Divorce (10 000 persons)	其 中 of which 民政部门批准 Approved by the Civil Administration	法院调判 Mediated by the Court
1990	10.77	19.49	2.04	1.06	3.27	1.45	1.82
1995	8.40	14.61	2.19	1.09	4.54	1.97	2.57
1996	8.96	14.98	2.31	1.24	4.93	2.14	2.79
1997	8.84	15.12	2.57	1.27	5.46	2.38	3.08
1998	8.57	14.48	2.67	1.28	5.92	2.85	3.07
1999	9.05	15.07	2.46	1.24	6.24	3.39	2.85
2000	9.31	15.08	2.89	1.45	6.36	3.52	2.84
2001	9.30	15.23	2.68	1.40	6.29	3.36	2.93
2002	9.10	14.60	3.05	1.40	5.92	3.08	2.84
2003	10.82	17.20	3.97	2.31	6.60	3.97	2.63
2004	12.49	20.27	4.18	2.05	7.26	5.35	1.91
2005	10.27	16.44	4.09	2.05	7.86	6.21	1.65
2006	16.56	27.29	5.83	2.93	9.43	7.55	1.88
2007	12.01	18.10	5.93	2.95	9.38	7.49	1.88
2008	14.16	22.04	6.28	3.17	9.35	7.44	1.91
2009	14.99	23.33	6.65	3.31	9.65	7.83	1.82
2010	13.03	20.10	5.96	2.98	9.34	7.62	1.72
2011	14.89	23.94	5.84	2.90	9.57	7.85	1.72
2012	14.42	22.96	5.88	2.86	10.57	8.83	1.74

表 2.10 主要年份涉外婚姻情况
CHINESE-FOREIGN MARRIAGE IN MAIN YEARS

年 份 Year	涉外婚姻(对) Chinese-Foreign Marriage (couple)	在涉外婚姻中的国内公民（人） In Chinese-Foreign Marriage Chinese Citizens (person)	在国内公民中 Among the Chinese Citizens 男 性 Male	女 性 Female
1990	1 345	1 345	136	1 209
1995	3 033	3 030	274	2 756
1996	3 107	3 105	307	2 798
1997	2 839	2 838	298	2 540
1998	2 926	2 923	293	2 630
1999	2 872	2 869	343	2 526
2000	3 187	3 182	374	2 808
2001	3 447	3 438	399	3 039
2002	2 705	2 690	67	2 623
2003	2 418	2 418	367	2 051
2004	2 636	2 623	417	2 206
2005	2 407	2 385	372	2 013
2006	2 943	2 943	540	2 403
2007	2 495	2 483	109	2 374
2008	2 626	2 553	428	2 125
2009	2 492	2 416	305	2 111
2010	2 231	2 144	414	1 730
2011	2 225	2 125	474	1 651
2012	2 195	2 064	473	1 591

注：本页数据由市民政局提供。
Note: This table is provided by Shanghai Civil Affairs Bureau.

表2.11 主要年份在沪外国常住人口
RESIDENT FOREIGNERS IN SHANGHAI IN MAIN YEARS

单位:人(person)

行 业	Sector	2005	2010	2011	2012
总 计	**Total**	**100 011**	**162 481**	**164 359**	**174 192**
居留许可外国人	**Residence Permitted Foreigners**	**95 384**	**159 303**	**163 124**	**172 551**
按国别(地区)分	Grouped by Country and Region				
#日 本	Japan	27 812	35 075	37 223	39 091
韩 国	Republic of Korea	14 047	21 073	20 297	20 456
新加坡	Singapore	5 547	7 545	6 955	6 935
德 国	Germany	4 591	8 023	8 040	8 680
英 国	United Kingdom	2 904	5 591	5 728	6 196
加拿大	Canada	4 279	7 306	7 407	7 669
美 国	United States	14 329	24 358	16 805	26 000
澳大利亚	Australia	3 729	6 165	6 207	6 545
法 国	France	4 181	8 238	8 751	9 472
按类别分	By Types				
#留学人员及家属	Overseas Students and Relatives	10 224	16 064	14 203	14 467
驻华机构代表及家属	Delegate and Relatives of Institutions Stationed in China	9 769	8 933	6 480	6 174
外资企业工作人员及家属	Employees and Relatives at Foreign Ventures	60 137	95 623	88 114	95 303
外国专家及家属	Foreign Experts and Relatives	4 586	6 638	6 817	7 528
永久居留外国人	Permanent Resident Foreigners		948	1 181	1 587
半年以上长期签证外国人	Long-term Vise Foreigners Above Half Year		2 230	54	54

上 / 海 / 统 / 计 / 年 / 鉴

主要统计指标解释

■ 人　口

人口数为每年12月31日的年末总人口。根据统计口径的不同，分为户籍人口和常住人口。户籍人口是指在公安部门办理了户籍登记的人口。常住人口是指实际上经常居住在一个地方（住所）的人口，一般都以在其住所居住半年以上者为常住人口。

■ 出生率

出生率（又称粗出生率）指在一定时期内（通常为一年）一定地区的出生人数与同期平均人数(或期中人数)之比，一般用千分率表示。计算公式：

$$\text{出生率}=\frac{\text{年出生人数}}{\text{年平均人数}}\times 1000‰$$

出生人数是指活产婴儿，即胎儿脱离母体时(不管怀孕月数)，有过呼吸或其他生命现象。年平均人数是年初、年底人口数的平均数，也可用年中人口数代替。

■ 死亡率

死亡率（又称粗死亡率）指在一定时期内（通常为一年）一定地区的死亡人数与同期平均人数（或期中人数）之比，一般用千分率表示。计算公式：

$$\text{死亡率}=\frac{\text{年死亡人数}}{\text{年平均人数}}\times 1000‰$$

■ 人口自然增长率

指在一定时期内（通常为一年）人口自然增加数（出生人数减死亡人数）与该时期内平均人数（或期中人数）之比，一般用千分率表示。计算公式：

$$\text{人口自然增长率}=\frac{\text{本年出生人数}-\text{年死亡人数}}{\text{年平均人数}}\times 1000‰$$

人口自然增长率＝人口出生率－人口死亡率

■ 户籍人口期望寿命

指在一定年龄组的死亡率水平下，该年龄组人群日后平均可能继续生存的年（岁）数。通常所说的平均期望寿命是指刚出生的一批人平均一生可能存活的年数。

SHANGHAI STATISTICAL YEARBOOK

EXPLANATORY NOTES TO MAJOR STATISTICAL INDICATORS

□ Population

Population refers to the total population by December 31 every year. According to different statistical approaches, there are two definitions of population named as population with registered residence and population with permanent residence. The former refers to the population with registration in the police while the latter refers to the population that actually reside in a place (residence) permanently, usually longer than half a year.

□ Birth Rate

Birth Rate (or gross birth rate) means the ratio of the number of births in a certain period (usually a year) to the average population in the same period (or mid–year figure). It is usually calculated in terms of permillage and its calculating formula is:

$$\text{Birth Rate} = \frac{\text{Number of Births}}{\text{Average Number of Population}} \times 1000‰$$

Number of Births refers to live births, when babies have showed any vital phenomena regardless of the length of pregnancy.

Average Number of Population is the average of the number of population at the beginning of the year and, at the end of the year and sometimes is substituted for with mid–year population.

□ Death Rate

Death Rate (or Gross Death Rate) refers to the ratio of number of deaths to the average population (or mid–year population) during a certain period of time (usually a year), which is often presented as permillage. Its calculating formula is :

$$\text{Death Rate} = \frac{\text{Number of Deaths}}{\text{Average Number of Population}} \times 1000‰$$

□ Natural Growth Rate of Population

Natural Growth Rate of Population refers to the ratio of natural increase in population (number of births minus number of deaths) in a certain period of time (usually a year) to the average population (or mid–year population) of the same period, which is often presented as permillage. The following formula are applied:

$$\text{Natural Growth Rate of Population} = \frac{\text{Number of Births} - \text{Number of Deaths}}{\text{Average Number of Population}} \times 1000‰$$

Natural Growth Rate of Population = Birth Rate–Death Rate

□ Life Expectancy of Registered Population

Life Expectancy of Registered Population refers to the average age that an age group may possibly live at a certain mortality rate of the group, in the common knowledge, the average age that a group of new–borns may possibly live.

第三篇

CHAPTER 3

从业人员和职工工资

EMPLOYMENT AND WAGES

简 要 说 明

一、本篇资料的主要内容

本篇资料反映上海市劳动经济方面的基本情况。如：从业人员、职工人数，城镇登记失业人数和城镇登记失业率，新增就业岗位，离退休、退职职工人数，工资总额，平均工资及离退休、退职人员养老金情况等。

二、本篇资料的统计范围

《劳动统计报表制度》的调查范围为上海市国民经济各行业法人单位及其所属的产业活动单位。

《私营单位劳动统计报表制度》的调查范围为上海市全部私营法人单位。

上海市人力资源和社会保障局有关统计报表的统计范围为上海市国民经济各行业法人单位及其所属的产业活动单位。

三、本篇的资料来源

1. 从业人员、职工人数以及工资总额等资料，是由上海市统计局人口和就业统计处根据《劳动统计报表制度》和《私营单位劳动统计报表制度》搜集资料，加工整理汇总取得。

2. 城镇登记失业人数和城镇登记失业率，新增就业岗位，离退休、退职职工人数，离退休、退职人员养老金情况，由上海市人力资源和社会保障局提供。

四、本篇的统计调查方法

劳动统计报表采用全面调查方法，由区县统计局和主管单位收集资料，汇总上报；私营单位统计报表采用抽样调查方法，由区县统计局收集资料，汇总上报。人力资源社会保障的资料采用全面调查方法，由市人力资源社会保障部门收集相关数据资料加工整理取得。

BRIEF INTRODUCTION

I. Main Contents

Data in this chapter reflect the basic conditions of Shanghai's labor economy, such as number of employed people, the urban registered unemployed people and unemployment rate, the number of new jobs, the number of retired people, total wages, average wages and pension situations.

II. Scope and Coverage of Statistics

The Reporting Form System on Labor Statistics covers various corporate units with legal person status and their subordinated business units in Shanghai's economic and social development.

The Reporting Form System on Labor Statistics in Private Enterprises covers all corporate units with legal person status in Shanghai's private enterprises.

The reporting forms provided by the Shanghai Human Resources and Social Security Bureau cover various corporate units with legal person status and their subordinated business units in Shanghai's economic and social development.

III. Sources of Data

(1)Data on basic conditions including employment and total wages are collected, prepared and compiled through The Reporting Form System on Labor Statistics and The Reporting Form System on Labor Statistics in Private Enterprises by the Department of Population and Employment Statistics at the Shanghai Statistics Bureau.

(2)Data on the urban registered unemployed people and unemployment rate, the number of new jobs, the number of retired people and pension situations are provided by the Shanghai Human Resources and Social Security Bureau.

IV. Methodology of Survey

The reporting form system on labor statistics, with materials collected, prepared and compiled by the statistical bureaus in districts and counties, is the result of a comprehensive survey. The reporting form system in private enterprises, with materials collected and compiled by the statistical bureaus in districts and counties, takes the sampling method in the survey. Data on human resources and social security is produced out of a comprehensive survey, with materials collected and compiled by the Shanghai Human Resources and Social Security Bureau.

表3.1 全社会各行业从业人员(2010～2012)
QUANTITY OF WHOLE SOCIAL EMPLOYEES IN DIFFERENT SECTORS

单位:万人(10 000 persons)

行业	Sector	2010	2011	2012
总计	**Total**	**1 090.76**	**1 104.33**	**1 115.50**
按产业分	**Grouped by Industry**			
第一产业	Primary Industry	37.09	37.28	45.70
第二产业	Secondary Industry	443.74	445.08	439.96
第三产业	Tertiary Industry	609.93	621.97	629.84
按行业分	**Grouped by Sector**			
农、林、牧、渔业	Farming, Forestry, Animal Husbandry and Fishery	37.09	37.28	45.70
采矿业	Mining	0.09	0.05	0.05
制造业	Manufacturing	341.42	341.41	336.86
电力、热力、燃气及水的生产和供应业	Electricity, Heat, Gas and Water Production and Supply Industry	6.14	6.27	5.99
建筑业	Construction	96.09	97.35	97.06
批发和零售业	Retail and Wholesale	180.69	181.66	185.81
交通运输、仓储和邮政业	Transportation, Warehousing and Post Industries	54.97	58.14	60.11
住宿和餐饮业	Hoteling and Catering	47.52	47.23	48.89
信息传输、软件和信息技术服务业	Information Transmission, Software and IT Services	20.03	27.57	28.12
#信息传输	Information Transmission	2.97	3.05	2.87
金融业	Finance	24.11	28.41	30.05
房地产业	Real Estate	35.94	35.59	33.36
租赁和商务服务业	Leasing and Business Service Industries	58.86	62.31	64.64
科学研究和技术服务业	Scientific and Technical Services	33.11	29.99	29.02
水利、环境和公共设施管理业	Water Conservancy, Environment and Public Facility Management	11.94	11.20	11.60
#公共设施管理业	Public Facility Management	2.60	2.49	6.46
居民服务、修理和其他服务业	Resident Services, Repairs and Other Services	62.75	58.86	57.93
教育	Education	29.02	30.31	30.11
卫生和社会工作	Health and Social Work	20.41	20.65	20.13
文化、体育和娱乐业	Culture, Sports and Entertainment	11.91	10.65	9.58
公共管理、社会保障和社会组织	Public Administration, Social Security and Social Organizations	18.67	19.40	20.49

表 3.2 各行业职工人数(2012)
QUANTITY OF STAFF AND WORKERS IN DIFFERENT SECTORS

单位:万人(10 000 persons)

行业	Sector	职工人数 Staff and Workers	按登记注册类型分 Classified by Registration Categories: 国有单位 State-owned Units	集体单位 Collective-owned Units	港澳台及外商投资单位 Units with Investment from Hong Kong, Macao, Taiwan and Foreign Countries	其他单位 Other Ownership Units
总 计	**Total**	**944.47**	**141.61**	**12.55**	**223.88**	**566.43**
按产业分	**Grouped by Industry**					
第一产业	Primary Industry	2.61	0.48	0.03	0.01	2.09
第二产业	Secondary Industry	462.40	22.24	5.05	161.61	273.50
第三产业	Tertiary Industry	479.46	118.89	7.47	62.26	290.84
按行业分	**Grouped by Sector**					
农、林、牧、渔业	Farming, Forestry, Animal Husbandry and Fishery	2.61	0.48	0.03	0.01	2.09
采矿业	Mining	0.05	0.01			0.04
制造业	Manufacturing	367.21	12.60	3.44	159.56	191.61
电力、热力、燃气及水的生产和供应业	Electricity, Heat, Gas and Water Production and Supply Industry	5.92	3.93	0.09	0.37	1.53
建筑业	Construction	89.22	5.70	1.52	1.68	80.32
批发和零售业	Retail and Wholesale	145.01	3.87	1.05	33.45	106.64
交通运输、仓储和邮政业	Transportation, Warehousing and Post Industries	57.41	18.23	0.61	2.03	36.54
住宿和餐饮业	Hoteling and Catering	36.55	2.64	0.47	8.11	25.33
信息传输、软件和信息技术服务业	Information Transmission, Software and IT Services	20.07	1.97		4.95	13.15
#信息传输	Information Transmission	2.88	1.49		0.97	0.42
金融业	Finance Inductry	29.29	5.07	0.02	3.62	20.58
房地产业	Real Estate	25.17	3.17	0.33	4.36	17.31
租赁和商务服务业	Leasing and Business Service Industries	52.06	9.55	2.06	3.01	37.44
科学研究和技术服务业	Scientific and Technical Services	24.18	7.89	0.11	1.44	14.74
水利、环境和公共设施管理业	Water Conservancy, Environment and Public Facility Management	6.24	4.34	0.30	0.03	1.57
#公共设施管理业	Public Facility Management	5.42	3.65	0.30	0.02	1.45
居民服务、修理和其他服务业	Resident Services, Repairs and Other Services	12.93	0.59	0.22	0.84	11.28
教 育	Education	27.16	24.59	0.18	0.04	2.35
卫生和社会工作	Health and Social Work	17.29	14.35	1.59	0.05	1.30
文化、体育和娱乐业	Culture, Sports and Entertainment	6.64	3.58	0.15	0.33	2.58
公共管理、社会保险和社会组织	Public Administration, Social Security and Social Organizations	19.46	19.05	0.38		0.03

注:本表包括全部城镇私营企业职工。
Note: Data in this table has included those of employees work for private enterprises.

表 3.3 主要年份城镇登记失业人数和城镇登记失业率
QUANTITY OF URBAN REGISTERED UNEMPLOYED AND URBAN REGISTERED UNEMPLOYMENT RATE IN MAIN YEARS

指标	Indicators	2000	2010	2011	2012
城镇登记失业人数(万人)	Registered Urban Unemployment (10 000 persons)	20.08	27.73	27.33	27.05
区	District	18.86	26.97	26.58	26.30
县	County	1.22	0.76	0.75	0.75
城镇登记失业率(%)	Registered Urban Unemployment Rate (%)	3.5	4.2	4.2	4.2

表 3.4 主要年份新增就业岗位
NEWLY ADDED WORKING POST IN MAIN YEARS

指标	Indicators	2003	2010	2011	2012
新增就业岗位(万个)	Newly Added Working Post (10 000 units)	46.20	63.15	64.16	61.38
#农村富余劳动力实现非农就业	Non-agricultural Working Post Gained by Surplus Rural Labor Force	12.50	12.18	13.03	11.02

表 3.5 主要年份离休、退休及退职职工人数
QUANTITY OF RETIRED AND RESIGNED PERSONS IN MAIN YEARS

单位:万人(10 000 persons)

指标	Indicators	2000	2010	2011	2012
总 计	**Total**	**234.23**	**352.02**	**363.95**	**378.40**
国有单位	State-owned Units	165.55	166.38	164.54	165.99
离 休	Retired Veteran Cadres	3.39	1.82	1.71	1.60
退 休	Retired	161.03	160.53	158.97	160.65
退 职	Resigned	1.13	4.03	3.86	3.74
集体单位	Collective-owned Units	50.22	46.97	45.63	46.40
离 休	Retired Veteran Cadres	0.10	0.04	0.04	0.04
退 休	Retired	48.40	45.15	43.92	44.73
退 职	Resigned	1.72	1.78	1.67	1.63
其他单位	Other Ownership Units	18.46	138.67	153.78	166.01
离 休	Retired Veteran Cadres	0.21	0.68	0.65	0.60
退 休	Retired	18.05	132.29	146.95	158.91
退 职	Resigned	0.20	5.70	6.18	6.50

表3.6 从业人员工资总额(1978～2012)
TOTAL WAGES OF EMPLOYEES

年 份 Year	从业人员工资总额(亿元) Total Wages of Employees (100 million yuan)	按产业分 Grouped by Industry			按登记注册类型分 Classified According to the Categories of Registration.		
		第一产业 Primary Industry	第二产业 Secondary Industry	第三产业 Tertiary Industry	国有单位 State-owned Units	集体单位 Collective-owned Units	其他单位 Other Ownership Units
1978	28.18	1.31	17.18	9.69	23.88	4.30	
1979	32.90	1.44	20.43	11.03	27.77	5.13	
1980	38.26	1.66	23.42	13.18	31.71	6.55	
1981	39.76	1.61	24.40	13.75	32.55	7.21	
1982	41.55	1.59	25.15	14.81	33.83	7.72	
1983	43.21	1.48	26.07	15.66	35.07	8.14	
1984	54.13	1.63	33.29	19.21	43.39	10.29	0.45
1985	69.63	2.10	42.86	24.67	55.96	13.18	0.49
1986	84.89	2.45	51.70	30.74	68.32	15.84	0.73
1987	96.36	2.64	58.18	35.54	78.15	17.46	0.75
1988	117.04	3.18	70.35	43.51	94.78	20.91	1.35
1989	134.04	3.60	81.41	49.03	106.57	25.17	2.30
1990	150.48	4.02	89.48	56.98	121.56	25.64	3.28
1991	177.55	4.64	105.25	67.66	142.00	30.24	5.31
1992	223.36	2.47	135.49	85.40	179.43	35.40	8.53
1993	290.42	2.57	157.10	130.75	212.10	39.56	38.76
1994	374.44	3.11	186.81	184.52	268.19	48.59	57.66
1995	465.67	3.53	232.10	230.04	324.72	56.99	83.96
1996	521.63	3.72	250.94	266.97	359.56	60.18	101.89
1997	547.87	3.69	245.59	298.59	366.61	60.11	121.15
1998	535.51	3.47	255.43	276.61	330.70	45.11	159.70
1999	612.85	3.35	277.11	332.39	366.55	43.62	202.68
2000	647.55	3.32	283.20	361.03	369.65	38.88	239.02
2001	716.95	3.25	301.93	411.77	389.26	36.91	290.78
2002	788.55	3.76	333.64	451.15	404.89	34.18	349.48
2003	873.06	2.53	373.19	497.34	434.93	32.43	405.70
2004	925.33	2.69	383.84	538.80	435.30	31.00	459.03
2005	1 245.44	3.21	478.97	763.26	474.39	30.28	740.77
2006	1 598.09	3.92	656.41	937.76	559.02	31.15	1 007.92
2007	1 976.54	4.35	796.03	1 176.16	704.35	35.94	1 236.25
2008	2 399.63	4.68	934.34	1 460.61	797.29	36.40	1 565.94
2009	2 902.66	5.28	1 060.30	1 837.08	938.66	38.70	1 925.30
2010	3 320.86	5.76	1 224.97	2 090.13	1 055.50	38.39	2 226.97
2011	4 831.06	9.17	1 974.35	2 847.54	1 213.64	53.88	3 563.54
2012	5 688.56	10.03	2 352.83	3 325.70	1 275.72	64.09	4 348.75

①按国家统计局制度规定，2011年起，从业人员报酬改为从业人员工资(下表同)。
②本表"其他单位"包括港澳台及外商企业。
❶According to regulations of National Bureau of Statistics system, since 2011, compensation of Employees has been changed to Wages of Employees(same as follows).
❷"Other Ownership Units" in this table includes foreign invested and HongKong, Macau and Taiwan funded enterprises.

表 3.7　从业人员平均工资（2012）
AVERAGE WAGES OF EMPLOYEES

单位:元(yuan)

行业	Sector	合计 Total	其中 of which 国有单位 State-owned Units	集体单位 Collective-owned Units	港澳台及外商投资单位 Units with Investment from Hong Kong, Macao, Taiwan and Foreign Countries	其他单位 Other Ownership Units
全　市	**Total**	**56 648**	**89 739**	**52 786**	**76 890**	**41 500**
按产业分	**Grouped by Industry**					
第一产业	Primary Industry	33 237	58 477	74 686	24 635	28 103
第二产业	Secondary Industry	48 012	80 474	42 069	64 314	36 974
第三产业	Tertiary Industry	65 067	91 421	60 398	107 405	45 918
按行业分	**Grouped by Sector**					
农、林、牧、渔业	Farming, Forestry, Animal Husbandry and Fishery	33 237	58 477	74 686	24 635	28 103
工　业	Industry	50 359	85 974	43 500	63 889	37 135
采矿业	Mining	103 785	48 945			120 487
制造业	Manufacturing	49 381	73 826	42 889	63 762	36 677
电力、热力、燃气及水的生产和供应业	Electricity, Heat, Gas and Water Production and Supply Industry	111 490	118 030	59 083	120 396	96 332
建筑业	Construction	39 656	67 034	39 310	91 392	36 639
批发和零售业	Wholesale and Retail	50 857	84 721	49 085	116 521	30 735
批发业	Wholesale	60 050	104 659	56 500	148 039	31 906
零售业	Retail	35 760	58 164	42 967	58 485	28 853
交通运输、仓储和邮政业	Transportation, Warehousing and Post	57 434	74 632	37 901	83 604	48 312
#交通运输	Transportation	56 284	74 043	35 951	91 401	48 179
邮政业	Postal	81 973	84 912	48 449	69 775	37 360
住宿和餐饮业	Hoteling and Catering	33 808	51 570	33 031	35 002	31 458
#餐饮业	Catering	29 366	42 968	33 496	31 293	28 112
信息传输、软件和信息技术服务业	Information Transmission, Software and IT Services	85 088	141 018		130 209	60 101
#信息传输	Information Transmission	127 160	144 843		115 924	88 283
金融业	Financial Industries	172 077	197 964	111 658	237 606	154 381
房地产业	Real Estate	48 475	64 219	50 015	70 721	40 999
租赁和商务服务业	Leasing and Business Services	50 884	65 915	64 978	160 054	38 860
科学研究和技术服务业	Scientific and Technical Services	81 937	113 227	76 455	193 838	57 615
水利、环境和公共设施管理业	Water Conservancies, Environment and Public Facilities Management	48 327	53 146	37 633	68 017	36 916
居民服务、修理和其他服务业	Resident Services, Repairs and Other Services	25 937	57 465	44 896	27 281	23 557
教　育	Education	83 074	86 623	60 988	133 048	51 572
卫生和社会工作	Health and Social Work	98 556	106 517	81 739	152 031	37 204
卫　生	Healthcare	99 844	108 200	82 688	152 031	37 285
社会工作	Social Welfare	59 595	61 639	36 876		21 312
文化、体育和娱乐业	Culture, Sports and Entertainment	68 136	90 808	63 948	44 488	38 689
文　化	Culture	95 615	97 719	63 569	72 176	91 104
体　育	Sports	49 151	58 806	80 226	30 132	43 405
娱乐业	Entertainment	35 783	99 700		115 286	28 533
公共管理、社会保障和社会组织	Public Administration, Social Security and Social Organizations	90 622	91 474	51 882		60 632
#社会保障	Social Security	63 786	63 605	65 163		36 444

表 3.8 职工工资总额和平均工资(1978～2012)
TOTAL WAGES AND AVERAGE ANNUAL WAGES OF STAFF AND WORKERS

年份 Year	职工工资总额(亿元) Total Wages of Staff and Workers (100 million yuan)	其中 of which 国有单位 State-owned Units	集体单位 Collective-owned Units	其他单位 Other Ownership Units	职工平均工资(元) Average Annual Wages of Staff and Workers (yuan)	其中 of which 国有单位 State-owned Units	集体单位 Collective-owned Units	其他单位 Other Ownership Units
1978	28.12	23.82	4.30		672	716	500	
1979	32.73	27.63	5.10		784	834	590	
1980	38.10	31.59	6.51		873	918	702	
1981	39.59	32.42	7.17		870	910	727	
1982	41.34	33.71	7.63		883	920	750	
1983	42.91	34.93	7.98		897	935	763	
1984	53.72	43.19	10.08	0.45	1 110	1 160	938	1 149
1985	68.99	55.50	13.00	0.49	1 416	1 467	1 227	1 628
1986	83.35	67.49	15.15	0.71	1 689	1 752	1 443	2 029
1987	94.78	77.19	16.87	0.72	1 893	1 960	1 623	2 510
1988	114.47	93.62	19.55	1.30	2 277	2 354	1 951	2 715
1989	131.10	105.08	23.77	2.25	2 608	2 691	2 259	3 235
1990	146.78	119.26	24.30	3.22	2 917	3 037	2 394	3 611
1991	172.84	139.12	28.51	5.21	3 375	3 487	2 817	4 363
1992	217.21	175.95	32.89	8.37	4 273	4 451	3 363	5 486
1993	279.33	206.12	36.60	36.61	5 650	5 784	4 253	7 043
1994	357.89	259.78	44.73	53.38	7 401	7 529	5 389	9 617
1995	440.75	314.69	51.61	74.45	9 279	9 578	6 309	11 518
1996	492.70	348.96	54.92	88.82	10 663	11 015	7 051	13 186
1997	510.10	353.69	53.69	102.72	11 425	11 733	7 329	14 313
1998	510.35	330.10	44.13	136.12	12 059	12 361	7 138	14 430
1999	583.54	366.21	43.22	174.11	14 147	14 419	7 935	16 736
2000	614.53	371.39	39.35	203.79	15 420	15 737	8 041	17 942
2001	678.29	389.91	35.79	252.59	17 764	17 820	8 525	20 865
2002	733.31	404.44	31.54	297.33	19 473	19 777	8 707	21 886
2003	803.84	430.92	30.52	342.40	22 160	22 541	9 844	24 359
2004	837.39	428.49	29.36	379.53	24 398	24 726	11 539	26 270
2005	1 146.97	463.24	28.44	655.29	26 823	28 803	12 819	26 792
2006	1 475.93	539.88	28.41	907.64	29 569	36 010	15 209	27 459
2007	1 802.17	673.20	32.75	1 096.22	34 707	46 426	19 244	30 687
2008	2 184.20	753.44	31.72	1 399.04	39 502	53 554	21 787	35 180
2009	2 594.20	889.50	34.24	1 670.46	42 789	62 390	25 390	37 104
2010	3 018.55	994.05	33.62	1 990.88	46 757	70 585	28 225	40 397
2011	4 505.57	1 185.91	50.60	3 269.06	51 968	79 541	42 010	46 314
2012	5 347.99	1 245.58	60.73	4 041.68	56 300	86 042	45 990	51 035

①2009 年起，职工工资总额和平均工资包括城镇私营企业职工工资。
② 本表"其他单位"包括港澳台及外商企业。
❶Total and average wages of staff and workers has included urban private enterprises since 2009.
❷"Other Ownership Units" in this table includes foreign invested and HongKong, Macan and Taiwan funded enterprises.

表3.9 职工工资总额(2012)
TOTAL WAGES OF STAFF AND WORKERS

单位:亿元(100 million yuan)

行 业	Sectors	合 计 Total	国有单位 State-owned Units	集体单位 Collective-owned Units	港澳台及外商投资单位 Units with Investment from Hong Kong, Macao, Taiwan and Foreign Countries	其他单位 Other Ownership Units
全 市	**Total**	**5 347.99**	**1 245.58**	**60.73**	**1 651.47**	**2 390.21**
按产业分	**Grouped by Industry**					
第一产业	Primary Industry	8.96	2.62	0.20	0.03	6.11
第二产业	Secondary Industry	2 216.79	161.85	20.37	1 001.72	1 032.85
第三产业	Tertiary Industry	3 122.24	1 081.11	40.16	649.72	1 351.25
按行业分	**Grouped by Sector**					
农、林、牧、渔业	Farming, Forestry, Animal Husbandry and Fishery	8.96	2.62	0.20	0.03	6.11
工 业	Industry	1 854.37	125.33	13.86	984.76	730.42
采矿业	Mining	0.56	0.06			0.50
制造业	Manufacturing	1 787.67	78.41	13.24	980.41	715.61
电力、热力、燃气及水的生产和供应业	Electricity, Heat, Gas and Water Production and Supply Industry	66.14	46.86	0.62	4.35	14.31
建筑业	Construction	362.42	36.52	6.51	16.96	302.43
批发和零售业	Wholesale and Retail	711.26	29.52	3.51	352.47	325.76
批发业	Wholesale	520.21	20.81	1.80	287.63	209.97
零售业	Retail	191.05	8.71	1.71	64.85	115.78
交通运输、仓储和邮政业	Transportation, Warehousing and Post	330.22	132.24	1.49	16.55	179.94
#交通运输	Transportation	299.20	108.24	1.26	13.35	176.35
邮政业	Postal	17.28	16.73	0.03	0.10	0.42
住宿和餐饮业	Hoteling and Catering	128.08	13.04	1.50	34.93	78.61
#餐饮业	Catering	82.05	1.15	0.79	26.85	53.26
信息传输、软件和信息技术服务业	Information Transmission, Software and IT Services	168.42	28.11		62.76	77.55
#信息传输	Information Transmission	36.46	21.82		10.96	3.68
金融业	Financial Industries	504.99	97.42	0.07	79.77	327.73
房地产业	Real Estate	129.06	20.07	1.45	29.66	77.88
租赁和商务服务业	Leasing and Business Services	238.53	42.99	11.06	41.82	142.66
科学研究和技术服务业	Scientific and Technical Services	200.82	90.69	0.85	26.32	82.96
水利、环境和公共设施管理业	Water Conservancies, Environment and Public Facilities Management	32.45	25.05	1.15	0.19	6.06
居民服务、修理和其他服务业	Resident Services, Repairs and Other Services	32.51	3.42	1.07	2.65	25.37
教 育	Education	237.98	224.82	1.19	0.25	11.72
卫生和社会工作	Health and Social Work	179.31	159.54	13.90	0.83	5.04
卫 生	Healthcare	175.92	156.25	13.80	0.83	5.04
社会工作	Social Welfare	3.39	3.28	0.10		0.01
文化、体育和娱乐业	Culture, Sports and Entertainment	42.51	30.36	0.84	1.52	9.79
文 化	Culture	29.10	24.79	0.82	0.13	3.36
体 育	Sports	5.56	3.94	0.02	0.79	0.81
娱乐业	Entertainment	7.85	1.62		0.60	5.63
公共管理、社会保障和社会组织	Public Administration, Social Security and Social Organizations	186.10	183.84	2.08		0.18
#社会保障	Social Security	4.09	3.30	0.78		0.01

表 3.10 职工平均工资(2012)
AVERAGE ANNUAL WAGES OF STAFF AND WORKERS

单位:元(yuan)

行业	Sectors	合计 Total	国有单位 State-owned Units	集体单位 Collective-owned Units	港澳台及外商投资单位 Units with Investment from Hong Kong, Macao, Taiwan and Foreign Countries	其他单位 Other Ownership Units
全 市	**Total**	**56 300**	**86 042**	**45 990**	**73 598**	**42 115**
按产业分	**Grouped by Industry**					
第一产业	Primary Industry	33 432	53 462	74 145	24 191	28 394
第二产业	Secondary Industry	47 385	70 348	37 921	61 694	37 276
第三产业	Tertiary Industry	65 128	89 151	51 442	104 777	46 867
按行业分	**Grouped by Sector**					
农、林、牧、渔业	Farming, Forestry, Animal Husbandry and Fishery	33 432	53 462	74 145	24 191	28 394
工 业	Industry	49 026	72 238	37 199	61 272	37 181
采矿业	Mining	100 194	41 860			121 640
制造业	Manufacturing	48 021	58 641	36 484	61 140	36 715
电力、热力、燃气及水的生产和供应业	Electricity, Heat, Gas and Water Production and Supply Industry	111 672	118 206	64 468	119 784	95 433
建筑业	Construction	40 455	64 551	39 553	102 770	37 508
批发和零售业	Wholesale and Retail	49 776	74 393	31 056	107 279	31 043
批发业	Wholesale	57 964	94 375	34 351	136 974	31 805
零售业	Retail	35 948	49 398	28 201	54 691	29 750
交通运输、仓储和邮政业	Transportation, Warehousing and Post	56 639	71 643	22 089	78 555	48 549
#交通运输	Transportation	55 477	70 695	20 020	84 809	48 425
邮政业	Postal	81 192	83 970	73 618	53 681	37 452
住宿和餐饮业	Hoteling and Catering	34 932	49 072	31 342	42 326	31 100
#餐饮业	Catering	30 997	38 043	31 468	39 891	27 760
信息传输、软件和信息技术服务业	Information Transmission, Software and IT Services	86 176	140 997		123 276	62 244
#信息传输	Information Transmission	126 450	144 180		115 419	87 488
金融业	Financial Industries	170 945	193 516	34 687	226 934	156 280
房地产业	Real Estate	50 172	60 354	41 689	67 285	44 144
租赁和商务服务业	Leasing and Business Services	44 994	41 640	50 820	137 843	38 062
科学研究和技术服务业	Scientific and Technical Services	84 726	114 331	74 862	184 036	58 313
水利、环境和公共设施管理业	Water Conservancies, Environment and Public Facilities Management	51 218	55 980	38 079	67 686	39 591
居民服务、修理和其他服务业	Resident Services, Repairs and Other Services	26 390	57 455	45 994	30 685	23 869
教 育	Education	86 506	90 009	62 773	58 841	50 923
卫生和社会工作	Health and Social Work	103 072	110 481	86 368	155 989	38 996
卫 生	Healthcare	104 276	112 067	87 122	155 989	39 037
社会工作	Social Welfare	64 445	66 001	39 402		22 727
文化、体育和娱乐业	Culture, Sports and Entertainment	64 151	82 721	56 623	45 990	39 521
文 化	Culture	86 612	87 285	56 121	74 869	94 297
体 育	Sports	49 931	59 547	80 226	29 814	43 712
娱乐业	Entertainment	36 450	96 976		122 959	29 032
公共管理、社会保障和社会组织	Public Administration, Social Security and Social Organizations	93 867	94 688	54 113		67 524
#社会保障	Social Security	66 912	67 407	65 564		36 444

表 3.11 主要年份离退休、退职人员养老金
PENSION FOR NONWORKING STAFF AND WORKERS IN MAIN YEARS

单位:亿元(100 million yuan)

指标	Indicators	2000	2010	2011	2012
离退休、退职人员养老金	**Pension for Nonworking Staff and Workers**	**205.14**	**783.42**	**912.71**	**1 018.79**
离休职工的离休费	Pensions for Retired Veteran Cadres	7.32	11.41	11.67	10.20
退休职工的退休费	Pensions for Retired	195.90	763.44	891.76	998.20
退职人员的退职生活费	Living Expenses for the Resigned	1.92	8.57	9.28	10.39

表 3.12 离退休、退职人员养老金(2012)
PENSION FOR NONWORKING STAFF AND WORKERS

单位:亿元(100 million yuan)

指标	Indicators	合计 Total	国有单位 State-owned Units	集体单位 Collective-owned Units	其他单位 Other Ownership Units
离退休、退职人员养老金	**Pension for Nonworking Staff and Workers**	**1 018.79**	**462.80**	**118.16**	**437.83**
离休职工的离休费	Pensions for Retired Veteran Cadres	10.20	7.39	0.16	2.65
退休职工的退休费	Pensions for Retired	998.20	451.08	116.02	431.10
退职人员的退职生活费	Living Expenses for the Resigned	10.39	4.33	1.98	4.08

注：本表"其他单位"包括港澳台及外商企业。
Note: "Other Ownership Units" in this table includes foreign invested and HongKong,Maca and Taiwan funded enterprises.

上 / 海 / 统 / 计 / 年 / 鉴

主要统计指标解释

从业人员

指从事一定社会劳动并取得工资或其他形式劳动报酬的人员，包括在岗职工、劳务派遣人员、再就业的离退休人员、私营业主、个体户主、私营和个体从业人员、乡镇企业从业人员、农村从业人员、其他从业人员(包括民办教师、宗教职业者、现役军人等)。这一指标反映了一定时期内全部劳动力资源的实际利用情况，是研究我国基本国情国力的重要指标。

各单位的从业人员指在各级国家机关、政党机关、社会团体及企业、事业单位中工作，取得工资或其他形式的劳动报酬的全部人员。包括在岗职工、劳务派遣人员、再就业的离退休人员、民办教师以及在各单位中工作的外方人员和港澳台方人员、兼职人员、借用的外单位人员和第二职业者。不包括离开本单位仍保留劳动关系的职工。各单位的就业人员反映了各单位实际参加生产或工作的全部劳动力。

职工

指在国有、城镇集体、联营、股份制、外商和港、澳、台投资、其他单位及其附属机构工作，并由其支付工资的各类人员。不包括下列人员：(1)乡镇企业就业人员；(2)城镇个体劳动者；(3)离休、退休、退职人员；(4)再就业的离、退休人员；(5)民办教师；(6)在城镇单位中工作的外方及港、澳、台人员；(7)其他按有关规定不列入职工统计范围的人员。

城镇登记失业人员

指有非农业户口，在一定的劳动年龄内(16 岁以上及男 50 岁以下、女 45 岁以下)，有劳动能力，无业而要求就业，并在当地就业服务机构进行求职登记的人员。

城镇登记失业率

指城镇登记失业人员同城镇单位就业人员、城镇私营企业及个体就业人员(扣除使用的农村劳动力、聘用的离退休人员、港澳台及外方人员)和城镇登记失业人员、城镇单位中的不在岗职工之和的比。计算公式为：

城镇登记失业率 = 城镇登记失业人员 / （城镇单位就业人员 − 使用的农村劳动力 − 聘用的离退休人员 − 聘用的港澳台及外方人员 + 不在岗职工 + 城镇私营企业及个体就业人员 + 城镇登记失业人员）× 100%

从业人员工资总额

根据《关于工资总额组成的规定》(1990 年 1 月 1 日国家统计局发布的一号令)进行修订，本单位在一定时期内(一季度、一年)直接支付给本单位全部从业人员的劳动报酬总额。包括计时工资、计件工资、奖金、津贴和补贴、加班加点工资、特殊情况下支付的工资。是在岗职工工资总额、劳务派遣人员工资总额和其他从业人员工资总额之和。

职工工资总额

指在报告期内直接支付给本单位职工的劳动报酬或生活费。职工工资总额包括在岗职工工资和离岗职工生活费两部分。

职工平均工资

指企业、事业、机关单位的职工在一定时期内平均每人所得的货币工资额。它表明一定时期职工工资收入的高低程度，是反映职工工资水平的主要指标。计算公式为：

职工平均工资 = 报告期实际支付的全部职工工资总额 / 报告期全部职工平均人数

SHANGHAI STATISTICAL YEARBOOK

EXPLANATORY NOTES TO MAJOR STATISTICAL INDICATORS

□ Employees

Employees refer to the persons who are engaged in social working and receive wages and other forms of remuneration payment, including total staff and workers, labor dispatched personnel, re-employed retirees, employers of private enterprises, self-employed workers, employees in private enterprises and individual economy, employees in township enterprises, employed persons in the rural areas , and other employed persons (including teachers in the schools run by the local people, people engaged in religious profession and the servicemen, etc.). This indicator reflects the actual utilization of total labour force during a certain period of time and is often used for the research on China's economic situation and national power.

Employees in Various Units refer to all the persons working in government agencies of various levels, political and party organizations, social organizations, enterprises and institutions, and receiving wages or other forms of payment. They include fully-employed staff and workers, labor dispatched personnel, re-employed retirees, teachers in schools run by the local people, foreigners and Chinese compatriots from Hong Kong, Macao, and Taiwan working in various units, part -time employees, employees of other units working temporarily at current posts, and employees holding the second job, but exclude staff and workers who have left their working units while keeping their labor contract (employment relation) unchanged. This indicator reflects the total number of laborers actually engaged in production or other operations in various units.

□ Staff and Workers

Staff and Workers refer to persons working in, and receive payment from units of state ownership, collective ownership, joint ownership, share holding ownership, foreign ownership, and ownership by entrepreneurship from Hong Kong, Macao, and Taiwan, and other types of ownership and their affiliated units. They do not include 1) persons employed in township enterprises, 2) urban self-employed persons, 3) retirees, 4) re-employed retirees, 5) teachers in the schools run by the local people, 6) foreigners and persons from Hong Kong, Macao and Taiwan who work in urban units, and 7) other persons not to be included by relevant regulations.

□ Registered Urban Unemployment

Registered Urban Unemployment refers to those non-agricultural population within working age (16-50 years for male and 16-45 years for females),who are able and willing to work but unemployed and have registered for job in local employment service agencies.

□ Registered Urban Unemployment Rate

Registered Urban Unemployment Rate refers to the ratio of the number of the registered unemployed to the sum of the number of persons employed in various units (minus the rural labour force, retirees, and Hong Kong, Macao, Taiwan and foreign employees they employ) laid-off workers in urban units, urban self-employed individuals and the registered urban unemployed persons. The formula is as follows:

Registered Urban Unemployment Rate = Number of Registered Urban Unemployed Persons ÷ (Number of Persons Employed in Urban Units − rural labour force employed− retirees employed − Hong Kong, Macao, Taiwan and foreign employees + laid-off workers + Self-employed Individuals in Urban Areas + Number of Registered Urban Unemployed Persons) × 100%.

□ Total Wages of Employees

Revised by Provisions on the composition of Total Wages (No.1 Order issued by National Bureau of Statistics in January 1, 1990), Total Wages of Employees refers to the total remuneration payment to employees in various units during a certain period of time (one quarter or one year). It contains hourly wages, piece rate wages, bonuses, allowances and subsidies, overtime wages, wages paid in special circumstances. It is the sum of total wages of staff and workers on duty, total wages of labour dispatched personnel and total wages of other employees.

□ Total Wages of Staff and Workers

Total Wages of Staff and Workers refer to the compensation for services of living cost a unit pays to its employees on the payroll, including the living cost paid to those not on duty.

EXPLANATORY NOTES TO MAJOR STATISTICAL INDICATORS

□ Average Wages of Staff and Workers

Average Wages of Staff and Workers refers to the average wage in money terms per person during a certain period of time for staff and workers in enterprises, institutions, and government agencies, which reflects the general level of wage income during a certain period of time and is calculated as follows:

Average Wages of Staff and Workers = Total Wages of Staff and Workers at Reference Time /Average Number of Staff and Workers at Reference Time.

第四篇

CHAPTER 4

国民经济核算

NATIONAL ECONOMIC ACCOUNTING

简要说明

生产总值(简称 GDP)核算采取国家和地区分级核算制度,上海市生产总值由上海市统计局核算处核算,主要包括:(1)初步核算数。我国按照季度开展 GDP 核算,1~4 季度 GDP 的初步核算数即为年度 GDP 初步核算数,于次年 1 月 20 日左右公布;(2)初步核实数,根据专业统计年报、财政决算资料和行政记录资料计算,在次年《上海市统计年鉴》公布。由于基础资料和核算方法的不同,年度 GDP 初步核算数和初步核实数会有所差异。除上述核算程序外,在国家开展普查和重点行业调查,或计算方法、分类标准发生变化时,上海市统计局须根据国家统计局的有关要求对 GDP 当期或历史数据进行调整,并在《上海市统计年鉴》上公布。

本年鉴所公布的 GDP 核算数据包括:(1)按照当年价格计算的总量;(2)可比增长及指数。GDP 总量变动受到价格变化和物量变化共同影响,在比较不同时期的 GDP 总量时要剔除价格变化的影响,以反映生产活动成果的实际变动。本年鉴公布的 GDP 及相关指标的增速为剔除价格变动影响的可比增速,并在此基础上计算指数。本篇 GDP 核算行业分类标准采用的仍是《国民经济行业分类》(GB/T 4754-2002)。

BRIEF INTRODUCTION

The gross domestic product, or GDP, uses nation–level and city–level classification system for calculation. Shanghai's GDP is produced by the Department of Accounting at the Shanghai Statistics Bureau. It covers (1) Preliminary figure: China calculates quarterly GDP figures, and the yearly preliminary GDP, which is published around January 20 in the following year, equals the preliminary rate for the four quarters combined. (2) Verified figure: it is calculated based on professional statistical report, fiscal accounts data and administrative records, published in the following year's Shanghai Statistical Yearbook. Because of differences in basic information and method of calculation, preliminary figure of the annual GDP and its verified figure may be different. In addition to the above–mentioned calculation procedure, the Shanghai Statistics Bureau modifies related GDP figures when China carries out national census or surveys in key industries, or when calculation methods or classification criteria change. The results should be published on The Shanghai Statistical Yearbook.

GDP data published in this yearbook include: (1) The total output based on the year's prices; (2) Comparable growth and indices. The total output of GDP changes with the prices and volumes, so the comparison of GDP in different periods should exclude the effect of price changes to reflect the actual movement in production activities. Growth of GDP data and related indicators in this yearbook has excluded the effect of price changes and is thus comparable. The indices are based on such comparable data as well. The calculation of GDP on industry Classification still uses The Classification of National Economic Industries (GB/T 4754–2002).

表 4.1 上海市生产总值(1978～2012)
GROSS DOMESTIC PRODUCT

年 份 Year	上海市生产总值(亿元) Gross Domestic Product (100 million yuan)	其 中 of which				
		第一产业 Primary Industry	第二产业 Secondary Industry	其 中 of which 工 业 Industry	其 中 of which 建筑业 Construction	第三产业 Tertiary Industry
1978	272.81	11.00	211.05	207.47	3.58	50.76
1979	286.43	11.39	221.21	216.62	4.59	53.83
1980	311.89	10.10	236.10	230.87	5.23	65.69
1981	324.76	10.58	244.34	237.12	7.22	69.84
1982	337.07	13.31	249.32	240.75	8.57	74.44
1983	351.81	13.52	255.32	246.26	9.06	82.97
1984	390.85	17.26	275.37	263.19	12.18	98.22
1985	466.75	19.53	325.63	311.12	14.51	121.59
1986	490.83	19.69	336.02	318.89	17.13	135.12
1987	545.46	21.60	364.38	336.54	27.84	159.48
1988	648.30	27.36	433.05	399.53	33.52	187.89
1989	696.54	29.63	466.18	432.92	33.26	200.73
1990	781.66	34.24	505.60	469.83	35.77	241.82
1991	893.77	34.06	550.64	514.79	35.85	309.07
1992	1 114.32	34.16	677.39	636.68	40.71	402.77
1993	1 519.23	37.82	902.38	846.71	55.67	579.03
1994	1 990.86	47.61	1 148.45	1 074.37	74.08	794.80
1995	2 499.43	59.82	1 419.41	1 308.20	111.21	1 020.20
1996	2 957.55	68.72	1 596.72	1 452.79	143.93	1 292.11
1997	3 438.79	72.03	1 774.02	1 598.91	175.11	1 592.74
1998	3 801.09	73.84	1 871.89	1 670.19	201.70	1 855.36
1999	4 188.73	74.49	1 984.64	1 787.98	196.66	2 129.60
2000	4 771.17	76.68	2 207.63	1 998.96	208.67	2 486.86
2001	5 210.12	78.00	2 403.18	2 166.74	236.44	2 728.94
2002	5 741.03	79.68	2 622.45	2 368.02	254.43	3 038.90
2003	6 694.23	81.02	3 209.02	2 941.24	267.78	3 404.19
2004	8 072.83	83.45	3 892.12	3 593.25	298.87	4 097.26
2005	9 247.66	90.26	4 381.20	4 036.85	344.35	4 776.20
2006	10 572.24	93.81	4 969.95	4 575.30	394.65	5 508.48
2007	12 494.01	101.84	5 571.06	5 154.42	416.64	6 821.11
2008	14 069.87	111.80	6 085.84	5 576.79	509.05	7 872.23
2009	15 046.45	113.82	6 001.78	5 408.75	593.03	8 930.85
2010	17 165.98	114.15	7 218.32	6 536.21	682.11	9 833.51
2011	19 195.69	124.94	7 927.89	7 208.59	719.30	11 142.86
2012	20 181.72	127.80	7 854.77	7 097.76	757.01	12 199.15

表4.2　上海市生产总值比上年增长(1978～2012)
GROWTH RATE OF GROSS DOMESTIC PRODUCT RAISED PRECEDING YEAR

单位:%

年份 Year	上海市生产总值 Gross Domestic Product	其中 of which 第一产业 Primary Industry	第二产业 Secondary Industry	其中 of which 工业 Industry	建筑业 Construction	第三产业 Tertiary Industry
1978	15.8	27.0	16.6	15.8	89.8	10.6
1979	7.4	-0.7	8.6	8.8	-2.2	3.1
1980	8.4	-0.6	6.0	6.1	1.6	22.2
1981	5.6	0.3	4.9	4.1	39.2	8.9
1982	7.2	26.2	4.6	4.2	18.7	13.4
1983	7.8	平	7.5	7.5	8.9	9.8
1984	11.6	25.2	10.0	9.7	19.3	14.7
1985	13.4	-22.2	14.9	15.0	11.1	14.7
1986	4.4	-0.2	4.0	3.7	11.7	6.0
1987	7.5	-2.7	7.4	6.8	22.3	8.9
1988	10.1	4.6	9.4	9.3	12.1	12.6
1989	3.0	0.3	1.6	1.9	-4.4	7.1
1990	3.5	4.3	2.8	2.7	5.1	5.3
1991	7.1	0.4	6.9	8.8	-18.7	8.6
1992	14.8	0.4	17.2	17.7	7.7	12.0
1993	15.1	-2.7	16.7	16.9	13.8	13.7
1994	14.5	2.9	14.2	14.2	14.1	16.2
1995	14.3	6.4	14.8	14.3	25.0	13.7
1996	13.1	5.0	11.1	10.4	24.9	18.1
1997	12.8	4.2	10.6	10.2	16.9	17.9
1998	10.3	2.2	8.2	7.8	14.8	14.8
1999	10.4	2.1	9.0	9.6	-0.6	13.4
2000	11.0	3.4	9.8	10.2	3.0	13.5
2001	10.5	3.0	12.0	12.1	10.9	9.4
2002	11.3	3.0	12.1	12.7	6.4	10.9
2003	12.3	2.3	16.1	17.6	1.3	9.0
2004	14.2	-5.0	14.9	16.1	0.8	14.1
2005	11.4	-9.7	10.5	10.5	10.2	12.8
2006	12.7	0.8	12.0	11.8	14.5	13.6
2007	15.2	2.0	11.5	12.2	4.0	18.8
2008	9.7	0.7	7.5	7.6	5.7	11.7
2009	8.2	-1.1	3.5	2.9	11.7	12.2
2010	10.3	-6.6	16.8	17.5	8.0	5.7
2011	8.2	-0.7	6.3	7.4	-3.5	9.6
2012	7.5	0.5	3.1	2.8	6.1	10.6

表4.3 上海市生产总值指数(以1978年为100，1978～2012)
INDEX OF GROSS DOMESTIC PRODUCT (1978＝100)

年份 Year	上海市生产总值 Gross Domestic Product	其中 of which				
		第一产业 Primary Industry	第二产业 Secondary Industry	其中 of which		第三产业 Tertiary Industry
				工业 Industry	建筑业 Construction	
1978	100	100	100	100	100	100
1979	107.4	99.3	108.6	108.8	97.8	103.1
1980	116.4	98.7	115.1	115.4	99.4	126.0
1981	122.9	99.0	120.7	120.1	138.4	137.2
1982	131.7	124.9	126.3	125.1	164.3	155.6
1983	142.0	124.9	135.8	134.5	178.9	170.8
1984	158.5	156.4	149.4	147.5	213.4	195.9
1985	179.7	121.7	171.7	169.6	237.1	224.7
1986	187.6	121.5	178.6	175.9	264.8	238.2
1987	201.7	118.2	191.8	187.9	323.9	259.4
1988	222.1	123.6	209.8	205.4	363.1	292.1
1989	228.8	124.0	213.2	209.3	347.1	312.8
1990	236.8	129.3	219.2	215.0	364.8	329.4
1991	253.7	129.8	234.3	233.9	296.6	357.7
1992	291.2	130.3	274.6	275.3	319.4	400.6
1993	335.2	126.8	320.5	321.8	363.5	455.5
1994	383.8	130.5	366.0	367.5	414.8	529.3
1995	438.7	138.9	420.2	420.1	518.5	601.8
1996	496.2	145.8	466.8	463.8	647.6	710.7
1997	559.7	151.9	516.3	511.1	757.0	837.9
1998	617.3	155.2	558.6	551.0	869.0	961.9
1999	681.5	158.5	608.9	603.9	863.8	1 090.8
2000	756.5	163.9	668.6	665.5	889.7	1 238.1
2001	835.9	168.8	748.8	746.0	986.7	1 354.5
2002	930.4	173.9	839.4	840.7	1 049.8	1 502.1
2003	1 044.8	177.9	974.5	988.7	1 063.4	1 637.3
2004	1 193.2	169.0	1 119.7	1 147.9	1 071.9	1 868.2
2005	1 329.2	152.6	1 237.3	1 268.4	1 181.2	2 107.3
2006	1 498.0	153.8	1 385.8	1 418.1	1 352.5	2 393.9
2007	1 725.7	156.9	1 545.2	1 591.1	1 406.6	2 844.0
2008	1 893.1	158.0	1 661.1	1 712.0	1 486.8	3 176.7
2009	2 048.3	156.3	1 719.2	1 761.6	1 660.8	3 564.3
2010	2 259.3	146.0	2 008.0	2 069.9	1 793.7	3 767.5
2011	2 444.6	145.0	2 134.5	2 223.1	1 730.9	4 129.2
2012	2 627.9	145.7	2 200.7	2 285.3	1 836.5	4 566.9

表4.4 上海市生产总值构成(1978～2012)
STRUCTURE OF GROSS DOMESTIC PRODUCT

单位:%

年份 Year	上海市生产总值 Gross Domestic Product	其中 of which				
		第一产业 Primary Industry	第二产业 Secondary Industry	其中 of which		第三产业 Tertiary Industry
				工业 Industry	建筑业 Construction	
1978	100	4.0	77.4	76.1	1.3	18.6
1979	100	4.0	77.2	75.6	1.6	18.8
1980	100	3.2	75.7	74.0	1.7	21.1
1981	100	3.3	75.2	73.0	2.2	21.5
1982	100	3.9	74.0	71.4	2.6	22.1
1983	100	3.8	72.6	70.0	2.6	23.6
1984	100	4.4	70.5	67.4	3.1	25.1
1985	100	4.2	69.8	66.7	3.1	26.0
1986	100	4.0	68.5	65.0	3.5	27.5
1987	100	4.0	66.8	61.7	5.1	29.2
1988	100	4.2	66.8	61.6	5.2	29.0
1989	100	4.3	66.9	62.1	4.8	28.8
1990	100	4.4	64.7	60.1	4.6	30.9
1991	100	3.8	61.6	57.6	4.0	34.6
1992	100	3.1	60.8	57.1	3.7	36.1
1993	100	2.5	59.4	55.7	3.7	38.1
1994	100	2.4	57.7	54.0	3.7	39.9
1995	100	2.4	56.8	52.3	4.5	40.8
1996	100	2.3	54.0	49.1	4.9	43.7
1997	100	2.1	51.6	46.5	5.1	46.3
1998	100	1.9	49.3	44.0	5.3	48.8
1999	100	1.8	47.4	42.7	4.7	50.8
2000	100	1.6	46.3	41.9	4.4	52.1
2001	100	1.5	46.1	41.6	4.5	52.4
2002	100	1.4	45.7	41.3	4.4	52.9
2003	100	1.2	47.9	43.9	4.0	50.9
2004	100	1.0	48.2	44.5	3.7	50.8
2005	100	1.0	47.4	43.7	3.7	51.6
2006	100	0.9	47.0	43.3	3.7	52.1
2007	100	0.8	44.6	41.3	3.3	54.6
2008	100	0.8	43.2	39.6	3.6	56.0
2009	100	0.7	39.9	36.0	3.9	59.4
2010	100	0.7	42.0	38.0	4.0	57.3
2011	100	0.7	41.3	37.6	3.7	58.0
2012	100	0.6	39.0	35.2	3.8	60.4

表4.5 上海市人均生产总值(1978～2012)
PER CAPITA GROSS DOMESTIC PRODUCT

年 份 Year	上海市生产总值(亿元) Gross Domestic Product (100 million yuan)	人均生产总值(按人民币计算)(元) Per Capita Gross Domestic Product (yuan)	人均生产总值指数 Per Capita Gross Domestic Product Index 以1978年为100 (1978=100)	以上年为100 (preceding year=100)	人均生产总值(按美元计算)(美元) Per Capita Gross Domestic Product (USD)
1978	272.81	2 485	100.0	114.9	1 445
1979	286.43	2 556	105.3	105.3	1 787
1980	311.89	2 725	111.8	106.2	1 829
1981	324.76	2 800	116.5	104.2	1 642
1982	337.07	2 864	123.0	105.6	1 513
1983	351.81	2 947	130.7	106.3	1 492
1984	390.85	3 232	144.0	110.2	1 389
1985	466.75	3 811	161.3	112.0	1 298
1986	490.83	3 956	166.1	103.0	1 146
1987	545.46	4 340	176.2	106.1	1 166
1988	648.30	5 080	191.0	108.4	1 365
1989	696.54	5 362	193.3	101.2	1 424
1990	781.66	5 911	196.6	101.7	1 236
1991	893.77	6 661	207.6	105.6	1 251
1992	1 114.32	8 208	235.6	113.5	1 488
1993	1 519.23	1 1061	268.1	113.8	1 920
1994	1 990.86	14 328	303.2	113.1	1 662
1995	2 499.43	17 779	342.3	112.9	2 129
1996	2 957.55	20 647	380.0	111.0	2 483
1997	3 438.79	23 397	417.6	109.9	2 822
1998	3 801.09	25 206	448.9	107.5	3 045
1999	4 188.73	27 071	483.0	107.6	3 270
2000	4 771.17	30 047	522.6	108.2	3 630
2001	5 210.12	31 799	559.7	107.1	3 842
2002	5 741.03	33 958	603.9	107.9	4 103
2003	6 694.23	38 486	658.9	109.1	4 650
2004	8 072.83	44 839	727.4	110.4	5 417
2005	9 247.66	49 648	781.2	107.4	6 061
2006	10 572.24	54 858	851.5	109.0	6 882
2007	12 494.01	62 040	939.2	110.3	8 159
2008	14 069.87	66 932	987.1	105.1	9 637
2009	15 046.45	69 165	1 032.5	104.6	10 125
2010	17 165.98	76 074	1 098.6	106.4	11 238
2011	19 195.69	82 560	1 153.5	105.0	12 784
2012	20 181.72	85 373	1 219.3	105.7	13 524

①1978 年～1992 年的人均生产总值按户籍人口计算，1993 年以后按半年以上常住人口计算。
②2001～2009 年的人均生产总值根据第六次人口普查结果调整后的年末常住人口数计算。
❶Per Capita Gross Domestic Product from 1978 to 1992 were calculated by registared population ,and resident population above half year after 1993.
❷Data of Per Capita Gross Domestic Product from 2001 to 2009 are calculated by resident population at year-end which have been adjusted according to the result of the sixth National Plpulation Census.

表4.6　主要年份上海市生产总值(按三次产业分)
GROSS DOMESTIC PRODUCT (CLASSIFIED BY THREE INDUSTRIES) IN MAIN YEARS

单位:亿元(100 million yuan)

指　标	Indicators	2001	2010	2011	2012
上海市生产总值	**Gross Domestic Product**	**5 210.12**	**17 165.98**	**19 195.69**	**20 181.72**
第一产业	Primary Industry	78.00	114.15	124.94	127.80
第二产业	Secondary Industry	2 403.18	7 218.32	7 927.89	7 854.77
工　业	Industry	2 166.74	6 536.21	7 208.59	7 097.76
建筑业	Construction	236.44	682.11	719.30	757.01
第三产业	Tertiary Industry	2 728.94	9 833.51	11 142.86	12 199.15
交通运输、仓储和邮政业	Transportation, Warehousing and Post	345.99	834.40	868.31	895.31
信息传输、计算机服务和软件业	Information Transmission, Computer Servcie and Software Industries	176.72	675.98	784.77	918.83
批发和零售业	Retail and Wholesale Industries	555.06	2 594.34	3 040.99	3 291.93
住宿和餐饮业	Hoteling and Catering	104.30	266.45	279.34	298.40
金融业	Financial Industry	529.26	1 950.96	2 277.40	2 450.36
房地产业	Real Estate Industry	328.59	1 002.50	1 019.68	1 147.04
租赁和商务服务业	Leasehold and Business in Services	136.97	776.13	912.60	1 065.56
科学研究、技术服务和地质勘查业	Scientific Research, Technology Service and Geological Prospecting	114.91	391.28	447.02	503.80
水利、环境和公共设施管理业	Water Conservancy, Environment and Public Facility Management Industries	32.59	50.19	53.40	60.00
居民服务和其他服务业	Community Service and Other Service Industries	46.16	179.98	205.06	221.88
教　育	Education	136.53	400.36	437.09	462.34
卫生、社会保障和社会福利业	Health, Social Security and Welfare Industries	72.27	250.41	286.89	328.43
文化、体育和娱乐	Culture, Sports and Entertainment	43.96	93.98	115.21	120.10
公共管理和社会组织	Public Administration and Social Organizations	105.63	366.55	415.10	435.17

表 4.7 主要年份上海市生产总值比上年增长(按三次产业分)
GROWTH RATE OF GROSS DOMESTIC PRODUCT IN MAIN YEARS(CLASSIFIED BY THREE INDUSTRIES)

单位:%

指 标	Indicators	2001	2010	2011	2012
上海市生产总值	**Gross Domestic Product**	**10.5**	**10.3**	**8.2**	**7.5**
第一产业	Primary Industry	3.0	-6.6	-0.7	0.5
第二产业	Secondary Industry	12.0	16.8	6.3	3.1
工 业	Industry	12.1	17.5	7.4	2.8
建筑业	Construction	10.9	8.0	-3.5	6.1
第三产业	Tertiary Industry	9.4	5.7	9.6	10.6
交通运输、仓储和邮政业	Transportation, Warehousing and Post	8.9	16.0	5.4	5.0
信息传输、计算机服务和软件业	Information Transmission, Computer Servcie and Software Industries	18.1	11.2	17.8	16.5
批发和零售业	Retail and Wholesale Industries	15.7	15.6	12.6	11.5
住宿和餐饮业	Hoteling and Catering	7.8	6.8	-0.3	2.6
金融业	Financial Industry	-9.1	5.1	9.4	12.6
房地产业	Real Estate Industry	20.4	-29.3	-2.4	4.7
租赁和商务服务业	Leasehold and Business in Services	29.5	15.7	15.9	12.3
科学研究、技术服务和地质勘查业	Scientific Research, Technological Service and Geological Prospecting	9.9	5.1	10.1	13.2
水利、环境和公共设施管理业	Water Conservancy, Environment and Public Facility Management Industries	23.9	9.2	3.2	13.9
居民服务和其他服务业	Community Service and Other Services Industries	18.8	12.5	12.8	7.1
教 育	Education	14.4	4.6	7.7	8.2
卫生、社会保障和社会福利业	Health, Social Security and Welfare Industries	14.0	6.2	10.3	16.7
文化、体育和娱乐	Culture, Sports and Entertainment	13.8	6.4	19.9	4.1
公共管理和社会组织	Public Administration and Social Organizations	14.5	9.5	8.5	9.2

表 4.8 上海市生产总值收入法项目(1978 ~ 2012)
GROSS DOMESTIC PRODUCT(BY INCOME ITEM)

单位:亿元(100 million yuan)

年 分 Year	上海市生产总 值 Gross Domestic Product	劳动者报酬 Compensation of Employees	生产税净额 Net Taxes on Production	固定资产折旧 Depreciation of Fixed Assets	营业盈余 Operating Surplus
1978	272.81	62.03	45.53	10.60	154.65
1979	286.43	68.15	45.61	11.13	161.54
1980	311.89	74.47	49.49	13.05	174.88
1981	324.76	78.99	54.52	14.70	176.55
1982	337.07	85.00	57.09	16.30	178.68
1983	351.81	90.36	57.51	18.73	185.21
1984	390.85	108.79	68.74	20.81	192.51
1985	466.75	125.99	87.36	26.16	227.24
1986	490.83	141.95	86.31	33.42	229.15
1987	545.46	163.88	98.61	40.73	242.24
1988	648.30	197.69	126.95	71.85	251.81
1989	696.54	223.35	136.01	79.79	257.39
1990	781.66	244.03	149.35	92.93	295.35
1991	893.77	302.94	170.42	126.62	293.79
1992	1 114.32	397.72	207.40	160.36	348.84
1993	1 519.23	563.59	257.30	159.93	538.41
1994	1 990.86	692.40	356.32	245.26	696.88
1995	2 499.43	901.83	430.67	339.77	827.16
1996	2 957.55	1 065.85	576.01	376.70	938.99
1997	3 438.79	1 195.63	716.02	425.04	1 102.10
1998	3 801.09	1 341.22	809.04	514.85	1 135.98
1999	4 188.73	1 518.26	902.10	615.28	1 153.09
2000	4 771.17	1 724.29	1 124.30	679.43	1 243.15
2001	5 210.12	1 934.27	1 184.62	769.59	1 321.64
2002	5 741.03	2 205.79	1 219.35	850.69	1 465.20
2003	6 694.23	2 452.32	1 265.89	975.24	2 000.78
2004	8 072.83	2 771.77	1 313.83	1 265.16	2 722.07
2005	9 247.66	3 312.31	1 459.39	1 488.54	2 987.42
2006	10 572.24	3 846.06	1 729.03	1 721.21	3 275.94
2007	12 494.01	4 481.91	2 142.97	1 931.76	3 937.37
2008	14 069.87	5 417.93	2 662.86	2 132.75	3 856.33
2009	15 046.45	5 901.84	2 916.92	2 229.19	3 998.50
2010	17 165.98	6 742.05	3 298.73	2 275.95	4 849.25
2011	19 195.69	7 709.62	3 713.40	2 298.34	5 474.33
2012	20 181.72	8 389.14	4 022.74	2 460.38	5 309.46

表 4.9　上海市生产总值收入法项目构成(1978～2012)
STRUCTURE OF GROSS DOMESTIC PRODUCT(BY INCOME ITEM)

单位:%

年 份 Year	上海市生产总 值 Gross Domestic Product	劳动者报酬 Compensation of Employees	生产税净额 Net Taxes on Production	固定资产折旧 Depreciation of Fixed Assets	营业盈余 Operating Surplus
1978	100	22.7	16.7	3.9	56.7
1979	100	23.8	15.9	3.9	56.4
1980	100	23.9	15.8	4.2	56.1
1981	100	24.3	16.8	4.5	54.4
1982	100	25.2	17.0	4.8	53.0
1983	100	25.7	16.4	5.3	52.6
1984	100	27.8	17.6	5.3	49.3
1985	100	27.0	18.7	5.6	48.7
1986	100	28.9	17.6	6.8	46.7
1987	100	30.0	18.1	7.5	44.4
1988	100	30.5	19.6	11.1	38.8
1989	100	32.1	19.5	11.5	36.9
1990	100	31.2	19.1	11.9	37.8
1991	100	33.9	19.1	14.1	32.9
1992	100	35.7	18.6	14.4	31.3
1993	100	37.1	16.9	10.5	35.5
1994	100	34.8	17.9	12.3	35.0
1995	100	36.1	17.2	13.6	33.1
1996	100	36.0	19.5	12.7	31.8
1997	100	34.8	20.8	12.4	32.0
1998	100	35.3	21.3	13.5	29.9
1999	100	36.3	21.5	14.7	27.5
2000	100	36.1	23.6	14.2	26.1
2001	100	37.1	22.7	14.8	25.4
2002	100	38.4	21.3	14.8	25.5
2003	100	36.6	18.9	14.6	29.9
2004	100	34.3	16.3	15.7	33.7
2005	100	35.8	15.8	16.1	32.3
2006	100	36.3	16.4	16.3	31.0
2007	100	35.9	17.1	15.5	31.5
2008	100	38.5	18.9	15.2	27.4
2009	100	39.2	19.4	14.8	26.6
2010	100	39.3	19.2	13.3	28.2
2011	100	40.2	19.3	12.0	28.5
2012	100	41.6	19.9	12.2	26.3

表 4.10 主要年份上海市生产总值(按所有制分)
GROSS DOMESTIC PRODUCT(BY OWNERSHIP) IN MAIN YEARS

年份 Year	上海市生产总值 Gross Domestic Product	其中 of which				
		公有制经济 Public-owned	其中 of which 国有经济 State-owned	集体经济 Collective-owned	非公有制经济 Non-public-owned	其中 of which #私营和个体 Private
绝对值(亿元)	Absolute Volume(100million yuan)					
1990	781.66	746.03	556.87	189.16	35.63	22.39
1995	2 499.43	2 047.57	1 489.06	558.51	451.86	192.66
2000	4 771.17	3 409.97	2 626.33	783.64	1 361.20	623.84
2001	5 210.12	3 554.56	2 773.76	780.80	1 655.56	830.27
2002	5 741.03	3 703.46	2 888.57	814.89	2 037.57	1 055.48
2003	6 694.23	4 171.16	3 360.21	810.95	2 523.07	1 258.15
2004	8 072.83	4 810.32	4 069.95	740.37	3 262.51	1 293.56
2005	9 247.66	5 256.49	4 471.92	784.57	3 991.17	1 944.55
2006	10 572.24	5 812.87	4 994.48	818.39	4 759.37	2 281.10
2007	12 494.01	6 674.98	5 852.65	822.33	5 819.03	2 804.01
2008	14 069.87	7 341.75	6 452.92	888.83	6 728.12	3 313.18
2009	15 046.45	7 769.86	6 864.01	905.85	7 276.59	3 571.19
2010	17 165.98	8 662.92	7 755.35	907.57	8 503.06	4 139.07
2011	19 195.69	9 585.12	8 660.23	924.89	9 610.57	4 598.84
2012	20 181.72	9 954.95	9 000.30	954.65	10 226.77	4 887.86
构成(%)	Composition(%)					
1990	100	95.4	71.2	24.2	4.6	2.9
1995	100	81.9	59.6	22.3	18.1	7.7
2000	100	71.4	55.0	16.4	28.6	13.1
2001	100	68.2	53.2	15.0	31.8	15.9
2002	100	64.5	50.3	14.2	35.5	18.4
2003	100	62.3	50.2	12.1	37.7	18.8
2004	100	59.6	50.4	9.2	40.4	19.7
2005	100	56.9	48.4	8.5	43.1	21.0
2006	100	55.0	47.3	7.7	45.0	21.6
2007	100	53.4	46.8	6.6	46.6	22.4
2008	100	52.2	45.9	6.3	47.8	23.5
2009	100	51.6	45.6	6.0	48.4	23.7
2010	100	50.5	45.2	5.3	49.5	24.1
2011	100	49.9	45.1	4.8	50.1	24.0
2012	100	49.3	44.6	4.7	50.7	24.2

表4.11 主要年份非公有制经济增加值(按产业分)
ADDED VALUE OF NON-PUBLIC-OWNED (GROUPED BY INDUSTRY) IN MAIN YEARS

单位:亿元(100 million yuan)

年份 Year	非公有制经济增加值 Added Value of Non-public-owned	其中 of which			
		第一产业 Primary Industry	第二产业 Secondary Industry	其中 of which 工业 Industry	第三产业 Tertiary Industry
1978	2.71	1.64	0.07	0.40	0.40
1990	35.63	9.01	15.22	13.74	11.40
1991	44.72	8.10	22.20	20.62	14.41
1992	73.41	7.65	42.13	39.85	23.63
1993	133.93	8.98	77.02	72.81	47.93
1994	250.63	10.88	154.62	148.31	85.13
1995	451.86	13.29	285.73	274.64	152.84
1996	655.39	14.31	424.30	407.69	216.78
1997	790.60	13.42	503.69	470.23	273.49
1998	940.64	13.25	561.66	518.25	365.72
1999	1 124.96	13.56	635.83	585.76	475.57
2000	1 361.20	14.25	773.50	715.18	573.45
2001	1 655.56	14.77	924.21	857.62	716.58
2002	2 037.57	14.34	1 085.12	1 004.78	938.11
2003	2 523.07	13.04	1 459.67	1 378.21	1 050.36
2004	3 262.51	10.44	1 921.74	1 757.96	1 330.33
2005	3 991.17	11.12	2 228.18	2 054.78	1 751.87
2006	4 759.37	11.41	2 634.01	2 438.40	2 113.95
2007	5 819.03	11.98	3 044.61	2 831.64	2 762.44
2008	6 728.12	13.35	3 294.60	3 039.51	3 420.17
2009	7 276.59	13.09	3 213.99	2 925.50	4 049.50
2010	8 503.06	13.13	3 928.43	3 575.67	4 561.50
2011	9 610.57	14.39	4 338.15	3 960.36	5 258.03
2012	10 226.77	14.72	4 312.21	3 882.90	5 899.84

表 4.12　上海市生产总值(支出法)(1978～2012)
GROSS DOMESTIC PRODUCT(BY EXPENDITURE APPROACH)

年　份 Year	上海市生产总值(亿元) Gross Domestic Product (100 million yuan)	其中 of which 货物和服务净流出 Net Outflows of Goods and Services	本市使用的生产总值 Gross Domestic Product Used	其中 of which 最终消费支出 Final Consumption	资本形成总额 Gross Capital Formation	上海市生产总值构成(%) Composition of GDP(%) #最终消费支出 Final Consumption	#资本形成总额 Gross Capital Formation	可供投资率(%) Available Investment Rate(%)
1978	272.81	165.79	107.02	59.06	47.96	21.6	17.6	78.4
1979	286.43	171.48	114.95	71.34	43.61	24.9	15.2	75.1
1980	311.89	164.13	147.76	81.24	66.52	26.0	21.3	74.0
1981	324.76	158.35	166.41	89.73	76.68	27.6	23.6	72.4
1982	337.07	153.90	183.17	92.90	90.27	27.6	26.8	72.4
1983	351.81	178.76	173.05	101.19	71.86	28.8	20.4	71.2
1984	390.85	171.97	218.88	117.25	101.63	30.0	26.0	70.0
1985	466.75	122.47	344.28	155.15	189.13	33.2	40.5	66.8
1986	490.83	80.97	409.86	181.74	228.12	37.0	46.5	63.0
1987	545.46	103.70	441.76	200.74	241.02	36.8	44.2	63.2
1988	648.30	57.32	590.98	255.42	335.56	39.4	51.8	60.6
1989	696.54	46.24	650.30	298.62	351.68	42.9	50.5	57.1
1990	781.66	91.87	689.79	358.45	331.34	45.9	42.4	54.1
1991	893.77	167.68	726.09	386.06	340.03	43.2	38.0	56.8
1992	1 114.32	150.12	964.20	476.57	487.63	42.7	43.8	57.2
1993	1 519.23	75.60	1 443.63	699.52	744.11	46.0	49.0	54.0
1994	1 990.86	-90.46	2 081.32	919.83	1 161.49	46.2	58.3	53.8
1995	2 499.43	-218.64	2 718.07	1 150.35	1 567.72	46.0	62.7	54.0
1996	2 957.55	-348.05	3 305.60	1 348.76	1 956.84	45.6	66.2	54.4
1997	3 438.79	-210.99	3 649.78	1 600.83	2 048.95	46.6	59.6	53.4
1998	3 801.09	32.25	3 768.84	1 758.09	2 010.75	46.3	52.9	53.7
1999	4 188.73	259.37	3 929.36	1 959.12	1 970.24	46.8	47.0	53.2
2000	4 771.17	356.93	4 414.24	2 244.52	2 169.72	47.0	45.5	53.0
2001	5 210.12	377.21	4 832.91	2 476.20	2 356.71	47.5	45.2	52.5
2002	5 741.03	418.68	5 322.35	2 791.06	2 531.29	48.6	44.1	51.4
2003	6 694.23	399.96	6 294.27	3 217.59	3 076.68	48.1	46.0	51.9
2004	8 072.83	457.99	7 614.84	3 832.59	3 782.25	47.5	46.9	52.5
2005	9 247.66	548.33	8 699.33	4 480.34	4 218.99	48.4	45.6	51.6
2006	10 572.24	523.75	10 048.49	5 175.15	4 873.34	49.0	46.1	51.0
2007	12 494.01	604.04	11 889.97	6 170.38	5 719.59	49.4	45.8	50.6
2008	14 069.87	753.38	13 316.49	7 172.67	6 143.82	51.0	43.7	49.0
2009	15 046.45	411.80	14 634.65	7 868.64	6 766.01	52.3	45.0	47.7
2010	17 165.98	333.91	16 832.07	9 424.29	7 407.78	54.9	43.2	45.1
2011	19 195.69	645.45	18 550.24	10 821.18	7 729.06	56.4	40.3	43.6
2012	20 181.72	978.32	19 203.40	11 528.58	7 674.82	57.1	38.0	42.9

注：2011 年起，本表至表 4.15 中的数据根据第六次人口普查结果调整后的人口数计算，与历史数据不可比。
Note: The data in table 4.12 to 4.15 have been adjusted according to the sixth National Population Census since 2010, and is uncomparable to historical data.

表4.13 最终消费支出及构成(1978～2012)
FINAL CONSUMPTION AND COMPOSITION

年份 Year	最终消费支出(亿元) Final Consumption (100 million yuan)					最终消费支出构成(%) Composition of Final Consumption (%)	
	合计 Total	居民消费支出 Household Consumption	其中 of which 农村居民 Rural Residents	其中 of which 城镇居民 Urban Residents	政府消费支出 Government Consumption	居民消费支出 Household Consumption	政府消费支出 Government Consumption
1978	59.06	48.25	12.82	35.43	10.81	81.7	18.3
1979	71.34	58.80	17.02	41.78	12.54	82.4	17.6
1980	81.24	66.31	19.43	46.88	14.93	81.6	18.4
1981	89.73	73.69	23.25	50.44	16.04	82.1	17.9
1982	92.90	75.02	26.41	48.61	17.88	80.8	19.2
1983	101.19	81.64	26.91	54.73	19.55	80.7	19.3
1984	117.25	94.56	31.10	63.46	22.69	80.6	19.4
1985	155.15	124.78	38.35	86.43	30.37	80.4	19.6
1986	181.74	145.73	42.49	103.24	36.01	80.2	19.8
1987	200.74	161.09	47.23	113.86	39.65	80.2	19.8
1988	255.42	211.04	55.97	155.07	44.38	82.6	17.4
1989	298.62	244.60	61.15	183.45	54.02	81.9	18.1
1990	358.45	284.79	66.15	218.64	73.66	79.5	20.5
1991	386.06	311.09	72.17	238.92	74.97	80.6	19.4
1992	476.57	366.09	84.86	281.23	110.48	76.8	23.2
1993	699.52	555.45	110.30	445.15	144.07	79.4	20.6
1994	919.83	732.71	130.08	602.63	187.12	79.7	20.3
1995	1 150.35	926.54	152.90	773.64	223.81	80.5	19.5
1996	1 348.76	1 080.79	168.13	912.66	267.97	80.1	19.9
1997	1 600.83	1 262.12	176.50	1 085.62	338.71	78.8	21.2
1998	1 758.09	1 379.41	178.52	1 200.89	378.68	78.5	21.5
1999	1 959.12	1 528.95	176.73	1 352.22	430.17	78.0	22.0
2000	2 244.52	1 756.27	176.79	1 579.48	488.25	78.2	21.8
2001	2 476.20	1 910.44	181.22	1 729.22	565.76	77.2	22.8
2002	2 791.06	2 134.79	185.58	1 949.21	656.27	76.5	23.5
2003	3 217.59	2 437.44	187.78	2 249.66	780.15	75.8	24.2
2004	3 832.59	2 869.26	186.78	2 682.48	963.33	74.9	25.1
2005	4 480.34	3 332.99	194.59	3 138.40	1 147.35	74.4	25.6
2006	5 175.15	3 858.54	223.98	3 634.56	1 316.61	74.6	25.4
2007	6 170.38	4 609.59	245.82	4 363.77	1 560.79	74.7	25.3
2008	7 172.67	5 290.40	275.91	5 014.49	1 882.27	73.7	26.3
2009	7 868.64	5 782.88	303.57	5 479.31	2 085.76	73.5	26.5
2010	9 424.29	7 281.88	339.11	6 942.77	2 142.41	77.3	22.7
2011	10 821.18	8 239.76	441.77	7 797.99	2 581.42	76.1	23.9
2012	11 528.58	8 721.25	468.25	8 253.00	2 807.33	75.6	24.4

表4.14 居民消费水平及指数(1978～2012)
HOUSEHOLD CONSUMPTION LEVEL AND INDEX

年 份 Year	居民消费水平(元) Household Consumption Level(yuan)			指数(以1978年为100) Index(1978 = 100)		
	全 市 Total	其 中 of which		全 市 Total	其 中 of which	
		农村居民 Rural Households	城镇居民 Urban Households		农村居民 Rural Households	城镇居民 Urban Households
1978	442	283	555	100.0	100.0	100.0
1979	527	379	627	117.2	129.1	111.6
1980	582	437	675	123.1	141.9	114.2
1981	638	521	712	133.1	167.2	118.7
1982	640	589	672	133.5	168.9	118.6
1983	688	600	741	142.8	192.9	122.9
1984	788	697	842	160.8	219.5	137.2
1985	1 031	938	1 078	182.0	252.2	153.1
1986	1 190	1 058	1 254	197.7	266.6	167.6
1987	1 298	1 102	1 401	199.9	257.5	173.3
1988	1 680	1 316	1 867	220.3	269.9	194.3
1989	1 927	1 449	2 165	221.4	271.5	194.7
1990	2 225	1 576	2 542	216.1	249.5	193.7
1991	2 420	1 726	2 755	234.3	283.9	206.7
1992	2 842	2 042	3 222	249.5	306.0	219.1
1993	3 923	2 737	4 394	287.4	311.8	255.9
1994	5 081	3 371	5 706	325.3	357.0	286.1
1995	6 310	4 120	7 050	379.3	402.7	333.3
1996	7 228	4 680	8 033	416.5	438.1	364.0
1997	8 289	5 086	9 234	449.0	462.2	391.3
1998	8 896	5 344	9 871	480.4	480.7	417.5
1999	9 683	5 497	10 753	515.9	495.1	448.0
2000	10 922	5 705	12 168	557.7	509.0	484.3
2001	[illegible]1 807	6 052	13 114	604.5	543.6	523.0
2002	[illegible]3 137	6 464	14 569	673.4	580.6	582.1
2003	[illegible]4 247	6 914	15 631	721.9	616.0	617.0
2004	16 470	7 715	17 883	815.0	671.4	689.8
2005	18 741	9 683	19 895	906.0	817.1	750.1
2006	21 475	11 228	22 755	1 019.2	926.5	842.4
2007	25 099	11 845	26 787	1 148.5	934.7	956.6
2008	2[illegible] 242	13 166	30 140	1 245.9	993.1	1 038.1
2009	3[illegible] 358	13 979	32 466	1 345.3	1 055.3	1 123.4
2010	3[illegible] 271	13 609	34 588	1 478.5	1 133.4	1 233.5
2011	3[illegible] 439	17 757	37 558	1 574.6	1 295.5	1 305.0
2012	36 893	18 512	39 095	1 669.1	1 375.8	1 383.3

注：1993年以前为年平均户籍人口数，1993年起为年平均常住人口数。

Note：Data in this table refer to yearly average registered population before 1993, and yearly average resident population after 1993.

表 4.15 资本形成总额和指数(1978～2012)
GROSS CAPITAL FORMATION AND INDEX

年份 Year	资本形成总额(亿元) Gross Capital Formation(100 million yuan)			资本形成总额指数(以1978年为100) Index of Gross Capital Formation (1978 = 100)		
	合计 Total	固定资本形成总额 Fixed Capital Formation	存货增加 Inventory Change	总指数 Indices	固定资本形成总额 Fixed Capital Formation	存货增加 Inventory Change
1978	47.96	31.69	16.27	100	100	100
1979	43.61	39.05	4.56	90.3	119.7	36.9
1980	66.52	45.57	20.95	134.6	133.5	136.7
1981	76.68	55.10	21.58	156.4	164.4	138.1
1982	90.27	70.49	19.78	178.8	210.5	107.6
1983	71.86	74.51	-2.65	150.7	223.7	-12.5
1984	101.63	90.70	10.93	210.0	262.7	91.9
1985	189.13	116.70	72.43	387.6	308.1	564.0
1986	228.12	144.41	83.71	431.8	352.5	607.4
1987	241.02	183.79	57.23	380.0	415.9	298.8
1988	335.56	236.92	98.64	449.2	474.1	392.1
1989	351.68	232.22	119.46	423.1	419.6	429.7
1990	331.34	248.46	82.88	338.1	430.5	131.1
1991	340.03	276.08	63.95	334.0	447.7	109.0
1992	487.63	382.01	105.62	435.2	561.5	162.1
1993	744.11	624.31	119.80	530.1	731.0	154.5
1994	1 161.49	996.48	165.01	726.8	1 019.1	196.1
1995	1 567.72	1 380.85	186.87	950.6	1 373.7	218.8
1996	1 956.84	1 711.46	245.38	1 158.8	1 660.8	279.5
1997	2 048.95	1 795.83	253.12	1 175.0	1 700.6	268.3
1998	2 010.75	1 804.81	205.94	1 129.2	1 695.5	201.2
1999	1 970.24	1 801.59	168.65	1 098.7	1 683.7	164.0
2000	2 169.72	1 933.01	236.71	1 152.5	1 746.0	191.0
2001	2 356.71	2 099.99	256.72	1 263.2	1 906.6	216.1
2002	2 531.29	2 366.10	165.19	1 387.0	2 192.6	148.9
2003	3 076.68	2 643.07	433.61	1 588.1	2 365.8	299.4
2004	3 782.25	3 239.04	543.21	1 804.1	2 680.5	347.3
2005	4 218.99	3 775.55	443.44	1 962.0	3 024.4	279.9
2006	4 873.34	4 383.33	490.01	2 210.4	3 427.9	299.0
2007	5 719.59	5 192.50	527.09	2 575.3	4 030.2	319.5
2008	6 143.82	5 614.47	529.35	2 708.2	4 235.3	338.4
2009	6 766.01	6 447.52	318.49	2 899.7	4 741.8	119.2
2010	7 407.78	6 380.33	1 027.45	3 094.0	4 533.2	383.5
2011	7 729.06	6 801.78	927.28	3 174.4	4 642.0	399.2
2012	7 674.82	7 012.53	662.29	3 266.5	4 957.7	295.4

表 4.16 主要年份旅游产业增加值
VALUE ADDED OF TOURISM INDUSTRY IN MAIN YEARS

指 标	Indicators	2005	2010	2011	2012
增加值(亿元)	**Value Added (100 million yuan)**	**584.26**	**1 360.80**	**1 411.26**	**1 497.68**
按行业分	Grouped by Sectors				
#旅行社服务业	Travel Agency	9.02	17.50	17.99	21.08
旅游宾(饭)馆业	Hotel	91.78	212.34	169.44	169.75
旅游运输业	Travel Transportation	120.86	159.67	160.29	164.63
邮电通信业	Post and Telecommunication	25.21	38.60	42.49	48.02
旅游商业	Tourism Commerce	96.17	529.28	576.50	597.82
餐饮业	Catering	68.92	67.17	79.05	95.26
城市交通业	Urban Traffic	45.96	93.18	101.84	114.95
园林文化业	Gardening	92.42	169.98	188.22	60.31
旅游产业增加值占上海市生产总值比重(%)	**Ratio of Value Added of Tourism Industry to GDP (%)**	**6.4**	**8.1**	**7.4**	**7.5**

表 4.17 主要年份信息产业增加值
VALUE ADDED OF INFORMATION INDUSTRY IN MAIN YEARS

指 标	Indicators	2000	2010	2011	2012
增加值(亿元)	**Value Added (100 million yuan)**	**338.18**	**1 672.14**	**1 891.36**	**2 030.24**
信息产品制造业	Information Products Manufacturing	195.82	690.76	707.11	701.12
信息产品销售业	Information Products Distribution	12.59	54.62	61.28	95.33
信息服务业	Information Services	129.77	926.76	1 122.96	1 233.79
结 构(%)	**Composition(%)**				
信息产品制造业	Information Products Manufacturing	57.9	41.3	37.4	34.5
信息产品销售业	Information Products Distribution	3.7	3.3	3.2	4.7
信息服务业	Information Services	38.4	55.4	59.4	60.8
信息产业增加值占上海市生产总值比重(%)	**Ratio of Value Added of Information Industry to GDP(%).**	**7.1**	**9.7**	**9.9**	**10.1**

表4.18 全员劳动生产率(1978～2012)
OVERALL LABOUR PRODUCTIVITY

单位:元/人

年 份 Year	合 计 Total	第一产业 Primary Industry	第二产业 Secondary Industry	第三产业 Tertiary Industry
1978	3 960	455	7 001	3 488
1979	4 060	490	6 931	3 500
1980	4 322	462	6 886	4 096
1981	4 386	508	6 697	4 177
1982	4 452	667	6 532	4 234
1983	4 590	729	6 431	4 510
1984	5 080	1 055	6 641	5 140
1985	6 041	1 408	7 493	6 098
1986	6 299	1 653	7 444	6 473
1987	6 944	2 019	7 913	7 314
1988	8 205	2 796	9 301	8 288
1989	8 833	3 258	10 011	8 655
1990	9 940	3 892	10 863	10 382
1991	11 272	4 011	11 737	12 940
1992	13 885	4 270	14 382	16 013
1993	19 060	4 957	19 485	22 473
1994	25 308	6 327	25 626	30 192
1995	31 634	7 791	32 503	36 878
1996	37 269	8 717	37 813	44 181
1997	43 497	8 895	44 461	51 279
1998	47 816	9 071	49 227	55 670
1999	52 130	9 191	52 397	61 961
2000	58 443	9 754	59 909	67 345
2001	64 298	8 843	70 375	71 696
2002	70 790	9 295	81 306	75 456
2003	79 488	10 257	94 726	80 210
2004	88 087	11 836	98 278	91 065
2005	94 967	14 069	102 494	99 058
2006	107 089	16 125	119 732	107 174
2007	123 120	18 679	132 409	126 429
2008	135 445	21 690	143 753	139 607
2009	142 104	23 250	141 687	152 331
2010	159 300	26 664	166 557	163 512
2011	174 897	33 600	178 391	180 905
2012	181 831	30 803	177 501	194 904

上 / 海 / 统 / 计 / 年 / 鉴

主要统计指标解释

生产总值(原国内生产总值)

指按市场价格计算的一个地区所有常住单位在一定时期内生产活动的最终成果。生产总值有三种表现形态,即价值形态、收入形态和产品形态。从价值形态看,它是所有常住单位在一定时期内所生产的全部货物和服务价值超过同期投入的全部非固定资产货物和服务价值的差额,即所有常住单位的增加值之和;从收入形态看,它是所有常住单位在一定时期内所创造并分配给常住单位和非常住单位的初次收入之和;从产品形态看,它是所有常住单位在一定时期内最终使用的货物和服务减去货物和服务的进口价值。在实际核算中,生产总值有三种计算方法,即生产法、收入法和支出法。三种方法分别从不同的方面反映生产总值及其构成。根据国务院和国家统计局有关我国 GDP 核算和数据发布制度的规定,上海国内生产总值自 2004 年起更名为"上海市生产总值",简称"上海市 GDP"。

三次产业

三次产业的划分是国际上常用的产业结构分类。第一产业是指产品直接取自自然界的部门,第二产业是指对初级产品进行再加工的部门,第三产业是指为生产和消费提供各种服务的部门。

第一产业包括农业、林业、畜牧业、渔业和农林牧渔服务业。

第二产业包括采矿业、制造业、电力、燃气及水的生产和供应业、建筑业。

第三产业是除第一、第二产业以外的其他行业。

劳动者报酬

指劳动者因从事生产活动所获得的全部报酬。包括劳动者获得的各种形式的工资、奖金和津贴,既包括货币形式的,也包括实物形式的,还包括劳动者所享受的公费医疗和医药卫生费、上下班交通补贴、单位支付的社会保险费、住房公积金等。对于个体经济来说,其所有者所获得的劳动报酬和经营利润不易区分,这两部分统一作为劳动者报酬处理。

生产税净额

指生产税减生产补贴后的余额。生产税指政府对生产单位从事生产、销售和经营活动以及因从事生产活动使用某些生产要素(如固定资产、土地、劳动力)所征收的各种税、附加费和规费。生产补贴与生产税相反,指政府对生产单位的单方面转移支出,因此视为负生产税,包括政策亏损补贴、价格补贴等。

固定资产折旧

指一定时期内为弥补固定资产损耗按照规定的固定资产折旧率提取的固定资产折旧,或按国民经济核算统一规定的折旧率虚拟计算的固定资产折旧。它反映了固定资产在当期生产中的转移价值。各类企业和企业化管理的事业单位的固定资产折旧是指实际计提的折旧费;不计提折旧的政府机关、非企业化管理的事业单位和居民住房的固定资产折旧是按照统一规定的折旧率和固定资产原值计算的虚拟折旧。原则上,固定资产折旧应按固定资产当期的重置价值计算,但是目前我国尚不具备对全社会固定资产进行重估价的基础,所以暂时只能采用上述办法。

营业盈余

指常住单位创造的增加值扣除劳动者报酬、生产税净额和固定资产折旧后的余额。它相当于企业的营业利润加上生产补贴,但要扣除从利润中开支的工资和福利等。

支出法生产总值

是从最终使用的角度反映一个国家(或地区)一定时期内生产活动最终成果的一种方法,包括最终消费支出、资本形成总额及货物和服务净出口三部分。计算公式为:

支出法生产总值 = 最终消费支出 + 资本形成总额 + 货物和服务净出口

最终消费支出

指常住单位在一定时期内对于货物和服务的全部最终消费支出,也就是常住单位为满足物质、文化和精神生活的需要,从本国经济领土和国外购买的货物和服务的支出;不包括非常住单位在本国经济领土内的消费支出。最终消费分为居民消费和政府消费。

主要统计指标解释

居民消费支出

指常住住户在一定时期内对货物和服务的全部最终消费支出。居民消费按市场价格计算，即按居民支付的购买者价格计算。购买者价格是购买者取得货物所支付的价格，包括购买者支付的运输和商业费用。居民消费除了直接以货币形式购买货物和服务的消费之外，还包括以其他方式获得的货物和服务的消费支出，即所谓的虚拟消费支出。居民虚拟消费支出包括以下几种类型：单位以实物报酬及实物转移的形式提供给劳动者的货物和服务；住户生产并由本住户消费了的货物和服务，其中的服务仅指住户的自有住房服务；金融机构提供的金融媒介服务；保险公司提供的保险服务。

政府消费支出

指一定时期内政府部门为全社会提供公共服务的消费支出和免费或以较低价格向住户提供的货物和服务的净支出。前者等于政府服务的产出价值减去政府单位所获得的经营收入的价值，政府服务的产出价值等于它的经常性业务支出加上固定资产折旧；后者等于政府部门免费或以较低价格向住户提供的货物和服务的市场价值减去向住户收取的价值。

资本形成总额

指常住单位在一定时期内获得的，并减去处置的固定资产，加上存货的变动，包括固定资本形成总额和存货增加。

固定资本形成总额

指生产者在一定时期内获得的固定资产减处置的固定资产的价值总额。固定资产是通过生产活动生产出来的，且其使用年限在一年以上、单位价值在规定标准以上的资产，不包括自然资产。可分为有形固定资本形成总额和无形固定资本形成总额。有形固定资本形成总额包括一定时期内完成的建筑工程、安装工程和设备工器具购置(减处置)价值，以及土地改良、新增役、种、奶、毛、娱乐用牲畜和新增经济林木价值。无形固定资本形成总额包括矿藏的勘探、计算机软件等获得减处置。

存货增加

指常住单位在一定时期内存货实物量变动的市场价值，即期末价值减期初价值的差额，再扣除当期由于价格变动而产生的持有收益。存货增加可以是正值，也可以是负值，正值表示存货上升，负值表示存货下降。存货包括生产单位购进的原材料、燃料和储备物资等存货，以及生产单位生产的产成品、在制品和半成品等存货。

货物和服务净流出

指货物和服务流出减货物和服务流入的差额。流出包括常住单位向非常住单位出售或无偿转让的各种货物和服务的价值；流入包括常住单位从非常住单位购买或无偿得到的各种货物和服务的价值。地区核算净流出，除包括本地区对外贸易及国外非贸易往来的净出口额，还包括地区间货物和服务流出减流入后的净额。

信息产业

是指与电子信息相关联的各种活动的集合，包括信息产品的制造、销售和信息服务等活动。由于信息产业增加值是依据若干行业的有关资料进行跨行业核算的，因此不宜将其与上海市生产总值中其他行业的增加值进行加总，否则会造成重复计算。

旅游产业

指本市与旅游相关的各行业，为境内外旅游者提供旅游服务的产业。这些服务包括：旅行社服务、交通运输服务、住宿服务、电讯服务、娱乐服务、餐饮服务、商品零售服务等。由于旅游产业增加值是依据相关行业的有关资料进行跨行业核算的，因此不宜将其与上海市生产总值中其他行业的增加值进行加总，否则会造成重复计算。

SHANGHAI STATISTICAL YEARBOOK

EXPLANATORY NOTES TO MAJOR STATISTICAL INDICATORS

□ Gross Regional Product(former Gross Domestic Product)

Gross Regional Product refers to the final products at market prices by (of) all resident units of a region during a certain period of time. Gross product is expressed in three different forms, i.e value, income, and products respectively. The form of value added refers to the total value of all products and services produced by all resident units during a certain period of time minus the total value of inputs of non–fixed–assets products and services or the summation of the value added of all resident units; the form of income includes all the income items produced by all resident units and distributed primarily to all resident and non–resident units; the form of product refers to all final goods and services minus the value of imports of goods and services. In the practice of national accounting, it is calculated by three approaches, i.e. product approach, income approach, and expenditure approach, respectively, to reflect Gross Product and its composition of different aspects. According to the regulations of GDP national accounting and data release issued by the State Council and National Bureau of Statistics, since 2004 Shanghai Gross Domestic Product has been renamed as Shanghai Gross Product Value, for short Shanghai GDP.

□ Three Industries

Classification of economic activities into three strata of industry is a common practice in the world. Primary industry refers to extraction of natural resources; secondary industry involves processing of primary products; and tertiary industry provides services of various kinds for production and consumption.

Primary industry includes farming, forestry, animal husbandry, fishery industry and service industry for farming, forestry, animal husbandry and fishery.

Secondary industry includes mining, manufacturing, power, steam and water production and supply and construction.

Tertiary industry refers to all other industries not included in primary or secondary industries.

□ Labourers Remuneration

Labourers Remuneration refers to the whole payment of various forms earned by the labourers from the productive activities they are engaged in. It includes wages, bonuses and allowances the labourers earned in monetary form and in kind. It also includes the free medical services provided to the labourers and the medicine expenses, traffic subsidies and social insurance, housing fund paid by the employers. As the individual economy is concerned, since the labourers remuneration is not easily distinguished from the operating profit, both are treated as labourers remuneration.

□ Net Taxes on Production

Net Taxes on Production refers to the difference of the taxes on production minus the subsidies on production. The taxes on production refers to the various taxes, extra charges and fees levied on the production units on their production, sale and business activities as well as on the use of some factors of production, such as fixed assets, land and labour force in the production activities they are engaged in. In contrast to the taxes on production, the subsidies on production refer to the unilateral government transfer to the production units and are therefore regarded as negative taxes on production. They include subsidies on the loss due to implementation of government policies, price subsidies, etc.

□ Depreciation of Fixed Assets

Depreciation of Fixed Assets refers to the depreciation of fixed assets of a given period, drawn in accordance with the stipulated depreciation rate for the purpose of compensating the wear loss of the fixed assets or the depreciation of fixed assets calculated in a fictitious way in accordance with the stipulated unified depreciation rate in the national economic accounting system. It reflects the value of transfer of the fixed assets in the production of the current period. The depreciation of fixed assets in various enterprises and institutions managed as enterprises refers to the depreciation expenses actually drawn. In government agencies and institutions not managed as enterprises which do not draw the depreciation expenses, as well as for the houses of residents, the depreciation of fixed assets is the imputed depreciation, which is calculated in accordance with the stipulated unified depreciation rate. In principle, the depreciation of fixed assets should be calculated on the basis of the re–purchased value of the fixed assets. However, there is no actual condition to re–evaluate all the fixed assets in China. Therefore, the above–mentioned methods are

EXPLANATORY NOTES TO MAJOR STATISTICAL INDICATORS

temporarily adopted at present.

□ Operating Surplus

Operating Surplus refers to the balance of the value added created by the resident units deducting the labourers remuneration, net taxes on production and the depreciation of fixed assets. It is equivalent to the business profit of the enterprises plus subsidies on production, but the wages and welfare expenses paid from the profits should be deducted.

□ GDP by Expenditure Approach

GDP by Expenditure Approach refers to the method of measuring the final results of production activities of a country (region) during a given period from the perspective of final use. It includes final consumption, total capital formation and net export of goods and services, i.e.:

GDP by expenditure approach = final consumption + total capital formation + net export of goods and services

□ Final Consumption

Final Consumption refers to the total expenditure of resident units on final consumption of goods and services in a certain period, namely the expenditure of the resident units for purchases of goods and services from domestic economic territory and abroad to meet the requirements of material, cultural and spiritual life. It excludes the expenditure of non-resident units on consumption in the economic territory of the country. The final consumption is classified into household consumption and government consumption.

□ Household Consumption

Household Consumption refers to the total expenditure of resident households on the final consumption of goods and services in a certain period of time. The households consumption is calculated at market prices, namely the purchasers prices which the households pay; the purchasers prices of goods are the prices the households pay when they obtain the goods, including the transport and commercial expenses paid by the households. In addition to the consumption of goods and services bought by the households directly with money, the expenditure on goods and services obtained by the households in other ways, i.e. the so-called imputed expenditure on consumption, is also included in the households consumption. The imputation expenditure of the households on consumption includes the following types: (a) the goods and services provided to the households by the units in the form of payment in kind and transfer in kind; (b) the goods and services produced and consumed by the households themselves, in which the services refer only to the services provided by the residential buildings owned by the households; (c) the services of financial intermediary provided by the financial institutions; (d) the insurance services provided by the insurance companies.

□ Government Consumption

Government Consumption refers to the expenditure on the consumption of the public services provided by the government to the whole society and the net expenditure on the goods and services provided by the government to the households at free charge or lower prices in a certain period of time. The former equals to the output value of the government services minus the value of operating income obtained by the government departments. (The output value of the government services equals to its current operating expenditure plus depreciation of fixed assets). The latter equals to the market value of the goods and services provided by the government free of charge or at low prices to the households minus the value received by the government from the households.

□ Total Capital Formation

Total Capital Formation refers to the fixed assets acquired minus those disposed and the change in inventory, including the total fixed capital assets formation and the increase in inventory.

□ Total Fixed Capital Formation

Total Fixed Capital Formation refers to the value of fixed assets acquired minus those disposed of during a given period. Fixed assets are the assets produced through production activities with specified unit value which could be used for over one year, excluding natural assets. Total fixed capital formation can be categorized into total tangible capital formation and total intangible capital formation. The total tangible capital formation include the value of the construction projects, installation projects completed and the equipment, apparatus and instruments purchased as well as the value of land improved, the value of draught animals, breeding stock, animals for milk, wool and for recreational purpose, and the newly increased forest with economic value during a given period. The total intangible capital formation includes the prospecting of minerals, the acquisition of computer software minus the disposal of them.

EXPLANATORY NOTES TO MAJOR STATISTICAL INDICATORS

□ Increase in Inventory

Increase in Inventory refers to the market value of the change in inventory of resident units during a given period, i.e. the difference of value between the beginning and the end of the period minus the current gains due to the change in prices. The increase in inventory can be positive or negative. A positive value indicates the increase in inventory while a negative value indicates the decrease in stock. The inventory includes the raw materials, fuels and reserve materials purchased by the production units as well as the inventory of finished products, semi-finished products, work-in-progress, etc.

□ Net Outflow of Goods and Services

Net Outflow of Goods and Service refers to difference of outflow of goods and service minus inflow of goods and service. The outflow includes the value of various goods and service sold or gratuitously transferred by resident unit to non-resident unit, and the inflow includes the value of various goods and service sold or gratuitously transferred by non-resident unit to resident unit. The net outflow of district, include the net outflow of foreign trade or non-trade of local district, and also the difference of outflow minus inflow of goods and service between domestic districts.

□ Information Industry

Information Industry refers to the aggregation of all kinds of activities related to electronic information, including manufactory and distribution of information-related products and information service. As accounted by referring to relevant documents of several industries, the value added of the information industry shall not be counted together with that of other industries in the Shanghai GDP to avoid repetitive computation.

□ Tourism Industry

Tourism Industry refers to those tourism-related industries that provide tourism services to domestic and overseas tourists, including: travel agency service, transportation service, hostelling service, telecommunication service, entertainment service, catering service and retailing service, etc.. As accounted by referring to relevant cross-industry data of several industries, the value added of the tourism industry shall not be counted together with that of other industries in the Shanghai GDP to avoid repetitive computation.

第五篇

CHAPTER 5

财政收支

FISCAL REVENUE AND EXPENDITURE

简要说明

本篇反映上海市地方财政收支和税收收入情况，资料来源于上海市财政局、上海市国家税务局和上海市地方税务局。

有关财政收支方面的资料，根据财政收支总表、财政收入明细表、财政支出明细表和区县财政收支完成情况表等的数据加工整理编制，其中，地方财政收支由市本级财政收支和区县级财政收支组成。有关税收收入方面的资料，根据全市税收收入情况表的数据加工整理编制。

BRIEF INTRODUCTION

The data in this chapter reflect government revenue, expenditure, and tax income situations. The data are collected, provided and complied by the Shanghai Finance Bureau and the Shanghai State Tax Bureau as well as the Shanghai Local Taxation Bureau.

Data on government revenue and expenditure are prepared, collected and compiled on the basis of information from the city's balance sheet of government revenue and expenditures, tables of government revenue and expenditure at city level, and tables of government revenue and expenditure at district and county level. Among them, local fiscal revenue and expenditure is comprised by revenue and expenditure in the city as well as in districts and counties. The data on tax income is prepared, collected and compiled on the base of information on Shanghai's tax income table.

表 5.1 地方财政收支(1978 ~2012)
LOCAL FISCAL REVENUES AND EXPENDITURES

单位:亿元 (100 million yuan)

年 份 Year	地方财政收入 Local Fiscal Revenue	其中 of which 税收收入 Taxes	其中 of which 非税收入 Non-taxes	地方财政支出 Local Fiscal Expenditure
1978	169.22	51.51	117.71	26.01
1979	172.69	53.73	118.96	27.06
1980	174.73	57.59	117.14	19.18
1981	174.35	62.93	111.42	19.06
1982	167.99	65.79	102.20	20.68
1983	156.39	110.05	46.34	22.39
1984	163.96	137.67	26.29	30.32
1985	184.23	185.76	-1.53	46.07
1986	179.46	177.90	1.56	59.08
1987	168.97	167.26	1.71	53.85
1988	161.62	182.42	-20.80	65.88
1989	166.88	190.21	-23.33	73.31
1990	166.99	183.31	-16.32	75.56
1991	175.53	182.88	-7.35	86.05
1992	185.56	188.61	-3.05	94.99
1993	242.34	252.99	-10.65	129.26
1994	175.33	196.60	-21.27	196.98
1995	227.30	240.06	-12.76	267.89
1996	288.49	308.26	-19.77	342.66
1997	352.33	369.23	-16.90	428.92
1998	392.22	406.73	-14.51	480.70
1999	431.85	427.23	4.62	546.38
2000	497.96	484.00	13.96	622.84
2001	620.24	589.91	30.33	726.38
2002	719.79	657.70	62.09	877.84
2003	899.29	796.87	102.42	1 102.64
2004	1 119.72	1 036.23	83.49	1 395.69
2005	1 433.90	1 238.40	195.50	1 660.32
2006	1 600.37	1 393.97	206.40	1 813.80
2007	2 102.63	1 975.48	127.15	2 201.92
2008	2 382.34	2 223.43	158.91	2 617.68
2009	2 540.30	2 368.45	171.85	2 989.65
2010	2 873.58	2 707.80	165.78	3 302.89
2011	3 429.83	3 172.72	257.11	3 914.88
2012	3 743.71	3 426.79	316.92	4 184.02

表5.2 主要年份地方财政收入
LOCAL FISCAL REVENUE IN MAIN YEARS

指 标	Indicators	2000	2010	2011	2012
地方财政收入(亿元)	**Local Fiscal Revenue (100 million yuan)**	**497.96**	**2 873.58**	**3 429.83**	**3 743.71**
#增值税	Value-added Tax	93.55	388.62	416.70	667.13
营业税	Business Tax	153.81	933.91	1 041.49	897.92
企业所得税	Enterprise Income Tax	103.03	606.05	731.05	806.77
个人所得税	Personal Income Tax	60.24	261.20	314.95	318.10
契 税	Deed	14.37	173.58	180.67	145.96
#市级财政收入	Fiscal Revenue at Municipal Level	215.81	1 393.23	1 675.79	1 831.64
区县级财政收入	Fiscal Revenue at District (County) Level	282.15	1 480.35	1 754.05	1 912.07
地方财政收入构成(%)	**Compostion of Local Fiscal Revenue (%)**	**100**	**100**	**100**	**100**
#增值税	Value-added Tax	18.8	13.5	12.1	17.8
营业税	Business Tax	30.9	32.5	30.4	24.0
企业所得税	Enterprise Income Tax	20.7	21.1	21.3	21.6
个人所得税	Personal Income Tax	12.1	9.1	9.2	8.5
契 税	Deed	2.9	6.0	5.3	3.9
#市级财政收入	Fiscal Revenue at Municipal Level	43.3	48.5	48.9	48.9
区县级财政收入	Fiscal Revenue at District (County) Level	56.7	51.5	51.1	51.1

表 5.3　主要年份区县级财政收支
FISCAL REVENUE AND EXPENDITURES OF DISTRICTS AND COUNTIES IN MAIN YEARS

单位:亿元 (100 million yuan)

地　区	District	地方财政收入 Local Fiscal Revenue			地方财政支出 Local Fiscal Expenditure		
		2000	2010	2012	2000	2010	2012
总　计	**Total**	**282.15**	**1 364.69**	**1 912.07**	**331.15**	**1 886.71**	**2 659.18**
浦东新区	Pudong New Area	64.53	425.40	550.30	79.45	524.06	666.63
黄 浦 区	Huangpu	21.91	64.36	144.13	22.80	80.73	171.81
卢 湾 区	Luwan	11.37	51.30		11.32	56.69	
徐 汇 区	Xuhui	15.40	90.43	109.08	19.10	99.29	125.40
长 宁 区	Changning	13.74	72.08	99.26	14.80	85.50	113.67
静 安 区	Jing'an	11.00	65.96	79.28	11.27	71.43	91.23
普 陀 区	Putuo	12.70	51.97	68.00	14.56	78.57	103.46
闸 北 区	Zhabei	11.89	46.30	64.95	13.95	68.55	99.17
虹 口 区	Hongkou	14.20	48.36	58.20	16.35	74.52	98.63
杨 浦 区	Yangpu	11.52	50.07	70.97	14.70	82.65	111.64
闵 行 区	Minhang	18.98	125.30	148.68	20.65	156.60	188.13
宝 山 区	Baoshan	16.17	70.35	94.10	17.60	114.43	144.77
嘉 定 区	Jiading	13.33	82.96	121.60	16.12	112.84	152.73
金 山 区	Jinshan	8.16	30.75	44.69	13.61	70.98	107.79
松 江 区	Songjiang	12.12	77.33	88.26	13.34	103.55	134.30
青 浦 区	Qingpu	13.24	58.95	75.16	15.36	88.40	117.78
奉 贤 区	Fengxian	6.53	40.43	58.41	8.04	77.12	119.49
崇 明 县	Chongming	5.36	28.04	36.98	8.13	78.21	112.56

注：2012 年起，原卢湾区并入黄浦区。
Note: Former Luwan District has been merged into Huangpu District since 2012.

表5.4　地方财政支出(2010～2012)
LOCAL FISCAL EXPENDITURES

指标	Indicators	2010	2011	2012
地方财政支出（亿元）	**Local Fiscal Expenditure(100 million yuan)**	**3 302.89**	**3 914.88**	**4 184.02**
#一般公共服务	General Public Services	226.02	236.11	251.47
公共安全	Public Security	187.25	206.11	221.08
教　育	Education	417.28	549.24	648.95
社会保障和就业	Social Security and Jobs	362.56	417.50	443.01
医疗卫生	Medical and Health Care	160.07	190.03	197.34
城乡社区事务	Urban and Country Community Affairs	475.47	579.29	627.44
#市级财政支出	Fiscal Expenditure at Municipal Level	1 278.76	1 508.46	1 524.84
区县级财政支出	Fiscal Expenditure at District (County) Level	2 024.13	2 406.42	2 659.18
地方财政支出比重（%）	**Percentage of the Local Fiscal Expenditure (%)**	**100**	**100**	**100**
#一般公共服务	General Public Services	6.8	6.0	6.0
公共安全	Public Security	5.7	5.3	5.3
教　育	Education	12.6	14.0	15.5
社会保障和就业	Social Security and Jobs	11.0	10.7	10.6
医疗卫生	Medical and Health Care	4.8	4.9	4.7
城乡社区事务	Urban and Country Community Affairs	14.4	14.8	15.0
#市级财政支出	Fiscal Expenditure at Municipal Level	38.7	38.5	36.4
区县级财政支出	Fiscal Expenditure at District (County) Level	61.3	61.5	63.6

表5.5　主要年份全市税收收入
TAXATION (TAX SCOPE) IN MAIN YEARS

单位:亿元(100 million yuan)

指标	Indicators	2000	2010	2011	2012
全市税收总收入	**Taxation**	**1 479.21**	**8 003.43**	**9 595.01**	**10 409.00**
#证券交易印花税	Stamp Tax of Stock Transaction	245.49	305.26	248.29	158.97
海关代征	Custom Taxation	313.04	2 082.92	2 766.33	2 883.40
国内增值税	Domestic Value Added Tax	380.21	1 575.00	1 682.41	2 115.29
国内消费税	Domestic Excise	69.71	499.58	570.35	633.49
营业税	Business Tax	171.42	933.93	1 041.54	897.92
企业所得税	Enterprise Income Tax	142.47	1 567.31	1 964.57	2 115.87
个人所得税	Personal Income Tax	67.79	653.01	787.38	795.24

上 / 海 / 统 / 计 / 年 / 鉴

主要统计指标解释

■ 地方财政收入

地方财政收入是指根据现行财政管理体制规定，划归地方财政的税收收入和非税收入。

■ 税收收入

地方财政收入中的税收收入主要包括营业税、房产税、城镇土地使用税、车船税、土地增值税、耕地占用税、契税等固定收入，以及增值税、企业所得税、个人所得税等共享收入部分。

■ 地方财政支出

地方财政支出是指按照现行中央政府与地方政府事权的划分，经地方人大批准，用于保障地方经济社会发展的各项财政支出。主要包括一般公共服务，公共安全，教育，科学技术，文化体育与传媒，社会保障和就业，医疗卫生，环境保护，城乡社区事务，农林水事务，交通运输等支出。

SHANGHAI STATISTICAL YEARBOOK

EXPLANATORY NOTES TO MAJOR STATISTICAL INDICATORS

□ Local Fiscal Revenue

Local Fiscal Revenue refers to the tax revenue and non–tax revenue collected by the local government as defined by the finance management system.

□ Tax Revenue

Tax Revenue of local fiscal revenue mainly includes business tax, house property tax, urban land use tax, tax on vehicles and boat operation, land appreciation tax, farm land occupation tax, deed tax, etc and the share part of value added tax, corporate income tax, individual income tax, etc.

□ Local Fiscal Expenditure

Local Fiscal Expenditure refers to the fiscal expenditure demarcated on the basis of the classification of the affairs administration rights between the central government and local government. It is approved by the local people's congress and used for the development of local economy and society. Local fiscal expenditure mainly includes the expenditure for general public services, public security, education, science and technology, culture, sport and media, social safety and employment, medical and health care, environment protection, urban and rural community affairs, agriculture, forestry and water conservancy and transportation, etc.

第六篇

CHAPTER 6

能源与环境

ENERGY AND ENVIRONMENT PROTECTION

简要说明

一、本篇资料的主要内容

本篇主要包含两部分内容:能源生产、消费和环境保护治理。

能源生产、消费的主要内容有能源消耗基本情况,能源消费弹性系数,人均、日均能源消费量,分行业、分主要能源品种的时间序列能源消费量,综合能源平衡表和主要能源品种的单项平衡表,电力建设情况等。

环境保护治理的主要内容有环保投入,工业固体废弃物防治,水环境保护,大气环境保护,环境空气状况、声环境及治理和城市环境卫生情况等。

二、本篇资料的统计范围

本篇资料的统计范围为全社会。

三、本篇的资料来源

能源生产、消费的资料来源:电力建设情况由市电力公司提供,其他表的数据均来自历年能源平衡表。

环境保护治理的资料来源:环保投入、工业固体废弃物防治、大气环境保护、环境空气状况和声环境及治理由上海市环境保护局提供;水环境保护由上海市水务局提供;城市环境卫生情况是由上海市绿化和市容管理局提供。

四、关于数据口径与计算方法的说明

(一)能源生产、消费

1. 单位能耗和单位电耗所需的2005~2010年GDP和工业增加值数据按2005年可比价计算,2011年起按2010年可比价计算。

2. 自2011年起,能源消费比上年增长按2010年能源消费量调整后的基数计算。

(二)环境保护治理

1. 2008年起工业废气排放量按新排放系数计算。

2. 2011年起,烟尘排放总量统计口径变更为烟(粉)尘排放量。

3. 2011年起,废水排放总量中增加了农业源和集中式治理设施排放的废水。

BRIEF INTRODUCTION

I. Main Contents

Data in this chapter cover mainly energy production, energy consumption, and environment protection and governance.

Energy production and consumption include basic energy consumption situations, elasticity coefficient of energy consumption, average energy consumption per capita, average daily energy consumption, energy consumption in time series by industry and main energy categories, comprehensive energy balance sheet, single balance sheet of main energy categories and electric power construction.

Environment protection and governance include investment in environment protection, prevention of industrial solid waste, water environment protection, air protection, governance of air and acoustic environment, and management of urban sanitation situations.

II. The Scope of Data

The scope of data in this chapter covers the whole city.

III. Sources of Data

Sources of data on energy production and consumption: Data on electric power construction are provided by the Shanghai Electric Power Company, and the rest are collected from the energy balance sheets over the years.

Sources of data on environment protection and governance: Data on investment in environment protection, prevention of industrial solid waste, air protection, and governance of air and acoustic environment are provided by the Shanghai Environmental Protection Bureau; data on water environment protection are provided by the Shanghai Water Authority; data on urban sanitation situations are provided by the Shanghai Greening & City Appearance Bureau.

IV. Notes on Coverage and Compilation of Data

(1)Energy production and consumption

(a)Unit energy consumption and unit power consumption required for GDP and industrial production between 2005 and 2010 are calculated on comparable prices in 2005, and are calculated on comparable prices in 2010 starting from 2011.

(b) Annual growth of energy consumption is calculated on the base of adjusted energy consumption data in 2010 starting from 2011.

(2)Environment protection and governance

(a) Industrial emission is calculated on new emission coefficient since 2008.

(b) Coverage of dust discharge changes to dust (smoke) discharge since 2011.

(c) Coverage of wastewater discharge started to include agricultural wastewater and wastewater from centralized treatment facilities from 2011.

表 6.1 主要年份能源消耗基本情况
ENERGY CONSUMPTION IN MAIN YEARS

年 份 Year	能源消费量（万吨标准煤）Energy Consumption (10 000 tons SCE)	其中 of which #工业 Industry	电力消耗（亿千瓦时）Electricity Power Consumption (100 million kwh)	其中 of which #工业 Industry
1990	3 191.06	2 462.21	264.74	220.97
1995	4 465.87	3 512.49	403.27	307.01
1996	4 626.21	3 484.47	430.40	318.18
1997	4 758.82	3 498.83	454.26	333.79
1998	4 874.11	3 452.96	482.94	343.60
1999	5 119.19	3 608.67	501.20	358.31
2000	5 499.48	3 778.76	559.42	393.13
2001	5 894.78	3 931.58	592.99	413.33
2002	6 249.34	3 988.13	645.71	447.46
2003	6 796.34	4 304.81	745.97	507.00
2004	7 405.64	4 518.82	821.44	555.12
2005	8 225.05	5 105.04	921.97	617.59
2006	8 875.70	5 371.06	990.15	656.10
2007	9 670.45	5 722.05	1 072.38	705.90
2008	10 207.36	5 886.83	1 138.22	727.13
2009	10 367.38	5 763.27	1 153.38	701.59
2010	11 201.13	6 290.10	1 295.87	786.61
2011	11 270.48	6 297.15	1 339.62	805.76
2012	11 362.15	6 151.11	1 353.45	786.25

表 6.1 续表 1 continued

年 份 Year	单位生产总值能耗（吨标准煤/万元）Energy Consumption of GDP (ton SCE/10 000 yuan)	单位生产总值电耗（千瓦时/万元）Electricity Power Consumption of GDP (kwh/10 000 yuan)	单位工业增加值能耗（吨标准煤/万元）Energy Consumption of Value Added in Industry (ton SCE/10 000 yuan)	单位工业增加值电耗（千瓦时/万元）Electricity Power Consumption of Value Added in Industry (kwh/10 000 yuan)
1990	4.082	3 386.89	5.241	4 703.19
1995	1.787	1 613.45	2.685	2 346.81
1996	1.564	1 455.26	2.398	2 190.13
1997	1.384	1 320.99	2.188	2 087.61
1998	1.282	1 270.53	2.067	2 057.25
1999	1.222	1 196.54	2.018	2 003.99
2000	1.153	1 172.50	1.890	1 966.67
2001	1.131	1 138.15	1.815	1 907.61
2002	1.089	1 124.73	1.684	1 889.60
2003	1.015	1 114.35	1.464	1 723.76
2004	0.917	1 017.54	1.258	1 544.90
2005	0.889	996.98	1.261	1 529.88
2006	0.851	949.69	1.187	1 453.81
2007	0.805	892.62	1.127	1 394.24
2008	0.775	863.64	1.080	1 334.46
2009	0.727	808.50	1.028	1 251.81
2010	0.712	823.18	0.953	1 194.05
2011	0.618	721.53	0.889	1 146.70
2012	0.570	678.41	0.849	1 089.46

注：单位能耗和单位电耗 2005 ~ 2010 按 2005 年可比价计算，2011 年起按 2010 年可比价计算。

Note: Energy Intensity and Electricity Intensity by GDP have been calculated by comparable prices of 2005 from 2005 to 2010, and Since 2011, it is calculated by comparable prices of 2010.

表 6.2 能源消费弹性系数(1978~2012)
ELASTICITY OF ENERGY CONSUMPTION

年份 Year	能源消费比上年增长(%) Growth Rate of Energy Consumption over Preceding Year(%)	电力消费比上年增长(%) Growth Rate of Electric Power Consumption over Preceding Year(%)	能源消费弹性系数 Elasticity of Energy Consumption	电力消费弹性系数 Elasticity of Electric Power Consumption
1978	6.6	10.8	0.42	0.68
1979	1.5	3.0	0.20	0.41
1980	-0.6	3.4		0.40
1981	1.0	6.4	0.18	1.14
1982	2.6	4.4	0.36	0.61
1983	2.5	4.2	0.32	0.54
1984	2.5	4.1	0.22	0.35
1985	4.9	3.9	0.37	0.74
1986	9.0	6.8	2.05	1.34
1987	5.7	4.1	0.77	0.81
1988	1.3	2.5	0.13	0.51
1989	4.4	1.3	1.46	0.83
1990	2.6	5.8	0.73	2.09
1991	8.6	9.0	1.22	1.28
1992	5.5	10.0	0.37	0.67
1993	7.9	9.0	0.52	0.59
1994	5.8	9.1	0.40	0.63
1995	6.9	6.9	0.48	0.48
1996	3.6	6.7	0.27	0.51
1997	2.9	5.5	0.22	0.43
1998	2.4	6.3	0.24	0.61
1999	5.0	3.8	0.48	0.36
2000	7.4	11.6	0.68	1.06
2001	7.2	6.0	0.68	0.57
2002	6.0	8.9	0.53	0.79
2003	8.8	15.5	0.71	1.26
2004	9.0	10.1	0.63	0.71
2005	11.1	12.2	0.97	1.07
2006	7.9	7.4	0.62	0.58
2007	9.0	8.3	0.59	0.55
2008	5.6	6.1	0.57	0.63
2009	1.6	1.3	0.19	0.16
2010	8.0	12.4	0.78	1.24
2011	2.4	3.4	0.30	0.41
2012	0.8	1.0	0.11	0.14

注：2011 年能源消费量比上年增长按 2010 年能源消费量调整后的基数计算。
Note: The year-on-year increases of Energy Consumption in 2011 are calculated according to the adjusted base of Energy Consumption in 2010.

表 6.3 主要年份能源消费总量
FINAL CONSUMPTION OF ENERGY IN MAIN YEARS

单位：万吨标准煤（10 000 tons SCE）

年 份 Year	能源消费总量 Energy Consumption	能源终端消费量 Final Consumption of Energy	加工转换投入（－）产出（＋）量 Processing Conversion Input (－) and Output (＋)	损失量 Loss Volume
1990	3 191.06	3 098.82	－52.20	40.04
1995	4 465.87	4 250.45	－74.67	140.75
1996	4 626.21	4 376.37	－98.48	151.36
1997	4 758.82	4 505.70	－117.53	135.59
1998	4 874.11	4 608.13	－108.22	157.76
1999	5 119.19	4 899.60	－83.98	135.60
2000	5 499.48	5 226.79	－89.20	183.49
2001	5 894.78	5 549.69	－133.94	211.16
2002	6 249.34	5 898.56	－132.17	218.62
2003	6 796.34	6 394.49	－158.30	243.55
2004	7 405.64	7 055.08	－131.85	218.71
2005	8 225.05	7 895.17	－140.59	189.29
2006	8 875.70	8 514.40	－167.58	193.73
2007	9 670.45	9 314.77	－147.01	208.67
2008	10 207.36	9 750.47	－227.60	229.28
2009	10 367.38	9 951.81	－181.67	233.90
2010	11 201.13	10 842.33	－108.68	250.13
2011	11 270.48	10 943.46	－73.23	253.79
2012	11 362.15	11 020.30	－77.17	264.69

表 6.4 主要年份平均每人生活用能源
ANNUAL RESIDENT ENERGY CONSUMPTION PER CAPITA IN MAIN YEARS

品 名	Items	2000	2010	2011	2012
生活消费能源总计（千克标准煤）	**Total Resident Energy Consumption (kg of SCE)**	**290.49**	**446.28**	**457.05**	**482.97**
煤 炭（千克）	Coal (kg)	87.85	20.67	18.64	17.42
天然气（立方米）	Natural Gas (cu. m)	4.53	34.52	37.12	42.01
液化石油气（千克）	Liquefied Petroleum Gas (kg)	13.31	14.65	14.71	14.92
煤 气（立方米）	Gas (cu. m)	97.49	27.88	23.14	16.54
电 力（千瓦时）	Electric Power (kwh)	335.05	748.74	753.61	792.66

注：本表按年平均人口数计算。
Note: Data in this table are calculated by average annual population.

表 6.5 平均每天各种能源消费量（2009～2012）
AVERAGE DAILY ENERGY CONSUMPTION BY VARIETY

能源品种	Items	2009	2010	2011	2012
合 计（万吨标准煤）	**Total (10 000 tons of SCE)**	**28.40**	**30.69**	**30.88**	**31.13**
煤 炭（万吨）	Coal (10 000 tons)	11.47	13.14	13.67	12.73
焦 炭（万吨）	Coke (10 000 tons)	1.86	1.96	1.96	1.84
燃料油（万吨）	Fuel Oil (10 000 tons)	2.04	2.04	1.85	1.75
汽 油（万吨）	Gasoline (10 000 tons)	1.06	1.14	1.30	1.42
煤 油（万吨）	Kerosene (10 000 tons)	0.97	1.09	1.10	1.10
柴 油（万吨）	Diesel Oil (10 000 tons)	1.32	1.39	1.42	1.56
天然气（亿立方米）	Natural Gas (100 million cu. m)	0.09	0.12	0.15	0.18
电 力（亿千瓦时）	Electricity (100 million kwh)	3.16	3.55	3.67	3.71

表6.6　主要年份能源终端消费量
FINAL CONSUMPTION OF ENERGY IN MAIN YEARS

单位:万吨标准煤(10 000 tons SCE)

年　份 Year	能源终端消费量 Final Consumption of Energy	其　中　of which 第一产业 Primary Industry	第二产业 Secondary Industry	第三产业 Tertiary Industry	生活消费 Living Consumption
1980	2 130.56	71.04	1 655.92	194.64	208.96
1990	3 098.82	58.49	2 387.88	403.47	248.98
1995	4 250.45	77.12	3 339.73	517.05	316.53
1996	4 376.37	102.18	3 291.05	626.39	356.78
1997	4 505.70	90.53	3 312.18	715.31	387.72
1998	4 608.13	91.06	3 261.21	828.84	427.02
1999	4 899.6	98.01	3 467.49	915.48	418.62
2000	5 226.79	103.37	3 592.86	1 069.32	461.24
2001	5 549.69	113.84	3 698.28	1 282.08	455.49
2002	5 898.56	109.13	3 802.12	1 508.46	478.85
2003	6 394.49	111.83	4 063.76	1 690.50	528.40
2004	7 055.08	108.35	4 339.27	2 016.48	590.98
2005	7 895.17	61.44	4 940.24	2 249.12	644.37
2006	8 514.40	59.16	5 183.29	2 555.08	716.87
2007	9 314.77	60.70	5 547.36	2 902.64	804.07
2008	9 750.47	62.81	5 636.03	3 153.79	897.85
2009	9 951.81	62.71	5 587.85	3 351.64	949.60
2010	10 842.33	63.48	5 960.72	3 592.77	1 007.02
2011	10 943.46	65.16	6 221.16	3 594.47	1 062.67
2012	11 020.30	68.68	6 065.65	3 744.25	1 141.72

表6.7　主要年份工业能源终端消费量
FINAL CONSUMPTION OF ENERGY INDUSTRY IN MAIN YEARS

年　份 Year	工业能源终端消费量(万吨标准煤) Final Consumption Energy of Industry (10 000 tons SCE)	原　煤(万吨) Coal (10 000 tons)	焦　炭(万吨) Coke (10 000 tons)	燃料油(万吨) Fuel Oil (10 000 tons)	电　力(亿千瓦时) Electric power (100 million kwh)
1980	1 645.20	535.03	211.52	122.41	136.85
1990	2 369.99	596.14	419.24	136.09	209.21
1991	2 591.11	641.71	516.28	140.06	226.69
1992	2 731.13	630.83	651.49	112.47	247.75
1993	2 988.03	700.97	617.24	170.97	262.75
1994	3 053.73	661.10	625.62	165.55	270.54
1995	3 297.07	694.31	687.98	154.76	282.87
1996	3 234.63	726.24	637.73	149.69	293.04
1997	3 245.71	698.14	653.75	147.70	309.74
1998	3 186.98	723.59	660.40	132.93	318.12
1999	3 389.09	792.14	658.28	120.21	335.01
2000	3 506.06	733.65	676.06	139.67	362.94
2001	3 586.48	790.51	654.79	136.93	381.64
2002	3 637.35	676.60	571.92	112.19	413.61
2003	3 902.97	675.58	573.94	117.11	464.74
2004	4 168.27	731.30	552.68	118.77	510.63
2005	4 775.16	843.73	603.16	130.94	568.29
2006	5 009.75	869.58	617.92	118.85	604.59
2007	5 366.37	790.10	691.38	91.99	649.82
2008	5 449.51	787.01	684.92	74.98	667.59
2009	5 376.05	825.59	658.32	71.92	641.58
2010	5 960.72	854.71	705.21	63.12	718.63
2011	6 008.4	813.06	706.34	62.86	735.27
2012	5 850.9	730.71	673.17	40.23	714.46

表6.8 主要年份能源平衡表(标准量)
BALANCE SHEET OF ENERGY IN MAIN YEARS (STANDARD EQUIVALENT)

单位:万吨标准煤(10 000 tons SCE)

指 标	Indicators	2000	2010	2011	2012
可供本地区消费的能源量	**Volume of Energy Available for Local Consumption**	**5 462.45**	**11 161.94**	**11 267.71**	**11 363.73**
库存差	Inventory Change	-69.09	-54.92	-47.65	-10.12
一次能源生产量	Primary Energy Production	103.40	72.39	63.69	65.61
回收能	Recovery of Energy	62.06	186.77		15.08
外省(市)调入量	Inflow from Other Provinces(Autonomous Region and Municipalities)	8 533.76	13 802.64	13 685.60	14 016.17
进口量	Imports	1 475.48	3 335.53	3 745.63	4 173.18
我轮.机在外国加油量	China Airplanes&ships Refueling in Abroad	40.15	860.33	899.22	666.14
本市调出量	Outflow from Shanghai (Autonomous Region of Municipality)	-4 438.19	-6 668.81	-6 646.56	-7 246.74
出口量	Exports	-179.95	-175.45	-79.58	-77.31
外轮.机在我国加油量(-)	Foreign Airplanes&ships Refueling in China	-65.14	-196.53	-352.63	-223.18
加工转换投入(-)产出(+)量	**Processing Conversion Input (-) and Output (+)**	**-89.2**	**-108.68**	**-73.23**	**-77.17**
#火力发电	Fuel Power Generation	-0.49			-32.85
供 热	Heating Supply		-37.11	-34.68	-28.49
炼 焦	Coke Making	-57.93	-34.77	-39.34	-24.04
炼 油	Oil Refining	-20.63	-4.96	-6.64	-6.88
制 气	Gas Making	-9.79	1.07	-1.79	15.08
损失量	**Loss Volume**	**183.49**	**250.17**	**253.79**	**264.69**
#运输和输配损失	Loss in Transportation and Distribution	183.49	250.17	253.79	264.69
终端消费量	**Final Consumption**	**5 226.79**	**10 802.03**	**10 943.46**	**11 020.30**
第一产业	Primary Industry	103.37	63.49	65.16	68.68
第二产业	Secondary Industry	3 592.87	6 154.82	6 221.16	6 065.65
工 业	Industry	3 506.07	5 936.45	6 008.40	5 850.90
建筑业	Construction	86.80	218.37	212.76	214.75
第三产业	Tertiary Industry	1 069.32	3 576.70	3 594.47	3 744.25
#交通运输、仓储和邮政业	Transportation, Storage and Post	598.09	2 062.90	2 009.09	2 045.91
批发、零售贸易业和住宿、餐饮业	Wholesale, Retail Sales and Hotel, Restaurants	130.08	491.36	507.23	530.66
生活消费	Living Consumption	461.24	1 007.02	1 062.67	1 141.72
城 镇	Urban	345.20	842.91	890.38	969.30
乡 村	Rural	116.03	164.11	172.29	172.42
平衡差额	**Balance**	**-37.03**	**1.07**	**-2.78**	**1.57**
能源消费总量	**Total Energy Consumption**	**5 499.48**	**11 160.87**	**11 270.48**	**11 362.15**

表6.9 能源终端消费量(2012)
FINAL CONSUMPTION OF ENERGY

单位:万吨(10 000 tons)

行 业	Sectors	原 煤 Coal	焦 炭 Coke	燃料油 Fuel Oil
总 计	**Total**	**870.13**	**673.17**	**631.3**
生产消费	**Production Consumption**	**828.94**	**673.17**	**631.30**
第一产业	Primary Industry	2.67		
第二产业	Secondary Industry	741.20	673.17	48.31
#工 业	Industry	730.71	673.17	40.23
第三产业	Tertiary Industry	85.07		582.99
#交通运输、仓储和邮政业	Transportation, Storage and Post	1.91		577.58
批发、零售贸易业和住宿、餐饮业	Wholesale, Retail Sales and Hotel, Restaurants	38.54		3.62
生活消费	**Living Consumption**	**41.19**		

表6.9 续表1 continued

单位:万吨(10 000 tons)

行 业	Sectors	汽 油 Gasoline	煤 油 Kerosene	柴 油 Diesel Oil
总 计	**Total**	**517.35**	**402.74**	**568.19**
生产消费	**Production Consumption**	**348.49**	**402.74**	**525.60**
第一产业	Primary Industry	17.80		13.79
第二产业	Secondary Industry	57.75	3.35	101.43
#工 业	Industry	31.31	3.34	67.75
第三产业	Tertiary Industry	272.94	399.39	410.38
#交通运输、仓储和邮政业	Transportation, Storage and Post	112.98	399.34	197.87
批发、零售贸易业和住宿、餐饮业	Wholesale, Retail Sales and Hotel, Restaurants	62.41	0.01	86.22
生活消费	**Living Consumption**	**168.86**		**42.59**

表6.9 续表2 continued

行 业	Sectors	其他石油制品(万吨) Other Petroleum Products (10 000 tons)	热 力(万百万千焦) Thermopower (10 000 million K.J)	电 力(亿千瓦时) Electric Power (100 million kwh)
总 计	**Total**	**224.80**	**7 661.82**	**1 281.66**
生产消费	**Production Consumption**	**224.80**	**7 661.82**	**1 094.28**
第一产业	Primary Industry			6.85
第二产业	Secondary Industry	224.80	7 492.66	744.29
#工 业	Industry	224.80	7 471.54	714.46
第三产业	Tertiary Industry		169.16	343.14
#交通运输、仓储和邮政业	Transportation, Storage and Post		65.69	38.74
批发、零售贸易业和住宿、餐饮业	Wholesale, Retail Sales and Hotel, Restaurants		43.21	74.72
生活消费	**Living Consumption**			**187.38**

表6.10 煤炭、石油、电力平衡表（2012）
COAL,PETROLEUM,ELECTRICITY BALANCE SHEEET

指　标	Indicators	煤　炭（万吨）Coal (10 000 tons)	石　油（万吨）Crude Oil (10 000 tons)	电　力（亿千瓦时）Electricity (100 million kwh)
可供本地区消费的能源量	**Total Energy Available for Consumption**	**5 701.89**	**3 259.93**	**1 353.45**
库存差	Inventory Changes in the Year	-27.4	7.98	
生产量	Energy Production		5.27	973.02
外省(市)调入量	Inflow from Other Provinces	7 806.58	4 052.59	476.18
进 口 量	Imports	544.01	2 378.60	
我轮、机在外国加油量	China Airplanes&ships Refueling in Abroad		494.79	
本市调出量(－)	Outflow from Shanghai	-2 621.30	-3 475.61	-95.75
出口量(－)	Exports		-52.01	
外轮、机在我国加油量(－)	Foreign Airplanes&ships Refueling in China		-151.68	
消费量	**Total Energy Consumption**	**5 703.22**	**3 259.99**	**1 353.45**
按行业分	**Consumption by Sectors**			
农、林、牧、渔业	Farming,Forestry,Animal Husbandry,Fishery and Water Conservancy	2.67	31.64	6.85
工　业	Industry	5 563.80	1 100.36	786.25
建筑业	Construction	10.49	82.10	29.83
交通运输、仓储和邮政业	Transport,Storage and Post	1.91	1 326.58	38.74
批发、零售业和住宿、餐饮业	Wholesale,Retail Trade and Hotel, Restaurants	38.54	169.47	74.72
其　他	Others	44.62	275.00	229.68
生活消费	Residential Consumption	41.19	274.84	187.38
按用途分	**Consumption by Usage**			
终端消费	Final Consumption	975.26	3 248.46	1 281.66
#工　业	Industry	835.84	1 088.83	714.46
用于加工转换	Processing and Conversion	4 715.83	11.53	
损失量	Others Losses	12.13		71.79
平衡差额	**Balanced Difference**	**-1.33**	**-0.06**	

表6.11 电力建设情况(2009～2012)
STATISTICS OF ELECTRIC POWER COUSTRUCTION

指 标	Indicators	2009	2010	2011	2012
发电量(亿千瓦时)	**Electric Power Generated(100 million kwh)**	**781.79**	**942.96**	**1 025.62**	**966.65**
线损率(%)	Electricity Loss Rate on Lines(%)	6.05	6.05	6.05	6.15
年末发电设备容量(万千瓦)	Power Generating Equipment Capacity (year-end)(10 000kw)	1 654.94	1 855.38	1 962.52	2 145.99
架空线长度(公里)	Length of Overhead Lines(km)	8 558.49	8 549.50	9 108.62	9 426.75
500KV(公里)	500KV(km)	798.24	992.91	1 231.65	1 231.34
220KV(公里)	220KV(km)	2 928.84	2 956.08	3 220.74	3 475.20
110KV(公里)	110KV(km)	738.13	702.60	749.39	800.29
35KV(公里)	35KV(km)	3 986.70	3 791.78	3 800.70	3 813.79
电缆长度(公里)	**Length of Cable(km)**	14 965.05	7 846.98	8 031.27	8 327.17
220KV(万千伏安)	220KV(10 000kva)	636.00	516.44	537.30	550.30
110KV(万千伏安)	110KV(10 000kva)	1 161.00	962.54	979.20	1 011.86
35KV(万千伏安)	35KV(10 000kva)	13 168.05	6 336.76	6 483.52	6 733.36
公用变电容量(万千伏安)	**Public Transformer Capacity(10 000kva)**	**10 418.65**	**11 657.19**	**12 443.17**	**13 051.90**
500KV(万千伏安)	500KV(10 000kva)	2 841.40	3 116.40	3 641.40	3 824.84
220KV－35KV(万千伏安)	220KV－35KV(10 000kva)	7 102.87	7 827.75	8 088.73	8 514.02
用电最高负荷(万千瓦)	**Peak Electric Power Consumption Load (10 000kw)**	**2 379.90**	**2 621.20**	**2 548.90**	**2 591.50**

注：本表数据由市电力公司提供。
Note: Data in this table is provided by Shanghai Electric Power Corporation.

表6.12 主要年份环保投入
INVESTMENT ON ENVIRONMENT PROTECTION IN MAIN YEARS

单位:亿元(100 million yuan)

年 份 Year	环境保护投资 Investment on Environment Protection	其中 of which 城市环境基础设施建设投资 Urban Environment Infrastructure Investment	环境保护投资相当于GDP(%) Investment on Environment Protection as Percentage of Gross Domestic Product(%)	自然保护区覆盖率(%) Coverage Rate of Natural Preservation Areas(%)
1990			2.06	
1995	46.49		1.86	
1996	68.83		2.33	
1997	82.35		2.39	
1998	102.13		2.69	
1999	111.57		2.66	
2000	141.91		2.97	7.8
2001	152.93		2.94	10.5
2002	162.39	126.99	2.83	11.8
2003	191.53	144.05	2.86	11.8
2004	225.37	166.90	2.79	11.8
2005	281.18	201.01	3.04	11.8
2006	310.85	177.81	2.94	11.8
2007	366.12	233.22	2.93	12.1
2008	422.37	284.30	3.00	12.1
2009	460.42	282.74	3.06	12.1
2010	507.54	294.73	2.96	12.1
2011	557.92	316.79	2.91	12.1
2012	570.49	286.26	2.83	11.8

表6.13 主要年份工业固体废弃物防治
PREVENTION AND CURE OF INDUSTRIAL SOLID WASTES IN MAIN YEARS

指 标	Indicators	2000	2010	2011	2012
工业固体废弃物产生量(万吨)	Volume of Industrial Solid Wastes Produced (10 000 tons)	1 354.74	2 448.36	2 442.20	2 198.81
#危险废物	Dangerous Wastes	28.32	51.25	56.36	54.96
工业废弃物综合利用量(万吨)	Volume of Industrial Wastes Treated and Utilized (10 000 tons)	1 515.90	2 366.90	2 358.11	2 140.36
#危险废物	Dangerous Wastes	27.05	28.47	30.13	30.34
工业废弃物综合利用率(%)	Ratio of Industrial Wastes Treated and Utilized (%)	93.26	96.16	96.56	97.34
工业固体废物处置量(万吨)	Volume of Industrial Solid Wastes Disposed (10 000 tons)	90.96	93.86	74.89	55.86
#危险废物	Dangerous Wastes	1.08	23.44	26.01	24.60

表6.14 水环境保护(1995～2012)
WATER ENVIRONMENT PROTECTION

年 份 Year	废水排放总量(亿吨) Total Waste Water Discharged (100 million tons)	其中 of which 工 业 Industrial Waste Water	废水化学需氧量排放总量(万吨) Total Emission of Oxygen of Waste Water Needed by Chemistry (10 000 tons)	其中 of which 工 业 Industrial Waste Water	工业重复用水量(万吨) Volume of Interative Used Water by Industry (10 000 tons)	污水处理厂数(座) Quantity Sewage Disposal Plants (unit)	污水处理厂污水处理量(万吨) Volume of Sewage Disposed by Sewage Disposal Plants (10 000 tons)
1995	22.45	11.61		12.29	445 391	17	14 665
1996	22.85	11.41	27.46	12.16	486 278	20	12 876
1997	21.10	9.99	38.55	11.70	495 622	22	14 790
1998	20.81	9.00	36.55	9.63	475 656	22	15 605
1999	20.28	8.52	34.98	8.92	605 772	22	17 479
2000	19.37	7.25	31.87	6.93	592 055	27	23 028
2001	19.50	6.80	30.48	5.27	709 913	26	29 487
2002	19.21	6.49	32.96	4.78	654 133	27	30 658
2003	18.22	6.11	28.38	4.38	690 068	30	39 891
2004	19.34	5.64	29.38	3.76	750 803	37	95 301
2005	19.97	5.11	30.44	3.66	886 503	42	117 833
2006	22.37	4.83	30.20	3.53	843 970	43	155 726
2007	22.66	4.76	29.44	3.38	899 098	45	152 886
2008	22.60	4.41	26.67	2.76	946 198	47	177 090
2009	23.05	4.12	24.34	2.90	1 004 672	51	171 609
2010	24.82	3.67	21.98	2.16	1 047 970	52	189 654
2011	19.86	4.46	24.90	2.74	747 893	53	193 354
2012	22.05	4.77	24.26	2.62	778 841	53	200 685

注：2011 年起，废水排放总量中增加了农业源和集中式治理设施排放的废水。
Note: Since 2011, waste water discharged from the agricultural source and centralized treatment facilities has been added in Total Waste Water Discharged.

表6.15 大气环境保护（1995～2012）
ATMOSPHERE ENVIRONMENT PROTECTION

年 份 Year	工业废气排放总量(亿标立方米) Industrial Waste Gas Emission (100 million cu. m)	烟尘排放总量(万吨) Total Emission of Smoke and Dust (10 000 tons)	其中 of which 工 业 Industrial Sector	其中 of which 生活及其他 Residential Sector and Others	废气二氧化硫排放总量(万吨) Total Emission of SO_2 (10 000 tons)	其中 of which 工 业 Industrial Sector	其中 of which 生活及其他 Residential Sector and Others
1995	4 625	20.78	13.33	7.45	53.41	38.15	15.26
1996	4 757	15.78	14.77	1.01	51.00	43.30	7.70
1997	4 755	17.08	13.38	3.70	50.85	43.62	7.23
1998	4 912	15.63	10.74	4.89	48.89	39.09	9.80
1999	4 947	13.57	9.00	4.57	40.31	31.09	9.22
2000	5 755	14.12	8.32	5.80	46.49	32.68	13.81
2001	6 964	13.52	6.23	7.29	47.26	30.00	17.26
2002	7 440	10.74	5.60	5.14	44.66	32.49	12.17
2003	7 799	11.54	4.97	6.57	43.54	30.07	13.47
2004	8 834	12.27	5.25	7.02	47.31	34.95	12.36
2005	8 482	11.52	4.95	6.57	51.28	37.52	13.76
2006	9 428	11.29	4.73	6.56	50.80	37.43	13.37
2007	9 591	10.60	4.04	6.56	49.78	36.44	13.34
2008	10 436	10.63	4.06	6.57	44.61	29.80	14.81
2009	10 059	10.18	3.64	6.54	37.89	23.93	13.96
2010	12 969	10.21	4.18	6.03	35.81	26.32	9.49
2011	13 692	8.98	6.64	2.34	24.01	21.01	3.00
2012	13 361	8.71	6.37	2.34	22.82	19.34	3.48

①2008 年起工业废气排放量按新排放系数计算。
②2011 年起，烟尘排放总量统计口径变更为烟(粉)尘排放量。
❶The Volume of Industrial Exhaust Emission in 2008 was calculated by new emission coefficient.
❷Since 2011, the statistics caliber of Total Emission of Smoke and Dust has been changed to Total Emission of Smoke(Powder) and Dust.

表6.16　主要年份环境空气状况
AMBIENT AIR CONDITION IN MAIN YEARS

	指　标 Indicators	2000	2010	2011	2012
中心城区二氧化硫年日平均值（毫克/立方米）	Annual Daily Mean Concentration of SO_2 in Urban Area（mg/m^3）	0.045	0.029	0.029	0.023
中心城区二氧化氮年日平均值（毫克/立方米）	Annual Daily Mean Concentration of NO_2 in Urban Area（mg/m^3）	0.090	0.050	0.051	0.046
中心城区可吸入颗粒平均浓度（毫克/立方米）	Mean Concentration of Inhalable Particulate in Urban Area（mg/m^3）		0.079	0.080	0.071
降水PH平均值	Rain PH Value	5.19	4.66	4.72	4.64
酸雨频率(%)	Frequency of Acid Rain（%）	26.0	73.9	67.5	80.0
环境空气质量优良天数(天)	Quantity of Days with Good Ambient Air Quality（day）	295	336	337	343
环境空气质量优良率(%)	Rate of Good Ambient Air Quality（%）	80.8	92.1	92.3	93.7

表6.17　主要年份声环境及治理
NOISE ENVIRONMENT AND TREATMENT IN MAIN YEARS

	指　标 Indicators	2000	2010	2011	2012
区域环境噪声平均等效声级	**Average Equivalent Sound Level of Area Ambient Noise**				
昼间时段(LeqdB(A))	Daytime（LeqdB(A)）	56.6	55.8	55.0	54.7
夜间时段(LeqdB(A))	Nighttime（LeqdB(A)）	49.2	48.3	48.0	48.2
交通环境噪声平均等效声级	**Average Equivalent Sound Level of Traffic Noise**				
昼间时段(LeqdB(A))	Daytime（LeqdB(A)）	70.5	69.8	70.0	69.3
夜间时段(LeqdB(A))	Nighttime（LeqdB(A)）	64.1	64.3	64.5	64.4

表 6.18 城市环境卫生情况(1978～2012)
URBAN ENVIRONMENTAL SITUATION

年份 Year	垃圾产生量 (万吨) Garbage Produced (10 000 tons)	其中 of which		清运粪便 (万吨) Night Soil Disposal Cleared (10 000 tons)
		生活垃圾 Residential Garbage	建筑垃圾 Construction Garbage	
1978	214	108	106	418
1979	250	125	126	374
1980	272	131	141	331
1981	272	146	126	329
1982	296	169	127	325
1983	280	166	113	311
1984	308	185	123	272
1985	305	196	109	252
1986	328	226	102	263
1987	325	229	97	262
1988	329	240	89	249
1989	344	250	94	246
1990	382	279	103	243
1991	393	296	97	229
1992	428	301	127	242
1993	488	335	152	234
1994	558	358	200	240
1995	668	372	296	216
1996	736	419	317	217
1997	755	454	301	227
1998	824	470	353	218
1999	767	500	267	172
2000	858	641	217	256
2001	901	644	257	219
2002	760	467	293	238
2003	800	585	215	251
2004	802	610	192	258
2005	777	622	155	254
2006	805	658	146	247
2007	852	702	150	232
2008	841	678	153	220
2009	870	710	160	221
2010	890	732	158	201
2011	1 142	704	438	207
2012	11 728	716	11 012	200

注：2012 年起，建筑垃圾中增加了工程渣土清运量。
Note: Since 2012, Construction Garbage Contains Volume of Construction Drdgs Clearance.

表 6.19 环境卫生设施（1978～2012）
URBAN ENVIRONMENTAL SANITATION

年份 Year	公共厕所 （座） Public lawatories(unit)	生活垃圾收集点（处） Collection Points of Residential Garbage(unit)	废物箱 （只） Trash Cans(unit)	倒粪站 （座） Excrements Stations(unit)	化粪池 （只） Septic Tanks(unit)
1978	706	13 840	2 333	3 303	25 540
1979	696	12 695	3 151	3 382	25 915
1980	713	15 707	3 402	3 445	26 754
1981	740	17 905	2 546	3 464	27 407
1982	760	18 824	2 821	3 484	28 652
1983	778	17 859	2 733	3 467	29 977
1984	798	20 384	3 890	3 481	30 943
1985	952	22 870	5 700	3 470	33 477
1986	950	31 142	5 983	3 537	39 175
1987	978	37 751	6 341	3 587	40 042
1988	992	42 802	5 117	3 342	41 171
1989	1 057	46 149	5 276	3 107	41 349
1990	1 016	46 368	4 921	2 973	43 655
1991	1 033	40 309	4 980	3 006	43 089
1992	1 048	44 752	4 961	2 655	43 694
1993	1 104	46 741	5 756	2 732	43 323
1994	1 100	50 292	6 993	2 739	43 125
1995	1 100	48 563	9 019	2 532	43 151
1996	1 112	51 456	9 522	2 412	38 657
1997	1 120	53 643	12 735	2 207	44 440
1998	1 203	59 498	15 968	2 127	41 760
1999	1 311	66 067	17 326	2 192	44 694
2000	2 215	22 470	23 189	2 045	46 921
2001	2 406	17 694	24 672	1 890	47 500
2002	3 776	26 787	29 517	1 846	49 220
2003	3 468	27 814	31 272	1 709	48 831
2004	3 640	28 649	34 571	1 611	47 579
2005	3 640	28 388	39 539	1 689	47 424
2006	3 746	29 812	44 888	2 253	46 217
2007	5 415	29 538	47 739	2158	45 841
2008	5 866	29 965	56 485	2 064	45 537
2009	5 633	30 584	67 465	2 257	43 775
2010	6 026	30 645	74 658	1 900	43 170
2011	5 768	30 648	78 213	1 868	42 652
2012	6 340	31 625	82 454	1 837	42 306

上 / 海 / 统 / 计 / 年 / 鉴

主要统计指标解释

能源消费总量

能源消费总量指一定时期内全国(地区)物质生产部门、非物质生产部门和生活消费的各种能源的总和,是观察能源消费水平、构成和增长速度的总量指标。能源消费总量包括原煤和原油及其制品、天然气、电力,但不包括低热值燃料、生物质能和太阳能等的利用。能源消费总量分为三部分,即终端能源消费量、能源加工转换损失量和能源损失量。

(1)终端能源消费量指一定时期内全国(地区)物质生产部门、非物质生产部门和生活消费的各种能源在扣除了用于加工转换二次能源消费量和损失量以后的数量。

(2)能源加工转换损失量指一定时期内全国(地区)投入加工转换的各种能源数量之和与产出各种能源产品之和的差额。它是观察能源在加工转换过程中损失量变化的指标。

(3)能源损失量指一定时期内能源在输送、分配、储存过程中发生的损失和由客观原因造成的各种损失量。不包括各种气体能源放空、放散量。

能源生产弹性系数

能源生产弹性系数反映能源生产量的增长与国民经济增长之间的比值。计算公式:

$$能源生产弹性系数=\frac{能源生产总量年平均增长速度}{国民经济年平均增长速度}$$

电力生产弹性系数

电力生产弹性系数反映电力生产量的增长与国民经济增长之间的比值。计算公式:

$$电力生产弹性系数=\frac{电力生产量年平均增长速度}{国民经济年平均增长速度}$$

能源消费弹性系数

能源消费弹性系数反映能源消费增长速度与国民经济增长速度之间比例关系的指标:

$$能源消费弹性系数=\frac{能源消费量年平均增长速度}{国民经济年平均增长速度}$$

电力消费弹性系数

电力消费弹性系数反映电力消费增长速度与国民经济增长速度之间比例关系的指标。计算公式为:

$$电力消费弹性系数=\frac{电力消费量年平均增长速度}{国民经济年平均增长速度}$$

能源加工转换效率

能源加工转换效率指一定时期内能源经过加工转换后,产出的各种能源产品的数量与投入加工转换的各种能源数量的比率。它是观察能源加工转换装置和生产工艺先进与落后、管理水平高低等的重要指标。计算公式为:

$$能源加工转换效率=\frac{加工转换产出量}{加工转换投入量}\times 100\%$$

“三废”综合利用产品产值

指报告期内利用“三废”作为主要原料生产的产品价值(现行价);已经销售或准备销售的应计算产品价值,留作生产自用的不应计算产品价值。

自然保护区

指对有代表性的自然生态系统、珍稀濒危野生动植物物种的天然分布区、水源涵养区、有特殊意义的自然历史遗迹等保护对象所在的陆地、陆地水体或海域,依法划出一定面积进行特殊保护和管理的区域。以县及县以上各级人民政府正式批准建立的自然保护区为准(包括“六五”以前由部门或“革委会”批准且现仍存在的自然保护区)。风景名胜区、文物保护区不计在内。自然保护区分国家级、省级、地市级和县级。按主管部门分属:环保、林业、农业、地矿、海洋、水利和其他部门。

工业固体废弃物产生量

指报告期内企业在生产过程中产生的固体状、半固体状和高浓度液体状废弃物的总量,包括危险废物、冶炼废渣、粉煤灰、炉渣、煤矸石、尾矿、放射性废物和其他废物等;不包括矿山开采的剥离废石和掘进废石(煤矸石和呈酸性或碱性的废石除外)。酸性或碱性废石指采掘的废石其流经水、雨淋水的pH值小于4或pH值大于10.5

上 / 海 / 统 / 计 / 年 / 鉴

者。

■ 危险废物

指列入国家危险废物名录或根据国家规定的危险废物鉴别标准和鉴别方法认定的,具有爆炸性、易燃性、易氧化性、毒性、腐蚀性、易传染疾病等危险特性之一的废物。

■ 工业废弃物综合利用量

指报告期内企业通过回收、加工、循环、交换等方式,从废弃物中提取或者使其转化为可以利用的资源、能源和其他原材料的废弃物量 (包括当年利用往年的工业废弃物贮存量),如用作农业肥料、生产建筑材料、筑路等。综合利用量由原产生废弃物的单位统计。

■ 工业废弃物综合利用率

指工业废弃物综合利用量占工业废弃物产生量 (包括综合利用往年贮存量)的百分率。计算公式为:

$$\text{工业废弃物综合利用率}=\frac{\text{工业废弃物综合利用量}}{\text{工业废弃物产生量}+\text{综合利用往年贮存量}}\times 100\%$$

■ 工业固体废物处置量

指报告期内企业将固体废物焚烧或者最终置于符合环境保护规定要求的场所,并不再回取的工业固体废物量(包括当年处置往年的工业固体废物贮存量)。处置方式有填埋(其中危险废物应安全填埋)、焚烧、专业贮存场(库)封场处理、深层灌注、回填矿井及海洋处置(经海洋管理部门同意投海处置)等。

■ 工业废水排放量

指经过企业厂区所有排放口排到企业外部的工业废水量。包括生产废水、外排的直接冷却水、超标排放的矿井地下水和与工业废水混排的厂区生活污水,不包括外排的间接冷却水(清污不分流的间接冷却水应计算在内)。

■ 工业废水排放达标量

指报告期内废水中各项污染物指标都达到国家或地方排放标准的外排工业废水量,包括未经处理外排达标的,经废水处理设施处理后达标排放的,以及经污水处理厂处理后达标排放的。

■ 工业废水排放达标率

指工业废水排放达标量占工业废水排放量的百分率,计算公式为:

$$\text{工业废水排放达标率}=\frac{\text{工业废水排放达标量}}{\text{工业废水排放量}}\times 100\%$$

■ 工业废气排放量

指企业厂区内燃料燃烧和生产工艺过程中产生的各种排入空气的含有污染物的气体总量,按标准状态〔273K,101 325Pa〕计算。测算公式为:

工业废气排放量 = 燃料燃烧过程中废气排放量 + 生产工艺过程中废气排放量

■ 工业二氧化硫排放总量

指报告期内企业在燃料燃烧和生产工艺过程中排入大气的 SO_2 总量,计算公式为:

工业二氧化硫排放量 = 燃料燃烧过程中二氧化硫排放量 + 生产工艺过程中二氧化硫排放量

■ 工业烟尘排放量

指企业厂区内燃料燃烧过程中产生的烟气中夹带的颗粒物排放量。

■ 酸雨频率

指酸雨出现的次数占降水出现次数的比例,通常称PH 值小于 5.6 的降水为酸雨。

SHANGHAI STATISTICAL YEARBOOK

EXPLANATORY NOTES TO MAJOR STATISTICAL INDICATORS

□ Total Energy Consumption

Total Energy Consumption refers to the total energy consumption of various forms by material production departments, non-material production departments and households in the country (region) in a given period of time. It is a comprehensive indicator to observe the scale, composition and development of energy consumption. The total energy consumption includes raw coal, crude petroleum and their products, natural gas and electricity, but excludes fuel of low calorific value, bioenergy and solar energy. Total domestic energy consumption can be divided into three parts:

(1) Final Energy Consumption refers to the total energy consumption by material production departments, non-material production departments and households in the country (region) in a given period of time, after deducting the secondary energy consumption and loss during the process of energy conversion.

(2) Loss During the Process of Energy Conversion refers to the total input of various forms for conversion, minus the total output of energy of various forms in the country in a given period of time. It is an indicator to observe the loss that occurs during the process of energy conversion.

(3) Loss refers to the total loss of energy due to mistakes or any objective reasons during the course of energy transport, distribution and storage in a given period of time. The loss of various kinds of gas due to gas discharges and stocktaking is excluded.

□ Elasticity of Energy Production

Elasticity of Energy Production is an indicator to show the relationship between the growth rate of energy production and the growth rate of the national economy. The formula is :

$$\text{Elasticity of Energy Production} = \frac{\text{average annual growth rate of energy production}}{\text{average annual growth rate of national economy}}$$

□ Elasticity of Electricity Production

Elasticity of Electricity Production is an indicator to show the relationship between the growth rate of electricity production and the growth rate of the national economy. The formula is :

$$\text{Elasticity of Electricity Production} = \frac{\text{average annual growth rate of electrictity production}}{\text{average annual growth rate of national economy}}$$

□ Elasticity of Energy Consumption

Elasticity Ratio of Energy Consumption is an indicator to show the relationship between the growth rate of energy consumption and the growth rate of the national economy. The formula is:

$$\text{Elasticity of Energy Consumption} = \frac{\text{average annual growth rate of energy consumption}}{\text{average annual growth rate of national economy}}$$

□ Elasticity of Electricity Consumption

Elasticity Ratio of Electricity Consumption is an indicator to show the relationship between the growth rate of electricity consumption and the growth rate of the national economy. The formula is:

$$\text{Elasticity of Electricity Consumption} = \frac{\text{average annual growth rate of electricity consumption}}{\text{average annual growth rate of national economy}}$$

□ Efficiency of Energy Transformation

Efficiency of Energy Transformation refers to the ratio of the total output of energy products after transformation and the total input of energy for transformation in the same reference period .It is an indicator to show the current conditions of energy processing and conversion equipment, production technique and management. The formula is:

$$\text{Efficiency of Energy Transformation} = \frac{\text{output of enery from transformation}}{\text{Input of energy for transformation}}$$

□ Output Value of Products Made from Waste Gas, Waste Water and Solid Wastes

Output Value of Products Made from Waste Gas, Waste Water and Solid Wastes refers current value of products with waste gas, waste water and solid wastes as main materials of production. Products sold and ready to sell shall be included while those produced for own use shall not be included.

□ Natural Reserves

Natural Reserves refer to all the land, water areas on land and sea areas are under special protection or management due to the

EXPLANATORY NOTES TO MAJOR STATISTICAL INDICATORS

possess ion of representative natural ecological system, natural distribution of rare and dying out animal zones, water-resource conservation areas, and natural historical relics. Also included are natural reserves formally approved by people's governments at various levels at and above county level (including those approved before the Sixth-five-year Program and still active natural reserves).Scenic spots and historical sites and zones for preservation of cultural relics are not included. Natural reserves are classified as national level, provincial level, prefecture level and county level ones. They are under the jurisdiction of different departments, such as: environment protection, forestry, agriculture, geological and mining, oceanic and water conservancy and so on.

□ Industrial Solid Wastes Produced

Industrial Solid Wastes Produced refers to total volume of solid, semi-solid and high concentration liquid residues produced by industrial enterprises from production process in a given period of time, including hazardous wastes, slag, coal ash, gangue, tailings, radioactive residues and other wastes, but excluding stones stripped or dug out in mining (gangue and acid or alkaline stones not included). A stone is acid or alkaline depending on the pH value of the water below 4 or above 10.5 when the stone is in, or soaked by, the water.

□ Hazardous Wastes

Hazardous Wastes refers to those included in the national hazardous wastes catalogue or specified as any one of the following properties in the national hazardous wastes identification standards: explosive, ignitable, oxidizable, toxic, corrosive or liable to cause infectious diseases or lead to other dangers.

□ Industrial Wastes Utilized

Industrial Wastes Utilized refers to volume of wastes from which useful materials can be extracted or which can be converted into usable resources, energy or other materials by means of reclamation, processing, recycling and exchange (including utilizing in the year the stocks of industrial wastes of the previous year). Examples of such utilizations include fertilizers, building materials and road materials. The information shall be collected by the producing units of the wastes.

□ Ratio of Industrial Wastes Utilized

Ratio of Industrial Wastes Utilized refers to the percentage of industrial wastes utilized over industrial wastes produced (including stocks of the previous years). It is calculated as:

Ratio of industrial wastes utilized = volume of industrial wastes utilized / (industrial wastes produced + stock of previous years) × 100%

□ Industrial Solid Wastes Disposed

Industrial Solid Wastes Disposed refers to quantity of industrial solid wastes which are burnt or placed ultimately in the sites meeting the requirements for environmental protection and not salvaged or recycled (including disposition in the year of those wastes of previous years). The disposition includes landfill (Safe landfills should be conducted for hazardous wastes), incineration, containment spaces, deep underground disposal, backfill in mining pits and disposal at sea.

□ Volume of Industrial Waste Water Discharged

Volume of Industrial Waste Water Discharged refers to the volume of industrial waste water discharged, through all outlets, to the outside of industrial enterprises, including waste water produced, direct-cooling water, underground water from mines that does not meet the standard of discharge, and the domestic sewage mixed up with industrial waste water when discharged, but excluding discharged indirect-cooling water.

□ Industrial Waste Water Meeting Discharge Standards

Industrial Waste Water Meeting Discharge Standards refers to volume of industrial waste water discharge which, with or without treatment, reaches national or local standards with regard to all pollutants.

□ Ratio of Standard Waste Water Discharged to the Total Discharge

Ratio of Standard Waste Water Discharged to the Total Discharge refers to the share of the volume of waste water up to the standard for discharge of the total volume. The formula is as follows:

Ratio of Standard Waste Water Discharged to the Total Discharge

$$\frac{\text{average annual growth rate of electricity consumption}}{\text{average annual growth rate of national economy}} \times 100\%$$

□ Volume of Waste Industrial Gas Emission

Industrial Waste Air Emission refers to discharge into atmosphere of waste air containing pollutants generated from fuel burning and production process in enterprises within a given period of

EXPLANATORY NOTES TO MAJOR STATISTICAL INDICATORS

time. It is calculated at standard status (273K, 101325Pa) as:

Industrial waste air emission = emission through fuel burning + emission through production process

□SO_2 Emission through Industrial Activities

SO_2 Emission through Industrial Activities refers to volume of sulphur dioxide emission from fuel burning and production process by enterprises during a given period of time. It is calculated as:

SO_2 emission through industrial activities = SO_2 emission from fuel burning + SO_2 emission from production process

□Industrial Soot Emission

Industrial Soot Emission refers to volume of soot in smoke emitted in process of fuel burning in premises of enterprises.

□Acid Rain Frequency

Acid Rain Frequency refers to the proportion of frequencies of acid rainfall to the total rainfall times. Rainfall is defined as acid rain when the PH value of its rainwater is small than 5.6.

第七篇

CHAPTER 7

固定资产投资

INVESTMENT IN FIXED ASSETS

简要说明

一、本篇资料的主要内容

本篇资料通过对一定时期全社会建造和购置固定资产活动的数量方面的描述，反映报告期内固定资产投资的规模、速度和内部结构情况，固定资产投资的资金来源及房屋施、竣工面积情况等。

二、本篇资料的统计范围

固定资产投资统计的范围包括：城镇和农村非农户建设项目投资，房地产开发投资及农户投资。

三、本篇的资料来源

城镇和农村非农户建设项目投资的统计资料来自上海市统计局投资建设统计处的固定资产投资统计调查；房地产开发投资的统计资料来自上海市统计局投资建设统计处的房地产开发、经营统计调查；农户投资的统计资料来自国家统计局上海调查总队农村住户调查处的农户固定资产统计调查。

四、本篇的统计调查方法

除农户固定资产投资统计采用抽样调查方法外，其他均为全面统计报表。

五、统计口径的变化

自 1997 年起，固定资产投资的统计起点由 5 万元及以上提高到 50 万元及以上。

自 2011 年起，固定资产投资项目的统计起点由计划总投资 50 万元及以上提高到 500 万元及以上。

BRIEF INTRODUCTION

I. Main Contents

Statistics in this chapter describe activities on the construction and purchase of fixed assets of the whole society during a given period of time, and reflect the size, growth, internal structure, source of funds of fixed asset investment and floor space of buildings under construction or completed.

II. Scope of Statistics

Statistics on the investment in fixed assets cover investments in construction projects of urban and rural non–farm households, investments in real estate development, and investment of farm households.

III. Sources of Data

Data on the investments in construction projects of urban and rural non–farm households are from the surveys of investment in fixed assets from Department of Investment and Construction Statistics of the Shanghai Municipal Bureau of Statistics. Data on the real estate investments are from surveys of real estate development and management conducted by Department of Investment and Construction Statistics of the Shanghai Municipal Bureau of Statistics. Data on the investment of farm households are from surveys conducted by Department of Rural Household Survey of the Survey Office of NBS in Shanghai

IV. Methodology of Data Collection

All data on investment in fixed assets are collected by the system of reporting form with complete enumeration, except data on individual investments in fixed assets in rural areas, which are collected through sample surveys.

V. Changes in Statistical Scope

Since 1997 the cut–off point of statistics of investment in fixed assets is raised from 50000 yuan to 500000 yuan.

Since 2011, the cut–off point of projects covered by statistics of investment in fixed assets is raised from an investment of 500000 yuan to 5000000 yuan.

表7.1 全社会固定资产投资总额(按投资类别分)(1978~2012)
TOTAL INVESTMENT IN FIXED ASSETS(GROUPED BY TYPE OF INVESTMENT)

单位:亿元(100 million yuan)

年 份 Year	本年完成投资合 计 Investment Completed Total	其 中 of which				
		建设项目 Construction Project	其 中 of which		房地产开发 Investment in Real Estate	农户投资 Farmers' Investment
			城 镇 Town	农村非农户 Rural Non-agricultural		
1978	27.91	26.88	23.92	2.96		0.79
1979	35.58	34.39	32.22	2.17		0.94
1980	45.43	43.45	40.44	3.01		1.41
1981	54.60	49.85	45.20	4.65		3.97
1982	71.34	65.97	61.91	4.06		4.32
1983	75.94	70.21	65.26	4.95		4.48
1984	92.30	83.11	76.04	7.07		7.28
1985	118.56	103.16	96.12	7.04		12.00
1986	146.93	132.44	122.64	9.80		10.30
1987	186.30	167.88	154.04	13.84	0.97	12.66
1988	245.27	219.90	197.71	22.19	1.68	16.90
1989	214.76	194.64	177.70	16.94	1.85	14.32
1990	227.08	199.05	184.67	14.38	8.16	15.96
1991	258.30	232.34	208.72	23.62	7.59	14.17
1992	357.38	318.93	263.51	55.42	12.71	17.00
1993	653.91	610.80	505.98	104.82	22.04	5.33
1994	1 123.29	971.68	830.45	141.23	117.43	10.40
1995	1 601.79	1 097.68	958.11	139.57	466.20	13.10
1996	1 952.05	1 238.85	1 080.53	158.32	657.79	20.00
1997	1 977.59	1 322.92	1 156.76	166.16	614.23	16.80
1998	1 964.83	1 361.41	1 224.01	137.40	577.12	12.76
1999	1 856.72	1 325.84	1 191.51	134.33	514.83	5.54
2000	1 869.67	1 284.08	1 122.47	161.61	566.17	10.36
2001	1 994.73	1 354.22	1 181.09	173.13	630.73	9.28
2002	2 187.06	1 430.69	1 262.77	167.92	748.89	6.87
2003	2 452.11	1 544.38	1 374.38	170.00	901.24	6.49
2004	3 084.66	1 903.33	1 722.51	180.82	1 175.46	5.86
2005	3 542.55	2 288.61	1 984.61	304.00	1 246.86	7.08
2006	3 925.09	2 643.53	2 246.93	396.60	1 275.59	5.96
2007	4 458.61	3 145.87	2 775.81	370.06	1 307.53	5.21
2008	4 829.45	3 459.38	3 044.46	414.92	1 366.87	3.20
2009	5 273.33	3 807.62	3 384.31	423.31	1 464.18	1.53
2010	5 317.67	3 334.95	2 858.56	476.39	1 980.68	2.03
2011	5 067.09	2 893.95	2 519.48	374.47	2 170.31	2.83
2012	5 254.38	2 870.04	2 559.12	310.92	2 381.36	2.98

注：自2011年起，全社会固定资产投资由建设项目投资、房地产开发投资和农户投资三部分组成；建设项目投资由城镇投资和农村非农户投资两部分组成，其中城镇投资包括原来的基本建设、更新改造、其他投资和城镇私人建房投资。

Note: Since 2011, total investment in fixed assets was composed of construction project investment, investment in real estate development and investment of rural households; construction project investment was composed of investment in urban areas and rural non-agricultural investment, in which investment in urban areas was composed of fundamental construction, renovation, other investments and urban private housing investment.

表 7.2 全社会固定资产投资总额(按经济类型分)(1978~2012)
TOTAL INVESTMENT IN FIXED ASSETS (GROUPED BY ECONOMIC TYPES)

单位:亿元(100 million yuan)

年份 Year	本年完成投资合计 Investment Completed Total	其中 of which			
		#国有经济 State-owned	#集体经济 Collective-owned	#股份制经济 Share-holding	#外商、港澳台经济 Hong Kong, Macao, Taiwan and Foreign Funded
1978	27.91	23.83	3.20		
1979	35.58	32.08	2.42		
1980	45.43	40.27	3.58		
1981	54.60	45.00	5.43		
1982	71.34	61.62	5.11		
1983	75.94	65.01	6.20		
1984	92.30	75.80	8.98		
1985	118.56	95.92	10.44		
1986	146.93	122.46	13.99		
1987	186.30	154.45	18.65		
1988	245.27	198.68	29.03		
1989	214.76	178.81	21.00		
1990	227.08	192.24	18.29		
1991	258.30	215.61	27.82		
1992	357.38	275.67	64.16		
1993	653.91	419.22	124.18	32.83	61.61
1994	1 123.29	721.37	189.75	76.99	101.78
1995	1 601.79	935.92	247.11	150.17	208.30
1996	1 952.05	1 048.27	239.47	165.57	340.18
1997	1 977.59	1 148.69	257.10	118.80	367.50
1998	1 964.83	1 087.94	208.84	203.81	405.17
1999	1 856.72	986.82	227.19	268.68	325.58
2000	1 869.67	829.98	156.34	421.53	319.05
2001	1 994.73	760.58	136.81	580.75	362.25
2002	2 187.06	742.72	101.33	631.70	369.96
2003	2 452.11	811.85	116.63	647.27	468.20
2004	3 084.66	955.12	146.58	667.52	851.39
2005	3 542.55	1 240.27	131.07	916.27	640.31
2006	3 925.09	1 460.09	159.31	910.31	725.85
2007	4 458.61	1 779.43	121.51	1 169.49	711.35
2008	4 829.45	2 295.74	104.86	1 026.67	748.14
2009	5 273.33	2 618.61	132.30	1 174.81	617.90
2010	5 317.67	2 234.12	183.07	1 200.26	686.95
2011	5 067.09	1 875.48	133.33	1 349.65	726.57
2012	5 254.38	1 855.24	112.41	1 417.80	758.08

表 7.3 主要年份全社会固定资产投资主要指标
MAJOR INDICATORS OF TOTAL INVESTMENT IN FIXED ASSETS IN MAIN YEARS

单位：亿元(100 million yuan)

指 标	Indicators	2000	2010	2011	2012
本年完成投资合计	**Investment Completed Total**	**1 869.67**	**5 317.67**	**5 067.09**	**5 254.38**
按隶属关系分	**Grouped by Administrative Relationship**				
中央项目	Central Government Projects	257.67	761.06	550.00	671.46
地方项目	Local Projects	1 612.00	4 556.61	4 517.09	4 582.92
按构成分	**Grouped by Use of Funds**				
建筑安装工程	Construction and Installation	882.91	2 820.17	2 991.95	3 097.79
设备、工器具购置	Purchase of Equipment and Instruments	482.47	991.10	834.17	851.13
其他费用	Others	504.29	1 506.40	1 240.97	1 305.46
按建设性质分	**Grouped by Type of Construction**				
#新 建	New Construction	730.76	2 052.69	1 764.74	1 715.93
改建和技术改造	Reconstruction and Technical Transformation	216.40	513.80	413.81	427.08
扩 建	Expansion	216.71	368.07	343.73	368.51
单纯购置	Simply Purchase	39.02	373.43	335.81	333.23
按产业分	**Grouped by Type of Industry**				
第一产业	Primary Industry	7.87	16.40	17.97	11.20
第二产业	Secondary Industry	615.94	1 435.37	1 290.89	1 294.14
第三产业	Tertiary Industry	1 245.86	3 865.90	3 758.23	3 949.04
按经济类型分	**Grouped by Economic Types**				
国有经济	State-owned	829.98	2 234.12	1 875.48	1 855.24
非国有经济	Non-state-owned	1 039.69	3 083.55	3 191.61	3 399.14
集体经济	Collective-owned	156.34	183.07	133.33	112.41
私营经济	Private	83.29	992.16	946.02	1 090.09
联营经济	Joint Owned	41.20	11.52	10.62	8.99
股份制经济	Share-holding	421.53	1 200.26	1 349.65	1 417.80
外商经济	Foreign Funded	222.86	439.28	473.28	528.06
港澳台经济	Hong Kong, Macao and Taiwan Funded	96.19	247.67	253.29	230.02
其他经济	Others	18.28	9.58	25.42	11.77
新增固定资产	**Newly Increased Fixed Assets**	**1 493.35**	**3 179.40**	**2 816.59**	**2 911.34**
固定资产交付使用率（%）	Rate of Fixed Assets Transfered and in Use(%)	79.9	59.8	55.6	55.4
房屋建筑面积(万平方米)	**Floor Space of Buildings (10 000 sq. m)**				
施工面积	Floor Space Under Construction	8 636.31	15 020.76	16 553.86	16 874.72
#住 宅	Residential Housing	4 804.12	7 344.07	8 423.11	8 350.83
竣工面积	Floor Space Completed	3 266.52	2 776.21	2 913.78	2 838.97
#住 宅	Residential Housing	1 724.02	1 415.44	1 568.83	1 626.73

注：按建设性质分组中不包括房地产开发投资和农户投资。 自2012年起固定资产投资项目行业代码采用新的分类标准(GB/T 4754－2011)，本表中的2011年产业分类数据参照新行业标准进行相应调整(下表同)。

Note: In "Type of Construction" the investment in real estate development and rural household invsetment are excluded. Since 2012, the industry investment in fixed assets project code using the new classfication standard (GB/T 4754－2011), 2011 Industrial Classification data in this table has been adjusted by the new industry standard(same as follows).

表 7.4　地方固定资产投资主要指标(2011～2012)
MAJOR INDICATORS OF LOCAL INVESTMENT IN FIXED ASSETS

单位:亿元(100 million yuan)

指　标	Indicators	2011	2012
本年完成投资合计	**Investment Completed Total**	**4 517.09**	**4 582.92**
按构成分	**Grouped by Use of Funds**		
建筑安装工程	Construction and Installation	2 764.62	2 840.92
设备、工器具购置	Purchase of Equipment and Instruments	591.64	594.62
其他费用	Others	1 160.82	1 147.38
按建设性质分	**Grouped by Type of Construction**		
#新　建	New Construction	1 604.86	1 447.72
改建和技术改造	Reconstruction and Technical Transformation	326.20	351.94
扩　建	Expansion	235.86	238.79
单纯购置	Simply Purchase	215.08	218.78
按产业分	**Grouped by Type of Industry**		
第一产业	Primary Industry	17.88	11.20
第二产业	Secondary Industry	1 040.92	1 051.48
第三产业	Tertiary Industry	3 458.29	3 520.24
按行业分	**Grouped by Sectors**		
#工　业	Industry	1 038.33	1 051.26
批发和零售业	Wholesale and Retail	52.80	62.10
交通运输、仓储和邮政业	Transportation, Storage, Postal and Telecommunications	492.48	371.03
住宿和餐饮业	Hotel and Catering	36.23	36.99
信息传输、软件和信息技术服务业	Transmission of Information, Software and Information Technology Services	16.27	28.98
金融业	Finance	14.85	13.77
房地产业	Real Estate	2 201.58	2 318.78
租赁和商务服务业	Leasing and Business Service	54.06	105.72
科学研究和技术服务业	Scientific Research and Technology Service and Geological Prospecting	39.49	27.82
水利、环境和公共设施管理业	Water Conservancy, Environment and Public Facility Management	371.92	340.94
居民服务、修理和其他服务业	Residents Service, Repair and Other Services	6.54	4.94
教　育	Education	37.70	38.60
卫生和社会工作	Health and Social Work	64.87	55.29
文化、体育和娱乐业	Culture, Sports and Entertainment	39.73	100.36
公共管理、社会保障和社会组织	Public Administration and Social Organizations	29.78	14.92
新增固定资产	**Newly Increased Fixed Assets**	**2 573.06**	**2 418.52**
固定资产交付使用率(%)	Rate of Fixed Assets Transfered and in Use(%)	57.0	52.8
房屋建筑面积(万平方米)	**Floor Space of Buildings (10 000 sq. m)**		
施工面积	Floor Space Under Construction	15 849.45	16 286.55
#住　宅	Residential Housing	8 002.26	8 071.41
竣工面积	Floor Space Completed	2 871.51	2 747.57
#住　宅	Residential Housing	1 568.59	1 553.05

表7.5 建设项目固定资产投资主要指标(2012)
MAJOR INDICATORS OF INVESTMENT IN FIXED ASSETS OF THE CONSTRUCTION PROJECT

单位:亿元(100 million yuan)

指 标	Indicators	全 市 Total	#地 方 Local Projects
本年完成投资合计	**Investment Completed Total**	**2 870.04**	**2 282.52**
按建设性质分	**Grouped by Type of Construction**		
#新 建	New Construction	1 715.93	1 447.72
改建和技改	Reconstruction and Technical Transformation	427.08	351.94
扩 建	Expansion	368.51	238.79
单纯购置	Simply Purchase	333.23	218.78
按产业分	**Grouped by Type of Industry**		
第一产业	Primary Industry	10.81	10.81
第二产业	Secondary Industry	1 294.13	1 051.48
第三产业	Tertiary Industry	1 565.10	1 220.23
按行业分	**Grouped by Economic Sectors**		
#工 业	Industry	1 292.61	1 051.26
批发和零售业	Wholesale and Retail	62.10	62.10
交通运输、仓储和邮政业	Transportation, Storage, Postal and Telecommunications	510.57	371.03
住宿和餐饮业	Hotel and Catering	37.09	36.99
信息传输、软件和信息技术服务业	Transmission of Information, Software and Information Technology Services	121.34	28.98
金融业	Finance	49.15	13.77
房地产业	Real Estate	20.58	18.78
租赁和商务服务业	Leasing and Business Service	151.73	105.72
科学研究和技术服务业	Scientific Research and Technology Service	39.47	27.82
水利、环境和公共设施管理业	Water Conservancy, Environment and Public Facility Management	341.49	340.94
居民服务、修理和其他服务业	Residents Service, Repair and Other Services	4.94	4.94
教 育	Education	52.07	38.60
卫生和社会工作	Health and Social Work	56.90	55.29
文化、体育和娱乐业	Culture, Sports and Entertainment	102.75	100.36
公共管理、社会保障和社会组织	Public Administration and Social Organizations	14.92	14.92
新增固定资产	**Newly Increased Fixed Assets**	**1 520.03**	**1 071.16**
固定资产交付使用率(%)	Rate of Fixed Assets Transfered and in Use(%)	53.0	46.9
房屋建筑面积(万平方米)	**Floor Space of Buildings (10 000 sq.m)**		
施工面积	Floor Space Under Construction	3 606.36	3 374.53
#住 宅	Residential Housing	17.55	17.55
竣工面积	Floor Space Completed	515.52	490.42

表7.6 工业各行业固定资产投资主要指标(2012)
MAIN INDICATORS OF INVESTMENT IN FIXED ASSETS OF VARIOUS INDUSTRIES

行业	Sectors	施工项目(个) Projects Under Construction (unit)	本年投产项目(个) Projects Completed and Put into Production (unit)	建成投产率(%) Rate of Projects Completed and Put into Use(%)	本年完成投资合计(亿元) Construction Transformation Investment (100 million yuan)
总 计	**Total**	**2 331**	**772**	**33.1**	**1 292.61**
采矿业	**Excavation**	**1**			**0.44**
开采辅助活动	Mining Support Activities	1			0.44
制造业	**Manufacturing**	**2 059**	**618**	**30.0**	**1 122.17**
农副食品加工业	Farm and Sideline Products Processing	25	7	28.0	7.42
食品制造业	Food Manufacturing	34	11	32.4	20.97
酒、饮料和精制茶制造业	Wine, Drinks and Purified Tea Manufacturing	2	1	50.0	1.03
烟草制品业	Tabacco Manufacturing	7	1	14.3	16.04
纺织业	Textile	26	10	38.5	5.62
纺织服装、服饰业	Textiles and Clothing Industry	38	14	36.8	7.43
皮革、毛皮、羽毛及其制品和制鞋业	Leather, Fur, Wool Products, and Shoes Manufacturing	8	4	50.0	1.46
木材加工和木、竹、藤、棕、草制品业	Timber Processing and Timber, Bamboo, Rattan, Coir and Straw Products Manufacturing	15	6	40.0	6.85
家具制造业	Furniture Manufacturing	20	8	40.0	3.27
造纸和纸制品业	Paper-making and Paper Products Manufacturing	26	11	42.3	11.63
印刷业和记录媒介复制业	Printing and Record Duplicating	29	10	34.5	10.47
文教、工美、体育和娱乐用品制造业	Culture, Education, Industrial Arts, Sports and Entertainment Goods Manufacturing	18	2	11.1	6.59
石油加工、炼焦和核燃料加工业	Oil Processing, Coking and Nuclear Fuel Processing	15	6	40.0	36.86
化学原料和化学制品制造业	Raw Chemical Materials and Chemical Products Manufacturing	170	56	32.9	81.86
医药制造业	Medicine Manufacturing	85	20	23.5	51.06
化学纤维制造业	Chemical Fiber Manufacturing	9	2	22.2	5.82
橡胶和塑料制品业	Rubber and Plastic Products Manufacturing	74	23	31.1	26.24
非金属矿物制品业	Non-metallic Mineral Products Manufacturing	51	24	47.1	21.12
黑色金属冶炼和压延加工业	Ferrous Metal Smelting and Rolling Processing Industry	255	104	40.8	63.07
有色金属冶炼和压延加工业	Nonferrous Metal Smelting and Rolling Processing Industry	24	4	16.7	9.59
金属制品业	Metal Products Manufacturing	117	44	37.6	40.88
通用设备制造业	General Equipment Manufacturing	190	55	28.9	84.07
专用设备制造业	Special Purpose Equipment Manufacturing	132	27	20.5	63.40
汽车制造业	The Automotive Manufacturing	170	33	19.4	134.02
铁路、船舶、航空航天和其他运输设备制造业	The Railroad, Marine, Aerospace and Other Transportation Equipment Manufacturing	49	10	20.4	60.68
电气机械和器材制造业	Electric Machinery Equipments and Manufacturing	146	42	28.8	61.47
计算机、通信和其他电子设备制造业	Computer, Communications and Other Electronic Equipment Manufacturing	159	34	21.4	180.15
仪器仪表制造业	Instrumentation Manufacturing	23	10	43.5	25.13
其他制造业	Other Manufacturing	137	37	27.0	74.96
废弃资源综合利用业	Comprehensive Utilization of Waste Resources	3			1.03
金属制品、机械和设备修理业	Metal Products, Machinery and Equipment Repair Industry	2	2	100.0	1.98
电力、热力、燃气及水生产和供应业	**Electricity, Heat, Gas and Water Production and Supply Industry**	**271**	**154**	**56.8**	**170.00**
电力、热力生产和供应业	Power and Heat Production and Supply	209	134	64.1	113.55
燃气生产和供应业	Gas Production and Supply	19	11	57.9	15.70
水的生产和供应业	Water Production and Supply	43	9	20.9	40.75

注：单纯购置项目和筹建项目固定资产投资不计算施工项目和本年投产项目个数。

Note: The investment in fixed assets of purchasing and preparatory project doesn't be calculated in projects under construction or projects completed and put into production in this year.

表 7.7 六大重点发展工业行业固定资产投资额(2011 ~2012)
FIXED ASSETS INVESTMENT IN SIX KEY INDUSTRIES

单位:亿元(100 million yuan)

指标	Indicators	2011	2012
工业六大重点行业	**Six Key Industries**	**706.19**	**740.35**
电子信息产品制造业	Electronic Information Product Manufacturing	239.13	207.29
汽车制造业	Automobile Manufacturing	106.19	134.02
石油化工及精细化工制造业	Petrochemical and Fine Chemical Products Manufacturing	74.39	95.46
精品钢材制造业	Fine Steel Manufacturing	62.53	62.16
成套设备制造业	Equipment Complex Manufacturing	177.12	176.86
生物医药制造业	Bio-medicine Manufacturing	48.14	65.33

注:自 2012 年起固定资产投资项目行业代码采用新的分类标准(GB/T 4754 – 2011),本表中的 2011 年产业分类数据参照新行业标准进行相应调整。由于个别投资项目同时属于六大重点发展工业行业中的两类,故各分类投资数直接相加大于合计数。

Note: Since 2012, the industry investment in fixed assets project code use the new classification standard (GB/T 4754 – 2011) and 2011 Industrial Classification data in this table are adjusted according to the new industry standard. Because individual investment projects belong to two categories of six key industries at the same time, the sum of classification number is greater than the total number.

表 7.8 主要年份新增固定资产
NEWLY INCREASED FIXED ASSETS IN MAIN YEARS

年份 Year	新增固定资产(亿元) Newly Increased Fixed Assets (100 million yuan)	其中 of which #房地产开发 Investment in Real Estate Development	固定资产交付使用率(%) Rate of Fixed Assets Transferred and in Use(%)
1990	222.99	4.97	98.2
1995	826.94	127.08	51.6
2000	1 493.35	477.39	79.9
2005	2 547.02	1 054.02	71.9
2006	2 680.85	1 058.94	68.3
2007	2 466.68	1 048.47	55.3
2008	2 773.14	994.10	57.4
2009	2 686.43	932.24	50.9
2010	3 179.40	964.27	59.8
2011	2 816.59	1 250.88	55.6
2012	2 911.34	1 388.45	55.4

表 7.9 主要年份固定资产投资资金来源
CAPITAL SOURCES OF FIXED ASSETS INVESTMENT IN MAIN YEARS

单位:亿元(100 million yuan)

指标	Indicators	2000	2010	2012
本年实际到位资金合计	**Total Actual Funds This Year**	**2 061.66**	**7 997.62**	**8 749.17**
上年末结余资金	Balance at End of Previous Year	241.05	1 440.57	1 635.40
本年实际到位资金小计	Sub-total Actual Funds this Year	1 820.61	6 557.05	7 113.77
国家预算资金	State Budgetary Funds	48.30	116.71	406.08
国内贷款	Domestic Loans	379.21	1 568.79	1 554.53
债 券	Bonds	4.85	10.06	
利用外资	Foreign Investment	161.83	239.18	165.89
#外商直接投资	Foreign Direct Investment	73.71	139.72	109.97
自筹资金	Self-Financed Capital	905.46	3 273.11	3 348.77
其他资金	Other Capital	320.96	1 349.21	1 638.50
本年各项应付款合计	The Total Payment of This Year	310.42	997.93	1 059.79
#工程款	Project Funds	76.52	438.19	536.12

注:自 2012 年起,国家预算资金和自筹资金统计口径调整,与历史数据不可比。

Note: Since 2012, the state budget funds and self-financing statistical standard has been adjusted, so the data is not comparable with the historical data.

表7.10 全社会房屋施工面积、竣工面积(1985～2012)
TOTAL FLOOR SPACE OF CONSTRUCTION AND COMPLETED BUILDINGS

年份 Year	施工面积(万平方米) Floor Area of Construction (10 000 sq. m)	其中 of which: #住宅 Residential Housing	其中 of which: 占全社会房屋施工面积比重(%) As Percentage of Total Floor Space Of Construction	竣工面积(万平方米) Floor Area Completed (10 000 sq. m)	房屋建筑面积竣工率(%) Construction Completion Rate (%)
1985	4 162.15	2 651.52	63.7	2 909.58	69.9
1986	4 874.44	2 469.27	50.7	2 493.93	51.2
1987	4 382.40	2 658.05	60.7	2 700.96	61.6
1988	4 369.20	2 667.00	61.0	2 457.34	56.2
1989	3 683.77	2 048.20	55.6	1 941.80	52.7
1990	3 801.46	2 269.06	59.7	2 138.44	56.3
1991	3 611.53	2 157.46	59.7	1 923.92	53.3
1992	4 709.52	2 463.79	52.3	2 608.20	55.4
1993	4 724.30	2 142.39	45.3	2 031.76	43.0
1994	6 720.70	3 520.27	52.4	2 519.09	37.5
1995	10 566.42	6 195.12	58.6	3 093.93	29.3
1996	10 730.85	5 874.26	54.7	3 254.57	30.3
1997	9 955.21	5 450.13	54.7	3 614.19	36.3
1998	9 364.36	5 113.52	54.6	3 364.43	35.9
1999	8 364.48	4 608.49	55.1	3 257.57	38.9
2000	8 636.31	4 804.12	55.6	3 266.52	37.8
2001	8 588.49	5 236.93	61.0	3 215.12	37.4
2002	9 425.42	5 994.70	63.6	3 102.54	32.9
2003	11 023.24	6 974.27	63.3	3 582.34	32.5
2004	12 291.81	7 873.44	64.1	4 932.57	40.1
2005	14 477.85	8 267.24	57.1	4 873.82	33.7
2006	14 596.49	8 085.28	55.4	4 901.46	33.6
2007	14 979.37	7 789.91	52.0	5 068.46	33.8
2008	14 083.52	7 060.19	50.1	3 828.79	27.2
2009	13 553.64	6 581.16	48.6	2 970.92	21.9
2010	15 020.76	7 344.07	48.9	2 776.21	18.5
2011	16 553.86	8 423.11	50.9	2 913.78	17.6
2012	16 874.72	8 350.83	49.5	2 838.97	16.8

表7.11 住宅投资和竣工建筑面积(1978~2012)
INVESTMENT IN RESIDENTIAL HOUSING AND FLOOR SPACE OF BUILDINGS COMPLETED

年 份 Year	住宅投资额 (亿元) Investment in Residential Housing (100 million yuan)	其 中 of which # 房地产 Real Estate	占全社会固定资产投资总额比重(%) As Percentage of Total Floor Space Of Construction	住宅竣工建筑面积(万平方米) Floor Area of Residence Building Completed (10 000 sq. m)	住宅建筑面积竣工率(%) Construction Completion Rate
1978	2.67		9.6	199.61	
1979	3.31		9.3	215.99	
1980	5.82		12.8	304.32	
1981	10.02		18.4	1 380.70	78.3
1982	11.03		15.5	1 363.63	77.7
1983	11.18		14.7	1 347.79	77.2
1984	15.88		17.2	1 788.44	80.9
1985	25.47		21.5	2 112.04	79.7
1986	28.24		19.2	1 790.01	72.5
1987	36.28		19.5	1 874.90	70.5
1988	44.84		18.3	1 758.29	65.9
1989	35.82	1.85	16.7	1 246.58	60.9
1990	42.94	7.26	18.9	1 339.02	59.0
1991	48.92	7.31	18.9	1 160.61	53.8
1992	61.23	11.73	17.1	1 379.18	56.0
1993	77.14	13.96	11.8	1 017.54	47.5
1994	300.65	106.31	26.8	1 349.24	38.3
1995	433.76	280.38	27.1	1 746.82	28.2
1996	466.99	356.01	23.9	1 872.65	31.9
1997	458.22	334.07	23.2	2 179.68	40.0
1998	404.96	320.66	20.6	1 963.51	38.4
1999	378.82	324.49	20.4	1 731.55	37.6
2000	443.90	408.82	23.7	1 724.02	35.9
2001	466.71	439.17	23.4	1 743.90	33.3
2002	584.51	567.76	26.7	1 880.50	31.4
2003	694.30	676.28	28.3	2 280.79	32.7
2004	922.61	900.67	29.9	3 270.43	41.5
2005	936.36	920.84	26.4	2 819.35	34.1
2006	854.15	835.65	21.8	2 746.80	34.0
2007	853.13	837.53	19.1	2 843.62	36.5
2008	871.52	843.63	18.0	1 899.40	26.9
2009	922.81	918.68	17.5	1 522.07	23.1
2010	1 232.96	1 229.83	23.2	1 415.44	19.3
2011	1 403.13	1 398.75	27.7	1 568.83	18.6
2012	1 457.64	1 451.94	27.7	1 626.73	19.5

注：1981 年以前住宅投资额和住宅竣工建筑面积数据不包括城乡私人建房和农村投资，从 1981 年开始为全社会口径。

Note: Before 1981, investments and floor area of residential housing completed in this table didn't cover private-built houses in urban and rural areas and rural investment, the whole society is covered since 1981.

上 / 海 / 统 / 计 / 年 / 鉴

主要统计指标解释

全社会固定资产投资

固定资产投资是国民经济再生产活动的一个重要部分。固定资产投资额是以货币形式表现的在一定时期内建造和购置固定资产的工作量以及与此有关的费用总称。它是反映固定资产投资规模、结构和发展速度的综合性指标。按照现行国家统计制度，全社会固定资产投资包括建设改造、房地产开发、城乡集体经济单位、城乡私人建房和其他经济单位投资。

自1997年起，固定资产投资统计起点为50万元（含50万元）以上项目；自2011年起，固定资产投资统计起点为500万元（含500万元）以上项目。

房地产开发投资

指各种登记注册类型的房地产开发公司、商品房建设公司及其他房地产开发法人单位和附属于其他法人单位实际从事房地产开发或经营活动的单位统一开发的包括统代建、拆迁还建的住宅、厂房、仓库、饭店、宾馆、度假村、写字楼、办公楼等房屋建筑物和配套的服务设施，土地开发工程（如道路、给水、排水、供电、供热、通讯、平整场地等基础设施工程）的投资；不包括单纯的土地交易活动。

固定资产投资按国民经济行业分

固定资产投资按国民经济行业分是根据建设项目建成投产后的主要产品或主要用途及社会经济活动性质来确定国民经济行业。一般情况下，一个建设项目或一个企业、事业单位只能属于一种国民经济行业。

固定资产投资按隶属关系分

固定资产投资按隶属关系分是按建设单位或企业、事业、行政单位的主管上级机关确定的。

（1）中央 是指中共中央、人大常委会和国务院各部、委、局、总公司以及直属机构直接领导的建设项目和企业、事业、行政单位。这些单位的固定资产投资计划由国务院各部门直接编制和下达，建设中所需物资、主要设备以及建设中的问题都由中央有关部门安排和解决。

（2）地方 是由省（自治区、直辖市）、地区（州、盟、省辖市）、县（旗、县级市）三级政府及业务主管部门直接领导和管理的建设项目、企业、事业、行政单位。地方项目还包括不隶属以上各级政府及主管部门的建设项目和企业、事业单位，如外商投资企业和无主管部门的企业等。

固定资产投资按构成分

固定资产投资按构成分是按其工作内容和实现方式来划分的，主要分为建筑安装工程，设备、工具、器具购置，其他费用三个部分。

（1）建筑安装工程(建筑安装工作量)：指各种房屋、建筑物的建造工程和各种设备、装置的安装工程。包括各种房屋建造工程；各种用途设备基础和各种工业窑炉的砌筑工程及金属结构工程；为施工而进行的各种准备工作和临时工程以及完工后的清理工作等；铁路、道路的铺设，矿井的开凿及石油管道的架设等；水利工程；防空地下建筑等特殊工程；列入房屋工程预算内的暖气、卫生、通风、照明、煤气等设备的价值及装设油饰工程；列入建筑工程预算内的各种管道(蒸汽、压缩空气、石油、给排水等管道)、电力、电讯电缆导线等的敷设工程；以及各种机械设备的安装工程；为测定安装工程质量，对设备进行的试运工作；房地产开发单位进行的商品房屋开发建设工程、土地开发工程。

在安装工程中，不包括被安装设备本身的价值。

（2）设备、工具、器具购置：指建设单位或企、事业单位购置或自制的，达到固定资产标准的设备、工具、器具的价值。新建单位及扩建单位的新建车间，按照设计或计划要求购置或自制的全部设备、工具、器具，不论是否达到固定资产标准均计入“设备、工具、器具购置”中。

（3）其他费用：指在固定资产建造和购置过程中发生的，除上述几项内容以外的各种应分摊计入固定资产的费用。

固定资产投资的资金来源

固定资产投资的资金来源是根据固定资产投资的资金来源不同，分为国家预算资金、国内贷款、债券、利用外资、自筹资金和其他资金来源。

（1）国家预算资金：自2011年起，按照全国人大和国务院的要求，各级财政的所有资金，包括税收和非税收入，均必须纳入预算管理，我国已不存在预算外资金的概念，因此各级政府用于固定资产投资的财政资金均为预算资金。旧的国家预算内资金的内容和现中央预算资金的内容基本一致。国家预算包括一般预算、政府性基金预

主要统计指标解释

算、国有资本经营预算和社保基金预算。各类预算中用于固定资产投资的资金全部作为国家预算资金填报。

（2）国内贷款：指报告期内企、事业单位向银行及非银行金融机构借入的用于固定资产投资的各种国内借款。包括银行利用自有资金及吸收的存款发放的贷款、上级主管部门拨入的国内贷款、国家专项贷款(包括煤代油贷款、劳改煤矿专项贷款等)、地方财政专项资金安排的贷款、国内储备贷款、周转贷款等。

（3）债券：是企业（公司）或金融机构通过发行各种债券，筹集用于固定资产投资的资金。包括由银行代理国家专业投资公司发行的重点企业债券和基本建设债券。

（4）利用外资：指报告期内收到的用于固定资产投资的国外资金，包括统借统还、自借自还的国外贷款，中外合资项目中的外资，以及对外发行债券和股票等。国家统借统还的外资指由我国政府出面同外国政府、团体或金融组织签订贷款协议、并负责偿还本息的国外贷款。

（5）自筹资金：指固定资产投资单位在报告期收到的，由各企事业单位筹集用于固定资产投资的资金，包括各类企事业单位的自有资金和从其他单位筹集的用于固定资产投资的资金，但不包括各类财政性资金、从各类金融机构借入资金和国外资金。

（6）其他资金来源：指在报告期收到的除以上各种资金之外的用于固定资产投资的资金。包括社会集资、个人资金、无偿捐赠的资金及其他单位拨入的资金等。

■ 固定资产投资按建设性质分

建设项目的性质一般分为新建、改建、扩建和单纯建造生活设施。

（1）新建：一般指从无到有“平地起家”开始建设的企业、事业和行政单位或独立的工程。现有企业、事业、行政单位一般不属于新建。但如有的单位原有基础很小，经过建设后新增的固定资产价值超过该企、事业、行政单位原有固定资产价值(原值)三倍以上的也应作为新建。

（2）改建和技术改造：是指现有企业、事业单位对原有设施进行技术改造或更新（包括相应配套的辅助性生产、生活福利设施）的建设项目。改建项目包括现有企业、事业单位为适应市场变化的需要，而改变企业的主要产品种类（如军工企业转民用品等）的建设项目，原有产品生产作业线由于各工序（车间）之间能力不平衡，为填平补齐充分发挥原有生产能力而增建不增加本企业主要产品设计能力的车间的建设项目。技术改造是指企业、事业单位在现有基础上，用先进的技术代替落后的技术，用先进的工艺和装备代替落后的工艺和装备，以改变企业落后的技术经济面貌，实现以内涵为主的扩大再生产，达到提高产品质量、促进产品更新换代、节约能源、降低消耗、扩大生产规模、全面提高社会经效益的目的。技术改造具体包括以下内容：机器设备和工具的更新改造；生产工艺改革、节约能源和原材料的改造；厂房建筑和公共设施的改造；保护环境进行的“三废”治理改造；劳动条件和生产环境的改造等。

（3）扩建：指在厂内或其他地点，为扩大原有产品的生产能力(或效益)或增加新的产品生产能力，而增建主要的生产车间(或主要工程)、分厂、独立的生产线。行政、事业单位在原单位增建业务用房(如学校增建教学用房、医院增建门诊部、病房等)也作为扩建。

现有企、事业单位为扩大原有主要产品生产能力或增加新的产品生产能力，增建一个或几个主要生产车间(或主要工程)、分厂，同时进行一些更新改造工程的，也应作为扩建。

（4）单纯建造生活设施：是指企（事）业及行政单位在不扩建、改建生产性工程和业务用房的情况下，单纯建造职工住宅、托儿所、子弟学校、医务室、浴室、食堂等生活福利设施。

■ 新增固定资产

新增固定资产又称交付使用的固定资产，是指已经完成建造和购置过程，并已交付生产或使用单位的固定资产价值。新增固定资产是表示固定资产投资成果的价值量指标，也是反映建设进度、计算固定资产投资效果的必要数据。

■ 固定资产交付使用率

指一定时期新增固定资产与同期完成投资额的比率。该指标是反映固定资产动用速度，衡量建设过程中宏观投资效果的综合指标。由于新增固定资产是较长时期内形成的结果，而投资额则是当年完成的，因此，该指标一般适宜于反映较长时期内固定资产的动用情况。

■ 施工项目

指报告期内正式进行过建筑或安装施工活动的建设项目。凡是报告期内施过工的建设项目，不论施工时间长短，均作为施工项目统计。施工项目个数可以反映一定时期固定资产投资的实际规模，与同期建成投产的建设项目个数相比，可以从建设速度的角度反映固定资产投资的效果。根据建设项目施工活动的不同性质，施工项目又分为：本年新

主要统计指标解释

开工项目　以前年度开工跨入本年继续施工项目，本年全部投产项目　以前年度全部停缓建在本年恢复施工的项目和本年进行过施工又在本年内全部停缓建的项目。

■ 全部投产项目

指报告期内按设计文件规定建成主体工程和相应配套的辅助设施，形成生产能力或工程效益，经过验收合格，并且已正式投入生产或交付使用的建设项目。
全部投产的工业项目是指设计文件规定形成生产能力的主体工程及其相应配套的辅助设施全部建成，经负荷试运转，证明具备生产设计规定合格产品的条件，并经过验收鉴定合格或达到竣工验收标准，与生产性工程配套的生活福利设施可以满足近期正常生产的需要，正式移交生产的建设项目。

■ 建成投产率

指一定时期内全部投产项目个数与同期施工项目个数的比率。该指标是从建设单位建设速度的角度反映投资效果的指标。

■ 房屋建筑面积竣工率

指一定时期内房屋竣工面积占同期房屋施工面积的比率。该指标从房屋建筑施工速度的角度反映投资效果的指标。

EXPLANATORY NOTES TO MAJOR STATISTICAL INDICATORS

□ Total Investment in Fixed Assets

Investment in Fixed Assets constitutes an important portion of the national economic reproduction. Fixed assets investment is a general term for both the work volume of production and purchase of fixed assets and relevant expenditure, in the form of currency, during a certain period. It is a comprehensive indicator of scale, structure and development speed of fixed assets investment. As stipulated in the current national statistics regulations, the social fixed assets investment includes the investment into infrastructure and reformation, real estate development, urban and rural collective economic bodies, private house construction in urban and rural areas and other economic bodies.

From 1997, the fixed assets items only include those with investment of 0.5 million yuan and above. From 2011, the fixed assets items only include those with investment of 5 million yuan and above.

□ Investment in Real Estate Development

Investment in Real Estate Development refers to the investment by the real estate development companies, commercial buildings construction companies and other real estate development units of various types of ownership in the construction of house buildings, such as residential buildings, factory buildings, warehouses, hotels, guesthouses, holiday villages, office buildings, and the complementary service facilities and land development projects, such as roads, water supply, water drainage, power supply, heating, telecommunications, land leveling and other projects of infrastructure. It excludes the activities in pure land transactions.

□ Investment in Fixed Assets by Sector

Investment in Fixed Assets by Sector refers to determining the classification of construction projects by the major products or the purpose of the projects when they are put into production or use, and by the nature of their social economic activities. In general, one project or one enterprise or institution can only be classified into one sector.

□ Investment in Fixed Assets by Jurisdiction of Management

Investment in Fixed Assets by Jurisdiction of Management refers to the classification of investment by the competent authorities under which investment is made by construction units, enterprises, institutions or administrative units.

(1) Central investment refers to the investment in projects or by enterprises, institutions or administrative units which are under the direct leadership and management of the CPC Central Committee, the NPC Standing Committee, the State Council and of the national commissions, ministries, agencies and state-owned large corporations. Various ministries and departments of the State Council prepare and implement plans for investment in fixed assets by those departments, and arrange and ensure the supply of materials and key equipment required for the projects.

(2) Local investment refers to the investment in projects or by enterprises, institutions or administrative units which are under the direct leadership and management of departments under the provincial, prefecture and county governments. Also included are projects by foreign-invested enterprises and enterprises without competent managing authorities.

□ Investment in Fixed Assets by Structure

Investment in Fixed Assets by Structure is classified by their contents. It is mainly classified into 3 categories, i.e. construction and installation, purchase of equipment and instrument, and other expenses.

(1) Construction and installation (work volume of construction and installation) refers to the construction of various houses and buildings and installation of various kinds of equipment and instruments. They include construction of various houses; equipment foundations, industrial kilns and stoves, and metal structure work; preparation works for project construction, and clearing up works post project construction; pavement of railways and roads, drilling of mines and putting up of oil pipes; construction of projects of water conservancy; construction of underground air-raid shelters and construction of other special projects; value of equipment for heating, sanitation, ventilation, lighting, gas, painting, etc. that are covered by the budget of housing projects; laying out of various pipelines (for steam, compressed air, petroleum, tap water and sewage) and lines for electric power and for communications; installation of various machinery equipment, testing operation for pre-testing the quality of installation projects, and land

EXPLANATORY NOTES TO MAJOR STATISTICAL INDICATORS

and other development work conducted by real estate developers for commercial housing. The value of equipment installed is not included in the value of installation projects.

(2) Purchase of equipment and instruments refers to the total value of equipment, tools, and instruments purchased or self-produced which come up to standards for fixed assets by the construction units or investing enterprises or institutions. Equipment, tools and instruments purchased or self-produced for new workshops by newly established or expanded units are categorized as "purchase of equipment and instruments" no matter whether they come up to the standards for fixed assets.

(3) Other expenses refer to expenses occurring during the construction or purchase of fixed assets other than those mentioned above.

□ Sources of Capital for Investment in Fixed Assets

Sources of capital for Investment in Fixed Assets include state budget funds, domestic loans, bond, foreign investment, self-raised funds, and others.

(1)State state budget funds. Since 2011, according to the requirement of the NPC and the State Council, all levels of financial resources, including tax and non-tax revenue, must be included in the budget management, extra-budgetary didn't exist any longer, all levels of government for fixing asset investment funds are budget funds. The old state budget funds were basically the same with the central budget funds. State budget includes the general budget, the government fund budget, the state capital budget and the social security fund budget. All kinds of budgets for all funds invested in fixed assets were reported as state budget funds.

(2)Domestic loans refers to various funds borrowed by enterprises and institutions from banks and non-bank financial institutions during the reference period for the purpose of investment in fixed assets, including loans issued by banks from their self-owned funds and deposit, loans appropriated by higher responsible authorities, special loans by government (including loan for replacing petroleum with coal, special loan for reform-through-labour coal mines), loans arranged by local government from special funds, domestic reserve loan, and working loan, etc.

(3) Bond refers to company and finance institutions raising funds for investment in fixed assets by issuing various bond, including key-son enterprise bond and infrastructure bond issued by banks as agency of national professional investment company.

(4) Foreign Investment refers to foreign funds received during the reference period for the purpose of investment in fixed assets, including foreign funds borrowed and managed by the government, by individual units, foreign fund in joint venture program, and issue of bonds and stocks at the international financial markets. The foreign funds borrowed and managed by the government refer to foreign loans borrowed by the government from foreign governments, organizations, or financial institutions under official agreements signed by both parties, under which government is responsible for the repayment of both the principal and interests of the foreign loans.

(5)Self-raised funds refers to the fixed asset investment units received during the reporting period, by the enterprises and institutions to raise funds for investment in fixed assets, including various types of enterprises and institutions of its own funds and from other units raised funds for investment in fixed assets, but does not include all kinds of financial funds, borrowed funds from various financial institutions and foreign capital.

(6) Other sources of funding refers to the reporting period, in addition to all of these funds received outside funding for investment in fixed assets. Including social funds raised from individuals, donations, funds and funds transferred from other units.

□ Investment in Fixed Assets by Type of Construction

The construction projects in general can be classified, by the type of construction, into new construction, expansion, reconstruction and construction of living facilities.

(1) New construction in general refers to newly constructed enterprises, institutions, administrative agencies or independent projects from scratch. Construction in the existing enterprises, institutions or agencies is not considered as new construction. In case the asset of the existing unit is quite small, and the value of newly added fixed assets exceeds the original value of assets by three times, the expansion will be considered as new construction.

(2)Reconstruction and technical transformation refers to construction projects by existing enterprises or institutions in innovation or technical transformation of the old facilities (including auxiliary production equipment and welfare facilities). Also considered as Reconstruction and Technical Transformation is the construction of new workshops by the existing enterprises or institutions to change the variety of products to meet the market demand (such as the production of civil products by defense industries), or to bring the designed production capacity into full play

EXPLANATORY NOTES TO MAJOR STATISTICAL INDICATORS

through a more balanced production process on production lines. Technical transformation refers to replacement of old technology and equipment by new technology and equipment, in order to expand the reproduction through improvement of technology contents in production, to improve product quality, to promote new products, to save energy, to reduce consumption, to expand the production scale and to improve overall social-economic efficiency. Technical transformation contains the following contents: updating of machinery, equipment and tools; reforming production process by using energy or material saving technology; construction of workshops and transformation of public facilities; improvement of working conditions and environment, etc.

(3) Expansion refers to construction of new major production workshop, branch factory or independent production line within a factory or in other locations, for the purpose of increasing the production capacity (or improving efficiency) of the original products. Newly constructed houses for the operation of institutions and administrative organizations (such as the newly constructed buildings for teaching in schools, buildings for clinics or wards in hospitals, etc.) are also classified as expansion.

Also included in the expansion are investments by existing enterprises or institutions in building major production line (s) or branch factory (ies) along with some work on innovation, for the purpose of expending the production capacity of original products or producing new products.

(4) Simply constructing establishment for life refers to enterprises and administrative unit simply construct the employee's residence, nursery, children school, infirmary, bathroom and eatery, without expanding or rebuilding the productive engineering and operation houses.

□ Newly Increased Fixed Assets

Newly Increased Fixed Assets, also called fixed assets put into operation, refers to the value of fixed assets that has been put into production or handed over to the production units after the completion of the process of construction and purchase. The newly increased fixed asset is an value indicator of the result of investment. It is also the necessary data for reflecting the construction process and the result of investment in fixed assets.

□ Rate of Projects of Fixed Assets Completed and Put into Operation

Rate of Projects of Fixed Assets Completed and Put into Operation refers to the ratio of the newly increased fixed assets to the total investment made in the same period. This is a comprehensive indicator reflecting the speed of the employment of fixed assets and the investment efficiency at the macro-level. As the newly increase fixed assets is the result of a long period while the investment is completed in the current year, this indicator is expected to be used to reflect the employment of fixed assets over a long period of time.

□ Projects under Construction

Projects under Construction refer to projects with construction and installation activities undertaken in the reference period. All projects that have construction activities undertaken during the reference period are reported as projects under construction irrespective of the length of construction work. The number of projects under construction can reflect the actual size of investment in fixed assets during a given period, and when compared with the number of projects completed and put into use during the same period, it demonstrates the results of investment in fixed assets. Depending on the nature of construction activities, projects under construction can also be classified into projects under construction in current year, winding-up projects in current year and stopped or suspended projects in previous years (with preservation work in current year).

□ Projects Completed and Put into Use

Projects Completed and Put into Use Industrial projects refer to the major projects and accessory facilities completed which result in forming production capacity and have been checked and accepted while the living and welfare facilities have been completed and can ensure normal production and formally put into production. Non-industrial projects refer to the major projects and accessory facilities completed which possess the designed capacity and have been checked, accepted and formally put into production.

□ Rate of Construction Projects Completed and Put into Use

Rate of Construction Projects Completed and Put into Use refers to the ratio of the number of construction projects completed and put into use in certain period of time to the number of projects under construction in the same period. This reflects the investment efficiency from the perspective of the speed of projects construction.

EXPLANATORY NOTES TO MAJOR STATISTICAL INDICATORS

□ Completion Rate of Floor Space of Buildings

Completion Rate of Floor Space of Buildings refers to the ratio of the floor space of buildings completed in certain period of time to the floor space of buildings under construction in the same period. This indicator reflects the investment result from the perspective of the speed of construction.

第八篇

CHAPTER 8

对外经济贸易和旅游

FOREIGN ECONOMIC RELATIONS, TRADE AND TOURISM

简要说明

本篇资料综合反映主要年份上海市对外贸易、进出口商品检验、外商直接投资、对外直接投资、对外经济合作和旅游等方面的概况。

一、对外贸易部分

对外贸易统计范围是按照联合国国际贸易统计原则,采用专门贸易记录制,对凡能引起区域内物质资源存量增加或减少的进出口货物,除制度另有规定外,均列入统计。

主要内容包括:上海关区和上海货物进出口的金额、国别、贸易方式、企业性质、产品类别等项目。

在按国别(地区)分的进、出口总额表中,出口货物按中华人民共和国关境外最终目的国(地区)统计,进口货物按中华人民共和国关境外原产国(地区)统计。

统计资料来源于上海海关,调查方法是全面调查。

二、进出口商品检验部分

进出口商品检验统计范围是涉及安全、卫生和环境保护等检验、检疫进出口商品目录范围内的所有商品。

主要内容包括:进口和出口商品检验批数、金额,不合格商品检验批数、金额等。

资料来源上海市出入境检验检疫局,调查方法是全面调查。

三、外商直接投资部分

外商直接投资统计范围是凡经上海工商行政管理机关核准登记,经各级商务部门批准设立的中外合资经营企业、合作经营企业、外资企业、外商投资股份制企业、合作开发项目等具有法人资格的独立核算企业(包括港澳台地区投资企业),在上海从事经营活动的外国及港澳台地区企业及外国公司在中国境内设立的分支机构。

主要内容包括:外商直接投资方式、投资产业和国别地区等情况。

资料来源于上海市商务委员会,调查方法是全面调查。

四、对外直接投资部分

对外直接投资统计范围是境内投资主体通过直接投资在境外设立的各类公司型企业和非公司型企业。

主要内容包括:境内投资主体的单位数、核准投资额。

资料来源是上海市商务委员会,调查方法是全面调查。

五、对外经济合作部分

对外经济合作统计范围是经各级商务主管部门批准的从事对外承包和劳务合作业务并具有法人地位的对外承包、劳务合作企业。

主要内容包括:对外承包工程合同金额、完成营业额和对外劳务合作派出人员等。

资料来源是上海市商务委员会,调查方法是全面调查。

六、旅游部分

旅游统计范围是旅行社、星级饭店和旅游者。

主要内容包括:旅行社接待经营情况、旅游景点和星级饭店基本情况、国际旅游入境人数、国内旅游来沪人数和人均消费支出等。

统计调查方法:国内旅游者来沪人数和人均消费支出指标采取抽样调查方法,其余数据均为全面调查。

资料来源是上海市旅游局、上海市出入境边防检查总站。

BRIEF INTRODUCTION

Data in this chapter reflect Shanghai's foreign trade, inspection of imports and exports, foreign direct investment, outbound direct investment, economic cooperation with foreign countries or territories as well as tourism in main years.

I. Foreign Trade

The scope of foreign trade statistics is in accordance with the United Nations' principles on international trade statistics, i.e.: all imports or exports that will lead to stock changes of material resources with the monitored territory; excluding goods by escape clause.

Data on foreign trade include: value of imports and exports through Shanghai ports, imports and exports by countries (regions), mode of trade, nature of trading companies, and product categories.

In the table on the total imports and exports classified by countries and regions, the exports are calculated at the Customs of the countries (regions) of destination and the imports are calculated at the Customs of the countries (regions) of origin.

Sources of data on foreign trade are complied from the Shanghai Customs through a comprehensive reporting system.

II. Inspection of Imports and Exports

The scope of imports and exports inspection includes all commodities that are under the catalog of imports and exports quarantine, related to safety, sanitation and environment protection issues

Data on inspection of imports and exports include: lot number and value of imports and exports, lot number of ineligible commodities and their value.

Sources of data are from the Shanghai Entry–Exit Inspection and Quarantine Bureau through a comprehensive reporting system.

III. Foreign Direct Investment

The statistics of foreign direct investment cover all the Sino–foreign joint ventures, Sino–foreign cooperative enterprises, wholly–owned foreign enterprise, foreign–funded stock companies, Sino–foreign cooperative development projects (including the enterprises funded by the entrepreneurs from Hong Kong, Macao and Taiwan) with independent accounting system and legal person status, and all foreign enterprises or enterprises funded by the entrepreneurs from Hong Kong Macao and Taiwan which engaged in business activities in Shanghai, and branches of foreign companies which have been approved to be set up within the boundaries of the People's Republic of China after verification and registration through Shanghai's administrative authorities for industry and commerce, and approval by the department of commerce at various levels.

Foreign direct investment includes: mode of foreign direct investment, investment by industry and countries (regions).

Sources of data are from the Shanghai Commission of Commerce through a comprehensive reporting system.

IV. Outbound Direct Investment

Outbound direct investment covers all types of overseas corporate and non–corporate enterprises set up by domes–

tic investors through direct investment.

It includes numbers of domestic investors and approved investment capital.

Data are from the Shanghai Commission of Commerce through comprehensive survey.

V. Foreign Economic Cooperationt

The scope of foreign economic cooperation covers enterprises engaged in contracted projects and labor services cooperation with foreign countries with approvals from the department of commerce at various levels.

Data on foreign economic cooperation include: contracted value of project, its revenue and labor services cooperation.

Data on foreign economic cooperation are from the Shanghai Commission of Commerce through a comprehensive reporting system.

VI. Tourism

The scope of tourism covers travel agencies, star-rated hotels and tourists.

Data on tourism include: operating conditions of the travel agencies, tourist attractions and star-rated hotels, the number of international tourists, the number of domestic tourists to Shanghai and consumption expenditure per capita.

Methodologies: sample survey method is used for domestic tourists to Shanghai and consumption expenditure per capita, and the rest are through a comprehensive reporting system.

Data are from the Shanghai Tourism Bureau and the Shanghai Entry-Exit Frontier Inspection Station.

表8.1　主要年份上海关区出口总额
TOTAL EXPORT TRADE VOLUME THROUGH CUSTOMS IN MAIN YEARS

单位:亿美元（100 million USD）

年　份 Year	关区出口总　额 Export Trade Volume Through Customs	其　中　of which				
		#一般贸易 Ordinary Trade	#来料加工装配贸易 Processing and Assembly Trade with Customers' Materials	#进料加工贸易 Processing Trade with Imported Materials	#对外承包工程货物 Construction Projects in Foreign Countries	#出料加工贸易 Outward Processing Trade
1990	86.62	51.39	3.20	30.67	0.41	0.45
1995	256.07	149.16	14.31	90.12	0.63	0.06
1996	272.13	146.05	25.42	97.69	1.01	
1997	334.51	178.93	37.17	115.17	0.71	
1998	374.58	199.24	44.13	127.55	0.79	
1999	442.88	234.43	55.08	149.68	0.59	
2000	615.72	341.02	64.21	205.13	1.25	
2001	680.07	380.43	61.09	228.43	1.26	0.13
2002	818.03	473.13	66.88	266.72	1.44	0.13
2003	1 123.06	618.90	78.81	408.79	1.18	0.12
2004	1 612.68	824.92	126.99	623.27	3.18	0.14
2005	2 124.30	1 057.68	195.83	813.26	6.37	0.16
2006	2 665.65	1 319.56	212.77	1 058.07	9.45	0.14
2007	3 284.80	1 659.44	228.77	1 273.71	20.55	0.17
2008	3 936.50	2 050.49	240.91	1 467.78	53.92	0.23
2009	3 251.28	1 647.82	175.38	1 252.87	69.78	0.13
2010	4 233.40	2 183.98	178.52	1 639.70	60.55	0.09
2011	4 999.64	2 691.93	151.78	1 846.59	77.70	0.11
2012	4 911.56	2 722.62	137.52	1 718.06	72.14	0.12

表8.2　主要年份上海关区进口总额
TOTAL IMPORT TRADE VOLUME THROUGH CUSTOMS IN MAIN YEARS

单位:亿美元（100 million USD）

年　份 Year	关区进口总　额 Import Trade Volume Through Customs	其　中　of which				
		#一般贸易 Oridinary Trade	#来料加工装配贸易 Processing and Assembly Trade with Customers' Materials	#进料加工贸易 Processing Trade with Imported Materials	#外商投资企业进口设备 Imported Equipment of Foreign Funded Enterprise	#租赁贸易 Leasing Trade
1990	86.27	51.79	2.40	19.70	6.11	
1995	225.30	93.79	13.49	65.96	45.16	0.11
1996	256.57	85.64	20.48	69.33	70.09	3.10
1997	252.32	83.02	27.64	79.79	45.86	3.65
1998	261.80	93.24	29.63	80.37	40.52	2.63
1999	318.63	137.56	35.72	82.84	30.36	4.55
2000	477.39	212.65	44.87	125.13	40.26	2.47
2001	524.81	245.94	47.38	123.39	47.46	2.45
2002	606.98	267.66	48.12	160.91	54.95	1.89
2003	888.95	377.21	54.47	243.24	66.32	2.36
2004	1 213.07	472.16	89.47	338.57	99.72	4.70
2005	1 382.48	502.49	133.69	409.30	74.76	7.85
2006	1 621.89	574.40	122.52	497.41	73.72	23.74
2007	1 924.29	719.30	154.88	528.03	75.22	24.46
2008	2 129.07	848.23	174.86	525.68	76.91	22.21
2009	1 903.61	883.20	121.40	428.62	38.92	4.36
2010	2 613.05	1 209.42	169.36	552.83	43.81	18.56
2011	3 123.50	1 558.35	135.68	610.32	51.18	13.69
2012	3 101.54	1 516.96	123.06	553.38	33.00	10.79

注：自2009年起，原口岸进出口商品总额改为上海关区进出口总额。
Note：Since 2009, Total Value of Port Imports and Exports have been changed to Total Trade Volume through Customs.

表8.3 主要年份按国别(地区)分的上海关区出口总额

TOTAL EXPORT TRADE VOLUME THROUGH CUSTOMS BY COUNTRIES AND REGIONS IN MAIN YEARS

单位:亿美元 (100 million USD)

国别(地区)	Country (Region)	2005	2010	2011	2012
总 计	**Total**	**2 124.30**	**4 233.40**	**4 999.64**	**4 911.56**
# 亚 洲	**Asia**	**898.90**	**1 653.96**	**2 022.89**	**2 023.25**
# 中国香港	Hong Kong, China	160.72	210.46	249.36	239.09
中国台湾	Taiwan, China	59.81	112.52	133.45	125.52
日 本	Japan	298.78	442.82	544.99	551.98
韩 国	Republic of Korea	78.66	138.83	170.70	168.69
新加坡	Singapore	48.69	94.80	107.85	113.29
马来西亚	Malaysia	38.27	73.08	81.19	83.96
泰 国	Thailand	22.39	61.18	79.57	91.27
菲律宾	Philippines	16.58	29.43	29.70	30.09
巴基斯坦	Pakistan	8.07	16.12	19.13	20.95
科威特	Kuwait	1.40	4.05	5.19	3.48
沙特阿拉伯	Saudi Arabia	8.84	19.92	33.13	33.76
阿拉伯联合酋长国	United Arab Emirates	23.24	44.97	52.44	54.77
非 洲	**Africa**	**53.42**	**130.79**	**156.71**	**161.27**
# 埃 及	Egypt	5.89	12.11	11.94	13.79
苏 丹	Sudan	2.35	4.39	3.58	2.85
欧 洲	**Europe**	**505.52**	**1 095.67**	**1 199.80**	**1 068.67**
# 德 国	Germany	99.69	214.67	216.84	205.00
法 国	France	44.84	110.42	100.99	77.25
意大利	Italy	42.81	118.34	120.53	85.39
荷 兰	Netherlands	75.62	154.89	185.24	162.35
英 国	United Kingdoms	59.10	117.88	129.79	123.49
瑞 典	Sweden	9.42	20.26	21.86	19.72
俄罗斯	Russia	18.60	59.95	77.35	88.38
美 洲	**America**	**618.05**	**1 234.11**	**1 470.82**	**1 513.00**
# 美 国	United States	501.11	910.54	1 058.72	1 087.47
加拿大	Canada	42.58	74.81	82.07	83.86
巴 西	Brazil	14.61	75.44	100.92	99.17
智 利	Chile	7.26	20.47	25.89	26.79
大洋洲及太平洋岛屿	**Oceanic and Pacific Island**	**48.41**	**118.87**	**149.42**	**145.37**
# 澳大利亚	Australia	41.94	95.45	125.09	126.57
新西兰	New Zealand	5.50	9.87	11.52	12.03

注：其他为无国别数(以下同)。
Note: Others refer to regions without sovereignty (Same as follows).

表8.4 主要年份按国别(地区)分的上海关区进口总额
TOTAL IMPORT TRADE VOLUME THROUGH CUSTOMS BY COUNTRIES AND REGIONS IN MAIN YEARS

单位:亿美元 (100 million USD)

国别(地区)	Country (Region)	2005	2010	2011	2012
总　计	**Total**	**1 382.48**	**2 613.05**	**3 123.50**	**3 101.54**
#亚　洲	**Asia**	**873.45**	**1 477.09**	**1 684.84**	**1 662.77**
#中国香港	Hong Kong, China	17.41	17.05	17.55	11.38
中国台湾	Taiwan, China	155.56	210.86	215.90	209.29
日　本	Japan	267.91	473.84	539.98	493.03
韩　国	Republic of Korea	163.95	279.87	283.29	263.45
新加坡	Singapore	44.30	51.61	65.70	65.87
马来西亚	Malaysia	43.88	117.63	158.56	169.17
泰　国	Thailand	36.53	63.19	76.11	66.35
菲律宾	Philippines	36.08	36.47	42.39	48.04
巴基斯坦	Pakistan	2.15	3.24	4.21	5.64
科威特	Kuwait	0.23	0.71	0.87	1.06
沙特阿拉伯	Saudi Arabia	4.01	8.28	11.81	12.62
阿拉伯联合酋长国	United Arab Emirates	0.95	1.85	4.22	5.19
非　洲	**Africa**	**13.76**	**41.85**	**45.79**	**44.04**
#埃　及	Egypt	0.44	1.31	1.85	1.63
南　非	South Africa	6.62	16.60	18.71	16.11
欧　洲	**Europe**	**264.89**	**619.42**	**810.26**	**807.58**
#德　国	Germany	103.93	248.28	310.64	297.20
法　国	France	28.81	53.72	71.57	85.68
意大利	Italy	23.91	51.07	68.52	61.58
荷　兰	Netherlands	8.17	15.19	19.64	19.64
英　国	United Kingdoms	15.62	37.69	51.03	57.64
瑞　典	Sweden	11.94	28.75	38.18	37.94
俄罗斯	Russia	8.30	22.93	31.09	28.18
美　洲	**America**	**202.70**	**420.66**	**505.50**	**506.52**
#美　国	United States	139.52	268.76	301.50	289.65
加拿大	Canada	14.89	27.89	39.02	32.00
巴　西	Brazil	13.08	19.03	30.47	32.16
智　利	Chile	18.42	63.82	77.21	86.96
大洋洲及太平洋岛屿	**Oceanic and Pacific Island**	**27.50**	**53.73**	**76.64**	**80.18**
#澳大利亚	Australia	23.79	45.35	65.13	66.46
新西兰	New Zealand	3.04	8.33	11.14	13.34
其　他	**Others**	**0.18**	**0.30**	**0.47**	**0.45**

表8.5 主要年份上海市进出口总额
TOTAL VALUE OF FOREIGN TRADE IMPORTS AND EXPORTS IN MAIN YEARS

年 份 Year	上海市进出口总额（亿美元） Total Value of Foreign Trade Imports and Exports (100 million USD)	上海市进口总额（亿美元） Total Value of Foreign Trade Imports (100 million USD)	上海市出口总额（亿美元） Total Value of Foreign Trade Exports (100 million USD)	进出口差 额（亿美元） Balance (100 million USD)	进出口总额相当于生产总值的比例(%) Foreign Trade Imports and Export as Percentage of Gross Domestic Product(%)	出口总额相当于生产总值的比例(%) Foreign Trade Export as Percentage of Gross Domestic Product(%)
1990	74.31	21.10	53.21	32.11	47.0	33.6
1995	190.25	74.48	115.77	41.29	63.6	38.7
1996	222.63	90.25	132.38	42.13	62.6	37.2
1997	247.64	100.40	147.24	46.84	59.7	35.5
1998	313.44	153.88	159.56	5.68	68.3	34.8
1999	386.04	198.19	187.85	-10.34	76.3	37.1
2000	547.10	293.56	253.54	-40.02	94.9	44.0
2001	608.98	332.70	276.28	-56.42	96.7	43.9
2002	726.64	406.09	320.55	-85.54	104.8	46.2
2003	1 123.97	639.15	484.82	-154.33	139.0	59.9
2004	1 600.26	865.06	735.20	-129.86	164.1	75.4
2005	1 863.65	956.23	907.42	-48.81	166.6	81.1
2006	2 274.89	1 139.16	1 135.73	-3.43	174.9	87.3
2007	2 829.73	1 390.45	1 439.28	48.83	179.3	91.2
2008	3 221.38	1 527.88	1 693.50	165.62	163.3	85.9
2009	2 777.31	1 358.17	1 419.14	60.97	127.3	65.1
2010	3 688.69	1 880.85	1 807.84	-73.01	148.0	72.5
2011	4 374.36	2 276.47	2 097.89	-178.58	147.2	70.6
2012	4 367.58	2 299.51	2 068.07	-231.44	136.6	64.7

注：1999 年以前外贸进口、出口商品总额为外经贸委统计口径，1999 年以后为海关统计的上海企业进口、出口总额(以下同)。

Note: Before 1999, the figures of Shanghai's foreign trade imports and exports were based on statistics from Shanghai Foreign Trade and Economic Cooperation Commission. Since 1999, the figures representing imports and exports are made by Shanghai enterprises through Shanghai Custom. Same as follows.

表8.6 主要年份上海市出口总额
TOTAL VALUE OF FOREIGN TRADE EXPORTS IN MAIN YEARS

单位：亿美元 (100 million USD)

	指 标 Indicators	2000	2010	2011	2012
出口总额	**Total Value of Exports**	**253.54**	**1 807.84**	**2 097.89**	**2 068.07**
按企业性质分	**Grouped by Different Enterprises**				
#国有企业	State-owned Enterprises	106.78	307.67	348.53	324.81
外商投资企业	Foreign-funded Enterprises	142.61	1 259.74	1 424.43	1 387.67
按贸易方式分	**Grouped by Trade**				
#一般贸易	Original Trade	101.72	632.74	771.55	789.29
加工贸易	Processing Trade	147.83	1 003.74	1 090.56	1 015.29
按产品类别分	**Grouped by Different Products**				
#机电产品	Electrical and Mechanical Products	121.43	1 311.14	1 484.14	1 454.37
#高新技术产品	High-tech Products		841.11	933.63	906.64

表8.7 主要年份按国别(地区)分的上海市出口总额
TOTAL VALUE OF FOREIGN TRADE EXPORTS BY COUNTRIES AND REGIONS IN MAIN YEARS

单位:亿美元 (100 million USD)

国别(地区)	Country (Region)	2000	2010	2011	2012
总 计	**Total**	**253.54**	**1 807.84**	**2 097.89**	**2 068.07**
亚 洲	**Asia**	**129.10**	**725.93**	**876.75**	**882.26**
#中国香港	Hong Kong, China	23.02	134.09	161.46	159.69
中国台湾	Taiwan, China	5.67	56.54	61.90	57.01
日 本	Japan	60.81	196.46	239.74	249.62
韩 国	Republic of Korea	10.59	58.92	74.18	69.45
新加坡	Singapore	7.88	59.01	67.50	68.63
马来西亚	Malaysia	2.59	42.52	40.86	36.47
泰 国	Thailand	2.48	24.14	32.19	36.06
巴基斯坦	Pakistan	0.55	3.08	3.97	5.24
科威特	Kuwait	0.20	1.53	1.92	1.04
沙特阿拉伯	Saudi Arabia	1.14	5.72	7.89	11.07
阿拉伯联合酋长国	United Arab Emirates	1.79	20.67	23.42	25.89
非 洲	**Africa**	**5.63**	**40.98**	**49.28**	**43.76**
#埃 及	Egypt	0.44	3.28	3.26	3.40
苏 丹	Sudan	0.22	1.21	0.94	1.10
阿尔及利亚	Algeria	0.09	1.29	1.30	1.48
摩洛哥	Morocco	0.20	0.97	0.73	1.05
欧 洲	**Europe**	**45.62**	**450.72**	**473.58**	**435.94**
#德 国	Germany	9.48	86.05	86.21	94.34
法 国	France	4.50	60.97	46.44	28.55
意大利	Italy	4.98	36.99	36.88	29.47
荷 兰	Netherlands	6.16	77.61	88.52	80.49
比利时	Belgium	2.95	16.70	20.98	16.01
英 国	United Kingdoms	7.07	43.11	47.82	50.01
俄罗斯	Russia	0.37	21.15	25.52	32.63
美 洲	**America**	**67.82**	**532.30**	**626.15**	**639.07**
#美 国	United States	56.25	409.91	483.94	501.59
加拿大	Canada	4.04	27.80	28.14	30.71
巴 西	Brazil	1.06	26.95	29.40	27.82
古 巴	Cuba	0.07	0.90	0.66	0.79
大洋洲及太平洋岛屿	**Oceanic and Pacific Island**	**5.37**	**57.91**	**72.13**	**67.04**
#澳大利亚	Australia	4.74	45.59	56.63	57.98

表 8.8 主要年份按国别(地区)分的上海市进口总额
TOTAL VALUE OF FOREIGN TRADE IMPORTS BY COUNTRIES AND REGIONS IN MAIN YEARS

单位:亿美元 (100 million USD)

国别(地区)	Country (Region)	2000	2010	2011	2012
总 计	**Total**	**293.56**	**1 880.85**	**2 276.47**	**2 299.51**
亚 洲	**Asia**	**161.59**	**1 041.98**	**1 232.7**	**1 227.93**
#中国香港	Hong Kong, China	16.68	12.61	10.47	8.54
中国台湾	Taiwan, China	19.44	150.05	150.09	145.26
日 本	Japan	70.43	308.71	346.54	323.49
韩 国	Republic of Korea	20.63	146.41	185.01	175.08
新加坡	Singapore	9.39	39.42	48.08	47.89
马来西亚	Malaysia	6.49	107.75	149.47	158.70
泰 国	Thailand	4.35	53.09	59.48	51.24
菲律宾	Philippines	1.83	33.44	38.31	44.27
科威特	Kuwait	0.22	0.94	0.62	1.73
沙特阿拉伯	Saudi Arabia	0.78	7.23	11.28	10.81
阿拉伯联合酋长国	United Arab Emirates	0.40	2.11	4.90	5.50
非 洲	**Africa**	**1.89**	**28.19**	**31.96**	**30.90**
欧 洲	**Europe**	**63.36**	**400.75**	**543.13**	**582.86**
#德 国	Germany	26.59	140.61	178.80	192.25
法 国	France	7.95	42.54	55.87	69.20
意大利	Italy	4.81	36.46	47.23	45.56
荷 兰	Netherlands	2.43	11.06	15.83	17.00
比利时	Belgium	2.83	25.08	35.85	33.39
英 国	United Kingdoms	3.76	23.43	43.12	57.46
瑞 士	Switzerland	2.22	29.87	42.41	40.87
瑞 典	Sweden	4.53	15.77	19.34	18.69
美 洲	**America**	**58.60**	**344.63**	**380.77**	**373.86**
#美 国	United States	40.11	202.75	212.60	200.19
加拿大	Canada	7.03	20.90	24.66	23.60
巴 西	Brazil	4.11	40.89	51.90	43.19
大洋洲及太平洋岛屿	**Oceanic and Pacific Island**	**8.07**	**65.13**	**87.55**	**83.67**
#澳大利亚	Australia	6.68	56.25	77.43	71.50
新西兰	New Zealand	1.25	7.48	9.29	11.53
其 他	**Others**	**0.05**	**0.17**	**0.36**	**0.29**

表8.9 主要年份进出口商品检验情况
IMPORTS AND EXPORTS INSPECTION IN MAIN YEARS

	指 标 Indicators	2000	2010	2011	2012
进口商品检验	**Imports Inspection**				
检验批数(批)	Groups of Inspection(group)	51 940	1 205 446	1 218 832	1 419 820
检验金额(亿美元)	Values of Inspection(100 million USD)	76.16	1 326.68	1 600.34	1 735.93
不合格批数(批)	Unqualified Groups (group)	1 539	5 562	12 035	21 141
占检验批数比重(%)	Percentage in Total (%)	3.0	0.5	1.0	1.5
不合格金额(亿美元)	Unqualified Values (100 million USD)	0.99	9.75	15.84	48.08
占检验金额比重(%)	Percentage in Total (%)	1.3	0.7	1.0	2.8
出口商品检验	**Exports Inspection**				
检验批数(批)	Groups of Inspection(group)	344 138	728 946	707 495	755 610
检验金额(亿美元)	Values of Inspection(100 million USD)	100.86	238.80	309.58	341.99
不合格批数(批)	Unqualified Groups (group)	564	202	200	214
不合格金额(亿美元)	Unqualified Values (100 million USD)	0.11	0.06	0.05	0.05

表8.10 主要年份直接吸收外资情况
FOREIGN DIRECT INVESTMENT IN MAIN YEARS

	指 标 Indicators	2000	2010	2011	2012
签订合同项目(个)	**Number of Signed Contracts (item)**	**1 814**	**3 906**	**4 329**	**4 043**
#合资经营	Joint Ventures	441	445	511	592
合作经营	Cooperative Ventures	226	14	13	8
独资经营	Sole-foreign Funded Enterprises	1 146	3 443	3 801	3 437
签订合同金额(亿美元)	**Contracted Foreign Capital (100 million USD)**	**63.90**	**153.07**	**201.03**	**223.38**
#合资经营	Joint Ventures	13.86	21.54	23.85	39.76
合作经营	Cooperative Ventures	5.86	1.11	14.85	7.29
独资经营	Sole-foreign Funded Enterprises	44.14	128.17	160.22	172.16
实际吸收外资金额(亿美元)	**Foreign Investment Actually Absorbed (100 million USD)**	**31.60**	**111.21**	**126.01**	**151.85**
#合资经营	Joint Ventures	12.94	17.84	19.87	27.18
合作经营	Cooperative Ventures	2.99	1.69	2.58	5.76
独资经营	Sole-foreign Funded Enterprises	15.67	90.71	102.07	118.29

表8.11 外商直接投资合同项目和金额（2012）
NUMBER OF CONTRACTS SIGNED AND VALUES OF FOREIGN DIRECT INVESTMENT PROJECTS

类别	Types	签订合同项目(个) Number of Contracts Signed(item)		签订合同金额(亿美元) Contracted Foreign Capital (100 million USD)		实际吸收外资金额(亿美元) Foreign Investment Actually Absorbed (100 million USD)	
		2012	至2012年底累计 Total by the End of 2012	2012	至2012年底累计 Total by the End of 2012	2012	至2012年底累计 Total by the End of 2012
总计	**Total**	**4 043**	**67 869**	**223.38**	**2 175.65**	**151.85**	**1 342.13**
#1 000万美元以上项目	**Projects of Over 10 Million USD**	**286**		**194.49**			
#工业	Industry	33		31.31			
按投资方式分	**Grouped by Investment Mode**						
#合资经营	Joint Ventures	592	17 686	39.76	478.77	27.18	362.97
合作经营	Cooperative Ventures	8	5 112	7.29	158.47	5.76	100.17
独资经营	Sole-foreign Funded Enterprises	3 437	44 982	172.16	1 489.68	118.29	848.16
按产业分	**Grouped by Industry**						
第一产业	Primary Industry	4	304	0.39	5.32	0.17	3.94
第二产业	Secondary Industry	221	26 127	35.86	868.44	24.89	491.46
#工业	Industry	206	25 216	35.32	848.99	24.55	485.06
第三产业	Tertiary Industry	3 818	41 438	187.13	1 301.89	126.79	846.73
按主要国别(地区)分	**Grouped by Country and Region**						
#中国香港	Hong Kong, China	1 436	20 618	120.65	814.91	68.43	436.05
中国澳门	Macao, China	8	261	0.69	4.80	0.04	1.69
中国台湾	Taiwan, China	328	7 278	3.65	62.01	4.34	42.88
日本	Japan	536	9 336	25.05	224.08	18.10	161.93
韩国	Republic of Korea	192	2 480	1.97	29.28	2.05	17.35
新加坡	Singapore	203	3 481	13.86	134.11	9.75	76.77
泰国	Thailand	11	250	0.09	2.92	0.08	2.70
德国	Germany	157	1 671	3.24	76.67	2.53	55.39
英国	United Kingdoms	81	1 128	0.94	28.69	0.79	23.12
法国	France	46	714	1.77	29.54	2.84	19.81
意大利	Italy	72	792	0.65	8.68	0.68	4.76
美国	United States	279	7 219	13.21	161.57	7.02	99.43
加拿大	Canada	48	1 101	0.30	9.72	0.14	5.14
澳大利亚	Australia	62	1 198	0.41	12.33	0.25	6.38

表8.12 主要年份引进技术设备实际到货金额
ARRIVED CAPITAL THROUGH IMPORTED TECHNOLOGY AND EQUIPMENT IN MAIN YEARS

单位：万美元（10 000 USD）

国 别(地区)	Country(Region)	2000	2010	2011	2012
总 计	**Total**	**104 558**	**3 903 807**	**5 002 120**	**4 929 346**
#中国香港	Hong Kong, China	10 746	17 414	15 604	14 602
日 本	Japan	10 069	886 132	1 052 104	916 493
德 国	Germany	16 314	814 006	1 058 792	1 123 554
意大利	Italy	622	123 823	143 158	123 447
美 国	United States	49 431	427 275	483 624	463 255
瑞 士	Switzerland	1 862	126 605	183 448	154 699
英 国	United Kingdoms	712	85 649	253 862	395 491
瑞 典	Sweden	639	72 594	95 979	81 685
奥地利	Austria	1 162	31 804	41 174	40 255
法 国	France	1 926	98 172	123 395	208 099

表8.13 对外承包工程和劳务合作(2011～2012)
OVERSEAS CONTRACTED PROJECTS AND LABOR SERVICES COOPERATION

指 标	Indicators	2011	2012
对外承包工程	**Overseas Contracted Projects**		
签订合同金额（万美元）	Value of Contract (10 000 USD)	1 234 673	1 031 056
实际营业额（万美元）	Actual Business Volume (10 000 USD)	594 113	681 188
派出人员(人次)	Dispatched Persons (person-time)	5 559	3 477
对外劳务合作	**Overseas Labor Services Cooperation**		
派出人员(人次)	Dispatched Persons (person-time)	8 749	17 767

表8.14 海外企业情况(2011～2012)
ENTERPRISES ABROAD

指 标	Indicators	2011 年新增 Established in 2011	至 2011 年底累计 Total by the End of 2011	2012 年新增 Established in 2012	至 2012 年底累计 Total by the End of 2012
项 目(个)	Number of Projects(unit)	172	1 680	249	1 929
投资额(万美元)	Investment Value (10 000 USD)	265 824	1 034 119	324 335	1 358 454

表8.15 国际会展(2010～2012)
INTERNATIONAL CONFERENCE AND EXHIBITION

指 标	Indicators	2010	2011	2012
举办国际会展个数(个)	International Exhibit(time)	232	227	265
国际会展展出总面积(万平方米)	Total Square of International Exhibit(10 000 sq. m)	577.50	689.32	826.90

表8.16 主要年份旅行社接待经营情况
TOURISTS RECEIVED BY TOUR AGENCIES IN MAIN YEARS

指 标	Indicators	2005	2010	2011	2012
接待境内外来沪旅游者(万人次)	**Overseas and Domestic Tourists(10 000 person-times)**	**750.89**	**1 239.28**	**962.88**	**1 018.27**
境外旅游者	Overseas Tourists	95.11	158.25	93.02	92.85
#外国人	Foreigners	90.01	147.79	81.88	80.68
中国香港	Tourists from Hong Kong, China	1.48	4.47	5.10	4.44
中国澳门	Tourists from Macao, China	0.01	0.08	2.01	2.26
中国台湾	Tourists from Taiwan, China	3.51	5.91	4.03	5.47
境内旅游者	Domestic Tourists	655.88	1 081.03	869.86	925.42
出境旅游者(万人次)	**Tourists Going Abroad (10 000 person-times)**	**51.71**	**116.86**	**132.44**	**175.40**
经营和财务状况	**Operation and Financial Status**				
营业收入(亿元)	Operational Revenues(100 million yuan)	132.43	341.88	433.78	574.28
利润总额(亿元)	Total Profits(100 million yuan)	1.61	4.02	6.39	8.34

表8.17 主要年份旅游景点基本情况
BASIC STATISTICS OF SCENIC SPOTS IN MAIN YEARS

指 标	Indicators	2005	2010	2011	2012
A级旅游景点数(家)	Scenic Spots of A Level and above(unit)	18	61	74	82
#5A级景点	AAAAA-Level		3	3	3
4A级景点	AAAA-Level	17	28	35	41
红色旅游基地数(个)	Red Travelling Base(unit)		30	33	34
#全国红色旅游基地	National Red Travelling Base		8	9	9

表8.18 主要年份国内旅游者来沪人数和人均消费支出
NUMBER OF DOMESTIC TOURISTS VISITING SHANGHAI AND PER CAPITA CONSUMPTION EXPENDITURES IN MAIN YEARS

指 标	Indicators	2005	2010	2011	2012
国内旅游者来沪人数(万人次)	**Number of Domestic Tourists Visiting Shanghai(10 000 person-times)**	**9 012**	**22 432**	**23 079**	**25 094**
外省市来沪旅游人数	Number of Tourists from other Provinces Visiting Shanghai	6 805	11 255	10 877	11 496
本市市民在本地旅游人数	Number of Local Tourists	2 207	11 177	12 202	13 598
国内旅游者人均消费支出(元)	**Consumption Expenditure Per Person (yuan)**	**1 452**	**1 175**	**1 207**	**1 285**
#长途交通费	Long-distance Traffic Expenditure	176	139	128	133
住宿费	Accommodation Expenditure	219	168	137	145
餐饮费	Food Expenditure	220	153	146	150
购物费	Shopping Expenditure	553	453	519	572
门票费	Ticket Expenditure	96	131	123	144
娱乐费	Entertainment Expenditure	30	42	34	38
市内交通费	Local Traffic Expenditure	88	53	47	48
邮电通信费	Post and Telecommunications Expenditure	37	14	8	8

注：本表为抽样调查资料。
Note: Data in this table are from the sampling survey.

表8.19 旅游星级饭店基本情况(2012)
BASIC STATISTICS OF STAR-RATED TOURISM HOTELS

指 标	Indicators	合 计 Total	五星级 Five-Star	四星级 Four-Star	三星级 Three-Star	二星级 Two-Star	一星级 One-Star
饭店数(个)	Number of Hotels(unit)	278	55	66	108	48	1
客房数(万间)	Number of Rooms (10 000 rooms)	6.49	2.43	1.99	1.66	0.40	0.01
床位数(万张)	Number of Beds (10 000 beds)	9.99	3.38	3.07	2.82	0.71	0.01
客房平均出租率(%)	Average Occupancy Rate (%)	56.9	59.1	59.6	49.8	60.4	57.3
营业收入(亿元)	Business Revenues (100 million yuan)	180.89	101.59	52.33	23.25	3.68	0.04
平均房价 (元/间天)	Average Room Rates (yuan/room. day)	627	956	534	322	217	111

表8.20 主要年份国际旅游入境人数
NUMBER OF OVERSEAS TOURISTS THROUGH SHANGHAI CUSTOM IN MAIN YEARS

指 标	Indicators	2000	2010	2011	2012
国际旅游入境人数(万人次)	**Number of Overseas Tourists Through Shanghai Custom(10 000 person-times)**	**181.40**	**851.12**	**817.57**	**800.40**
#外国人	Foreigner	139.14	665.63	648.31	633.03
#日 本	Japanese	53.76	152.47	147.94	136.05
新加坡	Singaporean	5.29	23.50	22.79	21.19
德 国	German	7.11	29.52	30.33	30.63
法 国	French	5.39	24.86	21.21	21.46
英 国	Briton	1.69	20.94	21.43	21.57
意大利	Italian	1.88	11.49	10.99	11.73
加拿大	Canadian	2.25	20.97	18.69	19.52
美 国	American	13.78	80.79	82.17	80.48
澳大利亚	Australian	3.23	21.33	21.52	21.47
港澳同胞	Hong Kong and Macao Chinese	17.62	77.47	66.34	63.33
台湾同胞	Taiwanese	19.88	108.02	102.92	104.04
平均每天来沪旅游人数(人次/天)	**Average Number of Tourists Visiting Shanghai Everyday (person-time/day)**	**4 970**	**23 382**	**22 399**	**21 929**
来沪旅游者平均逗留天数 (天/人)	**Average Time Tourists Staying in Shanghai (day/person)**	**3.92**	**3.51**	**3.42**	**3.34**
国际旅游(外汇)收入(亿美元)	**Foreign Exchange Earnings from International Tourism(100 million USD)**	**16.13**	**64.05**	**58.35**	**55.82**

上/海/统/计/年/鉴

主要统计指标解释

■ 关区进出口总额

指由海关统计的进出口商品总额。统计方法依据联合国的国际贸易统计原则，反映进出上海而引起物质资源储备增加或减少的商品运动。按上述原则应具备条件：实际进出上海（海关关境），不仅包括经商业交易行为的进出口货品，也包括援助、捐赠等未发生买卖关系的货品价值。出口按离岸价（FOB）统计，进口按到岸价（CIF）统计。

■ 上海市进出口总额

指海关统计中按经营单位即进出口企业在海关注册地的行政区域口径统计的数据，它反映的是上海行政辖区内各类具有进出口经营权企业（外贸企业）的进出口。它不包含外省市外贸企业途经上海口岸由上海海关结关放行及统计的进出口商品，但包含上海外贸企业经由非上海口岸进出口结关放行及统计的商品。

■ 外商直接投资

指外国企业和经济组织或个人（包括华侨、港澳台胞以及我国在境外注册的企业）按我国有关政策、法规，用现汇、实物、技术等在我国境内开办外商独资企业、与我国境内的企业或经济组织共同举办中外合资经营企业、合作经营企业或合作开发资源的投资（包括外商投资收益的再投资）以及企业投资总额内直接投资者对企业的贷款，即外方股东贷款(需在报告期内将相应合同及贷款协议报商务部备案核查)。

■ 引进技术

指通过贸易途径从国外获得发展我国国民经济和提高技术水平所需要的技术装备。引进方式有：许可证贸易（技术贸易）、生产线（包括成套设备）、单机（包括关键设备）、软硬件结合（同时引进技术和设备）和其他。

■ 对外承包工程

对外承包工程包括各对外承包公司以招标议标承包方式承揽的下列业务：(1) 承包国外工程建设项目。(2) 承包我国对外经济援助项目。(3) 承包我国驻外机构的工程建设项目。(4) 承包我国境内利用外资进行建设的工程项目。(5) 与外国承包公司合营或联合承包工程项目时我国公司分包部分。(6) 以服务成果向业主收费的技术服务项目（包括承担地形地貌测绘；地质资源勘探与普查；建设区域规划；提供设计文件、图纸、生产工艺技术资料和工程技术经济咨询；工程项目的可行性考察、研究和评估；进行技术指导和培训人员等）。(7) 对外承包兼营的房屋开发业务。对外承包工程的营业额是以货币表现的本期内完成的对外承包工程的工作量，包括以前年度签订的合同和本年度新签订的合同在报告期完成的工作量。

■ 对外劳务合作

指以收取工资的形式向业主或承包商提供技术和劳动服务的活动。上海对外承包公司在境外开办的合营企业，上海公司同时又提供劳务的，其劳务部分也纳入劳务合作统计。劳务合作营业额按报告期内向雇主提交的结算数（包括工资、加班费和奖金等）统计。

■ 国际旅游入境人数

指来上海参观、访问、旅行、探亲、访友、休养、考察、参加会议和从事经济、科技、文化、教育、体育、宗教等活动的外国人、华侨、港澳和台湾同胞的人数。不包括来上海常住1年以上的外国专家、留学生等。上海入境的境外旅游人数包括从上海口岸入境的境外旅游人数和从我国其他口岸入境的境外旅游人数。

■ 国际旅游（外汇）收入

指入境旅游的外国人、华侨、港澳台同胞在上海旅游过程中发生的一切旅游支出。

SHANGHAI STATISTICAL YEARBOOK

EXPLANATORY NOTES TO MAJOR STATISTICAL INDICATORS

□ Total Trade Volume Through Customs

Total Trade Volume through Customes refers to the aggregate volume of commodities that are imported or exported through Shanghai's ports. The statistics method follows the international trade statistics principles set by the United Nations. It reflects the fluctuation of Shanghai's material reserves caused by export or import. Requirements involved in the principle is: the commodities refer to those enter or leave Shanghai's ports, including not only the business trading activities but also the commodities value of the aid and donations that haven't been involved in sales . Exports are calculated according to FOB price, and imports are calculated according to CIF.

□ The Value of Foreign Trade Imports and Exports of Shanghai

Total Value of Foreign Trade Imports and Exports of Shanghai is offered by Customs authorities, covering the operation units, or the enterprises involved in import and export, that have registered in the administrative regions where the Customs operate. It reflects the import and export of all the enterprises with import and export rights (foreign trade enterprises) under the administration of Shanghai Municipality. It excludes those commodities of foreign trade enterprises from out of town that underwent customs clearance at Shanghai ports but includes commodities of foreign trade enterprises of Shanghai that underwent customs clearance in non-Shanghai ports.

□ Foreign Direct Investment

Foreign Direct Investment refers to the investments made inside China by foreign enterprises and economic organizations or individuals (including overseas Chinese, compatriots in Hong Kong, Macao and Chinese enterprises registered abroad), in line with the relevant policies and laws of China, for the establishment of wholly foreign-owned enterprises, and joint ventures or development projects launched in China (including re-investment of profits from foreign businesses), and the funds that enterprises borrow from abroad in the total investment of projects which are approved by the relevant departments of the governments and the loans from the direct investors within the total investment of the projects, i.e., foreign shareholders' loans. (The related contracts and loans agreements in the report period should be filed with the Ministry of Commerce)

□ Import of Technology

Import of Technology refers to technology and equipments obtained through the trade channel from other countries which are needed for advancing China's national economy and improving its technological level. The import form includes: licensing (technological trade), production lines (including complete plant), single machine (including key equipments), combination of hardware and software (importing technology and equipments simultaneously) and others.

□ Overseas Contracted Projects

Overseas Contracted Projects refer to projects undertaken by Chinese contractors (project contracting companies) through bidding process. They include: (1) overseas civil engineering construction projects financed by foreign investors. (2) overseas projects financed by the Chinese government through its foreign-aid programs. (3) construction projects of Chinese diplomatic missions, trade offices and other institutions stationed abroad. (4) construction projects in China financed by foreign investment. (5) sub-contracted projects to be taken by Chinese contractors through a joint umbrella project with foreign contractor(s). (6) technical assistance projects in the form of service results and chargeable to the owners (such as topographic surveying, geological prospecting, development zone programming, provision of documents, blueprint, materials on production process, technical consultation, project feasibility studies and evaluation, personnel training, etc.). and (7) housing development projects. The business turnover from international contracting is the work of contracted projects completed during the reporting period, expressed in monetary terms, including completed work on project contracts signed in previous years.

□ Overseas Labor Service Cooperation

Overseas Labor Service Cooperation refers to activities of providing technology and labor services to employers or contractors by collecting salaries and wages. Labor services provided by Shanghai's international contrasting corporations to their overseas

EXPLANATORY NOTES TO MAJOR STATISTICAL INDICATORS

joint ventures shall be included into the statistics of overseas services. The business turn over of overseas labor services is the settlement price (including salaries, overtime pay and bonuses) submitted to the employers during the reporting period.

□ Number of Overseas Tourists to Shanghai

Number of Overseas Tourists to Shanghai refers to the number of foreigners, overseas Chinese, and compatriots from Hong Kong, Macao and Taiwan coming to Shanghai for sightseeing, visits, tours, family reunions, meeting friends, vacations, study tours, attending meetings and other activities of an economic, scientific and technological, cultural, physical culture and religious nature. This does not include foreign experts and students residing in Shanghai for over 1 year. The number of overseas tourists to Shanghai includes those overseas tourists entering China through Shanghai customs and through customs other than Shanghai.

□ Foreign Exchange Earnings from International Tourism

Foreign Exchange Earnings from International Tourism refer to the total expenditures of foreigners, overseas Chinese, Chinese compatriots from Hong Kong, Macao and Taiwan during their stay in Shanghai.

第九篇

CHAPTER 9

价格水平

PRICES

简要说明

一、本篇资料的主要内容

本篇价格指数资料，反映生产、流通、消费、投资与交易等环节的价格变动趋势和变动幅度。主要包括居民消费价格指数、商品零售价格指数、工业生产者出产价格指数、工业生产者购进价格指数、固定资产投资价格指数、住宅租赁价格指数、土地交易价格指数等。

二、本篇的资料来源

价格指数编制由国家统计局上海调查总队组织实施，依据国家统计局统一制定的价格统计调查制度，由上海调查总队直接或通过区县调查队从基层采集原始价格数据汇总后上报。

三、居民消费、商品零售价格指数

编制居民消费、商品零售价格指数的资料采用抽样调查和重点调查相结合的方法取得，即在全市选择不同经济区域和分布合理的商品销售或服务网点，以及有代表性的商品或服务作为样本，对其市场价格进行定期调查，以样本推断总体。目前，居民消费、商品零售价格调查已涉及全市全部 17 个区县。

1. 价格调查点的抽选方法：对全市消费市场进行摸底调查、掌握市场的基本情况（经营品种、销售额等指标）基础上，将各种类型的商场（店）、超市、农贸市场、服务网点以销售额（成交额或经营规模）为标志，从高到低排队，依据所需调查点的数量进行等距抽样。选择经营品种齐全、销售额大的商场（店）、超市、农贸市场、服务网点作为价格调查点。

2. 代表规格品根据全市的消费情况确定，必须遵循以下原则：（1）选择消费量较大的消费项目；（2）价格变动趋势和变动程度有较强的代表性，即选中规格品与未选中规格品的价格变动特征愈相关愈好；（3）在市场销售份额大体相等的情况下，同一基本分类的规格品之间，性质差异愈大愈好，价格变动特征的相关性愈低愈好；（4）生产和销售前景较好；（5）选中的工业消费品必须是合格产品，工业产品包装上必须有注册商标、产地、规格等级等标识。

目前，居民消费价格调查分为 8 大类，262 个基本分类，全市每月共调查 1300 种以上的规格品价格；商品零售价格分为 16 个大类，229 个基本分类，全市每月调查 1000 种以上的规格品价格。

3. 价格调查方法：居民消费、商品零售价格调查是非全面调查，主要方法是定人、定点、定时直接调查。

4. 权数的确定：居民消费价格指数的权数主要根据全市城镇居民家庭消费支出构成确定；商品零售价格指数的权数主要根据全市社会商品零售额资料确定。

5. 指数计算方法：使用链式拉氏公式计算，固定基期为 2010 年。

四、工业生产者出厂价格指数

工业生产者出厂价格是工业品第一次出售时的出厂价格。该项调查采用重点调查与典型调查相结合的调查方法。重点调查对象为年主营业务收入 2000 万元及以上的工业法人企业;典型调查对象为年主营业务收入 2000 万元以下的工业法人企业。

1. 选择代表企业的原则:(1)按工业行业选择调查企业,各种类行业原则上都要有调查企业;(2)大型企业应尽量都选上(或占相当大比重);(3)选择生产正常、稳定的企业作为调查对象;(4)选择企业时要兼顾不同所有制形式。不仅选择国有企业,也要选择非国有企业。

2. 选择代表产品的原则:(1)按工业行业选择代表产品;(2)选择对国计民生影响大的产品;(3)选择生产较为稳定的产品;(4)选择有发展前景的产品;(5)选择具有地方特色的产品。

目前《工业生产者出厂价格调查目录》包括 11000 多种产品,并将其划分为 1702 个基本分类;《工业生产者购进价格调查目录》包括 6000 多种产品,并划分为 900 多个基本分类。上海根据全市的经济结构、产品结构和企业选报产品等情况,在工业生产者价格调查目录中编制规格品代码。上海编制工业生产者出厂价格指数选用近 700 个基本分类（1000 余种产品),工业生产者购进价格指数选用了近 500 个基本分类 (约 900 种产品)。

3. 价格调查方式采用企业网上直报形式,每月 1000 余家工业企业上报数据资料。

五、固定资产投资价格指数

固定资产投资价格调查采用重点调查与典型调查相结合的方法。固定资产投资价格调查所涉及的价格是构成固定资产投资额实体的实际购进价格或结算价格。调查的内容包括构成当年建筑工程实体的钢材、木材、水泥、地方材料(如砖、瓦、灰、沙、石等)、化工材料(如油漆等)等主要建筑材料价格;作为活劳动投入的劳动力价格(单位工资)和建筑机械使用费用;设备、工器具购置和其他费用投资价格。

1. 选择建筑安装工程调查点的原则:(1) 样本单位应具有一定覆盖面;(2) 投资经济活动代表性强;(3)兼顾不同登记注册类型;(4)选择重点工程;(5)兼顾国民经济各门类及不同工程类别。

2. 选择其他费用调查点的原则:在选择其他费用调查点时,所遵循的原则与建筑安装工程调查点的原则基本相同,特别是要注意选择那些投资额大的工程。但由于其他费用不易取得,所以在实际操作过程中,应同时在建设单位、施工单位开展重点调查,并辅以典型调查(从管理部门取得资料)。

3. 价格调查方式采用企业报表形式,每季度 120 余家调查企业上报数据资料。

六、住宅租赁价格指数

旅住宅租赁价格调查采用重点调查与典型调查相结合的方法。按月调查和收集全市住宅租赁的价格涨跌幅度、面积、金额等相关基础资料用于计算月度价格指数。

1. 选择调查单位的原则:(1)选取房地产经纪机构要注重代表性;(2)选取住宅样本要兼顾不同地理位置;(3)兼顾不同项目地段。

2. 价格调查方式采用企业报表形式。

七、土地交易价格指数

土地交易价格主要包括居住用地价格、工业用地价格、商业营业用地价格和其他用地价格等,土地交易方式主要包括拍卖、招标、挂牌销售、市场转让、市场抵押等。土地交易价格调查采用重点调查与典型调查相结合的方法。

1. 在选择调查单位的原则:(1)代表性强;(2)兼顾不同项目地段;(3)兼顾不同土地交易方式;(4)选中的调查单位对全部交易项目按房地产类型(编码)填报调查表。

2. 价格调查方式采用土地管理部门、土地交易中心提供方式。

BRIEF INTRODUCTION

I. Main Contents

Data on price indices in this chapter show the changing trends and the changing rates in the prices of production, trade, consumption, investment and transaction, mainly including consumer price indices, retail price indices, producer price indices, producer purchasing price indices, price indices for investment in fixed assets, residential rental indices and land transaction price indices.

II. Sources of Data

Statistics on price indices, organized and compiled by the Survey Office of the National Bureau of Statistics in Shanghai, are collected from the grassroots units or survey offices in districts and counties in accordance with the scheme of price survey system stipulated by the National Bureau of Statistics, and then statistics are tabulated and reported to the higher agencies.

III. Consumer Price Indices and Retail Price Indices

Data for compilation of the consumer price indices and the retail price indices in Shanghai are collected through a combination of sample surveys and surveys of key units. Areas distributed in the city's economic regions, representative commodities and representative services are selected as samples. Regular surveys are conducted to collect data on their market prices. Population parameters are inferred on the basis of the sample data. At present, 17 districts and counties in Shanghai are all included in the survey of the consumer price indices and the retail price indices.

(1) The selection of sample survey areas: Based on the basic conditions (including product varieties, their sales and etc) the city's consumer market, the city's consumer market, shops, supermarkets, wet markets and service outlets of different varieties are ranked by sales (turnover or scales) and then selected on the number of survey areas needed via systematic sampling method schemes. The price survey areas should be shops, supermarkets, wet markets and service outlets with a wide range of products and big sales.

(2) The goods are selected on the city's consumption conditions, following these principles: (a) goods sold in large quantities (b) Representative for the price changing trends and the changing rates, which means selected goods are highly relevant with those unselected (c) Under the conditions of similar market shares, the bigger the differences in nature among goods and the lower the price relevance, the better (d) Good production and sales outlook (e) Qualified industrial goods, with registered trademark, origin and grade printed on the packaging.

At present, data are collected on more than 1,300 specifications each month in the city under 262 basic headings in 8 categories in the consumer price surveys. For the retail price surveys, data are collected on more than 1,000 specifications each month under 229 basic headings in 16 categories.

(3) Method of data collection: Sample surveys are used for the consumer price indices and the retail price indices, with method of direct survey with fixed people, fixed location and fixed time period.

(4) Determination of the weights: The weights of the consumer price indices are determined according to the composition of the consumption expenditures of Shanghai's urban and rural households. The weights of the retail price indices are determined mainly according to the total retail sales of commodities in the city.

(5) Method of calculation: the approach of the chain Laspyres with 2010 being a base period.

IV. Producer Price Indices for industrial products

Producer prices for industrial products refer to the ex–factory price of manufactured goods when they are first sold. The survey program is a combined use of the key units' survey and typical units' survey methods. Key units refer to those industrial enterprises with annual revenue from the primary activities at and above 20 million yuan. Typical units refer to the industrial enterprises with annual revenue from the primary activities below 20 million yuan.

(1)Principles for selecting the representative enterprises: (a) Enterprises to be covered in the survey are selected by industrial sectors. In principle, every industry should have representative enterprises; (b) All (or a majority of) large–scale enterprises should be selected; (c) Enterprises selected should be those with normal and stable production. (d) Enterprises selected should include both state–owned and private companies to cover ownership of different nature.

(2)Principle for the selection of representative goods:

(a) The goods are selected by industrial sectors; (b) The selected goods should have great impact on the national economy and people's living conditions; (c) The production of the goods selected are relatively stable; (d) The prospects of the goods selected are promising; (e) The goods selected are local specialties.

The survey catalog of Producer Prices for Industrial Products includes over 11,000 goods, and they are divided into 1702 basic categories; Survey catalog of Purchasing Price for Industrial Producers includes over 6,000 goods, and they are divided into over 900 basic categories.

Based on the city's economic structure, product structure and the products selected by the enterprises, Shanghai compiles the code of specifications according to the Survey Catalog of Producer Price Indices for Industrial Products. More than 1,000 goods in 700 basic categories are selected to compile the city's producer price indices, and about 900 goods in 500 basic categories are chose to compile the city's purchasing price for industrial goods.

(3)Online direct reporting method is used for data collection. About 1,000 industrial enterprises report the price data every month.

V. Price Indices for Investment in Fixed Assets

Data on prices of investment in fixed assets are collected by a program involving the combined use of surveys on key units and surveys on typical units. The prices collected in the surveys of investment in fixed assets are the actual purchasing prices or settlement prices of entities of investment in fixed assets. The survey content includes the prices of main construction materials that constitute the architectural engineering entity in the year, such as steel, timber, cement, local construction materials (such as brick, tile, calcareous ashes, sand, stone, and etc.), chemical materials (such as oil paint, and etc.), the price of labor cost (wages), prices for renting of building machinery and equipment, the purchasing price of equipment, tools and instruments and the prices of others investments.

1. Principles for selecting the survey points of construction and installation: (1) Sample units should have a good coverage; (2) The economic activity of investment should have strong representativeness; (3) Different types of registration should be considered; (4) Key projects should be selected; (5) Inclusion of various sectors of the national economy and types of projects.

2. Principles for selecting price survey points of other charges or cost: The principles for selecting survey points of others charges or cost is in general the same as that of construction and installation, with special attention to include projects with huge investment value. Since it is not easy to obtain the other charges or cost, during the actual data gathering operations, survey on key construction owner units and building units should be conducted concurrently with survey on typical units (with information from administration units)

3. Enterprises reporting system is used as the method for the price survey. More than 120 enterprises should report their data in each quarter.

VI. Residential Rental Indices

Data on residential rental indices are collected by a program involving the combined use of surveys on key units and surveys on typical units. Data on fluctuations of the city's residential rental prices, the size of residential rental areas and their value are collected each month to calculate the monthly residential rental indices.

1. Principles for selecting enterprises: (1) Selected property agencies should be representative. (2) Sample residential buildings should cover different locations. (3) Cover projects in different locations.

2. Enterprises reporting system is used to carry out the survey.

VII. Land Transaction Price Indices

Land prices include primarily residential land prices, industrial land prices, commercial business land prices and prices of land for other uses. Transactions are settled in means such as auction, tender, public sales, transfer, collateral and etc. Data on land transaction price indices are collected by a program involving the combined use of surveys on key units and surveys on typical units.

1. The principles for selecting enterprises: (1) Strong representativeness; (2) Coverage of projects in different locations; (3) Coverage of different types of land transactions; (4) Selected enterprises should fill in the survey on all transactions with the property type code.

2. The method of survey is provided by the authorities of land administration and land transaction.

表 9.1 居民消费价格和商品零售价格指数(1978～2012)
OVERALL RESIDENTS CONSUMER PRICE INDEX AND RETAIL PRICE INDEX

年 份 Year	居民消费价格指数 Overall Residents Consumer Price Index		年 份 Year	商品零售价格指数 Retail Price Index	
	以上年价格为 100 preceding year = 100	以 1978 年价格为 100 1978 = 100		以上年价格为 100 preceding year = 100	以 1978 年价格为 100 1978 = 100
1978	100.5	100.0	1978	100.1	100.0
1979	100.9	100.9	1979	101.0	101.0
1980	105.9	106.9	1980	106.5	107.6
1981	101.4	108.3	1981	101.5	109.2
1982	100.3	108.7	1982	100.3	109.5
1983	100.2	108.9	1983	100.1	109.6
1984	102.2	111.3	1984	102.2	112.0
1985	115.2	128.2	1985	116.4	130.4
1986	106.3	136.3	1986	106.7	139.1
1987	108.1	147.3	1987	108.8	151.4
1988	120.1	176.9	1988	121.3	183.6
1989	115.9	205.1	1989	116.7	214.3
1990	106.3	218.0	1990	104.8	224.6
1991	110.5	240.9	1991	109.5	245.9
1992	110.0	265.0	1992	109.7	269.8
1993	120.2	318.5	1993	117.5	317.0
1994	123.9	394.6	1994	117.5	372.4
1995	118.7	468.4	1995	113.0	420.9
1996	109.2	511.5	1996	105.0	441.9
1997	102.8	525.8	1997	98.8	436.6
1998	100.0	525.8	1998	95.1	415.2
1999	101.5	533.7	1999	97.3	404.0
2000	102.5	547.0	2000	96.4	389.5
2001	100.0	547.0	2001	98.6	384.0
2002	100.5	549.8	2002	98.7	379.0
2003	100.1	550.3	2003	99.0	375.4
2004	102.2	562.2	2004	100.9	378.8
2005	101.0	567.6	2005	99.4	376.7
2006	101.2	574.5	2006	100.2	377.4
2007	103.2	592.6	2007	102.4	386.5
2008	105.8	626.8	2008	105.3	407.1
2009	99.6	624.3	2009	99.4	404.8
2010	103.1	643.6	2010	101.7	411.7
2011	105.2	677.0	2011	104.1	428.4
2012	102.8	696.2	2012	101.2	433.7

表 9.2 居民消费价格指数(1991 ~2012,以 1990 年价格为 100)
OVERALL RESIDENTS CONSUMER PRICE INDEX (1990 = 100)

年 份 Year	居民消费价格指数 Overall Residents Consumer Price Index	食 品 Food	烟 酒 Cigarettes and Liquors	衣 着 Clothing
1991	110.5	113.5	103.0	105.7
1992	121.6	128.7	113.0	115.7
1993	146.1	157.2	124.5	137.3
1994	181.0	207.1	139.5	158.8
1995	214.9	261.2	149.1	172.8
1996	234.6	288.6	149.1	187.8
1997	241.2	288.6	134.6	189.9
1998	241.2	282.3	129.2	178.5
1999	244.8	274.9	129.8	175.5
2000	250.9	270.0	126.1	167.2
2001	250.9	270.8	124.7	165.4
2002	252.2	278.6	123.4	161.2
2003	252.5	282.3	123.1	157.2
2004	257.8	305.6	121.0	148.1
2005	260.3	319.4	120.6	136.4
2006	263.4	327.5	120.9	145.2
2007	271.7	358.3	121.7	147.1
2008	287.4	413.1	123.7	149.5
2009	286.3	421.6	124.7	148.5
2010	295.2	454.1	126.1	146.4
2011	310.4	503.1	127.8	152.7
2012	319.2	532.4	129.6	157.2

注：2011 年起"烟酒及用品类"改为"烟酒类"。
Note: The type of Cigarettes, Liquors and Related Items is changed to the type of Cigarettes and Liquors since 2011.

表 9.2 续表 continued

年 份 Year	家庭设备用品及维修服务 Home Appliances and Repair Service	医疗保健和个人用品 Medicine, Medical Services and Personal Aricles	交通和通信 Transportation and Communication	娱乐教育文化用品及服务 Recreation, Education and Culture Articles	居 住 Residence
1991	112.5	113.1	108.5	96.9	129.3
1992	115.4	132.7	108.9	93.8	153.9
1993	126.4	151.8	127.5	115.7	206.8
1994	140.2	180.9	149.5	136.1	249.4
1995	145.5	199.0	171.5	158.2	300.0
1996	144.2	210.9	181.9	187.6	329.1
1997	131.8	215.4	210.3	205.6	396.9
1998	121.9	219.5	218.1	218.6	450.9
1999	117.5	223.6	245.1	244.1	477.5
2000	112.5	223.4	271.9	296.6	493.3
2001	109.3	217.6	266.7	302.8	504.6
2002	106.8	212.4	258.4	305.3	504.6
2003	105.1	212.4	248.9	306.2	510.2
2004	102.8	212.2	240.4	306.0	518.5
2005	103.6	212.9	234.3	300.8	533.7
2006	106.4	215.2	227.8	295.5	549.2
2007	109.9	215.7	220.8	287.4	573.9
2008	119.0	222.5	215.3	282.3	588.4
2009	120.8	221.3	210.0	276.5	568.1
2010	122.1	229.5	204.5	279.0	587.9
2011	130.8	238.8	204.8	276.7	619.6
2012	135.3	240.3	206.5	274.9	637.2

表9.3 居民消费价格指数(1991～2012,以上年价格为100)
OVERALL RESIDENTS CONSUMER PRICE INDEX(PRECEDING YEAR = 100)

年 份 Year	居民消费价格指数 Overall ResidentsConsumer Price Index	食 品 Food	烟 酒 Cigarettes and Liquors	衣 着 Clothing
1991	110.5	113.5	103.0	105.7
1992	110.0	113.4	109.7	109.5
1993	120.2	122.1	110.2	118.6
1994	123.9	131.8	112.0	115.7
1995	118.7	126.1	106.9	108.8
1996	109.2	110.5	100.0	108.7
1997	102.8	100.0	90.3	101.1
1998	100.0	97.8	96.0	94.0
1999	101.5	97.4	100.4	98.3
2000	102.5	98.2	97.2	95.3
2001	100.0	100.3	98.9	98.9
2002	100.5	102.9	98.9	97.5
2003	100.1	101.3	99.8	97.5
2004	102.2	108.3	98.3	94.2
2005	101.0	104.5	99.7	92.1
2006	101.2	102.5	100.2	106.4
2007	103.2	109.4	100.7	101.3
2008	105.8	115.3	101.7	101.6
2009	99.6	102.1	100.8	99.3
2010	103.1	107.7	101.1	98.6
2011	105.2	110.8	101.3	104.3
2012	102.8	105.8	101.4	103.0

表9.3 续表 continued

年 份 Year	家庭设备用品及维修服务 Home Appliances and Repair Service	医疗保健和个人用品 Medicine, Medical Services and Personal Aricles	交通和通信 Transportation and Communication	娱乐教育文化用品及服务 Recreation, Education and Culture Articles	居 住 Residence
1991	112.5	113.1	108.5	96.9	129.3
1992	102.6	117.3	100.4	96.8	119.0
1993	109.5	114.4	117.0	123.4	134.4
1994	110.9	119.2	117.3	117.6	120.6
1995	103.8	110.0	114.7	116.2	120.3
1996	99.1	106.0	106.1	118.6	109.7
1997	91.4	102.1	115.6	109.6	120.6
1998	92.5	101.9	103.7	106.3	113.6
1999	96.4	101.9	112.4	111.7	105.9
2000	95.7	99.9	110.9	121.5	103.3
2001	97.2	97.4	98.1	102.1	102.3
2002	97.7	97.6	96.9	100.8	100.0
2003	98.4	100.0	96.3	100.3	101.1
2004	97.8	100.0	96.5	99.9	101.6
2005	100.8	100.3	97.5	98.3	102.9
2006	102.7	101.1	97.3	98.2	102.9
2007	103.3	100.2	96.9	97.3	104.5
2008	108.3	103.1	97.5	98.2	102.5
2009	101.5	99.4	97.5	98.0	96.6
2010	101.1	103.7	97.4	100.9	103.5
2011	107.1	104.1	100.2	99.2	105.4
2012	103.5	100.6	100.8	99.3	102.8

表9.4 主要年份居民消费价格指数(以上年价格为100)
CLASSIFIED RESIDENTS CONSUMER PRICE INDEX IN MAIN YEARS(PRECEDING YEAR = 100)

类别	Types	2001	2010	2011	2012
居民消费价格指数	**Overall Residents Consumer Price Index**	**100.0**	**103.1**	**105.2**	**102.8**
#服务项目价格	Services Items Price	105.4	102.0	103.9	103.0
食 品	**Food**	**100.3**	**107.7**	**110.8**	**105.8**
粮 食	Grain	102.9	112.0	113.5	102.9
淀粉及制品	Starch and Its Products	103.6	95.5	106.6	109.5
干豆类及豆制品	Dry Beans and Bean Products	95.6	108.7	114.7	109.5
油 脂	Oil or Fat	84.5	105.6	117.5	103.8
肉禽及其制品	Meat Poultry and Their Products	99.3	104.3	119.9	105.1
蛋	Eggs	102.4	106.1	113.5	98.2
水产品	Aquatic Products	100.1	116.4	113.7	105.8
菜	Vegetables	108.9	111.0	99.8	111.1
#鲜 菜	Fresh Vegetables	110.2	111.5	98.3	113.3
调味品	Flavoring	99.2	106.5	107.7	103.5
糖	Sugars	101.4	103.8	104.8	103.5
茶及饮料	Tea and Beverages	98.4	103.9	105.1	103.1
干鲜瓜果	Dried and Fresh Fruits	104.3	112.0	114.5	102.8
#鲜瓜果	Fresh Fruits	105.8	113.9	117.5	100.8
糕点饼干面包	Cakes, Biscuits and Bread	100.5	100.5	108.8	102.8
液体乳及乳制品	Milk and Its Products	100.8	102.3	108.2	103.8
在外用膳食品	Dining Out	98.0	105.6	107.9	107.8
其他食品	Other Food	99.2	105.0	107.4	108.1
烟 酒	**Cigarettes and Liquors**	**98.9**	**101.1**	**101.3**	**101.4**
烟 草	Tobacco	99.2	101.0	100.3	100.0
酒	Liquors	98.2	101.6	103.9	105.0
衣 着	**Clothing**	**98.9**	**98.6**	**104.3**	**103.0**
服 装	Garments	96.4	99.9	105.4	103.9
男式服装	Men'Wear	99.0	102.8	103.7	103.9
女式服装	Women's Wear	94.7	98.3	107.4	103.8
儿童服装	Children's Wear	95.4	93.6	100.3	104.1
衣着材料	Clothing Materials	98.7	102.9	119.8	104.9
鞋袜帽	Shoes, Socks and Hats	106.2	93.6	99.0	99.3
#鞋	Shoes	106.6	92.4	98.5	99.0
衣着加工服务	Garment Processing Service	100.0	107.2	119.1	105.5

表9.4 续表 continued

类别	Types	2001	2010	2011	2012
家庭设备用品及维修服务	**Home Appliances and Repair Service**	**97.2**	**101.1**	**107.1**	**103.5**
耐用消费品	Durable Consumer Goods	94.7	99.6	102.8	103.0
室内装饰品	Interior Decorations	101.0	99.2	101.5	105.0
床上用品	Bed Articles	100.5	104.2	116.4	99.1
家庭日用杂品	Daily Use Household Articles	98.6	99.4	107.6	103.0
家庭服务及加工维修服务	Other Daily Use Articles	100.0	108.8	118.0	109.1
医疗保健和个人用品	**Medicine, Medical Services and Personal Aricles**	**97.4**	**103.7**	**104.1**	**100.6**
医疗保健	Medicine and Medical Services	96.5	100.8	100.6	99.9
#中药材及中成药	Herbs and Ready-made Traditional Chinese Medicine	105.5	105.5	105.8	102.3
西药	Western Medicine	92.0	99.6	94.6	95.6
保健器具及用品	Healthcare Equipment	95.4	98.6	104.9	106.9
医疗保健服务	Medical and Healthcare Service	100.0	103.7	103.1	99.8
个人用品及服务	Personal Aricles and Service	99.8	107.1	107.4	101.3
交通和通信	**Transportation and Communication**	**98.1**	**97.4**	**100.2**	**100.8**
交通	Transport	102.3	98.7	101.8	102.6
#交通工具	Transport Tools	97.9	99.5	101.6	99.3
通信	Communications	94.4	95.3	96.3	96.5
通信工具	Communications Tools	69.7	71.4	79.9	73.5
通信服务	Communications Service	103.1	100.0	99.7	100.3
娱乐教育文化用品及服务	**Recreation, Education and Culture Articles**	**102.1**	**100.9**	**99.2**	**99.3**
文娱用耐用消费品及服务	Durable Consumer Goods for Recreational Use	91.2	89.4	89.7	87.8
教育	Education	109.6	101.2	101.8	102.0
文化娱乐类	Recreation and Culture Articles	105.2	101.0	102.8	101.8
旅游	Tourism	96.2	115.9	99.9	102.1
居住	**Residence**	**102.3**	**103.5**	**105.4**	**102.8**
建房及装修材料	Construction and Decoration Materials	97.5	102.1	103.3	105.0
住房租金	Rents	111.0	106.8	105.6	100.2
自有住房	Self-owned House	99.8	103.0	107.1	103.2
水、电、燃料	Water, Electricity and Fuels	101.7	103.8	101.8	101.4
#水	Water	109.3	123.6	111.4	100.0
电	Electricity	100.0	100.0	100.0	102.4
液化石油气	LPG	118.4	117.2	106.0	105.1
管道燃气	Gas	100.0	100.0	100.0	100.0

表9.5 主要年份商品零售价格指数 (以上年价格为100)
CLASSIFIED RETAIL PRICE INDEX IN MAIN YEARS(PRECEDING YEAR =100)

类 别	Types	2001	2010	2011	2012
商品零售价格指数	**Overall Retail Price Index**	**98.6**	**101.7**	**104.1**	**101.2**
食 品	Food	98.4	107.6	111.0	105.9
粮 食	Grain	100.1	112.0	113.3	103.0
淀粉及制品	Starch and Its Products	100.4	95.5	106.6	109.5
干豆类及豆制品	Dry Beans and Bean Products	111.3	108.7	114.7	109.5
油 脂	Oil or Fat	81.4	105.6	117.3	103.8
肉禽及其制品	Meat Poultry and Their Products	100.4	104.2	119.9	105.1
蛋	Eggs	110.7	106.1	113.5	98.2
水产品	Aquatic Products	90.1	116.1	113.7	105.8
菜	Vegetables	107.1	111.0	99.8	111.1
调味品	Flavoring	99.5	106.5	107.5	103.5
糖	Sugars	104.4	103.8	104.8	103.5
干鲜瓜果	Dried and Fresh Fruits	107.3	112.1	114.5	102.8
糕点饼干面包	Cakes, Biscuits and Bread	99.8	100.5	108.8	102.8
液体乳及乳制品	Milk and Its Products	99.8	102.3	108.2	103.8
在外用膳食品	Dining Out	100.7	105.6	107.9	107.8
其他食品	Other Food	99.5	105.0	107.4	108.1
饮料、烟酒	Beverages, Tobacco and Liquor	98.4	101.9	102.3	102.1
服装、鞋帽	Garments, Shoes and Hats	107.7	98.4	103.9	102.9
纺织品	Textiles	98.8	103.9	117.6	99.5
家用电器及音像器材	Household Appliances and Audio-video Appliances	95.0	92.4	96.0	96.2
文化办公用品	Cultural Office Articles	98.7	97.7	94.7	94.1
日用品	Daily Use Articles	99.0	100.3	106.2	102.1
体育娱乐用品	Sports and Recreation Goods	99.1	95.9	103.8	100.0
交通、通信用品	Transportation and Communication Goods	97.4	94.0	98.3	95.4
家 具	Furniture	90.4	101.1	104.2	103.3
化妆品	Cosmetics	100.7	101.0	104.8	101.1
金银珠宝	Jewelry	87.2	111.7	107.9	99.2
中西药品及医疗保健用品	Traditional Chinese and Western Medicines	98.7	99.8	99.4	100.0
书报杂志及电子出版物	Newspapers and Magazines and Electronic Publications	99.5	103.2	102.1	102.1
燃 料	Fuels	111.4	112.8	107.2	102.0
建筑材料及五金电料	Building Materials and Hardwares	101.8	103.3	104.2	102.6

表9.6 工业生产者出厂价格指数(2005～2012,以2000年价格为100)
PRODUCER PRICE INDEX FOR INDUSTRIAL PRODUCTS (2000＝100)

类 别	Types	2005	2006	2007	2008
工业生产者出厂价格指数	**Producer Price Index for Industrial Products**	**99.6**	**100.2**	**101.4**	**103.6**
按轻重工业分	**Grouped by Light or Heavy Industries**				
轻工业	Light Industry	95.6	94.5	94.5	93.6
以农产品为原料	Using Farm Products as Raw Materials	103.3	103.9	107.1	111.0
以非农产品为原料	Using Non-farm Products as Raw Materials	89.4	87.8	87.0	85.2
重工业	Heavy Industry	102.2	104.7	107.1	112.7
采 掘	Mining and Guarrying	168.0	192.7	195.6	246.1
原 料	Raw Material	129.7	140.3	145.9	161.5
加 工	Manufacturing	92.8	93.1	94.7	97.4
按用途分	**Grouped by Use**				
生产资料	Means of Production	104.2	105.5	107.0	109.7
生活资料	Consumer Goods	90.5	89.5	89.7	90.9
#食 品	Food	107.4	107.9	113.1	119.1
衣 着	Clothing	103.0	103.4	105.2	107.5
一般日用品	Non-Durable Consumer Goods	95.6	96.5	97.5	99.6
耐用消费品	Durable Consumer Goods	78.4	74.8	71.5	69.5

表9.6 续表 continued

类 别	Types	2009	2010	2011	2012
工业生产者出厂价格指数	**Producer Price Index for Industrial Products**	**97.2**	**99.4**	**102.3**	**100.7**
按轻重工业分	**Grouped by Light or Heavy Industries**				
轻工业	Light Industry	88.7	86.1	89.5	90.1
以农产品为原料	Using Farm Products as Raw Materials	112.2	115.1	120.4	122.6
以非农产品为原料	Using Non-farm Products as Raw Materials	79.3	75.8	78.3	78.1
重工业	Heavy Industry	104.7	111.9	114.8	112.4
采 掘	Mining and Guarrying	203.0	237.3	272.9	273.2
原 料	Raw Material	148.3	173.2	191.0	189.3
加 工	Manufacturing	91.1	93.7	94.3	92.0
按用途分	**Grouped by Use**				
生产资料	Means of Production	101.0	103.7	106.6	104.6
生活资料	Consumer Goods	91.4	92.0	94.7	94.2
#食 品	Food	121.5	126.8	133.8	138.2
衣 着	Clothing	107.8	108.4	110.5	110.1
一般日用品	Non-Durable Consumer Goods	101.5	103.2	108.5	109.5
耐用消费品	Durable Consumer Goods	68.5	66.9	67.0	64.5

表9.7 工业生产者出厂价格指数（2005～2012，以2000年价格为100）（按国民经济行业分）
PRODUCER PRICE INDEX FOR INDUSTRIAL PRODUCTS(GROUPED BY NATIONAL INDUSTRIES, 2000 = 100)

类别	Types	2005	2006	2007	2008
工业生产者出厂价格指数	**Producer Price Index for Industrial Products**	**99.6**	**100.2**	**101.4**	**103.6**
按国民经济行业分	**Grouped by National Economy Industries**				
石油和天然气开采业	Petroleum and Natural Gas Exploiting	168.0	192.7	195.6	246.1
农副食品加工业	Farm and Sideline Products Processing	125.7	126.1	152.1	183.6
食品制造业	Food Manufacturing	103.1	104.2	107.0	114.3
酒、饮料和精制茶制造业	Wine, Beverage and Refined Tea Manufacturing	101.0	102.8	103.2	103.9
烟草制品业	Tabacco Manufacture	126.9	128.3	129.5	129.5
纺织业	Textile	99.8	100.1	100.8	101.5
纺织服装、服饰业	Textile and Garment, Apparel Industry	102.8	103.0	105.4	107.8
皮革、毛皮、羽毛及其制品和制鞋业	Leather, Fur, Feather and Its Products and Shoemaking Industry	100.4	101.4	101.6	101.9
木材加工和木、竹、藤、棕、草制品业	Timber Processing and Timber, Bamboo, Rattan, Coir and Straw Products Manufacturing	90.8	92.3	96.5	100.9
家具制造业	Furniture Manufacturing	97.0	97.6	98.6	98.7
造纸和纸制品业	Paper-making and Paper Products Manufacturing	86.4	86.1	86.3	89.6
印刷和记录媒介复制业	Printing and Record Duplicating Industry	93.8	91.2	89.0	91.0
文教、工美、体育和娱乐用品制造业	Stationary, Education ,Industrial Art, Sport and Entertainment Products Manufacturing	100.6	100.2	100.5	100.8
石油加工、炼焦和核燃料加工业	Oil Processing, Coking and Nuclear Fual Processing	166.3	188.6	197.8	242.1
化学原料和化学制品制造业	Raw Chemical Materials and Chemical Products Manufacturing	124.6	129.0	134.2	140.8
医药制造业	Medicine Manufacturing	86.9	85.8	88.5	93.5
化学纤维制造业	Chemical Fiber Manufacturing	112.9	111.9	113.8	114.3
橡胶和塑料制品业	Rubber and Plastic Products Manufacturing	98.7	100.8	101.7	101.8
非金属矿物制品业	Nonmetal Mineral Products	99.2	96.1	97.9	103.5
黑色金属冶炼和压延加工业	Smelting and Pressing of Ferrous Metals	156.8	152.3	165.6	188.9
有色金属冶炼和压延加工业	Smelting and Pressing of Nonferrous Metals	132.0	191.4	204.2	188.3
金属制品业	Metal Products Manufacturing	109.9	114.2	122.9	125.2
通用设备制造业	General Equipment Manufacturing	94.9	95.6	96.1	97.6
专用设备制造业	Special Purpose Equipment Manufacturing	93.6	92.4	92.1	93.1
汽车制造业	Automotive Industry				
铁路、船舶、航空航天和其他运输设备制造业	Railroads, Ships, Aerospace and other Transportation Equipment Manufacturing Industry				
电气机械和器材制造业	Electric Machinery Equipments and Manufacturing	87.9	93.0	95.1	96.4
计算机、通信和其他电子设备制造业	Computers, Cmmunications and Oher Electronic Equipment Manufacturing Industry	71.5	68.6	66.0	62.4
仪器仪表制造业	Instruments and Meters Manufacturing	85.6	83.9	83.2	83.3
其他制造业	Other manufacturing	102.7	111.6	113.8	126.5
废弃资源综合利用业	Comprehensive Utilization of Waste Resources	121.8	110.5	120.6	160.6
金属制品、机械和设备修理业	Metal Products, Machinery and Equipment Repair				
电力、热力生产和供应业	Production and Supply of Electricity and Thermal Power	102.2	103.2	103.9	106.0
燃气生产和供应业	Production and Supply of Gas	113.8	121.5	126.1	132.2
水的生产和供应业	Production and Supply of Water	117.8	117.9	117.9	119.4

注：废弃资源和废旧材料回收加工业以2002年价格为100。
Note: The price index of Waste Resources and Materials Recycling and Processing was 100 in 2002.

表9.7 续表 continued

类别	Types	2009	2010	2011	2012
工业生产者出厂价格指数	**Producer Price Index for Industrial Products**	**97.2**	**99.4**	**102.3**	**100.7**
按国民经济行业分	**Grouped by National Economy Industries**				
石油和天然气开采业	Petroleum and Natural Gas Exploiting	203.0	237.3	272.9	273.2
农副食品加工业	Farm and Sideline Products Processing	160.3	171.4	205.0	213.2
食品制造业	Food Manufacturing	119.2	124.9	133.3	138.2
酒、饮料和精制茶制造业	Wine, Beverage and Refined Tea Manufacturing	105.1	109.7	113.2	119.2
烟草制品业	Tabacco Manufacture	136.2	141.2	141.2	145.4
纺织业	Textile	101.9	104.1	108.6	106.8
纺织服装、服饰业	Textile and Garment, Apparel Industry	108.6	109.6	112.2	111.5
皮革、毛皮、羽毛及其制品和制鞋业	Leather, Fur, Feather and Its Products and Shoemaking Industry	100.9	100.9	101.0	100.4
木材加工和木、竹、藤、棕、草制品业	Timber Processing and Timber, Bamboo, Rattan, Coir and Straw Products Manufacturing	104.4	104.2	110.7	114.6
家具制造业	Furniture Manufacturing	97.1	90.4	92.9	93.2
造纸和纸制品业	Paper-making and Paper Products Manufacturing	94.7	95.2	100.0	101.1
印刷和记录媒介复制业	Printing and Record Duplicating Industry	90.8	90.6	91.9	91.3
文教、工美、体育和娱乐用品制造业	Stationary, Education ,Industrial Art, Sport and Entertainment Products Manufacturing	100.3	101.7	108.8	111.8
石油加工、炼焦和核燃料加工业	Oil Processing, Coking and Nuclear Fual Processing	230.2	279.0	325.6	333.1
化学原料和化学制品制造业	Raw Chemical Materials and Chemical Products Manufacturing	122.5	143.6	159.3	154.2
医药制造业	Medicine Manufacturing	94.2	94.5	97.4	99.2
化学纤维制造业	Chemical Fiber Manufacturing	100.8	116.6	132.5	120.8
橡胶和塑料制品业	Rubber and Plastic Products Manufacturing	103.9	105.5	113.5	113.4
非金属矿物制品业	Nonmetal Mineral Products	101.3	103.9	112.2	107.0
黑色金属冶炼和压延加工业	Smelting and Pressing of Ferrous Metals	150.4	173.1	190.6	167.7
有色金属冶炼和压延加工业	Smelting and Pressing of Nonferrous Metals	156.7	200.3	225.9	205.6
金属制品业	Metal Products Manufacturing	119.1	127.8	131.9	130.1
通用设备制造业	General Equipment Manufacturing	96.2	95.7	94.6	94.0
专用设备制造业	Special Purpose Equipment Manufacturing	94.9	94.6	95.1	95.7
汽车制造业*	Automotive Industry				96.3
铁路、船舶、航空航天和其他运输设备制造业*	Railroads, Ships, Aerospace and other Transportation Equipment Manufacturing Industry				98.5
电气机械和器材制造业	Electric Machinery Equipments and Manufacturing	93.1	93.9	94.7	92.9
计算机、通信和其他电子设备制造业	Computers, Cmmunications and Oher Electronic Equipment Manufacturing Industry	55.2	50.5	49.5	49.2
仪器仪表制造业	Instruments and Meters Manufacturing	81.6	81.3	82.4	81.4
其他制造业	Other manufacturing	126.2	141.5	164.6	165.4
废弃资源综合利用业	Comprehensive Utilization of Waste Resources	120.5	136.2	167.8	145.3
金属制品、机械和设备修理业*	Metal Products, Machinery and Equipment Repair				97.3
电力、热力生产和供应业	Production and Supply of Electricity and Thermal Power	109.9	111.7	112.7	115.4
燃气生产和供应业	Production and Supply of Gas	145.6	151.7	165.4	160.4
水的生产和供应业	Production and Supply of Water	144.4	162.7	179.1	180.5

注：＊为以2011年价格为100。
Note: The price index symbled "＊" was 100 in 2011.

表9.8 工业生产者出厂价格指数(2005~2012,以上年价格为100) PRODUCER PRICE INDEX FOR INDUSTRIAL PRODUCTS(PRECEDING YEAR =100)

类别	Types	2005	2006	2007	2008
工业生产者出厂价格指数	**Producer Price Index for Industrial Products**	**101.7**	**100.6**	**101.2**	**102.2**
按轻重工业分	**Grouped by Light or Heavy Industries**				
轻工业	Light Industry	100.6	98.8	100.0	99.1
以农产品为原料	Using Farm Products as Raw Materials	100.4	100.6	103.1	103.6
以非农产品为原料	Using Non-farm Products as Raw Materials	100.7	98.2	99.1	97.9
重工业	Heavy Industry	102.3	102.4	102.3	105.2
采　掘	Mining and Guarrying	124.5	114.7	101.5	125.8
原　料	Raw Material	109.7	108.2	104.0	110.7
加　工	Manufacturing	99.9	100.3	101.7	102.8
按用途分	**Grouped by Use**				
生产资料	Means of Production	103.2	101.2	101.4	102.5
生活资料	Consumer Goods	98.7	98.9	100.2	101.3
#食　品	Food	100.6	100.5	104.8	105.3
衣　着	Clothing	101.4	100.4	101.7	102.2
一般日用品	Non-Durable Consumer Goods	100.7	100.9	101.0	102.2
耐用消费品	Durable Consumer Goods	95.7	95.4	95.6	97.2

表9.8 续表 continued

类别	Types	2009	2010	2011	2012
工业生产者出厂价格指数	**Producer Price Index for Industrial Products**	**93.8**	**102.3**	**102.9**	**98.4**
按轻重工业分	**Grouped by Light or Heavy Industries**				
轻工业	Light Industry	94.8	97.1	103.9	100.7
以农产品为原料	Using Farm Products as Raw Materials	101.1	102.6	104.6	101.8
以非农产品为原料	Using Non-farm Products as Raw Materials	93.1	95.6	103.3	99.8
重工业	Heavy Industry	92.9	106.9	102.6	97.9
采　掘	Mining and Guarrying	82.5	116.9	115.0	100.1
原　料	Raw Material	91.8	116.8	110.3	99.1
加　工	Manufacturing	93.5	102.9	100.6	97.6
按用途分	**Grouped by Use**				
生产资料	Means of Production	92.1	102.7	102.8	98.1
生活资料	Consumer Goods	100.6	100.7	102.9	99.5
#食　品	Food	102.0	104.4	105.5	103.3
衣　着	Clothing	100.3	100.6	101.9	99.6
一般日用品	Non-Durable Consumer Goods	101.9	101.7	105.1	100.9
耐用消费品	Durable Consumer Goods	98.5	97.6	100.2	96.2

表9.9 工业生产者出厂价格指数(2005～2012,以上年价格为100)(按国民经济行业分)
PRODUCER PRICE INDEX FOR INDUSTRIAL PRODUCTS(GROUPED BY NATIONAL INDUSTRIES, PRECEDING YEAR = 100)

类别	Types	2005	2006	2007	2008
工业生产者出厂价格指数	**Producer Ex-factory Price Index**	**101.7**	**100.6**	**101.2**	**102.2**
按国民经济行业分	**Grouped by National Economy Industries**				
石油和天然气开采业	Petroleum and Natural Gas Exploiting	124.5	114.7	101.5	125.8
农副食品加工业	Farm and Sideline Products Processing	101.2	100.3	120.6	120.7
食品制造业	Food Manufacturing	101.1	101.1	102.7	106.8
酒、饮料和精制茶制造业	Wine, Beverage and Refined Tea Manufacturing	100.7	101.8	100.4	100.7
烟草制品业	Tabacco Manufacture	102.4	101.1	100.9	100.0
纺织业	Textile	100.4	100.3	100.7	100.7
纺织服装、服饰业	Textile and Garment, Apparel Industry	101.1	100.2	102.3	102.3
皮革、毛皮、羽毛及其制品和制鞋业	Leather, Fur, Feather and Its Products and Shoemaking Industry	100.7	101.0	100.2	100.3
木材加工和木、竹、藤、棕、草制品业	Timber Processing and Timber, Bamboo, Rattan, Coir and Straw Products Manufacturing	101.4	101.7	104.6	104.6
家具制造业	Furniture Manufacturing	101.1	100.6	101.0	100.1
造纸和纸制品业	Paper-making and Paper Products Manufacturing	98.5	99.6	100.2	103.8
印刷和记录媒介复制业	Printing and Record Duplicating Industry	100.0	97.2	97.6	102.2
文教、工美、体育和娱乐用品制造业	Stationary, Education ,Industrial Art, Sport and Entertainment Products Manufacturing	101.1	99.6	100.3	100.3
石油加工、炼焦和核燃料加工业	Oil Processing, Coking and Nuclear Fual Processing	120.1	113.4	104.9	122.4
化学原料和化学制品制造业	Raw Chemical Materials and Chemical Products Manufacturing	110.1	103.5	104.0	104.9
医药制造业	Medicine Manufacturing	99.4	98.7	103.1	105.6
化学纤维制造业	Chemical Fiber Manufacturing	107.6	99.1	101.7	100.4
橡胶和塑料制品业	Rubber and Plastic Products Manufacturing	102.0	102.1	100.9	100.1
非金属矿物制品业	Nonmetal Mineral Products	95.6	96.9	101.9	105.7
黑色金属冶炼和压延加工业	Smelting and Pressing of Ferrous Metals	111.0	97.1	108.7	114.1
有色金属冶炼和压延加工业	Smelting and Pressing of Nonferrous Metals	113.7	145.0	106.7	92.2
金属制品业	Metal Products Manufacturing	104.8	103.9	107.6	101.9
通用设备制造业	General Equipment Manufacturing	101.8	100.7	100.5	101.6
专用设备制造业	Special Purpose Equipment Manufacturing	99.0	98.7	99.7	101.1
汽车制造业	Automotive Industry				
铁路、船舶、航空航天和其他运输设备制造业	Railroads, Ships, Aerospace and other Transportation Equipment Manufacturing Industry				
电气机械和器材制造业	Electric Machinery Equipments and Manufacturing	101.8	105.8	102.3	101.4
计算机、通信和其他电子设备制造业	Computers, Cmmunications and Oher Electronic Equipment Manufacturing Industry	94.8	95.9	96.2	94.5
仪器仪表制造业	Instruments and Meters Manufacturing	98.1	98.0	99.2	100.1
其他制造业	Other manufacturing	102.4	108.7	102.0	111.2
废弃资源综合利用业	Comprehensive Utilization of Waste Resources	101.4	90.7	109.1	133.2
金属制品、机械和设备修理业	Metal Products, Machinery and Equipment Repair				
电力、热力生产和供应业	Production and Supply of Electricity and Thermal Power	101.3	101.0	100.7	102.0
燃气生产和供应业	Production and Supply of Gas	100.2	106.8	103.8	104.8
水的生产和供应业	Production and Supply of Water	100.0	100.1	100.0	101.3

表9.9 续表 continued

类　别	Types	2009	2010	2011	2012
工业生产者出厂价格指数	**Producer Price Index for Industrial Products**	**93.8**	**102.3**	**102.9**	**98.4**
按国民经济行业分	**Grouped by National Economy Industries**				
石油和天然气开采业	Petroleum and Natural Gas Exploiting	82.5	116.9	115.0	100.1
农副食品加工业	Farm and Sideline Products Processing	87.3	106.9	119.6	104.0
食品制造业	Food Manufacturing	104.3	104.8	106.7	103.7
酒、饮料和精制茶制造业	Wine, Beverage and Refined Tea Manufacturing	101.2	104.4	103.2	105.3
烟草制品业	Tabacco Manufacture	105.2	103.7	100.0	103.0
纺织业	Textile	100.4	102.2	104.3	98.3
纺织服装、服饰业	Textile and Garment, Apparel Industry	100.7	100.9	102.4	99.4
皮革、毛皮、羽毛及其制品和制鞋业	Leather, Fur, Feather and Its Products and Shoemaking Industry	99.0	100.0	100.1	99.4
木材加工和木、竹、藤、棕、草制品业	Timber Processing and Timber, Bamboo, Rattan, Coir and Straw Products Manufacturing	103.5	99.8	106.2	103.5
家具制造业	Furniture Manufacturing	98.4	93.1	102.8	100.3
造纸和纸制品业	Paper-making and Paper Products Manufacturing	105.7	100.5	105.0	101.1
印刷和记录媒介复制业	Printing and Record Duplicating Industry	99.8	99.8	101.4	99.3
文教、工美、体育和娱乐用品制造业	Stationary, Education ,Industrial Art, Sport and Entertainment Products Manufacturing	99.5	101.4	107.0	102.8
石油加工、炼焦和核燃料加工业	Oil Processing, Coking and Nuclear Fual Processing	95.1	121.2	116.7	102.3
化学原料和化学制品制造业	Raw Chemical Materials and Chemical Products Manufacturing	87.0	117.2	110.9	96.8
医药制造业	Medicine Manufacturing	100.8	100.3	103.1	101.8
化学纤维制造业	Chemical Fiber Manufacturing	88.2	115.7	113.6	91.2
橡胶和塑料制品业	Rubber and Plastic Products Manufacturing	102.1	101.5	107.6	99.9
非金属矿物制品业	Nonmetal Mineral Products	97.9	102.6	108.0	95.4
黑色金属冶炼和压延加工业	Smelting and Pressing of Ferrous Metals	79.6	115.1	110.1	88.0
有色金属冶炼和压延加工业	Smelting and Pressing of Nonferrous Metals	83.2	127.8	112.8	91.0
金属制品业	Metal Products Manufacturing	95.1	107.3	103.2	98.6
通用设备制造业	General Equipment Manufacturing	98.6	99.5	98.9	99.4
专用设备制造业	Special Purpose Equipment Manufacturing	101.9	99.7	100.5	100.6
汽车制造业	Automotive Industry				96.3
铁路、船舶、航空航天和其他运输设备制造业	Railroads, Ships, Aerospace and other Transportation Equipment Manufacturing Industry				98.5
电气机械和器材制造业	Electric Machinery Equipments and Manufacturing	96.6	100.9	100.8	98.1
计算机、通信和其他电子设备制造业	Computers, Cmmunications and Other Electronic Equipment Manufacturing Industry	88.4	91.5	98.1	99.4
仪器仪表制造业	Instruments and Meters Manufacturing	98.0	99.6	101.4	98.8
其他制造业	Other manufacturing	99.8	112.1	116.3	100.5
废弃资源综合利用业	Comprehensive Utilization of Waste Resources	75.0	113.0	123.2	86.6
金属制品、机械和设备修理业	Metal Products, Machinery and Equipment Repair				97.3
电力、热力生产和供应业	Production and Supply of Electricity and Thermal Power	103.7	101.6	100.9	102.4
燃气生产和供应业	Production and Supply of Gas	110.1	104.2	109.0	97.0
水的生产和供应业	Production and Supply of Water	120.9	112.7	110.1	100.8

表9.10　工业生产者购进价格指数（2005～2012，以2000年价格为100）
PRODUCER PURCHASING PRCIE INDEX（2000＝100）

类　别	Types	2005	2006	2007	2008
工业生产者购进价格指数	**Producer Purchasing Price Index**	**127.5**	**133.6**	**139.1**	**153.4**
燃料、动力类	Fuels and Power	169.3	187.8	195.9	265.6
黑色金属材料类	Ferrous Metals	165.1	153.0	163.1	190.8
#钢　材	Rolled-steel	142.4	136.6	142.6	162.7
有色金属材料类	Nonferrous Metals	122.2	170.0	182.2	175.6
化工原料类	Chemical Raw Materials	114.2	117.9	124.0	131.3
木材及纸浆类	Wood and Paper Pulps	94.2	94.5	96.4	98.9
建筑材料类及非金属矿类	Building Materials and Nonmetal Minerals	103.0	102.8	105.6	115.1
其他工业原材料及半成品类	Other Industrial Raw and Processed Materials	99.7	103.0	105.3	107.7
农副产品类	Farm and Sideline Products	116.8	122.8	131.0	141.0
纺织原料类	Textile Raw Material	99.7	100.2	102.0	105.3

表9.10　续表　continued

类　别	Types	2009	2010	2011	2012
工业生产者购进价格指数	**Producer Purchasing Price Index**	**137.8**	**153.2**	**164.7**	**156.0**
燃料、动力类	Fuels and Power	201.9	260.5	307.1	303.7
黑色金属材料类	Ferrous Metals	165.4	188.4	208.9	178.0
#钢　材	Rolled-steel	142.9	150.0	158.9	148.7
有色金属材料类	Nonferrous Metals	151.5	196.0	223.0	202.9
化工原料类	Chemical Raw Materials	114.9	133.3	147.3	142.0
木材及纸浆类	Wood and Paper Pulps	95.2	98.4	101.9	100.1
建筑材料类及非金属矿类	Building Materials and Nonmetal Minerals	113.5	119.6	138.7	130.0
其他工业原材料及半成品类	Other Industrial Raw and Processed Materials	104.1	106.5	107.5	104.4
农副产品类	Farm and Sideline Products	141.0	152.6	170.5	174.8
纺织原料类	Textile Raw Material	104.5	111.2	123.0	121.9

表9.11 工业生产者购进价格指数 (2005～2012,以上年价格为100)
PRODUCER PURCHASING PRICE INDEX(PRECEDING YEAR =100)

类别	Types	2005	2006	2007	2008
工业生产者购进价格指数	**Producer Purchasing Price Index**	**106.8**	**104.8**	**104.1**	**110.3**
燃料、动力类	Fuels and Power	124.1	110.9	104.3	135.6
黑色金属材料类	Ferrous Metals	103.2	92.7	106.6	117.0
#钢　材	Rolled-steel	109.9	95.9	104.4	114.1
有色金属材料类	Nonferrous Metals	112.2	139.1	107.2	96.4
化工原料类	Chemical Raw Materials	111.1	103.2	105.2	105.9
木材及纸浆类	Wood and Paper Pulps	101.5	100.3	102.0	102.6
建筑材料类及非金属矿类	Building Materials and Nonmetal Minerals	88.9	99.8	102.7	109.0
其他工业原材料及半成品类	Other Industrial Raw and Processed Materials	99.3	103.3	102.2	102.3
农副产品类	Farm and Sideline Products	98.1	105.1	106.7	107.6
纺织原料类	Textile Raw Material	101.8	100.5	101.8	103.2

表9.11 续表 continued

类别	Types	2009	2010	2011	2012
工业生产者购进价格指数	**Producer Purchasing Price Index**	**89.8**	**111.2**	**107.5**	**94.7**
燃料、动力类	Fuels and Power	76.0	129.0	117.9	98.9
黑色金属材料类	Ferrous Metals	86.7	113.9	110.9	85.2
#钢　材	Rolled-steel	87.8	105.0	105.9	93.6
有色金属材料类	Nonferrous Metals	86.3	129.4	113.8	91.0
化工原料类	Chemical Raw Materials	87.5	116.0	110.5	96.4
木材及纸浆类	Wood and Paper Pulps	96.3	103.4	103.6	98.2
建筑材料类及非金属矿类	Building Materials and Nonmetal Minerals	98.6	105.4	116.0	93.7
其他工业原材料及半成品类	Other Industrial Raw and Processed Materials	96.7	102.3	100.9	97.1
农副产品类	Farm and Sideline Products	100.0	108.2	111.7	102.5
纺织原料类	Textile Raw Material	99.2	106.4	110.6	99.1

表9.12 固定资产投资价格指数(2001～2012,以2000年价格为100)
PRICE INDEX OF INVESTMENT IN FIXED ASSETS (2000 = 100)

年 份 Year	固定资产投资价格指数 Price Index of Fixed Asset Investment	建筑安装工程 Building Project Price Index	#人工费 Manpower Cost Price Index	#材料费 Material Price Index	#机械使用费 Machinery Used Price Index	设备、工器具购置 Equipment and Instrument Price Index	其他费用投资 Other Investment Price Index
2001	100.7	102.4	109.0	101.2	99.7	96.5	101.3
2002	101.0	104.3	120.4	101.0	102.5	93.3	101.6
2003	103.4	109.7	125.8	106.6	107.5	91.0	103.0
2004	110.3	121.3	133.0	119.4	116.9	90.5	107.8
2005	111.2	122.4	139.4	118.7	123.4	88.1	111.2
2006	111.3	122.5	146.1	117.0	127.0	85.7	113.4
2007	115.2	128.1	156.8	122.0	130.0	85.2	118.0
2008	124.3	143.6	170.6	139.0	136.4	84.8	124.4
2009	120.6	136.1	181.2	126.6	138.9	81.5	127.1
2010	125.2	144.4	193.7	134.8	142.2	80.4	130.2
2011	133.3	159.7	213.5	150.4	148.0	80.2	133.7
2012	132.5	157.6	230.8	144.1	152.9	79.1	135.8

表9.13 固定资产投资价格指数(1995～2012,以上年价格为100)
PRICE INDEX OF INVESTMENT IN FIXED ASSETS(PRECEDING YEAR = 100)

年 份 Year	固定资产投资价格指数 Price Index of Fixed Asset Investment	建筑安装工程 Building Project Price Index	#人工费 Manpower Cost Price Index	#材料费 Material Price Index	#机械使用费 Machinery Used Price Index	设备、工器具购置 Equipment and Instrument Price Index	其他费用投资 Other Investment Price Index
1995	103.1	101.9	108.7	99.5		104.8	107.0
1996	107.0	108.9	114.2	97.4	118.5	101.7	107.7
1997	100.5	101.4	109.0	98.7	104.5	97.8	100.8
1998	98.4	98.9	96.0	98.3	99.7	96.1	99.6
1999	98.1	97.8	103.4	96.1	100.5	96.9	99.8
2000	100.0	101.5	100.6	101.8	99.8	97.0	99.9
2001	100.7	102.4	109.0	101.2	99.7	96.5	101.3
2002	100.3	101.9	110.5	99.8	102.8	96.7	100.3
2003	102.4	105.2	104.5	105.5	104.9	97.5	101.4
2004	106.7	110.6	105.7	112.0	108.7	99.4	104.7
2005	100.8	100.9	104.8	99.4	105.6	97.4	103.2
2006	100.1	100.1	104.8	98.6	102.9	97.3	102.0
2007	103.5	104.6	107.3	104.3	102.4	99.4	104.1
2008	107.9	112.1	108.8	113.9	104.9	99.5	105.4
2009	97.0	94.8	106.2	91.1	101.8	96.1	102.2
2010	103.8	106.1	106.9	106.5	102.4	98.6	102.4
2011	106.5	110.6	110.2	111.6	104.1	99.7	102.7
2012	99.4	98.7	108.1	95.8	103.3	98.6	101.6

表9.14 房屋租赁和土地交易价格指数 (2005～2012,以2000年价格为100)
PRICE INDEX OF HOUSE AND RESIDENCE(2000 = 100)

类别	Types	2005	2006	2007	2008
房屋租赁价格指数	**Price Index of House and Residence Leasing**	**115.9**	**120.6**	**126.7**	**132.6**
#商品住宅	Commercial Residence	113.7	116.4	123.9	129.2
土地交易价格指数	**Price Index of Land Exchange**	**153.0**	**154.8**	**166.9**	**180.0**
#居住用地	Residential	170.6	169.7	177.2	189.5
工业用地	Workshops	88.3	90.8	103.4	110.9

表9.14 续表 continued

类别	Types	2009	2010	2011	2012
房屋租赁价格指数	**Price Index of House and Residence Leasing**	**133.4**	**139.3**	**148.6**	**157.2**
#商品住宅	Commercial Residence	129.6	135.9	145.0	153.4
土地交易价格指数	**Price Index of Land Exchange**	**184.0**	**218.7**	**255.9**	**267.4**
#居住用地	Residential	195.0	246.5	279.5	289.8
工业用地	Workshops	112.8	129.8	154.6	161.4

注：按照国家统计局新的调查制度规定，从2008年开始，土地交易价格指数中工业仓储用地改为"工业用地"；从2011年开始，取消房屋租赁价格指数中非住宅租赁价格指数(下表同)。

Note: According to the new investigation system regulation of NBS, since year of 2008, Land for Workshops and Warehouses had been changed into Land for Workshops in the price index of land exchange. Since 2011, price indices of non residential leasing in the Price Index of Real Estate Leasing are canceled(same as follows).

表9.15 房屋租赁和土地交易价格指数（2005～2012，以上年价格为100）
PRICE INDEX OF HOUSE AND RESIDENCE(Preceding Year = 100)

类别	Types	2005	2006	2007	2008
房屋租赁价格指数	**Price Index of House and Residence Leasing**	**103.6**	**104.0**	**105.1**	**104.6**
#商品住宅	Commercial Residence	103.3	102.3	106.5	104.2
土地交易价格指数	**Price Index of Land Exchange**	**106.9**	**101.2**	**107.8**	**107.9**
#居住用地	Residential	105.4	99.5	104.4	106.9
工业用地	Workshops	103.7	102.9	113.8	107.3

表9.15 续表 continued

类别	Types	2009	2010	2011	2012
房屋租赁价格指数	**Price Index of House and Residence Leasing**	**100.6**	**104.4**	**106.7**	**105.8**
#商品住宅	Commercial Residence	100.3	104.9	106.7	105.8
土地交易价格指数	**Price Index of Land Exchange**	**102.2**	**118.9**	**117.0**	**104.5**
#居住用地	Residential	102.9	126.4	113.4	103.7
工业用地	Workshops	101.7	115.1	119.1	104.4

注：从2011年开始分别取消办公楼和商业营业用房租赁价格指数，办公楼和商业营业用房物业管理价格指数。

Note: Since 2011, offices and Commercial and Business Housing had been abandoned in the price index of estate leasing.

上/海/统/计/年/鉴

主要统计指标解释

■ 居民消费价格指数

居民消费价格指数是度量一组代表性消费商品及服务项目价格水平随着时间而变动的相对数，反映居民家庭购买的消费品及服务价格水平的变动情况。它是宏观经济分析和决策、价格总水平监测和调控以及国民经济核算的重要指标。其按年度计算的变动率通常被用来作为反映通货膨胀或紧缩程度的指标。

现行的居民消费价格指数按用途分为八个大类，包括食品、烟酒、衣着、家庭设备用品及维修服务、医疗保健和个人用品、交通和通信、娱乐教育文化用品及服务、居住。

■ 商品零售价格指数

商品零售价格指数是反映一定时期内城乡商品零售价格变动趋势和程度的相对数。商品零售价格的变动直接影响城乡居民的生活支出和国家的财政收入，影响居民购买力和市场供需的平衡，影响消费与积累的比例关系。因此，该指数可以从一个侧面对上述经济活动进行观察和分析。

■ 工业生产者出厂价格指数

从2011年起工业品出厂价格改为工业生产者出厂价格指数，它是反映一定时期内全部工业产品出厂价格总水平的变动趋势和程度的相对数，包括工业企业售给本企业以外所有单位的各种产品和直接售给居民用于生活消费的产品。该指数可以观察出厂价格变动对工业总产值及增加值的影响。

■ 工业生产者购进价格指数

从2011年起原材料、燃料和动力购进价格改为工业生产者购进价格指数，它是反映工业企业作为生产投入，从物资交易市场和能源、原材料生产企业购买原材料、燃料和动力产品时，所支付的价格水平变动趋势和程度的统计指标，是扣除工业企业物质消耗成本中的价格变动影响的重要依据。

目前，上海编制的工业生产者购进价格指数所调查的产品包括燃料动力、黑色金属、有色金属、化工、建材等九大类的近960种产品。

■ 固定资产投资价格指数

固定资产投资价格指数是反映一定时期内固定资产投资品及项目的价格变动趋势和程度的相对数。固定资产投资额是由建筑安装工程投资完成额、设备工器具购置投资完成额和其他费用投资完成额三部分组成的。编制固定资产投资价格指数应首先分别编制上述三部分投资的价格指数，然后采用加权算术平均法求出固定资产投资价格总指数。

该指数可以准确地反映固定资产投资中涉及的各类投资品和收费项目价格变动趋势和变动幅度，消除按现价计算的固定资产投资指标中的价格变动因素，真实地反映固定资产投资的规模、速度、结构和效益，为国家科学地制定、检查固定资产投资计划并提高宏观调控水平，为完善国民经济核算体系提供科学的、可靠的依据。

■ 房屋租赁价格指数

房屋租赁指以支付租金形式取得房屋使用权。房屋租赁价格指数是指房屋租赁价格总水平变动趋势和程度的相对数。

■ 土地交易价格指数

指房地产开发商或其他建设单位在进行开发之前，为取得土地使用权而实际支付的价格的变动趋势和程度的相对数。

SHANGHAI STATISTICAL YEARBOOK

EXPLANATORY NOTES TO MAJOR STATISTICAL INDICATORS

□ Consumer Price Index

The Consumer Price Index is an index that reflects the time-based change of prices of a group of representative consumption commodities and services. It is an important reference factor for macro-economic analysis and strategy, monitoring and adjustment of overall price level and the national economic budgeting. The year-on-year change of the index is often a norm reflecting the inflation or deflation.

The current CPI covers eight categories of goods and services: food; tobacco and liquor; garments; household facilities, articles and repair services; medical and health care and personal items; traffic and telecommunications; education, culture and recreation articles and services and residence.

□ Retail Price Index

Retail Price Indices reflect the trend and degree of change in retail prices of commodities during a given period. The change in retail prices of commodities directly affect the living expenditure of urban and rural residents, government revenue, purchasing power of residents and the equilibrium of market supply and demand, and the ratio of consumption to accumulation. Therefore, the retail price indices are useful to analyze the changes of the above economic activities.

□ Producer Ex-factory Price Index

Since 2011, Ex-factory Price Indices of Industrial Products have been changed into Producer Ex-factory Price Index. Producer Ex-factory Price Index reflects the trend and degree of changes in general ex-factory prices of all industrial products during a given period, including sales of industrial products by an industrial enterprise to all units outside the enterprise, as well as sales of consumer goods to residents. It can be used to analyze the impact of ex-factory prices on gross output value and value-added of the industrial sector.

□ Producer Purchasing Price Index

Since 2011 Indices of Purchasing Prices of Raw Materials, Fuels and Power have been changed into Producer Purchasing Price Index which reflects changes in the level and degree of prices paid by industrial enterprises when they purchase production input such as raw materials, fuels and power from the market or from other energy or raw materials producing enterprises. These indices provide important basis for measuring the material consumption of industrial enterprises after removing influence of price changes.

At present, close to 960 products in 9 categories, including fuels and power, ferrous metals, non-ferrous metals, chemicals, building materials, are covered in Shanghai for the survey to producer purchasing prices index.

□ Price Indices of Investment in Fixed Assets

Price Indices of Investment in Fixed Assets reflect the trend and degree of changes in prices of investment goods and projects in fixed assets during a given period. The investment in fixed assets consists of three components, namely the investment in construction and installation, the investment in purchases of equipment and instrument, and the investment in other items. Price indices of investment in fixed assets are calculated as the weighted arithmetic mean of the price indices of the three components of investment in fixed assets.

Removing the factor of price change in the aggregates of investment at current prices, this indicator shows the changes in the prices of commodities and fees involved in the investment of fixed assets, and can be used to observe the actual size, growth, structure, and efficiency of investment in fixed assets and provides reliable and scientific data for government planning, management, decision-making, and further improving the current national accounting system.

□ Price Indices of House and Residence Leasing

House and Residence leasing refer to the acquisition of the house and residence ownership by means of paying rent. The Price Indices of House and Residence Leasing are indicators of general trend and variation of the leasing price of house and residence.

□ Price Index of Land Exchange

Price Index of Land Exchange is an indicator of the general trend and variation of the paid price in order to obtain the ownership of the land by the real estate developer or other construction organizations before the development.

第十篇

CHAPTER 10

人民生活

LIVING STANDARDS

简要说明

一、本篇资料的主要内容

本篇资料反映上海市居民生活现状及变化情况,分为城市居民生活和农民居民生活两部分。

二、城市居民生活资料来源

城市居民生活状况的数据来源于国家统计局上海调查总队城镇住户抽样调查。调查内容主要包括家庭人口及其构成、家庭现金收支、主要商品购买数量及支出金额、劳动就业状况、居住状况和耐用消费品的拥有量等。

三、城镇住户调查方法

城镇住户调查的调查户的抽选工作分两步进行。第一步进行一次性的大样本调查;第二步从大样本调查中抽出一个小样本,作为经常性调查户,开展记帐工作。

大样本调查每三年进行一次,其目的主要为经常性调查提供抽样框和为经常性调查数据评估提供基础资料。在大样本调查中,采取分层、二阶段、与大小成比例(PPS 方法)的随机等距方法选取调查样本。即先按区(县)分层,在层内按照 PPS 方法随机等距抽选调查社区 / 居委会,在抽中社区 / 居委会内随机等距抽选调查住宅。对选出的大样本或一相样本开展调查,取得调查户家庭人口、就业人口、收入等辅助资料,然后,根据这些资料进行分组,从中按比例抽出一个小样本也称二相样本,作为经常性调查户。

在经常性调查中,首先向抽中的调查户每月发放帐本,由调查户采用日记帐方式对本家庭及每个成员的收支情况进行记录;再由专业的调查员每月在规定的时间将帐本回收并进行编码和审核;最后由国家统计局上海调查总队进行汇总得出人均可支配收入等数据资料。2003 年及之前,上海城市居民收支调查样本为 500 户;2004 年至 2012 年,调查样本增至 1000 户,分布于黄浦、徐汇、长宁、静安、普陀、闸北、虹口、杨浦、闵行、宝山、浦东等 11 个区。

四、农村居民生活资料来源

农村居民生活状况的数据来源于国家统计局上海调查总队的农村住户抽样调查。主要内容包括农村居民家庭生活基本情况、收入、生活消费支出、主要消费品消费量、耐用消费品拥有量等。

五、农村住户调查方法

农村居民收支调查是以农村常住户为调查对象,农村常住户指长期(半年以上)居住在行政村范围内的住户。户口不在本地而在本地居住半年及以上的住户也包括在本地农村常住户范围内;有本地户口,但举家外出谋生半年以上的住户,无论是否保留承包耕地都不包括在本地农村住户范围内。按国家统计局农村住户调查方案,采用抽样调查方法在全市郊区县抽取 1200 户农村居民家庭作为调查样本,分布于浦东、闵行、宝山、嘉定、金山、松江、青浦、奉贤、崇明 9 个区县的 120 个行政村。

为保证农村住户调查资料的准确性，农村住户调查在95%的概率把握程度下要求抽样误差不得超过±3%，本篇资料为2011年样本轮换后的样本数据。调查数据采用农村居民记账与一次性调查相结合的方法取得，调查户按照国家统计局上海调查总队统一编制的帐本和要求记账，现金收支帐、实物收支帐发生一笔记一笔，由区县调查员每月收取调查户的帐本，录入计算机，通过乡镇、区县、总队多级审核确保调查数据真实可靠。

BRIEF INTRODUCTION

I. Main Contents

Data in this chapter reflect the people's living conditions in Shanghai, consisting of two parts, on the life of urban and rural households respectively.

II. Sources of Data on the Living Conditions of Urban Residents

Data on the living conditions of urban residents come from the data collected through a sample survey on the urban households conducted by the Survey Office of the National Bureau of Statistics in Shanghai. The main contents of the survey include persons in the household and the household composition; cash income and expenditure of the household; quantity of major commodities purchased and expenditure; the employment of household members; the housing conditions; and the possession of durable consumer goods.

III. Methodology for Urban Household Survey

The selection of sample households in urban areas is done by two steps: the first step is to have a one-off large sample survey; the second step is to select a small sample from the large sample to be used as regular sample households for diaries.

The large sample survey is conducted every three years; the objective is to provide sample frame for regular surveys and basic information for data evaluation of regular surveys. In the large sample survey, samples in sample districts and counties are selected by systematic sampling method schemes, such as two-phase sampling and stratifying method, two-stage method and probability proportional to size (PPS) method. Namely, stratification is done at district (county) level, and then PPS systematic sampling method is used to select sample communities/resident's committees, finally the same method is used to select dwellings from the selected districts/resident's committees. A survey will be conducted to the large samples or the first phase samples to collect relevant information on household population, persons employed, income and so on. Then grouping is made based on the information collected, small samples or the second phase samples are selected according to proportions, which are regular sample households.

In regular surveys, selected households receive account books each month and keep diaries to record income and expenditure of the family and its individual members. Professional inspectors will then collect, encode and audit the data at fixed time each month, deliver them to the Survey Office of the National Bureau of Statistics to calculate data such as the average disposable income per capita. Shanghai's sample included 500 households before 2003; it increased to 1,000 households between 2004 and 2012, covering 11 districts of Huangpu, Xuhui, Changning, Jing'an, Putuo, Zhabei, Hongkou, Yangpu, Minhang, Baoshan and Pudong.

IV. Sources of Data on the Living Conditions of Rural Residents

Data on the living conditions of rural residents come from data collected through the sample survey on rural households, which is organized by the Survey Office of the National Bureau of Statistics in Shanghai. The main contents of the survey include the basic living conditions of rural households, income, consumption expenditure, consumption of major consumer goods, and the possession of durable consumer goods.

V. Methodology for Rural Household Survey

Data on the survey of income and expenditure of rural residents cover long-term residents in rural areas. Long-term residents refer to people living within the administered villages for more than half a year. Households without local registered residence are included given they have lived in the area for more than half a year. Households leaving the area for more than half a year are not included, even if they hold local registered residence or have contracted land. According to the scheme of the survey on rural living conditions proposed by the National Bureau of Statistics, the sampling approach is used to select 1,200 rural households as samples from 120 villages through 9 districts and counties of Pudong, Minhang, Baoshan, Jiading, Jinshan, Songjiang, Qingpu, Fengxian, and Chongming.

To guarantee accuracy of the data on the living conditions of rural households, it is required that the sampling error should not exceed ±3%, with a confidence probability as 95%. Data in this chapter are samples after 2011 when sample data were rotated. A combination of diaries kept by rural households and the one-time survey is used for collecting data. The households are keeping diaries on unified requirements compiled by the Survey Office of the National Bureau of Statistics in Shanghai. Income and expenditure of cash and real goods are recorded case by case. Data are collected by inspectors from districts and counties and compiled into computers. Inspectors from townships, counties, districts and the headquarters office will audit the data to make them accurate and reliable.

表 10.1 主要年份城乡居民家庭人均收入及恩格尔系数
PER CAPITA ANNUAL INCOME AND ENGEL'S COEFFICIENT OF URBAN AND RURAL HOUSEHOLDS

年 份 Year	城市居民家庭人均可支配收入（元） Average per Capita Disposable Income of Urban Households	农村居民家庭人均可支配收入（元） Average per Capita Disposable Income of Rural Households	城市居民家庭恩格尔系数（%） Engel Coefficient of Urban Households	农村居民家庭恩格尔系数（%） Engel Coefficient of Rural Households
1980	637	401	56.0	51.7
1985	1 075	806	52.1	43.8
1990	2 183	1 665	56.5	46.4
1995	7 172	4 246	53.4	44.3
1996	8 159	4 846	50.7	42.8
1997	8 439	5 277	51.7	41.5
1998	8 773	5 407	50.6	42.2
1999	10 932	5 481	45.2	43.1
2000	11 718	5 565	44.5	44.0
2001	12 883	5 850	43.4	40.3
2002	13 250	6 212	39.4	35.2
2003	14 867	6 658	37.2	35.4
2004	16 683	7 337	36.4	34.6
2005	18 645	8 342	35.9	36.8
2006	20 668	9 213	35.6	37.8
2007	23 623	10 222	35.5	36.8
2008	26 675	11 385	36.6	40.9
2009	28 838	12 324	35.0	37.1
2010	31 838	13 746	33.5	37.2
2011	36 230	15 644	35.5	40.1
2012	40 188	17 401	36.8	40.0

表 10.2 储蓄存款年末余额(1997～2012)
SAVINGS DEPOSITS AT YEAR-END

年 份 Year	储蓄存款余额(亿元) Savings Deposits (100 million yuan)	其 中 of which		人均储蓄存款余额（元） Average Deposits (yuan)
		定期储蓄 Time Account	活期储蓄 Current Account	
1997	2 109.18	1 843.25	265.93	14 165
1998	2 372.94	2 017.16	355.78	15 540
1999	2 597.12	2 119.82	477.30	16 574
2000	2 627.07	2 084.21	542.86	16 331
2001	3 109.50	2 301.33	808.17	19 266
2002	4 915.54	3 603.05	1 312.49	30 249
2003	6 054.60	4 260.87	1 793.73	35 386
2004	6 960.99	4 904.93	2 056.06	39 956
2005	8 432.49	6 071.83	2 360.66	47 416
2006	9 480.28	6 701.97	2 778.31	52 223
2007	9 326.45	6 185.85	3 140.60	50 194
2008	12 083.66	8 555.64	3 528.02	63 987
2009	14 357.65	9 733.13	4 624.53	74 728
2010	16 249.29	10 853.11	5 396.19	70 918
2011	17 958.22	12 032.83	5 925.39	77 989
2012	20 247.24	13 603.13	6 644.11	85 057

注：本表数据由中国人民银行上海总部提供。2000 年起储蓄存款余额为中外资金融机构本外币储蓄存款余额。

Note: Data in this table are provided by Shanghai Headquarters of the People's Bank of China. Since 2000, the savings deposits refered to all deposits in foreign and domestic currrency of foreign and domestic funded financial institutions.

表10.3 城市居民家庭生活基本情况(1980～2012)
BASIC STATISTICS OF URBAN HOUSEHOLDS

年份 Year	调查户数 (户) Number of Households Surveyed (household)	平均每户家庭人口 (人) Average Number Persons per Household (person)	平均每户就业人口 (人) Average Number of Employees per Household (person)	平均每户就业面 (%) Percentage of Emplyment per Household (%)	平均每一就业者负担人数 (人) Persons Supported by Each Employee (person)	平均每人可支配收入 (元) Average per Capita Disposable Income (yuan)
1980	500	4.06	2.41	59.4	1.68	637
1981	500	4.06	2.47	60.8	1.64	637
1982	500	4.03	2.48	61.5	1.63	659
1983	500	4.00	2.52	63.0	1.59	686
1984	500	3.94	2.53	64.2	1.56	834
1985	500	3.72	2.27	61.0	1.64	1 075
1986	500	3.66	2.30	62.8	1.59	1 293
1987	500	3.55	2.20	62.0	1.61	1 437
1988	500	3.38	2.08	61.5	1.63	1 723
1989	500	3.27	2.00	61.2	1.64	1 976
1990	500	3.25	1.98	60.9	1.64	2 183
1991	500	3.18	1.91	60.1	1.66	2 486
1992	500	3.11	1.84	59.2	1.69	3 009
1993	500	3.03	1.77	58.4	1.71	4 277
1994	500	3.07	1.69	55.0	1.82	5 868
1995	500	3.11	1.65	53.1	1.88	7 172
1996	500	3.07	1.58	51.5	1.94	8 159
1997	500	3.08	1.59	51.6	1.94	8 439
1998	500	3.09	1.58	51.1	1.96	8 773
1999	500	3.08	1.73	56.2	1.78	10 932
2000	500	3.04	1.64	53.9	1.85	11 718
2001	500	3.00	1.55	51.7	1.94	12 883
2002	500	2.90	1.52	52.4	1.91	13 250
2003	500	2.99	1.55	51.8	1.93	14 867
2004	1 000	3.04	1.53	50.3	1.99	16 683
2005	1 000	3.01	1.55	51.5	1.94	18 645
2006	1 000	3.02	1.60	53.0	1.89	20 668
2007	1 000	3.01	1.64	54.5	1.84	23 623
2008	1 000	2.97	1.63	54.9	1.82	26 675
2009	1 000	2.93	1.60	54.6	1.83	28 838
2010	1 000	2.90	1.60	55.2	1.81	31 838
2011	1 000	2.90	1.58	54.5	1.84	36 230
2012	1 000	2.89	1.55	53.6	1.86	40 188

注：2002年起，人均可支配收入不包括出售财物收入和个人交纳的社会保障支出。 其他年份按原口径计算。

Note: Incomes from selling properties and social security expenditure are excluded from disposable income since 2002. Other years follow the original caliber.

表 10.3 续表 continued

年 份 Year	平均每人消费支出（元） Average per Capita Consumption Expenditures (yuan)	其 中 of which #服务性消费支出 Service Consumption Expenditures	可支配收入比上年增长（%）（按当年价格） Growth Rate of Disposable Income on Preceding Year (at Current Price) (%)	消费支出比上年增长（%）（按当年价格） Growth Rate of Consumption Expenditure on Preceding Year (at Current Price) (%)	恩格尔系数（%） Engel Coefficient (%)	城镇居民人均住房居住面积（平方米） Dwelling Area per Capita (sq. m)
1980	553	75	32.5	28.8	56.0	4.4
1981	585	79	平	5.7	56.8	4.5
1982	576	82	3.5	-1.5	58.9	4.7
1983	615	87	4.0	6.9	58.5	4.9
1984	726	101	21.6	18.0	56.5	5.0
1985	992	121	28.9	36.6	52.1	5.4
1986	1 170	136	20.3	18.0	52.7	6.0
1987	1 282	161	11.1	9.6	54.4	6.2
1988	1 648	171	19.9	28.6	52.7	6.3
1989	1 812	190	14.6	9.9	55.8	6.4
1990	1 937	233	10.5	6.9	56.5	6.6
1991	2 167	294	13.9	11.9	56.9	6.7
1992	2 509	365	21.1	15.8	55.9	6.9
1993	3 530	568	42.2	40.7	53.1	7.3
1994	4 669	732	37.2	32.3	53.5	7.5
1995	5 868	889	22.2	25.7	53.4	8.0
1996	6 763	1 205	13.8	15.3	50.7	8.7
1997	6 820	1 173	3.4	0.8	51.7	9.3
1998	6 866	1 344	4.0	0.7	50.6	9.7
1999	8 248	1 781	24.6	20.1	45.2	10.9
2000	8 868	2 154	7.2	7.5	44.5	11.8
2001	9 336	2 393	9.9	5.3	43.4	12.5
2002	10 464	3 033	11.5	11.4	39.4	13.1
2003	11 040	3 369	12.2	5.5	37.2	13.8
2004	12 631	4 084	12.2	14.4	36.4	14.6
2005	13 773	4 447	11.8	9.0	35.9	14.9
2006	14 762	4 841	10.8	7.2	35.6	15.2
2007	17 255	5 595	14.3	16.9	35.5	15.5
2008	19 398	6 287	12.9	12.4	36.6	15.9
2009	20 992	6 656	8.1	8.2	35.0	16.4
2010	23 200	6 955	10.4	10.5	33.5	16.7
2011	25 102	7 721	13.8	8.2	35.5	17.0
2012	26 253	7 955	10.9	4.6	36.8	17.3

注：平均每人可支配收入和平均每人消费支出增长按同口径计算的。

Note: Growth of per Capita Disposable Income and growth of per Capita Consumption Expenditures are calculated by the same caliber.

表 10.4　城市居民家庭生活基本情况(2012，按收入水平分组)
BASIC STATISTICS OF URBAN HOUSEHOLD INCOME AND EXPENDITURES (2012, GROUPED BY INCOME LEVEL)

指　标	Indicators	总平均 Total Average	低收入户 Low Income	中低收入户 Medium-low Income
调查户数(户)	Number of Households Surveyed (household)	1 000	200	200
平均每户家庭人口(人)	Average Number of Persons per Household (person)	2.89	3.09	2.90
平均每户就业人口(人)	Average Number of Employees per Household (person)	1.55	1.43	1.38
平均每户就业面(%)	Percentage of Employment per Household (%)	53.6	46.3	47.6
平均每一就业者负担人数(人)	Persons Supported by Each Employee (person)	1.86	2.16	2.10
可支配收入(元)	Average per Capita Disposable Income (yuan)	40 188	19 059	27 597
工资性收入	Salaries	26 752	12 162	16 235
经营净收入	Net Income from Household Business	2 267	601	798
财产性收入	Property Income	576	101	271
转移性收入	Transferred Income	10 593	6 195	10 293
#养老金或离退休金	Pensions and Retirement Pay	9 477	5 365	9 811
出售财物收入(元)	Income from Selling Properties(yuan)	412	1 291	
借贷收入(元)	Borrowings and other Credit Items(yuan)	5 682	2 308	1 823
#住房贷款	Morgage Loans	243	645	
提取储蓄存款	Drawings of Saving Deposits	5 351	1 635	1 768
消费支出(元)	Average Per Capita Consumption Expenditures (yuan)	26 253	15 095	18 232
#服务性消费支出	Service Consumption Expenditure	7 955	4 385	5 216
购房与建房支出(元)	Buying and Building House Expenditure (yuan)	1 288	1 581	
转移性支出(元)	Transferred Expenditure (yuan)	3 784	982	1 915
社会保障支出(元)	Social Security Expenditure (yuan)	3 711	1 828	2 454
借贷支出(元)	Lendings and other Debit Items (yuan)	8 987	1 500	3 696

表 10.4 续表 continued

指 标	Indicators	中等收入户 Medium Income	中高收入户 Medium-high Income	高收入户 High Income
调查户数(户)	Number of Households Surveyed (household)	200	200	200
平均每户家庭人口(人)	Average Number of Persons per Household (person)	2.85	2.79	2.79
平均每户就业人口(人)	Average Number of Employees per Household (person)	1.49	1.62	1.82
平均每户就业面(%)	Percentage of Employment per Household (%)	52.3	58.1	65.2
平均每一就业者负担人数(人)	Persons Supported by Each Employee (person)	1.91	1.72	1.53
可支配收入(元)	Average per Capita Disposable Income (yuan)	34 351	44 474	78 522
工资性收入	Salaries	20 292	29 838	57 481
经营净收入	Net Income from Household Business	1 285	1 119	7 810
财产性收入	Property Income	361	682	1 536
转移性收入	Transferred Income	12 413	12 835	11 695
#养老金或离退休金	Pensions and Retirement Pay	11 651	11 988	8 966
出售财物收入(元)	Income from Selling Properties(yuan)	1	2	692
借贷收入(元)	Borrowings and other Credit Items(yuan)	3 818	4 117	16 936
#住房借贷	Morgage Loans			540
提取储蓄存款	Drawings of Saving Deposits	3 544	4 083	16 344
消费支出(元)	Average per Capita Consumption Expenditures (yuan)	22 946	29 575	47 092
#服务性消费支出	Service Consumption Expenditure	6 902	8 877	14 938
购房与建房支出(元)	Buying and Building House Expenditure(yuan)	683		4 214
转移性支出(元)	Transferred Expenditure(yuan)	3 226	3 445	9 766
社会保障支出(元)	Social Security Expenditure(yuan)	3 192	4 254	7 105
借贷支出(元)	Lendings and other Debit Items (yuan)	5 501	8 678	26 719

表 10.5 主要年份城市居民家庭人均可支配收入
PER CAPITA DISPOSABLE INCOME OF URBAN HOUSEHOLDS IN MAIN YEARS

单位:元(yuan)

年 份 Year	人均可支配收入 Average per Capita Disposable Income	工资性收入 Salaries	经营净收入 Net Income from Household Business	财产性收入 Property Income	转移性收入 Transferred Income
1980	637	551			86
1985	1 075	794	1		280
1990	2 183	1 548	1	21	613
1991	2 486	1 780		29	677
1992	3 009	2 138	3	44	824
1993	4 277	3 099	4	37	1 137
1994	5 868	4 224	28	54	1 562
1995	7 172	5 002	69	92	2 009
1996	8 159	5 889	87	61	2 122
1997	8 439	5 969	150	69	2 251
1998	8 773	6 004	98	57	2 614
1999	10 932	7 326	156	68	3 382
2000	11 718	7 832	120	65	3 701
2001	12 883	7 975	119	39	4 750
2002	13 250	7 915	436	94	4 805
2003	14 867	10 097	377	130	4 263
2004	16 683	11 422	507	215	4 539
2005	18 645	12 409	798	292	5 146
2006	20 668	13 962	959	300	5 447
2007	23 623	16 598	1 158	369	5 498
2008	26 675	18 909	1 399	369	5 998
2009	28 838	19 811	1 435	474	7 118
2010	31 838	21 745	1 628	511	7 954
2011	36 230	24 454	1 994	633	9 149
2012	40 188	26 752	2 267	576	10 593

表 10.6 主要年份城市居民家庭人均可支配收入与消费支出
PER CAPITA ANNUAL DISPOSABLE INCOME AND CONSUMPTION EXPENDITURES OF URBAN HOUSEHOLDS IN MAIN YEARS

单位:元(yuan)

指 标	Indicators	2000	2010	2011	2012
人均可支配收入	**Average per Capita Disposable Income**	**11 718**	**31 838**	**36 230**	**40 188**
低收入户	Low Income	6 840	14 996	17 206	19 059
中低收入户	Medium-low Income	8 815	21 780	24 824	27 597
中等收入户	Medium Income	10 529	27 484	31 414	34 351
中高收入户	Medium-high Income	12 892	35 120	40 771	44 474
高收入户	High Income	19 959	62 465	70 067	78 522
人均消费支出	**Average per Capita Consumption Expenditures**	**8 868**	**23 200**	**25 102**	**26 253**
低收入户	Low Income	6 272	12 555	13 700	15 095
中低收入户	Medium-low Income	7 516	15 970	18 449	18 232
中等收入户	Medium Income	8 555	21 611	23 228	22 946
中高收入户	Medium-high Income	9 445	26 773	30 387	29 575
高收入户	High Income	12 763	40 744	41 397	47 092

表 10.7 主要年份城市居民家庭人均消费支出
PER CAPITA CONSUMPTION EXPENDITURES OF URBAN HOUSEHOLDS IN MAIN YEARS

单位:元(yuan)

年 份 Year	消费支出 Total Consumption Expenditures	食 品 Food	衣 着 Clothing	家庭设备用品及服务 Household Facilities, Articles and Services	医 疗 保 健 Medicines and Medical Services	交通和通 信 Traffic and Communi-cations	教育文化娱乐服务 Education, Culture and Recreation Services	居 住 Residence	其他商品和服务 Other Commodities and Services
1980	553	310	79	50	7	20	49	26	12
1985	992	517	148	131	5	30	91	43	27
1990	1 937	1 095	208	196	11	58	231	90	48
1995	5 868	3 131	561	637	113	321	508	401	196
1996	6 763	3 429	590	614	148	496	827	416	243
1997	6 820	3 526	552	525	197	397	828	605	190
1998	6 866	3 477	472	453	261	406	893	674	230
1999	8 248	3 731	551	772	347	583	1 094	842	328
2000	8 868	3 947	567	683	501	759	1 287	794	330
2001	9 336	4 056	577	579	558	958	1 422	796	390
2002	10 464	4 120	613	653	734	1 115	1 668	1 189	372
2003	11 040	4 102	751	792	603	1 259	1 834	1 280	419
2004	12 631	4 593	797	780	762	1 703	2 195	1 327	474
2005	13 773	4 940	940	800	797	1 984	2 273	1 412	627
2006	14 762	5 249	1 027	877	763	2 333	2 432	1 436	645
2007	17 255	6 125	1 330	959	857	3 154	2 654	1 412	764
2008	19 398	7 109	1 521	1 182	755	3 373	2 875	1 646	937
2009	20 992	7 345	1 593	1 365	1 002	3 499	3 139	1 913	1 136
2010	23 200	7 777	1 794	1 800	1 006	4 076	3 363	2 166	1 218
2011	25 102	8 906	2 054	1 826	1 141	3 808	3 746	2 226	1 395
2012	26 253	9 656	2 111	1 906	1 017	4 564	3 724	1 790	1 485

表 10.8 主要年份城市居民家庭人均消费支出构成
COMPOSITION OF PER CAPITA CONSUMPTION EXPENDITURES OF URBAN HOUSEHOLDS IN MAIN YEARS

单位:%

年 份 Year	消费支出 Total Consumption Expenditures	食 品 Food	衣 着 Clothing	家庭设备用品及服务 Household Facilities Articles and Services	医 疗 保 健 Medicine and Medical Services	交通和通 信 Traffic and Communi-cations	教育文化娱乐服务 Education, Cultural and Recreation Services	居 住 Residence	其他商品和服务 Other Commodities and Services
1980	100	56.0	14.3	9.0	1.3	3.6	8.9	4.7	2.2
1985	100	52.1	14.9	13.2	0.5	3.0	9.2	4.4	2.7
1990	100	56.5	10.7	10.1	0.6	3.0	11.9	4.7	2.5
1995	100	53.4	9.6	10.8	1.9	5.5	8.7	6.8	3.3
1996	100	50.7	8.7	9.1	2.2	7.3	12.2	6.2	3.6
1997	100	51.7	8.1	7.7	2.9	5.8	12.1	8.9	2.8
1998	100	50.6	6.9	6.6	3.8	5.9	13.0	9.8	3.4
1999	100	45.2	6.7	9.3	4.2	7.1	13.3	10.2	4.0
2000	100	44.5	6.4	7.7	5.6	8.6	14.5	9.0	3.7
2001	100	43.4	6.2	6.2	6.0	10.3	15.2	8.5	4.2
2002	100	39.4	5.9	6.2	7.0	10.7	15.9	11.4	3.5
2003	100	37.2	6.8	7.2	5.4	11.4	16.6	11.6	3.8
2004	100	36.4	6.3	6.2	6.0	13.5	17.4	10.5	3.7
2005	100	35.9	6.8	5.8	5.8	14.4	16.5	10.2	4.6
2006	100	35.6	6.9	5.9	5.2	15.8	16.5	9.7	4.4
2007	100	35.5	7.7	5.5	5.0	18.3	15.4	8.2	4.4
2008	100	36.6	7.9	6.1	3.9	17.4	14.8	8.5	4.8
2009	100	35.0	7.6	6.5	4.8	16.7	14.9	9.1	5.4
2010	100	33.5	7.7	7.8	4.3	17.6	14.5	9.3	5.3
2011	100	35.5	8.2	7.3	4.5	15.2	14.9	8.9	5.5
2012	100	36.8	8.0	7.3	3.9	17.4	14.2	6.8	5.6

表 10.9　主要年份城市居民家庭人均消费支出
PER CAPITA CONSUMPTION EXPENDITURES OF URBAN HOUSEHOLD IN MAIN YEARS

单位:元(yuan)

类 别	Types	2000	2010	2011	2012
消费支出	**Total Consumption Expenditures**	**8 868**	**23 200**	**25 102**	**26 253**
食　品	Food	3 947	7 777	8 906	9 656
#粮　油	Grain and Oil	396	885	987	1 019
肉禽蛋水产品	Meat, Poultry, Eggs and Aquatic Products	1 324	2 071	2 401	2 609
蔬　菜	Vegetables	305	622	672	762
干鲜瓜果	Dry and Fresh Fruits	293	594	695	757
糕点、奶及奶制品	Cake, Milk and Dairy Products	315	615	700	766
在外饮食	Dining Out	710	1 925	2 275	2 598
衣　着	Clothing	567	1 794	2 054	2 111
#服　装	Garments	387	1 352	1 558	1 581
家庭设备用品及服务	Household Facilities, Articles and Services	683	1 800	1 826	1 906
#耐用消费品	Durable Consumer Goods	340	816	744	672
医疗保健	Medicines and Medical Services	501	1 006	1 141	1 017
#药品费	Medicines	244	430	486	413
医疗费	Medical Services	69	239	313	279
交通和通信	Traffic and Communications	759	4 076	3 808	4 564
交　通	Traffic	375	2 891	2 502	3 222
#交通费	Traffic Fees	335	749	902	916
通　信	Communications	384		1 306	1 342
#电信费	Telecommunication Fees	272	969	1 001	1 007
教育文化娱乐服务	Education, Culture and Recreation Articles and Services	1 287	3 363	3 746	3 724
教　育	Education	585	1 168	1 286	1 242
#学杂费	Tuition	365	456	430	405
家教及培训班	Family Education and Training		410	536	456
成人教育费	Adult Education Fee	78	124	154	223
文化娱乐服务	Culture and Recreation Services	147	1 139	1 406	1 565
文化娱乐用品	Culture and Recreation Articles	555	1 056	1 054	917
#家用电脑	Computers	197	289	350	270
书报杂志	Books, Newspapers and Magazines	73	76	79	74
居　住	Residence	794	2 166	2 226	1 790
#水　费	Water	72	119	135	141
电　费	Electricity	258	452	456	472
燃料费	Fuels	157	201	207	209
租赁房房租	Rent	142	265	266	230
物业管理费	Estate Management Fee	20	161	190	194
其他商品和服务	Other Commodities and Services	330	1 218	1 395	1 485

表 10.10 城市居民家庭人均消费支出(2012,按收入水平分组)
PER CAPITA CONSUMPTION EXPENDITURES OF URBAN HOUSEHOLDS (2012, GROUPED BY INCOME LEVEL)

单位:元(yuan)

类别	Types	总平均 Total Average	低收入户 Low Income	中低收入户 Medium-low Income
消费支出	**Total Consumer Expenditures**	**26 253**	**15 095**	**18 232**
食　品	Food	9 656	7 266	8 347
#粮　油	Grain and Oil	1 019	878	1 011
肉禽蛋水产品	Meat,Poultry,Eggs and Aquatic Products	2 609	2 189	2 557
蔬　菜	Vegetables	762	666	743
干鲜瓜果	Dry and Fresh Fruit	757	559	685
糕点、奶及奶制品	Cake,Milk and Dairy Products	766	600	658
在外饮食	Dining Out	2 598	1 450	1 704
衣　着	Clothing	2 111	1 070	1 434
#服　装	Garments	1 581	761	1 045
家庭设备用品及服务	Household Facilities Articles and Services	1 906	761	1 073
#耐用消费品	Durable Consumer Goods	672	218	300
医疗保健	Medicine and Medical Services	1 017	661	861
#药品费	Medicines	413	325	395
医疗费	Medical Services	279	233	285
交通和通信	Traffic and Communications	4 564	1 654	2 261
交　通	Traffic	3 222	652	1 194
#交通费	Traffic Fees	916	501	656
通　信	Telecommunications	1 342	1 002	1 067
#电信费	Communication Fees	1 007	826	857
教育文化娱乐服务	Education, Culture and Recreation Articles and Services	3 724	2 184	2 239
教　育	Education	1 242	1 147	875
#学杂费	Tuition	405	489	327
家教及培训班	Family Education and Training	456	322	300
成人教育费	Adult Education Fee	223	143	107
文化娱乐服务	Culture and Recreation Services	1 565	565	826
文化娱乐用品	Culture and Recreation Articles	917	472	538
#家用电脑	Computers	270	130	159
书报杂志	Books, Newspapers and Magazines	74	41	51
居　住	Residence	1 790	1 077	1 286
#水　费	Water	141	132	127
电　费	Electricity	472	408	414
燃料费	Fuels	209	195	200
租赁房房租	Rent	230	124	232
物业管理费	Estate Management Fee	194	85	117
其他商品和服务	Other Commodities and Services	1 485	422	731

表10.10 续表 continued

单位:元(yuan)

类别	Types	中等收入户 Medium Income	中高收入户 Medium-high Income	高收入户 High Income
消费支出	**Total Consumer Expenditures**	**22 946**	**29 575**	**47 092**
食品	Food	9 754	10 920	12 312
#粮油	Grain and Oil	1 049	1 122	1 053
肉禽蛋水产品	Meat, Poultry, Eggs and Aquatic Products	2 778	2 796	2 769
蔬菜	Vegetables	810	810	789
干鲜瓜果	Dry and Fresh Fruit	811	860	892
糕点、奶及奶制品	Cake, Milk and Dairy Products	798	887	911
在外饮食	Dining Out	2 285	3 166	4 558
衣着	Clothing	1 642	2 765	3 800
#服装	Garments	1 181	2 095	2 947
家庭设备用品及服务	Household Facilities Articles and Services	1 622	2 441	3 805
#耐用消费品	Durable Consumer Goods	606	805	1 500
医疗保健	Medicine and Medical Services	850	1 108	1 655
#药品费	Medicines	384	454	518
医疗费	Medical Services	248	292	345
交通和通信	Traffic and Communications	3 182	3 855	12 329
交通	Traffic	1 903	2 381	10 389
#交通费	Traffic Fees	850	1 126	1 506
通信	Telecommunications	1 279	1 474	1 940
#电信费	Communication Fees	995	1 059	1 322
教育文化娱乐服务	Education, Culture and Recreation Articles and Services	3 192	3 951	7 302
教育	Education	863	1 169	2 189
#学杂费	Tuition	223	304	680
家教及培训班	Family Education and Training	343	476	865
成人教育费	Adult Education Fee	206	249	424
文化娱乐服务	Culture and Recreation Services	1 590	1 731	3 258
文化娱乐用品	Culture and Recreation Articles	739	1 051	1 855
#家用电脑	Computers	194	347	544
书报杂志	Books, Newspapers and Magazines	69	76	139
居住	Residence	1 615	2 441	2 637
#水费	Water	144	137	169
电费	Electricity	465	500	586
燃料费	Fuels	198	205	246
租赁房房租	Rent	142	351	314
物业管理费	Estate Management Fee	182	240	362
其他商品和服务	Other Commodities and Services	1 089	2 094	3 252

表 10.11 城市居民家庭平均每人主要消费品消费量(2009～2012)
PER CAPITA CONSUMPTION OF MAJOR CONSUMER GOODS OF URBAN HOUSEHOLDS

商品名称	Name of Commodities	2009	2010	2011	2012
大　米(千克)	Grain(kg)	41.6	39.9	39.2	37.8
食用植物油(千克)	Edible Vegetable Oil(kg)	9.4	8.0	8.2	8.3
猪　肉(千克)	Pork(kg)	18.5	18.6	18.8	19.5
牛羊肉(千克)	Beef and Mutton(kg)	2.6	2.8	2.9	3.1
鸡(千克)	Poultry(kg)	6.6	6.9	7.1	6.9
鸭(千克)	Duck(kg)	2.6	2.5	2.7	3.0
鲜　蛋(千克)	Eggs(kg)	9.8	9.6	10.2	10.2
鱼(千克)	Fish(kg)	14.9	14.2	14.5	15.5
虾(千克)	Shrimp(kg)	5.3	4.4	4.3	4.8
鲜　菜(千克)	Vegetables(kg)	102.1	102.7	104.5	107.0
啤　酒(千克)	Beer(kg)	6.5	5.6	4.4	4.2
糕点类(千克)	Cake(kg)	5.9	5.5	5.5	5.8
鲜瓜果(千克)	Fresh Melon and Fruit(kg)	67.2	65.5	61.2	64.0
鲜乳品和酸奶(千克)	Fresh Milk and Yogurt (kg)	29.9	28.8	30.0	30.4
服　装(件)	Clothing (unit)	10.2	10.4	11.0	10.2
生活用水(立方米)	Household Water Consumption (cubic meters)	53.7	52.2	49.7	50.9
生活用电(千瓦时)	Household Power Consumption (kwh)	716.9	814.9	817.7	845.2
液化石油气(千克)	Liquified Petroleum Gas (kg)	1.0	0.8	0.8	0.7
管道燃气(立方米)	Pipeline Gas (cubic meters)	120.9	113.3	113.8	105.6

注：管道燃气包括管道煤气和管道天然气。
Note: Pipline Gas includes pipeline coal gas and pipeline natural gas.

表 10.12 主要年份平均每百户城市居民家庭年末耐用消费品拥有量
PER 100 URBAN HOUSEHOLDS YEAR-END POSSESSION OF DURABLE CONSUMER GOODS IN MAIN YEARS

商品名称	Name of Commodities	2000	2010	2011	2012
彩色电视机(台)	Color TV Set (unit)	147	188	191	192
照相机(架)	Camera (unit)	71	95	94	98
摄像机(架)	Video Camera (unit)	3	17	18	19
家用电脑(台)	Personal Computer (unit)	26	129	138	144
移动电话(部)	Mobile Phone (unit)	29	230	236	239
组合音响(台)	Music Center (unit)	32	52	48	49
家用空调器(台)	Household Air Conditioner (unit)	96	200	207	207
洗衣机(台)	Washing Machine (unit)	93	99	100	101
电冰箱(台)	Household Refrigerator (unit)	102	104	105	106
热水淋浴器(台)	Water Heater (unit)	64	98	101	100
微波炉(台)	Microwave Oven (unit)	78	98	98	99
消毒碗柜(台)	Dish-sterilization Boxes(unit)		16	17	17
家用汽车(辆)	Auto(unit)		17	18	20

表 10.13 农村居民家庭生活基本情况(1990~2012)
BASIC STATISTICS OF RURAL HOUSEHOLDS

年份 Year	调查户数 (户) Number of Households Surveyed (household)	平均每户人口 (人) Average Number of Person per Household (person)	平均每户劳动力 (人) Average Number of Labours per Household (person)	平均每一劳动力负担人数 (人) Persons Supported by Each Labourer (person)	平均每人总收入 (元) Average Gross Income per Capita (yuan)	平均每人可支配收入 (元) Average Disposable Income per Capita (yuan)
1990	1 000	3.68	2.46	1.49	1 990	1 665
1991	600	3.49	2.36	1.48	2 376	2 003
1992	600	3.43	2.36	1.46	2 581	2 226
1993	600	3.41	2.45	1.39	3 149	2 727
1994	600	3.41	2.51	1.36	3 940	3 437
1995	600	3.47	2.54	1.37	4 861	4 246
1996	600	3.40	2.54	1.34	5 506	4 846
1997	600	3.35	2.48	1.35	5 933	5 277
1998	600	3.33	2.50	1.33	5 965	5 407
1999	600	3.31	2.54	1.30	5 924	5 481
2000	600	3.31	2.53	1.31	6 400	5 565
2001	600	3.29	2.48	1.33	6 827	5 850
2002	600	3.33	2.52	1.32	7 080	6 212
2003	600	3.34	2.59	1.29	7 260	6 658
2004	600	3.33	2.54	1.31	7 994	7 337
2005	600	3.21	2.19	1.47	9 234	8 342
2006	600	3.20	2.24	1.43	10 225	9 213
2007	600	3.18	2.17	1.47	11 382	10 222
2008	600	3.15	2.15	1.46	12 662	11 385
2009	600	3.15	2.11	1.50	13 404	12 324
2010	600	3.11	2.11	1.48	15 346	13 746
2011	1 200	2.97	2.10	1.41	17 306	15 644
2012	1 200	2.93	2.06	1.43	19 293	17 401

注：2000 年前平均每人可支配收入按纯收入口径计算，平均每人总收入不包括内部亲友赠送。
Note: The Per Capita Disposable Income before 2000 refers to the Net Income. The Gross Income excludes the donations from relatives and friends.

表 10.13 续表 continued

年　份 Year	平均每人总支出（元） Average Expenditures Per Capita (yuan)	平均每人生活消费支出（元） Per Capita Consumpition Expenditures (yuan)	平均每人可支配收入指数（以 1990 年为 100） Index of Per Capita Disposable Income (1990 = 100)	平均每人生活消费支出指数（以 1990 年为 100） Index of Per Capita Consumption Expenditures (1990 = 100)	平均每人年底居住房屋面积（平方米） Average Per Capita Living Space Year-end (sq. m)
1990	1 592	1 262	100.0	100.0	37.08
1991	1 893	1 540	120.3	122.0	39.60
1992	2 322	1 967	133.7	155.9	42.07
1993	2 660	2 200	163.8	174.3	44.22
1994	3 320	2 715	206.4	215.1	44.15
1995	4 041	3 368	255.0	266.9	43.08
1996	4 581	3 868	291.1	306.5	45.47
1997	4 953	4 228	316.9	335.0	46.44
1998	4 924	4 207	324.7	333.4	47.24
1999	4 431	3 867	329.2	306.4	49.00
2000	5 578	4 138	334.2	327.9	53.58
2001	6 353	4 753	351.4	376.6	54.70
2002	6 988	5 311	373.1	420.8	57.08
2003	6 931	5 670	399.9	449.3	59.03
2004	7 580	6 329	440.7	501.5	59.84
2005	8 663	7 265	501.0	575.7	56.56
2006	9 344	8 006	553.3	634.4	59.99
2007	10 429	8 845	613.9	700.9	61.22
2008	10 840	9 115	683.8	722.3	62.30
2009	11 436	9 804	740.2	776.9	60.18
2010	11 988	10 225	825.6	810.2	59.68
2011	13 458	11 272	939.6	893.2	58.90
2012	14 853	12 096	1 045.1	958.5	60.42

表 10.14 主要年份农村居民家庭人均可支配收入
PER CAPITA DISPOSABLE INCOME OF RURAL HOUSEHOLDS IN MAIN YEARS

年 份 Year	人均可支配收入(元) Average Disposable Income Per Capita (yuan)	工资性收入 Wages	家庭经营纯收入 Household Business Income	转移性和财产性收入 Property and Transferred Income	比重(以人均可支配收入为100) Proportion(Average Disposable Income Per Capita = 100) 工资性收入 Wages	家庭经营纯收入 Household Business Income	转移性和财产性收入 Property and Transferred Income
1990	1 665	1 066	539	60	64.0	32.4	3.6
1995	4 246	2 734	1 183	329	64.4	27.9	7.7
2000	5 565	4 310	934	321	77.4	16.8	5.8
2001	5 850	4 491	967	392	76.8	16.5	6.7
2002	6 212	4 920	774	518	79.2	12.5	8.3
2003	6 658	5 284	813	561	79.4	12.2	8.4
2004	7 337	5 757	886	694	78.5	12.1	9.4
2005	8 342	6 364	811	1 167	76.3	9.7	14.0
2006	9 213	6 892	766	1 555	74.8	8.3	16.9
2007	10 222	7 498	754	1 970	73.3	7.4	19.3
2008	11 385	8 182	711	2 492	71.9	6.2	21.9
2009	12 324	8 721	590	3 013	70.8	4.8	24.4
2010	13 746	9 606	589	3 551	69.9	4.3	25.8
2011	15 644	10 493	877	4 274	67.1	5.6	27.3
2012	17 401	11 496	905	5 000	66.1	5.2	28.7

注：2000 年前是指每人可支配收入按纯收入口径计算。 2011 年，按可比口径计算，全年家庭经营纯收入增长为 22%；"土地征用补偿收入"不再列入财产性收入中。

Note: The per Capita Annual Disposable Income before 2000 refers to the Net Income. Since 2011, according to the calculation of comparable caliber, the growth rate of annual Household Business Income is 22%. Land Requisition Compensation Income is no longer included in the property income.

表 10.15 农村居民家庭人均可支配收入和人均生活消费支出(2000～2012)
PER CAPITA DISPOSABLE INCOME AND LIVING EXPENDITURES FOR CONSUMPTION OF RURAL HOUSEHOLDS

单位:元(yuan)

年 份 Year	总平均 Average	低收入户 Low Income	中低收入户 Medium-low Income	中等收入户 Medium Income	中高收入户 Medium-high Income	高收入户 High Income
人均可支配收入	**Average per Capita Disposable Income**					
2000	5 565	2 330	3 906	5 264	6 725	10 405
2001	5 850	2 351	4 078	5 649	7 122	10 930
2002	6 212	2 429	4 266	5 701	7 513	11 989
2003	6 658	2 761	4 621	6 213	7 972	12 777
2004	7 337	3 122	5 148	7 006	8 775	13 652
2005	8 342	3 347	5 594	7 612	9 755	15 309
2006	9 213	3 830	6 194	8 412	10 714	16 843
2007	10 222	4 321	7 098	9 442	11 807	18 443
2008	11 385	4 690	8 065	10 487	13 094	20 748
2009	12 324	5 279	8 785	11 184	14 039	22 465
2010	13 746	5 968	10 107	12 929	16 327	24 536
2011	15 644	7 018	11 772	14 568	18 145	27 227
人均生活消费支出	**Average per Capitor Consumption Expenditures**					
2000	4 138	2 390	3 387	3 887	5 487	5 880
2001	4 753	2 921	3 250	4 334	5 356	8 449
2002	5 311	2 350	4 341	4 834	5 873	9 683
2003	5 670	2 886	3 681	5 363	6 286	10 769
2004	6 329	4 076	4 914	5 309	6 992	10 971
2005	7 265	4 618	5 690	6 317	7 059	12 975
2006	8 006	4 788	6 001	6 951	8 015	15 058
2007	8 845	4 890	6 077	7 305	9 541	17 317
2008	9 115	5 024	6 280	9 555	10 700	14 517
2009	9 804	5 472	6 266	9 026	12 843	16 035
2010	10 225	5 026	7 881	8 739	15 103	15 187
2011	11 272	6 979	9 881	11 701	11 654	16 531
2012	12 096	7 784	8 813	10 802	13 725	19 773

表 10.16　主要年份农村居民家庭人均生活消费支出
PER CAPITA CONSUMPTION EXPENDITURES OF RURAL HOUSEHOLDS IN MAIN YEARS

单位:元(yuan)

年 份 Year	生活消费支出 Total Consumption Expenditures	食 品 Food	衣 着 Clothing	居 住 Residence	家庭设备用品及服务 Household Facilities, Articles and Services	交通和通 信 Traffic and Communi-cations	文教娱乐用品及服务 Education, Culture and Recreation Articles and Services	医 疗保 健 Medicines and Medical Services	其他商品和服务 Other Commodities and Services
1990	1 262	586	107	272	129	6	59	33	70
1995	3 368	1 491	233	761	284	159	256	73	111
2000	4 138	1 823	201	724	225	279	559	209	118
2001	4 753	1 915	226	890	294	340	673	265	150
2002	5 311	1 872	226	1 392	281	462	661	280	137
2003	5 670	2 004	250	1 437	297	587	676	333	86
2004	6 329	2 191	280	1 446	344	720	806	425	117
2005	7 265	2 676	367	1 323	458	739	936	562	204
2006	8 006	3 024	418	1 658	481	780	920	549	176
2007	8 845	3 259	476	2 097	452	884	857	571	249
2008	9 115	3 732	467	1 806	504	880	850	697	179
2009	9 804	3 639	496	2 103	481	1 212	943	739	191
2010	10 225	3 807	554	2 070	528	1 459	1 012	585	210
2011	11 272	4 517	644	1 806	649	1 309	1 139	909	299
2012	12 096	4 837	704	1 834	646	1 705	1 088	1 029	253

表 10.17　主要年份农村居民家庭人均生活消费支出构成
COMPOSITION OF PER CAPITA CONSUMER EXPENDITURES OF RURAL HOUSEHOLDS IN MAIN YEARS

单位:%

年 份 Year	生活消费支出 Total Consumption Expenditures	食 品 Food	衣 着 Clothing	居 住 Residence	家庭设备用品及服务 Household Facilities, Articles and Services	交通和通 信 Traffic and Communi-cations	文教娱乐用品及服务 Education, Culture and Recreation Articles and Services	医 疗保 健 Medicines and Medical Services	其他商品和服务 Other Commodities and Services
1990	100	46.4	8.5	21.6	10.2	0.5	4.7	2.6	5.5
1995	100	44.3	6.9	22.6	8.4	4.7	7.6	2.2	3.3
1996	100	42.8	6.6	21.1	9.4	5.2	9.0	2.8	3.1
1997	100	41.5	6.3	21.8	8.0	5.7	9.8	4.1	2.8
1998	100	42.2	5.7	20.8	8.8	5.4	11.0	4.0	2.1
1999	100	43.1	5.2	17.6	10.1	5.1	12.3	4.1	2.5
2000	100	44.0	4.9	17.5	5.4	6.7	13.5	5.1	2.9
2001	100	40.3	4.7	18.7	6.2	7.1	14.2	5.6	3.2
2002	100	35.2	4.3	26.2	5.3	8.7	12.4	5.3	2.6
2003	100	35.4	4.4	25.3	5.2	10.4	11.9	5.9	1.5
2004	100	34.6	4.4	22.9	5.4	11.4	12.7	6.7	1.9
2005	100	36.8	5.1	18.2	6.3	10.2	12.9	7.7	2.8
2006	100	37.8	5.2	20.7	6.0	9.7	11.5	6.9	2.2
2007	100	36.8	5.4	23.7	5.1	10.0	9.7	6.5	2.8
2008	100	40.9	5.1	19.8	5.5	9.7	9.3	7.7	2.0
2009	100	37.1	5.1	21.5	4.9	12.4	9.6	7.5	1.9
2010	100	37.2	5.4	20.2	5.2	14.3	9.9	5.7	2.1
2011	100	40.1	5.7	16.0	5.8	11.6	10.1	8.1	2.6
2012	100	40.0	5.8	15.2	5.3	14.1	9.0	8.5	2.1

表 10.18 农村居民家庭人均可支配收入(2012,按收入水平分组)
AVERAGE PER CAPITA DISPOSABLE INCOME OF RURAL HOUSEHOLDS (2011,GROUPED BY INCOME LEVEL)

单位:元(yuan)

指　标	Indicators	总平均 Total Average	低收入户 Low Income	中低收入户 Medium-low Income
平均每人可支配收入	**Average per Capita Disposable Income**	**17 401**	**7 707**	**13 071**
工资性收入	Wage	11 496	4 683	8 826
家庭经营纯收入	Household Business Income	905	512	700
#农业纯收入	Agricultural Income	436	265	295
财产性收入	Property Income	1 382	413	783
#利息收入	Interest Income	30	20	11
租金收入	Rental Income	920	290	454
转移性收入	Transferred Income	3 618	2 099	2 762
#离退休金、养老金	Pension	3 670	2 651	2 889

表 10.18 续表 continued

单位:元(yuan)

指　标	Indicators	中等收入户 Medium Income	中高收入户 Medium-high Income	高收入户 High Income
平均每人可支配收入	**Average per Capita Disposable Income**	**16 490**	**20 340**	**29 180**
工资性收入	Wage	10 622	13 532	20 057
家庭经营纯收入	Household Business Net Income	717	827	1 819
#农业纯收入	Agricultural Income	424	410	808
财产性收入	Property Net Income	1 332	1 672	2 565
#利息收入	Interest Income	9	27	90
租金收入	Rental Income	899	1 162	1 840
转移性收入	Transferred Income	3 819	4 309	4 739
#离退休金、养老金	Pension	3 853	4 207	4 394

表 10.19 农村居民家庭人均生活消费支出（2012，按收入水平分组）
PER CAPITA EXPENDITURES OF RURAL HOUSEHOLDS (2012, GROUPED BY INCOME LEVEL)

单位：元（yuan）

指 标	Indicators	总平均 Total Average	低收入户 Low Income	中低收入户 Medium-low Income	中等收入户 Medium Income	中高收入户 Medium-high Income	高收入户 High Income
生活消费支出	**Consumption Expenditures**	**12 096**	**7 784**	**8 813**	**10 802**	**13 725**	**19 773**
食 品	Food	4 837	3 784	4 010	4 665	5 489	6 308
衣 着	Clothing	704	314	588	592	817	1 226
居 住	Residence	1 834	866	937	1 073	2 311	4 136
家庭设备用品及服务	Household Faclities, Articles and Services	646	286	494	584	730	1 154
交通通信	Traffic and Communications	1 705	750	814	1 537	1 953	3 581
文教娱乐用品及服务	Education, Culture and Recreation Articles and Services	1 088	643	990	1 026	1 183	1 606
医疗保健	Medicine and Medical Services	1 029	1 007	828	1 065	924	1 353
其 他	Others	253	134	152	260	318	409

表10.20 主要年份农村居民家庭平均每人主要消费品消费量
PER CAPITA CONSUMPTION OF MAJOR CONSUMER GOODS OF RURAL HOUSEHOLDS IN MAIN YEARS

商品名称	Name of Commodities	2000	2010	2011	2012
粮　食（千克）	Grain (kg)	222.27	135.82	123.48	119.71
#稻　谷	Rice	205.25	130.52	113.15	109.00
油脂类（千克）	Edible Oil (kg)	7.99	7.46	10.25	10.36
蔬菜及菜制品（千克）	Vegetables and Their Products(kg)	92.41	65.01	69.26	72.23
肉禽及其制品（千克）	Meat, Poultry and Their Products (kg)	29.68	34.98	39.16	39.35
蛋类及蛋制品（千克）	Eggs and Their Products (kg)	10.71	8.07	8.58	8.92
奶及奶制品（千克）	Milk and Dairy Products(kg)	2.07	7.03	8.09	8.23
水产品（千克）	Aquatic Products (kg)	14.51	17.21	18.56	18.43
#鱼　类	Fish	10.11	11.29	12.68	12.37
虾、贝、蟹类	Shrimp,Testacean,Crab	2.61	4.34	4.32	4.66
水果及水果制品（千克）	Fruits and Their Products(kg)	36.94	29.04	25.98	26.35
食　糖（千克）	Suger (kg)	2.47	1.90	1.90	1.77
卷　烟（盒）	Cigarette (case)	44.49	46.70	58.55	60.14
酒（千克）	Liquor (kg)	15.68	15.07	18.57	18.02

表10.21 主要年份平均每百户农村居民家庭年末耐用消费品拥有量
PER 100 RURAL HOUSEHOLD YEAR-END POSSESSION OF DURABLE CONSUMER GOODS IN MAIN YEARS

商品名称	Name of Commodities	2000	2010	2011	2012
彩色电视机（台）	Color TV Set (unit)	97	198	188	190
电冰箱（台）	Household Refrigerator (unit)	74	103	99	101
洗衣机（台）	Washing Machine (unit)	69	95	88	90
影碟机（台）	VCD Player (unit)	27	22	14	14
生活用汽车（辆）	Moped and Motorcycle (vehicle)		6	10	14
家用空调器（台）	Household Air Conditioner (unit)	14	147	130	136
抽油烟机（台）	Cooking Soat Inducer (unit)	35	74	64	67
微波炉（台）	Microwave Oven (unit)	14	84	80	83
吸尘器（台）	Vacuam Cleaner (unit)	9	28	17	19
热水器（台）	Water Heater (unit)	44	96	90	91
移动电话（部）	Mobile Phone (unit)	19	194	189	200
家用电脑（台）	Personal Computer (unit)	5	60	50	49

上 / 海 / 统 / 计 / 年 / 鉴

主要统计指标解释

■ 城市居民可支配收入

指居民可用于最终消费支出和其他非义务性支出以及储蓄的总和，即居民家庭可以用来自由支配的收入。它是家庭总收入扣除交纳的所得税、个人交纳的社会保障费以及调查户的记账补贴后的收入。不包括出售财物和借贷收入。

■ 城市居民家庭消费支出

指城市居民家庭用于日常生活的全部支出。包括食品、衣着、家庭设备用品及服务、医疗保健、交通和通信、教育文化娱乐服务、居住、杂项商品和服务等八大类。

■ 城市居民家庭服务性消费支出

指调查户用于本家庭支付社会提供的各种文化和生活方面的非商品性服务费用。服务性消费的特点在于其劳动过程和消费过程在时间与空间上的统一。在居民家庭八大类消费中，服务性消费支出包括：1、食品类中加工服务费和部分在外饮食费用；2、衣着类中衣着加工服务费；3、家庭设备用品及服务类中家庭服务（如家政服务费用）；4、医疗保健类中医疗费（如诊疗费、上门出诊费、护工费用）；5、交通和通信类中交通工具服务费（如汽车使用、维修费用）、交通费中使用飞机、轮船、火车等交通工具费用、通信服务费（如电信费、邮费）；6、教育文化娱乐服务类中文化娱乐服务费（如参观、游览费用、健身活动费、团体旅游、其他文娱活动费）、文娱用品修理服务费、教育费（如义务、非义务教育支出）、成人教育支出、家教费、培训班费用、择校费；7、居住类中租赁费用、部分房屋装潢费用（人工费用）、居住服务费（如物业管理、维修费用）；8、杂项商品和服务（如美容、洗澡、理发费用，旅馆住宿等费用）。

■ 储蓄存款余额

指个人客户在其他存款性公司开立账户并存入资金或货币，由其他存款性公司出具存款凭证，个人客户凭存款凭证可以支取本金或利息的存款。

■ 农村居民可支配收入

指农村居民获得的经过初次分配与再分配后的收入。可支配收入可用于住户的最终消费、非义务性支出以及储蓄。

农村居民可支配收入＝总收入 － 家庭经营费用支出 － 税费支出 － 生产性固定资产折旧 － 财产性支出 － 转移性支出。

■ 农村居民家庭生活消费支出

指农村住户用于物质生活和精神生活方面的支出。包括食品，衣着，居住，家庭设备用品及服务，医疗保健，交通和通信，文化教育娱乐用品及服务，其他商品和服务等消费支出。

■ 财产性收入

指金融资产或有形非生产性资产的所有者向其他机构单位提供资金或将有形非生产性资产供其支配，作为回报而从中获得的收入。

■ 转移性收入

指农村住户和住户成员无须付出任何对应物而获得的货物、服务、资金或资产所有权等，不包括无偿提供的用于固定资本形成的资金。一般情况下，是指农村住户在二次分配中的所有收入。

SHANGHAI STATISTICAL YEARBOOK

EXPLANATORY NOTES TO MAJOR STATISTICAL INDICATORS

□ Disposable Income of Urban Households

Disposable Income of Urban Households refers to the actual income at the disposal of members of the households which can be used for final consumption, other non-compulsory expenditure and savings, which is part of the urban households' income that can be disposed by the urban households themselves. It is the income after deducting personal income tax, social insurance paid by individuals and investigation allowance from the total income of the households. The income from selling properties and borrowing are not included.

□ Consumption Expenditures of Urban Households

Consumption Expenditures of Urban Households refer to all the expenditures paid by urban households for consumption in daily life, including 8 categories as follows: food; clothing; household facilities, articles and services; medical care; traffic and telecommunication; education, culture and recreation services; housing; miscellaneous commodities and services.

□ Urbanities' Spending on Services

Urbanities'spending on services refers to urbanites pay for services rather than commodities. Services are offered and consumed at the same time and place. The service spending for an urban family falls into the following eight types: 1. Money paid for food processing and money spent while eating out; 2. Money paid for clothing processing; 3. Domestic services and services for home amenities; 4. Medical cost (including medical diagnosis and treatment, in-home medical services and nursing cost); 5. Transport tool service fees (such as for the use of a car and maintenance fee thereby arising, transport tools (plane, ship, train) fees, post and telecommunications fees; 6. Fees for culture and entertainment services (such as tour and fitness building), fees for repair of sports and entertainment items, education cost (spending on obligatory and non-obligatory education), adult education cost, tutor fees, training courses fees and extra money paid as sponsorship fee to a school a student outside his or her education community; 7. Housing rents, some interior decoration cost (for labor), residence service fees (such as for property management and repairs); 8. Fees for other services (such as at a beauty salon, bathhouse, hairdresser's and hotels).

□ Savings Deposits

Savings Deposits refers to the amount of the personal deposit account opened in other deposit-taking companies. The other deposit-taking companies issue the certificate of Savings Deposits to individual customers, by which the individual customers can withdraw principal or interest.

□ Disposable Income of Rural Households

Disposable Income of Rural Households refers to the actual income at the disposal of rural households after initial distribution and reallocation. Disposal Income can be used for final consumption, non-compulsory expenditure and savings.

Disposal Income of Rural Households=total household income-expenditure for household operations-taxes and fees-depreciation of productive fixed assets-expenses on properties-expenses on transfers.

□ Living Expenditures for Consumption of Rural Households

Living Expenditures for Consumption of Rural Households refer to expenditures of material and culture life of rural household, including expenses on food, clothing, housing, household appliances and service, medical and health care, traffic and communication items, cultural, education and recreation items and service and other commodities and service.

□ Income from Properties

Income from Properties refers to the income received as returns by owners of financial assets or tangible non-productive assets by providing capitals or tangible non-productive assets to other institutional units.

□ Income from Transfers

Income from Transfers refers to the receipt by rural households and their members of goods, services, capitals or rights of assets without giving or repaying accordingly, excluding capitals provided to them for the formation of fixed assets. In general, it refers to all income received by rural households through redistribution.service and other commodities and service.

第十一篇

CHAPTER 11

城市建设

URBAN CONSTRUCTION

简要说明

一、本篇资料的主要内容

本篇资料反映上海市城市建设的规模、速度及综合水平等基本情况，主要内容包括：市政道路、房屋建筑、供水排水、供气、城市绿化等城市建设情况。

二、本篇资料的来源

城市基础设施建设、公共事业和市政建设投资统计资料依据上海市统计局制定的《固定资产投资统计报表制度》收集整理提供。

房屋建筑统计资料由上海市住房保障和房屋管理局汇总整理提供。

市政工程部分统计资料和供气统计资料由上海市城乡建设和交通委员会汇总整理提供。

供水排水统计资料由上海市水务局汇总整理提供。

城市绿化统计资料由上海市绿化和市容管理局汇总整理提供。

三、本篇资料的统计范围

城市基础设施建设、公共事业和市政建设投资的统计资料执行范围同《固定资产投资篇》的执行范围。房屋建筑、市政工程、供水排水、供气、城市绿化的统计资料范围均是全市范围。

BRIEF INTRODUCTION

I. Main Contents

Data The data in this chapter reflect the basic conditions of the scale, growth rate, and overall level of urban construction of Shanghai. The main contents include municipal roads, house construction, water supply, drainage, gas supply, and urban afforestation.

II. Sources of data

Data on infrastructure construction, public facilities, urban construction investment are collected, prepared and provided by Shanghai Municipal Statistics Bureau in accordance with the Statistics Reporting Form System on the Fixed Asset Investment, which is stipulated by the Shanghai Municipal Statistics Bureau.

Data on house construction are collected, prepared, and provided by Shanghai Municipal Housing Security and Building Administration Bureau.

Data on urban construction projects and gas supply are collected, prepared, and provided by Shanghai Municipal Urban and Rural Construction and Transport Commission.

Data on water supply and drainage are collected, prepared, and provided by Shanghai Water Authority.

Data on urban afforestation are collected, prepared, and provided by Shanghai Municipal Afforestation & City Appearance and Environmental Sanitation Administration.

III. Scope and Coverage of Statistics

The Coverage of data on urban infrastructure construction, public facilities, and urban construction investment is the same with that in the chapter of Fixed Assets Investment. Data on house construction, urban construction projects, water supply, drainage, gas supply, and urban afforestation cover the whole city.

表 11.1 主要年份城市基础设施投资额
URBAN INFRASTRUCTURE INVESTMENT IN MAIN YEARS

单位:亿元(100 million yuan)

年份 Year	合计 Total	电力建设 Power Generation	运输邮电 Transportation, Postal and Telecommunications	其中 of which: 交通运输 Transportation	其中 of which: 邮电通信 Postal and Telecommunications	公用设施 Facilities for Public Use	其中 of which: 公用事业 Public Utilities	其中 of which: 市政建设 Civil Construction
1950～1978	60.08	19.71	23.25	19.41	3.84	17.12	6.85	10.27
1980	9.55	5.31	2.91	2.31	0.60	1.33	0.64	0.69
1985	23.49	3.97	6.75	5.52	1.23	12.77	7.88	4.89
1986	24.78	5.68	8.40	6.56	1.84	10.70	5.67	5.03
1987	32.64	9.31	12.39	10.02	2.37	10.94	5.36	5.58
1988	37.08	14.18	12.35	8.80	3.55	10.55	4.01	6.54
1989	36.09	11.69	9.96	6.16	3.80	14.44	6.84	7.60
1990	47.22	17.53	10.06	7.17	2.90	19.63	10.83	8.80
1991	61.38	19.79	19.07	14.49	4.58	22.52	9.15	13.37
1992	84.35	19.70	21.44	15.01	6.43	43.21	12.58	30.63
1993	167.94	25.77	46.44	31.75	14.69	95.73	37.91	57.82
1994	238.16	41.57	72.68	36.83	35.85	123.91	26.77	97.14
1995	273.78	57.33	79.36	25.94	53.42	137.09	35.03	102.06
1996	378.78	77.61	147.21	69.66	77.55	153.96	48.31	105.65
1997	412.85	80.24	146.10	85.06	61.04	186.51	52.24	134.27
1998	531.38	89.58	181.46	108.79	72.67	260.34	58.37	201.97
1999	501.39	83.05	166.16	102.24	63.92	252.18	64.20	187.98
2000	449.90	64.61	117.52	48.83	68.69	267.77	104.43	163.34
2001	510.78	72.22	168.42	60.72	107.70	270.14	92.25	177.89
2002	583.49	62.14	171.24	63.01	108.23	350.11	148.42	201.69
2003	604.62	66.00	350.35	273.77	76.58	188.28	36.91	151.36
2004	672.58	89.52	371.35	316.96	54.39	211.71	26.92	184.80
2005	885.74	124.22	443.90	385.58	58.32	317.62	41.33	276.28
2006	1 125.54	116.23	703.24	589.52	113.72	306.07	56.23	249.84
2007	1 466.33	163.30	942.03	840.46	101.57	361.01	60.90	300.11
2008	1 733.18	129.53	947.49	838.91	108.59	656.15	112.81	543.34
2009	2 113.45	253.39	1 100.90	978.24	122.66	759.16	135.95	623.21
2010	1 497.46	148.50	866.20	754.66	111.54	482.76	86.58	396.18
2011	1 157.34	118.81	668.52	595.75	72.76	370.01	54.22	315.80
2012	1 038.61	110.06	570.37	473.43	96.94	358.18	56.45	301.74

注：本表各项投资额均不包括住宅建设投资。从2003年起，交通运输投资包括公用设施中市内公共交通投资。2011年始，固定资产投资统计起点为500万元以上(含500万元)项目(下表同)。

Note: All items in this table exclude investment in residential housing. Since 2003, public traffic investment, which is belong to facilities for public use has been included in Transportation Investment. Since 2011, statistics of Investment in Fixed Assets only contain the projects with investment of 5 million yuan and above (same as follows).

表 11.2 用于公用事业和市政建设的投资额(1985 ~2012)
INVESTMENT IN PUBLIC UTILITIES AND CIVIL CONSTRUCTION

单位:亿元(100 million yuan)

年 份 Year	公 用 事 业 Public Utilities	其 中 of which 自来水 Tap Water	煤 气 Gas	市 政 建 设 Civil Construction	其 中 of which 园 林 绿 化 Parks and Green Areas	环 境 卫 生 Environmental Sanitation	市 政 工程建设 Administration of Civil Utilities	其 他 Others
1985	7.88			4.89				
1986	5.67	2.74	1.78	5.03	0.43	0.71	3.84	0.05
1987	5.36	2.53	1.79	5.58	0.30	0.34	4.94	…
1988	4.01	0.72	1.25	6.54	0.24	0.58	5.72	…
1989	6.84	1.52	0.90	7.60	0.01	0.52	7.02	0.05
1990	10.83	1.06	1.81	8.80	0.11	0.37	8.31	0.01
1991	9.15	2.34	2.35	13.37	0.15	0.45	12.77	…
1992	12.58	3.20	3.24	30.63	0.32	0.79	28.45	1.07
1993	37.91	6.90	16.72	57.82	0.52	1.06	56.24	…
1994	26.77	11.49	7.80	97.14	2.42	1.01	93.47	0.24
1995	35.03	13.12	12.97	102.06	4.27	1.26	96.21	0.32
1996	48.31	22.12	14.61	105.65	2.66	1.14	101.80	0.05
1997	52.24	27.08	10.03	134.27	5.11	1.62	127.41	0.13
1998	58.37	14.59	13.15	201.97	9.10	3.35	189.41	0.11
1999	64.20	6.41	9.89	187.98	28.62	2.97	155.73	0.66
2000	104.43	5.35	6.88	163.34	38.76	19.34	102.36	2.88
2001	92.25	5.97	5.83	177.89	32.92	2.97	140.63	1.37
2002	148.42	8.62	6.83	201.69	38.83	1.47	160.64	0.75
2003	36.91	22.89	14.02	151.36	33.85	9.25	107.73	0.53
2004	26.92	16.66	10.26	184.80	16.69	7.01	160.22	0.88
2005	41.33	29.66	11.67	276.28	13.88	15.36	246.58	0.46
2006	56.23	43.79	12.44	249.84	26.41	10.17	213.26	
2007	60.90	50.12	10.78	300.11	34.66	11.26	254.19	
2008	112.81	93.24	19.57	543.34	29.01	20.04	494.29	
2009	135.95	109.79	26.16	623.21	27.96	21.91	573.19	0.15
2010	86.58	61.63	24.95	396.18	35.87	10.80	349.27	0.25
2011	54.22	41.85	12.37	315.80	44.71	23.91	247.15	0.03
2012	56.45	40.75	15.70	301.74	20.99	23.74	256.73	0.26

表 11.3 主要年份各类房屋构成情况
COMPOSITION OF BUILDING IN MAIN YEARS

单位：万平方米（10 000 sq. m）

指 标	Indicators	2000	2010	2011	2012
总 计	**Total**	**34 206**	**93 591**	**98 092**	**105 152**
居住房屋	Residential Buildings	20 865	52 639	55 077	56 263
花园住宅	Villas	250	2 064	2 215	1 708
公 寓	Apartments	206	492	50 261	51 975
职工住宅	Staff Dwellings	17 939	47 951		
联列住宅	United Columns Residences			496	1 052
新式里弄	Improved Residential Blocks	428	527	525	311
旧式里弄	Old Residential Blocks	1 896	1 237	1 222	1 206
简 屋	Simple Housings	84	29	29	11
其 他	Others	62	339	329	
非居住房屋	Non-Residential Buildings	13 341	40 952	43 015	48 888
工 厂	Plants	5 739	18 524	19 223	22 233
学 校	Schools	1 417	3 172	3 251	2 976
仓库堆栈	Warehouses	650	1 654	1 711	1 671
办公楼	Offices	2 416	6 365	6 520	6 101
商场店铺	Stores	1 191	5 497	5 654	5 847
医 院	Hospitals	367	754	763	576
旅 馆	Hotels	376	931	997	1 087
影剧院	Theatres and Cinemas	47	75	77	55
其 他	Others	1 138	3 979	4 820	8 342

注：根据市住房保障和房屋管理局提供居住房屋分类的调整，2011 年起公寓数据包含职工住宅数据，2012 年起取消其他分类。
Note: According to the adjustment of residential houses classification provided by Shanghai Municipal Housing Security and Building Administration Bureau, since 2011, the apartment data contains data of the staff housing, and since 2012, other classifications are canceled.

表 11.4 主要年份八层以上房屋情况
BUILDINGS OVER EIGHT STOREYS IN MAIN YEARS

类 别	Types	单 位 Unit	2000	2010	2011	2012
总 计	**Total**	**幢（building）**	**3 529**	**20 579**	**22 998**	**32 022**
		万平方米（10 000 sq. m）	6 180	21 911	27 002	30 550
8～10 层	8～10 Storeys	幢（building）	536	2 744	2 966	4 367
		万平方米（10 000 sq. m）	451	2 430	2 544	2 911
11～15 层	11～15 Storeys	幢（building）	684	9 672	11 307	15 125
		万平方米（10 000 sq. m）	875	6 320	10 662	10 390
16～19 层	16～19 Storeys	幢（building）	831	4 247	4 594	7 484
		万平方米（10 000 sq. m）	1 100	4 449	4 700	6 690
20～29 层	20～29 Storeys	幢（building）	1 266	2 936	3 065	3 839
		万平方米（10 000 sq. m）	2 695	5 504	5 759	6 996
30 层以上	Over 30 Storeys	幢（building）	212	980	1 066	1 207
		万平方米（10 000 sq. m）	1 059	3 208	3 338	3 563

注：本页数据按建筑面积计算。
Note: Data on this page are calculated according to floor space of builings.

表 11.5 各区、县房屋建筑分布情况(2012)
DISTRIBUTION OF BUILDINGS IN DIFFERENT DISTRICTS AND COUNTIES

单位：万平方米(10 000 sq. m)

地区	District	建筑面积合计 Total	其中 of which 居住房屋 Residential	非居住房屋 Non-Residential
总计	**Total**	**105 152**	**56 263**	**48 888**
浦东新区	Pudong New Area	23 748	13 035	10 713
黄浦区	Huangpu	3 604	1 724	1 881
徐汇区	Xuhui	5 687	3 311	2 376
长宁区	Changning	3 926	2 426	1 500
静安区	Jing'an	1 745	848	897
普陀区	Putuo	5 637	3 487	2 150
闸北区	Zhabei	3 642	2 178	1 464
虹口区	Hongkou	3 502	2 227	1 275
杨浦区	Yangpu	5 275	3 215	2 060
闵行区	Minhang	11 694	6 766	4 928
宝山区	Baoshan	8 392	4 904	3 487
嘉定区	Jiading	6 421	2 903	3 518
金山区	Jinshan	3 533	1 281	2 252
松江区	Songjiang	7 859	3 489	4 370
青浦区	Qingpu	4 388	1 690	2 699
奉贤区	Fengxian	4 378	1 924	2 454
崇明县	Chongming	1 719	855	864

表11.6 各区、县各类房屋分布情况(2012)
DISTRIBUTION OF VARIOUS BUILDINGS IN DIFFERENT DISTRICTS AND COUNTIES

单位：万平方米(10 000 sq. m)

地区 District		居住房屋 Residential Buildings	其中 of which 花园住宅 Villas	公寓 Apartments	联列住宅 United Columns Residences
总计	**Total**	**56 263**	**1 708**	**51 975**	**1 052**
浦东新区	Pudong New Area	13 035	356	12 440	206
黄浦区	Huangpu	1 724	9	1 320	…
徐汇区	Xuhui	3 311	52	3 153	9
长宁区	Changning	2 426	56	2 308	1
静安区	Jing'an	848	21	677	1
普陀区	Putuo	3 487	11	3 397	17
闸北区	Zhabei	2 178		2 045	…
虹口区	Hongkou	2 227	7	1 948	…
杨浦区	Yangpu	3 215	1	3 042	6
闵行区	Minhang	6 766	317	6 315	126
宝山区	Baoshan	4 904	29	4 783	87
嘉定区	Jiading	2 903	85	2 713	91
金山区	Jinshan	1 281	17	1 188	28
松江区	Songjiang	3 489	356	2 824	288
青浦区	Qingpu	1 690	280	1 250	118
奉贤区	Fengxian	1 924	88	1 766	58
崇明县	Chongming	855	23	806	16

表 11.6 续表 1 continued

单位：万平方米(10 000 sq. m)

地 区	District	其 中 of which 新式里弄 Improved Residential Blocks	旧式里弄 Old Residential Blocks	简 屋 Simple Housings
总 计	**Total**	**311**	**1 206**	**11**
浦东新区	Pudong New Area	3	29	1
黄 浦 区	Huangpu	88	305	2
徐 汇 区	Xuhui	53	42	2
长 宁 区	Changning	18	43	…
静 安 区	Jing'an	76	72	…
普 陀 区	Putuo	4	58	…
闸 北 区	Zhabei	1	132	
虹 口 区	Hongkou	59	210	2
杨 浦 区	Yangpu	6	158	1
闵 行 区	Minhang	1	7	…
宝 山 区	Baoshan	…	6	…
嘉 定 区	Jiading		14	…
金 山 区	Jinshan	…	49	…
松 江 区	Songjiang	1	20	…
青 浦 区	Qingpu	…	42	
奉 贤 区	Fengxian	1	11	…
崇 明 县	Chongming	…	8	2

表 11.6 续表 2 continued

单位：万平方米(10 000 sq. m)

地 区	District	非居住房屋 Non-Residential Buildings	其中 of which 工厂 Plants	学校 Schools	仓库堆栈 Warehouses	办公楼 Offices
总 计	**Total**	**48 888**	**22 233**	**2 976**	**1 671**	**6 101**
浦东新区	Pudong New Area	10 713	4 512	573	375	1 291
黄浦区	Huangpu	1 881	151	105	26	680
徐汇区	Xuhui	2 376	519	322	64	662
长宁区	Changning	1 500	210	123	34	461
静安区	Jing'an	897	63	47	5	341
普陀区	Putuo	2 150	479	177	200	438
闸北区	Zhabei	1 464	416	103	54	282
虹口区	Hongkou	1 275	201	113	34	388
杨浦区	Yangpu	2 060	749	328	76	295
闵行区	Minhang	4 928	2 705	302	251	214
宝山区	Baoshan	3 487	1 550	154	286	225
嘉定区	Jiading	3 518	1 968	185	67	294
金山区	Jinshan	2 252	1 559	74	48	122
松江区	Songjiang	4 370	3 197	110	39	148
青浦区	Qingpu	2 699	1 916	76	41	93
奉贤区	Fengxian	2 454	1 625	113	27	109
崇明县	Chongming	864	411	71	43	58

表 11.6 续表 3 continued

单位：万平方米(10 000 sq. m)

地 区 District		其中 of which 商场店铺 Stores	医 院 Hospitals	旅 馆 Hotels	影剧院 Theatres and Cinemas	其 他 Others
总 计	**Total**	**5 847**	**576**	**1 087**	**55**	**8 342**
浦东新区	Pudong New Area	1 218	81	264	5	2 395
黄 浦 区	Huangpu	333	65	139	13	369
徐 汇 区	Xuhui	233	83	78	3	411
长 宁 区	Changning	195	35	104	2	335
静 安 区	Jing'an	101	26	78	2	234
普 陀 区	Putuo	353	25	65	3	410
闸 北 区	Zhabei	217	32	61	5	296
虹 口 区	Hongkou	188	28	56	6	261
杨 浦 区	Yangpu	223	38	32	3	316
闵 行 区	Minhang	532	44	17	4	861
宝 山 区	Baoshan	420	16	30	2	803
嘉 定 区	Jiading	452	23	45	1	484
金 山 区	Jinshan	294	22	19	1	112
松 江 区	Songjiang	428	20	37	…	390
青 浦 区	Qingpu	283	14	21	2	253
奉 贤 区	Fengxian	304	9	24	2	242
崇 明 县	Chongming	72	17	17	2	172

表11.7 各区、县八层以上房屋分布(2012)
DISTRIBUTION OF BUILDINGS OVER EIGHT STOREYS BY DISTRICTS AND COUNTIES

单位：万平方米(10 000 sq. m)

地区 District		合计 Total		8～10层 8～10 Storeys		11～15层 11～15 Storeys	
		幢 Building	面积 Floor Space	幢 Building	面积 Floor Space	幢 Building	面积 Floor Space
总计	**Total**	**32 022**	**30 550**	**4 367**	**2 911**	**15 125**	**10 390**
浦东新区	Pudong New Area	7 697	6 946	868	604	4 229	2 776
黄浦区	Huangpu	1 032	2 012	145	140	145	164
徐汇区	Xuhui	1 879	2 533	280	224	529	443
长宁区	Changning	1 232	1 830	242	155	353	339
静安区	Jing'an	564	1 092	82	54	61	57
普陀区	Putuo	1 886	2 348	213	128	619	496
闸北区	Zhabei	1 173	1 361	181	116	467	380
虹口区	Hongkou	1 085	1 461	176	123	274	229
杨浦区	Yangpu	1 692	1 732	238	197	679	513
闵行区	Minhang	4 739	3 284	755	522	3 040	2 020
宝山区	Baoshan	2 698	1 793	391	191	1 518	941
嘉定区	Jiading	1 971	1 388	186	106	897	603
金山区	Jinshan	449	310	76	46	312	194
松江区	Songjiang	2 032	1 443	240	172	1 182	776
青浦区	Qingpu	847	381	148	68	348	201
奉贤区	Fengxian	868	552	87	46	356	196
崇明县	Chongming	178	84	59	19	116	62

表 11.7 续表 continued

单位：万平方米(10 000 sq. m)

地 区 District		16～19 层 16～19 Storeys		20～29 层 20～29 Storeys		30 层以上 Over 30 Storeys	
		幢 Building	面 积 Floor Space	幢 Building	面 积 Floor Space	幢 Building	面 积 Floor Space
总 计	**Total**	**7 484**	**6 690**	**3 839**	**6 996**	**1 207**	**3 563**
浦东新区	Pudong New Area	1 736	1 499	657	1 255	207	812
黄 浦 区	Huangpu	196	290	348	813	198	605
徐 汇 区	Xuhui	458	546	452	899	160	421
长 宁 区	Changning	244	302	292	619	101	415
静 安 区	Jing'an	101	132	232	512	88	337
普 陀 区	Putuo	447	541	467	811	140	372
闸 北 区	Zhabei	205	238	228	436	92	191
虹 口 区	Hongkou	283	345	248	496	104	268
杨 浦 区	Yangpu	461	463	268	489	46	70
闵 行 区	Minhang	790	569	128	154	26	19
宝 山 区	Baoshan	626	495	132	136	31	30
嘉 定 区	Jiading	665	486	211	174	12	19
金 山 区	Jinshan	48	53	13	17		
松 江 区	Songjiang	522	367	87	126	1	2
青 浦 区	Qingpu	323	103	28	9		
奉 贤 区	Fengxian	377	260	47	48	1	2
崇 明 县	Chongming	2	1	1	2		

表 11.8 主要年份市政工程设施情况
CIVIL FACILITIES IN MAIN YEARS

指 标	Indicators	2000	2010	2011	2012
道路长度(公里)	Length of Roads(km)	6 641	16 687	16 792	17 316
道路面积(万平方米)	Area of Roads (10 000 sq. m)	8 147	25 607	26 176	26 813
城市桥梁(座)	Bridges (bridge)	4 432	11 849	12 149	12 544
防洪堤长度(公里)	Length of Floodwalls (km)	335	1 009	1 119	1 129
城市排水管道长度(公里)	Length of Sewage Pipelines (km)	3 920	11 483	17 599	18 191
污水处理厂污水处理能力(万吨/日)	Capacity of Sewage Treatment(10 000 tons/day)	463	684	694	701
防汛泵站(座)	Pumping Stations of Flood Prevention (bridge)	160	186	186	183

表 11.9 主要年份自来水情况
TAP WATER SUPPLY IN MAIN YEARS

指 标	Indicators	2000	2010	2011	2012
水厂个数(个)	Quantity of Water Works (unit)	218	105	90	78
水厂生产能力(万立方米/日)	Production Capacity (10 000 cu. m/day)	1 048	1 131	1 150	1 145
供水管道长度(公里)	Length of Water Supply Pipelines (km)	15 943	31 182	32 217	34 904
供水总量(亿立方米)	Volume of Water Supply (100 million cu. m)	24.00	30.90	31.13	30.97
售水总量(亿立方米)	Sales Volume of Tap Water (100 million cu. m)	19.75	24.44	24.41	24.35
#工业用水	Industrial Use	5.49	5.80	5.60	5.18
生活用水	Living Use	14.26	18.64	18.81	19.17
#居民生活用水	Living Use for Residents	6.82	9.80	9.70	9.96
人均日居民生活用水量(升)	Per Capita Daily Consumption of Water (liter)	114	117	113	115

表 11.10 主要年份用电量
ELECTRICITY POWER CONSUMPTION IN MAIN YEARS

	指 标 Indicators	2000	2010	2011	2012
用电量（亿千瓦小时）	Power Consumption（100 million kwh）	559.51	1 295.87	1 339.62	1 353.45
#农业用电	Agricultural Consumption	9.10	6.07	6.37	6.85
工业用电	Industrial Consumption	392.97	786.61	805.76	786.25
交通运输、仓储、邮政业	Transportation, Storage and Post Industry	5.94	34.11	38.00	38.74
商业、住宿和餐饮业	Commercial, Hotel and Eateries	41.81	69.44	72.04	74.72
金融、房地产、商务及居民服务业	Finance, Real Estate, Commerce and Residential Service	25.00	130.82	139.01	149.12
公共事业及管理组织	Public Affairs and Administrative Organization	23.18	76.64	78.48	82.77
城乡居民生活用电	Urban Residential Consumption	53.20	168.95	175.22	187.38

表 11.11 主要年份电力建设情况
ELECTRICITY POWER CONSTRUCTION IN MAIN YEARS

	指 标 Indicators	2001	2010	2011	2012
年末发电设备容量（万千瓦）	Year-end Capacity of Electricity Generating Equipment（10 000 KW）	1 121.09	1 855.38	1 962.52	2 145.99
架空线长度（公里）	Length of Trolly Wire（k. m.）	6 480.72	8 549.50	9 108.62	9 426.75
#220KV	220KV	1 756.74	2 956.08	3 220.74	3 475.20
电缆长度（公里）	Length of Cable（k. m.）	3 633.00	7 846.98	8 031.27	8 327.17
#220KV	220KV	145.00	516.44	537.30	550.30
公用变电容量（万千伏安）	Public Power Transformation Capacity（10 000 KVA）	4 601.08	11 657.19	12 443.17	13 051.90
#220KB ~ 35KV	220KB – 35KV	3 716.68	7 827.75	8 088.73	8 514.02

注：本页数据由市电力公司提供。
Note: Data on this page are provided by Shanghai Electric Power Corporation.

表 11.12 主要年份煤气、液化石油气、天然气情况
GAS, LIQUEFIED PETROLEUM GAS AND NATURAL GAS IN MAIN YEARS

指 标	Indicators	2000	2010	2011	2012
煤 气	**Gas**				
煤气生产能力(万立方米/日)	Production Capacity (10 000 cu. m/day)	984.30	817.40	817.40	567.40
煤气管线长度(公里)	Length of Gas Pipelines (km)	6 606	5 517	4 710	3 596
煤气销售总量(亿立方米)	Total Sales Volume (100 million cu. m)	18.40	12.85	10.82	8.18
#家庭用量	Household Consumption	11.46	6.28	5.32	3.91
家庭煤气用户数(万户)	Households Users (10 000 households)	255.89	132.89	101.78	75.70
液化石油气	**Liquefied Petroleum Gas (LPG)**				
液化石油气销售总量(万吨)	Sales of LPG (10 000 tons)	45.94	40.05	39.65	39.33
#家庭用量	Household Consumption	20.47	23.62	20.90	21.42
家庭液化石油气用户数(万户)	Household Users (10 000 households)	239.30	316.37	310.62	328.22
天然气	**Natural Gas**				
天然气销售总量(亿立方米)	Sales of Natural Gas (100 million cu. m)	2.16	42.66	51.47	60.01
#家庭用量	Household Consumption	0.45	7.79	8.63	9.93
天然气管线长度(公里)	Length of Natural Gas Pipelines (km)	1 742	17 316	19 068	21 283
家庭天然气用户数(万户)	Household Users of Natural Gas (10 000 households)	38.10	405.89	455.92	502.81

表 11.13 主要年份公共交通和轮渡情况
PUBLIC TRANSPORTATION AND FERRY IN MAIN YEARS

指 标	Indicators	2000	2010	2011	2012
公共汽电车	**Buses and Trolley Buses**				
公交运营线路长度(公里)	Length of Public Bus Operation Lines (km)	23 260	23 131	22 906	23 190
公交运营线路条数(条)	Number of Public Bus Operation Lines (line)	978	1 165	1 202	1 257
运营公交车辆数(辆)	Operating Public Transportation Vehicles (vehicle)	17 939	17 455	16 589	16 695
#公共汽车	Buses	17 358	17 038	16 235	16 336
客运总量(亿人次)	Passenger Volume(100million person-times)	26.49	28.08	28.11	28.04
出租汽车	**Taxi**				
运营车辆(辆)	Operating Vehicles (vehicle)	42 943	50 007	50 438	50 683
#小客车	Small Passenger Car	40 806	49 016	49 509	49 803
载客车次(万次)	Number of Carryings(10 000 times)	37 599.00	63 306.89	60 858.56	59 503.00
运营里程(亿公里)	Operation Length (100 million km)	46.48	64.85	64.29	63.77
#载客里程	Transport Lengths of Passengers	24.35	39.79	39.54	39.84
运营收入(亿元)	Operation Revenues(100 million yuan)	76.68	154.72	159.36	167.74
运营单位(个)	Operation Unit (unit)	1 178	3 301	3 282	3 201
轮 渡	**Ferry**				
年末轮渡船数(艘)	Year-end Number of Ferry Boats (ship)	95	42	38	54
乘客人数(亿人次)	Passenger Volume (100 million person-times)	1.85	0.89	0.78	0.72

注：本表数据由市交通运输和港口管理局提供。
Note: Data in this table are provided by Shanghai Municipal Transport and Port Authority.

表 11.14 轨道交通、城市快速路、黄浦江大桥和隧道基本情况（2009～2012）
BASIC FACTS OF RAILWAY COMMUNICATION, URBAN EXPRESSWAYS, BRIDGES ACROSS HUANGPU RIVER AND TUNNELS

指 标	Indicators	2009	2010	2011	2012
轨道交通	**Urban Metro**				
运营车辆(辆)	Operating Vehicles(car)	1 833	2 842	2 899	3 130
轨道交通线路条数(条)	Number of Operation Lines(line)	11	12	12	13
运营线路长度(公里)	Length of Operation Lines(km)	355.05	452.57	454.10	468.19
运营里程(万列·公里)	Operation Mileage(10 000 vehicle-km)	2 871	4 778	5 406	5 570
客运总量(万人次)	Volume of Passenger Traffic (10 000 person-times)	131 837	188 407	210 105	227 573
年末从业人数(人)	Year-end Number of Staff and Workers (person)	20 349	39 785	26 046	28 153
城市快速路、大桥和隧道	**Urban Expresswarys, Bridges and Tunnels**				
城市快速路长度(公里)	Length of Urban Expresswarys (km)	114	196	194	199
越江大桥数(座)	Number of Bridges Across Huangpu River (bridge)	8	10	10	10
越江隧道数(条)	Tunnels Across Huangpu River (tunnel)	9	12	13	13

①越江隧道中含外滩隧道。
②本表数据由市交通运输和港口管理局、市城乡建设和交通委员会提供。
❶The Bund Tunnel is contained in Tunnels Across Huangpu River.
❷Data in this table are provided by Shanghai Municipal Transport and Port Authority and Shanghai Municipal Urban and Rural.

表 11.15 主要年份城市设施水平
LEVEL OF URBAN FACILITIES IN MAIN YEARS

指 标	Indicators	2000	2010	2011	2012
人均日综合生活用水量(升)	Per Capita Daily Consumption of Water for Life (liter)	241	223	220	221
人均日居民生活用水量(升)	Per Capita Daily Consumption of Water (liter)	114	117	113	115
自来水普及率(%)	Percentage of Population with Access to Tap Water (%)	99.97	99.99	99.99	99.99
拥有道路长度(公里/万人)	Per Capita Length of Roads (km/10 000 persons)	5.84	11.82	11.83	12.19
人均拥有道路面积(平方米)	Per Capita Area of Roads (sq. m)	7.17	18.13	18.44	18.88
每万人拥有城市排水管道长度(公里)	Length of Sewage Pipelines Per 10 000 Persons (km)	2.96	8.13	12.39	12.75
每万人拥有公共交通车辆 (辆)	Number of Public Transportation Vehicles Per 10 000 Persons (vehicle)	12.08	12.46	11.79	11.91
每万人拥有出租汽车(辆)	Number of Taxi Per 10 000 Persons (vehicle)	25.61	21.72	21.49	21.29
人均公园绿地面积 (平方米)	Per Capita Park Green Areas (sq. m)	4.60	13.00	13.10	13.29
每万人拥有公共厕所(座)	Number of Public Lavatories Per 10 000 Persons (unit)	1.67	4.27	4.06	4.44

表 11.16 主要年份城市绿地情况
URBAN GREEN SPACE IN MAIN YEARS

单位：公顷(hectare)

年 份 Year	城市绿地面积 Urban Green Space	其 中 of which # 公园绿地 Public Green Area	其 中 of which 公园面积 Area of Parks	街道绿地 Roadside Green Area	# 附属绿地 Sub Green	# 生产绿地 Production Green
1990	3 570	983	712	271	2 255	294
1995	6 561	1 793	920	873	4 429	309
1996	7 231	2 008	933	1 076	4 889	305
1997	7 849	2 484	961	1 523	5 083	253
1998	8 855	3 117	976	2 141	5 456	253
1999	11 117	3 856	993	2 863	6 888	318
2000	12 601	4 812	1 153	3 658	7 346	388
2001	14 771	5 820	1 291	4 529	8 624	248
2002	18 758	7 810	1 411	6 399	9 591	267
2003	24 426	9 450	1 473	7 977	10 218	335
2004	26 689	10 979	1 481	9 498	10 921	335
2005	28 865	12 038	1 521	10 516	11 591	335
2006	30 609	13 307	1 525	11 782	12 202	331
2007	31 795	13 899	1 675	12 224	13 590	204
2008	34 256	14 777	1 686	13 091	14 739	189
2009	116 929	15 406	1 687	13 119	17 376	230
2010	120 148	16 053	1 915	13 418	18 589	230
2011	122 283	16 446	2 151	13 499	19 442	213
2012	124 204	16 848	2 217	13 865	20 084	269

注：根据《城市和村镇建设统计报表制度》，2009 年对绿地分类进行了调整。 城市绿地由公园绿地、生产绿地、防护绿地、附属绿地和其他绿地五大类构成。

Note: The Categories of Urban Green include Public Green Area, Production Green Area, Protection Green Area, Sub Green Area and Other Green Area, which have been adjusted by the Statistical Reporting Regulation of City and Town Construction since 2009.

表 11.16 续表 continued

年 份 Year	公园数 (个) Parks (unit)	游园人数 (万人次) Visitors to Parks and Zooes (10 000 person-times)	行道树实有数 (万株) Roadside Trees (10 000 trees)	新辟绿地面积(公顷) Greenlands Newly Created (hectare)	绿化覆盖率 (%) Coverage Rate of Urban Green Areas(%)
1990	83	8 474	23	186	12.4
1995	100	9 064	33	516	16.0
1996	105	9 797	41	587	17.0
1997	108	9 757	43	728	17.8
1998	111	9 285	48	1 077	19.1
1999	115	9 601	54	1 315	20.3
2000	122	8 184	57	1 458	22.2
2001	125	8 561	65	1 374	23.8
2002	133	8 796	68	2 600	30.0
2003	136	9 629	74	4 904	35.2
2004	136	13 381	80	2 434	36.0
2005	144	13 656	83	2 116	37.0
2006	144	16 652	86	1 691	37.3
2007	146	18 342	69	1 629	37.6
2008	147	22 119	73	1 190	38.0
2009	147	21 671	76	1 096	38.1
2010	148	21 794	81	1 223	38.2
2011	153	20 481	93	1 063	38.2
2012	157	22 231	98	1 038	38.3

表11.17　各区、县绿化面积(2012)
URBAN GREEN AREA IN DIFFERENT DISTRICTS AND COUNTIES

地区 District		城市绿地面积(公顷) Urban Green Space (hectare)	其中 of which #公园绿地面积 Park Green Areas	公园数(个) Quantity of Parks (unit)	公园游园人数(万人次) Visitors to Parks and Zoos (10 000 person-times)
总　计	**Total**	**124 204.43**	**16 848.02**	**157**	**22 231.29**
浦东新区	Pudong New Area	26 725.16	6 065.00	25	2 083.33
黄浦区	Huangpu	264.56	161.64	12	3 342.18
徐汇区	Xuhui	1 261.52	503.99	11	2 733.35
长宁区	Changning	1 041.66	449.55	13	1 668.52
静安区	Jing'an	106.62	47.07	3	319.69
普陀区	Putuo	1 180.25	527.85	17	2 325.15
闸北区	Zhabei	619.39	232.70	7	1 591.14
虹口区	Hongkou	407.04	153.39	9	1 985.67
杨浦区	Yangpu	1 377.71	462.54	14	1 990.77
闵行区	Minhang	8 398.76	2 238.85	10	891.72
宝山区	Baoshan	6 486.25	1 993.53	13	2 178.86
嘉定区	Jiading	7 918.69	1 196.78	5	285.03
金山区	Jinshan	8 779.29	617.14	7	123.22
松江区	Songjiang	12 797.64	710.87	5	350.56
青浦区	Qingpu	10 234.21	745.06	3	111.98
奉贤区	Fengxian	9 863.34	494.17	1	211.14
崇明县	Chongming	26 742.35	247.89	2	38.98

上 / 海 / 统 / 计 / 年 / 鉴

主要统计指标解释

■ 城市基础设施

城市基础设施包括电力建设、交通运输、邮电通信、公用事业和市政建设等。

■ 道路长度

指道路长度和与道路相通的桥梁、隧道的长度，按车行道中心线计算。

■ 城市绿地

指以自然植被和人工植被为主要存在形态的城市用地。它包含两个层次的内容：一是城市建设用地范围内用于绿化的土地；二是城市建设用地之外，对城市生态、景观和居民休闲生活具有积极作用、绿化环境较好的区域。

■ 绿地面积

指报告期末用作园林和绿化的各种绿地面积。包括公园绿地、生产绿地、防护绿地、附属绿地和其他绿地面积。

其中：公园绿地：指向公众开放的、以游憩为主要功能，有一定的游憩设施和服务设施，同时兼有健全生态、美化景观、防灾减灾等综合作用的绿化用地。它是城市建设用地、城市绿地系统和城市市政公用设施的重要组成部分。

■ 供水管道长度

指从送水泵至用户水表之间所有管道的长度。不包括新安装尚未使用的管道。

■ 供水总量

指报告期供水企业（单位）供出的全部水量。包括有效供水量和漏损水量。

■ 生活用水

生活用水包括城市公共用水和居民家庭用水。城市公共用水包括建筑业用水、公共服务用水及生态环境用水。建筑业用水指土木工程建筑业、线路管道和设备安装业、建筑安装业、建筑装饰业和其他建筑业用水。生态环境用水主要包括城镇绿化、环卫用水及深井回灌用水。公共服务用水指为城市社会公共生活服务的用水。包括行政事业单位、部队营区和公共设施服务、社会服务业、批发零售贸易业、旅馆饮食业以及其他公共服务业等单位的用水。居民家庭用水指城市范围内所有居民家庭的日常生活用水。包括城市居民、农民家庭、公共供水站用水。

■ 煤气生产能力

指报告期末煤气生产厂制气、净化、输送等环节的综合生产能力，不包括备用设备能力。一般按设计能力计算，如果实际生产能力大于设计能力时，应按实际测定的生产能力计算。测定时应以制气、净化、输送三个环节中最薄弱的环节为主。

■ 排水管道长度

指所有排水总管、干管、支管、检查井及连接井进出口等长度之和。

■ 运营公交车辆数

指年末公交企业(单位)用于运营业务的全部车辆数。以企业(单位)固定资产台帐中已投入运营的车辆数为准。

■ 污水日处理能力

指污水处理厂(或处理装置)每昼夜处理污水量的设计能力。

SHANGHAI STATISTICAL YEARBOOK

EXPLANATORY NOTES TO MAJOR STATISTICAL INDICATORS

□ Urban Infrastructure Facilities

Urban Infrastructure Facilities include facilities for power generating, transportation, post and telecommunication, public utilities, development of municipal engineering.

□ Length of Roads

The length of roads refers to the length of roads and of the bridges and tunnels connected to the roads, calculated by the center line of the roads.

□ Urban Green

Urban Green refers the urban land mainly used as natural vegetation and artificial vegetation. First, it includes the area of urban construction land for greening. Except the urban construction land, the green area which is beneficial for urban ecology, landscape and residents leisure is also included.

□ Green Space

Green Space includes all kinds of gardens and green at the end of reporting period. Park green area, production green area, protection green area, sub green area and other green area are all included.

Park green area refers to green areas open to the public for amusement and rest with the facilities of amusement, rest and services. Its function includes perfecting ecology, beautifying landscape, and preventing and reducing disaster. It is an important part of urban construction land, urban green and municipal public infrastructure in city.

□ Length of Water Supply Pipelines

Length of Water Supply Pipelines refers to the total length of all the pipelines between the water pumps and the user's water meters, excluding pipelines newly installed but not used yet.

□ Volume of Water Supply

Volume of Water Supply refers to the total volume of water supplied by water-works (units) during the reference period, including both the effective water supply and loss during the water supply.

□ Consumption of Water for Living Use

Consumption of Water for Linvin Use refers to the water consumption for city public and the water consumption of households for daily life. The water consumption for city public includes the water consumption of construction, the water consumption of public service facilities and the water consumption of city ecology. The water consumption of construction refers to the water consumption of civil engineering, line pipe and equipment installation, construction installation, construction decoration and other construction. The water consumption of city ecology mainly includes the consumption of urban green, urban Sanitation and deep well re-irrigation. The water consumption of public service facilities refers to the water consumption for urban public services, including the consumption of government agencies and public institutions, military barracks, public facilities, wholesale and retail outlets, restaurants, hotels, and other units providing public services. Household water consumption refers to consumption of water for daily life of all households in the boundary of cities, including households of urban residents and farmers, and public water supply stations.

□ Production Capacity of Gas

Production Capacity of Gas refers to the comprehensive production capacity of the urban gasworks in gas generation, purification and delivery at the end of the reference period, excluding capacity of the reserved facilities. In general, it is determined by the designed capacity, and when actual production capacity is larger than the designed capacity, the capacity is determined by the actual measurement on the weakest link in the production, purification and delivery.

□ Length of Sewage Pipes

Length of Sewage Pipes refers to the total length of general drainage, trunks, branch and inspection wells, connection wells, inlets and outlets, etc.

第十二篇

CHAPTER 12

农　　业

AGRICULTURE

简要说明

一、本篇资料的主要内容

本篇资料反映本市农业生产和农村经济的基本情况，内容主要包括农林牧渔业产值、耕地、农村户数和人口、农作物播种面积、主要农产品产量、农产品出口、农田水利投资、农村用电量、农业机械拥有量、农业技术应用和综合开发、市级农业园区基本情况等方面的统计资料。

二、本篇资料的统计范围

农业统计范围为上海市，包括闵行区、宝山区、嘉定区、松江区、金山区、青浦区、奉贤区、崇明县和浦东新区（农村）行政区域范围内所有建制乡镇、行政村和涉农街道、居委会辖区内的生产经营单位和农户；上海光明食品（集团）、上海水产（集团）总公司、青东农场、前卫农场、上实现代农业园区以及其他中央属、市属和军委系统的农业生产（经营）活动单位。

1. 农业：指对各种农作物的种植活动。包括谷物、豆类、薯类、棉花、油料、糖料、麻类、烟叶、蔬菜、园艺作物、水果、坚果、饮料和香料作物、中草药及其他作物的种植。

2. 林业：包括林木的栽培(不包括茶园、桑园和果园的栽培、管理和收获等活动),木材和竹材的采运，林产品的采集。

3. 畜牧业：包括牲畜饲养和放牧，家禽饲养以及野生动物的捕猎和饲养。

4. 渔业：包括水生动物和海藻类植物的养殖和捕捞。

5. 农、林、牧、渔服务业：指对农、林、牧、渔业生产活动进行的各种支持性服务。但不包括各种科学技术和专业性技术服务活动。

农村社会经济统计范围包括除城关镇以外所有乡镇的社会经济活动。

三、本篇的资料来源及统计调查方法

1. 农业生产基本情况（表 12.1 至 12.10、表 12.13 和表 12.15），由国家统计局上海调查总队根据《农村统计报表制度》的有关资料整理提供。

《农村统计报表制度》包括四部分内容：

一是农林牧渔业统计。包括农作物播种面积、主要农作物产量、耕地、农业机械等内容。这部分内容为全面统计报表制度，水果、林业、渔业和部分畜牧业数据来源为农委相关部门，调查方法由统计部门及资料来源相关部门确定。

二是农业产值综合统计。包括农林牧渔业产值、农林牧渔业中间消耗、农产品出口、种源农业等内容，调查方法由统计部门确定。

三是农村综合统计。包括乡镇社会经济基本情况、市级农业园区、行政村基本情况、郊区主要经济指标月报表、农业能源消费情况等内容。上海参照国家统计局《县域社会经济基本情况统计报表制度》充实部分指标进行调查。

四是农产量抽样调查。包括农户种植意向、全年实测粮食产量、农作物预计产量等内容。调查方法由统计部门确定。

2. 主要年份农田水利投资(表 12.11),主要来源于水务部门汇总的统计报表,调查方法由水务部门确定。

3. 主要年份农村用电量(表 12.12),主要来源于上海电力公司,调查方法由电力公司确定。

4. 主要年份农业技术应用和综合开发情况(表 12.14),由国家统计局上海调查总队根据《农村统计报表制度》和农委相关部分报表的有关资料整理提供。调查方法由统计部门及农委相关部门确定。

BRIEF INTRODUCTION

I. Main Contents

The data in this chapter reflect the basic conditions of agricultural production and rural economy in Shanghai. The main contents include output of agriculture, forestry, animal husbandry and fishery, cultivated land, number of rural households, rural population, sown area of farm crops, output of major agricultural products, agricultural products export, investment in facilities of water conservancy, electricity consumption in rural areas, ownership of agricultural machinery, application and comprehensive development of rural technology, and basic conditions of municipal agricultural zones.

II. Scope and Coverage of Statistics

Data on agriculture cover the whole Shanghai Municipality including Minhang, Baoshan, Jiading, Songjiang, Jinshan, Qingpu, Fengxian districts, Chongming County, and Pudong New Area (rural area). Included in agriculture statistics are production activities in agriculture by rural production units and by rural households; production activities of farms in counties, villages and rural communities; production activities in agriculture undertaken by Shanghai Bright Food (Group), Shanghai Fisheries (Group) Corporation, the Qingdong Farm, the Qianwei Farm, SIIC Modern Agriculture Park and agricultural production units owned by the central government, municipal government and military agencies.

(1) Agriculture: it refers to cultivation of farm crops, including cereals, beans, tuber crops, cotton, oil–bearing crops, sugar crops, hemp, tobacco leaves, vegetables, gardening plants, fruits, nuts, crops for beverages and spices, medicinal herbs and other farm crops.

(2) Forestry: it includes the planting of trees (excluding activities of planting, managing and harvesting of tea, mulberry fields and fruits), cutting and transport of timber and bamboo and collection of forest products.

(3) Animal husbandry: it includes the raising and grazing of domestic animals and poultry, and the hunting and raising of wild animals.

(4) Fishery: it includes cultivation and catching of aquatic animals and seaweed.

(5) Services in support of agriculture, forestry, animal husbandry and fishery: they include supporting services to production activities in agriculture, forestry, animal husbandry and fishery but do not include activities of science and technology and professional services.

Rural social and economic statistics cover social and economic activities in all townships except towns, where county governments are located.

III. Data Sources and Survey Methodology

(1) Data on basic conditions of agricultural production (Table 12.1 to Table 12.10, Table 12.13, and Table 12.15) are provided by the Survey Office of the National Bureau of Statistics in Shanghai using data from the Statistical Survey System on Rural Areas.

Statistical Survey System on Rural Areas consists of four parts:

First, it includes statistics on agriculture, forestry, animal husbandry and fishery, including agricultural production conditions, arable land, and agricultural machinery. Content in this part adopts the comprehensive reporting system, whose fruit, forestry, and part of animal husbandry data are provided by Shanghai Municipal Agriculture Commission.

Survey methodologies are determined by the statistics department and relevant providers of the data.

Second, it includes comprehensive statistics on value of agricultural output, including output of agriculture, forestry, animal husbandry, and fishery, intermediate consumption of agriculture, forestry, animal husbandry, and fishery, export of agricultural products, and seed industries. Survey methodologies are determined by the statistics department.

Third, it includes comprehensive statistics on rural areas. The data include basic conditions of social and economic activities at county, township and rural administrations, municipal agricultural zones, major monthly economic indicator of suburban areas, and energy consumptions of units engaged in agriculture, forestry, animal husbandry and fishery. Data are provided according to Statistical Reporting System on the Basic Condition of Social and Economic Activities of Counties with additional standards supplemented by Shanghai authorities.

Fourth, it includes sample surveys on agricultural output. The data include farmers' intention to plant, final measured crop output for the year, and expectations for crop output. Methodologies are determined by the statistics department.

(2) Investment in irrigation and reservoirs in main years (table 12.11) with data mainly provided by Shanghai Municipal Water Authority. Methodologies are determined by Shanghai Municipal Water Authority.

(3) Rural power consumption in main years (table 12.12) with data mainly provided by Shanghai Municipal Electric Power Company. Methodologies are determined by Shanghai Municipal Electric Power Company.

(4) Application and comprehensive development of agricultural technology in main years (table 12.14) with Data collected and provided by the Survey Office of the National Bureau of Statistics in Shanghai according to Statistical Survey System on Rural Areas and relevant materials submitted by Shanghai Municipal Agricultural Commission. Methodologies are determined by the statistics department.

表 12.1 农业总产值(1978～2012)
GROSS OUTPUT VALUE OF AGRICULTURE

单位:亿元(100 million yuan)

年份 Year	农业总产值 Gross Output Value of Agriculture	其中 of which				
		种植业 Planting	林业 Forestry	畜牧业 Animal Husbandry	渔业 Fishery	农林牧渔服务业 Service Industry for Agriculture
1978	18.26	13.49	0.06	3.67	0.86	
1979	20.41	15.10	0.04	4.22	0.90	
1980	18.90	11.40	0.06	6.27	0.97	
1981	20.33	11.91	0.21	6.38	1.23	
1982	23.97	13.80	0.23	7.81	1.56	
1983	22.68	12.59	0.20	7.80	1.29	
1984	26.59	16.41	0.21	8.06	1.40	
1985	31.38	15.63	0.21	12.25	2.82	
1986	33.76	16.83	0.24	12.75	3.45	
1987	38.84	17.69	0.34	15.48	4.79	
1988	53.07	22.47	0.45	22.18	7.43	
1989	60.63	25.53	0.39	26.41	7.88	
1990	68.16	29.09	0.37	30.25	8.04	
1991	73.65	30.51	0.39	33.38	8.97	
1992	80.01	32.80	0.43	37.19	9.18	
1993	96.20	40.52	0.41	42.95	12.31	
1994	140.24	60.19	0.49	62.04	17.52	
1995	182.47	77.71	0.45	81.48	22.83	
1996	200.95	87.64	0.67	85.46	27.18	
1997	204.41	85.20	0.47	88.37	30.37	
1998	206.75	89.10	0.84	87.27	29.54	
1999	206.90	87.86	0.98	86.35	31.71	
2000	216.50	89.81	1.41	87.35	37.92	
2001	227.61	95.53	3.52	88.43	40.13	
2002	233.57	97.21	7.75	83.48	45.13	
2003	247.29	98.17	13.05	81.13	49.21	5.73
2004	248.89	109.32	13.14	70.77	49.90	5.76
2005	233.39	111.25	11.11	54.34	51.64	5.05
2006	237.01	119.99	10.43	46.29	55.25	5.05
2007	255.98	126.74	10.05	58.00	54.19	7.00
2008	280.35	137.52	9.12	68.40	57.11	8.20
2009	283.15	147.53	8.99	64.61	53.53	8.49
2010	287.03	155.27	7.53	62.90	52.62	8.71
2011	314.58	165.07	7.62	77.44	54.72	9.73
2012	321.73	171.48	9.55	72.59	57.45	10.66

注：2003 年以前，农业总产值不包括农林牧渔服务业。

Note: The Gross Output Value of Agriculture did not include the output value of service industry for planting, forestry, animal husbandary and fishery before 2003.

表 12.2　农业总产值指数(以 1978 年为 100，1978～2012)
GROSS OUTPUT VALUE INDEX OF AGRICULTURE (1978 = 100)

年 份 Year	农业总产值指数 Index of Gross Output Value of Agriculture	其 中 of which				
		种植业 Planting	林 业 Forestry	牧 业 Animal Husbandry	渔 业 Fishery	农林牧渔服务业 Service Industry for Agriculture
1978	100.0	100.0	100.0	100.0	100.0	
1979	101.4	92.9	121.9	128.1	101.6	
1980	92.1	78.6	152.9	115.8	104.1	
1981	100.0	83.9	144.0	140.2	97.3	
1982	117.4	97.4	161.1	170.1	107.3	
1983	109.9	86.0	116.1	167.3	123.6	
1984	124.5	109.0	98.4	167.5	114.7	
1985	113.0	88.2	107.2	181.4	127.6	
1986	119.7	89.5	134.5	201.2	149.5	
1987	122.5	90.6	138.9	206.7	158.1	
1988	130.3	95.3	166.0	227.0	160.0	
1989	132.0	92.3	134.9	245.6	171.8	
1990	139.5	96.3	139.7	271.2	164.3	
1991	146.2	95.6	153.7	299.0	172.7	
1992	154.7	101.3	144.0	322.9	168.8	
1993	147.9	94.1	129.4	313.8	166.8	
1994	159.4	96.0	130.5	336.7	215.0	
1995	177.0	104.0	125.2	363.0	252.4	
1996	191.6	114.5	168.6	389.1	269.6	
1997	202.5	123.1	133.0	404.3	288.4	
1998	207.3	129.4	185.2	412.1	278.6	
1999	212.6	133.2	258.3	418.0	289.2	
2000	220.9	141.2	414.9	414.6	321.9	
2001	236.5	145.2	629.7	433.7	392.0	
2002	243.6	145.7	1 546.0	416.4	442.6	100.0
2003	246.3	135.3	2 062.4	395.5	544.4	102.6
2004	229.6	144.0	2 070.6	306.5	526.4	103.2
2005	205.5	136.7	1 613.0	221.6	555.4	91.4
2006	206.9	141.1	1 514.6	205.0	587.6	90.3
2007	210.0	142.9	1 458.6	214.2	573.5	121.6
2008	210.2	147.2	1 185.8	223.6	520.2	134.6
2009	209.1	145.1	1 147.9	238.6	481.7	140.0
2010	198.4	138.3	960.8	231.9	443.2	139.2
2011	197.2	139.1	914.7	237.2	407.3	147.8
2012	198.2	139.7	1 032.7	233.2	411.0	157.6

注：根据国家统计局方法制度规定，从 2006 年起，农业总产值指数按可比价计算，2006 年以前按不变价计算。

Note: According to the regulation of National Bureau of Statistics, since 2006, index of gross output value of agriculture has been calculated by comparable price, and before 2006, it was calculated by constant price.

表 12.3 耕地面积(1978 ~2012) AREAS UNDER CULTIVATION

年 份 Year	耕地面积（万公顷）Cultivated Area (10 000 hectares)	其中 of which 水 田 Paddy Fields	其中 of which 水浇地 Irrigated Land	平均每个农村人口占有耕地（平方米）Cultivated Area Per Rural Person (sq·m)	平均每个农村从业人员占有耕地（平方米）Cultivated Area Per Rural Employee (sq·m)
1978	36.01	31.88	4.14	800	1 240
1979	35.58	31.49	4.08	793	1 220
1980	35.41	31.26	4.15	787	1 193
1981	35.27	31.02	4.25	773	1 173
1982	35.17	30.96	4.21	767	1 173
1983	34.99	31.00	4.00	760	1 193
1984	34.58	30.89	3.69	760	1 207
1985	33.96	30.45	3.51	753	1 200
1986	33.30	29.75	3.56	740	1 200
1987	33.09	29.67	3.42	740	1 207
1988	32.72	29.28	3.44	740	1 213
1989	32.40	28.95	3.45	733	1 227
1990	32.32	28.54	3.78	773	1 293
1991	32.10	28.38	3.72	731	1 236
1992	31.78	28.03	3.75	718	1 303
1993	30.20	26.42	3.78	712	1 215
1994	29.38	25.81	3.58	735	1 262
1995	29.00	25.39	3.61	740	1 189
1996	30.06	27.16	2.89	753	1 051
1997	29.80	26.93	2.87	762	1 052
1998	29.38	26.67	2.71	758	1 087
1999	29.09	26.15	2.94	732	1 058
2000	28.59	25.74	2.85	731	1 048
2001	28.06	26.02	2.04	722	1 029
2002	27.04	25.06	1.98	693	986
2003	25.73	24.19	1.54	668	951
2004	24.57	22.88	1.69	654	918
2005	23.73	22.34	1.39	647	899
2006	20.80	18.83	1.97	583	901
2007	20.60	18.65	1.95	580	942
2008	20.50	17.51	2.99	550	884
2009	20.23	16.98	3.25	553	895
2010	20.10	15.32	4.78	598	969
2011	19.96	15.21	4.75	565	933
2012	19.90	13.82	6.08	623	963

表 12.4 主要年份农村户数、人口和从业人员
RURAL HOUSEHOLDS, POPULATION AND EMPLOYEES IN MAIN YEARS

指 标	Indicators	2000	2010	2011	2012
户 数(万户)	**Households (10 000 households)**	**115.17**	**114.22**	**119.02**	**112.08**
人 口(万人)	**Population (10 000 persons)**	**360.71**	**305.68**	**311.18**	**289.70**
从业人员(万人)	**Employees (10 000 persons)**	**253.45**	**188.70**	**188.32**	**187.45**
#农 业	Agriculture	81.45	34.06	33.38	44.87
工 业	Industry	108.75	100.85	97.87	92.61
建筑业	Construction	11.14	8.99	9.15	13.17
交通运输、仓储及邮政业	Transportation, Storage and Post	7.07	7.85	9.07	7.78
批发和零售业	Wholesale and Retail	13.49	6.16	7.11	9.02

注：从业人员包括农村国有经济的机关、团体、学校、企事业单位的集体户和户口在家而领取工资的国家职工。
Note: Employees have included salary taking state staff and workers who had local residential papers or registered in the collective residential papers of stateowned economic departments, organizations, schools, enterprises and institutions in rural areas.

表 12.5 主要年份农作物总播种面积
TOTAL SOWN AREA OF PLANTING IN MAIN YEARS

年 份 Year	总播种面积(万公顷) Total Sown Area (10 000 hectare)	粮食作物 Grain Crops		经济作物 Cash Crops	
		播种面积 Sown Area	占总播种面积(%) Percentage (%)	播种面积 Sown Area	占总播种面积(%) Percentage (%)
1990	63.11	41.71	66.1	21.40	33.9
1995	54.22	34.40	63.5	19.82	36.5
1996	57.01	35.38	62.1	21.63	37.9
1997	55.23	36.58	66.2	18.65	33.8
1998	55.64	35.25	63.4	20.39	36.6
1999	55.17	33.50	60.7	21.67	39.3
2000	52.15	25.88	49.6	26.27	50.4
2001	49.09	21.12	43.0	27.97	57.0
2002	47.67	18.77	39.4	28.90	60.6
2003	41.92	14.83	35.4	27.09	64.6
2004	40.44	15.47	38.3	24.97	61.7
2005	40.36	16.61	41.1	23.75	58.9
2006	40.14	16.55	41.2	23.59	58.8
2007	39.07	16.96	43.4	22.11	56.6
2008	38.84	17.45	44.9	21.39	55.1
2009	39.61	19.33	48.8	20.28	51.2
2010	40.12	17.92	44.7	22.20	55.3
2011	40.06	18.63	46.5	21.43	53.5
2012	39.00	18.76	48.1	20.24	51.9

表 12.6　主要年份农副产品产量
OUTPUT OF MAJOR FARM AND SIDELINE PRODUCTS IN MAIN YEARS

指　标	Indicators	2000	2010	2011	2012
农副产品	**Farm and Sideline Products**				
粮　食(万吨)(包括大豆)	Grain (10 000tons) (Including Soybean)	174.00	118.40	121.95	122.39
棉　花(万吨)	Cotton (10 000tons)	0.12	0.35	0.48	0.38
油　料(万吨)	Oil Plants (10 000tons)	16.37	2.29	1.86	1.73
#油菜籽	Rapeseed	15.71	2.04	1.64	1.51
蔬　菜(万吨)	Vegetables (10 000tons)	377.00	398.08	408.24	406.93
西甜瓜(万吨)	Watermelons and Muskmelons (10 000tons)	49.88	55.44	46.01	37.14
水　果(万吨)	Fruits (10 000tons)	22.54	44.16	40.22	48.15
#生　梨	Pear	1.74	3.84	3.17	3.74
柑　桔	Citrus Fruits	10.18	20.16	17.68	24.28
畜禽产品	**Livestock and Poultry**				
生猪出栏量(万头)	Quantity of Sold Hogs(10 000heads)	471.46	265.98	267.00	241.64
生猪年末圈存量(万头)	Hogs In Pens By Year-end (10 000heads)	241.60	171.87	180.65	172.71
奶牛年末头数(万头)	Cows In Pens By Year-end (10 000heads)	5.83	6.72	6.89	5.98
羊年末头数(万头)	Sheep In Pens By Year-end (10 000heads)	55.44	24.46	24.40	25.61
兔年末圈存量(万头)	Rabbits In Pens By Year-end (10 000heads)	88.90	12.17	7.42	8.08
猪　肉(万吨)	Pork (10 000tons)	25.96	17.87	19.12	17.57
牛羊肉(万吨)	Beef and Mutton (10 000tons)	0.79	0.54	0.55	0.58
家禽出栏量(万羽)	Quantity of Poultry Sold Birds (10 000fowls)	17 213	4 084	4 300	3 650
牛　奶(万吨)	Milk (10 000tons)	25.95	24.71	29.08	26.31
鲜　蛋(万吨)	Fresh Egg (10 000tons)	16.64	6.28	6.30	5.90
水产品	**Aquatic Products**				
海水产品(万吨)	Seawater Aquatic Products (10 000tons)	12.23	12.15	11.80	13.21
淡水产品(万吨)	Freshwater Aquatic Products (10 000tons)	16.64	16.82	16.57	14.00

表 12.7　农牧业特色种养产品产量(2011～2012)
OUTPUT OF SPECIAL PRODUCTS IN FARMING AND ANIMAL HUSBANDRY

指　标	Indicators	2011	2012	指　标	Indicators	2011	2012
桃　子(万吨)	Peach (10 000tons)	9.23	9.25	野　鸡(万只)	Pheasant (10 000 fowls)	19.82	11.18
葡　萄(万吨)	Graper (10 000tons)	9.54	10.29	野　鸭(万只)	mallard (10 000 fowls)	197.09	178.68
草　莓(万吨)	Strawberry (10 000tons)	1.72	1.89	肉　鸽(万只)	Meat Dove (10 000fowls)	918	971
枣(吨)	Date(ton)	1 312	1 113	甲　鱼(吨)	Soft-shelled Turtle (ton)	299	361
弥猴桃(吨)	Kiwi (ton)	661	852	河　蟹(万吨)	Hairy Crab (10 000tons)	1.51	1.50

表 12.8 主要农副产品产量与建国以来最高年产量的比较 (2012)
OUTPUT OF MAJOR FARM AND SIDELINE PRODUCTS IN COMPARISON WITH THE PEAK YEAR SINCE 1949

指 标	Indicators	2012	建国以来最高年 Peak Year Since 1949		2012 年为建国以来最高年份(%) 2012/Peak Year Since 1949
			年 份 Year	产 量 Output	
农产品	**Farm products**				
粮 食(万吨)	Grain (10 000tons)	122.39	1 978	260.88	46.9
棉 花(万吨)	Cotton (10 000tons)	0.38	1 978	12.10	3.1
油菜籽(万吨)	Rapeseed (10 000tons)	1.73	1 992	21.84	7.9
蔬 菜(万吨)	Vegetables (10 000tons)	406.93	2 008	46.12	104.4
西甜瓜(万吨)	Watermelons and Muskmelons (10 000tons)	37.14	2 003	76.50	48.6
水 果(万吨)	Fruits (10 000tons)	48.15	2 008	46.12	104.4
畜产品	**Animal Husbandry Products**				
猪年末圈存数(万头)	Quantity of Hogs in Pens (year-end) (10 000heads)	172.71	1 978	365.74	47.2
猪 肉(万吨)	Pork (10 000tons)	17.57	2 001	26.40	66.6
奶牛年末头数(万头)	Quantity of Milk Cow (year-end) (10 000heads)	5.98	1 991	7.31	81.8
牛 奶(万吨)	Milk (10 000tons)	26.31	2 002	27.98	94.0
家禽出栏量(万只)	Quantity of Poultry Sold(10 000fowls)	3 650	1 997	17 851	20.4
鲜 蛋(万吨)	Fresh Eggs (10 000tons)	5.90	2 001	16.87	35.0
水产品	**Aquatic Products**				
海水产品(万吨)	Seawater Aquatic Products (10 000tons)	13.21	2 006	19.44	68.0
淡水产品(万吨)	Freshwater Aquatic Products (10 000tons)	14.00	2 003	22.13	63.3

注：建国以来最高年份和产量均是指 2011 年及以前的年份和产量，不包括 2012 年在内。
Note: Peak year and output of peak year since 1949 refer to the years before 2011, excluding 2012.

表 12.9 主要年份农业商品产值和商品率
OUTPUT VALUE OF AGRICULTURAL COMMODITY AND COMMODITY RATE IN MAIN YEARS

指 标	Indicators	2000	2010	2011	2012
农业商品产值(亿元)	**Output Value of Agricultural Commodity (100 million yuan)**	**179.79**	**236.15**	**264.09**	**271.95**
#种植业	Planting	61.84	120.22	129.40	136.90
#粮食作物	Grain Crops	10.15	16.43	19.09	20.79
牧 业	Animal Husbandry	80.75	58.01	70.88	67.73
#猪	Hogs	29.82	30.38	40.89	37.52
禽	Poultry	33.41	8.95	9.49	8.39
蛋	Eggs	7.94	5.10	5.62	4.87
渔 业	Fishery	36.53	50.42	50.92	55.23
#淡水产品	Freshwater Aquatic Products	25.14	36.62	35.25	37.54
农业商品率(%)	**Agricultural Commodity Rate (%)**	**83.0**	**82.3**	**84.0**	**84.5**
#种植业	Planting	68.8	77.4	78.4	79.8
#粮食作物	Grain Crops	45.4	53.8	54.4	57.4
牧 业	Animal Husbandry	92.4	92.2	91.5	93.3
#猪	Hogs	95.8	94.7	95.9	96.5
禽	Poultry	91.9	86.5	80.7	85.8
蛋	Eggs	82.3	93.3	93.2	93.1
渔 业	Fishery	96.3	95.8	93.1	96.1
#淡水产品	Freshwater Aquatic Products	95.9	95.0	91.2	95.0

表 12.10 主要年份农产品出口情况
EXPORTS OF AGRICULTURAL PRODUCTS IN MAIN YEARS

单位:亿元(100 million yuan)

指 标	Indicators	2000	2010	2011	2012
农产品出口总额	**Output Value of Exports of Agricultural Products**	**7.88**	**11.28**	**12.62**	**12.70**
#农业产品	Farm Products	0.63	2.30	2.12	2.34
牧业产品	Animal Husbardry Products	1.71	0.16	0.10	0.17
渔业产品	Fishery Products	5.55	8.41	9.99	10.30
农产品直接出口总额	**Output Value of Direct Exports of Agricultural Products**	**6.82**	**9.50**	**10.56**	**11.07**
#农业产品	Farm Products	0.47	1.27	1.31	1.02
牧业产品	Animal Husbardry Products	0.99	0.07	0.10	0.17
渔业产品	Fishery Products	5.37	7.79	8.80	9.67
主要出口产品	**Main Products of Exports**				
蔬 菜	Vegetables	0.19	2.03	1.48	1.30
活 猪	Hogs	0.63	0.16	0.10	0.17
水产品	Aquatic Products	5.55	8.41	9.99	10.30
海水产品	Seawater Aquatic Products	5.29	7.37	8.60	9.03
淡水产品	Freshwater Aquatic Products	0.26	1.04	1.39	1.26

表 12.11 主要年份农田水利投资
INVESTMENT IN FARM WATER CONSERVANCY IN MAIN YEARS

单位：万元(10 000 yuan)

年 份 Year	合 计 Total	政府投资 Government Investment	其 中 of which #海 塘 Seadike	 #水 文 Hydrologic	 #基本建设 Capital Construction	其 他 Others
1990	26 143	15 959	907		1 506	10 184
1995	62 474	44 651	6 103		21 800	17 823
1996	76 467	56 421	6 470		20 693	20 046
1997	83 097	60 497	14 467		22 447	22 600
1998	108 565	83 596	9 660		37 780	24 969
1999	150 324	119 193	18 580	200	53 660	31 131
2000	184 102	151 539	22 063	100	53 532	32 563
2001	244 337	188 477	10 598	100	120 575	55 860
2002	382 935	264 370	23 548	203	140 875	118 565
2003	516 075	375 688	13 083	188	199 341	140 387
2004	576 050	219 506	7 317	254	97 328	356 544
2005	543 780	176 215	7 010	366	55 290	367 566
2006	467 449	202 815	2 603	316	30 423	264 634
2007	577 116	379 071	4 138	183	193 886	198 045
2008	623 627	443 344	14 774	754	175 652	180 283
2009	619 579	497 583	7 299	225	128 160	121 996
2010	534 195	433 825	11 455	2 113	17 623	100 370
2011	717 044	647 510	12 792	1 775	102 372	69 524
2012	727 380	712 654	17 166	1 277	56 189	14 726

注：2012 年起，因水利部门统计制度变更，国家投资变更为政府投资；自筹改为其他；农田水利工程投资口径变更为农田水利投资，包括水利专项维护投入。

Note: Since 2012, according to the regulations of water Resources Department, state investment is changed to government investment, funds raised is changed to others, water conservancy project investment is changed to water conservancy irvestment, including the maintenance input of water conservancy.

表 12.12 主要年份农村用电量
RURAL ELECTRICITY POWER CONSUMPTION IN MAIN YEARS

年 份 Year	农村用电量 （亿千瓦时） Rural Electricity Power Consumption (100 million kwh)	其 中 of which		
		机电排灌 Motorized Drainage and Irrigation	农、副业加工 Farming and Sideline Products Processing	乡村办工业 Rural Enterprises
1990	32.16	1.75	4.00	22.85
1995	58.19	2.00	7.26	41.24
1996	62.07	2.01	7.79	44.16
1997	64.98	1.94	6.92	47.55
1998	67.91	2.09	6.79	49.55
1999	70.89	2.09	6.34	52.67
2000	73.19	2.34	6.12	49.71
2001	79.66	1.51	3.57	62.51
2002	81.79	1.24	3.62	57.56
2003	89.70	1.12	3.24	61.53
2004	114.35	1.17	2.41	79.01
2005	124.53	0.99	2.70	99.72
2006	143.54	1.03	2.84	97.98
2007	171.68	0.85	2.44	108.11
2008	178.05	0.94	2.94	117.22
2009	191.80	0.86	2.94	141.97
2010	195.48	0.61	4.41	

表 12.12 续表 continued

年 份 Year	农村用电量 （亿千瓦时） Rural Electricity Power Consumption (100 million kwh)	其 中 of which					
		种植业 Planting	林 业 Forestry	畜牧业 Animal Husbandry	渔 业 Fishery	农林牧渔服务业 Services Industry for Agriculture	其 中 of which 排 灌 Drainage and Irrigation
2011	800.96	2.64	0.45	0.94	0.74	1.43	0.36
2012	819.71	3.00	0.45	1.01	0.84	1.47	0.41

注：因统计口径调整，2010 年起，乡村办工业用电量不再单独统计。
Note：Sine 2010, the Electricity Power Consumption of Rural Enterprises is no longer retained according to new statistical standard.

表 12.13　主要年份农业机械拥有量
POSSESSION OF AGRICULTURAL MACHINERY IN MAIN YEARS

机械名称	Name of Machinery	2000	2010	2011	2012
农业机械总动力（万千瓦）	**Total Power of Agricultural Machinery (10 000kw)**	**142.50**	**104.15**	**105.58**	**112.72**
耕作机械动力合计（万千瓦）	Total Power of Farming Machinery (10 000kw)	37.60	29.54	30.17	31.93
#大、中型拖拉机（台）	Large and Medium Tractors (set)	7844	5 796	6 412	6 431
（万千瓦）	(10 000 kw)	29.30	24.21	25.31	27.81
小型拖拉机（台）	Small Tractors (set)	9 253	5 788	5 245	4 514
（万千瓦）	(10 000kw)	8.30	5.34	4.85	4.12
排灌机械动力合计（万千瓦）	Total Power of Drainage and Irrigation Machinery (10 000 kw)	25.92	21.80	22.11	25.32
收获机械动力合计（万千瓦）	Total Power of Harvest Machinery (10 000kw)	33.30	12.19	12.95	14.49
#联合收割机（台）	Combined Harvesters (set)	4 991	2 230	2 380	2 557
（万千瓦）	(10 000 kw)	2.70	8.52	9.56	11.38
机动脱粒机（万台）	Motorized Threshers (10 000 sets)	11.34	0.75	0.63	0.28
（万千瓦）	(10 000 kw)	30.05	2.96	2.25	1.01
植物保护机械动力合计（万千瓦）	Total Power of Plant Protecting Machine (10 000 kw)	3.07	5.34	5.42	5.46
#机动喷雾器（万台）	Motorized Nebulizers (10 000 sets)	2.07	2.11	2.25	2.29
（万千瓦）	(10 000 kw)	3.07	4.72	5.14	5.13
渔业机械动力合计（万千瓦）	Total Power of Fishery Machinery (10 000 kw)	23.40	23.23	24.42	25.05
#机动渔船（艘）	Motorized Fishing Boats (ship)	2 905	1 788	1 644	1 477
（万千瓦）	(10 000 kw)	20.50	18.74	18.96	19.08
运输机械动力合计（万千瓦）	**Total Power of Transport Machinery (10 000kw)**	**8.11**	**0.83**	**0.79**	**1.10**
其他农业机械动力合计（万千瓦）	Total Power of Other Agricultural Machine (10 000kw)	11.13	11.05	9.59	9.37
#推土机（辆）	Bulldozers (automobile)	45	41	30	32
（万千瓦）	(10 000 kw)	0.25	0.24	0.19	0.20

表 12.14 主要年份农业技术应用和综合开发情况
TECHNOLOGY APPLICATIONS AND INTEGRATIVE EXPLOITATION IN AGRICULTURE IN MAIN YEARS

指标	Indicators	2000	2010	2011	2012
机耕面积（万公顷）	Areas of Motorized Cultivation (10 000 hectares)	23.46	39.47	39.97	38.61
机电排灌总控制面积（万公顷）	Total Area with Motorized Drainage and Irrigation Facilities (10 000 hectares)	28.59	17.61	19.76	19.70
粮食机种面积（万公顷）	Areas of Motorized Planting (10 000 hectares)	6.08	5.30	5.01	5.15
占粮食播种面积（%）	Percentage in Total Planting Area of Grain (%)	23.5	29.6	26.9	27.5
粮食机收面积（万公顷）	Areas of Motorized Harvesting (10 000 hectares)	16.42	16.57	17.13	17.71
占粮食收获面积（%）	Percentage in Total Harvesting Area of Grain (%)	63.4	92.5	92.2	94.4
喷、滴管灌面积（万公顷）	Areas of Irrigating by Insufflantion and Dripping Pipeline (10 000 hectares)	0.43	0.80	0.83	0.90
机械植保面积（万公顷）	Areas of Mechancial Protecting (10 000 hectares)	41.10	30.41	31.91	33.10
化肥施用面积（万公顷）	Areas of Chemical Fertilizing (10 000 hectares)	32.10	22.66	21.77	22.10
化肥施用量（实物量）（万吨）	Chemical Fertilizer Consumption (real) (10 000 tons)	82.54	44.89	41.44	39.43
化肥施用量（折纯量）（万吨）	Chemical Fertilizer Consumption (convert to pure amount) (10 000 tons)	19.33	11.84	11.62	10.99
农药施用面积（万公顷）	Areas of Farm Pesticides (10 000 hectares)	31.02	22.78	21.73	21.28
农药施用量(万吨)	Farm Pesticides Consumption (10 000 tons)	1.10	0.70	0.63	0.58
农用塑料薄膜使用量（万吨）	Agricultural Plastic Film Consumption (10 000 tons)	2.13	2.11	2.05	1.93
地膜覆盖面积（万公顷）	Areas Covered by Plastic Film (10 000 hectares)	2.05	2.62	2.40	2.34
科技兴农项目数（个）	Quantity of Scientific and Technological Agricultural Promotion Projects (unit)			76	84
科技兴农项目定向总额（亿元）	Value of Scientific and Technological Agricultural Promotion Projects (100 million yuan)			1.70	2.13
常年菜田面积（万公顷）	Areas of Perennial Vegetable Farmland (10 000 hectares)	1.25	3.29	4.81	3.83
#设施菜田	Established Vegetable Farmland	0.27	1.15	1.33	1.33
精养渔塘面积（万公顷）	Areas of Find-breed Ponds (10 000 hectares)	1.05	0.54	0.73	0.71

表 12.15 市级农业园区基本情况(2012)
MAJOR INDICATORS OF MUNICIPAL AGRICULTURAL ZONE

项 目	Item	园区规划面积(公顷) Planning Area of Zone (hectare)	已开发利用面积(公顷) Developed Area (hectare)	引进投资项目(个) Introduction of Investment Item (unit)	引进投资金额(万元) Value of Investment Item (10 000 yuan)	基础设施投资(万元) Infrastruture Investment (10 000 yuan)
总　计	**Total**	**33 798**	**20 403**	**784**	**1 213 813**	**419 154**
闵　行	Minhang	2 163	1 219	136	28 623	14 330
宝　山	Baoshan	2 000	947.3	8	16 560	13 247
嘉　定	Jiading	2 200	1 302	18	3 086	29 115
孙　桥	Sunqiao	932	346	88	70 377	19 352
临　空	Linkong	1 038	222	31	47 311	4 223
金　山	Jinshan	4 800	1 602	44	99 944	102 010
松　江	Songjiang	4 000	2 957	255	151 182	32 404
青　浦	Qingpu	1 707	631	59	37 243	23 801
南　汇	Nanhui	1 030	349	20	231 231	23 323
奉　贤	Fengxian	1 849	1 641	81	457 367	95 886
崇　明	Chongming	2 600	1 483	8	21 886	17 570
上　实	Shangshi	8 467	7 388	8	25 186	18 311
农工商	Nonggongshang	1 012	317	28	23 817	25 582

表 12.16 域外市属农场农业生产情况(2011～2012)
AGRICULTURAL PRODUCTION OF EXTERNAL MUNICIPAL FARM

指 标	Indicators	2011	2012
农业总产值(亿元)	**Gross Output Value of Agriculture(100 million yuan)**	**13.66**	**16.08**
#种植业	Planting	4.75	5.32
林 业	Forestry	0.11	0.22
畜牧业	Animal Husbandry	6.38	7.15
渔 业	Fishery	2.42	3.39
主要农产品产量	**Output of Major Farm Products**		
粮 食(万吨)	Grain(10 000 tons)	17.94	17.50
夏 粮	Summer Grain Crops	7.48	6.82
秋 粮	Autumn Grain Crops	10.46	10.68
棉 花(吨)	Cotton(ton)	210	135
油菜籽(吨)	Rapeseed(ton)	244	540
蔬 菜(吨)	Vegetables(ton)	1 338	10 140
园林水果(吨)	Fruits(ton)	280	300
西 瓜(吨)	Watermelon(ton)	5 828	515
茶 叶(吨)	Tea-leaves(ton)	12	12
生猪出栏(万头)	Quantity of Sold Hogs(10 000 heads)	25.30	30.70
牛 奶(万吨)	Milk(10 000 tons)	4.71	5.66
水产品(万吨)	Aquatic Products(10 000 tons)	2.30	2.65

注：域外市属农场是指上海光明食品(集团)有限公司所属的外地农场，其产量和产值不包括在全市总量中。

Note: External municipal farm refers to the nonlocal farms owned to Shanghai bright food (Group) Co., Ltd., whose output and gross output value are not included in the total of the city.

上 / 海 / 统 / 计 / 年 / 鉴

主要统计指标解释

■ 农村从业人员

指乡村人口中16岁以上实际参加生产经营活动并取得实物或货币收入的人员，既包括劳动年龄内实际参加劳动人员，也包括超过劳动年龄但实际参加劳动的人员，但不包括户口在家的在外学生、现役军人和丧失劳动能力的人，也不包括待业人员和家务劳动者。劳动者年龄为16岁以上。

■ 农业总产值

农业总产值是以货币表现的农、林、牧、渔业全部产品的总量和对农林牧渔生产活动进行的各种支持性服务活动的价值。它反映一定时期内农业生产的总规模和总成果。

农、林、牧、渔业的统计范围是：

(1)种植业　包括农作物种植业和其他农业。

农作物种植业包括谷物、豆类、薯类、棉、油料、糖料、麻类、烟叶、蔬菜、药材、瓜类和其他农作物的种植，以及茶园、桑园、果园的生产经营。

其他农业包括采集野生植物的果实、纤维、树胶、树脂、油料以及柴草、野生药材、菌类等及农民家庭兼营的商品性工业。

(2)林业　包括林木的栽培(不包括茶园、桑园和果园的栽培、管理和收获等活动)、林产品的采集和村及村以下合作经济组织和农户的竹木采伐。

(3)牧业　包括除渔业养殖以外的一切动物饲养和放牧，以及野生动物的捕猎和饲养。

(4)渔业　包括水生动物和海藻类植物的养殖和捕捞。

(5)农林牧渔服务业　包括农林牧渔业生产活动进行的各种支持性服务活动。但不包括各种科学技术和专业技术服务活动。

从所有制看，包括国有经济的各种专业农(农、林、牧、渔)场以及国家各级机关团体学校、科研机构、部队经营的农业；集体所有制的乡镇村各级办农场；农村各种经济组织经营的农、林、牧、渔业以及工矿企业家属集体经营的农业；农民家庭自营的农林牧渔业及兼营商品性工业等。

农业总产值的计算方法通常是按农林牧渔业产品及其副产品的产量分别乘以各自单位产品价格求得，少数生产周期较长、当年没有产品或产品产量不易统计的，则采用间接方法匡算其产值，然后将四业产品产值和服务业产值相加即为农业总产值。

1957年以前的农业总产值中包括了厩肥和农民自给性手工业(如农民自制衣服、鞋、袜，自己从事粮食初步加工等)。1958年及以后的农业总产值，林业中增加了村及村以下竹木采伐产值；牧业中取消了厩肥产值；副业中取消了农民自给性手工业产值，增加了村及村以下办的工业产值；渔业中增加了海洋捕捞水产品产值。1980年及以后的农业总产值，在副业中增加了农民家庭兼营工业商品部分的产值。从1984年起村及村以下办工业产值划归工业。从1993年起，取消副业。将野生动物的捕猎划入牧业，野生植物采集和农民家庭兼营商品性工业划归农业。从2003年起，农业总产值中包括了农林牧渔服务业产值。

■ 农业机械总动力

指用于农、林、牧、渔业生产的各种动力机械的动力总和。动力机械包括耕作、排灌、种植、植物保护、收获、农产品加工、运输、畜牧、渔业、农田水利等各种机械。不包括专门用于乡办工业、基本建设、非农业运输、科学试验和教学等非农业生产方面用的动力机械与作业机械的数量。

■ 农作物播种面积

指报告期内收获农产品的作物的实际播种或移植有农作物的面积。凡是实际种植农作物的面积，不论种植在耕地上还是种植在非耕地上，均包括在农作物播种面积中。在播种季节基本结束后，因遭灾而重新改种和补种的农作物面积，也包括在内。

■ 粮食产量

指全社会的产量。包括国有经济经营的、集体统一经营的和农民家庭经营的粮食产量，还包括工矿企业办的农场和其他生产单位的产量。粮食除包括稻谷、小麦、玉米、高粱、谷子及其他杂粮外，还包括薯类和豆类。其产量计算方法，豆类按去豆荚后的干豆计算；薯类(包括甘薯和马铃薯，不包括芋头和木薯)1963年以前按每4公斤鲜薯折1公斤粮食计算，从1964年开始改为按5公斤鲜薯折1公斤粮食计算。城市郊区作为蔬菜的薯类(如马铃薯等)按鲜品计算，并且不作粮食统计。其他粮食一律按脱

主要统计指标解释

粒后的原粮计算。1989 年以前粮食产量数据主要靠全面报表取得,1989 年开始使用抽样调查数据。

■ 棉花产量

指全社会的产量。包括春播棉和夏播棉。产量按皮棉计算。3 公斤籽棉折 1 公斤皮棉,不包括木棉。

■ 油料产量

指全部油料作物的生产量。包括花生、油菜籽、芝麻、向日葵籽、胡麻籽(亚麻籽)和其他油料。不包括大豆、木本油料和野生油料。花生以带壳干花生计算。

■ 水产品产量

指人工养殖的水产品和天然生长的水产品的捕捞量。包括海水的鱼类、虾蟹类、贝类和藻类以及内陆水域的鱼类、虾蟹类和贝类,不包括淡水生植物。水产品产量是通过各级水产和统计部门逐级上报取得数据。1995 年及以前,贝类中牡蛎按鲜肉计算;蚶、蛤、蛏按 5 斤鲜品折 1 斤计算。1996 年以后则统一按鲜品计算。

■ 猪、牛、羊肉产量

指当年出栏并已屠宰、除去头蹄下水后带骨肉(即胴体重)的重量。包括全社会范围内的产量。1996 年前为各级逐级上报数据。1996 年第一次农业普查以后,由于畜牧业产品年报数据与普查数据之间存在一定的差距,国家统计局农调总队对畜牧业年报数据与普查数据进行衔接。1999 年以后,国家统计局开展了猪、牛、羊、禽等主要畜禽品种的抽样调查,并用抽样数据作为国家定案数据使用。未开展抽样调查的品种,仍使用各级统计部门逐级上报数据。

EXPLANATORY NOTES TO MAJOR STATISTICAL INDICATORS

□ Employees in Rural Areas

Employees in Rural Areas refers to people in rural areas who are older than 16 years and engaged in production and business activities that generate incomes in cash or in practicality. It includes all working laborers, no matter whether they are within the working age or not, whereas students studying outside but with their registered residence at home, active serviceman, people who lost their ability to work, unemployed people, and those engaged in housework are not included. The working age is defined as older than 16 years.

□ Gross Output Value of Agriculture

Gross Output Value of Agriculture refers to the total volume of products of farming, forestry, animal husbandry and fishery expressed in the monetary terms and output value of all kinds of service activities that support farming, forestry, animal husbandry and fishery production. It reflects the overall scale and achievements of agricultural production during a given period of time.

The scope of statistics on farming, forestry, animal husbandry, and fishery are as follows:

(1) Farming includes cultivation of farm crops and other agricultural activities.

Cultivation of farm crops include cultivation of grain crops, legume crops tuber-crops, cotton, oil-bearing crops, sugar crops, bastfiber plants, tobacco, vegetables, medicinal herbs, melon crops, and cultivation and management of tea plantations, mulberry fields and orchards.

Other agricultural activities include harvesting wild fruits, fiber, tree gum, resin, oil-bearing plants, firewood, wild medicinal herbs, fungus, and rural-household commodity industries.

(2) Forestry refers to planting trees of various kinds (excluding tea plantations mulberry fields and orchards), collection of forestry products and cutting and felling of bamboo and trees by villages and other cooperative organizations under village level.

(3) Animal husbandry refers to raising and grazing of all kinds of farm animals except fishing and aquatic cultivating, and hunting and rising of wild animals.

(4) Fishery refers to cultivation and catching of fish and other aquatic products and cultivation and collection of seaweed and other aquatic plants.

(5) Service Industry for Farming, Forestry, Animal Husbandry and Fishery refers to all kinds of service activities that support farming, forestry, animal husbandry and fishery production, whereas activities of science, technology and professional service are not included.

In terms of ownership, China's agriculture includes specialized state farms (for farming, forestry, animal husbandry, fishery), farms managed by various government agencies, organizations, schools, research institutions, and army; farms managed by rural collective organizations at levels of the township, town, and village; farming, forestry, animal husbandry, fishery run by various rural collective organizations and farming run by collective family members' organizations of mining and industrial enterprises; farming, forestry, animal husbandry and fishery and some commodity industries run by individual farmers.

Gross output value of agriculture is obtained by first multiplying the output of products or by-products by their unit price. For a small number of products, annual output of which is not available or difficult to get due to the long production/growing process involved, the output value will be estimated through an indirect approach. The sum of output value of all products of farming, forestry, animal husbandry and fishery and output value of service activities will then and together to form gross output value of agriculture.

Before 1957, China's gross agricultural output value included the value of barnyard manure and handicraft products for self-consumption (clothes, shoes, stockings, and initial grain processing under-taken by peasants). After 1958, the output value of cutting and felling of bamboo and trees by villages and other cooperative organizations under villages have been included in forestry; value of barnyard manure has been excluded from animal husbandry; the value of self-consumed handicrafts has been excluded from sideline occupations, while output value of industries run by villages and cooperative organizations under village level has been included in sideline occupations and output value of fish catches by motor fishing boats has been added to fishery. Since 1980, the output value of handicraft products made for sale by farmer households has been added to sideline occupations. From 1984, industries run by villages and cooperative organizations under village level have been included in the sector of industry. After 1993, the category of sideline occupations has been canceled and hunting of

EXPLANATORY NOTES TO MAJOR STATISTICAL INDICATORS

wild animals has been classified into husbandry, and harvesting of wild vegetation and commodity industry run by rural households have been grouped into the category of agriculture. Since 2003, the output value of service industry for farming, forestry, animal husbandry and fishery is included in the gross output value of agriculture.

□ Total Power of Agricultural Machinery

Total Power of Agricultural Machinery refers to the total mechanical power of machinery used in farming, forestry animal husbandry and fishery, including machines used for ploughing, irrigation and drainage, crop growing, plant protection, harvesting, farm product processing, transport, stock breeding, fishery and water conservancy. Machinery employed for non–agricultural purposes such as township industry, capital construction, non–agricultural transport, scientific experiments and for teaching is excluded.

□ Sown Area of Planting

Sown Area of Planting refers to area of land sown or transplanted with crops that have been harvested during report period, regardless of being in cultivated area or non–cultivated area. Area of land re–sown due to natural disasters is also included.

□ Grain Output

Grain Output refers to the total output in the whole country including grains produced by state farms, collective units, rural households, as well as by farms affiliated to industrial and mining enterprises and other production units. Grain includes rice, wheat, corn, sorghum, millet and other miscellaneous grains as well as tubers and bean. Output of beans refers to dry beans without pods. The output of tubers (sweet potatoes and potatoes, not including taros and cassava) was converted into that of grain at the ratio 4:1, i.e. 4 kilograms of fresh tubers was equivalent to 1 kilogram of grain up to 1963. Since 1964 the ratio for conversion has been 5:1. Tubers supplied as vegetables (such as potatoes) in cities and suburbs are calculated as fresh vegetables and their output is not included in the output of grain. Output of all other grains refers to husked grain. Data on grain production before 1989 were obtained through Comprehensive Statistical Reporting System. Since 1989, data from sample surveys are used.

□ Cotton Output

Cotton Output refers to the cotton production in the whole country including cotton sown in spring and in autumn. Output is measured as the weight of ginned cotton. Three kilograms of seed–cotton are equivalent to 1 kilogram of ginned cotton, excluding ceiba.

□ Output of Oil–bearing Crops

Output of Oil–bearing Crops refers to the total production of oil–bearing crops of various kinds, including peanuts, (dry, in shell) rapeseeds, sesame, sunflower seeds, flax seeds, and other oil–bearing crops. Soybeans, oil–bearing woody plants, and wild oil–bearing crops are not included.

□ Output of Aquatic Products

Output of Aquatic Products refers to catches of both artificially cultured and naturally grown aquatic products, including fish, shrimps, crabs and shellfish in sea and inland water as well as seaweed. Freshwater plants are not included. Data on output of aquatic products are reported by aquatic product and statistical agencies level by level. Before 1995, among the shellfish, the oyster was counted as fresh meat; 5 kilograms of ark shell, clams and frogs are equivalent to 1 kilogram of fresh aquatic products; they are all counted as fresh aquatic products since 1996.

□ Output of Pork, Beef, and Mutton

Output of Pork, Beef, and Mutton refers to the meat of slaughtered hogs, cattle, sheep and goats with head, feet, and offal taken away. Data refers to the production of the whole country. The first agriculture census of China in 1996 revealed some discrepancy between the production of animal products from the annual reports and that from the census. Efforts were made by the Rural Socio–economic Survey Organization of NBS to adjust the output value of animal husbandry to make the figures from the annual reports consistent with the census data. Since 1999, NBS conducted sample survey for the major animal husbandry products, such as hogs, cattle, sheep and goats and fowls, and the data from sample surveys are used as national finalized data. Those products, which are not covered by the sample survey, are still reported by statistical agencies level by level.

第十三篇

CHAPTER 13

工　业

INDUSTRY

简要说明

一、本章资料的主要内容

本篇资料反映上海市工业经济方面的基本情况,主要内容包括:

1. 上海工业经济概况。规模以上工业企业主要经济指标,以及按地区、隶属关系、企业登记注册类型、轻重工业、企业规模和工业行业大类分组的主要经济指标;按隶属关系、轻重工业、企业规模分组和国有控股的主要经济效益指标。

2. 国有控股主要经济指标及其占全市比重。

3. 六个重点发展工业行业及信息产品制造业主要经济指标。

4. 高技术产业按登记注册类型和技术领域分组的主要经济指标。

5. 都市型工业按企业规模、登记注册类型和行业分组的主要经济指标。

6. 历年主要工业产品产量及 2012 年主要工业产品产、销量。

7. 大中小型工业企业按轻重工业、隶属关系、从业人员、工业总产值、固定资产原价分组的主要经济指标。

8. 国家级、市级工业园区主要经济指标。

二、本篇资料的统计范围

本篇资料除表 12.1 为全市工业企业以外,其余工业数据的统计范围如下:1998 年至 2006 年为全部国有和年主营业务收入 500 万元及以上的非国有工业企业;2007 至 2010 年为年主营业务收入 500 万元及以上的工业企业(即规模以上工业企业);从 2011 年开始,为年主营业务收入 2000 万元及以上的工业企业(即规模以上工业企业)。

本篇资料中工业行业分类按 2011 年《国民经济行业分类》标准划分;企业大中小微型划分按 2011 年《统计上大中小微型企业划分办法》标准执行。

三、本篇的资料来源和统计调查方法

本篇工业企业统计数据主要是根据工业统计年度报表中有关资料整理汇总的。

BRIEF INTRODUCTION

I. Main Contents

The Data in this chapter reflect the basic conditions of the industrial sector in Shanghai.

Major contents include:

(1) Basic conditions of industrial sectors in Shanghai; major economic indicators of industrial enterprises above designated sizes; as well as major economic indicators classified by regions, by subordination, by types of registration, by light and heavy industries, by size of enterprise, and by branch of industry; and major economic efficiency indicators classified by subordination, by light and heavy industries, by sizes of enterprise, and on state-controlled industrial enterprises.

(2) Major economic indicators of state-controlled industrial enterprises and their proportions of the city's total.

(3) Major economic indicators of six key industrial sectors and information technology manufacturing sector.

(4) Major economic indicators of high technology industries classified by types of registration and by technology areas.

(5) Major economic indicators of urban industries classified by sizes of enterprise, by type of registration, and by industrial sectors.

(6) Output of major industrial products in recent years, as well as output and sales of major industrial products in 2012

(7) Major economic indicators of large-, medium-, and small-size industrial enterprises classified by subordination, by types of registration, by number of employees, by gross output value of industry, and by original value of fixed assets.

(8) Major economic indicators of municipal and national industrial zones.

II. Scope and Coverage of Statistics

Except for table 12.1, which covers all industrial enterprises in the city, the scopes of industrial statistics were all state-owned industrial enterprises and non-state-owned industrial enterprises whose annual revenue from principal business was more than 5 million yuan from 1998 to 2006. For 2007 to 2010, the scopes of industrial statistics were all industrial enterprises whose annual revenue from principal business was more than 5 million yuan, (i.e., the industrial enterprises above designated size). Since 2011, the scope is adjusted to all industrial enterprises whose annual revenue from principal business was more than 20 million yuan (i.e. industrial enterprises above designated size).

Branches of industry in this chapter are based on the 2002's National Industrial Classification of all Economic Activities, and data by size of enterprise are based on 2011 Standards of Enterprises by Size.

Ⅲ. Sources of Data and Methodology of Survey

The data of industrial enterprises statistics in this Chapter are collected mainly from the relevant data in the annual industrial statistics reporting forms.

表 13.1 工业总产值及指数(1978 ~2012)
GROSS OUTPUT VALUE OF INDUSTRY AND INDEX

年 份 Year	工业总产值(亿元) Gross Output Value of Industry(100 million yuan)			工业总产值指数(以 1978 年为 100) Indices of Gross Output Value of Industry(1978 = 100)		
	合 计 Total	轻工业 Light Industry	重工业 Heavy Industry	总指数 Index	轻工业 Light Industry	重工业 Heavy Industry
1978	514.01	266.02	247.99	100.0	100.0	100.0
1979	556.30	290.78	265.52	108.6	109.7	107.6
1980	598.75	331.13	267.62	115.7	123.4	108.3
1981	620.12	360.12	260.00	120.0	135.9	104.6
1982	634.65	359.62	275.03	125.6	139.9	111.9
1983	663.53	363.92	299.61	134.4	147.6	121.8
1984	728.12	395.60	332.52	147.7	163.3	132.7
1985	862.73	456.59	406.14	167.7	184.3	151.9
1986	952.21	493.09	459.12	177.0	192.2	162.6
1987	1 073.84	556.96	516.88	188.9	206.3	172.4
1988	1 304.66	679.17	625.49	208.8	227.2	191.4
1989	1 524.67	789.57	735.10	215.0	233.6	197.3
1990	1 642.75	846.63	796.12	223.6	241.8	206.7
1991	1 947.18	976.34	970.84	255.2	269.2	241.9
1992	2 429.96	1 132.75	1 297.21	306.7	306.4	306.6
1993	3 327.04	1 401.33	1 925.71	368.2	352.7	380.1
1994	4 255.19	1 890.12	2 365.06	435.3	429.9	437.6
1995	5 349.53	2 432.67	2 916.86	510.9	504.2	513.9
(1995)	(4 547.47)	(2 092.89)	(2 454.57)			
1996	5 126.22	2 334.29	2 791.73	590.1	568.7	606.4
1997	5 649.93	2 528.19	3 121.74	675.7	640.4	704.1
1998	5 763.67	2 527.56	3 236.11	728.5	657.7	788.7
1999	6 213.24	2 679.71	3 533.53	805.1	709.1	887.5
2000	7 022.98	2 903.40	4 119.59	913.7	782.2	1 027.7
2001	7 806.18	2 986.59	4 819.59	1 063.8	865.2	1 234.8
2002	8 730.00	3 169.30	5 560.70	1 219.1	934.7	1 463.2
2003	11 708.49	3 550.80	8 157.68	1 601.9	1 064.0	2 061.3
2004	14 595.29	3 871.33	10 723.97	1 927.1	1 268.2	2 492.2
2005	16 876.78	4 299.31	12 577.48	2 195.0	1 395.0	2 873.5
2006	19 631.23	4 747.28	14 883.94	2 500.1	1 494.0	3 341.9
2007	23 108.63	5 318.85	17 789.78	2 892.6	1 641.9	3 926.7
2008	25 968.38	5 839.41	20 128.96	3 126.9	1 770.0	4 244.8
2009	24 888.08	5 663.34	19 224.74	3 227.0	1 716.9	4 457.0
2010	31 038.57	6 692.35	24 346.22	3 966.0	2 025.9	5 540.1
2011	33 834.44	7 420.92	26 413.52	4 227.8	2 194.0	5 878.0
2012	33 186.41	7 507.02	25 679.39	4 215.1	2 222.6	5 836.9

注：从 1996 年开始，工业总产值按新规定计算，括号内数为 1995 年新规定数(以下同)。
Note: Since 1996, new regulations have been adopted in calculating total industrial gross output value of industry. The figures of 1995 in brackets are calculated in line with the new regulations (same as follows).

表 13.2　各区、县工业企业主要指标(2012)
MAJOR INDICATIORS OF INDUSTRIAL ENTERPRISES IN DISTRICTS AND COUNTIES

地　区 District		单位数(个) Number of Enterprises (unit)	从业人员(万人) Employees (10 000 persons)	工业总产值(亿元) Gross Output Value of Industry (100 million yuan)	年末资产总计(亿元) Total Assets (year-end) (100 million yuan)	主营业务收入(亿元) Prime Operating Revenue (100 million yuan)	利润总额(亿元) Total Pre-tax Profits (100 million yuan)
总　计	**Total**	**9 772**	**264.97**	**31 896.88**	**31 160.89**	**34 096.29**	**2 149.42**
浦东新区	Pudong New Area	1 885	65.79	9 199.76	10 058.00	10 400.96	704.83
黄浦区	Huangpu	28	1.50	182.85	235.19	245.55	10.20
徐汇区	Xuhui	164	4.51	620.01	502.75	692.22	54.83
长宁区	Changning	43	1.04	68.66	111.01	67.86	7.27
静安区	Jing'an	7	0.13	15.02	38.20	16.34	3.00
普陀区	Putuo	125	3.17	213.38	300.72	253.33	23.23
闸北区	Zhabei	69	2.12	159.38	269.04	175.75	2.36
虹口区	Hongkou	27	0.51	41.65	92.82	51.15	8.31
杨浦区	Yangpu	93	3.13	989.67	1 373.57	995.32	175.44
闵行区	Minhang	1 169	34.03	3 626.05	3 519.23	3 805.29	231.91
宝山区	Baoshan	558	13.23	2 361.47	2 870.93	2 842.49	196.58
嘉定区	Jiading	1 307	34.59	4 273.96	3 059.51	4 368.15	433.03
金山区	Jinshan	723	14.41	1 682.09	1 219.84	1 721.57	15.41
松江区	Songjiang	1 372	40.66	3 571.68	2 698.34	3 583.87	113.71
青浦区	Qingpu	938	20.59	1 492.51	1 359.28	1 486.93	81.51
奉贤区	Fengxian	1 087	19.01	1 594.61	1 488.15	1 545.90	53.05
崇明县	Chongming	138	4.81	378.82	570.41	382.46	2.96
其　他	Others	39	1.78	1 425.32	1 393.91	1 461.14	31.80

表 13.3 规模以上工业企业主要指标(2012)
MAJOR INDICATORS OF THE CITY'S INDUSTRIAL ENTERPRISES ABOVE THE SET SCALE

类别	Types	单位数（个）Quantity of Enterprises (unit)	从业人员（万人）Employees (10 000 persons)
总计	**Total**	**9 772**	**264.97**
按隶属关系分	**Grouped by Subordination**		
#中央工业	Central Government	162	16.95
市(局)属工业	Municipality	576	34.29
区属工业	District	310	6.99
乡属工业	Township	46	1.29
村委会属工业	Village	210	4.16
按登记注册类型分	**Grouped by Registration Categories**		
内资	Domestic Funded	5 407	107.21
#国有	State-owned	174	8.20
集体	Collective-owned	155	2.65
有限责任公司	Companies with Limited Liabilities	916	29.05
股份有限公司	Share-holding Companies with Limited Liabilities	151	10.09
私营	Private	3 712	51.96
港澳台商投资	Hong Kong, Macao and Taiwan Funded	1 208	42.03
#港澳台商独资	Sole Funded	739	26.79
港澳台商投资股份有限公司	Share-holding Companies Ltd.	34	2.90
外商投资	Foreign Funded	3 157	115.73
#中外合资经营	Joint-venture	807	32.58
外资企业	Sole Funded	2 148	75.42
外商投资股份有限公司	Share-holding Companies Ltd.	39	2.88
按轻、重工业分	**Grouped by Light and Heavy Industry**		
轻工业	Light Industry	3 429	85.86
重工业	Heavy Industry	6 343	179.11
按企业规模分	**Grouped by Size of Enterprises**		
大型	Large	325	96.08
中型	Medium	1 498	80.73
小型	Small	7 949	88.17
按工业行业分	**Grouped by Sectors**		
采矿业	**Mining Industry**	**1**	**0.02**
石油和天然气开采业	Petroleum and Natural Gas Exploiting	1	0.02
制造业	**Manufacture Industry**	**9 695**	**260.52**
农副食品加工业	Farm and Sideline Products Processing	137	3.08
食品制造业	Food Manufacturing	225	8.26

工业总产值（亿元）Gross Output Value of Industry (100 million yuan)	年末资产总计（亿元）Total Assets (year-end) (100 million yuan)	固定资产净值（亿元）Net Value of Fixed Assets (100 million yuan)	流动资产合计（亿元）Current Assets (100 million yuan)
3[illegible] 896.88	**31 160.89**	**7 772.52**	**18 144.55**
[illegible] 806.16	8 103.02	2 998.50	3 351.74
[illegible] 260.07	7 305.09	1 441.27	4 099.01
706.94	630.56	133.52	401.95
116.85	92.37	19.58	65.36
293.32	194.73	33.86	145.57
1[illegible] 480.23	15 895.81	4 147.92	8 227.27
1 296.84	2 385.89	1 458.22	614.65
174.80	119.10	18.96	87.62
4 598.60	5 454.71	1 279.04	3 241.94
2 658.34	4 489.77	801.22	1 857.38
3 327.11	3 090.51	542.31	2 148.93
4 [illegible]44.57	3 624.72	901.16	2 216.62
3 [illegible]83.99	1 980.24	439.49	1 397.33
[illegible]59.24	732.14	218.81	258.62
14 [illegible]72.08	11 640.36	2 723.44	7 700.67
6 [illegible]79.69	4 745.48	1 038.58	3 109.88
7 [illegible]44.99	5 664.09	1 431.57	3 787.42
[illegible]71.59	931.43	192.12	587.56
6 [illegible]24.54	6 757.10	1 348.18	4 395.54
24 [illegible]72.33	24 403.79	6 424.35	13 749.01
17 [illegible]25.89	16 873.11	4 466.36	8 922.70
7 138.89	6 748.91	1 651.90	4 201.55
7 332.10	7 538.88	1 654.26	5 020.30
9.92	**35.35**	**0.09**	**26.82**
9.92	35.35	0.09	26.82
3[illegible] 0[illegible]0.09	**28 363.50**	**5 791.98**	**17 775.65**
3[illegible]8.20	210.16	35.85	149.93
6[illegible].46	566.67	140.52	326.13

表 13.3 续表 1 continued

类别	Types	单位数(个) Quantity of Enterprises (unit)	从业人员(万人) Employees (10 000 persons)
酒、饮料和精制茶制造业	Wine, Beverage and Refined Tea Manufacturing	44	1.55
烟草制品业	Tobacco Manufacturing	2	0.41
纺织业	Textile	243	4.35
纺织服装、服饰业	Textiles and Clothing Industry	537	13.69
皮革、毛皮、羽毛及其制品和制鞋业	Leather, Fur, Wool Products and Shoes Manufacturing	135	3.69
木材加工和木、竹、藤、棕、草制品业	Timber Processing and Timber, Bamboo, Rattan, Coir and Straw Products Manufacturing	79	1.19
家具制造业	Furniture Manufacturing	168	4.53
造纸和纸制品业	Paper-making and Paper Products Manufacturing	208	3.68
印刷和记录媒介复制业	Printing and Record Duplicating	183	3.39
文教、工美、体育和娱乐用品制造业	Culture, Education, Industrial Arts, Sports and Entertainment Goods Manufacturing	147	3.83
石油加工、炼焦和核燃料加工业	Oil Processing, Coking and Nuclear Fuel	39	2.09
化学原料和化学制品制造业	Raw Chemical Materials and Chemical Products Manufacturing	754	11.70
医药制造业	Medicine Manufacturing	205	6.30
化学纤维制造业	Chemical Fiber Manufacturing	29	0.39
橡胶和塑料制品业	Rubber and Plastic Products Manufacturing	735	14.14
非金属矿物制品业	Non-metallic Mineral Products Manufacturing	414	6.80
黑色金属冶炼和压延加工业	Ferrous Metal Smelting and Rolling Processing Industry	142	4.58
有色金属冶炼和压延加工业	Nonferrous Metal Smelting and Rolling Processing Industry	164	2.53
金属制品业	Metal Products Manufacturing	780	16.37
通用设备制造业	General Equipment Manufacturing	1 228	24.05
专用设备制造业	Special Purpose Equipment Manufacturing	643	12.75
汽车制造业	The Automotive Manufacturing	552	22.78
铁路、船舶、航空航天和其他运输设备制造业	The Railroad, Marine, Aerospace and Other Transportation Equipment Manufacturing	156	6.91
电气机械和器材制造业	Electric Machinery Equipments and Manufacturing	933	23.52
计算机、通信和其他电子设备制造业	Computer, Communications and Other Electronic Equipment Manufacturing	500	46.77
仪器仪表制造业	Instrumentation Manufacturing	200	4.29
其他制造业	Other Manufacturing	50	1.08
废弃资源综合利用业	Comprehensive Utilization of Waste Resources	29	0.21
金属制品、机械和设备修理业	Metal Products, Machinery and Equipment Repair Industry	34	1.60
电力、热力、燃气及水生产和供应业	**Electricity, Heat, Gas and Water Production and Supply Industry**	**76**	**4.43**
电力、热力生产和供应业	Production and Supply of Electricity and Thermal Power	35	2.14
燃气生产和供应业	Production and Supply of Gas	16	1.07
水的生产和供应业	Production and Supply of Water	25	1.23

工业总产值 (亿元) Gross Output Value of Industry (100 million yuan)	年末资产总计 (亿元) Total Assets (year-end) (100 million yuan)	固定资产净值 (亿元) Net Value of Fixed Assets (100 million yuan)	流动资产合计 (亿元) Current Assets (100 million yuan)
[illegible]7.63	121.99	46.27	62.70
7[illegible]5.05	979.83	46.02	736.93
2[illegible]9.74	257.57	42.84	157.11
5[illegible]2.80	502.78	63.50	379.83
1[illegible]3.58	166.29	14.65	143.26
74.94	75.58	12.91	51.55
25[illegible].78	197.32	28.45	151.99
30[illegible].94	277.84	94.26	153.91
19[illegible].17	222.27	71.78	124.72
395.06	198.13	28.73	148.23
1 605.55	582.58	246.58	244.09
2 546.55	2 293.03	753.17	1 192.73
513.[illegible]2	637.27	119.54	400.23
37.[illegible]3	44.56	14.44	23.39
8[illegible]9.[illegible]8	941.47	236.33	582.91
5[illegible]2.[illegible]8	699.01	136.16	466.68
1 585.[illegible]5	2 067.75	551.96	788.05
457.[illegible]	323.65	67.26	214.24
963.[illegible]	899.18	203.91	602.01
2 45[illegible].6[illegible]	2 948.36	509.88	2 088.11
1 09[illegible].9[illegible]	1 469.45	233.74	1 071.80
4 296.8[illegible]	4 419.99	618.77	2 524.83
761.51	1 233.82	280.32	744.50
2 122.80	1 961.36	305.84	1 424.64
5 745.38	3 389.09	744.45	2 373.65
298.67	301.52	40.29	234.18
53.39	61.63	19.18	37.23
31.[illegible]1	27.60	8.75	15.86
79.[illegible]8	285.74	75.63	160.23
1 846.[illegible]7	**2 762.04**	**1 980.46**	**342.09**
1 636.[illegible]3	2 170.20	1 687.88	215.46
157.75	262.45	78.25	85.22
53.08	329.39	214.32	41.40

表 13.3 续表 2 continued

类 别	Types	年末负债合计 Total Liabilities (year-end)	年末所有者权益 Owners' Equity (year-end)
总 计	**Total**	**15 772.54**	**15 350.79**
按隶属关系分	**Grouped by Subordination**		
#中央工业	Central Government	3 500.28	4 601.92
市(局)属工业	Municipality	3 609.98	3 679.43
区属工业	District	317.88	312.26
乡属工业	Township	47.81	44.53
村委会属工业	Village	109.06	85.47
按登记注册类型分	**Grouped by Registration Categories**		
内 资	Domestic Funded	7 228.27	8 658.42
#国 有	State-owned	880.65	1 504.76
集 体	Collective-owned	65.73	53.26
有限责任公司	Companies with Limited Liabilities	2 825.92	2 626.87
股份有限公司	Share-holding Companies with Limited Liabilities	1 486.20	3 002.89
私 营	Private	1 811.02	1 273.91
港澳台商投资	Hong Kong, Macao and Taiwan Funded	2 030.83	1 590.09
#港澳台商独资	Sole Funded	1 194.32	783.30
港澳台商投资股份有限公司	Share-holding Companies Ltd.	350.55	381.59
外商投资	Foreign Funded	6 513.44	5 102.28
#中外合资经营	Joint-venture	2 636.48	2 092.20
外资企业	Sole Funded	3 158.36	2 498.70
外商投资股份有限公司	Share-holding Companies Ltd.	572.69	358.71
按轻、重工业分	**Grouped by Light and Heavy Industry**		
轻工业	Light Industry	2 974.76	3 761.80
重工业	Heavy Industry	12 797.78	11 588.99
按企业规模分	**Grouped by Size of Enterprises**		
大 型	Large	8 290.90	8 578.89
中 型	Medium	3 543.73	3 198.84
小 型	Small	3 937.92	3 573.06
按工业行业分	**Grouped by Sectors**		
采矿业	**Mining Industry**	**5.11**	**30.25**
石油和天然气开采业	Petroleum and Natural Gas Exploiting	5.11	30.25
制造业	**Manufacture Industry**	**14 659.10**	**13 667.34**
农副食品加工业	Farm and Sideline Products Processing	109.09	100.81
食品制造业	Food Manufacturing	304.24	262.43

单位：亿元(100 million yuan)

主营业务收入 Prime Operating Revenue	利润总额 Total Pre-tax Profits	税金总额 Total Tax and Duties	成本费用总额 Total Cost and Expenses
3[illegible] 096.29	**2 149.42**	**1 660.52**	**31 766.98**
[illegible] 152.71	341.44	849.50	6 298.53
[illegible] 559.53	862.22	391.68	6 895.70
808.35	37.01	16.39	781.71
117.85	5.51	3.25	113.74
322.98	14.06	7.04	310.53
13 389.43	887.19	1 004.70	12 332.97
1 390.74	35.59	54.27	1 373.62
175.69	6.10	5.42	172.81
4 815.54	290.05	683.04	4 070.81
3 181.57	374.75	155.84	3 045.63
3 405.79	161.03	92.52	3 266.35
4 944.59	195.14	127.89	4 743.58
3 [illegible]78.11	117.67	35.80	2 980.14
954.82	3.93	67.91	911.24
15 762.27	1 067.09	527.93	14 690.43
7 [illegible]98.94	733.24	364.92	6 425.81
7 [illegible]06.48	317.61	144.44	7 415.96
[illegible]64.14	-4.88	6.19	475.93
7 [illegible]28.27	635.36	821.22	6 215.80
26 [illegible]68.01	1 514.06	839.30	25 551.18
[illegible]8 [illegible]50.68	1 312.87	1 249.45	17 311.20
7 [illegible]51.29	436.28	201.05	7 088.79
7 [illegible]54.32	400.27	210.02	7 366.99
10.64	**2.47**	**1.69**	**6.19**
10.64	2.47	1.69	6.19
32 [illegible]97.32	**2 082.80**	**1 590.53**	**29 908.30**
357.64	16.39	4.48	350.32
685.48	50.87	38.58	643.56

表 13.3 续表 3　continued

类别	Types	年末负债合计 Total Liabilities (Year-end)	年末所有者权益 Owners Equity (Year-end)
酒、饮料和精制茶制造业	Wine, Beverage and Refined Tea Manufacturing	59.06	62.91
烟草制品业	Tabacco Manufacturing	80.97	898.86
纺织业	Textile	112.98	144.30
纺织服装、服饰业	Textiles and Clothing Industry	266.19	235.26
皮革、毛皮、羽毛及其制品和制鞋业	Leather, Fur, Wool Products and Shoes Manufacturing	58.24	108.04
木材加工和木、竹、藤、棕、草制品业	Timber Processing and Timber, Bamboo, Rattan, Coir and Straw Products Manufacturing	43.50	32.08
家具制造业	Furniture Manufacturing	117.24	79.99
造纸和纸制品业	Paper-making and Paper Products Manufacturing	137.85	139.09
印刷和记录媒介复制业	Printing and Record Duplicating	94.22	127.87
文教、工美、体育和娱乐用品制造业	Culture, Education, Industrial Arts, Sports and Entertainment Goods Manufacturing	114.61	83.32
石油加工、炼焦和核燃料加工业	Oil Processing, Coking and Nuclear Fuel	331.96	250.59
化学原料和化学制品制造业	Raw Chemical Materials and Chemical Products Manufacturing	1 141.53	1 149.89
医药制造业	Medicine Manufacturing	277.90	359.16
化学纤维制造业	Chemical Fiber Manufacturing	20.54	24.00
橡胶和塑料制品业	Rubber and Plastic Products Manufacturing	498.88	441.02
非金属矿物制品业	Non-metallic Mineral Products Manufacturing	409.93	287.96
黑色金属冶炼和压延加工业	Ferrous Metal Smelting and Rolling Processing Industry	806.56	1 260.74
有色金属冶炼和压延加工业	Nonferrous Metal Smelting and Rolling Processing Industry	193.78	129.75
金属制品业	Metal Products Manufacturing	483.06	414.29
通用设备制造业	General Equipment Manufacturing	1 709.68	1 234.99
专用设备制造业	Special Purpose Equipment Manufacturing	840.45	628.57
汽车制造业	The Automotive Manufacturing	1 939.43	2 479.48
铁路、船舶、航空航天和其他运输设备制造业	The Railroad, Marine, Aerospace and Other Transportation Equipment Manufacturing	891.17	341.93
电气机械和器材制造业	Electric Machinery Equipments and Manufacturing	1 109.17	849.65
计算机、通信和其他电子设备制造业	Computer, Communications and Other Electronic Equipment Manufacturing	2 141.67	1 229.44
仪器仪表制造业	Instrumentation Manufacturing	134.94	166.22
其他制造业	Other Manufacturing	21.85	39.78
废弃资源综合利用业	Comprehensive Utilization of Waste Resources	17.39	10.22
金属制品、机械和设备修理业	Metal Products, Machinery and Equipment Repair Industry	191.03	94.70
电力、热力、燃气及水生产和供应业	**Electricity, Heat, Gas and Water Production and Supply Industry**	**1 108.33**	**1 653.21**
电力、热力生产和供应业	Production and Supply of Electricity and Thermal Power	809.92	1 359.79
燃气生产和供应业	Production and Supply of Gas	112.97	149.47
水的生产和供应业	Production and Supply of Water	185.44	143.95

单位:亿元(100 million yuan)

主营业务收入 Prime Operating Revenue	利润总额 Total pre-tax Profits	税金总额 Total Tax and Duties	成本费用总额 Total Cost and Expenses
117.07	6.02	8.48	110.25
753.06	191.15	586.68	112.07
2[illegible]4.85	13.18	6.59	233.76
5[illegible]8.44	33.86	21.82	529.57
161.01	9.89	6.55	151.96
80.43	2.78	2.65	78.13
257.88	28.06	6.56	237.53
313.11	17.84	12.19	298.98
19[illegible].89	18.47	8.65	180.02
47[illegible].96	21.67	4.14	461.64
1 51[illegible].89	-25.42	167.64	1 508.10
2 541.11	124.56	71.68	2 536.46
517.04	67.68	36.32	464.66
37.68	1.46	0.58	37.68
[illegible]81.35	46.55	22.46	841.10
541.46	23.95	18.17	525.04
2 037.54	128.00	20.22	1 998.42
484.41	7.69	5.84	478.24
995.72	66.14	26.28	940.67
2 511.62	158.96	85.76	2 369.37
1 105.05	73.03	29.72	1 041.68
5 3[illegible]0.56	769.18	303.47	4 745.05
7[illegible]8.34	-7.95	10.84	714.74
2 184.[illegible]7	103.74	47.35	2 092.64
5 842.[illegible]1	97.96	23.39	5 764.88
320.00	29.56	8.53	293.72
52.91	4.97	2.11	48.75
35.03	0.84	0.64	34.89
8[illegible].67	1.73	2.17	84.42
1 88[illegible].33	**64.15**	**68.30**	**1 852.49**
1 63[illegible].9[illegible]	67.35	62.76	1 584.41
19[illegible].1[illegible]	-1.11	2.83	201.94
57.2[illegible]	-2.09	2.72	66.14

表 13.4 工业企业销售产值(2012)
SALES VALUE OF INDUSTRIAL ENTERPRISES

单位:亿元(100 million yuan)

类别	Types	工业销售产值 Sales Value of Industry	其中 of which #出口交货值 Delivery Value of Industry Export
总　计	**Total**	**31 559.60**	**8 102.79**
按隶属关系分	**Grouped by Subordination**		
#中央工业	Central Government	6 693.18	667.86
市(局)属工业	Municipality	6 275.21	586.94
区属工业	District	701.59	78.26
乡属工业	Township	117.09	25.49
村委会属工业	Village	293.29	29.71
按登记注册类型分	**Grouped by Registration Categories**		
内　资	Domestic Funded	12 361.06	1 047.49
#国　有	State-owned	1 301.15	24.70
集　体	Collective-owned	171.57	9.37
有限责任公司	Companies with Limited Liabilities	4 587.97	459.17
股份有限公司	Share-holding Companies with Limited Liabilities	2 650.35	233.31
私　营	Private	3 233.28	296.16
港澳台商投资	Hong Kong, Macao and Taiwan Funded	4 898.59	2 289.08
#港澳台商独资	Sole Funded	3 051.89	1 920.57
港澳台商投资股份有限公司	Share-holding Companies Ltd.	954.76	84.51
外商投资	Foreign Funded	14 299.95	4 766.22
#中外合资经营	Joint-venture	6 097.80	769.45
外资企业	Sole Funded	7 364.42	3 705.87
外商投资股份有限公司	Share-holding Companies Ltd.	465.23	204.81
按轻、重工业分	**Grouped by Light and Heavy Industry**		
轻工业	Light Industry	6 869.06	1 329.68
重工业	Heavy Industry	24 690.54	6 773.11
按企业规模分	**Grouped by Size of Enterprises**		
大　型	Large	17 159.27	5 616.16
中　型	Medium	7 090.67	1 381.37
小　型	Small	7 309.66	1 105.25
按工业行业分	**Grouped by Sectors**		
采矿业	**Mining Industry**	**10.64**	
石油和天然气开采业	Petroleum and Natural Gas Exploiting	10.64	
制造业	**Manufacture Industry**	**29 703.53**	**8 102.79**
农副食品加工业	Farm and Sideline Products Processing	335.83	8.72
食品制造业	Food Manufacturing	609.74	29.79

表 13.4 续表 continued

单位:亿元(100 million yuan)

类别	Types	工业销售产值 Sales Value of Industry	其中 of which #出口交货值 Delivery Value of Industry Export
酒、饮料和精制茶制造业	Wine, Beverage and Refined Tea Manufacturing	104.53	7.02
烟草制品业	Tabacco Manufacturing	764.71	8.53
纺织业	Textile	245.26	46.37
纺织服装、服饰业	Textiles and Clothing Industry	545.47	155.08
皮革、毛皮、羽毛及其制品和制鞋业	Leather, Fur, Wool Products and Shoes Manufacturing	161.49	48.10
木材加工和木、竹、藤、棕、草制品业	Timber Processing and Timber, Bamboo, Rattan, Coir and Straw Products Manufacturing	75.58	12.73
家具制造业	Furniture Manufacturing	251.32	76.57
造纸和纸制品业	Paper-making and Paper Products Manufacturing	295.55	24.12
印刷和记录媒介复制业	Printing and Record Duplicating	187.93	20.83
文教、工美、体育和娱乐用品制造业	Culture, Education, Industrial Arts, Sports and Entertainment Goods Manufacturing	388.80	79.76
石油加工、炼焦和核燃料加工业	Oil Processing, Coking and Nuclear Fuel	1 593.50	26.79
化学原料和化学制品制造业	Raw Chemical Materials and Chemical Products Manufacturing	2 433.53	274.86
医药制造业	Medicine Manufacturing	491.36	47.37
化学纤维制造业	Chemical Fiber Manufacturing	38.32	11.09
橡胶和塑料制品业	Rubber and Plastic Products Manufacturing	860.04	230.42
非金属矿物制品业	Non-metallic Mineral Products Manufacturing	518.40	71.66
黑色金属冶炼和压延加工业	Ferrous Metal Smelting and Rolling Processing Industry	1 580.58	149.24
有色金属冶炼和压延加工业	Nonferrous Metal Smelting and Rolling Processing Industry	453.87	60.07
金属制品业	Metal Products Manufacturing	949.96	292.29
通用设备制造业	General Equipment Manufacturing	2 446.50	528.04
专用设备制造业	Special Purpose Equipment Manufacturing	1 081.95	269.25
汽车制造业	The Automotive Manufacturing	4 323.11	207.76
铁路、船舶、航空航天和其他运输设备制造业	The Railroad, Marine, Aerospace and Other Transportation Equipment Manufacturing	752.53	346.06
电气机械和器材制造业	Electric Machinery Equipments and Manufacturing	2 089.86	576.79
计算机、通信和其他电子设备制造业	Computer, Communications and Other Electronic Equipment Manufacturing	5 658.83	4 346.99
仪器仪表制造业	Instrumentation Manufacturing	299.27	105.19
其他制造业	Other Manufacturing	52.88	5.91
废弃资源综合利用业	Comprehensive Utilization of Waste Resources	32.69	0.18
金属制品、机械和设备修理业	Metal Products, Machinery and Equipment Repair Industry	80.14	35.19
电力、热力、燃气及水生产和供应业	**Electricity, Heat, Gas and Water Production and Supply Industry**	**1 845.42**	
电力、热力生产和供应业	Production and Supply of Electricity and Thermal Power	1 635.94	
燃气生产和供应业	Production and Supply of Gas	158.19	
水的生产和供应业	Production and Supply of Water	51.30	

表 13.5 工业企业经济效益指标(2012)
ECONOMIC EFFICIENCY INDICATORS OF INDUSTRIAL ENTERPRISES

类 别	Types	工业经济效益综合指数 Industrial Economic Benefit Synthetic Index	总资产贡献率(%) Total Assets Contribution Ratio (%)	资产保值增值率(%) Ratio of Capital Hold and Rise (%)	资产负债率(%) Asset-debt Ratio (%)
总 计	**Total**	**255.89**	**12.61**	**111.31**	**50.62**
#国有控股企业	Enterprises with the State Holding Major Shares	514.03	16.69	111.46	44.98
按隶属关系分	**Grouped by Subordination**				
中央工业	Central Government	705.77	15.00	107.44	43.20
地方工业	Municipality	224.65	11.77	113.04	53.22
按轻、重工业分	**Grouped by Light and Heavy Industry**				
轻工业	Light Industry	287.10	21.92	113.51	44.02
重工业	Heavy Industry	247.06	10.04	110.60	52.44
按企业规模分	**Grouped by Size of Enterprise**				
大 型	Large	359.20	15.29	111.60	49.14
中 型	Medium	203.72	10.23	109.73	52.51
小 型	Small	184.22	8.76	112.04	52.23

表 13.5 续表 continued

类 别	Types	工业全员劳动生产率(元/人) Overall Industrial Labor Productivity (yuan/person)	流动资产周转次数(次) Turnover of Current Assets (time)	成本费用利润率(%) Ratio of pre-tax Profits to Cost and Expenses(%)	工业产品销售率(%) Sales Rate of Industrial Products(%)
总 计	**Total**	**244 419**	**1.93**	**6.61**	**98.94**
#国有控股企业	Enterprises with the State Holding Major Shares	639 548	2.14	8.95	99.30
按隶属关系分	**Grouped by Subordination**				
中央工业	Central Government	984 370	2.17	5.33	98.34
地方工业	Municipality	193 968	1.87	6.93	99.11
按轻、重工业分	**Grouped by Light and Heavy Industry**				
轻工业	Light Industry	249 774	1.69	9.94	99.20
重工业	Heavy Industry	241 810	2.00	5.80	98.87
按企业规模分	**Grouped by Size of Enterprise**				
大 型	Large	397 480	2.18	7.40	99.04
中 型	Medium	171 668	1.83	5.98	98.63
小 型	Small	151 669	1.56	5.35	99.02

表 13.6　国有控股企业主要指标占全市比重(2012)
PROPORTION OF THE MAJOR INDICATORS OF ENTERPRISES WITH THE STATE HOLDING MAJOR SHARES

指　标	Indicators	合　计 Total	国有控股企业 Enterprises with the State Holding Major Shares	占全市比重(%) Proportion of City(%)
企业单位数(个)	Number of Enterprises (unit)	9 772	776	7.9
从业人员(万人)	Year-end Employees (10 000 persons)	264.97	46.34	17.5
工业总产值(亿元)	Gross Output Value of Industry (100 million yuan)	31 896.88	11 846.84	37.1
年末资产总计(亿元)	Total Assets (year-end) (100 million yuan)	31 160.89	14 132.78	45.4
流动资产合计(亿元)	Current Assets (100 million yuan)	18 144.55	6 541.83	36.1
固定资产净值(亿元)	Net Value of Fixed Assets (100 million yuan)	7 772.52	4 175.94	53.7
年末负债合计(亿元)	Total Liabilities (year-end) (100 million yuan)	15 772.54	6 356.50	40.3
年末所有者权益(亿元)	Owners Equity (year-end) (100 million yuan)	15 350.79	7 774.77	50.6
主营业务收入(亿元)	Prime Operating Revenue (100 million yuan)	34 096.29	13 556.68	39.8
主营业务税金及附加(亿元)	Product Sales Tax and Addition (100 million yuan)	804.16	762.53	94.8
利润总额(亿元)	Total Pre-Tax Profits (100 million yuan)	2 149.42	1 123.26	52.3
税金总额(亿元)	Total Tax and Duty (100 million yuan)	1 660.52	1 200.69	72.3
亏损企业数(个)	Number of Loss-making Enterprises (unit)	1 952	160	8.2
亏损企业亏损额(亿元)	Total Losses Made by Enterprises-in-red (100 million yuan)	313.01	137.17	43.8

表 13.7 六个重点发展工业行业主要指标(2012)
MAJOR INDICATORS OF SIX KEY INDUSTRIES ABOVE THE SET SCALE

行 业	Sectors	单位数(个) Quantity of Enterprises (unit)	平均从业人员(万人) Average Employees (10 000 persons)	工业总产值(亿元) Gross Output Value of Industry (100 million yuan)
总 计	**Total**	**4 160**	**141.75**	**21 063.56**
电子信息产品制造业	Electronic Information Product Manufacturing	1 062	58.40	6 755.12
汽车制造业	Automobile Manufacturing	552	22.69	4 296.82
石油化工及精细化工制造业	Petrochemical and Fine Chemical Products Manufacturing	679	12.41	3 944.10
精品钢材制造业	Fine Steel Manufacturing	101	3.90	1 548.32
成套设备制造业	Equipment Complex Manufacturing	1 398	34.82	3 773.28
生物医药制造业	Bio-medicine Manufacturing	368	9.53	745.93
六个重点发展工业行业占全市比重(%)	Percentage of the Six Key Industries in Shanghai (%)	42.6	53.5	66.0

表 13.7 续表 1 continued

行 业	Sectors	工业销售产值(亿元) Sales Value of Industry (100 million yuan)	年末资产总计(亿元) Total Property (year-end) (100 million yuan)
总 计	**Total**	**20 782.66**	**19 513.56**
电子信息产品制造业	Electronic Information Product Manufacturing	6 637.41	4 298.50
汽车制造业	Automobile Manufacturing	4 323.11	4 419.99
石油化工及精细化工制造业	Petrochemical and Fine Chemical Products Manufacturing	3 818.21	2 596.52
精品钢材制造业	Fine Steel Manufacturing	1 543.94	2 037.13
成套设备制造业	Equipment Complex Manufacturing	3 736.51	5 226.34
生物医药制造业	Bio-medicine Manufacturing	723.49	935.09
六个重点发展工业行业占全市比重(%)	Percentage of the Six Key Industries in Shanghai (%)	65.9	62.6

表 13.7 续表 2 continued

行 业	Sectors	主营业务收入(亿元) Prime Operating Revenue (100 million yuan)	利润总额(亿元) Total Pre-tax Profits (100 million yuan)	税金总额(亿元) Total Tax and Duties (100 million yuan)
总 计	**Total**	**22 781.00**	**1 383.78**	**743.11**
电子信息产品制造业	Electronic Information Product Manufacturing	6 872.97	155.51	42.78
汽车制造业	Automobile Manufacturing	5 360.56	769.13	303.47
石油化工及精细化工制造业	Petrochemical and Fine Chemical Products Manufacturing	4 027.93	85.35	231.48
精品钢材制造业	Fine Steel Manufacturing	2 000.99	126.58	18.94
成套设备制造业	Equipment Complex Manufacturing	3 758.23	151.50	102.86
生物医药制造业	Bio-medicine Manufacturing	760.32	95.62	43.58
六个重点发展工业行业占全市比重(%)	Percentage of the Six Key Industries in Shanghai (%)	66.8	64.4	44.8

表13.8 信息产品制造业主要指标(2012)
MAJOR INDICATORS OF INFORMATION PRODUCTS MANUFACTURING INDUSTRY

单位:亿元(100 million yuan)

行 业	Sectors	工业总产值 Gross Output Value of Industry	工业销售产值 Sales Value of Industry	年末资产总计 Total Assets (year-end)
总 计	**Total**	**6 755.12**	**6 637.41**	**4 298.50**
通信设备制造	Communications Equipment	723.43	708.45	554.95
雷达及配套产品制造	Radar ane Supported Product	1.02	1.02	0.94
广播电视设备制造	Broadcast and Television Equipment	12.66	12.71	10.86
电子计算机制造	Computer	3 513.57	3 463.42	1 244.60
家用视听设备制造	Household Seeing and Hearing Equipment	199.13	197.44	95.24
电子测量仪器制造	Geodesic Equipment of Electron	153.68	152.53	146.25
电子专用设备制造	Special Equipment of Electron	240.98	235.78	225.85
电子元件制造	Electronic Component	663.70	656.22	631.92
电子器件制造	Electronic Equipment	635.94	622.61	901.49
#集成电路制造	Integrated Circuit	326.16	323.95	569.03
电子机电产品制造	Machinery and Electronic Products of Electron	581.87	558.73	445.60
电子专用材料制造	Special Materials of Electron	29.14	28.52	40.78

表13.8 续表 continued

单位:亿元(100 million yuan)

行 业	Sectors	主营业务收入 Prime Operating Revenue	利润总额 Total Pre-tax Profits	税金总额 Total Tax and Duty
总 计	**Total**	**6 872.97**	**155.51**	**42.78**
通信设备制造	Communications Equipment	715.09	13.46	2.42
雷达及配套产品制造	Radar ane Supported Product	1.02	0.06	0.08
广播电视设备制造	Broadcast and Television Equipment	12.84	0.35	0.26
电子计算机制造	Computer	3 607.63	18.43	8.63
家用视听设备制造	Household Seeing and Hearing Equipment	202.60	2.75	0.79
电子测量仪器制造	Geodesic Equipment of Electron	161.53	18.31	4.26
电子专用设备制造	Special Equipment of Electron	240.46	12.35	4.88
电子元件制造	Electronic Component	663.93	30.75	8.99
电子器件制造	Electronic Equipment	642.06	30.98	3.96
#集成电路制造	Integrated Circuit	326.04	19.20	2.34
电子机电产品制造	Machinery and Electronic Products of Electron	597.28	26.96	8.04
电子专用材料制造	Special Materials of Electron	28.52	0.94	0.46

表 13.9 高技术产业主要指标(2011～2012)
MAIN FACT ABOUT HIGH TECHNOLOGY INDUSTRY

类 别	Types	工业总产值(亿元) Gross Output Value of Industry (100 million yuan) 2011	2012
总 计	**Total**	**7 060.47**	**6 824.99**
占全市比重(%)	**Proportion (%)**	**21.8**	**21.4**
按登记注册类型分	**Grouped by Registration Categories**		
国 有	State-owned	68.03	73.55
集 体	Collective-owned	1.59	2.48
股份合作企业	Cooperative	3.86	3.40
股份制企业	Share Holding	438.59	494.97
外商投资企业	Foreign Funded	6 509.92	6 203.23
其 他	Others	38.48	47.37
按技术领域分	**Grouped by Technology Areas**		
信息化学品制造	Information Chemical Product	39.09	27.16
医药制造业	Medical and Pharmaceutical Product	448.95	513.22
航空航天器制造	Aviation and Aircraft Manufaturing	59.94	91.09
电子及通信设备制造业	Electron and Communicate Equipments	2 321.69	2 231.80
电子计算机及办公设备制造业	Electronic Computers and Office Equipments	3 806.01	3 575.65
医疗设备及仪器仪表制造业	Medical Treatment Instrument and Meter	384.78	386.07

表 13.9 续表 1 continued

类 别	Types	工业销售产值(亿元) Sales Value of Industry (100 million yuan) 2011	2012	年末资产总计(亿元) Total Property (year-end) (100 million yuan) 2011	2012
总 计	**Total**	**6 950.67**	**6 714.23**	**4 469.12**	**4 657.39**
占全市比重(%)	**Proportion(%)**	**21.7**	**21.3**	**15.2**	**14.9**
按登记注册类型分	**Grouped by Registration Categories**				
国 有	State-owned	67.26	72.71	110.94	112.95
集 体	Collective-owned	1.58	2.43	5.38	5.90
股份合作企业	Cooperative	3.67	3.87	4.43	4.56
股份制企业	Share Holding	429.60	482.33	677.55	738.10
外商投资企业	Foreign Funded	6 412.53	6 108.08	3 636.02	3 752.27
其 他	Others	36.03	44.81	34.81	43.61
按技术领域分	**Grouped by Technology Areas**				
信息化学品制造	Information Chemical Product	37.49	26.48	46.95	40.03
医药制造业	Medical and Pharmaceutical Product	424.48	491.36	572.13	637.27
航空航天器制造	Aviation and Aircraft Manufaturing	59.36	88.73	149.04	164.28
电子及通信设备制造业	Electron and Communicate Equipments	2 302.03	2 195.41	2 055.58	2 144.49
电子计算机及办公设备制造业	Electronic Computers and Office Equipments	3 745.06	3 524.56	1 295.15	1 281.79
医疗设备及仪器仪表制造业	Medical Treatment Instrument and Meter	382.25	387.68	350.26	389.51

表13.9 续表2 continued

类 别	Types	主营业务收入(亿元) Prime Operating Revenue (100 million yuan)		利润总额(亿元) Total Pre-tax Profits (100 million yuan)	
		2011	2012	2011	2012
总 计	**Total**	**7 106.23**	**6 941.65**	**225.07**	**212.07**
占全市比重(%)	**Proportion (%)**	**20.7**	**20.4**	**10.0**	**9.9**
按登记注册类型分	**Grouped by Registration Categories**				
国 有	State-owned	68.65	70.28	5.44	7.03
集 体	Collective-owned	2.41	2.32	0.25	0.32
股份合作企业	Cooperative	3.93	3.96	0.27	0.47
股份制企业	Share Holding	458.31	510.67	39.47	45.17
外商投资企业	Foreign Funded	6 535.78	6 307.45	178.56	157.22
其 他	Others	37.15	46.96	1.09	1.85
按技术领域分	**Grouped by Technology Areas**				
信息化学品制造	Information Chemical Product	42.67	26.47	3.10	0.91
医药制造业	Medical and Pharmaceutical Product	449.24	517.04	57.66	67.68
航空航天器制造	Aviation and Aircraft Manufaturing	58.74	89.58	2.05	1.58
电子及通信设备制造业	Electron and Communicate Equipments	2 337.50	2 234.78	98.82	79.53
电子计算机及办公设备制造业	Electronic Computers and Office Equipments	3 821.99	3 668.51	23.19	21.61
医疗设备及仪器仪表制造业	Medical Treatment Instrument and Meter	396.09	405.28	40.25	40.76

表13.9 续表3 continued

类 别	Types	税金总额(亿元) Total Tax and Duties (100 million yuan)		产品销售率(%) Sales Rate of Industrial Products(%)	
		2011	2012	2011	2012
总 计	**Total**	**57.17**	**72.77**	**98.4**	**98.4**
占全市比重(%)	**Proportion (%)**	**3.7**	**4.4**		
按登记注册类型分	**Grouped by Registration Categories**				
国 有	State-owned	2.36	1.92	98.9	98.9
集 体	Collective-owned	0.14	0.22	99.4	98.0
股份合作企业	Cooperative	0.34	0.30	95.2	114.0
股份制企业	Share Holding	17.44	21.72	97.9	97.4
外商投资企业	Foreign Funded	35.49	46.58	98.5	98.5
其 他	Others	1.40	2.03	93.6	94.6
按技术领域分	**Grouped by Technology Areas**				
信息化学品制造	Information Chemical Product	0.58	0.42	95.9	97.5
医药制造业	Medical and Pharmaceutical Product	28.07	36.32	94.5	95.7
航空航天器制造	Aviation and Aircraft Manufaturing	0.62	0.76	99.0	97.4
电子及通信设备制造业	Electron and Communicate Equipments	16.14	14.76	99.2	98.4
电子计算机及办公设备制造业	Electronic Computers and Office Equipments	1.70	9.09	98.4	98.6
医疗设备及仪器仪表制造业	Medical Treatment Instrument and Meter	10.06	11.42	99.3	100.4

表 13.10 都市型工业主要指标(2011 ~2012)
MAIN STATISTICS OF URBAN INDUSTRIES

类别	Types	单位数(个) Quantity of Enterprises (unit)		从业人员(万人) Employees (10 000 persons)		工业总产值(亿元) Gross Output Value of Industry(100 million yuan)	
		2011	2012	2011	2012	2011	2012
总 计	**Total**	**2 082**	**2 034**	**56.09**	**56.21**	**3 441.14**	**3 590.63**
按企业规模分	**Grouped by Size of Enterprises**						
大 型	Large	63	70	14.83	16.29	1 011.16	1 068.15
中 型	Medium	419	377	22.06	20.54	1 230.60	1 288.80
小 型	Small	1 600	1 587	19.19	19.39	1 199.38	1 233.68
按登记注册类型分	**Grouped by Registration Categories**						
内 资	Domestic Funded	1 040	1 046	20.51	20.80	1 258.55	1 371.42
#国 有	State-owned	30	26	0.73	0.69	32.05	29.94
集 体	Collective-owned	19	16	0.23	0.18	8.19	6.51
有限责任公司	Companies with Limited Liabilities	150	169	4.20	4.55	389.72	454.40
股份有限公司	Share-holding Companies with Limited Liabilities	26	30	2.37	2.12	220.44	248.04
私 营	Private	777	746	12.46	12.33	556.01	563.94
港澳台商投资	Hong Kong, Macao and Taiwan Funded	347	313	11.47	10.15	668.57	598.42
#与港澳台商合资经营	Joint-venture	101	84	3.76	3.33	191.76	190.12
港澳台商独资	Sole Funded	208	190	5.89	5.38	332.27	272.43
外商投资	Foreign Funded	695	675	24.11	25.27	1 514.02	1 620.78
#中外合资经营	Joint-venture	166	169	5.02	5.55	289.03	365.51
外资企业	Sole Funded	470	449	16.77	17.43	1 091.08	1 123.63
按行业分	**Grouped by Sectors**						
服装服饰业	Garment and Trappings	588	517	15.55	13.07	564.86	480.53
食品加工制造业	Food Processing	358	368	10.73	12.29	925.49	991.11
包装、印刷业	Packaging and Printing	258	260	4.86	4.78	267.20	278.01
室内装饰用品制造业	Indoor Decoration Materials and Equipments Manufacturing	359	397	8.27	9.13	459.76	595.49
化妆品及清洁洗涤用品制造业	Cosmetics and Cleaning Manufacturing	152	132	3.19	2.82	338.04	314.31
工艺美术品、旅游用品制造业	Art Crafts and Tourism Equipments Manufacturing	207	178	5.89	5.21	439.07	447.73
小型电子信息产品制造业	Small Electronic Information Products Manufacturing	160	182	7.60	8.92	446.72	483.46

表13.10 续表1　continued

单位:亿元(100 million yuan)

类　别	Types	工业销售产值 Sales Value of Industry		年末资产总计 Total Assets (year-end)		主营业务收入 Prime Operating Revenue	
		2011	2012	2011	2012	2011	2012
总　计	**Total**	**3 395.85**	**3 552.02**	**2 891.28**	**3 081.77**	**3 648.96**	**3 812.74**
按企业规模分	**Grouped by Size of Enterprises**						
大　型	Large	1 005.39	1 057.71	834.85	916.93	1 102.10	1 154.90
中　型	Medium	1 196.68	1 284.24	1 004.20	1 044.21	1 277.89	1 346.09
小　型	Small	1 193.78	1 210.06	1 052.23	1 120.64	1 268.97	1 311.75
按登记注册类型分	**Grouped by Registration Categories**						
内　资	Domestic Funded	1 242.96	1 362.41	1 033.29	1 166.09	1 394.12	1 533.37
#国　有	State-owned	31.81	30.11	45.27	39.13	40.92	37.64
集　体	Collective-owned	7.90	6.26	7.33	6.49	8.83	7.11
有限责任公司	Companies with Limited Liabilities	386.26	454.88	257.91	307.04	453.20	531.32
股份有限公司	Share-holding Companies with Limited Liabilities	217.26	253.44	292.72	333.58	288.46	341.78
私　营	Private	547.79	549.62	403.26	441.12	550.70	547.28
港澳台商投资	Hong Kong, Macao and Taiwan Funded	648.80	585.39	570.35	546.20	667.39	596.53
#与港澳台商合资经营	Joint-venture	187.90	185.41	154.29	168.60	192.79	188.97
港澳台商独资	Sole Funded	323.92	267.67	300.18	259.66	330.05	274.15
外商投资	Foreign Funded	1 504.09	1 604.22	1 287.64	1 369.49	1 587.45	1 682.84
#中外合资经营	Joint-venture	303.43	358.07	267.53	310.78	321.32	377.58
外资企业	Sole Funded	1 065.48	1 117.10	902.28	944.11	1 117.42	1 165.20
按行业分	**Grouped by Sectors**						
服装服饰业	Garment and Trappings	555.49	485.37	501.40	432.05	589.62	497.20
食品加工制造业	Food Processing	909.94	985.44	744.26	838.06	1 011.60	1 093.04
包装、印刷业	Packaging and Printing	263.86	273.43	304.52	305.47	282.43	280.97
室内装饰用品制造业	Indoor Decoration Materials and Equipments Manufacturing	456.48	581.14	361.61	481.83	462.71	597.38
化妆品及清洁洗涤用品制造业	Cosmetics and Cleaning Manufacturing	339.66	309.64	325.69	327.89	350.27	327.63
工艺美术品、旅游用品制造业	Art Crafts and Tourism Equipments Manufacturing	428.33	440.60	285.21	269.24	500.94	536.93
小型电子信息产品制造业	Small Electronic Information Products Manufacturing	442.08	476.39	368.58	427.24	451.40	479.58

表13.10 续表2 continued

单位:亿元(100 million yuan)

类别	Types	利润总额 Total Pre-tax Profits		税金总额 Total Tax and Duties	
		2011	2012	2011	2012
总计	**Total**	**239.29**	**245.63**	**121.14**	**120.75**
按企业规模分	**Grouped by Size of Enterprises**				
大型	Large	89.06	90.02	46.30	46.77
中型	Medium	81.12	82.57	45.01	41.50
小型	Small	69.11	73.04	29.83	32.47
按登记注册类型分	**Grouped by Registration Categories**				
内资	Domestic Funded	92.32	91.24	42.57	46.06
#国有	State-owned	2.64	2.63	1.49	1.35
集体	Collective-owned	0.29	0.39	0.32	0.32
有限责任公司	Companies with Limited Liabilities	23.76	29.07	9.62	11.11
股份有限公司	Share-holding Companies with Limited Liabilities	32.47	31.98	14.00	15.71
私营	Private	30.61	25.13	16.05	16.31
港澳台商投资	Hong Kong, Macao and Taiwan Funded	57.17	51.58	19.92	16.97
#与港澳台商合资经营	Joint-venture	17.44	22.41	6.28	6.24
港澳台商独资	Sole Funded	30.49	18.34	12.35	8.68
外商投资	Foreign Funded	89.79	102.82	58.65	57.72
#中外合资经营	Joint-venture	16.41	30.93	7.89	8.39
外资企业	Sole Funded	64.36	64.21	45.34	44.06
按行业分	**Grouped by Sectors**				
服装服饰业	Garment and Trappings	50.11	23.06	21.30	15.53
食品加工制造业	Food Processing	54.23	67.74	48.01	49.32
包装、印刷业	Packaging and Printing	21.86	23.79	9.53	11.16
室内装饰用品制造业	Indoor Decoration Materials and Equipments Manufacturing	35.99	47.78	9.63	13.82
化妆品及清洁洗涤用品制造业	Cosmetics and Cleaning Manufacturing	22.37	27.83	20.55	18.07
工艺美术品、旅游用品制造业	Art Crafts and Tourism Equipments Manufacturing	26.82	27.81	6.73	6.26
小型电子信息产品制造业	Small Electronic Information Products Manufacturing	27.90	27.62	5.39	6.59

表 13.11 主要年份工业产品产量
OUTPUT OF INDUSTRIAL PRODUCTS IN MAIN YEARS

年 份 Year	化学纤维（万吨）Chemical Fibers (10 000 tons)	食用植物油（万吨）Vegetable Oil (10 000 tons)	啤 酒（亿升）Beer (100 million litres)	罐 头（万吨）Can (10 000 tons)	彩色电视机（万部）Color TV Set (10 000 units)
1978	11.59	7.32	0.50	4.75	0.24
1980	15.15	6.77	0.66	5.46	0.55
1985	22.49	11.13	0.83	6.84	71.75
1990	25.74	13.42	1.66	4.97	81.48
1995	37.83	39.94	2.16	3.50	111.77
1996	38.61	17.38	2.00	3.43	42.59
1997	39.26	12.35	2.61	3.72	70.42
1998	40.93	19.46	2.69	3.70	107.80
1999	37.38	8.03	2.65	3.49	152.05
2000	47.15	11.55	3.04	3.26	147.97
2001	45.46	10.32	3.33	3.70	108.30
2002	51.67	9.65	3.62	3.79	137.02
2003	54.17	8.64	3.99	4.02	158.15
2004	48.45	3.51	5.92	4.51	135.08
2005	49.78	45.11	7.05	4.99	145.46
2006	50.60	72.86	7.17	5.78	251.67
2007	51.48	85.24	7.30	7.20	158.37
2008	43.00	96.88	7.27	4.96	185.78
2009	37.91	92.27	6.74	3.71	195.51
2010	49.00	85.31	6.54	4.06	254.03
2011	51.34	84.56	5.09	3.90	224.63
2012	48.24	101.70	5.95	4.29	142.87

表 13.11 续表 1 continued

年 份 Year	家用洗衣机（万台）Household Washing Machines (10 000 units)	家用电冰箱（万台）Household Refrigerators (10 000 units)	房间空气调节器（万台）Household Airconditioners (10 000 units)	燃气热水器（万台）Water Heaters (10 000 units)	服 装（亿件）Garments (10 000 million cases)
1980	0.81	0.42	0.10		1.19
1985	113.85	20.49	0.74		2.33
1990	101.29	53.36	1.83		2.43
1995	144.80	128.72	62.46		6.30
1996	141.52	93.12	86.75	37.90	7.14
1997	124.81	30.72	88.20	36.25	5.63
1998	72.55	38.61	113.98	36.52	5.50
1999	57.03	43.03	180.70	35.07	5.26
2000	62.11	43.12	186.08	32.27	4.45
2001	70.79	43.44	223.57	27.86	4.35
2002	95.92	35.97	217.57	36.32	4.84
2003	134.27	34.46	239.72	37.24	4.91
2004	165.67	33.14	399.16	51.86	4.63
2005	183.26	42.68	358.57	65.64	6.72
2006	288.74	101.08	410.60	69.89	6.73
2007	289.68	100.66	395.21	80.46	6.60
2008	234.63	123.21	387.12	67.89	6.10
2009	207.79	189.15	317.78	59.35	3.91
2010	216.57	218.55	400.41	103.70	5.72
2011	218.96	185.19	619.91	104.44	5.06
2012	197.12	151.63	584.10	106.49	5.04

表 13.11 续表 2 continued

年 份 Year	机制纸及纸板(万吨) Machine-Made Paper and Paperboards (10 000 tons)	粗 钢 (万吨) Steel (10 000 tons)	成品钢材 (万吨) Rolled-Steel Products (10 000 tons)	生 铁 (万吨) Pig Iron (10 000 tons)
1978	27.34	476.52	360.08	149.86
1980	29.57	521.61	412.63	171.12
1985	41.29	570.16	451.18	215.37
1990	46.49	914.62	609.59	526.90
1995	47.08	1 006.92	738.08	664.04
1996	38.85	1 441.92	1 175.74	964.03
1997	40.00	1 532.42	1 296.48	1 054.56
1998	45.46	1 603.75	1 417.58	1 208.57
1999	45.42	1 668.62	1 486.08	1 337.75
2000	43.54	1 778.70	1 544.46	1 473.00
2001	41.35	1 874.71	1 641.11	1 468.91
2002	42.61	1 719.42	1 626.98	1 276.12
2003	44.40	1 726.65	1 710.80	1 300.24
2004	35.96	1 823.65	1 818.41	1 356.47
2005	35.73	1 927.96	1 964.16	1 582.89
2006	85.87	1 902.82	2 129.78	1 639.13
2007	83.76	2 081.58	2 144.16	1 790.00
2008	80.46	1 992.09	2 074.95	1 735.87
2009	71.03	2 032.24	2 181.37	1 787.48
2010	86.94	2 214.27	2 475.95	1 901.39
2011	87.28	2 225.48	2 482.81	1 947.48
2012	91.46	1 970.91	2 340.76	1 800.44

表 13.11 续表 3 continued

年 份 Year	轮胎外胎 (万条) Tires (10 000 tires)	水 泥 (万吨) Cement (10 000 tons)	乙 烯 (万吨) Ethylene (10 000 tons)	发电设备 (万千瓦) Power Generating Equipments (10 000 kw)
1978	149.59	139.47	12.69	109.80
1980	174.85	161.28	13.59	58.20
1985	219.00	219.31	14.02	133.00
1990	318.78	230.30	21.95	210.20
1995	375.31	433.22	8.20	496.50
1996	942.69	443.77	46.51	494.30
1997	829.57	338.47	45.44	541.60
1998	957.75	330.95	50.36	403.85
1999	804.43	251.14	59.26	314.55
2000	830.66	311.69	59.05	179.00
2001	545.97	334.75	63.10	336.20
2002	704.80	351.58	80.00	461.90
2003	846.92	568.24	94.83	1 013.70
2004	927.17	665.01	95.60	1 520.30
2005	932.27	719.97	160.44	2 138.05
2006	1 055.47	818.28	193.83	2 944.71
2007	932.54	786.24	187.24	2 845.59
2008	866.65	765.46	182.03	2 831.10
2009	849.07	754.19	180.30	2 440.70
2010	915.22	670.80	226.72	2 555.60
2011	908.26	805.56	197.53	2 889.59
2012	1 004.37	794.71	195.57	2 886.30

表13.11 续表4 continued

年 份 Year	发电量（亿千瓦时）Electric Power Generation (100 million kwh)	硫 酸（万吨）Sulfuric (10 000 tons)	金属切削机床（台）Metal-cutting Machines (unit)	微型计算机设备（万部）Personal Computers (10 000 units)
1978	199.32	34.49	17 384	
1980	206.41	38.76	16 949	
1985	256.25	35.22	19 408	
1990	284.10	40.04	13 796	0.77
1995	403.42	31.03	15 833	4.07
1996	428.64	36.24	15 379	6.20
1997	458.48	36.79	18 700	40.39
1998	482.16	32.59	11 916	21.16
1999	498.01	38.38	17 822	40.09
2000	553.09	34.22	22 346	42.04
2001	572.86	36.15	21 839	47.13
2002	608.92	30.41	27 252	75.25
2003	684.99	31.41	33 497	734.68
2004	766.15	33.67	13 975	996.09
2005	728.74	33.32	13 158	2 176.17
2006	710.96	30.37	13 372	2 670.09
2007	737.80	30.46	14 440	4 478.78
2008	773.54	26.06	16 430	5 767.97
2009	778.20	27.02	5 641	7 320.15
2010	876.19	28.66	13 386	9 388.44
2011	946.96	27.98	14 813	10 162.53
2012	886.19	18.15	29 012	9 804.83

表13.11 续表5 continued

年 份 Year	移动通信基站设备（万信道）Mobile Communication Facilities (10 000 channels)	集成电路（万块）Semi-conduct IC (10 000 units)	汽 车（万辆）Motor Vehicles (10 000 vehicles)	其中 of which #轿 车 Cars
1978			1.04	0.26
1980			1.47	0.53
1985			1.22	0.86
1990		1 167	2.81	2.46
1995		15 290	16.27	16.07
1996		11 624	20.17	20.02
1997		88 098	23.30	23.15
1998		92 908	23.64	23.50
1999		170 001	25.58	25.42
2000	1.60	239 330	25.29	25.15
2001	39.49	225 315	29.00	28.88
2002	24.82	339 494	39.19	39.05
2003	28.20	397 313	59.58	58.84
2004	57.67	548 727	55.96	54.99
2005	115.03	677 003	48.45	48.09
2006	174.16	640 483	65.28	64.47
2007	307.46	891 138	82.12	81.15
2008	343.58	830 487	80.65	80.00
2009	198.76	722 883	125.03	122.46
2010	299.44	1 134 629	169.89	159.77
2011	490.40	1 663 143	191.57	174.20
2012	148.75	1 602 978	202.43	180.68

注：2000 年开始移动通信基站设备不包括手机。

Note: The figure of mobile communication facilities has excluded mobile phones since 2000.

表 13.12 主要工业产品生产、销售总量(2012)
OUTPUT AND SALES OF MAIN INDUSTRIAL PRODUCTS

产品名称	Product	单 位 Unit	生产量 Output	销售量 Sales
发电量	Electric Power Generation	亿千瓦时 (100 million kwh)	886.19	719.71
啤 酒	Beer	亿升 (100 million liters)	5.95	5.96
无酒精饮料（软饮料）	Non-alcoholic Beverage	万吨 (10 000 tons)	284.15	282.55
卷 烟	Cigarettes	亿支(100 million pieces)	916.92	915.59
化学纤维	Chemical Fibers	万吨 (10 000 tons)	48.24	47.52
纱	Yarn	万吨 (10 000 tons)	3.80	3.39
布	Cloth	亿米 (100 million m)	1.71	1.55
蚕丝及交织机织物	Silk Products	万米 (10 000 m)	220.04	211.72
服 装	Garments	亿件 (100 million cases)	5.04	5.20
皮革鞋靴	Leather Shoes	万双 (10 000 pairs)	1 980.73	2 005.38
机制纸及纸版	Paperboard	万吨 (10 000 tons)	91.46	83.98
汽 油	Gasoline	万吨 (10 000 tons)	305.03	308.00
柴 油	Diesel Oil	万吨 (10 000 tons)	822.14	806.78
焦 炭	Coke	万吨 (10 000 tons)	632.60	62.64
硫 酸	Sulphuric Acid	万吨 (10 000 tons)	18.15	14.11
烧 碱	Caustic Soda	万吨 (10 000 tons)	72.75	72.39
化学农药原药	Chemical Pesticides	万吨 (10 000 tons)	1.53	1.55
乙 烯	Ethylene	万吨 (10 000 tons)	195.57	33.18
合成橡胶	Synthetic Rubber	万吨 (10 000 tons)	24.76	24.20
合成洗涤剂	Synthetic Detergents	万吨 (10 000 tons)	29.89	30.00
轮胎外胎	Tires	万条 (10 000 tires)	1 004.37	996.63
水 泥	Cement	万吨 (10 000 tons)	794.71	794.07
铜 材	Copper Materials	万吨 (10 000 tons)	26.72	26.10
生 铁	Pig Iron	万吨 (10 000 tons)	1 800.44	1.06
粗 钢	Steel	万吨 (10 000 tons)	1 970.91	32.00
金属切削机床	Metal-cutting Machines	台(unit)	29 012	29 517
#数控金属切削机床	Digital Machine Tools	台(unit)	4 066	4 124
金属集装箱	Metal Container	万立方米 (10 000 cu. m)	779.21	760.56
卫生陶瓷	Sanitary Ceramics	万件 (10 000 pieces)	219.01	195.37

表 13.12 续表 continued

产品名称	Product	单位 Unit	生产量 Output	销售量 Sales
涂　料	Coating	万吨 (10 000 tons)	138.00	137.50
#建筑涂料	Construction Coating	万吨 (10 000 tons)	79.16	78.97
集成电路	Integrated Circuits	亿块 (100 million units)	160.30	159.30
乳制品	Dairy Product	万吨 (10 000 tons)	58.17	58.30
成品钢材	Rolled-steel Products	万吨 (10 000 tons)	2 340.76	2 328.02
发动机	Engines	万千瓦 (10 000 kw)	18 078.59	8 291.78
缝纫机	Sewing Machines	万台 (10 000 units)	92.68	92.86
汽　车	Motor Vehicles	万辆 (10 000 vehicles)	202.43	206.12
#轿　车	Cars	万辆 (10 000 vehicles)	180.68	184.35
摩托车	Motorcycles	万辆 (10 000 vehicles)	102.85	101.09
两轮脚踏自行车	Bicycles	万辆 (10 000 vehicles)	446.35	450.20
民用钢质船舶	Civil Steel Ships	万载重吨 (10 000 syn-tons)	1 044.37	1 044.37
发电设备	Power Generating Equipments	万千瓦 (10 000 kw)	2 886.30	3 593.45
电力电缆	Electric Cable	万公里 (10 000 km)	102.19	102.34
家用洗衣机	Household Washing Machines	万台 (10 000 units)	197.12	203.09
家用电冰箱	Household Refrigerators	万台 (10 000 units)	151.63	152.91
房间空气调节器	Household Air-conditioners	万台 (10 000 units)	584.10	604.34
家用吸排油烟机	Range Hoods	万台 (10 000 units)	4.95	5.08
微波炉	Microwave Oven	万台 (10 000 units)	397.94	398.16
电饭锅	Electric Rice Cookers	万个 (10 000 units)	408.13	426.03
家用吸尘器	Vacuum Cleaners	万台 (10 000 units)	18.51	18.08
燃气热水器	Water Heaters	万台 (10 000 units)	106.49	105.48
程控交换机	Program-controlled Exchanges	万线 (10 000 lines)	121.90	121.90
集成电路圆片	Wafer	万片 (10 000 units)	308.85	306.59
微型计算机设备	Personal Computers	万部 (10 000 units)	9 804.83	9 803.58
彩色电视机	Color Television Sets	万部 (10 000 units)	142.87	142.75
移动通信基站设备	Mobile Communication Base Station Facilities	万信道 (10 000 channels)	148.75	148.75
糖　果	Candy	万吨 (10 000 tons)	16.55	17.57
实木木地板	Solid Wood Flooring	万平方米 (10 000 sq·m)	580.66	610.87
复合木地板	Flooring	万平方米 (10 000 sq·m)	2 709.47	2 713.90

表 13.13 大型工业企业主要指标(2012)
MAJOR INDICATORS OF LARGE SIZED INDUSTRIAL ENTERPRISES

类别	Types	单位数（个）Quantity of Enterprises (unit)	从业人员（万人）Employees (10 000 persons)	工业总产值（亿元）Gross Output Value of Industry (100 million yuan)	工业销售产值（亿元）Sales Value of Industry Products (100 million yuan)
总　计	**Total**	**325**	**96.08**	**17 325.89**	**17 159.27**
按轻、重工业分	**Grouped by Light and Heavy Industry**				
轻工业	Light Industry	106	22.64	2 731.43	2 739.48
重工业	Heavy Industry	219	73.43	14 594.46	14 419.79
按隶属关系分	**Grouped by Subordination**				
中央工业	Central Government	34	13.19	5 617.66	5 502.20
地方工业	Local Government	291	82.89	11 708.23	11 657.07
按从业人员分	**Grouped by Number of Employees**				
1 万人及以上	10 000 persons and above	9	24.81	6 434.62	6 387.81
5 000 ~ 9 999 人	5 000 ~ 9 999 persons	24	15.00	2 463.15	2 487.21
3 000 ~ 4 999 人	3 000 ~ 4 999 persons	38	14.97	2 908.20	2 914.90
3 000 人以下	Below 3 000 persons	254	41.30	5 519.91	5 369.35
按工业总产值分	**Grouped by Gross Output Value of Industry**				
10 亿元及以上	1 000 million yuan and above	213	78.11	16 630.73	16 454.72
5 ~ 9.99 亿元	500 ~ 999 million yuan	82	13.49	570.37	575.62
5 亿元以下	Below 500 million yuan	30	4.48	124.79	128.93
按固定资产原价分	**Grouped by Original Value of Fixed Assets**				
10 亿元及以上	1 000 million yuan and above	108	55.31	13 392.12	13 266.89
1 ~ 9.99 亿元	100 ~ 999 million yuan	191	36.23	3 093.92	3 052.07
5 000 ~ 9 999 万元	50 ~ 99.99 million yuan	17	2.75	593.65	588.80
5 000 万元以下	Below 50 million yuan	9	1.79	246.18	251.51

实收资本(股本)(亿元) Paid-in Capital (fixed capital stock) (100 million yuan)	年末资产总计(亿元) Total Assets (year-end) (100 million yuan)	年末负债合计(亿元) Total Liabilities (year-end) (100 million yuan)	主营业务收入(亿元) Prime Operation Revenue (100 million yuan)	利润总额(亿元) Total Pre-tax Profits (100 million yuan)	税金总额(亿元) Total Tax and Duties (100 million yuan)	成本费用总额(亿元) Total Costs and Expenses (100 million yuan)
3 162.63	**16 873.11**	**8 290.90**	**18 950.68**	**1 312.87**	**1 249.45**	**17 311.20**
422.69	2 711.71	914.12	2 885.47	368.38	684.38	2 083.55
2 739.94	14 161.40	7 376.78	16 065.21	944.49	565.07	15 227.65
1 120.34	7 139.55	2 952.07	5 878.61	294.17	811.53	5 065.48
2 041.79	9 733.56	5 338.83	13 072.06	1 018.70	437.92	12 245.72
479.94	5 021.68	2 381.66	6 794.60	368.18	266.21	6 383.30
590.40	3 574.77	1 746.29	3 483.74	392.27	120.82	3 265.55
484.2[illegible]	2 395.41	870.23	2 950.50	226.91	717.99	2 192.55
1 608.0[illegible]	5 881.24	3 292.72	5 721.83	325.51	144.42	5 469.79
2 789.08	15 740.95	7 693.36	18 144.64	1 275.01	1 225.82	16 527.00
246.51	776.54	406.35	629.11	30.87	18.23	612.85
127.04	355.62	191.19	176.92	7.00	5.39	171.36
2 498.89	13 898.87	6 644.46	14 804.38	1 074.73	1 149.02	13 369.28
532.14	2 518.81	1 391.74	3 287.15	213.21	89.44	3 107.23
54.36	323.22	203.99	595.51	23.58	8.47	574.14
77.24	132.20	50.70	263.63	1.35	2.52	260.56

表 13.13 续表 continued

类　别	Types	单位数（个）Quantity of Enterprises (unit)	从业人员（万人）Employees (10 000 persons)	工业总产值（亿元）Gross Output Value of Industry (100 million yuan)
按工业行业分	**Grouped by Sectors**			
制造业	**Manufacture Industry**	**314**	**93.22**	**16 498.68**
农副食品加工业	Farm and Sideline Products Processing	4	0.75	42.21
食品制造业	Food Manufacturing	14	3.64	249.21
酒、饮料和精制茶制造业	Wine, Beverage and Refined Tea Manufacturing	3	0.66	38.52
烟草制品业	Tabacco Manufacturing	1	0.36	752.08
纺织业	Textile	5	0.73	61.62
纺织服装、服饰业	Textiles and Clothing Industry	8	2.09	163.54
皮革、毛皮、羽毛及其制品和制鞋业	Leather, Fur, Wool Products and Shoes Manufacturing	2	0.67	72.70
家具制造业	Furniture Manufacturing	5	1.44	99.76
造纸和纸制品业	Paper-making and Paper Products Manufacturing	4	0.62	80.03
印刷和记录媒介复制业	Printing and Record Duplicating	2	0.30	28.63
文教、工美、体育和娱乐用品制造业	Culture, Education, Industrial Arts, Sports and Entertainment Goods Manufacturing	6	1.08	62.76
石油加工、炼焦和核燃料加工业	Oil Processing, Coking and Nuclear Fuel Processing	2	1.77	1 504.87
化学原料和化学制品制造业	Raw Chemical Materials and Chemical Products Manufacturing	16	2.60	849.98
医药制造业	Medicine Manufacturing	10	2.02	185.56
橡胶和塑料制品业	Rubber and Plastic Products Manufacturing	7	2.05	169.69
非金属矿物制品业	Non-metallic Mineral Products Manufacturing	5	0.72	54.08
黑色金属冶炼和压延加工业	Ferrous Metal Smelting and Rolling Processing Industry	4	2.73	1 200.87
有色金属冶炼和压延加工业	Nonferrous Metal Smelting and Rolling Processing Industry	2	0.38	37.92
金属制品业	Metal Products Manufacturing	10	3.40	161.05
通用设备制造业	General Equipment Manufacturing	27	5.55	973.14
专用设备制造业	Special Purpose Equipment Manufacturing	11	1.86	249.15
汽车制造业	The Automotive Manufacturing	39	10.49	3 121.48
铁路、船舶、航空航天和其他运输设备制造业	The Railroad, Marine, Aerospace and Other Transportation Equipment Manufacturing	11	4.14	605.22
电气机械和器材制造业	Electric Machinery Equipments and Manufacturing	34	6.90	718.99
计算机、通信和其他电子设备制造业	Computer, Communications and Other Electronic Equipment Manufacturing	72	34.51	4 899.57
仪器仪表制造业	Instrumentation Manufacturing	5	0.85	72.88
其他制造业	Other Manufacturing	1	0.26	18.61
金属制品、机械和设备修理业	Metal Products, Machinery and Equipment Repair Industry	4	0.67	24.55
电力、热力、燃气及水生产和供应业	**Electricity, Heat, Gas and Water Production and Supply Industry**	**11**	**2.86**	**827.20**
电力、热力生产和供应业	Production and Supply of Electricity and Thermal Power	3	1.48	745.44
燃气生产和供应业	Production and Supply of Gas	5	0.78	53.49
水的生产和供应业	Production and Supply of Water	3	0.60	28.27

工业销售产值（亿元）Sales Value of Industry Products (100 million yuan)	实收资本（股本）（亿元）Paid-in Capital (fixed capital stock) (100 million yuan)	年末资产总计（亿元）Total Assets (year-end) (100 million yuan)	年末负债合计（亿元）Total Liabilities (year-end) (100 million yuan)	主营业务收入（亿元）Prime Operation Revenue (100 million yuan)	利润总额（亿元）Total Pre-tax Profits (100 million yuan)	税金总额（亿元）Total Tax and Duties (100 million yuan)	成本费用总额（亿元）Total Costs and Expenses (100 million yuan)
16 331.78	**2 975.87**	**15 162.95**	**7 757.29**	**18 090.89**	**1 298.16**	**1 211.04**	**16 447.85**
41.01	13.43	22.66	8.70	38.65	1.14	1.24	37.84
248.00	51.80	230.43	124.43	326.28	24.86	20.31	305.06
38.83	12.69	40.96	17.57	45.90	3.11	2.56	44.44
761.73	17.40	974.18	79.97	760.13	190.55	586.21	109.75
59.22	8.60	50.19	17.82	57.62	6.85	2.34	50.80
175.37	19.20	172.59	78.58	175.40	22.29	12.11	154.33
72.70	0.58	100.30	20.79	72.44	7.51	4.77	64.57
97.32	12.82	76.74	40.84	97.56	18.26	2.66	87.34
77.06	15.63	63.73	26.46	88.15	7.02	5.72	81.05
28.05	12.53	26.99	3.59	27.81	4.51	1.82	23.43
60.01	9.59	38.90	16.99	55.52	4.99	0.86	50.69
1 494.31	158.99	524.56	309.02	1 497.26	-31.25	165.37	1 397.22
746.75	376.71	782.08	389.11	892.95	9.40	19.55	892.02
176.70	56.37	206.28	117.09	195.23	14.97	13.75	185.31
167.53	35.85	191.41	126.11	176.87	10.62	3.38	167.92
55.98	22.26	72.41	39.15	63.39	5.82	1.41	58.07
1 198.03	280.82	1 801.60	662.09	1 520.46	125.01	10.61	1 481.29
36.82	13.97	53.11	35.88	35.35	1.11	1.00	34.52
155.56	31.32	134.08	66.12	163.33	18.71	2.62	146.63
977.24	185.68	1 396.11	913.06	987.76	53.34	37.13	937.26
237.72	52.43	328.88	220.41	231.04	10.80	5.06	219.39
3 149.30	485.99	3 416.19	1 405.12	4 144.16	682.92	272.44	3 607.75
595.37	184.94	1 045.22	793.14	576.27	-15.19	6.33	557.04
726.00	104.31	525.12	303.95	737.99	44.25	16.53	695.84
4 835.97	745.75	2 584.71	1 758.44	4 991.72	67.21	12.78	4 934.76
72.80	15.16	64.25	39.71	80.91	3.62	1.05	78.26
18.61	5.96	27.01	2.99	18.61	2.90	1.30	15.70
27.75	45.08	212.26	140.14	32.14	2.82	0.11	29.57
827.49	**186.76**	**1 710.16**	**533.61**	**859.79**	**14.71**	**38.41**	**863.35**
745.44	84.86	1 452.97	369.11	744.28	18.90	35.29	737.70
53.91	45.82	83.88	55.18	86.22	-0.58	1.89	88.82
28.15	56.08	173.31	109.31	29.30	-3.62	1.23	36.83

表 13.14 中型工业企业主要指标(2012)
MAJOR INDICATORS OF MEDIUM SIZED INDUSTRIAL ENTERPRISES

类 别	Types	单位数（个）Quantity of Enterprises (unit)	从业人员（万人）Employees (10 000 persons)	工业总产值（亿元）Gross Output Value of Industry (100 million yuan)	工业销售产值（亿元）Sales Value of Industry Products(100 million yuan)
总 计	**Total**	**1 498**	**80.73**	**7 188.89**	**7 090.67**
按轻、重工业分	**Grouped by Light and Heavy Industry**				
轻工业	Light Industry	590	31.26	2 029.61	2 003.48
重工业	Heavy Industry	908	49.47	5 159.28	5 087.19
按隶属关系分	**Grouped by Subordination**				
中央工业	Central Government	42	2.60	1 002.97	1 004.88
地方工业	Local Government	1 456	78.13	6 185.92	6 085.79
按从业人员分	**Grouped by Number of Employees**				
1 000 人及以上	1 000 persons and above	62	8.79	149.14	146.72
500 ~ 999 人	500 ~ 999 persons	572	39.08	3 444.82	3 398.22
500 人以下	Below 500 persons	864	32.86	3 594.93	3 545.73
按工业总产值分	**Grouped by Gross Output Value of Industry**				
10 亿元及以上	1 000 million yuan and above	130	7.76	3 322.32	3 265.40
5 ~ 9.99 亿元	500 ~ 999 million yuan	225	13.24	1 522.40	1 511.72
1 ~ 4.99 亿元	100 ~ 499 million yuan	871	48.64	2 159.37	2 127.59
5 000 ~ 9 999 万元	50 ~ 99.99 million yuan	210	8.58	162.02	162.52
5 000 万元以下	Below 50 million yuan	62	2.52	22.77	23.44
按固定资产原价分	**Grouped by Original Value of Fixed Assets**				
10 亿元及以上	1 000 million yuan and above	35	2.27	1 353.06	1 349.70
1 ~ 9.99 亿元	100 ~ 999 million yuan	627	36.81	3 599.62	3 565.30
5 000 ~ 9 999 万元	50 ~ 99.99 million yuan	348	17.88	1 145.98	1 117.54
1 000 ~ 4 999 万元	10 ~ 49.99 million yuan	397	18.40	901.39	871.05
1 000 万元以下	Below 10 million yuan	91	5.38	188.83	187.07

实收资本（股本）（亿元）Paid-in Capital (fixed capital stock) (100 million yuan)	年末资产总计（亿元）Total Assets (year-end) (100 million yuan)	年末负债合计（亿元）Total Liabilities (year-end) (100 million yuan)	主营业务收入（亿元）Prime Operation Revenue (100 million yuan)	利润总额（亿元）Total Pre-tax Profits (100 million yuan)	税金总额（亿元）Total Tax and Duties (100 million yuan)	成本费用总额（亿元）Total Costs and Expenses (100 million yuan)
1 802.60	**6 748.91**	**3 543.73**	**7 451.29**	**436.28**	**201.05**	**7 088.79**
544.51	1 971.01	965.76	2 093.04	145.25	74.83	1 977.84
1 258.09	4 777.90	2 577.97	5 358.25	291.03	126.22	5 110.94
238.54	735.17	425.87	1 046.34	37.50	30.38	1 012.65
1 564.05	6 013.74	3 117.86	6 404.95	398.79	170.67	6 076.13
65.62	171.94	84.60	147.72	2.12	7.14	147.74
935.10	3 429.77	1 706.00	3 565.96	209.21	106.19	3 397.46
801.88	3 147.20	1 753.13	3 737.60	224.95	87.73	3 543.58
499.62	2 205.49	1 333.81	3 457.48	183.07	80.86	3 293.90
402.13	1 665.47	794.77	1 579.00	133.16	42.83	1 460.56
792.20	2 581.39	1 272.05	2 215.78	117.85	70.57	2 132.71
92.90	252.68	114.57	169.82	2.96	5.55	171.43
15.76	43.89	28.53	29.22	-0.75	1.24	30.19
398.64	1 117.21	654.45	1 360.04	44.00	38.27	1 323.13
1 062.27	3 891.12	1 859.12	3 730.07	258.36	102.71	3 520.49
189.79	933.91	513.35	1 240.45	82.93	28.98	1 168.13
132.33	697.45	440.11	929.62	44.72	23.75	890.27
19.57	109.22	76.70	191.11	6.27	7.34	186.77

表 13.14 续表 continued

	类 别 Types	单位数（个）Quantity of Enterprises (unit)	从业人员（万人）Employees (10 000 persons)	工业总产值（亿元）Gross Output Value of Industry (100 million yuan)
按工业行业分	**Grouped by Sectors**			
制造业	**Manufacture Industry**	**1 477**	**79.61**	**6 389.73**
农副食品加工业	Farm and Sideline Products Processing	23	1.19	118.38
食品制造业	Food Manufacturing	57	2.74	225.27
酒、饮料和精制茶制造业	Wine, Beverage and Refined Tea Manufacturing	9	0.48	28.55
烟草制品业	Tabacco Manufacturing	1	0.05	2.98
纺织业	Textile	27	1.40	54.32
纺织服装、服饰业	Textiles and Clothing Industry	104	5.83	164.94
皮革、毛皮、羽毛及其制品和制鞋业	Leather, Fur, Wool Products and Shoes Manufacturing	29	1.63	45.80
木材加工和木、竹、藤、棕、草制品业	Timber Processing and Timber, Bamboo, Rattan, Coir and Straw Products Manufacturing	12	0.50	27.39
家具制造业	Furniture Manufacturing	27	1.39	83.84
造纸和纸制品业	Paper-making and Paper Products Manufacturing	23	1.02	71.30
印刷和记录媒介复制业	Printing and Record Duplicating	25	1.26	58.08
文教、工美、体育和娱乐用品制造业	Culture, Education, Industrial Arts, Sports and Entertainment Goods Manufacturing	31	1.44	213.44
石油加工、炼焦和核燃料加工业	Oil Processing, Coking and Nuclear Fuel Processing	3	0.13	37.77
化学原料和化学制品制造业	Raw Chemical Materials and Chemical Products Manufacturing	58	3.04	578.64
医药制造业	Medicine Manufacturing	42	2.31	176.80
化学纤维制造业	Chemical Fiber Manufacturing	2	0.07	1.93
橡胶和塑料制品业	Rubber and Plastic Products Manufacturing	95	5.08	241.58
非金属矿物制品业	Non-metallic Mineral Products Manufacturing	49	2.66	186.48
黑色金属冶炼和压延加工业	Ferrous Metal Smelting and Rolling Processing Industry	12	0.59	231.90
有色金属冶炼和压延加工业	Nonferrous Metal Smelting and Rolling Processing Industry	21	0.90	192.71
金属制品业	Metal Products Manufacturing	93	5.31	284.87
通用设备制造业	General Equipment Manufacturing	130	7.06	639.06
专用设备制造业	Special Purpose Equipment Manufacturing	103	5.24	443.24
汽车制造业	The Automotive Manufacturing	135	7.10	735.32
铁路、船舶、航空航天和其他运输设备制造业	The Railroad, Marine, Aerospace and Other Transportation Equipment Manufacturing	24	1.35	58.69
电气机械和器材制造业	Electric Machinery Equipments and Manufacturing	163	8.64	753.45
计算机、通信和其他电子设备制造业	Computer, Communications and Other Electronic Equipment Manufacturing	138	8.64	603.16
仪器仪表制造业	Instrumentation Manufacturing	26	1.54	103.77
其他制造业	Other Manufacturing	7	0.39	9.84
金属制品、机械和设备修理业	Metal Products, Machinery and Equipment Repair Industry	8	0.62	16.20
电力、热力、燃气及水生产和供应业	**Electricity, Heat, Gas and Water Production and Supply Industry**	**21**	**1.11**	**799.16**
电力、热力生产和供应业	Production and Supply of Electricity and Thermal Power	9	0.45	762.72
燃气生产和供应业	Production and Supply of Gas	3	0.19	20.81
水的生产和供应业	Production and Supply of Water	9	0.47	15.63

工业销售产值(亿元) Sales Value of Industry Products (100 million yuan)	实收资本(股本)(亿元) Paid-in Capital (fixed capital stock) (100 million yuan)	年末资产总计(亿元) Total Assets (year-end) (100 million yuan)	年末负债合计(亿元) Total Liabilities (year-end) (100 million yuan)	主营业务收入(亿元) Prime Operation Revenue (100 million yuan)	利润总额(亿元) Total Pre-tax Profits (100 million yuan)	税金总额(亿元) Total Tax and Duties (100 million yuan)	成本费用总额(亿元) Total Costs and Expenses (100 million yuan)
6 293.13	**1 602.12**	**6 101.80**	**3 130.87**	**6 645.13**	**403.82**	**179.27**	**6 312.42**
118.10	15.53	69.36	34.88	137.36	4.29	1.26	133.53
225.59	50.47	193.95	101.62	221.04	16.63	12.99	209.07
23.49	25.47	39.79	18.15	29.65	0.77	3.41	27.46
2.98	2.90	5.64	1.00	2.93	0.60	0.46	2.32
54.05	24.29	84.86	29.60	53.97	2.44	1.63	52.05
158.77	49.45	156.27	84.46	165.13	5.54	4.58	160.73
44.64	8.38	32.09	17.63	44.82	1.93	0.95	43.68
27.49	8.56	33.60	16.53	29.53	1.09	1.03	28.70
82.2	8.79	47.72	30.97	84.97	5.60	1.72	79.34
69.75	16.12	71.36	31.64	72.19	5.65	2.78	67.98
57.64	19.20	77.13	30.65	64.03	5.95	2.86	60.39
216.02	14.57	86.41	53.21	237.72	12.31	1.67	228.99
36.61	3.37	11.48	7.36	49.78	2.20	0.74	47.43
564.35	131.33	465.26	263.07	587.14	34.14	18.48	557.75
168.20	65.57	242.98	81.05	172.75	32.96	14.65	147.03
1.92	4.27	5.69	0.40	1.92	0.62	0.03	2.14
237.29	83.08	308.77	143.83	238.22	17.01	7.02	224.09
185.93	77.36	293.26	162.82	196.76	10.56	5.55	190.53
232.22	77.87	123.07	56.36	315.69	2.44	6.42	314.23
191.26	41.00	138.43	73.52	189.23	5.81	2.78	185.04
282.95	64.65	291.19	157.60	295.56	20.21	9.16	280.26
636.74	138.12	620.95	316.75	664.69	55.58	23.19	614.73
441.36	147.22	629.22	338.49	457.23	35.68	11.88	425.11
732.61	122.81	618.13	317.87	750.64	59.25	18.85	694.34
59.08	30.56	80.32	37.61	65.45	2.06	1.25	64.88
722.23	161.86	696.94	387.63	779.15	35.13	14.51	752.03
583.98	163.29	519.00	257.75	602.18	15.45	5.00	593.15
104.65	21.30	105.76	43.02	109.19	13.98	3.01	96.60
10.03	3.70	10.24	5.05	10.21	0.43	0.35	9.78
16.01	21.04	42.93	30.34	16.01	-2.50	1.05	19.07
797.54	**200.49**	**647.11**	**412.86**	**806.16**	**32.47**	**21.78**	**776.37**
762.72	136.06	486.41	327.44	762.66	32.64	20.46	730.84
20.81	20.82	43.39	27.62	24.63	-0.27	0.23	25.12
14.00	43.60	117.31	57.80	18.87	0.09	1.09	20.41

表 13.15 小型工业企业主要指标(2012)
MAJOR INDICATORS OF SMALL SIZED INDUSTRIAL ENTERPRISES

类 别	Types	单位数(个) Quantity of Enterprises (unit)	从业人员(万人) Employees (10 000 persons)	工业总产值(亿元) Gross Output Value of Industry (100 million yuan)	工业销售产值(亿元) Sales Value of Industry Products(100 million yuan)
总 计	**Total**	**7 949**	**88.17**	**7 382.10**	**7 309.66**
按轻、重工业分	**Grouped by Light and Heavy Industry**				
轻工业	Light Industry	2 733	31.96	2 163.50	2 126.09
重工业	Heavy Industry	5 216	56.21	5 218.60	5 183.56
按隶属关系分	**Grouped by Subordination**				
中央工业	Central Government	86	1.16	185.53	186.10
地方工业	Local Government	7 863	87.01	7 196.57	7 123.55
按从业人员分	**Grouped by Number of Employees**				
200 人及以上	200 persons and above	1 116	26.94	2 178.28	2 148.83
100 ~ 199 人	100 ~ 199 persons	2 717	38.45	2 790.22	2 767.90
100 人以下	Below 100 persons	4 116	22.78	2 413.60	2 392.92
按工业总产值分	**Grouped by Gross Output Value of Industry**				
5 亿元及以上	500 million yuan and above	138	2.46	1 542.00	1 521.78
1 ~ 4.99 亿元	100 ~ 499 million yuan	1 639	26.05	3 115.96	3 072.91
5 000 ~ 9 999 万元	50 ~ 99.99 million yuan	2 129	25.95	1 485.49	1 472.46
5 000 万元以下	Below 50 million yuan	4 043	33.70	1 238.66	1 242.51
按固定资产原价分	**Grouped by Original Value of Fixed Assets**				
10 亿元及以上	1 000 million yuan and above	17	0.28	389.35	387.60
1 ~ 9.99 亿元	100 ~ 999 million yuan	506	8.83	1 458.36	1 450.67
5 000 ~ 9 999 万元	50 ~ 99.99 million yuan	734	11.99	1 049.99	1 040.51
1 000 ~ 4 999 万元	10 ~ 49.99 million yuan	3 358	40.69	2 707.17	2 673.01
1 000 万元以下	Below 10 million yuan	3 334	26.37	1 777.23	1 757.88

实收资本（股本）（亿元）Paid-in Capital (fixed capital stock) (100 million yuan)	年末资产总计（亿元）Total Assets (year-end) (100 million yuan)	年末负债合计（亿元）Total Liabilities (year-end) (100 million yuan)	主营业务收入（亿元）Prime Operation Revenue (100 million yuan)	利润总额（亿元）Total Pre-tax Profits (100 million yuan)	税金总额（亿元）Total Tax and Duties (100 million yuan)	成本费用总额（亿元）Total Costs and Expenses (100 million yuan)
2 250.29	**7 538.88**	**3 937.92**	**7 694.32**	**400.27**	**210.02**	**7 366.99**
649.18	2 074.38	1 094.89	2 249.77	121.73	62.01	2 154.41
1 601.11	5 464.50	2 843.03	5 444.55	278.54	148.02	5 212.58
87.[illegible]8	228.30	122.34	227.75	9.77	7.59	220.40
2 163.11	7 310.57	3 815.58	7 466.57	390.50	202.43	7 146.59
605.99	2 110.15	1 120.35	2 260.35	127.37	58.96	2 145.17
906.9[illegible]	2 987.71	1 545.80	2 876.64	144.85	80.80	2 759.28
737.39	2 441.01	1 271.77	2 557.34	128.05	70.26	2 462.54
350.85	1 190.13	568.50	1 644.38	99.85	33.07	1 550.84
846.32	3 116.93	1 628.08	3 138.59	208.85	83.77	2 967.48
506.09	1 637.65	885.15	1 535.68	60.66	48.15	1 488.45
547.04	1 594.16	856.19	1 375.67	30.91	45.03	1 360.22
206.55	519.77	239.50	390.36	22.34	12.59	368.88
691.15	1 797.99	898.64	1 564.41	87.12	38.97	1 496.03
372.31	1 185.87	613.86	1 072.36	56.32	29.35	1 031.21
693.46	2 700.49	1 416.80	2 844.47	157.31	80.19	2 715.55
286.81	1 334.75	769.12	1 822.72	77.18	48.92	1 755.31

表 13.15 续表 continued

类 别	Types	单位数（个） Quantity of Enterprises (unit)	从业人员（万人） Employees (10 000 persons)	工业总产值（亿元） Gross Output Value of Industry (100 million yuan)
按工业行业分	**Grouped by Sectors**			
采矿业	**Mining Industry**	**1**	**0.02**	**9.92**
石油和天然气开采业	Petroleum and Natural Gas Exploiting	1	0.02	9.92
制造业	**Manufacture Industry**	**7 904**	**87.69**	**7 151.69**
农副食品加工业	Farm and Sideline Products Processing	110	1.13	177.61
食品制造业	Food Manufacturing	154	1.89	135.98
酒、饮料和精制茶制造业	Wine, Beverage and Refined Tea Manufacturing	32	0.40	40.56
纺织业	Textile	211	2.23	133.80
纺织服装、服饰业	Textiles and Clothing Industry	425	5.77	214.32
皮革、毛皮、羽毛及其制品和制鞋业	Leather, Fur, Wool Products and Shoes Manufacturing	104	1.39	45.07
木材加工和木、竹、藤、棕、草制品业	Timber Processing and Timber, Bamboo, Rattan, Coir and Straw Products Manufacturing	67	0.69	47.55
家具制造业	Furniture Manufacturing	136	1.70	73.18
造纸和纸制品业	Paper-making and Paper Products Manufacturing	181	2.04	150.60
印刷和记录媒介复制业	Printing and Record Duplicating	156	1.84	104.45
文教、工美、体育和娱乐用品制造业	Culture, Education, Industrial Arts, Sports and Entertainment Goods Manufacturing	110	1.31	118.86
石油加工、炼焦和核燃料加工业	Oil Processing, Coking and Nuclear Fuel Processing	34	0.19	62.90
化学原料和化学制品制造业	Raw Chemical Materials and Chemical Products Manufacturing	680	6.06	1 117.93
医药制造业	Medicine Manufacturing	153	1.97	150.86
化学纤维制造业	Chemical Fiber Manufacturing	27	0.32	35.99
橡胶和塑料制品业	Rubber and Plastic Products Manufacturing	633	7.01	458.41
非金属矿物制品业	Non-metallic Mineral Products Manufacturing	360	3.43	282.22
黑色金属冶炼和压延加工业	Ferrous Metal Smelting and Rolling Processing Industry	126	1.26	153.08
有色金属冶炼和压延加工业	Nonferrous Metal Smelting and Rolling Processing Industry	141	1.26	226.49
金属制品业	Metal Products Manufacturing	677	7.66	522.49
通用设备制造业	General Equipment Manufacturing	1 071	11.44	843.40
专用设备制造业	Special Purpose Equipment Manufacturing	529	5.66	407.57
汽车制造业	The Automotive Manufacturing	378	5.19	440.02
铁路、船舶、航空航天和其他运输设备制造业	The Railroad, Marine, Aerospace and Other Transportation Equipment Manufacturing	121	1.42	97.60
电气机械和器材制造业	Electric Machinery Equipments and Manufacturing	736	7.98	650.36
计算机、通信和其他电子设备制造业	Computer, Communications and Other Electronic Equipment Manufacturing	290	3.62	242.65
仪器仪表制造业	Instrumentation Manufacturing	169	1.89	122.02
其他制造业	Other Manufacturing	42	0.43	24.94
废弃资源综合利用业	Comprehensive Utilization of Waste Resources	29	0.21	31.71
金属制品、机械和设备修理业	Metal Products, Machinery and Equipment Repair Industry	22	0.30	39.03
电力、热力、燃气及水生产和供应业	**Electricity, Heat, Gas and Water Production and Supply Industry**	**44**	**0.46**	**220.50**
电力、热力生产和供应业	Production and Supply of Electricity and Thermal Power	23	0.20	127.86
燃气生产和供应业	Production and Supply of Gas	8	0.10	83.46
水的生产和供应业	Production and Supply of Water	13	0.15	9.18

工业销售产值（亿元）Sales Value of Industry Products (100 million yuan)	实收资本（股本）（亿元）Paid-in Capital (fixed capital stock) (100 million yuan)	年末资产总计（亿元）Total Assets (year-end) (100 million yuan)	年末负债合计（亿元）Total Liabilities (year-end) (100 million yuan)	主营业务收入（亿元）Prime Operation Revenue (100 million yuan)	利润总额（亿元）Total Pre-tax Profits (100 million yuan)	税金总额（亿元）Total Tax and Duties (100 million yuan)	成本费用总额（亿元）Total Costs and Expenses (100 million yuan)
10.64	**9.00**	**35.35**	**5.11**	**10.64**	**2.47**	**1.69**	**6.19**
10.64	9.00	35.35	5.11	10.64	2.47	1.69	6.19
7 078.62	**2 090.35**	**7 098.75**	**3 770.94**	**7 461.30**	**380.82**	**200.23**	**7 148.03**
176.71	24.26	118.14	65.51	181.63	10.95	1.98	178.95
136.15	58.65	142.28	78.18	138.16	9.38	5.28	129.43
37.16	32.80	41.24	23.34	41.52	2.15	2.51	38.35
131.98	42.85	122.52	65.56	133.25	3.88	2.62	130.91
211.33	41.66	173.91	103.14	217.91	6.02	5.13	214.51
44.[illegible]5	11.47	33.91	19.82	43.75	0.45	0.83	43.71
48.[illegible]9	11.40	41.98	26.97	50.90	1.69	1.62	49.43
71.79	17.95	72.86	45.43	75.36	4.20	2.18	70.86
148.74	57.04	142.74	79.75	152.77	5.17	3.70	149.95
102.24	35.53	118.15	59.97	103.04	8.00	3.98	96.21
112.77	15.74	72.82	44.40	184.73	4.36	1.61	181.96
62.58	7.60	46.55	15.58	66.85	3.64	1.53	63.45
1 122.44	361.89	1 045.69	489.36	1 161.02	81.02	33.65	1 086.69
146.47	61.09	188.01	79.76	149.06	19.75	7.92	132.32
36.40	16.29	38.87	20.14	35.76	0.84	0.55	35.54
455.22	152.51	441.29	228.94	466.76	18.93	12.05	449.09
276.49	97.22	333.33	207.96	281.31	7.57	11.22	276.43
150.34	41.60	143.09	88.11	201.39	0.55	3.19	202.90
225.80	33.57	132.12	84.39	259.83	0.77	2.05	258.68
511.45	117.50	473.91	259.33	536.83	27.22	14.49	513.78
832.5[illegible]	246.40	931.30	479.86	859.16	50.04	25.45	817.38
402.86	127.57	511.36	281.55	416.78	26.54	12.77	397.18
441.20	90.33	385.68	216.43	465.76	27.01	12.17	442.97
98.08	27.27	108.27	60.42	96.62	5.18	3.26	92.82
641.63	207.52	739.30	417.58	667.04	24.37	16.32	644.76
238.88	94.43	285.39	125.48	248.50	15.29	5.60	236.97
121.82	35.92	131.51	52.21	129.90	11.97	4.47	118.85
24.25	6.84	24.37	13.81	24.10	1.64	0.46	23.27
32.69	8.67	27.60	17.39	35.08	0.84	0.64	34.89
36.39	6.75	30.54	20.54	36.52	1.41	1.01	35.78
220.39	**150.94**	**404.77**	**161.87**	**222.38**	**16.98**	**8.11**	**212.77**
127.78	90.40	230.82	113.36	128.99	15.80	7.01	115.87
83.47	51.09	135.18	30.18	84.32	-0.26	0.71	88.00
9.15	9.45	38.78	18.33	9.08	1.43	0.39	8.90

表 13.16 国家级、市级工业园区主要经济指标(2012)
MAJOR ECONOMIC INDICATORS OF MUNICIPAL AND NATIONAL INDUSTRIAL ZONE

指 标	Indicators	国家级开发区 National Level Develop Zone	其 中 of which	
			外高桥保税区 Waigaoqiao Free Trade Zone	金桥出口加工区 Jinqiao Export Processing Zone
单位数(个)	Quantity of Enterprises (unit)	1 301	136	179
从业人员(万人)	Employees (10 000 persons)	64.56	4.42	12.57
工业总产值(亿元)	Gross Output Value of Industry(100 million yuan)	8 707.12	726.48	1 924.87
出口交货值(亿元)	Delivery Value of Industry Exports(100 million yuan)	3 791.96	166.08	332.90
实收资本(股本)(亿元)	Paid-in Capital(Fixed capital stock)(100 million yuan)	2 130.16	74.64	473.17
年末资产总计(亿元)	Total Assets (year-end)(100 million yuan)	8 417.82	441.1	1 770.82
流动资产合计(亿元)	Total Current Assets(100 million yuan)	5 207.77	342.48	1 265.03
固定资产合计(亿元)	Total Fixed Assets(100 million yuan)	1 783.91	88.17	291.59
固定资产原价(亿元)	Original Value of Fixed Assets(100 million yuan)	3 662.61	175.38	755.87
年末负债合计(亿元)	Total Liabilities (year-end)(100 million yuan)	4 305.21	279.15	954.25
年末流动负债合计(亿元)	Total Current Liabilities (year-end)(100 million yuan)	3 784.37	258.60	913.13
长期负债合计(亿元)	Total Long-term Liabilities(100 million yuan)	500.21	19.31	34.68
年末所有者权益(亿元)	Owners' Equity (year-end)(100 million yuan)	4 092.87	161.84	802.09
主营业务收入(亿元)	Prime Operating Revenue(100 million yuan)	9 856.08	750.54	2 904.48
利润总额(亿元)	Total Pre-tax Profits(100 million yuan)	689.49	27.96	255.80
税金总额(亿元)	Total Tax and Duties(100 million yuan)	245.41	5.26	124.14
亏损总额(亿元)	Total Loss(100 million yuan)	73.88	3.76	14.02

其 中 of which						
张江高科技园区 Zhangjiang Hi-Tec Park	漕河泾新兴技术开发区 Caohejing Hi-tec Park	漕河泾出口加工区 Caohejing Export Processing Zone	闵行经济技术开发区 Minhang Hi-tec Park	松江出口加工区 Songjiang Export Processing Zone	闵行出口加工区 Minhang Export Processing Zone	青浦出口加工区 Qingpu Export Processing Zone
98	122	11	64	47	9	10
5.56	3.71	2.92	3.78	12.02	0.74	0.29
609.55	350.40	678.80	473.71	1 611.32	96.91	49.17
220.04	118.03	660.62	80.88	1 572.70	90.55	44.37
436.18	115.13	19.29	105.85	71.28	11.58	14.36
2 005.49	393.66	200.25	450.41	678.08	56.02	41.38
926.74	237.20	163.14	354.82	561.57	45.61	26.58
209.79	83.61	34.68	72.38	106.87	9.59	13.77
619.57	190.72	71.01	157.24	193.72	12.99	18.77
520.64	179.15	169.78	266.84	541.98	46.39	25.60
369.70	159.78	168.48	264.57	532.88	46.12	18.98
150.82	17.89	0.08	1.98	9.10	0.27	6.62
1 485.85	214.49	29.03	183.54	136.11	9.62	15.78
687.29	371.63	679.69	480.45	1 575.14	91.48	46.03
211.52	42.23	4.74	43.87	6.65	-3.69	1.56
25.71	10.48	0.01	24.78		0.02	0.01
7.81	2.19	0.01	1.74	3.89	4.26	0.12

表13.16 续表1 continued

指标	Indicators	其中 of which 陆家嘴金融贸易区 Lujiazui Financial Trade Zone	虹桥经济技术开发区 Hongqiao Economic and Technological Development Zone	佘山国家旅游度假区 Sheshan State Holiday Resort
单位数(个)	Qiantity of Enterprises (unit)	9	2	2
从业人员(万人)	Employees (10 000 persons)	0.96	0.07	0.03
工业总产值(亿元)	Gross Output Value of Industry(100 million yuan)	152.91	1.04	2.60
出口交货值(亿元)	Delivery Value of Industry Exports(100 million yuan)	2.86	0.63	0.34
实收资本(股本)(亿元)	Paid-in Capital(Fixed capital stock)(100 million yuan)	62.65	0.10	0.61
年末资产总计(亿元)	Total Assets (year-end)(100 million yuan)	240.42	1.70	2.04
流动资产合计(亿元)	Total Current Assets(100 million yuan)	164.44	0.87	1.22
固定资产合计(亿元)	Total Fixed Assets(100 million yuan)	40.55	0.37	0.38
固定资产原价(亿元)	Original Value of Fixed Assets(100 million yuan)	64.69	0.72	0.65
年末负债合计(亿元)	Total Liabilities (year-end)(100 million yuan)	150.28	0.95	1.13
年末流动负债合计(亿元)	Total Current Liabilities (year-end)(100 million yuan)	133.94	0.95	1.13
长期负债合计(亿元)	Total Long-term Liabilities(100 million yuan)	16.18		
年末所有者权益(亿元)	Owners' Equity (year-end)(100 million yuan)	90.14	0.75	0.90
主营业务收入(亿元)	Prime Operating Revenue(100 million yuan)	159.61	1.04	2.66
利润总额(亿元)	Total Pre-tax Profits(100 million yuan)	6.68	0.11	0.03
税金总额(亿元)	Total Tax and Duties(100 million yuan)	4.98	0.02	0.02
亏损总额(亿元)	Total Loss(100 million yuan)	0.02		0.01

其中 of which			市级开发区 Municipal Level Development Zone	其中 of which		
上海紫竹高新技术产业开发区 Zizhu High and New Technical Industrial Development Zone	上海化学工业经济技术开发区 Chemical Industry Economic and Technological Development Zone	上海松江经济技术开发区 Songjiang Economic and Technological Development Zone		上海宝山工业园区 Haibaoshan Industrial Park	上海月杨工业园区 Yueyang Industrial Park	上海富盛经济开发区 Fusheng Economic Development Zone
[illegible]	27	578	2 946	183	93	2
0.51	0.71	16.15	79.88	4.07	1.89	0.02
118.54	715.90	1 194.93	7 672.32	304.46	200.50	0.91
23.95	66.81	411.19	2 450.25	56.87	12.56	0.34
27.37	303.04	414.91	1 670.82	101.68	43.21	0.23
148.37	706.00	1 281.08	6 647.33	388.01	189.04	0.76
103.64	188.14	826.31	4 457.75	244.05	137.77	0.45
34.62	436.07	361.46	1 508.51	81.61	34.26	0.05
62.16	713.96	625.16	2 446.82	111.28	55.02	0.10
93.17	422.43	653.46	3 662.35	207.09	110.11	0.45
86.16	246.44	583.50	3 343.06	192.08	103.23	0.45
6.44	175.99	60.84	277.57	10.97	5.69	
55.19	283.57	623.96	2 978.78	180.19	78.13	0.31
123.02	743.06	1 239.98	7 909.75	333.31	234.98	0.78
3.27	16.27	72.50	482.35	24.49	11.19	0.05
6.89	15.95	27.13	186.45	10.57	4.40	0.02
4.57	17.10	14.39	60.87	3.90	0.71	

表 13.16 续表 2 continued

指 标	Indicators	其中 of which 上海浦东空港工业园区 Pudong Konggang Industrial Park	上海嘉定工业园区 Jiading Industrial Park	上海嘉定汽车产业园区 Jiading Automobile Industrial Park
单位数(个)	Quantity of Enterprises (unit)	129	446	199
从业人员(万人)	Employees (10 000 persons)	2.97	11.94	6.64
工业总产值(亿元)	Gross Output Value of Industry(100 million yuan)	198.86	1128.15	664.07
出口交货值(亿元)	Delivery Value of Industry Exports(100 million yuan)	41.76	317.91	67.76
实收资本(股本)(亿元)	Paid-in Capital(Fixed capital stock)(100 million yuan)	32.23	255.51	90.64
年末资产总计(亿元)	Total Assets (year-end)(100 million yuan)	172.72	982.91	455.50
流动资产合计(亿元)	Total Current Assets(100 million yuan)	118.57	635.72	325.07
固定资产合计(亿元)	Total Fixed Assets(100 million yuan)	38.99	232.97	95.33
固定资产原价(亿元)	Original Value of Fixed Assets(100 million yuan)	56.80	406.80	159.36
年末负债合计(亿元)	Total Liabilities (year-end)(100 million yuan)	96.18	493.29	257.44
年末流动负债合计(亿元)	Total Current Liabilities (year-end)(100 million yuan)	92.51	434.02	246.49
长期负债合计(亿元)	Total Long-term Liabilities(100 million yuan)	3.41	54.80	8.39
年末所有者权益(亿元)	Owners' Equity (year-end)(100 million yuan)	76.48	489.34	197.33
主营业务收入(亿元)	Prime Operating Revenue(100 million yuan)	187.49	1 162.82	681.71
利润总额(亿元)	Total Pre-tax Profits(100 million yuan)	9.80	91.59	52.59
税金总额(亿元)	Total Tax and Duties(100 million yuan)	6.00	21.21	15.62
亏损总额(亿元)	Total Loss(100 million yuan)	1.74	6.70	1.84

其中 of which						
上海市莘庄工业园区 Xinzhuang Industrial Park	上海青浦工业园区 Qingpu Industrial Park	上海西郊工业园区 Xijiao Economic Development Zone	上海松江经济开发区 Songjiang Economic Development Zone	上海奉贤经济开发区 Fengxian Economic Development Zone	上海金山工业园区 Jinshan Industrial Park	上海枫泾工业园区 Fengjing Industrial Park
271	353	132	150	128	248	110
9.03	8.92	3.25	2.26	3.61	4.20	1.81
927.04	735.83	209.08	137.31	330.74	359.25	121.46
269.02	144.77	76.29	27.66	84.66	58.69	10.13
248.84	216.25	79.93	40.39	102.09	106.37	30.76
1 045.33	660.25	216.49	143.51	364.11	355.47	125.10
717.47	427.88	139.92	104.70	229.69	207.37	84.95
215.72	178.91	62.26	27.28	87.20	106.55	25.84
377.74	279.88	107.42	46.68	124.26	141.93	40.26
582.35	310.36	113.34	69.22	193.67	208.90	60.65
521.01	283.94	107.43	63.24	180.16	175.14	57.50
57.68	20.09	4.31	4.84	11.21	22.58	2.76
461.92	349.47	103.06	74.07	170.40	146.39	64.37
974.52	707.66	216.19	135.13	349.88	380.79	119.75
81.21	49.51	7.33	9.39	24.96	13.33	7.58
30.18	26.80	7.47	3.92	11.48	6.88	3.96
11.16	6.71	2.66	0.89	3.60	4.53	0.73

表 13.16 续表 3 continued

指标	Indicators	其中 of which 上海朱泾工业园区 Zhujing Industrial Park	上海市市北高新技术服务业园区 Shibei Hi-Tech Park	上海崇明工业园区 Congming Industrial Park
单位数(个)	Qiantity of Enterprises (unit)	73	25	16
从业人员(万人)	Employees (10 000 persons)	1.09	0.61	0.24
工业总产值(亿元)	Gross Output Value of Industry(100 million yuan)	66.03	36.22	11.36
出口交货值(亿元)	Delivery Value of Industry Exports(100 million yuan)	9.23	6.73	0.23
实收资本(股本)(亿元)	Paid-in Capital(Fixed capital stock)(100 million yuan)	13.63	17.88	3.07
年末资产总计(亿元)	Total Assets (year-end)(100 million yuan)	58.40	55.05	13.42
流动资产合计(亿元)	Total Current Assets(100 million yuan)	38.45	44.58	8.06
固定资产合计(亿元)	Total Fixed Assets(100 million yuan)	13.47	5.65	4.21
固定资产原价(亿元)	Original Value of Fixed Assets(100 million yuan)	22.55	14.60	6.29
年末负债合计(亿元)	Total Liabilities (year-end)(100 million yuan)	35.33	32.69	7.64
年末流动负债合计(亿元)	Total Current Liabilities (year-end)(100 million yuan)	31.82	32.03	7.52
长期负债合计(亿元)	Total Long-term Liabilities(100 million yuan)	2.94	0.59	0.12
年末所有者权益(亿元)	Owners' Equity (year-end)(100 million yuan)	23.05	22.36	5.72
主营业务收入(亿元)	Prime Operating Revenue(100 million yuan)	65.30	40.01	11.09
利润总额(亿元)	Total Pre-tax Profits(100 million yuan)	0.03	0.60	0.43
税金总额(亿元)	Total Tax and Duties(100 million yuan)	1.02	1.87	0.45
亏损总额(亿元)	Total Loss(100 million yuan)	1.32	1.84	0.19

其中 of which						
上海星火工业园区 Xinghuo Industrial Park	上海浦东康桥工业园区 Pudong Kangqiao Industial Park	上海新杨工业园区 Xinyang Industrial Park	上海浦东合庆工业园区 Pudong Heqing Industrial Park	上海南汇工业园区 Nanhui Industrial Park	上海奉城工业园区 Fengcheng Industrial Park	上海未来岛高新技术产业园区 Weilai Island High and New Technical Industrial Park
40	142	12	57	80	50	7
1.02	11.57	0.26	1.74	1.66	0.78	0.28
209.02	1 683.39	23.91	138.07	113.21	35.83	37.62
36.90	1 137.49	0.54	40.52	37.11	6.78	6.28
63.53	143.31	6.98	35.98	27.55	6.88	3.86
175.83	833.50	36.93	182.01	137.21	28.49	27.30
95.00	628.49	20.12	120.07	90.25	19.14	19.99
71.40	131.51	6.01	43.13	34.18	7.34	4.64
121.13	229.98	9.24	68.87	45.98	11.87	8.73
100.82	555.53	11.59	100.21	85.59	15.75	14.14
74.34	531.36	11.23	86.97	81.64	14.82	14.14
26.48	23.37	0.36	13.21	2.89	0.87	
75.01	277.00	25.34	81.34	51.62	12.73	13.16
205.86	1 756.30	25.01	137.18	112.25	35.41	36.33
0.64	70.26	2.47	15.53	3.62	0.44	5.33
2.11	24.94	0.95	2.33	2.06	0.80	1.41
5.02	3.29	0.18	0.65	2.31	0.85	0.06

上/海/统/计/年/鉴

主要统计指标解释

■ 工　业

指从事自然资源的开采，对采掘品和农产品进行加工和再加工的物质生产部门。具体包括：(1)对自然资源的开采，如采矿、晒盐等(但不包括禽兽捕猎和水产捕捞)；(2)对农副产品的加工、再加工，如粮油加工、食品加工、缫丝、纺织、制革等；(3)对采掘品的加工、再加工，如炼铁、炼钢、化工生产、石油加工、机器制造、木材加工等，以及电力、自来水、煤气的生产和供应等；(4)对工业品的修理、翻新，如机器设备的修理、交通运输工具(包括小卧车)的修理等。

工业统计调查单位为独立核算法人工业企业。

独立核算法人工业企业指从事工业生产经营活动的单位。独立核算法人工业企业应同时具备以下条件：①依法成立，有自己的名称、组织机构和场所，能够承担民事责任；②独立拥有和使用资产，承担负债，有权与其他单位签订合同；③独立核算盈亏，并能够编制资产负债表。

■ 轻工业

指主要提供生活消费品和制作手工工具的工业。按其所使用的原料不同，可分为两大类：(1)以农产品为原料的轻工业，是指直接或间接以农产品为基本原料的轻工业。主要包括食品制造、饮料制造、烟草加工、纺织、缝纫、皮革和毛皮制作、造纸以及印刷等工业；(2)以非农产品为原料的轻工业，是指以工业品为原料的轻工业。主要包括文教体育用品、化学药品制造、合成纤维制造、日用化学制品、日用玻璃制品、日用金属制品、手工工具制造、医疗器械制造、文化和办公用机械制造等工业。

■ 重工业

指为国民经济各部门提供物质技术基础的主要生产资料的工业。按其生产性质和产品用途，可以分为下列三类：(1)采掘(伐)工业，是指对自然资源的开采，包括石油开采、煤炭开采、金属矿开采、非金属矿开采等工业；(2)原材料工业，指向国民经济各部门提供基本材料、动力和燃料的工业。包括金属冶炼及加工、炼焦及焦炭、化学、化工原料、水泥、人造板以及电力、石油和煤炭加工等工业；(3)加工工业，是指对工业原材料进行再加工制造的工业。包括装备国民经济各部门的机械设备制造工业、金属结构、水泥制品等工业，以及为农业提供的生产资料如化肥、农药等工业。

根据上述划分原则，修理业中以重工业产品为修理作业对象的划为重工业，反之划为轻工业。

■ 工业总产值

(1)定义：工业总产值是以货币形式表现的，工业企业在一定时期内生产的工业最终产品或提供工业性劳务活动的总价值量。它反映一定时间内工业生产的总规模和总水平。

(2)计算原则：

工业生产的原则，即凡是企业在报告期生产的经检验合格的产品，不管是否在报告期销售，均包括在内。

最终产品的原则，即凡是计入工业总产值的产品，必须是本企业生产的经检验合格的，不需要再进行任何加工的最终产品。如果企业有中间产品(半成品)对外销售，则对外销售的中间产品应视为企业的最终产品。

工厂法原则，即工业总产值是以工业企业作为基本计算(核算)单位，即按企业的最终产品计算工业总产值。按这种方法计算的工业总产值，不允许同一产品价值在企业内部重复计算，不能把企业内部各个车间(分厂)生产的成果相加，但允许企业间的重复计算。

(3)内容及计算方法：

1995年全国工业普查对工业总产值(原规定)的内容及计算原则和方法做了某些修订，修订后的工业总产值(新规定)包括三项内容：即本期生产成品价值、对外加工费收入、在制品半成品期末期初差额价值三部分。

本期生产成品价值：指企业本期生产，并在报告期内不再进行加工，经检验、包装入库的全部工业成品(半产品)价值合计，包括企业生产的自制设备及提供给本企业在建工程、其他非工业部门和福利部门等单位使用的成品价值。本期生产成品价值为按自备原材料生产的产品的数量乘以本期不含增值税(销项税额)的产品实际销售平均单价计算；会计核算中按成本价格转帐的自制设备和自产自用的成品，按成本价格计算生产成品价值。生产成品价值中不包括用定货者来料加工的成品（半产品)价值。

对外加工费收入：指企业在报告期内完成的对外承接的工业品加工(包括用定货者来料加工产品)的加工费收入和对外工业修理作业所取得的加工费收入。对外加

主要统计指标解释

工费收入要不含增值税(销项税额)的价格计算,可根据会计"产品销售收入"科目的有关资料取得。

对于本企业对内非工业部门提供的加工修理、设备安装的劳务收入,如果企业会计核算基础较好,能取得这部分资料,而且这部分价值所占比重较大,应包括在对外加工费收入中。

自制半成品在制品期末期初差额价值：指企业报告期在制品期末减期初的差额价值，本指标一般可以从会计核算资料中取得。如果会计产品成本核算中不计算半成品、在制品的成本,则总产值中也不包括这部分价值,反之则包括。

(4)工业总产值统计范围变化和计算方法修订情况：

1984年以前工业总产值不包括村办工业,村办工业总产值划归农业。1984年以后工业总产值包括村办工业。

1995年工业普查对工业总产值计算方法做了修订,即从1995年始按新修订(新规定)方法计算工业总产值。新规定与原规定的区别如下：

全价与加工费的计算原则不同：新规定为凡自备原材料,不论其生产繁简程度如何,一律按全价计算工业总产值;凡来料加工,允许按加工费计算工业总产值。原规定则视生产加工的繁简程度不同,规定哪些行业按全价,哪些行业按加工费计算工业总产值。

自制半成品、在产品期末期初差额价值的计算原则不同:新规定要求,凡会计产品成本核算时计算了成本的差额价值,总产值中就应包括,否则可不包括;原规定则按生产周期六个月的界限区分，凡生产周期六个月以上的企业,总产值计算中应包括这部分差额价值,否则可不包括。

计算价格不同:新规定按不含增值税(销项税额)的价格计算;原规定则按含增值税(销项税额)的价格计算。

■ 大、中、小、微型企业

大中小微型企业划分标准:自2011年年报起,大中小型企业划分标准执行"关于印发中小企业划型标准规定的通知"(工信部联企业〔2011〕300号)。即大型企业必须同时达到从业人员≥1000人、营业收入≥40000万元;中型企业必须同时达到1000人>从业人员≥300人、40000万元>营业收入≥2000万元;小型企业必须同时达到300人>从业人员≥20人、2000万元>营业收入≥300万元；其余的均为微型企业。

■ 资产总计

资产是指企业拥有或者控制的能以货币计量的经济资源,包括各种财产、债权和其他权利。资产按其流动性(即资产的变现能力和支付能力)划分为:流动资产、长期投资、固定资产、无形资产、递延资产和其他资产。

■ 流动资产

指企业可以在一年内或者超过一年的一个生产周期内变现或者耗用的资产，包括现金及各种存款、短期投资,应收及预付款项、存货等。根据会计"资产负债表"中"流动资产合计"项的期末数填列。

指企业可以在一年内或者超过一年的一个生产周期内变现或者耗用的资产，包括现金及各种存款、短期投资,应收及预付款项、存货等。

■ 固定资产净值

固定资产净值指固定资产原价减去累计折旧后的净额。该指标根据"资产负债表"中"固定资产原价"、"累计折旧"指标的期初、期末数计算填列。

计算公式为：

固定资产净值 = 固定资产原价 − 累计折旧

■ 负债合计

指企业所承担的能以货币计量,将以资产或劳务偿付的债务总计。负债一般按偿还期长短分为流动负债和长期负债。流动负债合计是指企业在一年内或超过一年的一个营业周期内偿还的债务;长期负债合计是指偿还期在一年以上或者超过一年的一个营业周期内偿还债务。

■ 所有者权益

指企业投资人对企业净资产的所有权。企业净资产等于企业全部资产减去全部负债后的余额,包括企业投资人对企业的最初投入的实际到位的资产及资本公积金、盈余公积金和未分配利润。所有者权益合计数小于零,表示企业资不抵债。

■ 利润总额

指企业生产经营活动的最终成果，是企业在一定时期内实现的盈亏相抵后的利润总额(亏损以"−"号表示),它等于营业利润加上补贴收入加上投资收益加上营业外净收入再加上以前年度损益调整。

主要统计指标解释

总资产贡献率

反映企业全部资产的获利能力，是企业经营业绩和管理水平的集中体现，是评价和考核企业盈利能力的核心指标。计算公式为：

总资产贡献率(%)= 利润总额 + 税金总额 + 利息支出 / 平均资产总额 × 100%

公式中：税金总额为产品销售税金及附加与应缴增值税之和；平均资产总额为期初期末资产之和的算术平均值。

资产负债率

该指标既反映企业经营风险的大小，也反映企业利用债权人提供的资金从事经营活动的能力。计算公式为：

资产负债率(%)= 负债总额 / 资产总额 × 100%

资产与负债均为报告期期末数。

流动资产周转次数

指一定时期内流动资产完成的周转次数，反映投入工业企业流动资金的周转速度。计算公式为：

流动资产周转次数 = 主营业务收入 / 全部流动资产平均余额

公式中：全部流动资产平均余额为期初和期末的流动资产之和的算术平均值。

成本费用利润率

反映企业投入的生产成本及费用的经济效益，同时也反映企业降低成本所取得的经济效益。计算公式为：

成本费用利润 (%)= 利润总额 / 成本费用总额 × 100%

公式中：成本费用总额为主营业务成本、销售费用、管理费用、财务费用之和。

产品销售率

该指标反映工业产品已实现销售的程度，是分析工业产销衔接情况、研究工业产品满足社会需求的指标。计算公式为：

产品销售率 (%)= 工业销售产值 / 工业总产值 (现价) × 100%

资产保值增值率

该指标反映企业净资产的变动状况，是企业发展能力的集中体现。计算公式为：

资本保值增值率＝报告期期末所有者权益 / 上年同期期末所有者权益

所有者权益等于资产总计减负债总计。

全员劳动生产率

该指标反映企业的生产效率和劳动投入的经济效益。计算公式为：

$$全员劳动生产率(元/人)= \frac{工业增加值}{全部从业人员平均人数}$$

SHANGHAI STATISTICAL YEARBOOK

EXPLANATORY NOTES TO MAJOR STATISTICAL INDICATORS

□ Industry

Industry refers to the material production sector which is engaged in extraction of natural resources and processing and reprocessing of minerals and agricultural products, including (1) extraction of natural resources, such as mining, salt production (but not including hunting and fishing); (2) processing and reprocessing of farm and sideline produces, such as rice husking, flour milling, wine making, oil pressing, silk reeling, spinning and weaving, and leather making; (3) manufacture of industrial products, such as steel making, iron smelting, chemicals manufacturing, petroleum processing, machine building, timber processing; water and gas production and electricity generation and supply; (4)repairing of industrial products such as the repairing of machinery and means of transport (including cars).

Units of industrial statistics survey corporate industrial enterprises with independent accounting system.

Corporate industrial enterprises with independent accounting system refer to enterprises engaging in industrial production activities, which meet the following requirements: ①They are established legally, having their own names, organizations, location, able to take civil liability; ②They possess and use their assets independently, assume liabilities, and are entitled to sign contracts with other units; ③They are financially independent and compile their own balance sheets.

□ Light Industry

Light Industry refers to the industry that produces consumer goods and hand tools. It consists of two categories, depending on the materials used:

(1)Industries using farm products as raw materials. These are branches of light industry which directly or indirectly use farm products as basic raw materials, including the manufacture of food and beverages, tobacco processing, textile, clothing, fur and leather manufacturing, paper making, printing, etc.

(2)Industries using non farm products as raw materials. These are branches of light industry which use manufactured goods as raw materials, including the manufacture of cultural, educational articles and sports goods, chemicals, synthetic fiber, chemical products for daily use, glass products for daily use, metal products for daily use, hand tools, medical apparatus and instruments, and the manufacture of cultural and clerical machinery.

□ Heavy Industry

Heavy Industry refers to the industry which produces capital goods, and provides various sectors of the national economy with necessary material and technical basis. It consists of the following three branches according to the purpose of production or the use of products:

(1) Mining, quarrying and logging industry refers to the industry that extracts natural resources, including extraction of petroleum, coal, metal and non-metal ores.

(2) Raw materials industry refers to the industry that provides various sectors of the national economy with raw materials, fuels and power. It includes smelting and processing of metals, coking and coke chemistry, chemical materials and building materials such as cement, plywood, and power, petroleum refining and coal dressing.

(3) Manufacturing industry refers to the industry that processes raw materials. It includes machine building industry which equips sectors of the national economy, industries of metal structure and cement products, industries producing means of agricultural production, such as chemical fertilizers and pesticides. According to the above principle of classification, the repairing trades which are engaged primarily in repairing products of heavy industry are classified into heavy industry while these engaged in repairing products of light industry are classified into light industry.

ed into light industry.

□ Gross Output Value of Industry

(1)Definition: Gross industrial output value is the total volume of final industrial products produced and industrial services provided during a given period. It reflects the total achievements and overall scale of industrial production during a given period.

(2) Principles for calculation:

Statistics on industrial production follow the principle that all products produced by the enterprises and accepted during the reference period are to be included no matter whether they are sold or not during the reference period.

Determination of final products follow the principle that all products that are included in the calculation of grow industrial

EXPLANATORY NOTES TO MAJOR STATISTICAL INDICATORS

output value are the final products of the enterprise which have been accepted through quality check and require no further processing. If an enterprise has intermediate (semi-finished) products to sell, these intermediate products are considered as the final products of the enterprise.

Gross industrial output value is calculated following the principle of factory approach, i.e. industrial enterprise is used as the basic accounting unit in calculating the gross industrial output value. By this approach, value of the same product is not to be double counted, and the output value of different workshops (branch factories) should not be added. However, this approach does not exclude the possibility of double counting between enterprises.

(3) Content and calculation method:

The old definition of gross industrial output value was modified during the national industrial census in 1995. The revised (new) definition of gross industrial output value consists of 3 components: value of the finished products during the reference period, income from external processing, and value of change in semi-finished products at the end and at the beginning of the reference period.

Value of the finished products during the reference period: refers to the value of all finished (semi-finished) industrial products that are produced during the reference period without the need for further processing, checked for acceptance, packed and put into the warehouse of the enterprise, including the value of own-produced equipment and the value of products provided to the projects under construction of the enterprise, and to other non-industrial or welfare units. Value of finished products during the reference period is calculated by the quantity of products produced using own materials multiplied by the average unit prices at which products are sold (excluding value-added tax). Own-produced equipment and products produced for own use are value at cost prices as in the case of enterprise accounting. Value of finished products does not include the value of finished products (semi-finished products) that are produced using the materials from the clients who make the orders.

Income from external processing: refers to income from contracted external processing of industrial products (including processing of industrial products using materials from the clients), and the income from industrial repairing work provided to other units. Income from external processing is calculated using information from the item "products sales income" in the enterprise accounting at the prices excluding value-added tax. For income from services such as processing, repairing and installation of equipment provided to non-industrial units within the enterprise, if the accounting work of the enterprise is good enough to separate it from other records, and the share of such services is significant, it should also be included in the income from external processing.

Value of change in semi-finished products at the end and at the beginning of the reference period: refers to the value of change in semi-finished products at the end and at the beginning of the reference period, which generally can be obtained from accounting records of enterprises. If the enterprise accounting excludes the cost of semi-finished products, then it should not be included in the gross industrial output value, and vice versa.

(4) Changes in the coverage and method of calculation of gross industrial output value

Prior to 1984, the value of rural industry run by villages was classified into agriculture instead of industry. Since 1984, it has been included in the gross industrial output value.

Method of calculation for the gross industrial output value was modified in the industrial census in 1995. The difference in the new method as compared with the old one is outlined below:

Principle in using full value vs. processing fee: The new method stipulates that all products produced using own materials are to be calculated with full value in reporting the gross industrial output value irrespective of sophistication of production, and for external processing, it allows calculation using processing fee. In the old method, however, the use of full value or processing fee was determined by the degree of sophistication of production in different branches of industries.

Principle in determining the value of change in semi-finished products: The new method requires that value of the change in semi-finished products should be included in the gross industrial output value if it is included in the accounting record of the enterprise, otherwise it should not be included. By the old method, it is determined by the type of enterprises in terms of production cycle. If the production cycle is over 6 months, the value of change in semi-finished products is included in the gross industrial output value, otherwise it is excluded.

Difference in prices: The new method uses prices excluding value-added tax in the calculation of gross industrial output value, while the old method used prices including value-added tax

□ Large, Medium、Small and Micro Enterprises

Large, Medium, Small and Micro Enterprises division criteri-

EXPLANATORY NOTES TO MAJOR STATISTICAL INDICATORS

a: Since 2011 annual report, criteria for classifying Large, Medium and Small Enterprises follow the Notice On the issuance of small and medium enterprises designated standards (MIIT Joint on Enterprise, [2011] No.300). Under the new classification criteria, an enterprise could be entitled Large Enterprise only when it has more than 1000 employees, its operating revenue exceeds 400 million yuan, simultaneously. An enterprise could be entitled Medium Enterprise only when its employee number ranges from 300 to 1000, its operating revenue ranges from 20 million and 400 million yuan, simultaneously. An enterprise could be entitled Small Enterprise only when its employee number ranges from 20 to 300, its operating revenue ranges from 3 million and 200 million yuan, simultaneously. All other enterprises should be entitled Micro Enterprise.

□ Aggregate Assets

Total Assets refer to all economic resources, in monetary terms, that is owned or controlled by enterprises, including properties, creditors equity and other economic rights of all forms. Classified by the degree of equitability, total assets include circulating assets, long-term investment, fixed assets, intangible assets and deferred assets, and other assets.

□ Working Capital

Working Capital refers to capital that an enterprise can cash or use during one year or one production cycle that may exceed one year, including cash and savings deposits of various forms, short-term investment, money receivable and prepaid money, inventories, etc.

□ Net Value of Fixed Assets

Net value of fixed assets refers to the original value of fixed assets minus depreciation over years, i.e.:

Information on this indicator can be obtained from the beginning and ending figures of the original value of fixed assets and cumulative depreciation from the Assets and Liability Table of enterprise.

Net value of fixed assets=original value of fixed assets- cumulative depreciation.

□ Aggregate Liabilities

Aggregate liabilities refer to the total debts of an enterprise which can be calculated in monetary term and will be repaid in the forms of assets or service. Usually, the debts are divided into liquid liability and long-term debt according to the length of the payback period. The liquid liability is the debt that an enterprise will pay back during an operation cycle which is either shorter or longer than a year. The long-term debt refers to a debt whose payback period is longer than a year or which will be repaid during an operation cycle that is longer than a year.

□ Creditors' Equity

Creditors' Equity refers to investors ownership of net assets of the enterprise, which is equal to the total assets of the enterprise minus its total liabilities, including the primary input actually received at the enterprise from investors, capital accumulation fund, surplus accumulation fund and undistributed profit. When the total of creditors' equity is less than zero, that indicates the liability of the enterprise is larger that its assets.

□ Total Profits

Total Profits refer to the final achievements of production and operation of the enterprises, represented by the total profits after deducting losses (loss is expressed by the negative figure). It is the sum of profits from operation, income from subsidies, investment earnings, net income from activities other than operation, and adjustment of profits and losses of previous years.

□ Ratio of Profits, Taxes and Interests to Average Assets

Ratio of Profits, Taxes and Interests to Average Assets reflects the profit-making capability of all assets of the enterprise and is a key indicator manifesting the performance and management and evaluating the profit-making potential of the enterprise. It is calculated as follows:

Ratio of Profits, Taxes and Interests to Average Assets (%) = [(total profits + total taxes + interest payment) / average assets] × 100%

In the above formula, total taxes is the sum of tax and extra charges on the sales of products and value-added tax payable; and average assets is the arithmetic mean of the sum of beginning assets and ending assets.

□ Ratio of Debts to Assets

Ratio of Debts to Assets reflect both the operation risk and the capability of the enterprise in making use of the capital from the creditors. It is calculated as follows:

Ratio of Debts to Assets (%) = (total debts / total assets) × 100%

EXPLANATORY NOTES TO MAJOR STATISTICAL INDICATORS

Both assets and debts are figures at the end of the reference period.

□ Turnover of Working Capital

Turnover of Working Capital refers to the number of times of turnover of working capital in a given period of time, which reflects the speed of the turnover of working capital of industrial enterprises, and is calculated as follows:

Turnover of Working Capital= (prine operating revenue) / (average balance of total working capital)

In the above formula, average balance of total working capital refers to the arithmetic mean of the sum of working capital at the beginning and at the end of the reference period.

□ Ratio of Profits to Total Industrial Costs

Ratio of Profits to Total Industrial Costs refers to the ratio of profits realized in a given period to the total costs in the same period, which reflects the economic efficiency of input cost and is calculated as follows:

Ratio of Profits to Total Industrial Cost(%)=(total profits/ total costs) × 100%

Total costs in the above formula is the sum of prime operating costs, marketing cost, management cost and financial cost.

□ Ratio of Sales to Gross Output Value

Ratio of Sales to Gross Output Value reflects the degree at which industrial products are sold. It helps to analyze the linkage between production and sales and the extent of the needs of the society that has been met by the supply of industrial products. It is calculated as follows:

Ratio of Sales to Gross Output Value= (Industrial sales / Gross industrial output value at current prices) × 100%

□ Capital Maintenance and Appreciation Rate

Capital Maintenance and Appreciation Rate reflects the changes of an enterprise's net assets. It epitomizes the growth capability of an enterprise. Its calculating formula is:

Capital maintenance and appreciation rate = Ownership equity at the end of the reporting period/Ownership equity at the same period of the previous year. Ownership equity is the result of total assets minus total liabilities.

□ Overall Labour Productivity

Overall Labour Productivity is an indicator reflecting the production efficiency of an enterprise and the economic efficiency of its labour input, calculated by the formula:

Overall Labour Productivity (yuan/person)=industrial value-added/average of all persons engaged.

第十四篇

CHAPTER 14

建筑业

CONSTRUCTION

简 要 说 明

一、本章资料的主要内容

本篇资料反映上海市建筑业概况和发展情况。包括建筑业企业基本情况和生产经营情况。主要指标有企业个数、从业人员数、建筑业签订的合同额、建筑业总产值、房屋建筑面积、劳动生产率和主要财务指标等。此外,还包括本市各区县主要建筑业指标完成情况。

二、本篇资料的统计范围

根据建筑业发展的实际情况,建筑业统计范围从2002年年报起由原具有建筑业资质等级四级及四级以上的独立核算的建筑业企业调整为具有建筑业资质的独立核算建筑业企业。

三、本篇的资料来源及统计调查方法

本篇建筑业企业统计数据是根据国家统计局制定的《建筑业统计报表制度》整理汇总的。建筑业统计报表是上海市统计局根据企业实际情况采取全面调查的方法布置、收集,由各资质内建筑业企业通过联网直报上报的全面报表。

BRIEF INTRODUCTION

I. Main Contents

Data in this chapter show a general situation and development of the construction industry in Shanghai. They cover the situation of production and management of the construction enterprises, including the number of enterprises; number of employed persons; construction contracts signed; gross output value of construction industry; floor space of buildings under construction; labor productivity and main financial indicators etc. They also cover the performance of main construction indicators in districts and counties.

II. Scope of Statistics

In view of the development of the construction industry, since 2002, the scope of construction statistics has been adjusted to include all the construction enterprises of various types of ownership with qualification certificates and independent accounting systems, replacing the previous criteria that required construction enterprises of various types of ownership to have qualification certificates at or above Class 4 with independent accounting systems.

III. Sources of Data and Methods of Survey

Data on construction enterprises are collected in accordance with the Reporting Form System of Construction Statistics stipulated by the NBS. The annual reporting forms on construction statistics are designed by the Shanghai Municipal Statistics Bureau in accordance with local situations for comprehensive collection by the qualified construction enterprises through the comprehensive network straight report.

表 14.1 建筑业主要指标(1978 ~2012)
MAJOR INDICATORS OF CONSTRUCTION INDUSTRY

年 份 Year	年末从业人员 (万人) Year-end Employees (10 000 persons)	总产值 (亿元) Output Value (100 million yuan)	房屋竣工面积 (万平方米) Floor Space of Building Completed (10 000 sq. m)	平均每个职工房屋竣工面积 (平方米/人) Area of Completed Building for Every Staff and Worker (sq. m/person)	全员劳动生产率 (按总产值计算) (元/人) Overall Labor Productivity (In Term of Output Value) (yuan/person)
1978	10.07	5.55	234.03	26.32	6 005
1979	23.35	13.98	564.62	26.10	6 226
1980	27.27	17.07	607.91	24.13	6 513
1981	30.21	18.03	649.93	22.28	5 941
1982	30.73	21.56	684.61	22.90	6 928
1983	33.35	24.64	736.34	22.46	7 189
1984	32.94	30.62	799.40	23.10	8 402
1985	33.35	36.73	819.24	23.78	10 070
1986	35.53	49.91	867.08	22.87	12 147
1987	35.83	59.45	872.25	22.66	14 455
1988	36.70	68.83	836.73	21.26	16 251
1989	34.43	74.75	758.34	19.70	18 053
1990	34.01	75.62	747.88	20.01	18 569
1991	34.62	84.30	775.63	20.14	21 022
1992	36.33	117.68	860.49	19.92	26 221
1993	36.90	193.00	1 144.16	26.10	44 020
1994	39.95	309.68	1 557.87	29.33	58 305
1995	41.10	391.42	1 485.87	25.44	67 023
1996	36.19	450.41	1 514.58	26.95	80 161
1997	37.40	564.37	1 777.41	29.60	93 995
1998	40.88	593.11	1 913.55	33.08	102 531
1999	39.01	573.06	1 950.76	33.86	99 473
2000	35.91	631.64	1 909.11	33.02	109 244
2001	35.52	730.33	2 434.73	39.55	118 641
2002	41.97	822.27	2 596.95	42.23	133 698
2003	50.52	1 195.80	3 609.20	71.44	153 910
2004	74.26	1 724.40	4 672.53	62.92	168 719
2005	72.23	1 889.25	5 648.85	78.21	182 299
2006	73.44	2 285.38	6 506.41	88.59	208 368
2007	69.33	2 524.18	6 090.22	87.84	228 710
2008	80.79	3 245.77	5 723.90	70.85	293 520
2009	88.88	3 830.53	5 719.93	64.36	312 360
2010	96.09	4 300.19	6 217.15	64.70	344 720
2011	96.86	4 586.28	5 984.74	61.79	359 232
2012	88.08	4 843.44	6 476.07	73.52	451 564

表 14.2 建筑业主要指标（2012）
MAJOR INDICATORS OF CONSTRUCTION INDUSTRY

类别	Types	企业数（个）Quantity of Enterprises (unit)	年末从业人员（万人）Year-end Employees (10 000 persons)	竣工产值（亿元）Output Value of Construction Completed (100 million yuan)
总　计	**Total**	**3 179**	**88.08**	**2 545.78**
按登记注册类型分	**By Registration Categories**			
内　资	Domestic Funded	3 044	85.45	2 406.93
#国　有	State-owned	120	3.48	171.68
集　体	Collective Owned	72	1.35	32.34
股份合作	Stock-holding Cooperative	21	0.15	4.15
联　营	Joint Owned	15	0.28	5.46
有限责任公司	Limited Liability Companies	544	32.62	1 067.69
股份有限公司	Stock-holding Companies Ltd.	61	4.88	356.66
私　营	Private	2 211	42.69	768.94
港澳台商投资	Hong Kong, Macao and Taiwan Funded	77	1.05	40.23
外商投资	Foreign Funded	58	1.58	98.63
按行业分	**By Sectors**			
房屋建筑业	Housing Construction Industry	965	61.34	1 584.24
土木工程建筑业	Civil Engineering Industry	605	11.45	487.62
建筑安装业	Construction and Installation Industry	743	7.79	243.66
建筑装饰和其他建筑业	Construction and Decoration Industry and Other Construction Industry	866	7.49	230.26
按资质标准分	**By Qualification Standard**			
施工总承包	Chief Construction Contract	1 453	73.98	2 121.44
专业承包	Professional Contract	1 726	14.09	424.35

表 14.2 续表 1 continued

类 别	Types	总产值（亿元）Output Value (100 million yuan)	其中 of which #建筑工程 Construction	#安装工程 Installation
总 计	**Total**	**4 843.44**	**4 021.24**	**680.70**
按登记注册类型分	**By Registration Categories**			
内 资	Domestic Funded	4 578.54	3 848.38	607.76
#国 有	State-owned	395.00	326.76	45.21
集 体	Collective Owned	52.72	42.20	6.69
股份合作	Stock-holding Cooperation	5.71	5.37	0.27
联 营	Joint Owned	16.10	12.54	1.29
有限责任公司	Limited Liability Companies	2 246.00	1 988.66	218.54
股份有限公司	Stock-holding Companies Ltd.	453.89	344.80	107.17
私 营	Private	1 409.12	1 128.05	228.59
港澳台商投资	Hong Kong, Macao and Taiwan Funded	129.52	78.40	44.51
外商投资	Foreign Funded	135.37	94.47	28.43
按行业分	**By Sectors**			
房屋建筑业	Housing Construction Industry	2 755.76	2 506.19	183.18
土木工程建筑业	Civil Engineering Industry	1 162.00	1 012.23	127.79
建筑安装业	Construction and Installation Industry	438.02	89.19	318.24
建筑装饰和其他建筑业	Construction and Decoration Industry and Other Construction Industry	487.66	413.64	51.49
按资质标准分	**By Qualification Standard**			
施工总承包	Chief Construction Contract	4 023.02	3 464.63	460.49
专业承包	Professional Contract	820.42	556.61	220.21

表 14.2　续表 2　continued

类别	Types	房屋建筑面积(万平方米) Floor Space of Buildings (10 000 sq. m) 施工面积 Under Construction	竣工面积 Completed
总　计	**Total**	**27 961.55**	**6 476.07**
按登记注册类型分	**By Registration Categories**		
内　资	Domestic Funded	27 671.14	6 367.70
#国　有	State-owned	664.25	91.00
集　体	Collective Owned	306.97	188.07
股份合作	Stock-holding Cooperation	1.91	1.91
联　营	Joint Owned	61.65	9.83
有限责任公司	Limited Liability Companies	15 367.89	2 734.39
股份有限公司	Stock-holding Companies Ltd.	3 626.24	872.08
私　营	Private	7 642.24	2 470.41
港澳台商投资	Hong Kong, Macao and Taiwan Funded	79.35	
外商投资	Foreign Funded	211.06	108.37
按行业分	**By Sectors**		
房屋建筑业	Housing Construction Industry	27 148.00	6 266.75
土木工程建筑业	Civil Engineering Industry	550.29	131.16
建筑安装业	Construction and Installation Industry	128.95	69.91
建筑装饰和其他建筑业	Construction and Decoration Industry and Other Construction Industry	134.32	8.26
按资质标准分	**By Qualification Standard**		
施工总承包	Chief Construction Contract	27 672.74	6 397.47
专业承包	Professional Contract	288.81	78.60

表 14.3　各区、县建筑业主要指标(2012)
MAIN CONSTRUCTION INDICATORS OF DISTRICTS AND COUNTIES

地　区	District	企业数(个) Quantity of Enterprises (unit)	年末从业人员(万人) Year-end Employees (10 000 persons)	总产值(亿元) Output Value (100 million yuan)
总　计	**Total**	**3 179**	**88.08**	**4 843.44**
浦东新区	Pudong New Area	616	25.64	1 197.06
黄 浦 区	Huangpu	190	2.37	225.35
徐 汇 区	Xuhui	220	5.97	403.92
长 宁 区	Changning	162	4.07	208.93
静 安 区	Jing'an	82	1.66	40.75
普 陀 区	Putuo	256	5.83	325.65
闸 北 区	Zhabei	103	3.79	383.19
虹 口 区	Hongkou	172	3.67	364.34
杨 浦 区	Yangpu	253	5.43	263.23
闵 行 区	Minhang	164	5.71	246.10
宝 山 区	Baoshan	223	6.68	596.80
嘉 定 区	Jiading	170	2.96	107.14
金 山 区	Jinshan	115	2.70	89.55
松 江 区	Songjiang	131	3.90	134.80
青 浦 区	Qingpu	74	2.53	86.05
奉 贤 区	Fengxian	202	3.87	130.74
崇 明 县	Chongming	46	1.30	39.85

表 14.3 续表 Continued

地 区	District	房屋施工面积（万平方米）Floor Space of Buildings Under Construction (10 000 sq. m)	房屋竣工面积（万平方米）Floor Space of Buildings Completed (10 000 sq. m)	其中 of which #住宅房屋 Residence
总 计	**Total**	**27 961.55**	**6 476.07**	**3 371.72**
浦东新区	Pudong New Area	9 778.33	1 613.68	841.44
黄浦区	Huangpu	429.89	82.62	26.64
徐汇区	Xuhui	703.55	144.47	109.14
长宁区	Changning	2 148.79	484.62	279.32
静安区	Jing'an	830.37	15.16	12.00
普陀区	Putuo	2 484.15	620.68	442.40
闸北区	Zhabei	853.54	245.38	162.82
虹口区	Hongkou	2 166.74	494.80	312.18
杨浦区	Yangpu	960.66	278.17	125.04
闵行区	Minhang	2 048.14	555.18	323.95
宝山区	Baoshan	2 145.26	592.65	142.58
嘉定区	Jiading	745.54	303.19	193.31
金山区	Jinshan	261.51	95.20	11.31
松江区	Songjiang	976.24	436.70	94.85
青浦区	Qingpu	572.25	145.43	51.56
奉贤区	Fengxian	650.01	274.78	186.84
崇明县	Chongming	206.59	93.36	56.33

表 14.4 建筑业主要财务指标(2012)
MAJOR ACCOUNTING INDICATORS OF CONSTRUCTION INDUSTRY

指 标	Indicators	合 计 Total	内 资 Domestic Investment
施工企业单位数（个）	Quantity of Construction Enterprises (unit)	3 179	3 044
固定资产原价（亿元）	Fixed Assets (Original Value) (100 million yuan)	659.92	641.02
固定资产净值（亿元）	Fixed Assets (Net Value) (100 million yuan)	359.52	347.81
自有机械设备台数（万台）	Machinery and Equipment (10000 units)	16.07	15.41
自有机械设备净值（亿元）	Machinery and Equipment (Net Value) (100 million yuan)	153.29	152.41
自有机械设备总功率（万千瓦）	Capacity of Machinery and Equipment (10 000 kw)	371.90	365.27
总产值（亿元）	Output Value(100 million yuan)	4 843.44	4 578.54
资产合计（亿元）	Assets at Year-end (100 million yuan)	6 632.79	6 330.52
#流动资产	Current Assets	5 342.37	5 068.27
固定资产	Fixed Assets	414.29	396.25
无形资产	Intangible Assets	35.98	35.58
负债合计（亿元）	Total Liabilities at Year-end (100 million yuan)	5 002.01	4 760.90
流动负债	Current Liabilities	4 661.84	4 438.92
非流动负债	Non-current Liabilities	282.23	273.86
所有者权益（亿元）	Total Owners Equity (100 million yuan)	1 627.54	1 566.41
企业总收入（亿元）	Total Revenue of Enterprises (100 million yuan)	5 960.28	5 632.99
主营业务收入	Prime Operating Revenue	5 907.25	5 583.16
其他业务收入	Other Revenue	53.03	49.83
房屋施工面积（万平方米）	Floor Space of Building Under Construction (10 000 sq. m)	27 961.55	2 7671.14
房屋竣工面积（万平方米）	Floor Space of Building Completed (10 000 sq. m)	6 476.07	6 367.70
利润总额（亿元）	Total Profits (100 million yuan)	163.57	147.16
全员劳动生产率（元/人）（按总产值计算）	Overall Labor Productivity (yuan/person) (In Term of Output Value)	451 564	441 608
技术装备率（元/人）	Per Capita Machinery Value (yuan/person)	17 404	17 836
动力装备率（千瓦/人）	Per Capita Machinery Capacity (kw/person)	4.2	4.3
房屋建筑面积竣工率（%）	Rate of Buiding Completed (%)	23.2	23.0
产值利润率（%）	Ratio of Profit/Gross Output Value (%)	3.4	3.2
产值利税率（%）	Ratio of Profit and Taxes/Gross Output Value (%)	3.2	3.3

其中 of which					
#国有 Stateowned	集体 Collective Owned	股份合作 Stock-holding Cooperation	联营 Joint Owned	有限责任公司 Companies With Limited Liabilition	股份有限公司 Stock-holding Companies Liabilities
120	72	21	15	544	61
75.64	3.65	1.01	0.49	326.50	82.21
38.41	1.72	0.59	0.29	180.65	44.10
1.15	0.32	0.02	0.07	5.68	0.75
25.0[illegible]	0.69	0.04	0.14	81.64	18.10
52.45	4.34	0.35	3.85	176.14	24.52
395.0[illegible]	52.72	5.71	16.10	2 246.00	453.89
712.38	52.51	8.17	9.20	3 158.03	738.29
493.16	49.38	7.33	8.03	2 536.18	521.11
45.88	1.25	0.77	0.43	201.00	48.15
6.12	0.13			19.30	3.05
531.32	35.67	5.97	5.95	2 579.59	540.36
462.01	33.12	5.62	5.92	2 437.63	482.35
64.89	1.80	0.03		133.77	54.96
180.38	16.84	2.19	3.25	577.81	197.94
511.12	60.22	4.95	17.47	2 716.39	789.39
494.52	60.04	4.91	17.41	2 704.90	783.39
16.60	0.18	0.04	0.06	11.49	6.00
664.25	306.97	1.91	61.65	15 367.89	3 626.24
91.00	188.07	1.91	9.83	2 734.39	872.08
14.75	0.89	0.07	0.14	81.95	16.65
643 371	283 956	503 425	396 907	551 023	377 414
72 027	5 111	2 780	5 170	25 032	37 095
15.1	3.2	2.4	13.7	5.4	5.0
13.7	61.3	100.0	15.9	17.8	24.0
3.7	1.7	1.2	0.9	3.6	3.7
3.0	3.6	2.8	3.4	3.4	3.2

表 14.4　续表 Continued

指　标	Indicators	其中 of which #私营 Private	港澳台商投资 Hong Kong, Macao and Taiwan Funded	外商投资 Foreign Funded
施工企业单位数（个）	Quantity of Construction Enterprises (unit)	2 211	77	58
固定资产原价（亿元）	Fixed Assets (Original Value) (100 million yuan)	151.50	9.83	9.08
固定资产净值（亿元）	Fixed Assets (Net Value) (100 million yuan)	82.04	6.41	5.31
自有机械设备台数（万台）	Machinery and Equipment (10 000 units)	7.41	0.30	0.37
自有机械设备净值（亿元）	Machinery and Equipment (Net Value) (100 million yuan)	26.70	0.45	0.43
自有机械设备总功率（万千瓦）	Capacity of Machinery and Equipment (10 000 kw)	103.61	3.59	3.03
总产值（亿元）	Output Value(100 million yuan)	1 409.12	129.52	135.37
资产合计（亿元）	Assets at Year-end (100 million yuan)	1 651.94	144.12	158.15
#流动资产	Current Assets	1 453.06	124.34	149.76
固定资产	Fixed Assets	98.76	12.64	5.39
无形资产	Intangible Assets	6.98	0.22	0.17
负债合计（亿元）	Total Liabilities at Year-end (100 million yuan)	1 062.04	109.42	131.69
流动负债	Current Liabilities	1 012.27	104.85	118.06
非流动负债	Non-current Liabilities	18.41	4.47	3.90
所有者权益（亿元）	Total Owners, Equity (100 million yuan)	587.99	34.67	26.45
企业总收入（亿元）	Total Revenue of Enterprises (100 million yuan)	1 533.45	159.90	167.38
主营业务收入	Prime Operating Revenue	1 517.99	157.72	166.37
其他业务收入	Other Revenue	15.46	2.18	1.01
房屋施工面积（万平方米）	Floor Space of Building Under Construction (10 000 sq. m)	7 642.24	79.35	211.06
房屋竣工面积（万平方米）	Floor Space of Building Completed (10 000 sq. m)	2 470.41		108.37
利润总额（亿元）	Total Profits (100 million yuan)	32.71	10.65	5.77
全员劳动生产率（元/人）（按总产值计算）	Overall Labor Productivity (yuan/person) (In Term of Output Value)	332 522	103 6778	580 724
技术装备率（元/人）	Per Capita Machinery Value (yuan/person)	6 254	4 313	2 703
动力装备率（千瓦/人）	Per Capita Machinery Capacity (kw/person)	2.4	3.4	1.9
房屋建筑面积竣工率（%）	Rate of Buiding Completed (%)	32.3		51.3
产值利润率（%）	Ratio of Profit/Gross Output Value (%)	2.3	8.2	4.3
产值利税率（%）	Ratio of Profit and Taxes/Gross Output Value (%)	3.2	2.5	2.5

表 14.5　建筑业签订合同情况(2012)
S TUATION OF CONSTRUCTION CONTRACTS

单位:亿元(100 million yuan)

类　别	Types	签订合同额 Signed Contract Value	上年结转合同额 Value from Contracts Signed in 2011	本年新签合同额 Value from New Contracts Signed in 2012
总　计	**Total**	**11 246.87**	**5 035.18**	**6 211.69**
按经济类型分	**Grouped by Registration Categories**			
内　资	Domestic Funded	10 583.01	4 820.67	5 762.34
#国　有	State-owned	729.73	314.91	414.82
集　体	Collective Owned	66.15	20.93	45.22
股份合作	Stock-holding Cooperation	6.11	1.90	4.20
联　营	Joint Owned	16.12	5.55	10.58
有限责任公司	Limited Liability Companies	5 893.36	2 588.68	3 304.69
股份有限公司	Stock-holding Companies Ltd.	1 669.76	935.40	734.36
私　营	Private	2 201.78	953.31	1 248.48
港澳台商投资	Hong Kong, Macao and Taiwan Funded	365.35	86.34	279.00
外商投资	Foreign Funded	298.52	128.17	170.34
按隶属关系分	**Grouped by Subordination**			
#中央属	Central Government	4 236.65	1 768.33	2 468.33
市　属	Municipality	2 591.45	1 480.58	1 110.88
区(县)属	District and County	681.77	218.54	463.23
按资质等级分	**Grouped by Quarlification Level**			
#特　级	Special Grade	5 072.19	2 384.82	2 687.37
一　级	First Grade	4 157.66	1 836.26	2 321.40
二　级	Second Grade	1 420.83	621.55	799.28
三　级	Third Grade	571.63	180.37	391.26
按行业类别分	**Grouped by Sector**			
房屋建筑业	Housing Construction Industry	7 025.42	3 295.31	3 730.11
土木工程建筑业	Civil Engineering Industry	2 776.21	1 298.74	1 477.47
建筑安装业	Construction and Installation Industry	791.02	253.06	537.97
建筑装饰和其他建筑业	Construction and Decoration Industry and Other Construction Industry	654.22	188.08	466.14
按资质标准分	**Grouped by Qualification**			
施工总承包	Chief Construction Contract	10 170.67	4 705.38	5 465.28
专业承包	Professional Contract	1 076.20	329.80	746.40

表 14.6 建筑业承包工程完成情况(2012)
COMPLETION OF CONTRACTED PROJECTS BY CONSTRUCTION ENTERPRISES

单位:亿元(100 million yuan)

类别	Types	直接从建设单位承揽工程完成产值 Completed Output Value of Projects Contracted Directly form Investors	其中 of Which: 自行完成施工产值 Own-completed Output Value	其中 of Which: 分包出去工程的产值 Output Value of Out-sourced Projects	从建设单位外承揽工程完成产值 Completed Output Value of Projects Contracted from Non-investors
总 计	**Total**	**5 121.29**	**4 389.64**	**731.65**	**453.80**
按经济类型分	**Grouped by Registration Categories**				
内 资	Domestic Funded	4 826.68	4 157.22	669.47	421.33
#国 有	State-owned	425.12	363.44	61.68	31.56
集 体	Collective Owned	51.59	51.19	0.40	1.53
股份合作	Stock-holding Cooperation	5.37	5.33	0.04	0.38
联 营	Joint Owned	14.15	14.15		1.95
有限责任公司	Limited Liability Companies	2 314.95	2 085.87	229.09	160.13
股份有限公司	Stock-holding Companies Ltd.	695.80	369.51	326.28	84.38
私 营	Private	1 319.70	1 267.72	51.98	141.40
港澳台商投资	Hong Kong, Macao and Taiwan Funded	136.62	118.96	17.66	10.57
外商投资	Foreign Funded	157.99	113.47	44.52	21.90
按隶属关系分	**Grouped by Subordination**				
#中央属	Central Government	1 607.88	1 523.31	84.57	72.52
市 属	Municipality	1 029.68	543.99	485.70	151.51
区(县)属	District and County	410.60	403.61	6.99	14.59
按资质等级分	**Grouped by Quarlification Level**				
#特 级	SpecialGrade	1 727.27	1 322.39	404.88	106.11
一 级	First Grade	2 113.32	1 871.90	241.42	212.62
二 级	Second Grade	870.68	805.21	65.46	87.61
三 级	Third Grade	400.27	381.26	19.01	46.68
按行业类别分	**Grouped by Sector**				
房屋建筑业	Housing Construction Industry	3 041.29	2 504.40	536.89	251.36
土木工程建筑业	Civil Engineering Industry	1 203.50	1 065.64	137.86	96.36
建筑安装业	Construction and Installation Industry	432.82	390.17	42.65	47.85
建筑装饰和其他建筑业	Construction and Decoration Industry and Other Construction Industry	443.69	429.44	14.25	58.22
按资质标准分					
施工总承包	Chief Construction Contract	4 381.05	3 693.00	688.05	330.02
专业承包	Professional Contract	740.24	696.65	43.59	123.78

上 / 海 / 统 / 计 / 年 / 鉴

主要统计指标解释

建筑业总产值

建筑业总产值是以货币表现的建筑业企业在一定时期内生产的建筑业产品和服务的总和。建筑业总产值包括:

(1)建筑工程产值:指列入建筑工程预算内的各种工程价值。

(2)安装工程产值:指设备安装工程价值,不包括被安装设备本身价值。

(3)其他产值:建筑业总产值中除建筑工程、安装工程以外的产值。包括房屋构筑物修理产值、非标准设备制造产值、总包企业向分包企业收取的管理费以及不能明确划分的施工活动所完成的产值。

a.房屋构筑物修理产值:指房屋和构筑物修理所完成的产值,但不包括被修理房屋、构筑物本身价值和生产设备的修理产值。

b.非标准设备制造产值:指加工制造没有定型的非标准生产设备的加工费和原材料价值(如化工厂、炼油厂用的各种罐、槽,矿井生产统一使用的各种漏斗、三角槽、阀门等)以及附属加工厂为本企业承建工程制作的非标准设备的价值。

按建筑业总产值计算的全员劳动生产率

即平均每个从事建筑业生产活动的人员的建筑业总产值,计算公式为:

按建筑业总产值计算的全员劳动生产率 = 建筑业总产值 / 计算建筑业劳动生产率的平均人数

计算建筑业劳动生产率的平均人数指建筑业企业报告期实际拥有的、与建筑施工活动有关的人员的平均人数,包括参加本企业建筑施工活动的非本企业人员,但不包括企业内部社会服务性机构的人员以及由本企业支付工资但所从事的工作与本企业生产基本无关的人员。

房屋建筑面积

指房屋全部平面面积的总和。它从房屋的外墙线算起,包括可供使用的有效面积和墙柱等结构占用面积。多层房屋按各层(包括地下室)面积总和计算。旧房加层或改造,只计算增加的建筑面积;旧房拆除重建,计算其全部面积;临时房屋不计算建筑面积。

房屋施工面积

指报告期内施过工的全部房屋建筑面积,包括本期新开工的房屋面积、上期跨入本期继续施工的房屋面积、上期停缓建在本期恢复施工的房屋面积、本期竣工的房屋面积及本期施工后又停缓建的房屋面积。

房屋竣工面积

指在报告期内房屋建筑按照设计要求已全部完工,达到了使用条件,经检查验收鉴定合格,正式移交使用单位的房屋建筑面积。

SHANGHAI STATISTICAL YEARBOOK

EXPLANATORY NOTES TO MAJOR STATISTICAL INDICATORS

□ Gross Output Value of Construction

Gross Output Value of Construction refers to total of construction products and services, expressed in money terms, produced of rendered by construction and installation enterprises during a given period of time. It includes:

(1) Output value of construction projects: the value of projects covered by the project budgets;

(2) Output value of installation projects: the value of the installation of equipments, (excluding the value of the equipment to be installed);

(3) Other output values: the output value of construction industry apart from that of construction projects and installation projects. It includes: output value of repair of buildings and structures; output value of non-standard equipment manufacturing; overhead expenses received by contracted enterprises from the sub-contracted enterprises and the complete output value of construction activities for which there is no clear definition.

a. Output value of repair of buildings and structures: the value created through the repair of buildings and structures. It doesn't include the value of buildings or structures being repaired and the value of the repair of production equipment;

b. Output value of manufactured non-standard equipment: the value of non-standard production equipment, including raw materials and manufacturing cost, made for the project (i.e., chemical plant; kettles or tanks used by refineries; various fillers, triangle tanks, valves used by mines). It also includes the output value of equipment manufactured by subsidiary workshops.

□ All-personnel Labor Productivity Calculated by Gross Output Value of Construction Industry

All-personnel labor productivity calculated by gross output value of construction industry refers to the average gross output value of construction industry by every personnel engaged in production activities in the construction industry.

All-personnel labor Productivity Calculated by Gross Output Value of Construction Industry = Gross Output Value of Construction Industry / Average Number of Construction Industry

Average Number of Construction Industry refers to average number of Persons that construction enterprises actually have and related to construction activities, includes those engaged in the construction activities of the enterprises but belong to other enterprises, and excludes those work for the social service institutions inside the enterprise and those paid by the enterprise but whose work has nothing do with the construction.

□ Floor Space of Buildings

Floor Space of Buildings under Construction refers to total floor space of the horizontal section of outer walls above the plinth of the building, including the effective area and the area occupied by the structure. Multi-storey building refers to the sum of each storey, including the basement. The old buildings with storey added or rebuild only calculate the floor space added. The old buildings after dismantling and reconstruction calculate the total floor space. The tabernacle calculates no floor space.

□ Floor Space of Buildings Under Construction

Floor Space of Buildings under Construction refers to floor space of buildings under construction during the reference period, including newly started buildings, buildings started earlier and continued during the reference period, and buildings suspended earlier but restarted during the reference period, buildings completed during the reference period, and buildings under construction and then suspended during the reference period.

□ Floor Space of Buildings Completed

Floor Space of Buildings Completed refers to the floor space of buildings that are completed in the reference period in accordance with the requirements of the design, up to the standard for putting them into use, and have been checked and accepted by concerned departments as qualified ones.

第十五篇

CHAPTER 15

交通运输、邮政和信息传输

TRANSPORTATION, POSTS AND INFORMATION TRANSMISSION

简要说明

一、本章资料的主要内容

本篇资料反映上海市交通运输、邮政业和信息传输业发展的基本状况。

交通运输、邮政业资料主要包括:运输线路长度、旅客发送量、旅客周转量、货物运输量、货物周转量、港口码头情况、港口货物吞吐量、集装箱吞吐量、邮轮经济、经营性停车场、民用车辆拥有量、邮政业务主要指标等内容。

信息传输业资料主要包括:电信业务开展情况、邮电通信水平、信息化基础设施情况、信息服务业经营情况、信息技术应用等方面资料。

二、本篇资料的统计范围和统计方式

1. 铁路资料:包括国家铁路(含控股合资)、地方铁路和非控股合资铁路运营情况,不含军用铁路及由厂矿企事业单位自建的铁路专用线和专用铁道。

2. 公路、水路、港口资料:(1)公路、水路运输量统计包括全面调查和非全面调查两种方式,统计范围为在上海市交通运输主管部门登记注册的从事公路、水路客、货运输的营业性的车辆和船舶所完成的运输量;(2)港口统计采用全面调查方式,统计范围为上海市全部沿海港口和内河港口。

3. 民用车辆拥有量资料:民用车辆拥有量由民用汽车拥有量和民用拖拉机拥有量组成。

4. 民航运输资料：统计范围为在上海市注册从事民用航空运输飞行和通用飞行的航空运输企业和定期航班通航机场,不包括在上海市从事运输飞行的外省市和外国航空公司。

5. 邮电业务量按业务种类分为邮政业务量和电信业务量：邮政业务量统计范围是上海市邮政业企业和年业务收入 200 万元以上的快递企业；邮政业基础设施资料统计范围是上海市境内提供国家邮政服务的机构和设施。

三、本篇的资料来源

本篇资料中的交通运输、邮政业资料由上海市统计局工业交通处负责整理、编辑。有关交通运输资料分别来源于上海市铁路局、上海市城市交通和港口管理局、上海机场(集团)有限公司、上海市公安局车辆管理所、上海市农机办、上海市邮政公司、上海市邮政局。

本篇资料中的信息传输资料由上海市统计局社会与科技统计处负责采集、整理和编辑。相关电信业务资料由上海市通信管理局提供,信息化基础设施、信息服务业、信息技术应用等方面资料由上海市经济和信息化委员会提供。

BRIEF INTRODUCTION

I. Main Contents

Data in this chapter reflect the basic conditions of transportation, postal services and telecommunications industries in Shanghai.

Data on the transportation and postal services industries cover mainly the length of the traffic lines, passenger departing volume, turnover volume of passenger traffic, freight traffic volume, turnover volume of freight traffic, conditions of ports, port freight throughput, container throughput, yacht economy, parking lots operation, civil motor vehicles, and postal services.

Data on the telecommunications industry cover mainly conditions of telecommunications services, telecommunications level, infrastructure of informatization, operation of information service industry, and application of information technology.

II. Scope and Methodology of Statistics

(1)Data on railway transportation: They include the operation and management of the national (including state-controlled joint ventures), local and non state-controlled joint-venture railways but exclude railways for military purpose, lines built by industrial and mining enterprises and special railways.

(2)Data on highways, waterways and ports: (a) Data on highway and waterway transportation are collected through both comprehensive reporting system and non-comprehensive reporting system. The statistical scope encompasses all the vehicles and ships registered with the transportation authorities in Shanghai and engaged in highway or waterway freight or passenger transportation business. (b) Data on ports are collected through comprehensive reporting system. The statistical scope encompasses all ports along the sea and the rivers.

(3)Data on civil motor vehicles: They include the numbers of civil automobiles and tractors.

(4)Data on civil aviation transportation: The targets of statistical collection are enterprises registered in Shanghai for engagement in civil aviation transportation flights and flights for general purposes and general aviation airports with scheduled flights. They exclude foreign companies and companies registered in other provinces and cities, which operate flights within the Shanghai territory.

(5)By types of business, the business volumes of postal and telecommunications sectors are divided into those of postal services and telecommunication services: Data on postal businesses include postal enterprises and express delivery companies with annual revenue above 2 million yuan. Data on postal infrastructure include institutions and facilities in Shanghai that provide state postal services.

III. Sources of Data

Data on transportation and postal services in this chapter are collected, processed and compiled by the Department of Industry and Transportations, Shanghai Municipal Statistics Bureau. Data on transportation are from the Shanghai Railway Bureau, Shanghai Municipal Transport and Port Authority, Shanghai Land-carriage Administration, Shanghai Airport Group, Civil Agricultural Engineering Office, Shanghai Post Corporation and Shanghai Municipal Post Bureau.

Data on information transmission in this chapter are collected, processed and complied by Department of Society and Technology Shanghai Municipal Statistics Bureau. Data on telecommunication businesses are provided by Shanghai Communications Administration. Data on infrastructure of informatization, information service industry, and application of information technology are provided by Shanghai Municipal Economic and InformatizationCommission.

表 15.1 主要年份运输线路长度
LENGTHS OF TRAFFIC LINES IN MAIN YEARS

指 标	Indicators	2000	2010	2011	2012
铁路运输	**Railway**				
运营里程(公里)	Operation Mileage (km)	257	414	453	457
正线延展里程(公里)	Mainline Railway Length Extended (km)	397	697	774	826
公路运输	**Highway**				
通车里程(公里)	Operation Mileage(km)	5 970	11 974	12 084	12 541
# 高速公路	High Speed Highways	98	775	806	806
内河航道	**Navigable Inland Waterways**				
航道里程(公里)	Length of Navigable Inland Waterways (km)	2 100	2 110	2 037	2 074

表 15.2 主要年份交通运输主要指标
MAJOR INDICATORS OF TRANSPORTATION IN MAIN YEARS

指 标	Indicators	2000	2010	2011	2012
公路运输	**Highway Transportation**				
营运汽车拥有量(辆)	Operating Vehicles (Vehicle)	155 860	185 531	193 897	198 055
载客汽车	Passenger Vehicles	30 757	20 386	20 662	21 508
载货汽车	Freight Trucks	125 103	165 145	173 235	176 547
载客汽车客位数(客位)	Seat of Passenger Vehicles(seat)	309 834	523 564	557 814	548 591
载货汽车吨位数(万吨)	Tonnage of Freight Trucks(10 000 tons)				
港 口	**Harbor**				
船舶平均在港停泊时间(天)	Average Days of Vessel Berthed at Harbor (day)	0.9	0.40	0.40	0.46
机 场	**Aviation**				
起降航班数(万架次)	Aircraft Movements(10 000 sortie-times)		55.11	57.39	59.67
进出港旅客人次(万人次)	Passenger Turnover(10 000 person-times)		7 187.74	7 456.01	7 870.84
# 国内航线	Domestic Flight		5 106.96	5 228.84	5 473.74
国际及地区航线	International and Regional Flight		2 080.78	2 227.17	2 397.09

表 15.3　主要年份旅客发送量
PASSENGER DEPARTING IN MAIN YEARS

单位：万人次（10 000 person-times）

年份 Year	旅客发送量 Passenger Departures	其中 of which			
		铁路 Railway	公路 Highway	港口 Harbor	民用航空 Civil Aviation
1990	3 835	2 476	605	555	199
1995	5 265	2 929	1 257	512	567
1996	5 822	2 804	1 974	422	622
1997	6 057	2 779	2 277	328	673
1998	6 139	2 760	2 006	678	695
1999	6 406	2 906	2 178	581	741
2000	6 893	2 980	2 482	539	892
2001	6 324	3 231	1 508	543	1 042
2002	7 326	3 518	2 046	526	1 236
2003	7 212	3 391	2 052	528	1 241
2004	8 968	4 076	2 465	621	1 806
2005	9 487	4 313	2 468	626	2 080
2006	9 619	4 458	2 784	68	2 309
2007	10 371	4 795	2 872	95	2 609
2008	10 927	5 343	2 934	89	2 565
2009	11 136	5 161	2 995	90	2 890
2010	13 456	6 095	3 634	85	3 642
2011	13 519	6 198	3 477	78	3 766
2012	14 547	6 758	3 748	66	3 974

①2000 年前旅客发送量是专业运输部门的数字，2001 年开始改为跨省市旅客运输的行业统计数字。
②港口旅客发送量从 2006 年起口径不包含海港到内河部分。
❶The passenger departures volume before 2000 is based on the figures for special traffic departments and the volume since 2001 is based on the figures for the inter-provincial passenger transport industries.
❷The Volume of Passenger Departures excludes those from seaports to freshwater since 2006.

表 15.4　主要年份旅客周转量
TURNOVER VOLUME OF PASSENGER TRAFFIC IN MAIN YEARS

单位：亿人·公里（100 million persons·km）

年份 Year	旅客周转量 Turnover Volume of Passenger Traffic	其中 of which			
		铁路 Railway	公路 Highway	水运 Waterway	民用航空 Civil Aviation
1990	113.94	26.85	8.42	40.84	37.84
1995	170.98	34.18	8.23	31.71	96.86
1996	171.81	31.49	8.83	24.13	107.36
1997	181.99	31.44	12.61	16.52	121.42
1998	199.15	30.68	12.07	9.97	146.43
1999	217.95	34.18	15.81	7.94	160.02
2000	234.72	35.40	16.44	6.77	176.11
2001	286.93	37.81	42.31	5.48	201.30
2002	332.12	39.48	50.43	4.41	237.80
2003	353.62	38.10	58.00	4.65	252.88
2004	599.62	46.35	72.09	4.49	476.70
2005	663.93	48.86	75.06	4.52	535.48
2006	742.87	51.23	86.85	4.52	600.28
2007	883.25	51.34	94.02	6.10	731.79
2008	869.07	53.22	94.07	6.73	715.09
2009	1 002.59	51.12	99.57	6.38	845.52
2010	1 214.25	60.16	115.44	3.69	1 034.96
2011	1 307.56	63.11	106.74	1.02	1 136.69
2012	1 223.05	68.38	112.72	0.99	1 040.97

表 15.5　主要年份货物运输量
FREIGHT TRAFFIC VOLUME IN MAIN YEARS

单位:万吨(10 000 tons)

年份 Year	货物运输量 Freight Traffic Volume	其中 of which				
		铁路 Railway	公路 Highway	水运 Waterway	其中 of which #远洋运输 Ocean Shipping	民用航空 Civil Aviation
1990	22 848	1 257	8 714	12 864	2 246	13
1995	22 531	1 376	6 273	14 845	2 778	37
1996	40 928	1 320	25 023	14 544	3 594	41
1997	41 373	1 252	25 991	14 082	4 201	48
1998	42 090	1 152	26 352	14 529	4 844	57
1999	44 485	997	27 171	16 241	5 783	76
2000	47 954	1 055	28 369	18 442	7 022	88
2001	49 545	1 080	28 869	19 496	7 129	100
2002	54 196	1 131	29 759	23 174	7 210	132
2003	58 669	1 208	30 678	26 621	7 832	162
2004	63 180	1 284	31 554	30 148	8 603	194
2005	68 741	1 278	32 684	34 557	10 091	222
2006	72 617	1 223	33 799	37 342	11 766	253
2007	78 108	1 143	35 634	41 041	12 575	290
2008	84 347	1 012	40 328	42 729	12 197	305
2009	76 967	941	37 745	37 983	11 916	298
2010	81 023	959	40 890	38 803	15 172	371
2011	93 318	888	42 685	49 389	16 044	356
2012	94 376	825	42 911	50 302	17 491	338

①2005 年起民航货物吞吐量不包括旅客行李。
②2008 年，公路货运量为交通部公路运输专项调查数据。
❶The Freight Traffic Volume of Civil Aviation in 2005 doesn't include the freight transportation volume.
❷The Highway Freight Traffic Volume of 2008 refers to the result of highway transportation special investigation hold by Ministry of Communications.

表 15.6　主要年份货物周转量
TURNOVER VOLUME OF FREIGHT TRAFFIC IN MAIN YEARS

单位:亿吨·公里(100 million tons·km)

年份 Year	货物周转量 Turnover Volume of Freight Traffic	其中 of which				
		铁路 Railway	公路 Highway	水运 Waterway	其中 of which #远洋运输 Ocean Shipping	民用航空 Civil Aviation
1990	3 359	111	11	3 236	1 957	1
1995	4 187	143	9	4 030	2 259	5
1996	3 814	133	49	3 627	2 721	5
1997	4 016	123	47	3 840	3 049	6
1998	4 838	117	49	4 665	3 794	7
1999	5 606	113	51	5432	4 020	10
2000	6 620	122	56	6 430	5 285	12
2001	6 992	113	60	6 808	5 511	11
2002	7 472	100	65	7 295	5 674	12
2003	8 587	118	69	8 385	6 376	15
2004	10 036	42	71	9 899	7 486	24
2005	12 132	47	73	11 986	9 285	27
2006	13 837	55	80	13 683	10 817	19
2007	15 949	35	85	15 789	12 039	40
2008	16 031	29	253	15 712	11 529	37
2009	14 436	25	244	14 118	10 596	49
2010	16 173	26	266	15 818	14 535	63
2011	20 367	21	284	20 005	15 654	57
2012	20 427	18	288	20 067	16 086	54

①2004 年起，上海铁路分局改为上海铁路局，货物周转量数据有所调整。
②2006 年民航货物周转量未包括中国货运航空公司的数据。
③2008 年，公路货物周转量为交通部公路运输专项调查数据。
❶Since 2004, Shanghai Railway Branch Bureau has been change into Shanghai Railway Bureau ,the Turnover Volume of Freight has been adjusted accordingly.
❷In 2006,the date of China Cargo Airlines wasn't included in the Turnover Volume of Freight of Aviation .
❸The Highway Freight Turnover Volume of 2008 refers to the result of highway transportation special investigation hold by Ministry of Communications.

表 15.7 主要年份港口码头情况
PORTS IN MAIN YEARS

年 份 Year	沿海码头长度 （万米） Length of Harbor （10 000 m）	沿海泊位 （个） Berths （unit）	其中 of which #万吨级 10 000 Tonnage	其中 of which #集装箱泊位 Container Berths
1990	1.77	122	64	7
1995	1.90	140	68	12
1996	1.90	138	69	12
1997	1.96	142	71	12
1998	7.58	1 108	109	13
1999	7.69	1 110	113	18
2000	7.64	1 098	111	18
2001	7.67	1 087	112	18
2002	7.92	1 096	115	20
2003	8.76	1 202	125	24
2004	8.90	1 198	123	24
2005	8.95	1 181	124	28
2006	9.16	1 140	131	32
2007	10.15	1 155	133	37
2008	11.49	1 203	137	42
2009	11.68	1 145	153	38
2010	11.92	1 218	157	45
2011	11.97	1 226	160	43
2012	12.29	1 245	162	43

注：1997 年以前，沿海码头长度、沿海泊位为原港务局数据，从 1998 年后，为全港数据。

Note: Before 1997, the figures of length of harbor and berths were from the ports belonged to Port Administration Bureau, and after 1998, data have been collected from all types of ports.

表 15.8 主要年份港口货物吞吐量
PORT FREIGHT THROUGHPUT IN MAIN YEARS

单位：万吨（10 000 tons）

年 份 Year	港口货物吞吐量 Port freight Throughput	其中 of which 内 贸 Internal Trade	其中 of which 外 贸 Foreign Trade	进 港 Arrival	其中 of which 内 贸 Internal Trade	其中 of which 外 贸 Foreign Trade	出 港 Departure	其中 of which 内 贸 Internal Trade	其中 of which 外 贸 Foreign Trade
1990	13 959	11 366	2 593	9 461	7 592	1 869	4 498	3 774	724
1995	16 567	12 481	4 086	12 097	9 492	2 605	4 470	2 989	1 481
1996	16 401	12 265	4 136	11 947	9 266	2 681	4 454	3 000	1 454
1997	16 397	11 684	4 713	11 852	8 921	2 931	4 545	2 763	1 782
1998	16 387	11 483	4 904	11 839	8 815	3 024	4 548	2 669	1 879
1999	18 641	12 356	6 285	12 936	9 037	3 899	5 705	3 319	2 386
2000	20 440	12 807	7 633	13 791	9 242	4 549	6 649	3 565	3 084
2001	22 099	13 446	8 653	14 922	9 706	5 216	7 177	3 740	3 437
2002	26 384	15 776	10 609	17 444	11 096	6 349	8 940	4 680	4 260
2003	31 621	18 653	12 968	20 606	12 999	7 607	11 015	5 654	5 361
2004	37 897	22 061	15 836	24 113	15 022	9 091	13 784	7 039	6 745
2005	44 317	25 825	18 492	27 539	17 441	10 098	16 778	8 384	8 394
2006	53 748	32 480	21 268	34 600	23 613	10 987	19 148	8 867	10 281
2007	56 144	30 574	25 570	35 479	22 619	12 860	20 665	7 956	12 709
2008	58 170	30 793	27 377	36 481	22 782	13 699	21 689	8 012	13 677
2009	59 205	33 394	25 811	39 000	24 920	14 080	20 205	8 474	11 731
2010	65 339	35 114	30 225	41 549	25 083	16 466	23 791	10 032	13 759
2011	72 758	38 980	33 778	45 525	27 173	18 352	27 233	11 807	15 426
2012	73 559	37 734	35 825	45 151	25 233	19 918	28 408	12 501	15 907

注：本表数据由上海港务集团提供。

Note: Data in this table is provided by Shanghai International Port Group.

表 15.9　主要年份国际集装箱吞吐量(按进出港分)
INTERNATIONAL CONTAINERS AND CARGO THROUGHPUT OF FOREIGN TRADE IN MAIN YEARS

年　份 Year	国际标准集装箱吞吐量重量(万吨) Weight of International Containers (10 000 tons)	国际标准集装箱吞吐量(万 TEU) International Containers (10 000 TEU)	其　中　of which	
			进　港 Input	出　港 Output
1990	446	45.6	22.4	23.2
1995	1 389	152.6	69.3	83.3
1996	1 785	197.1	92.4	104.7
1997	2 304	252.8	114.7	138.1
1998	2 766	306.6	141.1	165.5
1999	3 949	421.6	196.7	224.9
2000	5 170	561.2	266.1	295.1
2001	5 911	634.0	305.4	328.6
2002	7 822	861.2	414.1	447.1
2003	10 225	1 128.3	544.4	583.8
2004	13 294	1 455.4	699.6	755.8
2005	16 250	1 808.4	887.2	921.3
2006	19 595	2 171.9	1 064.4	1 107.5
2007	23 850	2 615.2	1 276.3	1 338.9
2008	25 992	2 800.6	1 397.8	1 402.8
2009	24 619	2 500.2	1 222.9	1 277.3
2010	27 992	2 906.9	1 436.1	1 470.8
2011	31 220	3 173.9	1 555.1	1 618.9
2012	32 480	3 252.9	1 605.1	1 647.9

注：TEU 是"折合 20 英尺标准箱"英文缩写语。
Note：TEU is the abbreviation, which refers to 20-foot equivalent unit.

表 15.10　邮轮经济发展情况(2011 ~2012)
CRUISE ECONOMIC DEVELOPMENT

指　标	Indicators	2011	2012
邮轮靠泊次数(次)	Cruise Berthing Times (time)	113	180
#以上海为母港靠泊次数	Homeport in Shanghai	81	128
邮轮旅客吞吐量(万人)	Cruise Passenger Throughput (10 000 persons)	20.44	35.03
#以上海为母港吞吐量	Homeport in Shanghai	13.80	25.58

注：本表数据由上海港码头管理中心提供。
Note: Data in this table are provided by Shanghai Port Manangement Center.

表 15.11 经营性停车场(库)营运情况(2010～2012)
STATISTICS OF PARKING LOTS (GARAGES) OPERATION

指 标	Indicators	2010	2011	2012
计时停放(万辆次)	Time Parking (10 000 vehicletimes)	8 585	10 053	11 259.06
包月停放(万辆次)	Monthly Parking (10 000 vehicletimes)	2 913	3 443	4 340.44
车辆停放总次合计(万辆次)	Quantity of Parking Times (10 000 vehicletimes)	11 498	14 053	17 231.21
经营车辆停放收入(亿元)	Revenue of Parking Lots (100 million yuan)	10.81	12.64	14.92

表 15.12 民用车辆拥有量(2010～2012)
CIVIL MOTOR VEHICLES

单位:万辆(10 000 vehicles)

指 标	Indicators	2010	2011	2012
总 计	**Total**	**309.70**	**329.17**	**260.90**
#汽 车	Civil Automobile	175.72	194.96	212.86
载客汽车	Passenger Vehicles	146.24	163.91	185.71
#轿 车	Cars	111.52	124.62	140.20
载货汽车	Freight Trucks	23.81	24.83	20.73
其他汽车	Other Automobile	5.67	6.21	6.41
摩托车	Motorcycle	129.12	128.89	42.53
拖拉机	Tractors	1.16	1.17	1.09

①本表不包括军用车辆和码头、机场等专用特种车辆。
②从 2012 年起，民用车辆拥有量的数据不含强制报废量(下表同)。
❶This table doesn't include the quantity of military vehicles and special vehicles for port and airport.
❷Since 2012, the civil vehicle ownership data does not contain mandatory retirement amount (the same as the following table).

表 15.13 个人民用车辆拥有量(2010～2012)
INDIVIDUAL CIVIL MOTOR VEHICLES

单位:万辆(10 000 vehicles)

指 标	Indicators	2010	2011	2012
总 计	**Total**	**229.83**	**245.88**	**182.57**
#汽 车	Civil Automobile	103.88	119.92	141.32
载客汽车	Passenger Vehicles	103.57	119.57	140.84
#轿 车	Cars	86.54	98.87	114.58
载货汽车	Freight Trucks	0.11	0.14	0.25
其它汽车	Other Automobile	0.20	0.22	0.23
摩托车	Motorcycle	125.95	125.95	41.23

表 15.14　邮政电信主要指标(2010 ~2012)
MAIN INDICATORS OF POST AND TELECOMMUNICATION

	指　标 Indicators	2010	2011	2012
邮电局、所(个)	Post Office (unit)	593	564	541
报刊图书销售点(个)	Publications Sales Outlet (unit)	1 868	1 714	1 659
邮政信筒信箱(个)	Mail Boxe (unit)	3 568	3 482	3 363
集邮品销售点(个)	Stamps Sales Outlet (unit)	376	351	195
邮政储蓄网点(个)	Postal Savings Office (unit)	371	368	370
邮路条数(条)	Number of Mail Route (route)	521	570	685
邮路总长度 (万公里)	Total Length of Mail Routes (10 000 km)	5.23	4.83	6.39
农村投递路线总长度 (万公里)	Length of Rural Delivery Routes (10 000 km)	2.36	2.62	2.27
长途电话业务电路 (2M)	Long-distance Call Line (2M)	272 645	425 247	482 027
长途光缆线路长度 (公里)	Long-distance Cable (km)	4 670	4 729	4 758

注：由于邮政速递物流公司成立，邮政公司的部分基础设施被拨出。
Note: The part of post infrastructure are transferred from Shanghai Post Corporation to newly established Shanghai Post Express and Logistics Corporation.

表 15.15　主要年份邮政业务主要指标
MAJOR INDICATORS OF POSTAL BUSINESS IN MAIN YEARS

	指　标 Indicators	2000	2010	2011	2012
邮政业务总量(亿元)	Volume of Postal Business (100 million yuan)	22.40	49.48	50.45	190.83
函　件 (亿件)	Mails (100 million units)	4.61	11.66	13.04	13.47
国内特快专递 (万件)	Domestic Express Mails (10 000 pieces)	709.90	25 708.85	43 312.09	55 975.40
国际及港澳台特快专递 (万件)	International and Hong Kong、Macao and Taiwan Express Mails (10 000 pieces)	52.10	3 088.01	3 039.32	3 929.90
邮政储蓄期末余额(亿元)	Postal Saving Deposit Balance (100 million yuan)	153.50	545.64	633.00	764.20
报纸、杂志累计订销数 (亿份)	Total Copies of Newspapers and Magazines Subscribed and Sold (100 million pieces)	11.30	11.99	11.25	12.37
集邮业务(万枚)	Stamp Collection Business (10 000 stamps)	9 467	5 156	4 918	4 172

①2010 年起，“国内特快专递”和“国际特快专递”数据包括邮政业企业和年业务收入 200 万元以上的快递企业。
②2012 年起，“邮政业务总量”包括国家邮政业务总量和非国家邮政业务总量。
❶Since 2010, data of Domestic Express Mails and International Express Mails are included post interprise and express corporation of annual revenue above 2 million yuan.
❷Since 2012, Volume of Postal Business Contains Volume of National Postal business and Volume of Non-national Postal-business.

表15.13　主要年份电信业务主要指标
MAJOR INDICATORS OF TELECOM BUSINESS IN MAIN YEARS

指　标	Indicators	2005	2010	2011	2012
电信业务总量(亿元)	Volume of Telecom Business (100 million yuan)	375.77	966.96	415.00	447.35
年末固定电话用户(万户)	Year-end Installed Telephones (10 000 households)	966.70	935.91	926.43	902.90
#住宅电话	Household Phones Installed	685.00	574.52	560.85	538.52
移动电话用户(万户)	Mobile Phone Subscribers Users (10 000 households)	1 444.20	2 361.55	2 620.61	3 008.30
#3G移动电话用户	3G Mobile Phone Users		197.32	464.66	748.15
长途通话时长(亿分钟)	Long-distance Call Lasting Time (100 million minutes)	110.10	205.77	244.26	261.83
固定电话长途通话时长	Installed Telephone Domestic Long-distance Call Lasting Time	31.20	38.84	56.67	60.14
国内长途电话通话时长	Domestic Trunk Calls	29.90	36.67	52.47	55.41
国际及港澳台电话通话时长	Overseas Calls	1.30	2.17	4.20	4.73
移动电话长途通话时长	Mobile Telephone Long-distance Call Lasting Time	19.60	37.37	187.59	214.76
国内长途电话通话时长	Domestic Trunk Calls	18.70	36.00	184.64	211.62
国际及港澳台电话通话时长	Overseas Calls	0.90	1.37	2.95	3.14
移动电话通话时长(亿分钟)	Mobile Calls (100 million minutes)	290.10	1 012.39	1 097.64	1 280.87
本地通话时长	Local Calls	270.50	975.02	910.05	1066.10
长途通话时长	Long-listanve	19.60	37.37	187.59	214.76
移动短信业务量(亿条)	Volume of Mobile Short Messages (100 million pieces)	180.60	371.54	316.49	336.11
局用交换机容量(含接入网设备容量)(万门)	Capacity of Office Telephone Exchanges(Including Access Network Capacity) (10 000 units)	1 357.00	1 338.61	1 328.03	1 280.52
移动电话交换机容量(万户)	Mobile Phone Exchange Capacity (10 000 households)	1 991	3 995	3 978	3 973

表 15.17 主要年份邮电通信水平
POSTAL AND TELECOM LEVEL IN MAIN YEARS

指 标	Indicators	2005	2010	2011	2012
固定电话普及率（%）	Popularity Rate of Telephone Line（%）	51.1	40.6	39.5	37.9
住宅电话普及率（%）	Popularity Rate of Household Telephone（%）	137.9	110.6	107.4	102.7
移动电话普及率(%)	Popularity Rate of Mobile Telephone（%）	76.4	102.6	111.6	126.4
平均每一邮政局所服务面积（平方公里）	Average Area Served by One Post Office（sq. km）	10.00	10.69	11.24	10.78
平均每一邮政局所服务人口(万人)	Average Population Served by Every Post Office(10 000 persons)	2.99	3.86	4.15	4.40
人均每年发函件数(件)	Average Number of Letters Mailed（piece）	52.00	50.89	55.54	56.71
人均每年购报刊数(份)	Average Number of Newspaper and Magazine Purchased（piece）	65.00	50.50	47.90	51.97

注：固定电话普及率及移动电话普及率为根据第六次人口普查调整后的数据。
Note：Data of Popularity Rate of Telephone Line and Popularity Rate of Mobile Telephone have been adjusted according to the sixth census.

表 15.18 主要年份信息化基础设施情况
INFRASTRUCTURE OF INFORMATIZATION IN MAIN YEARS

指 标	Indicators	2005	2010	2011	2012
信息通信管线长度(沟公里)	Length of Information Communication Pielines（channel km）	1 621	5 821	6 258	7 003
卫星站点(个)	Satellite Station（unit）	925	770	817	479
国际互联网用户(万人)	Users of Internet（10 000 persons）	803	1 560	1 691	1 750
互联网用户普及率(%)	Users of Internet per Hundred People（%）	46.6	68.1	72.0	73.5
宽带接入用户(万户)	Broadband Access Users（10 000 households）	247.40	517.40	550.70	626.82
#家庭宽带	Household Users of broadband access	222.66	440.00	455.00	476.74
家庭宽带接入用户普及率(%)	Household Users of broadband access per hundred household（%）	31.8	51.6	52.3	54.1
IPTV 用户(万户)	IPTV Users（10 000 households）		130	153	178
有线数字电视用户(万户)	Digital Cable TV Users（10 000 households）		220.0	262.2	365.5

①互联网用户普及率和家庭宽带接入用户普及率为根据第六次人口普查调整后的数据。
②因部门统计口径调整，2012 年起，卫星站点中不再包括仅有接收功能无发射功能的卫星站点。
❶Data of Users of Internet per Thousand People and Household Users of Broadband Access per Hundred Household have been adjusted according to the sixth census.
❷Due to departmental statistical adjustment, since 2012, satellite station no longer includes sites without transmitting function.

表 15.19　主要年份信息服务业经营情况
OPERATION OF INFORMATION SERVICE INDUSTRY IN MAIN YEARS

指　标	Indicators	2005	2010	2011	2012
信息服务业经营收入(亿元)	Operating Revenue of Information Service Industry (100 million yuan)	905.06	1 978.51	2 251.63	2 593.95
#软件和信息技术服务业	Computer Service & Software Industry	390.09	1 145.10	1 302.89	1 571.46
信息服务业从业人员(万人)	Employees of Information Service Industry (10 000 persons)	18.81	31.20	33.51	39.36
#软件和信息技术服务业	Computer Service & Software Industry	12.70	23.25	25.31	30.18

注：2012 年起，#软件和信息技术服务业为根据国民经济行业分类(GB/T 4754－2011)统计的行业数据。表中其他年份根据国民经济行业分类(GB/T 4754－2002)统计。

Note: Since 2012, industry data on #software and information technology services are according to National industry classification (GB/T 4754－2011), data before 2012 are according to National industry classification (GB/T 4754－2002).

表 15.20　信息技术应用(2009～2012)
APPLICATION OF INFORMATION TECHNOLOGY

指　标	Indicators	2009	2010	2011	2012
社会公共服务领域信息化	**Informatization of Public Service**				
"市民信箱"累计注册用户(万人)	Accumulative Registered Users of Citizen Mail Box (10 000 persons)	385.46	399.00	409.00	416.76
"付费通"业务平台交易量(万笔)	All-year Exchange Volum of FFT(10 000 units)	4 649.81	7 483.10	9 555.90	10 947.14
"付费通"业务平台交易额(亿元)	All-year Exchange Value of FFT(100 million yuan)	46.53	62.40	70.90	72.75
交通卡销售额(亿元)	All-year Sales Value of Traffic Card (100 million yuan)	11.94	26.00	13.60	14.39
银行卡累计发卡量(万张)	Accumulative Volum of Bank Card (10 000 pieces)	10 009.93	11 427.54	13 098.00	14 207.38
银行卡交易额(亿元)	All-year Exchange Value of Bank Card (100 million yuan)	9 517.10	11 306.30	13 887.70	16 608.12
#持卡消费金额	Consumption Value with Bank Card	4 200.08	4 963.76	6 425.12	8 843.11
社会信用体系	**Social Credit System**				
个人信用信息入库量(万条)	Newly Recorded Individual Credit Information (10 000 pieces)	1 110	1 138	1 156	1 157
个人信用信息累计查得量(万次)	Accumulative Provided Volum of Individual Credit Information Report (10 000 pieces)	911	928	943	959
企业信用信息入库量(万家)	Newly Recorded Enterprise Credit Information (10 000 units)	98	98	147	147

上/海/统/计/年/鉴

主要统计指标解释

■ 铁路运营里程

铁路运营里程又称营业长度(包括正式营业和临时营业里程)，指办理客货运输业务的铁路正线总长度。凡是全线或部分建成双线及以上的线路，以第一线的实际长度计算；复线、站线、段管线、岔线和特殊用途线以及不计算运费的联络线都不计算营业里程。铁路营业里程是反映铁路运输业基础设施发展水平的重要指标，也是计算客货周转量、运输密度和机车车辆运用效率等指标的基础资料。

■ 内河航道里程

内河航道里程也称内河通航里程，指在一定时期内，能通航运输船舶及排筏的天然河流、湖泊水库、运河及通航渠道的长度。包括全年季节性通航累计三个月以上的航道，不包括仅供零散流放竹、木排的河道。该指标可以反映内河水运网的规模、水平和发展情况。

■ 货物(旅客)周转量

指在一定时期内，由各种运输工具运送的货物(旅客)数量与其相应运输距离的乘积之总和，是反映运输业生产总成果的重要指标，也是编制和检查运输生产计划，计算运输效益、劳动生产率以及核算运输单位成本的主要基础资料。通常以吨公里和人公里为计算单位。计算货物周转量通常按发出站与到达站之间的最短距离，也就是计费距离计算。

■ 货(客)运量

指在一定时期内，各种运输工具实际运送的货物(旅客)数量。它是反映运输业为国民经济和人民生活服务的数量指标，也是制定和检查运输生产计划、研究运输发展规模和速度的重要指标。货运按吨计算，客运按人计算。货物不论运输距离长短、货物类别，均按实际重量统计。旅客不论行程远近或票价多少，均按一人一次客运量统计；半价票、小孩票也按一人统计。

■ 港口货物吞吐量

指经由水路进、出港区范围，并经过装卸的货物数量。按货物流向分为进港吞吐量和出港吞吐量，按货物贸易性质分为内贸和外贸吞吐量。按货物的类别分，可根据现行的交通行业标准《运输货物分类和代码》分类。

■ 国际标准集装箱吞吐量

凡经过水运进、出港区范围，并经过装卸的集装箱箱数和重量(含集装箱自重)，通常是按进港和出港分别统计。

TEU 是“折合 20 英尺标准箱”的英文缩写。它是指各种尺寸的国际标准集装箱的自然箱数，按各自的换算比例，折算为 20 英尺标准箱的换算箱数。其换算比例为：40 英尺箱 1：2；35 英尺箱 1：1.75；20 英尺箱 1：1；10 英尺箱 1：0.5。

■ 民用车辆拥有量

指报告期末，在公安交通管理部门按照《机动车注册登记工作规范》，已注册登记领有民用车辆牌照的全部汽车数量。汽车拥有量统计的主要分类：根据汽车结构分为载客汽车、载货汽车及其他汽车；根据汽车所有者不同分为个人(私人)汽车、单位汽车；根据汽车的使用性质分为营运汽车、非营运汽车和特种汽车；根据汽车大小规格不同载客汽车分为大型、中型、小型和微型，载货汽车分为重型、中型、轻型和微型。

■ 邮政业务总量

指以货币表现的邮政部门用于邮政服务的总数量。它综合反映了一定时期邮政工作的总成果，是研究邮政业务量构成和发展趋势的重要指标。它用各种邮政分类业务量，如函件件数、电报份数、订销报刊累计份数等，分别乘以相应的平均单位(不变价)，加总后再加上其他业务收入求得。

■ 住宅电话用户

指安装在居民住宅或农民家里并按照住宅电话用户登记注册和收费的电话用户。包括私人付费、单位付费和按规定免费安装的住宅电话用户。

主要统计指标解释

移动电话用户

指通过移动电话交换机进入移动电话网、占用移动电话号码的电话用户。用户数量以报告期末在移动电话营业部门实际办理登记手续进入移动电话网的户数进行计算，一部移动电话统计为一户。

局用交换机容量

指安装在电信企业用于接续本地固定电话的电话交换机容量。

EXPLANATORY NOTES TO MAJOR STATISTICAL INDICATORS

□ Operation Mileage of Railways

Operation Mileage of Railways refers to the total length of the trunk line under passenger and freight transportation (including both full operation and temporary operation). The calculation is based on the actual length of the first line even if this line has a full or partial double track or more tracks, excluding double tracks, station sidings, tracks under the charge of stations, branch lines, special-purpose lines and the non-payable connecting lines. The length of railways in operation is an important indicator to show the development of the infrastructure for the railway transport, and also the essential data to calculate volume of passenger freight transport, traffic density and utilization efficiency of the locomotives and carriages.

□ Length of Navigable Inland Waterways

Length of Navigable Inland Waterways it is an indicator reflecting the size and development of inland water network, it refers to the length of the natural rivers, lakes, reservoirs, canals, and ditches open to navigation during a given period, which enables the transport by ships and rafts. It includes the channels open to navigation for over an accumulative 3 months in a year, yet this does not include the river courses, which are only used to float odd logs and bamboo rafts. This indicator can reflect the scale, level and development situation of the inland waterway network.

□ Freight (Passenger) Turnover Volume

Freight (Passenger) Turnover Volume refers to the total of the product of the physical volume of transported cargo (passenger) by the transport distance, usually using ton/kilometer and person/kilometer as calculating units. Normally, the shortest distance between the departure point and the destination is the basis to calculate the freight turnover volume, that is to say, the payable distance. This is an important indicator to show the total results of the transport industry, to prepare and examine the transport plan and to measure the efficiency, the labor productivity and the unit cost of transport.

□ Freight (Passenger) Traffic

Freight (Passenger) Traffic refers to the volume of freight (passenger) transported with various means. The freight (passenger) traffic provides a quantitative measure to show how the transport industry serves the national economy and people, and is also an important indicator for planning the transport industry and for studying the development scale and speed of the transport industry. Freight transport is calculated in tons and passenger traffic is calculated in the number of persons. Despite the type of freight and travelling distance, the freight transport is calculated in the actual weight of the goods: and despite the travelling distance and ticket price, the passenger traffic is calculated by the principle that one person can be counted only once in one travel. The passenger who travels with a half price ticket or a child ticket is also calculated as one person.

□ Volume of Freight Handled in Ports

Volume of Freight Handled in Ports refers to the volume of cargo passing in and out of the harbour area of the major coastal ports and having been loaded and unloaded. The volume of freight handled may be classified by direction of flow as freight for import and freight for export, or by nature of cargo as freight for domestic trade and freight for foreign trade. The volume of freight handled maybe classified by the classification of cargo, or the current transport standard of The Classification and Code of Cargo Type.

□ International Container Throughput Capacity

International Container Throughput Capacity refers to number and weight of containers which are loaded or unloaded within port area via water carriage. It is often calculated by entering and leaving port, respectively. TEU was the abbreviation of twenty foot equivalent unit, which refers to converted number of all kinds of containers. The conversion method is based on respective conversion ratio and the number of all kinds of container is converted to the standard number of twenty foot equivalent unit. The conversion ratio is: 40 feet container 1 ∶ 2, 35 feet container 1 ∶ 1.75, 20 feet container 1 ∶ 1, 10 feet container 1 ∶ 0.5.

□ Individual Civil Motor Vehicles

Individual Civil Motor Vehicles refers to the total numbers of vehicles that are registered and received vehicles' license tags according to the Work Standard for Motor Vehicles Registration formulated by transport management office under department of

EXPLANATORY NOTES TO MAJOR STATISTICAL INDICATORS

public security at the end of reference period. They are divided into following categories according to the structure of motor vehicles: passenger vehicles, trucks and others; and private vehicles and vehicles for units use according to ownerships; working vehicles, non-working vehicles and special motor vehicles according to kind of usage; large passenger vehicles, medium passenger vehicles and small passenger vehicles, heavy trucks, light -heavy trucks and light trucks according to sizes of vehicles.

□ Volume of Post Business

Volume of Post Business refers to the total amount of post services provided by the post department, which reflects the total achievements by the post departments during a given period of time in a comprehensive way, and is an important indicator to study the composition and development of the post business. It is arrived by first multiplying the business volume of different types, such as number of letters, telegrams and accumulated number of newspaper and journals subscribed and sold, etc. by their respective average unit price (fixed price) and then adding these products together, plus the income from other business revenues.

□ Household Telephone Subscribers

Household Telephone Subscribers refer to telephone sets installed in the dwelling units of urban or rural residents, and registered as residence subscribers for payment, including 3 types of payment for the service: private payment, public payment and free service.

□ Mobile Phone Subscribers

Mobile Phone Subscribers refer to the persons who own mobile telephone numbers and are connected with the mobile telephone communication network through the mobile telephone switchboards. The number of subscribers is calculated by the subscribers who have completed registration at mobile communication business centers and entered into the mobile telephone network. One mobile telephone is taken as a user.

□ Capacity of Office Telephone Exchanges

Capacity of Office Telephone Exchanges refers to the capacity of telephone exchanges installed in the office of telecommunication service providers for communication between fixed telephones.

第十六篇

CHAPTER 16

批发和零售

WHOLESALE AND RETAIL

简要说明

一、本章资料的主要内容

本篇资料主要反映上海市批发和零售业、住宿和餐饮业的发展与经营状况，同时反映国内商品流通、商品消费、市场运行态势。主要内容包括：限额以上批发和零售业产业活动单位和从业人员、商品流转情况、财务状况；限额以上住宿餐饮业产业活动单位和从业人员、经营状况、财务状况；连锁经营情况；商品交易市场成交情况；社会消费品零售总额；商品销售总额等。

二、本篇资料的统计范围

批发和零售业、住宿和餐饮业的法人企业、产业活动单位、个体户，零售业、住宿和餐饮业连锁集团，商品交易市场。

三、本篇的资料来源

本篇资料是根据《批发和零售业统计报表制度》、《住宿和餐饮业统计报表制度》进行搜集和加工整理而得。

四、本篇的统计调查方法

本篇资料中限额以上批发和零售业、住宿和餐饮业法人企业、个体户、其他行业附营的限额以上批发和零售业、住宿和餐饮业产业活动单位资料，以及零售业、住宿和餐饮业连锁集团，商品交易市场采用全面调查的方法；限额以下企业及个体户等资料采用抽样调查方法推算。

BRIEF INTRODUCTION

I. Main Contents

Data in this chapter reflect the development and operation of Shanghai's wholesale and retail trade, hotels and catering trade. Data also reflect domestic commodity circulation, consumption, and market operation. Main contents include the basic conditions, employment, circulation of commodities, and financial status of wholesale and retail trades above the set scale; basic conditions, employment, business situation, and financial status of accommodation and catering services above the set scale; chain business conditions, transactions of commodities market, retail sales of main consumer goods, and total sales of consumer goods.

II. Scope of Statistics

Included in this chapter are the registered enterprises and self–employed individuals of wholesale and retail trade, hotels and catering trade; chain enterprises in retail, accommodation, and catering businesses; and commodities markets.

III. Sources of Data

Data in this chapter are collected and processed in accordance with The Statistical Reporting Form System on Wholesale and Retail Trades and The Statistical Reporting Form System on Hotel and Catering.

IV. Survey Methodology

Data on basic conditions for all corporate enterprises and self–employed individuals above the set scale of wholesale and retail trades, hotel, and catering businesses; affiliating establishments above the set scale of other industries involved in the wholesale and retail trades, hotels and catering businesses; chain enterprises of wholesale and retail trades; and commodities markets data are collected through comprehensive reporting? system. Data on enterprises and self–employed individuals below the set scale are collected by sample surveys.

表 16.1 批发零售贸易业、餐饮业从业人员(1978～2012)
EMPLOYEES OF WHOLESALES, RETAILERS AND CATERING

单位:万人(10 000 persons)

年 份 Year	从业人员 Employees	其 中 of which			
		批发零售贸易业 Wholesale and Retail	其 中 of which		餐饮业 Catering
			批发业 Wholesale	零售业 Retail	
1978	39.62	30.70	5.46	25.24	5.57
1979	44.70	32.94	7.87	25.07	5.82
1980	45.78	33.94	7.91	26.03	5.66
1981	48.47	35.31	8.41	26.90	6.25
1982	50.24	36.70	9.05	27.65	6.51
1983	51.30	37.64	8.86	28.78	6.51
1984	55.24	40.57	8.81	31.76	6.86
1985	62.64	45.41	8.99	36.42	7.66
1986	63.76	44.98	8.96	36.02	7.97
1987	66.13	45.98	8.85	37.13	8.18
1988	72.80	50.89	9.42	41.47	8.67
1989	77.31	52.20	9.67	42.53	9.35
1990	74.75	50.48	8.19	42.29	9.33
1991	75.41	52.47	8.53	43.94	10.71
1992	87.27	63.71	13.74	49.97	10.98
1993	109.98	98.44	29.68	68.76	11.54
1994	88.51	77.49	27.58	49.91	11.02
1995	111.24	94.78	34.31	60.47	16.46
1996	145.67	122.21	50.79	71.42	23.46
1997	149.97	125.64	53.68	71.96	24.33
1998	150.96	126.56	53.67	72.89	24.40
1999	153.90	128.18	53.93	74.25	25.72
2000	154.32	128.41	53.79	74.62	25.91
2001	165.68	138.73	56.33	82.40	26.95
2002	179.34	152.19	65.40	86.79	27.15
2003	174.93	147.91	59.31	88.60	27.02
2004	181.25	156.21	74.77	81.44	25.04
2005	195.92	169.60	84.71	84.89	26.32
2006	203.51	174.49	86.32	88.17	29.02
2007	204.46	175.50	86.23	89.27	28.96
2008	202.84	172.72	87.98	84.74	30.12
2009	205.49	175.32	90.36	84.96	30.17
2010	207.94	176.69	91.58	85.21	31.25
2011	215.57	184.61	96.96	87.65	30.96
2012	226.70	194.28	104.33	89.95	32.42

注：本表从业人员是指本行业的全部从业人员。
Note: Employees in this table refer to all the employees in the table.

表 16.2 限额以上批发贸易业产业活动单位和从业人员（2012）
QUANTITY OF BUSINESS UNITS AND EMPLOYEES OF WHOLESALE TRADE ABOVE THE SET SCALE

类别	Types	法人企业（个）Quantity of Corporations (unit)	产业活动单位数（个）Quantity of Business Units (unit)	从业人员（人）Quantity of Employees (person)
总计	**Total**	**5 073**	**8 246**	**384 765**
按登记注册类型分	**Grouped by Registration Categories**			
内资	Domestic Funded	3 585	5 554	172 460
国有	State-owned	193	419	14 413
集体	Collective-owned	48	67	2 103
股份合作	Share Holding Cooperative Enterprises	8	8	175
联营	Joint-Owned Enterprises	18	27	1 455
有限责任公司	Companies with Limited Liabilities	645	1 243	52 487
股份有限公司	Share Holding Companies with Limited Liabilities	58	757	16 873
私营	Private	2 574	2 979	82 322
其他	Others	41	54	2 632
港澳台商投资	Hong Kong, Macao and Taiwan Funded	403	837	69 031
外商投资	Foreign Funded	1 085	1 855	143 274
按行业分	**Grouped By Sectors**			
农、林、牧产品批发	Agriculture, Forestry and Animal Husbandry Products	36	42	1 732
食品、饮料及烟草制品批发	Food, Beverage and Tabacco	302	933	37 349
#米、面制品及食用油批发	Rice, Flour and Cooking Oil	49	100	4 337
烟草制品批发	Tabacco	22	495	7 178
纺织、服装及日用品批发	Textile Products, Garments and Commodity	715	1 303	113 196
#服装批发	Garments	235	509	43 970
文化、体育用品及器材批发	Culture & Sports Articles and Equipments	135	194	8 553
医药及医疗器材批发	Medicines and Special Appliances of Medicines	195	334	37 979
矿产品、建材及化工产品批发	Mineral Products, Materials of Construction and Chemical Products	1 984	2 978	62 028
#煤炭及制品批发	Coal	71	76	2 068
石油及制品批发	Petroleum	147	814	14 916
金属及金属矿批发	Metal Products and Metal Minerals	946	1 062	17 275
建材批发	Building Materials	134	157	3 850
机械设备、五金交电及电子产品批发	Mechinery Equipments, Hardwares, Electric Appliances and Eletronic Products	1 196	1 750	96 053
#汽车批发	Automobiles	35	48	8 252
汽车零配件批发	Spare and Component Parts for Automobiles	88	113	6 267
电气设备批发	Electrical Equipment	110	154	10 373
计算机、软件及辅助设备批发	Computers, Softwares and Accessorial Equipments	128	167	11 194
贸易经纪与代理	Trade Broker and Agent	194	255	9 785
其他批发	Others	316	457	18 090

表 16.3 限额以上零售贸易业产业活动单位和从业人员（2012）
QUANTITY OF BUSINESS UNITS AND EMPLOYEES OF RETAIL TRADE ABOVE THE SET SCALE

类别	Types	法人企业（个）Quantity of Corporations (unit)	产业活动单位数（个）Quantity of Business Units (unit)	从业人员（人）Quantity of Employees (person)
总　计	**Total**	**1 589**	**11 963**	**313 603**
按登记注册类型分	**Grouped by Registration Categories**			
内　资	Domestic Funded	1 380	9 388	201 225
国　有	State-owned	119	621	11 872
集　体	Collective-owned	45	214	2 398
股份合作	Share Holding Cooperative Enterprises	15	51	456
联　营	Joint-Owned Enterprises	40	49	872
有限责任公司	Companies with Limited Liabilities	453	5 028	101 313
股份有限公司	Share Holding Companies with Limited Liabilities	36	704	16 275
私　营	Private	654	2 624	66 655
其　他	Others	18	97	1 384
港澳台商投资	Hong Kong, Macao and Taiwan Funded	117	933	57 221
外商投资	Foreign Funded	92	1 642	55 157
按行业分	**Grouped By Sectors**			
综合零售	Comprehensive Retail Sale	249	5 709	122 932
#百货零售	Articles For Daily Use	105	276	19 311
超级市场零售	Retail Sale of Supermarket	101	1 605	75 129
食品、饮料及烟草制品专门零售	Food, Beverage and Tabacco	100	1 601	21 120
纺织、服装及日用品专门零售	Textile, Garments and Articles for Daily Use	173	1 601	68 147
#服装零售	Garments	102	981	53 526
文化、体育用品及器材专门零售	Culture & Sports Articles and Equipments	122	366	12 516
#体育用品及器材零售	Sporting Goods and Equipment	8	23	1 114
图书、报刊零售	Books, Newspapers and Periodicals	19	154	3 813
医药及医疗器材专门零售	Medicines and Special Appliances of Medicines	84	1 216	13 544
#药品零售	Medicine	75	1 130	12 663
汽车、摩托车、燃料及零配件专门零售	Automobiles, Motocycles, Fuels and Their Parts	605	736	36 279
#汽车零售	Automobiles	407	449	30 756
家用电器及电子产品专门零售	Household Electrical Appliances and Electronic Products	100	397	20 157
#家用视听设备零售	Home Audio-visual Equipment	7	41	3 184
日用家电设备零售	Household Appliances	24	149	7 456
计算机、软件及辅助设备零售	Computers, Softwares and Accessorial Equipments	34	40	1 683
通信设备零售	Telecommunication Appliances	16	69	2 330
五金、家具及室内装修材料专门零售	Hardwares, Furnitures and Materials of Decoration	80	176	6 162
货摊、无店铺及其他零售业	Stall, Non-store and Other Retailing	76	161	12 746
#互联网零售	Internet	17	19	9 956
邮购及电视、电话零售	Mail Order and TV, Telephone Sales	4	4	170

表 16.4 社会消费品零售总额(1978～2012)
TOTAL RETAIL SALES OF CONSUMER GOODS

单位:亿元(100 million yuan)

年 份 Year	社会消费品零售总额 Total Retail Sales of Consumer Goods	按商品用途分 by Use			
		食品类 Foods	衣着类 Clothing	用品类 Articles	燃料类 Fuels
1978	54.10	26.51	11.60	15.16	0.83
1979	68.28	30.05	16.07	21.28	0.88
1980	80.43	34.30	19.75	25.44	0.94
1981	88.73	38.78	21.27	27.73	0.95
1982	89.80	40.72	19.57	28.52	0.99
1983	100.68	44.20	22.31	33.18	0.99
1984	123.72	50.18	27.71	44.81	1.02
1985	173.39	64.08	35.51	72.70	1.10
1986	196.84	76.99	39.38	79.31	1.16
1987	225.25	91.01	42.52	90.41	1.31
1988	295.83	119.36	53.66	121.17	1.64
1989	331.38	140.03	51.95	137.70	1.70
1990	333.86	142.15	52.33	137.23	2.15
1991	382.06	162.82	52.91	163.30	3.03
1992	464.82	190.70	67.04	202.83	4.25
1993	675.92	259.93	101.30	309.26	5.43
1994	834.76	325.44	123.89	378.86	6.57
1995	1 050.96	407.44	153.74	481.96	7.82
1996	1 258.00	490.97	178.80	579.12	9.11
1997	1 435.38	564.62	200.62	659.61	10.53
1998	1 593.27	640.84	212.85	728.22	11.36
1999	1 722.33	694.03	228.18	787.62	12.50
2000	1 865.28	743.31	248.94	858.33	14.70
2001	2 016.37	802.53	266.31	931.02	16.51
2002	2 203.89	874.76	289.43	1 021.84	17.85
2003	2 404.45	939.29	309.70	1 135.27	20.19
2004	2 656.91	1 043.26	341.28	1 247.39	24.98
2005	2 979.50	1 026.70	335.30	1 563.15	54.35
2006	3 375.20	1 119.77	379.83	1 770.75	104.85
2007	3 873.30	1 204.70	435.88	2 032.07	200.65
2008	4 577.23	1 383.63	515.09	2 401.39	277.12
2009	5 173.24	1 609.01	582.17	2 714.06	268.00
2010	6 070.50	1 830.64	686.15	3 197.85	355.86
2011	6 814.80	2 036.14	760.31	3 590.39	427.96
2012	7 412.30	2 107.08	862.56	3 990.29	452.36

注：2005～2009 年社会消费品零售总额及分组依二经普数据，按国家统计局规定进行了修订。

Note: The Total Value of Retail Sales of Cosumer Goods from 2005～2009 are from Second Economic Census, and has been revised according to the regulations of NBS.

表 16.4 续表 1 continued

单位:亿元(100 million yuan)

年 份 Year	按经济类型分 by Type of Ownership				
	国有经济 State-owned	集体经济 Collective-owned	私营经济 Private-owned	个 体 Individual	其 他 Others
1978	39.50	14.41		0.19	
1979	46.47	21.32		0.20	0.29
1980	54.01	25.31		0.24	0.87
1981	56.57	30.28	0.04	0.29	1.55
1982	56.48	31.39	0.03	0.32	1.58
1983	63.17	34.55	0.02	0.70	2.24
1984	75.63	43.80	0.02	1.68	2.59
1985	102.59	59.49	0.18	6.42	4.71
1986	111.73	69.06	0.67	8.47	6.91
1987	123.05	80.38	0.88	11.46	9.48
1988	161.65	103.84	1.72	14.56	14.06
1989	176.07	119.97	1.76	16.16	17.42
1990	179.37	115.59	2.05	16.17	20.68
1991	200.25	135.30	2.72	18.70	25.09
1992	247.68	157.56	5.75	22.88	30.95
1993	250.97	202.05	0.51	41.45	180.94
1994	249.27	198.56	0.64	65.00	321.29
1995	247.10	193.03	0.86	76.44	533.54
1996	238.54	183.50	30.10	92.64	713.22
1997	225.35	173.85	21.83	114.88	899.47
1998	210.92	161.70	59.48	126.94	1 034.23
1999	180.33	141.83	62.77	141.16	1 196.24
2000	150.09	118.26	496.86	153.57	946.50
2001	135.69	105.90	596.21	172.66	1 005.91
2002	131.91	102.19	699.75	190.66	1 079.38
2003	133.36	102.68	803.74	208.45	1 156.22
2004	134.44	102.78	935.44	233.01	1 251.24
2005	157.98	51.63	814.31	443.31	1 512.28
2006	178.96	58.48	922.46	502.18	1 713.12
2007	205.37	67.11	1 058.59	576.29	1 965.93
2008	242.69	79.31	1 250.98	681.03	2 323.22
2009	263.80	87.08	1 438.99	776.37	2 607.00
2010	306.34	98.29	1 739.44	927.42	2 999.01
2011	300.63	108.44	1 903.77	1 029.44	3 472.53
2012	316.70	126.40	2 055.11	1 146.79	3 767.29

注：1997 年以前私营经济为合营。
Note: The figures of Private Owned before 1997 refer to these of Joint Owned.

表 16.4 续表 2 continued

单位:亿元(100 million yuan)

年 份 Year	社会消费品零售总额 Total Retail Sales of Consumer Goods	按行业分 by Sectors			
		批发零售贸易业 Wholesale and Retail Trade	住宿餐饮业 Hotels and Catering Trade	制造业 Manufacturing	其他行业 Others
1978	54.10	47.55	2.39	1.65	2.51
1979	68.28	59.02	2.82	2.54	3.90
1980	80.43	70.28	3.41	4.24	2.50
1981	88.73	77.53	3.68	4.61	2.91
1982	89.80	77.31	3.76	5.44	3.29
1983	100.68	84.93	4.26	7.72	3.77
1984	123.72	103.27	4.90	10.60	4.95
1985	173.39	150.03	7.58	8.41	7.37
1986	196.84	170.12	9.54	8.79	8.39
1987	225.25	193.50	11.09	10.47	10.19
1988	295.83	254.99	14.48	11.90	14.46
1989	331.38	265.87	15.66	16.84	33.01
1990	333.86	265.67	17.08	15.15	35.96
1991	382.06	300.26	20.91	17.70	43.19
1992	464.82	362.03	25.92	20.25	56.62
1993	675.92	559.56	35.47	29.24	51.65
1994	834.76	684.81	42.74	32.75	74.46
1995	1 050.96	864.01	52.61	38.05	96.29
1996	1 258.00	1 032.78	78.50	39.84	106.88
1997	1 435.38	1 173.94	93.49	44.38	123.57
1998	1 593.27	1 298.40	96.58	45.41	152.88
1999	1 722.33	1 391.08	114.93	47.22	169.10
2000	1 865.28	1 493.13	134.12	49.16	188.87
2001	2 016.37	1 619.13	148.88	50.78	197.58
2002	2 203.89	1 756.77	193.68	52.66	200.78
2003	2 404.45	1 920.20	225.83	53.87	204.55
2004	2 656.91	2 108.59	279.44	56.29	212.59
2005	2 979.50	2 637.29	342.21		
2006	3 375.20	2 987.54	387.66		
2007	3 873.30	3 428.43	444.87		
2008	4 577.23	4 051.51	525.72		
2009	5 173.24	4 575.50	597.74		
2010	6 070.50	5 391.59	678.91		
2011	6 814.80	6 100.99	713.81		
2012	7 412.30	6 653.10	759.20		

表 16.5 主要年份批发零售贸易业销售、库存总额
PURCHASE, SALES AND INVENTORY OF WHOLESALE AND RETAIL TRADE IN MAIN YEARS

单位:亿元(100 million yuan)

指 标	Indicators	2000	2010	2011	2012
商品销售总额	**Sales of Commodities**	**7 474.81**	**37 383.25**	**46 075.87**	**53 795.10**
零 售	Retail	1 723.31	5 199.12	6 018.57	6 598.46
批 发	Wholesale	5 751.50	32 184.13	40 057.30	47 196.64
年末库存总额	**Year-end Inventory**	**262.50**	**1 913.49**	**2 357.55**	**2 805.57**

注：本表为国内批发零售贸易业、物资供销业、对外贸易业统计口径。
Note: The figures in this table are based on the scope of wholesale and retail trade, purchase and sales of commodities and foreign trade.

表 16.6 批发零售贸易业商品销售、库存总额(2012)
PURCHASE, SALES AND INVENTORY OF WHOLESALE AND RETAIL TRADE

单位:亿元(100 million yuan)

类 别	Types	商品销售总额 Sales of Commodities	商品库存总额 Year-end Inventory
总 计	**Total**	**53 795.10**	**2 805.57**
限额以上单位	Above the Set Scale	45 381.85	2 605.68
限额以下单位	Below the Set Scale	8 413.25	199.89

表 16.7 汽车交易情况(2010～2012)
DISTRIBUTION OF AUTOMOBILE

单位:万辆(10 000 vehicles)

类 别	Types	2010	2011	2012
国产小型客车	Domestic Small Passenger Cars	24.11	25.72	27.18
#国产轿车	Domestic Cars	19.73	20.56	21.34
进口小型客车(含轿车)	Small Passerger Cars Imported(including cars)	3.02	3.95	4.43
二手车交易量	Dealing Number of Secondhand Cars	31.12	32.54	37.91
#轿 车	Saloon Cars	18.30	19.34	22.53

表16.8 限额以上批发贸易业商品购、销、存总额(2012)
PURCHASE, SALES AND INVENTORY OF WHOLESALE TRADE ABOVE THE SET SCALE

单位:亿元(100 million yuan)

类别	Types	商品购进总额 Purchase of Commodities	商品销售总额 Sales of Commodities	商品库存总额 Year-end Inventory
总计	**Total**	**37 385.07**	**42 530.96**	**2 427.57**
按登记注册类型分	**Grouped by Type of Registration**			
内资	Domestic Funded Enterprises	23 374.56	24 291.87	1 176.10
国有	State-Owned Enterprises	6 568.89	6 630.48	244.56
集体	Collective-Owned Enterprises	72.03	75.75	6.76
股份合作	Share Holding Cooperative Enterprises	85.77	87.78	3.86
联营	Joint-Owned Enterprises	152.96	161.24	14.53
有限责任公司	Companies with Limited Liabilities	7 218.50	7 570.35	384.50
股份有限公司	Share Holding Companies with Limited Liabilities	2 525.40	2 630.35	125.51
私营	Private Enterprises	6 648.15	7 017.78	390.13
其他	Others	102.85	118.14	6.24
港澳台商投资	Hong Kong, Macao and Taiwan Funded Enterprises	3 117.78	3 833.05	389.30
外商投资	Foreign Funded Enterprises	10 892.72	14 406.03	862.17
按行业分	**Grouped by Sector**			
农、林、牧产品批发	Agriculture, Forestry and Animal Husbandry Products	184.49	191.97	49.15
食品、饮料及烟草制品批发	Food, Beverage and Tabacco	1 480.33	1 784.07	156.69
#米、面制品及食用油批发	Rice, Flour and Cooking Oil	360.65	426.79	41.14
烟草制品批发	Tabacco	350.73	393.83	9.13

表16.8 续表 continued

单位:亿元(100 million yuan)

类别	Types	商品购进总额 Purchase of Commodities	商品销售总额 Sales of Commodities	商品库存总额 Year-end Inventory
纺织、服装及家庭用品批发	Textile, Clothing and Household Goods	2 928.79	3 663.22	363.86
#服装批发	Garments	769.12	954.92	149.19
文化、体育用品及器材批发	Culture & Sports Articles and Equipments	769.80	850.30	68.05
医药及医疗器材批发	Medicines and Special Appliances of Medicines	1 199.40	1 434.00	191.15
矿产品、建材及化工产品批发	Mineral Products, Materials of Construction and Chemical Products	20 453.14	20 901.50	777.32
#煤炭及制品批发	Coal	1 034.39	1 047.94	10.57
石油及制品批发	Petroleum	5 372.96	5 552.00	116.30
金属及金属矿批发	Metal Products and Metal Minerals	10 062.51	10 074.49	408.20
建材批发	Building Materials	561.45	563.02	53.05
化肥批发	Chemical Fertilizer	52.25	54.78	4.48
机械设备、五金交电及电子产品批发	Mechinery Equipments, Hardwares, Electric Appliances and Eletronic Products	8 619.23	11 659.85	635.23
#汽车批发	Automobiles	2 904.98	5 153.81	177.55
汽车零配件批发	Spare and Component Parts for Automobiles	566.44	638.33	38.67
电气设备批发	Electrical Equipment	310.33	376.15	33.27
计算机、软件及辅助设备批发	Computers, Softwares and Accessorial Equipments	1 188.04	1 271.58	83.07
贸易经纪与代理	Trade Broker and Agent	599.49	711.56	60.49
其他批发	Others	1 150.40	1 334.50	125.62

表 16.9 限额以上零售贸易业商品购、销、存总额(2012)
PURCHASE, SALES AND INVENTORY OF RETAIL TRADE ABOVE THE SET SCALE

单位:亿元(100 million yuan)

类别	Types	商品购进总额 Purchase of Commodities	商品销售总额 Sales of Commodities	商品库存总额 Year-end Inventory
总计	**Total**	**4 042.66**	**5 220.53**	**643.85**
按登记注册类型分	**Grouped by Type of Registration**			
内资	Domestic Enterprises	2 557.55	3 415.41	362.13
国有	State-Owned Enterprises	263.00	327.28	16.75
集体	Collective-Owned Enterprises	24.90	26.64	1.52
股份合作	Share Holding Cooperative Enterprises	6.36	6.76	0.41
联营	Joint-Owned Enterprises	28.91	34.03	1.88
有限责任公司	Companies with Limited Liabilities	1 079.80	1 422.76	126.28
股份有限公司	Share Holding Companies with Limited Liabilities	172.43	201.39	36.82
私营	Private Enterprises	966.76	1 376.53	176.65
其他	Others	15.40	20.04	1.82
港澳台商投资	Hong Kong, Macao and Taiwan Funded	799.12	1 013.52	144.78
外商投资	Foreign Funded Enterprises	685.99	791.60	136.94
按行业分	**Grouped by Sector**			
#综合零售	Comprehensive Retail Sale	1 186.02	1 471.64	142.84
食品、饮料及烟草制品专门零售	Food, Beverage and Tabacco	444.78	450.81	20.48
纺织、服装及日用品专门零售	Textile Products, Gaments and Commodity	290.95	550.05	114.88
文化、体育用品及器材专门零售	Culture & Sports Articles and Equipments	216.81	265.90	114.09
医药及医疗器材专门零售	Medicines and Special Appliances of Medicines	157.34	166.70	13.20
汽车、摩托车、燃料及零配件专门零售	Automobiles, Motocycles, Fuels and Their Parts	1 179.81	1 229.56	111.23
家用电器及电子产品专门零售	Household Electrical Appliances and Electronic Products	310.26	653.93	85.89
五金、家具及室内装修材料专门零售	Hardwares, Furnitures and Materials of Decoration	48.03	70.05	8.85

表 16.10 主要年份限额以上批发零售贸易业主要生产资料销售量
SALES OF MAJOR PRODUCT MATERIAL OF WHOLESALE AND RETAIL SALES TRADE ABOVE THE SET SCALE IN MAIN YEARS

单位:万吨(10 000 tons)

生产资料名称	Names of Product Material	2005	2010	2011	2012
钢材	Steels	1 807.99	5 579.00	5 712.05	6 916.37
铜	Cuprum	57.38	162.95	177.62	247.61
铝	Aluminium	21.34	152.32	205.46	214.17
煤炭	Coal	3 016.67	8 180.34	10 209.06	15 475.93
汽油	Gasoline	1 213.18	1 609.10	2 020.84	1 866.83
煤油	Coal Oil	502.88	870.56	779.36	810.45
柴油	Diesel Oil	2 961.25	3 896.15	3 457.19	2 926.06
水泥	Concrete	118.73	362.00	228.06	395.69

表 16.11 限额以上批发零售贸易业主要商品分类销售额(2012)
TOTAL SALES OF ENTERPRISES ABOVE THE SET SCALE IN WHOLESALE AND RETAIL TRADE BY CATEGORY OF MAIN COMMODITIES

单位:亿元(100 million yuan)

类别	Types	合计 Total	批发 Wholesale	零售 Retail
粮油、食品、饮料、烟酒类	Grain and Oil, Food, Beverages, Tobacco and Liquor	2 937.05	2 182.09	754.97
#粮油、食品类	Grain and Oil, and Food	1 723.82	1 219.54	504.28
#粮油类	Grain and Oil	559.49	444.38	115.10
肉禽蛋类	Meat, Poultry and Eggs	225.53	151.31	74.22
饮料类	Beverages	165.72	110.97	54.75
烟酒类	Tobacco and Liquor	1 047.52	851.58	195.94
服装、鞋帽、针纺织品类	Clothing, Shoes, Hats and Textiles	2 192.80	1 493.70	699.10
#服装类	Clothing	1 484.06	905.35	578.71
鞋帽类	Shoes and Hat	218.66	131.66	87.00
针、纺织品类	Knitwear and Textiles	490.08	456.68	33.40
化妆品类	Cosmetics	557.28	419.67	137.60
金银珠宝类	Gold, Silver and Jewelry	595.86	444.36	151.50
日用品类	Articles for Daily Use	974.45	692.81	281.64
#洗涤用品类	Washing Articles	66.29	36.43	29.87
儿童玩具类	Toys for Children	30.24	19.65	10.59
五金、电料类	Hardware and Electrical Materials	495.66	481.88	13.78
体育、娱乐用品类	Sports and Recreation Articles	61.96	32.44	29.52
书报杂志类	Newspapers and Magazines	29.37	10.28	19.09
电子出版物及音像制品类	E-journal and Video Products	6.36	3.10	3.26
家用电器和音像器材类	Household Appliances and Video Appliances	832.14	469.91	362.23
中西药品类	Traditional Chinese and Western Medicines	1 102.98	845.08	257.89
#西药类	Western Medicines	813.80	652.85	160.95
中草药及中成药类	Traditional Chinese Medicines	125.61	83.50	42.11
文化办公用品类	Cultural and Official Goods	1 442.49	1 292.86	149.62
家具类	Furniture	87.15	57.25	29.90
通讯器材类	Communication Appliances	1 374.94	1 298.80	76.14
煤炭及制品类	Coal and Related Product	1 435.88	1 432.57	3.31
木材及制品类	Lumber and Related Product	64.94	64.94	
石油及制品类	Oil and Related Product	5 795.22	5 343.18	452.04
化工材料及制品类	Chemical Material and Related Product	2 968.15	2 968.15	
#化肥类	Fertilizer	142.24	142.24	
金属材料类	Metal Material	9 942.24	9 942.24	
建筑及装潢材料类	Building and Decoration Materials	264.29	232.26	32.03
机电产品及设备类	Mechanical and Electrical Products	3 247.58	3 235.27	12.30
#农机类	Agriculture Machinery	30.28	30.28	
汽车类	Automobile	6 410.07	5 450.71	959.36
种子饲料类	Seed and Feedstuff	77.49	77.49	
棉麻类	Cotton and Hemp	62.95	62.95	
其他类	Others	2 147.02	2 030.51	116.51

表 16.12 商品交易市场成交情况(2012)
DEALS IN MERCHANDISE EXCHANGE MARKET

分 类	Types	年末出租摊位数(个) Quantity of Year-end booth Lent (unit)	成交额(亿元) Transaction Volume (100 million yuan)
总 计	**Total**	**163 988**	**10 959.15**
# 粮油、食品、饮料、烟酒类	Grain and Oil, Foodstuff, Beverage, Tobacco and Liquor	74 189	951.79
服装、鞋帽、针纺织品类	Garments, Shoes and Hats, Textile Products	24 560	117.60
化妆品类	Cosmetics	235	0.70
金银珠宝类	Jewelry	148	0.92
日用品类	Articles for Daily Use	4 090	326.92
五金、电料类	Hardware and Electrical Appliances	5 394	30.47
体育、娱乐用品类	Recreation and Sports Articles	432	4.42
书报杂志类	Books, Newspapers and Magazines	85	1.94
电子出版物及音像制品类	Electronic Publications and Audio-video Products	93	0.46
家用电器和音像器材类	Household Appliances and Audio-video Equipments	1 070	6.89
中西药品类	Medicines	308	5.30
文化办公用品类	Culture and Office Articles	2 360	30.78
家具类	Furnitures	3 403	24.66
通讯器材类	Telecommunication Appliances	2 010	2.75
木材及制品类	Woods and Woods Product	1 646	34.17
石油及制品类	Oil and Oil Product	553	1 406.95
化工材料及制品类	Chemical Material and Chemical Product	1 233	101.76
金属材料类	Mental and Mental Product	5 133	7 471.93
建筑及装潢材料类	Construct and Decorate Material	17 964	177.48
机电产品及设备类	Mechanical and Electrical Product and Equipments	898	9.17
汽车类	Automobile	3 832	271.10

表 16.13 主要年份限额以上批发零售贸易业主要财务指标
MAIN FINANCIAL INDICATORS OF WHOLESALE AND RETAIL SALES ABOVE THE SET SCALE IN MAIN YEARS

单位：亿元(100 million yuan)

指标	Indicators	2005	2010	2011	2012
流动资产	Current Assets	2 929.27	7 608.03	9 387.10	13 014.63
#存　货	Inventory	722.78	1 655.36	2 206.63	2 822.83
固定资产原价	Fixed Assets Original Value	546.78	790.06	891.16	1 147.93
累计折旧	Accumulative Depreciation	169.94	291.58	328.85	434.66
#本年折旧	Depreciation	31.20	55.82	52.62	86.53
资产总计	Total Assets	3 926.22	9 608.53	11 448.89	16 154.94
负债合计	Total Liabilities	2 727.25	6 710.76	8 511.34	11 624.39
所有者权益合计	Total Owner's Equities	1 198.97	2 897.78	3 337.06	4 530.40
实收资本	Paid-up Capital	862.49	1 464.26	1 657.35	2 216.31
#国家资本	State Capital	132.19	379.67	269.56	283.91
港澳台资本	Hong Kong, Macao and Taiwan Capital	38.17	137.69	185.86	263.67
外商资本	Foreign Capital	242.71	376.04	397.01	562.23
主营业务收入	Prime Operating Revenues	11 236.19	26 372.58	33 174.83	42 188.70
主营业务成本	Operating Costs	9 874.12	24 300.03	31 338.29	39 098.63
营业费用	Operating Expenses	501.98	1 135.41	1 355.99	1 966.19
主营业务税金及附加	Sales Taxes and Extra Charges	10.10	40.73	51.75	58.57
管理费用	Management Expenses	243.12	475.41	586.55	847.26
财务费用	Financial Expenses	24.09	47.93	64.52	107.64
营业利润	Operating Profits	248.71	535.95	710.81	790.50
利润总额	Total Profits	223.35	640.19	748.52	910.30
主营业务应付工资总额	Total Payable Salaries Involved in Major Business	130.25	258.66	367.46	655.58
主营业务应付福利费总额	Total Payable Welfare Involved in Major Business	21.89	17.63		

注：2011 年起，营业费用改为销售费用，取消主营业务利润科目，主营业务应付工资总额、主营业务应付福利费总额纳入应付职工薪酬(本年贷方累计发生额)统计，不再拆分(后表同)。

Note: Since 2011, Operating Expense is changed into Sales Expense, subject of prime operating profit is canceled, Total Payable Salaries Involved in Major Business and Total Payable Welfare Involved in Major Business are merged into Wages Owed to Employees (credit accumulative amount this year) for statistics, and the latter will no longer be divided.

表 16.14 主要年份限额以上餐饮业主要财务指标
MAIN FINANCIAL INDICATORS OF CATERING SECTOR ABOVE THE SET SCALE IN MAIN YEARS

单位:亿元(100 million yuan)

指 标	Indicators	2005	2010	2011	2012
流动资产	Current Assets	43.60	114.24	131.20	155.87
#存 货	Inventory	5.10	8.28	10.19	19.06
固定资产原价	Fixed Assets Original Value	44.76	81.97	74.61	99.81
累计折旧	Accumulative Depreciation	15.65	31.64	32.31	40.03
#本年折旧	Depreciation	3.83	6.63	5.68	5.70
资产总计	Total Assets	94.49	214.43	236.27	282.71
负债合计	Total Liabilities	64.13	156.19	175.25	214.21
所有者权益合计	Total Owner's Equities	30.36	58.25	60.97	68.49
实收资本	Paid-up Capital	31.05	62.42	76.57	77.91
#国家资本	State Capital	0.78	5.28	6.25	5.23
港澳台资本	Hong Kong, Macao and Taiwan Capital	6.95	13.36	11.28	15.76
外商资本	Foreign Capital	6.66	17.62	19.54	19.27
主营业务收入	Prime Operating Revenues	157.66	335.96	363.59	349.76
主营业务成本	Operating Costs	72.03	145.44	168.01	153.10
营业费用	Operating Expenses	53.86	123.32	122.50	146.92
主营业务税金及附加	Sales Taxes and Extra Charges	8.14	17.34	19.85	20.09
管理费用	Management Expenses	19.42	37.25	42.24	50.09
财务费用	Financial Expenses	1.15	3.47	3.90	5.47
营业利润	Operating Profits	5.49	10.96	11.03	7.23
利润总额	Total Profits	5.49	15.12	12.43	11.68
主营业务应付工资总额	Total Payable Salaries Involved in Major Business	17.54	41.08	50.77	59.04
主营业务应付福利费总额	Total Payable Welfare Involved in Major Business	2.26	2.51		

表 16.15 主要年份限额以上连锁零售业、住宿和餐饮业经营情况
BASIC STATISTICS OF CHAIN RETAIL, ACCOMMODATION AND CATERING ABOVE THE SET SCALE IN MAIN YEARS

指 标	Indicators	2005	2010	2011	2012
门店总数(个)	Quantity of Stores(unit)	15 775	20 977	21 166	21 105
营业面积(万平方米)	Operational Area(10 000 sq. m)	809.16	938.35	996.26	1 036.57
从业人数(万人)	Number of Persons Employed(10 000 person)	24.47	36.68	38.19	37.17
商品购进总额(亿元)	Purchase of Commodities(100 million yuan)	1 222.94	2 249.57	2 490.29	2 601.39
商品销售总额(亿元)	Sales of Commodities (100 million yuan)	1 815.32	3 071.67	3 327.36	3 403.58
#零售额	Retail Sales	1 201.03	2 241.97	2 436.34	2 393.05
餐饮业营业收入(亿元)	Total Operating Revenue (100 million yuan)	35.69	106.81	120.88	141.31

表 16.16 限额以上批发零售贸易业主要财务指标(2012)
MAIN FINANCIAL INDICATORS OF WHOLESALE AND RETAIL ENTERPRISES ABOVE THE SET SCALE

类别	Types	流动资产 Current Assets	固定资产原价 Fixed Assets Original Value	资产总计 Total Assets
总计	**Total**	**13 014.63**	**1 147.93**	**16 154.94**
按登记注册类型分	**Grouped by Type of Registration**			
批发贸易业	**Wholesale Trade**	**11 131.87**	**652.93**	**13 571.22**
内资	Domestic Funded Enterprises	5 660.34	388.30	7 289.83
国有	State-Owned Enterprises	931.04	68.25	1 216.23
集体	Collective-Owned Enterprises	32.09	3.19	40.55
股份合作	Share Holding Cooperative Enterprises	17.16	0.72	18.42
联营	Joint-Owned Enterprises	56.24	2.11	57.97
有限责任公司	Companies with Limited Liabilities	1 719.10	117.07	2 263.58
股份有限公司	Share Holding Companies with Limited Liabilities	565.70	72.29	818.32
私营	Private Enterprises	2 293.57	119.89	2 807.55
其他	Others	45.44	4.77	67.22
港澳台商投资	Hong Kong, Macao and Taiwan Funded Enterprises	1 323.12	62.82	1 490.11
外商投资	Foreign Funded Enterprises	4 148.41	201.81	4 791.29
零售贸易业	**Retail Trade**	**1 882.76**	**495.01**	**2 583.72**
内资	Domestic Funded Enterprises	1 170.63	304.55	1 584.77
国有	State-Owned Enterprises	80.02	54.41	132.78
集体	Collective-Owned Enterprises	7.90	4.74	14.38
股份合作	Share Holding Cooperative Enterprises	2.19	0.50	2.63
联营	Joint-Owned Enterprises	4.92	1.44	6.07
有限责任公司	Responsibility Co. Ltd.	430.94	121.40	559.76
股份有限公司	Share Holding Co. Ltd.	86.23	60.09	182.89
私营	Private Enterprises	549.99	61.42	676.83
其他	Others	8.43	0.55	9.44
港澳台商投资	Hong Kong, Macao and Taiwan Funded Enterprises	455.95	80.33	619.42
外商投资	Foreign Funded Enterprises	256.18	110.13	379.53

单位:亿元(100 million yuan)

负债合计 Total Liabilities	所有者权益合计 Total Owner's Equity	实收资本 Paid-up Capital	主营业务收入 Prime Operating Revenues	主营业务成本 Prime Operating Costs	利润总额 Total Profits
11 624.39	**4 530.40**	**2 216.31**	**42 188.70**	**38 525.17**	**910.30**
9 812.47	**3 758.60**	**1 793.92**	**37 884.89**	**34 888.98**	**825.48**
5 313.12	1 976.56	1 132.79	21 118.30	20 246.82	241.18
880.16	336.07	157.22	5 934.17	5 586.23	75.45
29.55	11.00	2.96	68.70	67.72	1.44
16.07	2.34	1.91	87.70	85.98	0.24
46.95	11.01	5.97	140.04	132.53	2.87
1 615.54	648.04	269.62	6 880.09	6 648.07	102.42
570.[illegible]3	247.70	312.63	1 273.14	1 238.28	17.67
2 111.88	695.51	367.53	6 625.74	6 386.15	35.00
42.32	24.89	14.95	108.71	101.87	6.09
1 027.30	462.81	168.56	3 602.32	3 121.10	145.02
3 472.05	1 319.23	492.57	13 164.28	11 521.05	439.27
1 811.92	**771.80**	**422.39**	**4 303.81**	**3 636.20**	**84.82**
1 071.18	513.59	203.12	2 708.84	2 388.66	43.83
94.10	38.68	18.71	300.22	262.63	8.14
8.02	6.36	3.56	27.61	25.38	0.40
1.03	1.60	0.25	6.47	5.79	0.22
3.42	2.65	0.81	31.87	29.72	0.97
450.00	109.76	70.80	1 187.97	1 052.76	23.21
77.58	105.31	33.27	170.49	138.53	16.17
427.57	249.25	74.68	965.00	857.24	-5.90
9.45	-0.02	1.03	19.20	16.62	0.62
439.82	179.60	114.32	901.01	707.21	36.97
300.92	78.61	104.94	693.96	540.33	4.02

表 16.16 续表 continued

类别	Types	流动资产 Current Assets	固定资产原价 Fixed Assets Original Value	资产总计 Total Assets
按行业分	Grouped by Sector			
批发贸易业	**Wholesale Trade**	**11 131.87**	**652.93**	**13 571.22**
农、林、牧产品批发	Agriculture, Forestry and Animal Husbandry Products	110.47	22.81	173.95
食品、饮料及烟草制品批发	Food, Beverage and Tabacco	768.24	69.81	986.12
纺织、服装及家庭用品批发	Textile, Clothing and Household Goods	1 316.60	111.78	1 632.51
文化、体育用品及器材批发	Culture & Sports Articles and Equipments	271.62	8.42	310.01
医药及医疗器材批发	Medicines and Special Appliances of Medicines	537.45	86.53	622.10
矿产品、建材及化工产品批发	Mineral Products, Materials of Construction and Chemical Products	3 933.98	195.49	4 984.74
机械设备、五金交电及电子产品批发	Mechinery Equipments, Hardwares, Electric Appliances and Eletronic Products	3 343.70	105.78	3 895.27
贸易经纪与代理	Trade Broker and Agent	276.67	11.59	306.58
其他批发	Others	573.12	40.71	659.95
零售贸易业	**Retail Trade**	**1 882.76**	**495.01**	**2 583.72**
综合零售	Comprehensive Retail Sale	477.02	273.04	771.23
食品、饮料及烟草制品专门零售	Food, Beverage and Tabacco	179.92	9.92	245.71
纺织、服装及日用品专门零售	Textile Products, Garments and Commodity	256.52	76.27	354.75
文化、体育用品及器材专门零售	Culture & Sports Articles and Equipments	141.40	19.45	178.50
医药及医疗器材专门零售	Medicines and Special Appliances of Medicines	47.24	4.92	52.68
汽车、摩托车、燃料及零配件专门零售	Automobiles, Motocycles, Fuels and Their Parts	320.06	51.00	402.42
家用电器及电子产品专门零售	Household Electrical Appliances and Electronic Products	332.66	17.35	395.49
五金、家具及室内装修材料专门零售	Hardwares, Furnitures and Materials of Decoration	30.39	23.42	60.56
货摊、无店铺及其他零售业	Stall, Non-store and Other Retailing	97.56	19.65	122.39

单位:亿元(100 million yuan)

负债合计 Total Liabilities	所有者权益合计 Total Owner's Equity	实收资本 Paid-up Capital	主营业务收入 Prime Operating Revenues	主营业务成本 Prime Operating Costs	利润总额 Total Profits
9 812.47	**3 758.60**	**1 793.92**	**37 884.89**	**34 888.98**	**825.48**
103.43	65.51	32.43	175.10	170.13	2.83
699.95	286.02	97.91	1 565.43	1 292.12	74.49
1 10[illegible].03	531.43	247.62	3 385.54	2 748.10	150.39
221.31	88.67	44.96	760.02	709.05	18.65
453.32	168.79	67.31	1 161.89	920.59	57.17
3 655.89	1 328.85	883.68	18 293.99	17 618.71	151.57
2 873.15	1 022.13	306.95	10 606.99	9 647.29	323.36
225.45	81.13	36.00	655.62	627.52	14.53
473.87	186.08	77.06	1 280.32	1 155.46	32.49
1 811.92	**771.80**	**422.39**	**4 303.81**	**3 636.20**	**84.82**
552.33	218.90	140.73	1 210.10	1 001.74	39.68
168.94	76.77	24.67	395.14	366.98	24.97
255.93	98.82	73.06	488.97	280.89	26.09
130.95	47.54	40.30	239.70	187.21	-2.73
42.43	10.20	5.30	136.61	119.20	3.97
297.13	105.27	63.51	1 131.37	1 062.89	10.45
203.73	191.76	40.58	311.05	270.09	-10.06
44.40	16.16	16.77	57.15	42.16	0.41
116.00	6.38	17.47	333.72	305.04	-7.96

表 16.17 限额以上住宿餐饮业主要财务指标（2012）
MAIN FINANCIAL INDICATORS OF ACCOMMODATION AND CATERING ENTERPRISES ABOVE THE SET SCALE

类 别	Types	流动资产 Current Assets	固定资产原价 Fixed Assets Original Value	资产总计 Total Assets
总 计	**Total**	**325.34**	**503.09**	**825.72**
按登记注册类型分	**Grouped by Type of Registration**			
住宿业	**Accommodation**	**169.47**	**403.27**	**543.01**
内 资	Domestic Enterprises	134.57	308.10	440.26
国 有	State-Owned Enterprises	48.16	137.80	190.30
集 体	Collective-Owned Enterprises	2.57	9.22	8.94
股份合作	Share Holding Cooperative Enterprises			
联 营	Joint-Owned Enterprises	0.38	4.00	3.36
有限责任公司	Companies with Limited Liabilities	37.88	111.02	138.51
股份有限公司	Share Holding Companies with Limited Liabilities	0.91	2.97	3.12
私 营	Private Enterprises	42.95	41.21	93.50
其 他	Others	1.73	1.88	2.53
港澳台商投资	Hong Kong, Macao and Taiwan Funded	9.35	41.06	45.36
外商投资	Foreign Funded Enterprises	25.56	54.11	57.39
餐饮业	**Catering**	**155.87**	**99.81**	**282.71**
内 资	Domestic Enterprises	105.78	55.12	181.35
国 有	State-Owned Enterprises	11.35	0.96	11.94
集 体	Collective-Owned Enterprises	1.02	1.13	2.13
股份合作	Share Holding Cooperative Enterprises	0.60	0.24	0.89
联 营	Joint-Owned Enterprises	0.01	0.07	0.22
有限责任公司	Responsibility Co. Ltd.	10.95	12.36	26.46
股份有限公司	Share Holding Co. Ltd.	12.34	2.34	24.10
私 营	Private Enterprises	68.92	37.38	114.03
其 他	Others	0.60	0.64	1.59
港澳台商投资	Hong Kong, Macao and Taiwan Funded	28.16	28.84	53.03
外商投资	Foreign Funded Enterprises	21.94	15.86	48.32
按行业分	**Grouped by Sector**			
住宿业	**Accommodation**	**169.47**	**403.27**	**543.01**
旅游饭店	Tiyrust Hotel	134.45	363.12	446.27
一般旅馆	Fonda	27.70	32.44	81.80
其他住宿服务	Others	7.32	7.71	14.95
餐饮业	**Catering**	**155.87**	**99.81**	**282.71**
正餐服务	Restaurant	128.50	70.01	225.57
快餐服务	Fast Food	14.39	22.39	34.66
饮料及冷饮服务	Beverages and Cold Drinks	9.81	4.54	17.27
茶馆服务	Teahouse	0.05	0.02	0.07
咖啡馆服务	Cafe	7.60	2.93	13.19
酒吧服务	Bar	0.03	0.04	0.06
其他饮料及冷饮服务	Others	2.13	1.55	3.96
其他餐饮业	Others	3.17	2.88	5.20
小吃服务	Refreshment	0.48	0.40	0.79
餐饮配送服务	Food Distribution	1.86	0.66	2.46
其他未列明餐饮业	Others	0.83	1.81	1.96

单位:亿元(100 million yuan)

负债合计 Total Liabilities	所有者权益合计 Total Owner's Equity	实收资本 Paid-up Capital	主营业务收入 Prime Operating Revenues	主营业务成本 Prime Operating Costs	利润总额 Total Profits
525.50	**300.41**	**375.79**	**553.51**	**209.53**	**14.32**
311.09	**231.92**	**297.89**	**203.75**	**56.43**	**2.64**
235.51	203.76	260.20	160.12	41.09	0.71
75.67	113.63	74.88	56.15	13.30	1.68
7.39	1.55	1.55	3.51	1.48	-0.45
3.0[illegible]	0.35	1.35	0.76	0.26	-0.18
70.32	68.19	62.41	50.66	14.30	0.04
1.74	1.38	1.49	1.84	0.41	-0.01
74.32	19.18	118.34	43.07	10.12	-1.45
3.06	-0.53	0.19	4.14	1.23	1.09
37.89	7.47	15.17	17.88	4.80	-0.30
36.69	20.69	22.52	25.75	10.54	2.24
214.21	**68.49**	**77.91**	**349.76**	**153.10**	**11.68**
141.79	39.56	33.57	205.66	101.72	3.62
11.21	0.73	0.73	4.47	2.28	0.14
1.36	0.77	0.23	2.36	1.22	0.08
0.58	0.30	0.07	0.72	0.28	0.07
0.08	0.14	0.15	0.06	0.02	0.00
18.[illegible]6	8.30	8.06	23.89	10.64	0.13
15.[illegible]2	8.79	2.27	13.43	7.41	2.33
93.80	20.22	21.78	158.86	78.70	0.89
1.27	0.32	0.28	1.89	1.18	-0.02
33.62	19.41	21.18	68.11	24.24	4.41
38.80	9.52	23.16	75.99	27.13	3.66
311.09	**231.92**	**297.89**	**203.75**	**56.43**	**2.64**
241.8[illegible]	204.38	279.65	157.34	46.50	-0.40
58.40	23.40	15.54	37.51	8.30	1.91
10.81	4.14	2.70	8.90	1.64	1.13
214.21	**68.49**	**77.91**	**349.76**	**153.10**	**11.68**
172.80	52.76	51.50	261.68	116.48	7.35
6.12	19.85	46.99	20.85	0.54	
9.58	7.70	2.74	30.94	9.12	4.02
0.08	-0.01	0.02	0.21	0.06	0.00
6.29	6.90	1.80	23.65	7.11	3.82
0.03	0.03	0.23	0.35	0.10	0.02
3.19	0.78	0.70	6.74	1.85	0.18
3.29	1.91	3.81	10.15	6.63	-0.24
0.75	0.04	1.32	1.52	0.69	-0.18
1.18	1.27	1.15	4.88	3.84	0.00
1.37	0.59	1.34	3.75	2.11	-0.06

上 / 海 / 统 / 计 / 年 / 鉴

主要统计指标解释

■ 社会消费品零售总额

指批发和零售业、餐饮业、新闻出版业、邮政业和其他服务业等，售予城乡居民用于生活消费的商品和社会集团用于公共消费的商品之总量。社会消费品零售总额包括：

一、批发和零售业企业(单位)：

1.售予城乡居民的各种生活消费品；

2.售予入境旅游的外国人、华侨、港澳台同胞的各类商品；

3.售予行政事业单位、社会团体、军队和武警等机构的商品，以及以零售方式售予各类企业的商品。具体包括：用于非生产和社会交往的办公用品，如通讯设备、计算器具和设备、电讯网络设备、文印设备、音像视听器材和设备、纸张、本册、文具及装订文印材料、家具、日用电器、针纺织品、清洁卫生用品、文体用品、奖品、纪念品、礼品等；供内部人员乘坐的交通工具和燃料；用于办公设施修缮的各类配件、材料、工具等；用于取暖和防暑降温的设备、燃料、材料及食品等；专用于教学的用品和设备；非营利医疗机构的中、西药品、中药材和医疗设备器材；非专用的劳动保护用品；不对外营业的内部食堂用的餐具、炊具、设备、清洁卫生工具和食品、燃料等；军队、武警用于其人员生活的衣着品和个人用品；其他各类非生产性设备和用品。

二、餐饮业出售的主食、菜肴、烟酒饮料和其他商品。

三、新闻出版业、邮政业售予城乡居民、企事业单位、军队和武警等机构的书报杂志、音像制品、邮品等。

四、其他服务业出售的食品、烟酒饮料、服装鞋帽、日常生活用品、医药保健用品、艺术品、工艺美术品、玩具、殡葬用品以及其他消费品。

■ 商品购进总额

指从本企业(单位)以外的单位和个人购进(包括从境外直接进口)作为转卖或加工后转卖的商品总额。它反映批发零售贸易业从国内、国外市场上购进商品的总量。商品购进总额包括：(1)从工农业生产者购进的商品；(2)从出版社、报社的出版发行部门购进的图书、杂志和报纸；(3)从各种登记注册类型的批发零售贸易企业（单位）购进的商品；(4)从其他单位购进的商品，如从机关、团体、企业等单位购进的剩余物资，从餐饮业、服务业购进的商品，从海关、市场管理部门购进的缉私和没收的商品，从居民手中收购的废旧商品等；(5)从国(境)外直接进口的商品。不包括企业(单位)为自身经营用和未通过买卖行为而收入的商品以及销售退回、商品升溢等。

■ 商品销售总额

指对本企业以外的单位和个人出售（包括对国（境）外直接出口）的商品。这个指标反映批发零售贸易业在上海市场以及上海以外市场上销售商品的总量。商品销售总额包括：(1) 售给城乡居民和社会集团消费用的商品；(2) 售给工业、农业、建筑业、运输邮电业、批发零售贸易业、餐饮业、服务业等作为生产、经营使用的商品；(3) 售给批发零售贸易业作为转卖或加工后转卖的商品；(4) 对国（境）外直接出口的商品。不包括：出售本企业自用的废旧包装用品，未通过买卖行为付出的商品，经本单位介绍，由买卖双方直接结算，本单位只收取手续费的业务，购货退出的商品以及商品损耗和损失等。

■ 主营业务收入

指企业在销售商品、提供劳务等日常活动中所产生的收入总额。

■ 主营业务成本

指企业已销商品应负担的进货原价和商品进价成本。

■ 营业费用

指批发零售贸易企业在购、销、存过程中发生的各项经营费用。包括运输费、装卸费、包装费、保险费、展览费、差旅费、广告费、商品损耗、进出口商品累计佣金、经营人员的工资及福利费等。

SHANGHAI STATISTICAL YEARBOOK

EXPLANATORY NOTES TO MAJOR STATISTICAL INDICATORS

□ Total Retail Sales of Consumer Goods

Total Retail Sales of Consumer Goods refer to the sum of retail sales of commodities sold by wholesale, retail, catering, publishing, post and telecommunications and other service industries to urban and rural households for private consumption and to social institutions for public consumption. Retail sales of consumer goods include:

Sales by wholesale and retail units:

of consumer goods sold to urban and rural households

of commodities sold to foreigners, overseas Chinese and Chinese compatriots from Hong Kong, Macau and Taiwan visiting in China

of commodities sold to government agencies, institutions, social organizations, military and armed police units, and commodities sold to enterprises in the form of retail sales. More specifically, they include: office facilities and articles for non-production purposes such as communications equipment, computing equipment and instruments, TV and network equipment, printing and copying equipment, audio-visual equipment and instruments, paper, notebook, stationeries, furniture, electric appliances, knitwear, sanitation and cleaning articles, cultural and sport articles, articles for prizes, souvenirs, etc.; transport vehicles and fuels for employees; materials, spare parts and tools for the maintenance of office facilities; equipment, fuels, materials and food for winter heating or summer cooling purposes; articles and equipment for teaching purpose; Chinese and western medicines and medical equipment and facilities purchased by non profit-making medical institute; non-specialized work safety articles; cooking utensils, tableware, equipment, cleaning articles, food and fuels purchased by internal cafeterias; clothes and personal articles purchased by military or armed police units for their officials and soldiers; and other equipment and articles for non-production purposes.

Sales of stable food, cooked dishes, beverages, tobaccos and other articles by catering units.

Sales of books, newspapers, magazines, audio-visual products and post products by publishing, post and telecommunications departments to urban and rural households and to enterprises, institutions, military and armed police units.

Sales of food, beverages, tobaccos, clothing, hats, footwear, articles for daily use, medicines, medical and health articles, work of art, handicrafts, toys, funeral articles and other articles by other service industries.

□ Total Purchase of Commodities

Purchase, Sales and Stock of Commodities by Wholesale and Retail Trades refer to the total volume of commodities purchased, total volume of sales and exports, and the stock of commodities by wholesale and retail enterprises (establishments) of different status of registration from domestic and overseas markets. This indictor reflects the relationship among purchase, sales and stock of commodities in the circulation of goods and reveals the existing problems.

□ Total Sales of Commodities

Total Sales of Commodities refer to the selling of commodities to other establishments and individuals (including direct export). Reflecting the total value of sales of commodities at Shanghai markets and out-of-Shanghai markets, this indicator includes: (1) commodities sold to urban and rural households and institutions for their consumption; (2) commodities sold to establishments in industry, agriculture, construction, transportation, post and telecommunications, wholesale and retail trade, catering and service trade and public utility for their production and operation; (3) commodities sold to wholesale and retail establishments for re-selling, with or without further processing; and (4) commodities for direct export to other countries. Excluded are selling of waste packaging materials used by enterprises themselves commodities transferred without buying or selling procedures, commission income from brokerage in transactions whose settlement is directly handled by buyers and sellers, rejected commodities in the purchase, loss in commodities, etc.

□ Prime Operating Revenue

Prime Operating Revenue refers to the earnings a corporation receives in daily activity such as selling goods and offering labor service.

SHANGHAI STATISTICAL YEARBOOK

□ Operating Cost

Operating Cost refers to the cost a corporation paid to buy and deliver the commodities.

□ Operating Expenses

Operating Expenses refer to the spendings that a wholesaler or retailer pays in buying, selling or stocking goods. It includes fees incurred in transport, loading and unloading, packaging, insurance, exhibition, business trip, advertisement, commodity wastage, commissions in import and export, salaries and bonus paid to workers involved.

第十七篇

CHAPTER 17

金融业

FINANCE

简要说明

本篇反映上海市金融业发展情况。由以下四部分组成:一是保费收支情况,数据由中国保险监督管理委员会上海监管局提供;二是金融机构存贷款余额及利率调整情况,数据由中国人民银行上海总部和上海公积金管理中心提供;三是金融业单位数,数据由中国银行业监督管理委员会上海监管局、中国保险监督管理委员会上海监管局、中国证券监督管理委员会上海监管局等部门提供;四是金融市场运行情况,数据由上海证券交易所、上海期货交易所、中国金融期货交易所、全国银行间同业拆借中心和上海黄金交易所提供。

BRIEF INTRODUCTION

Data in this chapter reflect the development of Shanghai's financial industries. The data consit of four parts: (1) Premium of primary insurance and payment. Data are provided by the China Insurance Regulatory Commission Shanghai Bureau. (2) The situations regarding the changes of deposit and loan balance, and adjustment of interest rates. Data are provided by the Shanghai Headquarters of People's Bank of China and the Shanghai Provident Fund Administration Center. (3) Quantity of financial institutions. Statistics are provided by the China Banking Regulatory Commission Shanghai Bureau, the China Insurance Regulatory Commission Shanghai Bureau, and the China Securities Regulatory Commission Shanghai Bureau. (4) Data on the activities of financial institutions. Data are provided by the Shanghai Stock Exchange, the Shanghai Futures Exchange, the China Financial Futures Exchange, the National Interbank Funding Center, and the Shanghai Gold Exchange.

表 17.1 原保险保费收入和赔付支出(1978～2012)
PREMIUM OF PRIMARY INSURANCE AND PAYMENT

年 份 Year	原保险保费收入 (亿元) Premium of Primary Insurance (100 million yuan)	其 中 of which 人身保险 Liability Insurance	其 中 of which 财产保险 Property Insurance	原保险赔付支出 (亿元) Payment of Primary Insurance (100 million yuan)	其 中 of which 人身保险 Liability Insurance	其 中 of which 财产保险 Property Insurance
1978	0.17			0.17		
1979	0.16			0.07		
1980	0.70			0.13		
1981	0.95			0.32		
1982	1.11			0.21		
1983	1.33			0.45		
1984	1.76			0.36		
1985	2.27			0.54		
1986	3.04			0.68		
1987	4.03			0.92		
1988	5.38			1.55		
1989	7.37			1.89		
1990	8.99			2.22		
1991	11.16			4.47		
1992	18.20			4.23		
1993	25.91			5.89		
1994	39.48			11.91		
1995	44.04	17.08	26.96	12.75		
1996	58.10	28.64	29.46	15.00		
1997	87.72	58.13	29.59	19.10		
1998	102.92	70.50	32.42	28.67		
1999	115.28	81.53	33.75	39.46		
2000	127.23	92.14	35.09	36.44	20.56	15.88
2001	180.25	140.30	39.95	38.82	19.61	19.21
2002	237.61	193.30	44.31	49.97	28.38	21.59
2003	289.93	232.50	57.43	61.97	34.87	27.10
2004	307.11	231.30	75.81	70.86	36.79	34.07
2005	333.62	245.76	87.86	87.46	40.20	47.26
2006	407.04	305.72	101.33	91.31	46.14	45.17
2007	482.64	363.22	119.43	139.82	86.79	53.03
2008	600.06	468.27	131.79	184.09	104.57	79.52
2009	665.03	513.22	151.81	176.74	98.24	78.50
2010	883.86	686.68	197.18	194.54	110.28	84.26
2011	753.11	519.71	233.39	260.71	156.39	104.32
2012	820.64	564.26	256.38	255.79	117.16	138.63

注：2010 年原保险保费收入为按财产险公司和寿险公司分类。
Note: Data of Premium of Primary Insurance of 2010 are classified by Property Insurance Company and Liability Insurance Company.

表 17.2 金融机构存贷款年末余额(2010～2012)
SAVING DEPOSIT AND LOAN BALANCE OF FINANCIAL INSTITUTIONS AT YEAR-END

单位:亿元(100 million yuan)

指 标	Indicators	2010	2011	2012
金融机构存款余额	**Saving Deposit Balance of Financial Institutions**	**52 190.04**	**58 186.48**	**63 555.25**
中资金融机构	Chinese Financial Institutions	48 118.64	53 089.19	58 287.02
人民币	RMB	46 678.13	51 315.12	55 732.05
外汇(折人民币)	Foreign Currencies(Converting into RMB)	1 440.51	1 774.07	2 554.97
外资金融机构	Foreign-funded Financial Institutions	4 071.40	5 097.29	5 268.23
外汇(折人民币)	Foreign Currencies (Converting into RMB)	902.70	1 139.25	1 107.53
人民币	RMB	3 168.70	3 958.04	4 160.70
金融机构贷款余额	**Loan Balance of Financial Institutions**	**34 154.17**	**37 196.79**	**40 982.48**
中资金融机构	Chinese Financial Institutions	29 970.80	32 863.85	36 784.99
人民币	RMB	27 970.18	30 644.58	33 814.10
外汇(折人民币)	Foreign Currencies (Converting into RMB)	2 000.62	2 219.27	2 970.89
外资金融机构	Foreign-funded Financial Institutions	4 183.36	4 332.93	4 197.49
外汇(折人民币)	Foreign Currencies (Converting into RMB)	1 580.23	1 617.41	1 525.69
人民币	RMB	2 603.13	2 715.52	2 671.80

表 17.3 中资金融机构人民币存款年末余额(2012)
RMB SAVING DEPOSIT OF CHINESE FINANCIAL INSTITUTIONS AT YEAR-END

单位:亿元(100 million yuan)

指 标	Indicators	2012	比 2012 年初增加 Increase from the Beginning of 2012
各项存款余额	**All Deposits**	**55 732.05**	**4 427.46**
单位存款	Unit Deposits	31 331.72	1 788.17
#活期存款	Current Deposits	9 672.72	-160.37
定期存款	Time Deposits	8 708.03	1 489.51
个人存款	Personal Deposits	20 110.51	2 487.16
#储蓄存款	Savings Deposits	18 905.95	2 178.65
财政性存款	Fiscal Deposits	1 629.76	-204.62
临时性存款	Temporary Deposits	72.96	20.04
委托存款	Entrusted Deposits	279.60	36.23
其他存款	Other Deposits	2 307.51	300.48

表 17.4 中资金融机构人民币贷款年末余额(2012)
RMB LOAN BALANCE OF CHINESE FINANCIAL INSTITUTIONS AT YEAR-END

单位:亿元(100 million yuan)

指标	Indicators	2012	比2012年初增加 Increase from the Beginning of 2012
各项贷款余额	**All Loans**	**33 814.10**	**3 149.28**
境内贷款	Domestic Loans	33 648.77	3 142.03
#短期贷款	Short-term Loans	9 037.27	1 176.32
#个人贷款及透支	Personal Loans and Overdrafts	831.93	198.01
单位普通贷款及透支	Common Unit Loans and Overdrafts	7 183.10	622.67
贸易融资	Trade Financing	985.25	353.41
中长期贷款	Mid and Long-term Loans	21 353.29	802.90
#个人贷款	Personal Loans	6 249.52	403.11
单位普通贷款	Common Unit Loans	11 581.75	-30.16
贸易融资	Trade Financing	162.53	3.00
融资租赁	Financing Leasing	1 569.99	633.75
票据融资	Bill Fianacing	1 643.23	493.44
境外贷款	Foreign Loans	165.33	7.25

表 17.5 个人消费贷款及公积金贷款(2010~2012)
PERSONAL CONSUMPTION LOAN AND ACCUMULATION FUND LOAN

指标	Indicators	2010	2011	2012
金融机构人民币个人消费贷款余额(亿元)	**Personal Consumption Loan from Domestic Funded Commercial banks(100 million yuan)**	**4 841.45**	**5 914.48**	**6 341.38**
#个人住房贷款	Housing Mortgage Loan	4 399.90	4 753.99	4 925.98
汽车消费贷款	Car Consumption Loan	134.29	662.65	822.05
个人住房贷款占金融机构人民币个人消费贷款额比重(%)	**Housing Mortgage Loan Percentage of Personal Consumption Loan**	**90.88**	**80.38**	**77.70**
公积金贷款余额(亿元)	**Accumulation Fund Loan(100 million yuan)**	**1 127.45**	**1 203.11**	**1 420.50**

表 17.6　年末金融业单位数(2011～2012)
QUANTITY OF FINANCIAL INSTITUTIONS

单位:家(unit)

指　标	Indicators	2011	2012
金融业单位数	Financial Institutions	1 048	1 124
# 货币金融	Monetary and Financial	160	510
资本市场	Capital Markets	149	193
保险业	Insurance Institutions	333	347
# 外资金融单位数	Foreign Financial Institutions Operating in Shanghai	173	208

注：金融业单位数统计中，货币金融单位统计至市分行及持牌运营中心；资本市场单位统计至证券公司市分公司、基金公司、期货公司、证券投资咨询公司、资信评级机构、证券市场机构和登记结算机构；保险业统计至保险公司市分公司、专业保险运营中心和保险中介机构。此外，金融单位统计包括各金融监管部门。

Note: Among the statistics of financial institutions, monetary and financial institutions includes the municipal branches and certified operating certers, capital markets institutions include the municipal branch company, coporate fundation, futures company; security investment consultant company, credit rating agency, security market institution and registration and settlment institution; insurance institutions include insurance group, municipal branches of insurance company, specail insurance operations center and insurance agency institutions. In addition, the statistics of financial institutions includes financial regulatary institutions as well.

表 17.7　主要金融市场成交概况(2010～2012)
DEAL STATISTICS OF MAIN FANANCIAL MARKET

单位:亿元(100 million yuan)

指　标	Indicators	2010	2011	2012
上海证券交易所	**Shanghai Stock Exchange**	**398 395.73**	**454 651.56**	**547 535.22**
上海期货交易所	**Shanghai Future Exchange**	**1 234 794.76**	**869 068.71**	**891 953.72**
中国金融期货交易所	**China Financial Futures Exchange**	**410 698.77**	**437 658.55**	**758 406.78**
全国银行间货币与债券市场	**Inter-bank Lending and Bond Market**	**1 798 225.10**	**1 966 399.84**	**2 636 302.88**
同业拆借	RMB Unsecured Loans	278 684.03	334 412.04	467 043.65
回购交易	Bonds Repurchase.	875 935.56	994 534.79	1 417 140.27
现券买卖	Spot Bond Trade (include Asset-backed Securities)	640 422.08	636 422.90	751 952.83
债券远期交易	Bond Forward Transactions	3 183.43	1 030.10	166.12
上海黄金交易所	**Total Gold Turnover**	**20 204.96**	**44 411.23**	**35 297.25**

注：本表数据除上海期货交易所和上海黄金交易所成交额按双向计算外，其他成交额数据均按单向计算。

Note: The turnover data in the table are calculated by buy or sell except Shanghai Futures Exchange and Shanghai Gold Exchange turnover calculated by buy and sell.

表 17.8 金融机构人民币存款基准利率(1990～2012)
BENCHMARK INTEREST RATE OF RMB DEPOSIT FOR FINANCIAL INSTITUTIONS

单位:年利率% (annual interest rate)

调整时间 Adjust Time	活期 Checking Deposit	定期 fixed deposit					
		3个月 3 Months	6个月 6 Months	1年 1 Year	2年 2 Year	3年 3 Year	5年 5 Year
1990.04.15	2.88	6.30	7.74	10.08	10.98	11.88	13.68
1990.08.21	2.16	4.32	6.48	8.64	9.36	10.08	11.52
1991.04.21	1.80	3.24	5.40	7.56	7.92	8.28	9.00
1993.05.15	2.16	4.86	7.20	9.18	9.90	10.80	12.06
1993.07.11	3.15	6.66	9.00	10.98	11.70	12.24	13.86
1996.05.01	2.97	4.86	7.20	9.18	9.90	10.80	12.06
1996.08.23	1.98	3.33	5.40	7.47	7.92	8.28	9.00
1997.10.23	1.71	2.88	4.14	5.67	5.94	6.21	6.66
1998.03.25	1.71	2.88	4.14	5.22	5.58	6.21	6.66
1998.07.01	1.44	2.79	3.96	4.77	4.86	4.95	5.22
1998.12.07	1.44	2.79	3.33	3.78	3.96	4.14	4.50
1999.06.10	0.99	1.98	2.16	2.25	2.43	2.70	2.88
2002.02.21	0.72	1.71	1.89	1.98	2.25	2.52	2.79
2004.10.29	0.72	1.71	2.07	2.25	2.70	3.24	3.60
2006.08.19	0.72	1.80	2.25	2.52	3.06	3.69	4.14
2007.03.18	0.72	1.98	2.43	2.79	3.33	3.96	4.41
2007.05.19	0.72	2.07	2.61	3.06	3.69	4.41	4.95
2007.07.21	0.81	2.34	2.88	3.33	3.96	4.68	5.22
2007.08.22	0.81	2.61	3.15	3.60	4.23	4.95	5.49
2007.09.15	0.81	2.88	3.42	3.87	4.50	5.22	5.76
2007.12.21	0.72	3.33	3.78	4.14	4.68	5.40	5.85
2008.10.09	0.72	3.15	3.51	3.87	4.41	5.13	5.58
2008.10.30	0.72	2.88	3.24	3.60	4.14	4.77	5.13
2008.11.27	0.36	1.98	2.25	2.52	3.06	3.60	3.87
2008.12.23	0.36	1.71	1.98	2.25	2.79	3.33	3.60
2010.10.20	0.36	1.91	2.20	2.50	3.25	3.85	4.20
2010.12.26	0.36	2.25	2.50	2.75	3.55	4.15	4.55
2011.02.09	0.40	2.60	2.80	3.00	3.90	4.50	5.00
2011.04.06	0.50	2.85	3.05	3.25	4.15	4.75	5.25
2011.07.07	0.50	3.10	3.30	3.50	4.40	5.00	5.50
2012.06.08	0.40	2.85	3.05	3.25	4.10	4.65	5.10
2012.07.06	0.35	2.60	2.80	3.00	3.75	4.25	4.75

注：本表数据摘自中国人民银行网站。
Note: Data in the table are from the web of People's Bank of China .

表 17.9 金融机构人民币贷款基准利率(1991～2012)
BENCHMARK INTEREST RATE OF RMB LOAN FOR FINANCIAL INSTITUTIONS

单位:年利率%(annual interest rate)

调整时间 Adjust Time	6 个月 6 Month	1 年 1 Year	1～3 年(含) 1～3 Years	3～5 年(含) 3～5 Years	5 年以上 Above 5 Years
1991.04.21	8.10	8.64	9.00	9.54	9.72
1993.05.15	8.82	9.36	10.80	12.06	12.24
1993.07.11	9.00	10.98	12.24	13.86	14.04
1995.01.01	9.00	10.98	12.96	14.58	14.76
1995.07.01	10.08	12.06	13.50	15.12	15.30
1996.05.01	9.72	10.98	13.14	14.94	15.12
1996.08.23	9.18	10.08	10.98	11.70	12.42
1997.10.23	7.65	8.64	9.36	9.90	10.53
1998.03.25	7.02	7.92	9.00	9.72	10.35
1998.07.01	6.57	6.93	7.11	7.65	8.01
1998.12.07	6.12	6.39	6.66	7.20	7.56
1999.06.10	5.58	5.85	5.94	6.03	6.21
2002.02.21	5.04	5.31	5.49	5.58	5.76
2004.10.29	5.22	5.58	5.76	5.85	6.12
2006.04.28	5.40	5.85	6.03	6.12	6.39
2006.08.19	5.58	6.12	6.30	6.48	6.84
2007.03.18	5.67	6.39	6.57	6.75	7.11
2007.05.19	5.85	6.57	6.75	6.93	7.20
2007.07.21	6.03	6.84	7.02	7.20	7.38
2007.08.22	6.21	7.02	7.20	7.38	7.56
2007.09.15	6.48	7.29	7.47	7.65	7.83
2007.12.21	6.57	7.47	7.56	7.74	7.83
2008.09.13	6.21	7.20	7.29	7.56	7.74
2008.10.09	6.12	6.93	7.02	7.29	7.47
2008.10.30	6.03	6.66	6.75	7.02	7.20
2008.11.27	5.04	5.58	5.67	5.94	6.12
2008.12.23	4.86	5.31	5.40	5.76	5.94
2010.10.20	5.10	5.56	5.60	5.96	6.14
2010.12.26	5.35	5.81	5.85	6.22	6.40
2011.02.09	5.60	6.06	6.10	6.45	6.60
2011.04.06	5.85	6.31	6.40	6.65	6.80
2011.07.07	6.10	6.56	6.65	6.90	7.05
2012.06.08	5.85	6.31	6.40	6.65	6.80
2012.07.06	5.60	6.00	6.15	6.40	6.55

注：本表数据摘自中国人民银行网站。
Note: Data in the table are from the web of People's Bank of China.

表 17.10 上海证券交易所上市公司股本结构(2010～2012)
CAPITAL STOCK STRUCTURE OF PUBLIC COMPANIES IN SHANGHAI STOCK EXCHANGE

单位:亿元(100 million yuan)

指 标	Indicators	2010	2011	2012
发行总股本	**Total**	**28 101.77**	**29 756.86**	**31 094.64**
尚未流通股份	Non-circulation Shares	5 908.20	5 472.85	5 096.29
国家拥有股份	State Shares	4 709.21	4 157.27	3 848.20
境内法人持有股份	Domestic Sponsoring Corporate Shares	235.79	191.3	249.80
外资法人持有股份	Foreign Corporate Shares	25.79	27.85	22.17
个人发起人股	Personal Sponsor Shares	20.61	27.13	79.66
募集法人股	Raised Corporate	4.53	3.23	3.23
机构配售	Agencies Placing	136.38	101.98	38.31
其 他	Others	775.89	964.08	854.91
已流通股份	Circulation Shares	22 193.57	24 284.01	25 998.35
境内上市的人民币普通股	A Shares	15 901.47	17 859.52	19 377.77
境内上市外资股	B Shares	129.84	134.28	143.56
境外上市外资股	H Shares	6 162.27	6 290.21	6 477.01

表 17.11 上海证券交易所市场概况(2010～2012)
SHANGHAI STOCK EXCHANGE MARKET

指 标	Indicators	2010	2011	2012
上市公司数(个)	Quantity of Public Company (unit)	894	931	954
上市证券数(个)	Quantity of Negotiable Securities(unit)	1 500	1 691	2 098
上市股票数(个)	Quantity of Listed Stock(unit)	938	975	998
股票发行股数(亿股)	Shares of Stocks Issued (100 million shares)	21 939.51	23 466.65	24 618
A 股	A Shares	21 809.67	23 332.37	24 474.06
B 股	B Shares	129.84	134.28	143.56
股票市价总值(亿元)	Aggregate Value of Stocks in Market Price (100 million yuan)	179 007.24	148 376.22	158 698.44
A 股	A Shares	178 000.02	147 692.76	157 912.65
B 股	B Shares	1 007.22	683.47	785.79
流通股数(亿股)	Shares in Circulation (100 million shares)	16 031.31	17 993.80	19 521.33
A 股	A Shares	15 901.47	17 859.52	19 377.77
B 股	B Shares	129.84	134.28	143.56
流通市值(亿元)	Value in Circulation (100 million yuan)	142 337.45	122 851.36	134 294.45
A 股	A Shares	141 330.23	122 167.89	133 508.66
B 股	B Shares	1 007.22	683.47	785.79
市场筹资额(亿元)	Funds Raised from Market (100 million yuan)	7 585.14	5 489.75	4 864.51
首次发行 A 股	IPO of A Shares	1 891.51	1 014.01	333.57
再次发行 A 股	Additional A Shares Issued	3 640.62	2 185.68	2 556.74
债 券	Convertible Loan Stock	2 053.00	2 293.80	1 974.20

表 17.12 主要年份上证综合指数 THE SHANGHAI COMPOSITE INDEX IN MAIN YEARS

年 份 Year	开 盘 Open	最 高 High	日 期 Date		最 低 Low	日 期 Date		收 盘 Close
1990	96.05	127.61	12月31日	31,Dec	95.79	12月19日	19,Dec	127.61
1995	637.72	926.41	5月22日	22,May	524.43	2月7日	7,Feb	555.29
1996	550.26	1 258.69	12月11日	11,Dec	512.83	1月19日	19,Jan	917.02
1997	914.06	1 510.18	5月12日	12,May	870.80	2月20日	20,Feb	1 194.10
1998	1 200.95	1 422.95	6月4日	4,June	1 043.02	8月18日	18,Aug	1 146.70
1999	1 144.89	1 756.18	6月30日	30,June	1 047.83	5月17日	17,May	1 366.58
2000	1 368.69	2 125.72	11月23日	23,Nov	1 361.21	1月4日	4,Jan	2 073.48
2001	2 077.08	2 245.44	6月14日	14,June	1 514.86	10月22日	22,Oct	1 645.97
2002	1 643.49	1 748.89	6月25日	25,June	1 339.20	1月29日	29,Jan	1 357.65
2003	1 347.43	1 649.60	4月16日	16,Apr	1 307.40	11月13日	13,Nov	1 497.04
2004	1 492.72	1 777.52	4月6日	6,Apr	1 260.32	9月13日	13,Sep	1 266.50
2005	1 260.78	1 318.27	3月8日	8, Mar	1 011.50	7月11日	11, July	1 161.06
2006	1 163.88	2 698.90	12月29日	29,Dec	1 161.91	1月4日	4,Jan	2 675.47
2007	2 728.19	6 124.04	10月16日	16,Oct	2 541.53	2月6日	6,Feb	5 261.56
2008	5 265.00	5 522.78	1月14日	14,Jan	1 664.93	10月28日	28,Oct	1 820.81
2009	1 849.02	3 478.01	8月4日	4,Aug	1 844.09	1月5日	5,Jan	3 277.14
2010	3 289.75	3 282.18	1月5日	5,Jan	2 363.95	7月5日	5,July	2 808.08
2011	2 825.33	3 057.33	4月18日	18,Apr	2 166.21	12月27日	27,Dec	2 199.42
2012	2 212.00	2 478.38	2月27日	27,Feb	1 949.46	12月4日	4,Dec	2 269.13

表 17.13 上证各类指数概况(2012) ALL KINDS OF INDEX OF SHANGHAI

	年 份 Year	最 高 High	日 期 Date		最 低 Low	日 期 Date		收 盘 Close
上证综指	Shanghai Composite Index	2 478.38	2月27日	27,Feb	1 949.46	12月4日	4,Dec	2 269.13
上证 180	Shanghai 180	5 808.99	5月4日	4,May	4 596.73	12月4日	4,Dec	5 550.09
上证 50	Shanghai 50	1 877.43	5月4日	4,May	1 528.28	12月4日	4,Dec	1 857.68
上证 380	Shanghai 380	3 519.95	3月14日	14,Mar	2 465.46	12月4日	4,Dec	2 944.82
红利指数	Dividend Index	2 005.82	3月5日	5,Mar	1 596.09	12月4日	4,Dec	1 906.03
治理指数	Governance Index	723.68	5月4日	4,May	568.51	11月30日	31,Nov	691.91
A 股指数	A Share Index	2 596.15	2月7日	7,Feb	2 041.16	12月4日	4,Dec	2 376.04
B 股指数	B Share Index	253.10	5月8日	8,May	195.09	7月31日	31,July	244.92
基金指数	Fund Index	4 014.86	5月7日	7,May	3 347.34	12月4日	4,Dec	3 921.09
国债指数	Bond Index	135.82	12月31日	31,Dec	131.44	1月4日	4,Jan	135.79
企业债指数	Corporate Bond Index	159.65	12月31日	31,Dec	148.22	1月6日	6,Jan	159.60

表 17.14 上海证券交易所有价证券成交总额(2009～2012)
TOTAL VOLUME OF PRICED SECURITIES TRADING IN SHANGHAI STOCK EXCHANGE

单位:亿元 (100 million yuan)

指 标	Indicators	2009	2010	2011	2012
总 计	**Total**	**441 875**	**398 396**	**454 652**	**547 535**
股 票	Stocks	346 512	304 312	237 560	164 545
#A 股	A Shares	345 443	303 216	236 814	164 047
B 股	B Shares	1 069	1 096	746	413
债 券	Bond	39 806	74 914	210 715	379 819
基金(含 ETF)	Fund	6 549	4 772	2 901	3 171
权 证	Warrant	49 008	14 398	3 475	

表 17.15 主要年份上海证券交易所股票账户开户情况
ACCOUNT-OPENING BY INVESTORS IN SHANGHAI STOCK EXCHANGE IN MAIN YEARS

单位:万户(10 000 households)

指 标	Indicators	2000	2010	2011	2012
年末开户总数	**Total Accounts Year-end**				
总 数	Total	2 957.84	8 154.23	8 705.02	8 996.40
个 人	Private	2 944.89	8 116.45	8 664.93	8 954.88
机 构	Institution	12.95	37.78	40.09	41.52
A 股开户数	**A Shares Accounts**				
总 数	Total	2 943.32	8 001.44	8 550.85	8 841.56
个 人	Private	2 931.20	7 965.48	8 512.71	8 802.09
机 构	Institution	12.12	35.96	38.14	39.47
B 股开户数	**B Shares Accounts**				
总 数	Total	14.52	152.78	154.17	154.84
个 人	Private	13.69	150.97	152.22	152.79
机 构	Institution	0.83	1.82	1.95	2.05
当年新开户总数	**Newly Opened Accounts During the Year**				
总 数	Total	676.72	748.86	550.79	291.38
个 人	Private	672.09	746.20	548.48	289.95
机 构	Institution	4.64	2.66	2.31	1.43
A 股新开户数	**Newly Opened Accounts of A Shares**				
总 数	Total	671.08	746.41	549.41	290.71
个 人	Private	666.52	743.86	547.23	289.38
机 构	Institution	4.56	2.55	2.18	1.33
B 股新开户数	**Newly Opened Accounts of B Shares**				
总 数	Total	5.64	2.45	1.38	0.67
个 人	Private	5.56	2.34	1.25	0.57
机 构	Institution	0.08	0.11	0.13	0.10

上/海/统/计/年/鉴

主要统计指标解释

■ 存　款

机构或个人在保留资金或货币所有权的条件下，以不可流通的存款凭证为依据，暂时让渡或接受资金使用权所形成的债权或债务。

■ 贷　款

机构或个人在保留资金或货币所有权的条件下，以不可流通的借款凭证或类似凭证为依据，暂时让渡或接受资金使用权所形成的债权或债务。

■ 上证综合指数

以在上海证券交易所上市的全部股票(A股和B股)作为样本计算的股票价格指数。

■ 市场筹资额

企业在上海证券交易所通过发行股票和债券所筹集的资金总额。

■ 原保险保费收入

指保险人与投保人之间直接签订的原保险合同中确认的保费收入，不包括再保险保费收入。

■ 原保险赔付支出

指保险企业根据保险人与投保人之间直接签订的原保险合同中确认的赔付款项，不包括再保险赔付支出。

SHANGHAI STATISTICAL YEARBOOK

EXPLANATORY NOTES TO MAJOR STATISTICAL INDICATORS

□ Deposit

Deposit refers to the creditor's rights or debt formed by temporary lending or receiving funds in condition of institutions or individuals to retain the ownership of funds or monetary and based on the non-negotiable certificates of deposits.

□ Loan

Loan refers to the creditor's rights or debt formed by temporary lending or receiving funds in condition of institutions or individuals to retain the ownership of funds or monetary and based on the non-negotiable certificates of loan or similar certificates.

□ SSE Composite Index

SSE Composite Index is a stock price index, which is calculated by the price of all stocks (including A stocks and B stocks) in Shanghai Stock Exchange.

□ Market Financing

Market Financing refers to the total amount of fund which enterprises raise by issuing shares or bonds in Shanghai Stock Exchange.

□ Premium of Primary Insurance

Premium of Primary Insurance includes the insurance premium which is entered into the original insurance contract signed directly between the insurer and the insured, and reinsurance premium is excluded.

□ Payment of Primary Insurance

Payment of Primary Insurance includes the insurance payment which is entered into the original insurance contract signed directly between the insurer and the insured, and reinsurance payment is excluded.

第十八篇

CHAPTER 18

房地产业

REAL ESTATE

简要说明

一、本章资料的主要内容

本篇资料反映上海市房地产业生产经营和发展情况。主要指标有房地产开发投资额、房屋施工面积、商品房销售面积、房屋拆迁户数、存量房买卖登记面积等。

二、本篇的资料来源

本篇中房地产开发投资和资金来源、房屋建筑面积和造价、商品房销售和出租统计资料根据上海市统计局制定的《房地产开发、经营统计报表制度》调查汇总提供。

本篇中房屋拆迁(征收)、存量房买卖登记统计资料由上海市住房保障和房屋管理局提供。

本篇中土地使用权出让统计资料由上海市规划和国土资源管理局提供。

三、本篇资料的统计调查方法

本篇中涉及房地产开发经营统计资料采用全面调查的方法，由全市房地产开发经营法人企业通过联网直报的方式上报取得。

BRIEF INTRODUCTION

I. Main Contents

Data in this chapter reflect business operation and development of real estate industry in Shanghai. Main indicators include investment in real estate development, floor area of construction, sold area of commodity, buildings resettlement, and exchance of second–hand houses.

II. Sources of statistics

Data on real estate development investment and capital source, construction area and cost of property development commodity housing sold and leased are compiled in accordance with Statistical Reporting System on Real Estate Development and Operation made by Shanghai Municipal Statistics Bureau.

Data on buildings resettlement and exchance of second–hand houses are provided by Shanghai Municipal Housing Security and Building Administration Bureau.

Data on lease of land plot tenure are provided by Shanghai Municipal Bureau of Planning and Land Resources.

III. Survey Methodology

Data on development and operation of real estate adopt comprehensive reporting system, being collected from data directly reported by the city's real estate development and operation enterprises with legal person status through the Internet.

表 18.1　主要年份房地产开发投资和经营情况
INVESTMENT AND OPERATION IN REAL ESTATE DEVELOPMENT IN MAIN YEARS

单位:亿元(100 million yuan)

指　标	Indicators	2000	2010	2011	2012
投资总额	**Total Investment**	**566.17**	**1 980.68**	**2 170.31**	**2 381.36**
在投资总额中	Of Total Investment				
住　宅	Residence	408.82	1 229.83	1 398.75	1 451.94
#别墅、高档公寓	Villas and Apartment	40.72	373.67	369.24	335.08
办公楼	Office Building	57.47	224.46	231.09	262.85
商业营业用房	Commercial Building	51.51	244.7	236.05	293.75
其　他	Others	48.38	281.69	304.43	372.81
新增固定资产	**Newly Increased Fixed Assets**	**477.39**	**964.27**	**1 250.88**	**1 388.45**
资金来源合计	**Total Capital Source**	**778.16**	**4 443.85**	**4 627.98**	**5 316.93**
上年末结余资金	Balance at End of Previous Year	113.48	1 214.56	1 421.05	1 348.42
本年资金来源小计	Sub-total Capital Source of this Year	664.68	3 229.29	3 206.93	3 968.51
国内贷款	Domestic Loans	155.37	819.57	741.18	975.78
利用外资	Foreign Capital Utilized	28.11	96.05	43.55	26.12
#外商直接投资	Foreign Direct Investment	16.24	65.52	41.01	26.12
自筹资金	Self-Financed Capital	211.86	1 070.88	1 192.87	1 385.96
其他资金	Other Capital	269.34	1 242.78	1 229.32	1 580.66

表18.2 主要年份房地产开发企业房屋建筑面积和造价
CONSTRUCTION AREA AND COST OF PROPERTY DEVELOPED BY REAL ESTATE COMPANIES IN MAIN YEARS

指 标	Indicators	2000	2010	2011	2012
房屋施工面积（万平方米）	**Floor Area of Construction（10 000 sq. m）**	**5 523.23**	**11 295.03**	**12 983.32**	**13 249.97**
住 宅	Residence	4 263.50	7 313.85	8 386.26	8 315.68
#别墅、高档公寓	Villas and Apartment	254.11	1 584.11	1 682.51	1 425.77
办公楼	Office Building	515.10	1 103.18	1 158.34	1 284.68
商业营业用房	Commercial Building	438.47	1 292.96	1 365.89	1 449.91
其 他	Others	306.16	1 585.04	2 072.83	2 199.69
房屋竣工面积（万平方米）	**Floor Area Completed（10 000 sq. m）**	**1 643.62**	**1 941.25**	**2 240.62**	**2 305.06**
住 宅	Residence	1 388.01	1 396.05	1 549.66	1 609.13
#别墅、高档公寓	Villas and Apartment	66.38	328.00	319.89	275.91
办公楼	Office Building	95.93	150.69	174.33	206.87
商业营业用房	Commercial Building	100.16	176.41	231.80	177.65
其 他	Others	59.52	218.09	284.83	311.41
房屋竣工价值（亿元）	**Value of Building Completed（100 million yuan）**	**355.79**	**779.93**	**1 011.57**	**1 060.07**
住 宅	Residence	270.29	536.66	646.06	692.63
#别墅、高档公寓	Villas and Apartment	20.66	178.27	199.44	183.52
办公楼	Office Building	45.41	74.23	118.45	135.49
商业营业用房	Commercial Building	24.29	87.13	137.63	106.09
其 他	Others	15.80	81.91	109.44	125.87
竣工房屋平均造价（元/平方米）	**Average Construction Cost（yuan/sq. m）**	**2 164**	**4 018**	**4 515**	**4 599**
住 宅	Residence	1 947	3 844	4 169	4 304
#别墅、高档公寓	Villas and Apartment	3 112	5 435	6 235	6 651
办公楼	Office Building	4 733	4 926	6 794	6 549
商业营业用房	Commercial Building	2 425	4 939	5 938	5 972
其 他	Others	2 654	3 756	3 842	4 042

表 18.3 主要年份商品房销售和出租情况
COMMODITY HOUSING SOLD AND LEASED IN MAIN YEARS

指 标	Indicators	2000	2010	2011	2012
商品房销售面积（万平方米）	**Sold Area of Commodity Housing(10 000 sq. m)**	**1 557.87**	**2 055.53**	**1 771.30**	**1 898.46**
住 宅	Residence	1 445.87	1 685.35	1 473.72	1 592.63
#别墅、高档公寓	Villas and Apartment	53.44	341.71	237.32	234.56
办公楼	Office Building	47.76	162.89	147.40	111.73
商业营业用房	Commercial Building	54.54	125.56	95.57	120.01
其 他	Others	9.70	81.72	54.61	74.10
商品房销售额（亿元）	**Sales Volume of Commodity Housing (100 million yuan)**	**555.45**	**2 959.94**	**2 568.88**	**2 669.49**
住 宅	Residence	480.97	2 395.35	1 981.91	2 208.96
#别墅、高档公寓	Villas and Apartment	32.65	852.62	637.27	661.35
办公楼	Office Building	44.05	307.67	371.81	234.62
商业营业用房	Commercial Building	27.87	197.57	181.66	194.62
其 他	Others	2.56	59.34	33.49	31.29
商品房出租面积（万平方米）	**Commodity Housing Leased (10 000 Sq. m)**	**358.38**	**1 262.47**	**1 305.47**	**1 355.20**
住 宅	Residence	59.29	85.72	87.68	92.43
#别墅、高档公寓	Villas and Apartment	37.43	76.18	75.40	73.26
办公楼	Office Building	156.15	516.18	578.23	643.83
商业营业用房	Commercial Building	62.04	373.34	392.70	396.45
其 他	Others	80.91	287.23	246.86	222.48

表 18.4 每百户城市居民家庭房屋产权构成(2009～2012)
PROPERTY RIGHT STRUCTURE OF TOWNSMAN TENEMENT PER HUNDRED HOUSEHOLDS

单位：%

类 别	Type	2009	2010	2011	2012
每百户城市居民家庭房屋产权构成	**Property Right Structure of Townsman Tenement per Hundred Households**	**100**	**100**	**100**	**100**
租赁公房	Leasehold Public Tenement	16.3	16.4	13.9	14.5
租赁私房	Leasehold Private Tenement	3.7	3.5	3.3	3.0
原有私房	Inhere Private Tenement	0.7	0.7	0.9	0.7
房改私房	Reformed Private Tenement	37.2	37.4	37.9	38.7
商品房	Commercial Tenement	41.3	41.1	43.3	42.7
其 他	Others	0.8	0.9	0.7	0.5

表 18.5 房屋征收(拆迁)情况(1995～2012)
BUILDINGS EXPROPRIATION(RESETTLEMENT)

年份 Year	征收(拆迁)户数(户) Quantity of Expropriation (Resettlements) (unit)	其中 of which #居民住宅 Residence	征收(拆迁)面积(万平方米) Floor Area Expropriated (Resettled) (10 000 sq. m)	其中 of which #居民住宅 Residence
1995	75 777	73 695	322.77	253.90
1996	89 132	86 481	342.95	258.86
1997	79 857	77 388	479.67	363.16
1998	78 205	75 157	452.22	343.94
1999	75 185	73 709	342.50	248.17
2000	70 606	68 293	365.77	288.35
2001	73 728	71 909	515.65	386.66
2002	101 097	98 714	644.53	485.00
2003	80 858	79 077	584.93	475.47
2004	42 415	41 552	308.40	232.52
2005	75 857	74 483	1 222.53	851.85
2006	81 126	76 874	1 516.85	848.35
2007	51 354	49 092	825.00	690.00
2008	53 583	51 288	1 028.53	753.71
2009	68 286	65 439	927.63	612.56
2010	39 721	38 441	585.70	389.87
2011	23 112	22 349	333.83	182.83
2012	21 910	21 262	219.42	127.27

注：1995～2010 年为拆迁数据，2011 年起为征收数据。
Note: Data in this table are buildings resettlement from 1995～2010, buildings expropriation since 2011.

表 18.6 各区房屋征收(拆迁)情况(2012)
BUILDINGS EXPROPRIATION(RESETTLEMENT) IN DIFFERENT DISTRICTS

地区	District	征收(拆迁)户数(户) Quantity of Expropriation (Resettlements) (unit)	其中 of which #居民住宅 Residence	征收(拆迁)面积(万平方米) Floor Area Expropriated (Resettld 10 000 sq. m)	其中 of which #居民住宅 Residence
总计	**Total**	**21 910**	**21 262**	**219.42**	**127.27**
#浦东新区	Pudong New Area	2 448	2 297	67.71	36.26
黄浦区	Huangpu	5 157	5 118	14.16	13.80
徐汇区	Xuhui	151	101	3.93	0.60
长宁区	Changning	1 936	1 907	6.68	5.46
静安区	Jing'an	381	258	7.17	0.91
普陀区	Putuo	1 872	1 872	12.09	12.09
闸北区	Zhabei	4 043	4 043	11.67	11.67
虹口区	Hongkou	755	739	3.49	2.48
杨浦区	Yangpu	3 331	3 301	10.34	9.34

表 18.7 土地使用权出让情况(2012)
LEASE OF LAND PLOT TENURE

指 标	Indicators	出让地块（幅）Leased Plot (piece)	出让面积（万平方米）Leased Area (10 000 sq. m)
总 计	**Total**	**843**	**3 226.35**
商业服务	Commercial Service	138	449.83
住 宅	Residence	208	1 240.69
工矿仓储	Storage of Industry	491	1 530.49
公共建筑	Public Buildings	6	5.35

注：本表数据由市规划和国土资源管理局提供基础资料，由市统计局整理。
Note: Basic data in this table are provided by Shanghai Municipal Bureau of Planning and Land Resources, and sorted by Shanghai Municipal Statistics Bureau.

表 18.8 存量房交易情况(1994～2012)
EXCHANGE OF SECOND-HAND HOUSES

年 份 Year	成交套数（套）Houses Traded (set)	成交面积（万平方米）Areas Traded (10 000 sq. m.)	其中 of which: 住 宅 Residence	办公楼 Office	商业营业用房 Commerce
1994	2 821	31.76	10.59		
1995	4 176	60.87	19.70		
1996	4 689	82.29	25.09		
1997	9 180	162.40	87.68	23.95	14.95
1998	24 501	315.23	197.56	21.49	18.28
1999	44 234	510.84	336.69	37.63	14.61
2000	96 348	778.52	648.23	39.48	21.65
2001	164 598	1 422.43	1 031.48	56.99	57.24
2002	204 239	1 790.50	1 341.60	65.70	91.80
2003	263 297	2 306.28	1 807.57	105.14	114.28
2004	303 291	2 726.70	2 222.24	117.12	121.39
2005	189 896	1 971.50	1 608.20	88.10	78.00
2006	184 194	1 706.81	1 375.22	67.35	46.53
2007	213 733	1 992.59	1 715.05	49.73	36.34
2008	142 224	1 413.41	1 107.17	40.61	42.04
2009	312 857	2 809.45	2 490.58	48.19	43.59
2010	202 511	1 966.86	1 522.21	68.31	70.61
2011	146 151	1 398.67	1 058.71	62.87	51.21
2012	157 585	1 446.77	1 136.17	57.34	46.71

上/海/统/计/年/鉴

主要统计指标解释

房地产开发投资

指报告期内房地产开发企业(单位)完成的全部用于房屋建设工程、土地开发工程的投资额以及公益性建筑和土地购置费等的投资。

施工面积

指报告期内施工的全部房屋建筑面积。包括本期新开工的面积和上期开工跨入本期继续施工的房屋面积，以及上期已停建在本期恢复施工的房屋面积。本期竣工和本期施工后又停缓建的房屋，其建筑面积仍计入本期房屋施工面积中。

竣工面积

指在报告期内房屋建筑按照设计要求已经全部完工,达到住人和使用条件,经验收鉴定合格(或达到竣工验收标准) 正式移交使用单位的各栋房屋建筑面积的总和。

房屋建筑面积竣工率

指一定时期内房屋竣工面积占同期房屋施工面积的比率。该指标从房屋建筑施工速度的角度反映投资效果的指标。

别墅、高档公寓

指建筑造价和销售价格明显高于一般商品住宅的商品住宅。别墅一般指地处郊区,独立成栋的商品住宅;高档公寓一般指地处市内高尚社区，高层或多层的商品住宅。别墅、高档公寓的确定标准:一是经有房地产投资计划审批权的主管部门审批建设的别墅、高档公寓开发项目;二是销售价格高于当地同等地段商品住宅平均销售价格一倍以上的别墅、公寓开发项目。该指标可以分析房地产投资结构,反映高收入家庭商品住宅的供求平衡情况。

SHANGHAI STATISTICAL YEARBOOK

EXPLANATORY NOTES TO MAJOR STATISTICAL INDICATORS

□ Investment in Real Estate Development

Investment in Real Estate Development refers to investment entirely used for building construction project and land development project by real estate development enterprises, and investment in public buildings and purchase costs of land.

□ Floor Area of Construction

Floor Area of Construction refers to total floor space of all buildings under construction during the reference period, including floor space of newly started buildings during the reference period, floor space of construction extended from the previous period to the current period, and floor space of construction suspended during the previous period and resumed in the current period. Floor space of construction completed in the current period, and floor space of construction started and then suspended in the current period are also included in the floor space under construction of the current year.

□ Floor Area Completed

Floor Area Completed refers to the floor space of all buildings completed in the reference period, which have been appraised and accepted (or come up to the designed standards) and have been transferred to the owners for use.

□ Completion Rate of Floor Space of Buildings

Completion Rate of Floor Space of Buildings refers to the ratio of the floor space of buildings completed in certain period of time to the floor space of buildings under construction in the same period. This indicator reflects the investment result from the perspective of the speed of construction.

□ Villas, High-Grade Apartments

Villas, High-Grade Apartments refers to commercial houses whose construction costs and marketing prices are significantly higher than ordinary housing. Villas are independent structures generally located in the suburbs; high-grade apartments are multi-story buildings located in elegant urban neighborhoods. Criteria for villas and high-grade apartments include: 1) projects for the construction of villas or high-grade apartments have to be approved by competent departments in charge of real estate development and investment plans, and 2) prices for projects on villas or high-grade apartments are higher by over 100% compared with the average prices of ordinary commercial housing projects in similar location. This indicator helps to analyze the investment structure of the real estate industry and the demand and supply of housing for high-income households.

第十九篇

CHAPTER 19

科学技术

SCIENCE AND TECHNOLOGY

简要说明

一、本章资料的主要内容

科技统计资料主要内容包括:全社会以及工业企业、政府部门属研究机构、高校的研究与试验发展(R&D)活动情况;技术市场交易情况;科技成果情况;民营科技企业状况;科协系统科技活动情况;专利申请和授权情况等。

二、本篇资料的统计范围

科技活动统计资料范围为全社会有研究与试验发展(R&D)活动的企事业单位,具体包括工业企业、政府部门属研究机构、普通高等学校以及研究与试验发展(R&D)活动相对密集行业(包括农、林、牧、渔业,建筑业,交通运输、仓储和邮政业,信息传输、计算机服务和软件业,金融业,租赁和商务服务业,科学研究、技术服务和地质勘查业,水利、环境和公共设施管理业,卫生、社会保障和社会福利业,文化、体育和娱乐业等)中从事研究与试验发展(R&D)活动的企事业单位。

三、本篇的资料来源

全市综合资料、企业及有关行业企事业单位的研究与试验发展(R&D)活动情况资料由上海统计局调查提供;政府部门属研究机构资料由上海市科学技术委员会、上海市经济和信息化委员会调查提供;科学研究、技术服务和地质勘查业企事业的研究与试验发展(R&D)活动情况资料,以及技术市场资料、科技成果、民营科技企业状况由上海市科学技术委员会调查提供;高校资料由上海市教育委员会调查提供;科协系统科技活动资料由上海市科学技术协会调查提供;专利资料由上海市知识产权局调查提供。

四、本篇的调查方法

研究与试验发展(R&D)活动情况采用全面调查取得;科协、专利资料采用抽样等多种调查方法取得。

五、统计资料口径变化

2000 年以前科技活动统计资料只包括大中型工业企业、政府部门属研究机构、普通高等学校,2000 年及以后年份扩大到了全社会范围。

BRIEF INTRODUCTION

I. Main Contents

Data on science and technology mainly include: data on scientific and technological activities, R&D activities all over the country, including industrial enterprises, scientific and technological institutions under government departments, universities and colleges; data on technological markets; data on science and technology achievements; data on scientific and technological research institutions run by local people; data on the scientific and technological activities in the system of associations for science and technology; patents application accepted and granted.

II. Statistical Range

Data on science and technology include research and development (R&D) activities of enterprises and institutions all over the country, mainly including industrial enterprises, scientific and technological institutions under government departments, universities, colleges and relatively R&D–intensive industries (such as agriculture, forestry, animal husbandry, fisher, construction, transport, storage and post, information transmission, computer services and software, financial intermediation, leasing and business services, scientific research, technical service and geologic prospecting, management of water conservancy, environment and public facilities, health, social security and social welfare, culture, sports and entertainment).

III. Data Sources

Data on national aggregates and R&D activities of various enterprises and institutions are from Shanghai Municipal Statistics Bureau; data on scientific and technological institutions under government departments are from Science and Technology Commission of Shanghai Municipality、Shanghai Municipal Commission of Economy and Informatization; data on R&D activities of scientific research、technical service、geologic prospecting, and technological markets, scientific and technical payoffs, scientific and technological research institutions run by local people are from Science and Technology Commission of Shanghai Municipality; data on scientific and technological activities in universities and colleges are from Shanghai Municipal Education Commission; data on the scientific and technological activities of associations for science and technology are from Science and Technology Commission of Shanghai Municipality; Shanghai Intellectual Property Administration provides data on patents.

IV. Statistical Methodology

Data on R&D activities are collected through complete surveys. Data on scientific and technological associations and patent applications are through sample surveys and other surveys.

V. Changes of the statistical coverage of data

Before 2000, data only included large and medium–sized industrial enterprises, scientific research institutions under government departments, and universities and colleges. Since 2000 (inclusive), data have covered all industries.

表 19.1 主要年份科技活动主要指标
MAIN INDICATORS OF SCIENTIFIC AND TECHNOLOGICAL ACTIVITIES IN MAIN YEARS

年 份 Year	科技活动人员 (万人) Personnel Engaged in Scientific and Technological Activities (10 000 persons)	研究与试验发展(R&D)人员全时当量(万人年) Full-time Equivalent of R&D Personnel (10 000 person-years)	研究与试验发展(R&D)经费内部支出(亿元) Expenditures on R&D (100 million yuan)	研究与试验发展经费支出相当于上海市生产总值比例(%) R&D as Percentage of Gross Domestic Product (%)	地方财政科技经费支出(亿元) Local Fiscal Expenditures on Scientific and Technological Research (100 million yuan)	科技经费支出占地方财政支出比重(%) Percentage of Expenditures on Scientific and Technological Research in Local Fiscal (%)
1990	19.34		10.13	1.30	2.44	3.2
1995	18.25		32.60	1.30	5.12	2.0
2000	20.17	6.31	76.73	1.61	10.08	1.6
2001	17.57	5.20	88.08	1.69	12.39	1.7
2002	17.89	5.02	102.36	1.78	15.25	1.7
2003	17.59	5.62	128.92	1.93	19.84	1.8
2004	18.25	5.73	170.28	2.11	39.32	2.8
2005	19.67	7.07	213.77	2.31	79.34	4.8
2006	20.07	8.01	258.84	2.45	94.89	5.2
2007	22.79	9.03	307.50	2.46	105.77	4.9
2008	23.08	9.75	362.30	2.58	120.27	4.6
2009	33.90	13.29	423.38	2.81	215.31	7.2
2010	33.46	13.50	481.70	2.81	202.03	6.1
2011	37.53	14.85	597.71	3.11	218.50	5.6
2012	38.89	15.59	679.46	3.37	245.43	5.9

注：本表部分数据由上海市财政局等部门提供。
Note: Data in this table are mainly provided by Shanghai Municipal Finance Bureau.

表 19.2 主要年份研究与试验发展(R&D)经费按执行部门分类
EXPENDITURES ON R&D GROUPED BY EXECUTIVE DEPARTMENT IN MAIN YEARS

单位:亿元(100 million yuan)

指 标	Indicators	2000	2010	2011	2012
总 计	**Total**	**76.73**	**481.70**	**597.71**	**679.46**
科研机构	Research Institutions	25.58	105.35	133.58	180.98
高等院校	Institutions of Higher Education	7.43	45.80	54.83	61.70
企 业	Enterprises	41.44	321.31	397.91	426.34
#工业企业	Industrial Enterprises	34.78	274.05	343.76	371.51
#大中型工业企业	Large and Medium Industrial Enterprises	30.98	237.75	288.84	317.48
其 他	Others	2.28	9.25	11.39	10.44

表 19.3 主要年份研究与试验发展(R&D)活动情况
RESEARCH AND DEVELOPMENT(R&D)ACTIVITIES IN MAIN YEARS

	指 标 Indicators	2000	2010	2011	2012
有 R&D 活动单位数(个)	**Quantity of Science and Technology Institutions (unit)**	**1 070**	**1 782**	**2 074**	**2 152**
#科研机构	Research Institutions	125	113	109	112
高等院校	Institutions of Higher Education	41	68	68	68
企 业	Enterprises	820	1 453	1 746	1 826
其 他	Others	84	148	151	146
R&D 人员投入情况	**Personnel Investment on R&D**				
R&D 人员(万人)	R&D Personnel(10 000 persons)		17.75	19.87	20.88
R&D 人员全时当量(万人年)	Full-time Equivalent of R&D Personnel(10 000 person-years)	6.31	13.50	14.85	15.34
基础研究	Basic Research	0.60	1.42	1.45	1.61
应用研究	Applied Research	1.92	2.29	2.49	2.44
试验发展	Experimental Development	3.79	9.79	10.91	11.29
R&D 经费投入情况	**Expenditure on R&D**				
R&D 经费内部支出(亿元)	Intramural Expenditure on R&D (100 million yuan)	76.73	481.70	597.71	679.46
#基础研究	Basic Research	4.98	31.05	37.78	49.16
应用研究	Applied Research	18.18	68.99	92.43	91.58
试验发展	Experimental Development	53.57	381.67	467.50	538.72
#政府资金	Government Funds	24.22	142.78	175.93	225.76
企业资金	Self-raised Funds by Enterprises	33.76	318.28	392.05	413.61
境外资金	Offshore Funds	4.79	6.80	10.23	7.19
其 他	Others	13.96	13.83	19.50	32.90
R&D 项目(课题)情况	**R&D project**				
项目(课题)数(万项)	Quantity of Projects (10 000 item)	2.07	5.56	6.18	6.58
项目(课题)参加人员(万人年)	Personnel Engaged in Projects (10 000 person-years)	5.42	11.89	13.14	13.94
项目(课题)经费内部支出(亿元)	Inner Expenditure on Projects (100 million yuan)	54.31	379.37	455.18	510.98
科技活动产出情况	**Output of Science and Technic Activities**				
新产品产值(亿元)	Production Value of New Product(100 million yuan)	1 401.62	5 870.02	7 142.05	6 652.92
新产品销售收入(亿元)	Sales Revenue of New Product(100 million yuan)	1 398.54	6 543.07	7 772.20	7 399.91
专利申请数(件)	Patent Applications(piece)	11 337	71 196	80 215	82 682
#发明专利	Invention Patents	4 713	26 165	32 142	37 139
专利授权数(件)	Patents Granted(piece)	4 050	48 215	47 960	51 508
#发明专利	Invention Patents	304	6 867	9 160	11 379
有效发明专利数(件)	Effective Invention Patents(piece)		23 843	31 117	40 309
发表科技论文数(篇)	Quantity of Science and Technic Papers Published(case)	37 216	87 971	90 352	91 088
出版科技著作(种)	Science and Technic Works Published(piece)	2 614	3 329	3 121	3 306
商标申请注册数(件)	Register Applications for Trade Marks (case)	9 455	60 243	83 998	91 867
商标核准注册数(件)	Registration approved for Trade Marks (case)	6 208	70 417	56 540	59 679
科技成果登记数(项)	Quantity of Achievements Registered in Scientific and Technological Activities(item)	1 102	2 318	2 388	2 415

注：本表部分数据由市知识产权局、市工商局和市科学技术委员会提供。

Note: Data in this table are partly provided by Shanghai Intellectual Property Service Center, Shanghai Administration of Industry and Commerce and Shanghai Municipal Science and Technology Commission.

表 19.4 国有企事业单位专业技术人员基本情况(2012)
PROFESSIONAL AND TECHNICAL PERSONNEL IN STATE-OWNED ENTERPRISES AND INSTITUTIONS

单位:万人(10 000 persons)

类别	Types	合计 Total	其中 of which	按学历分 by Education Background		
			#女性 Female	大学本专科以上 College and University above	中等专业 Specialized Secondary School	高中及以下 Senior Middle School and below
总计	**Total**	**89.91**	**43.77**	**80.36**	**6.16**	**3.38**
高级岗位	Senior	9.43	3.52	9.35	0.05	0.03
中级岗位	Medium	27.38	14.16	26.24	0.87	0.27
初级岗位	Junior	29.36	14.79	24.46	3.70	1.20
未聘人员	Not Appointed	23.73	11.30	20.31	1.54	1.88

表 19.4 续表 continued

单位:万人(10 000 persons)

类别	Types	合计 Total	其中 of which	按学历分 by Education Background		
			#女性 Female	大学本专科以上 College and University above	中等专业 Specialized Secondary School	高中及以下 Senior Middle School and below
总计	**Total**	**89.91**	**43.77**	**80.37**	**6.16**	**3.38**
工程技术人员	Engineering	24.53	5.13	21.91	1.53	1.08
农业技术人员	Agriculture	0.34	0.10	0.25	0.06	0.03
卫生技术人员	Scientific Research	2.50	0.86	2.46	0.03	0.02
科学研究人员	Medical Prlfessionals	10.63	7.64	8.78	1.76	0.10
教学人员	Teching	17.57	12.23	17.30	0.23	0.04
经济人员	Economic	22.77	11.27	19.67	1.60	1.49
财会人员	Financial Accounting	6.47	4.22	5.66	0.58	0.22
统计人员	Statistical	0.68	0.39	0.55	0.07	0.06
新闻出版、播音人员	Translator	0.12	0.07	0.12		
翻译人员	Media, Publishing & Announcer	0.87	0.47	0.83	0.02	0.02
艺术人员	Culture & Art	0.59	0.23	0.42	0.09	0.08
其他专业人员	Others	2.84	1.16	2.41	0.19	0.24

注:本页数据由市委组织部提供。
Note: Data on this page are provided by Shanghai Municipal Party Committee Orgonization Department.

表 19.5　主要年份各类技术合同项目
VARIOUS TECHNOLOGICAL CONTRACTS IN MAIN YEARS

单位:项(item)

年份 Year	项目 Item	其中 of which 技术开发 Technological Development	技术转让 Technological Transfer	技术咨询 Technological Consulting	技术服务 Technological Service
1991	25 023	3 038	1 992	3 203	16 790
1995	21 213	1 915	775	3 672	14 851
1996	20 074	1 841	823	3 821	13 589
1997	18 863	1 643	1 037	3 569	12 614
1998	18 364	1 206	919	3 235	13 004
1999	19 721	1 158	937	3 993	13 633
2000	20 974	1 561	888	3 905	14 620
2001	23 816	2 385	1 294	5 012	15 125
2002	26 010	2 984	1 156	4 983	16 887
2003	27 292	3 512	2 112	5 306	16 362
2004	27 327	4 398	2 453	4 814	15 662
2005	30 290	5 256	2 444	4 753	17 837
2006	28 191	6 165	2 172	3 592	16 262
2007	27 742	6 425	2 133	3 086	16 098
2008	28 713	7 154	1 749	3 873	15 937
2009	27 109	8 071	1 549	3 034	14 455
2010	26 185	8 894	1 370	2 685	13 236
2011	29 332	10 771	1 317	3 277	13 967
2012	27 998	10 974	1 170	3 026	12 828

表 19.6　主要年份各类技术合同成交金额
TOTAL CONTRACTED VALUE IN VARIOUS TECHNOLOGICAL CONTRACTS IN MAIN YEARS

单位:亿元(100 million yuan)

年份 Year	成交金额 Contracted Value	其中 of which 技术开发 Technological Development	技术转让 Technological Transfer	技术咨询 Technological Consulting	技术服务 Technological Service
1991	9.33	2.15	1.90	0.55	4.72
1995	23.04	4.14	1.57	2.12	15.21
1996	25.65	4.38	1.50	2.81	16.97
1997	28.76	5.72	2.14	3.28	17.61
1998	31.41	4.55	2.58	2.44	21.85
1999	36.63	3.68	3.50	3.24	26.21
2000	73.90	9.96	36.44	3.51	23.99
2001	106.16	28.24	50.71	4.63	22.58
2002	120.22	45.40	46.18	4.63	24.01
2003	142.78	50.96	50.79	6.11	34.92
2004	171.70	61.31	42.32	6.00	62.07
2005	231.73	87.47	110.08	6.42	27.76
2006	344.43	142.79	165.18	7.60	28.86
2007	432.64	181.50	212.49	5.50	33.15
2008	485.75	213.24	229.53	6.41	36.57
2009	489.86	266.30	174.34	5.39	43.83
2010	525.45	264.68	213.86	4.93	41.98
2011	550.32	328.25	164.49	5.40	52.18
2012	588.52	297.14	223.48	5.17	62.73

注：本页数据由市技术市场管理办公室提供。
Note: Data on this page are provided by Shanghai Technology Market Administrative Office.

表 19.7 科技成果（2000～2012）
ACHIEVEMENTS IN SCIENTIFIC AND TECHNICAL RESEARCH

单位：项(item)

年 份 Year	科技成果 Achievements in Science and Technology	按成果水平分 By Level of Achievements			
		# 国际领先 Being First Created in the World	# 国际先进 Attaining Advanced World Levels	# 国内领先 Being First Created in China	# 国内先进 Attaining Advanced Domestic Levels
2000	1 102	45	462	452	117
2001	1 338	78	542	444	116
2002	1 418	65	603	463	106
2003	1 508	71	532	481	155
2004	1 629	147	669	480	155
2005	1 701	123	629	588	189
2006	1 953	250	675	655	191
2007	2 396	180	761	938	254
2008	1 866	125	664	663	226
2009	2 166	260	651	831	247
2010	2 318	188	698	724	202
2011	2 388	211	598	568	158
2012	2 415	177	572	596	142

表 19.7 续表 continued

单位：项(item)

年 份 Year	按成果分 By Type of Achievements				
	基础理论成果 Fundamental Theory Research Results	应用技术成果 Application of Technological Achievements	其 中 of which		软科学成果 Soft Scientific Achievements
			已推广应用 Been Populized	未应用 Not Been Populized	
2000	79	953	809	144	70
2001	81	1 196	940	256	61
2002	110	1 250	961	289	58
2003	97	1 281	1 045	236	130
2004	70	1 488	1 204	284	71
2005	61	1 555	1 261	294	85
2006	52	1 799	1 506	293	102
2007	139	2 162	1 724	438	95
2008	115	1 695	1 337	358	56
2009	94	2 009	1 747	262	63
2010	152	2 104	1 824	280	62
2011	182	2 137	1 943	194	69
2012	218	2 112	1 914	198	85

表 19.8 主要年份科研机构研究与试验发展(R&D)活动情况
RESEARCH AND DEVELOPMENT(R&D)ACTIVITIES OF SCIENTIFIC RESEARCH INSTITUTIONS IN MAIN YEARS

指标	Indicators	2000	2010	2011	2012
有 R&D 活动单位数(个)	**Quantity of Science and Technology Institutions (unit)**	**125**	**113**	**109**	**112**
R&D 人员投入情况	**Personnel Investment on R&D**				
R&D 人员(人)	R&D Personnel(person)		26 550	28 082	30 076
R&D 人员全时当量(人年)	Full-time Equivalent of R&D Personnel(person-years)	19 802	23 241	25 256	27 199
#基础研究	Basic Research	2 675	3 781	4 254	4 922
应用研究	Applied Research	8 873	8 771	9 626	10 592
试验发展	Experimental Development	8 254	10 689	11 376	11 685
R&D 经费投入情况	**Expenditure on R&D**				
R&D 经费内部支出(亿元)	Intramural Expenditure on R&D (100 million yuan)	25.58	105.35	133.58	180.98
#基础研究	Basic Research	3.06	13.87	16.94	24.80
应用研究	Applied Research	9.84	34.51	42.37	49.34
试验发展	Experimental Development	12.68	56.97	74.27	106.84
#政府资金	Government Funds	18.89	88.98	111.65	147.53
企业资金	Self-raised Funds by Enterprises	1.09	6.61	6.85	3.85
境外资金	Offshore Funds	0.69	0.54	0.58	1.02
R&D 项目(课题)情况	**R&D project**				
R&D 项目(课题)数(项)	Quantity of Projects (10 000 item)	3 190	5 933	5 981	6 732
R&D 项目(课题)人员全时当量(人年)	Personnell Engaged in Projects (10 000 person-years)	14 015	18 799	20 070	24 380
R&D 项目(课题)经费内部支出(亿元)	Inner Expenditure on Projects (100 million yuan)	8.56	58.99	72.64	120.18
科技产出及成果情况	**Output of Science and Technic Activities**				
发表科技论文数(篇)	Quantity of Science and Technic Papers Published(case)	6 831	7 896	8 382	9 275
出版科技著作(种)	Works of Science and Technology Published(kind)	187	197	169	229
专利申请受理数(件)	Number of Patents Applications(piece)	425	1 864	2 296	3 168
#发明专利	Inventions	275	1 593	1 888	2 489
专利申请授权数(件)	Number of Patents Application Granted(piece)		817	1 183	1 513
#发明专利	Inventions		502	744	1 057
有效发明专利数(件)	Effective Invention Patents(piece)	779	2 732	3 084	4 201

表 19.9 主要年份获得科技成果奖励情况
ACHIEVEMENTS AWARDED IN SCIENTIFIC AND TECHNOLOGICAL RESEARCH IN MAIN YEARS

单位:项(item)

指 标	Indicators	2000	2010	2011	2012
科技成果获奖总数	**Quantity of Achievements Awarded**	**287**	**298**	**333**	**333**
获国家科技成果奖	**National Award**	**21**	**58**	**56**	**51**
#国家最高科学技术奖(人)	State Supreme Science Award		1		
国家自然科学奖	Natural Science Award	3	6	5	7
国家技术发明奖	Technological Invention Award	1	4	7	7
国家科学技术进步奖	Science and Technology Progress Award	17	46	41	36
国际科学技术合作奖(人)	International Science and Technology Cooperation Award		1	3	1
获上海科技进步奖	**Shanghai Award**	**266**	**240**	**277**	**282**

表 19.10 主要年份自然科学研究与技术开发机构课题情况
PROJECTS OF NATURAL SCIENCE RESEARCH AND TECHNOLOGICAL DEVELOPMENT INSTITUTIONS IN MAIN YEARS

年 份 Year	机构数 (个) Quantity of Institutions (unit)	课题数 (项) Quantity of Projects (item)	投入人力 (人年) Manpower Input (person-year)	投入经费 (万元) Funds Invested (10 000 yuan)
1990	229	8 339	23 279	33 061
1995	230	6 544	17 531	80 957
1996	233	5 538	17 434	90 504
1997	232	5 481	17 507	117 199
1998	230	5 554	16 713	122 513
1999	225	5 135	16 396	125 620
2000	229	4 879	17 104	148 846
2001	221	4 468	16 972	210 910
2002	218	4 393	15 523	251 837
2003	216	4 473	17 058	282 865
2004	212	4 540	17 299	330 063
2005	206	4 416	18 924	425 266
2006	202	4 585	19 008	494 657
2007	199	5 534	20 443	542 601
2008	194	6 006	21 111	719 082
2009	195	6 653	23 773	698 690
2010	191	7 141	26 080	992 896
2011	182	7 356	26 643	1 215 674
2012	180	8 031	29 745	1 324 384

表 19.11　自然科学研究与技术开发机构课题情况(2012)
STATISTICS OF PROJECTS OF NATURAL SCIENCE RESEARCH AND DEVELOPMENT INSTITUTIONS

类别	Types	机构数（个）Number of Institutions (unit)	课题数（项）Number of Projects (item)	投入人力（人年）Manpower Input (person-year)	投入经费（万元）Funds Invested (10 000 yuan)
总　计	**Total**	**180**	**8 031**	**29 745**	**1 324 384**
按学科分	**By Subject**				
自然科学	Natural Science	18	3 384	3 552	221 339
农业科学	Agriculture Science	19	721	930	26 734
医学科学	Medical Science	17	1 103	1 866	50 207
工程科学与技术	Engineering Science and Technology	122	2 802	23 335	1 025 089
社会与人文科学	Social Science and Humanities	4	21	62	1 013
按行业分	**By Sector**				
#制造业	Manufacturing	88	1 481	16 932	827 770
建筑业	Construction	4	143	319	11 383
交通运输、仓储和邮政业	Transportation, Warehousing and Post	4	30	102	2 445
科学研究和技术服务业	Scientific Research and Technical Service	44	4 933	10 046	433 902
水利、环境和公共设施管理业	Water Conservancy, Environment and Public Facility Management	8	245	473	5 821
卫生和社会工作	Health and Social Work	13	511	889	12 984

表 19.12　自然科学研究与技术开发机构论文与著作情况（2012）
PAPERS AND WORKS OF NATURAL SCIENCE RESEARCH AND TECHNOLOGICAL DEVELOPMENT INSTITUTIONS

类别	Types	论文（篇）Papers (piece)	其中 of which #国外发表 Issued Abroad	科技著作（种）Scientific and Technological Works (sort)
总　计	**Total**	**9 567**	**3 643**	**215**
按学科领域分	**By Subject**			
自然科学	Natural Science	2 614	1 648	38
农业科学	Agriculture Science	874	205	11
医学科学	Medical Science	1 576	830	35
工程科学与技术	Engineering Science and Technology	4 479	957	128
社会与人文科学	Social and Humanities Science	24	3	3
按行业分	**By Sector**			
#农、林、牧、渔业	Farming, Forestry, Animal Husbandry and Fishery	755	201	9
制造业	Manufacturing	2 524	393	123
电力、热力、燃气及水生产和供应业	Electric Power, Thermal, Steam and Water Production and Supply	321	2	1
建筑业	Construction	46	6	7
科学研究和技术服务业	Scientific Research and Technical Service	4 694	2 589	46
卫生和社会工作	Health and Social Work	871	385	23

表 19.13　区县级以上国有单位独立研究与开发机构人员(2012)
PERSONNEL OF STATE-OWNED INDEPENDENT RESEARCH AND DEVELOPMENT INSTITUTIONS ABOVE DISTRICT AND COUNTY LEVEL

单位:人(person)

类　别	Types	从事科技活动人员 Personnel Engaged in Scientific and Technological Activities	其　中　of which			
			#R&D 人员 R&D Personnel	#高中级技术职称人　员 Personnel with High and Medium Technic Titles	#研究生 Post-graduates	#大　学 University and College
总　计	**Total**	**45 715**	**37 974**	**27 101**	**18 354**	**17 858**
按隶属关系分	**By Subordination**					
中国科学院	The Chinese Academy of Science	7 624	11 303	5 447	4 625	1 889
国务院部门	Departments of the State Council	25 573	20 632	14 568	9 259	10 728
地　方	Local	12 518	6 039	7 086	4 470	5 241
按领域分	**By Subject**					
自然科学	Natural Science	43 470	37 286	25 513	17 381	17 026
社会与人文科学	Social Sciences and Humanities	1 133	677	899	728	245
科技信息文献	Scientific & Technological Information & Documents	1 112	11	689	245	587

表 19.14　主要年份区县级属研究与开发机构状况
RESEARCH AND DEVELOPMENT INSTITUTIONS AT DISTRICT AND COUNTY LEVEL IN MAIN YEARS

指　标	Indicators	2000	2010	2011	2012
机构数(个)	Quantity of Institutions (unit)	35	18	17	17
从业人员(人)	Quantity of Employees (person)	1 261	1 015	947	939
#从事科技活动人员	Personnel Engaged in Science and Technic Activities	736	764	727	777
科技活动经费内部支出(万元)	Inner Expenditures on Science and Technic Activities (10 000 yuan)	7 343	15 482	16 353	18 175

表 19.15 主要年份高等学校研究与试验发展(R&D)活动情况
RESERCH AND DEVELOPMENT(R&D) ACTIVITIES OF HIGHER EDUCATION IN MAIN YEARS

指标	Indicators	2000	2010	2011	2012
有 R&D 活动单位数(个)	**Quantity of Science and Technology Institutions (unit)**	**41**	**68**	**68**	**68**
#理工农医	Science, Engineering, Agriculture and Medicine		38	38	38
人文社科	Humanity and Social Science		30	30	30
R&D 人员投入情况	**Personnel Investment on R&D**				
R&D 人员(人)	R&D Personnel(person)		38 175	37 514	38 348
R&D 人员全时当量(人年)	Full-time Equivalent of R&D Personnel (person-year)	10 816	21 565	21 011	21 171
#基础研究	Basic Research	3 015	9 026	8 905	9 801
应用研究	Applied Research	6 378	10 387	10 523	9 867
试验发展	Experimental Development	1 423	2 152	1 583	1 502
R&D 经费投入情况	**Expenditure on R&D**				
R&D 经费内部支出(亿元)	Intramural Expenditure on R&D (100 million yuan)	7.43	45.80	54.83	61.70
#基础研究	Basic Research	1.44	15.19	18.84	22.52
应用研究	Applied Research	4.50	24.71	29.00	31.42
试验发展	Experimental Development	1.49	5.90	6.99	7.76
#政府资金	Government Funds	3.26	27.33	34.26	39.91
企业资金	Self-raised Funds by Enterprises	3.38	15.47	18.27	19.40
境外资金	Offshore Funds	0.31	0.67	0.54	0.30
R&D 课题情况	**R&D Projects**				
R&D 课题数(项)	Quantity of Projects(item)	12 525	36 656	39 629	42 572
R&D 课题人员全时当量(人年)	Full-time Equivalent of Personnel in Projects(person-year)	15 945	21 541	20 995	21 130
R&D 课题经费内部支出(亿元)	Inner Expenditure on Projects (100 million yuan)	7.28	32.96	38.08	43.49
科技产出及成果情况	**Output of Science and Technic Activities**				
发表科技论文(篇)	Quantity of Science and Technic Papers Published(case)	25 896	70 290	71 669	71 343
出版科技著作(种)	Works of Science and Technology Published(sort)	2 206	3 020	2 822	2 940
专利申请数(件)	Number of Patents Applications(piece)	527	6 828	8 003	8 770
#发明专利	Inventions	385	4 834	5 544	6 213
专利授权数(件)	Number of Patents Application Granted(piece)		4 035	4 780	6 316
#发明专利	Inventions		2 169	2 599	3 511
有效发明专利数(件)	Effective Invention Patents(piece)		11 558	14 010	11 013

表 19.16 高等学校科技活动人员（2012）
SCIENTIFIC AND TECHNOLOGICAL PERSONNEL OF INSTITUTIONS OF HIGHER EDUCATION

单位：人（person）

指标	Indicators	合计 Total	其中 of which 自然科学 Natural Science	工程与技术 Engineering and Technology	医学科学 Medical Science	农业科学 Agriculture Science	其他 Others
总计	**Total**	**45 339**	**5 038**	**14 040**	**21 363**	**375**	**4 523**
#科学家和工程师	Scientists and Engineers	43 099	4 966	13 666	20 248	362	3 857
按职称分	By Professional Title						
高级	Senior	15 384	2 854	6 400	5 172	186	772
中级	Medium	17 452	1 831	5 886	7 427	137	2 171
初级	Junior	10 263	281	1 380	7 649	39	914

表 19.17 高等学校研究机构和课题情况（2012）
RESEARCH INSTITUTIONS AND PROJECT OF HIGHER EDUCATION

指标	Indicators	合计 Total	其中 of which #自然科学 Natural Science	#工程与技术 Engineering and Technology	#医学科学 Medical Science	#农业科学 Agriculture Science
研究机构数（个）	Research Institutions(unit)	256	52	123	74	4
机构 R&D 人员（人）	Institutions Personnel of R&D(person)	8 003	1 823	4 133	1 899	83
机构 R&D 经费支出（亿元）	R&D expenditure of Institutions (100 million yuan)	8.49	1.95	5.15	1.22	0.15
课题数（个）	Quantity of Projects of R&D (unit)	28 910	4 864	14 964	8 315	767
课题投入人员（人年）	Project Personnel(person-year)	18 743.6	2 582.8	8 044.6	7 851.5	264.7
课题投入经费(亿元)	Project Funding(100 million yuan)	79.62	12.34	52.52	12.81	1.95
课题经费支出（亿元）	Project Expenditure(100 million yuan)	57.87	9.07	38.44	9.30	1.06

注：本页统计范围是指高等学校中理工农医类口径。
Note: Figures of this page refer to those of science, engineering, agriculture and medicine of higher education.

表 19.13 主要年份专利申请量和授权量
PATENT APPLICATIONS AND CERTIFIED IN MAIN YEARS

单位：件(item)

指 标	Indicators	2000	2010	2011	2012
专利申请量	**Patent Applications**	**11 337**	**71 196**	**80 215**	**82 682**
#发 明	Inventions	4 713	26 165	32 142	37 139
专利授权量	**Patent Certified**	**4 050**	**48 215**	**47 960**	**51 508**
#发 明	Inventions	304	6 867	9 160	11 379
有效发明专利	Effective Invention Patents		23 843	31 117	40 309
PCT 国际专利受理	PCT International Patent Application Accepted		735	847	1 024

表 19.19 科协系统出版物和科技服务情况(2012)
PUBLICATIONS AND CONSULTATIVE ACTIVITIES OF SCIENCE AND TECHNOLOGY ASSOCIATIONS

指 标	Indicators	合 计 Total	其中 of which: 市级科协 Municipal level Associations	区(县)级科协 District and County Level Associations	市级学会 Municipal Level Societies
出版物	**Publications**				
主办科技期刊(种)	Scientific Journals(sort)	83	1	6	76
科技期刊总印数(万册)	Total Printed (10 000 copies)	467	49	7	411
编著科技图书(种)	Science and Technology Books (sort)	282	262	1	19
科技图书总印数(万册)	Total Printed of Science and Technology Books (10 000 copies)	28	8	1	19
主办科技报纸(种)	Technology Newspaper (sort)	5	2		3
科技报纸总印数(万份)	Total Printed of Technology Newspaper (10 000 copies)	703	699		4
咨 询	**Consultation**				
提供决策咨询报告(篇)	Decision Consultation Reports (sheet)	323	25	123	175
#获上级领导批示报告(篇)	Marking by superiors (sheet)	62		33	29
举办决策咨询活动(次)	Decision Consultation Activities (time)	251	44	85	122
参加决策咨询活动专家数(人次)	Experts Participating in Decision Consultation Activities(person-time)	1 908	520	494	894

表 19.20 科协系统科普活动和科技培训情况（2012）
PROMOTING SCIENCE ACTIVITIES AND TRAINING PROGRAM ORGANIZED BY SCIENCE AND TECHNOLOGY ASSOCIATIONS

指 标	Indicators	合 计 Total	其中 of which 市级科协 Municipal level Associations	区(县)级科协 District and County Level Associations	市级学会 Municipal Level Societies
举办科普宣讲活动(次)	Science Propaganda Activities (time)	10 189	307	8 488	1 394
科普宣讲活动参加人次(万人次)	Participants in Science Propaganda Activities (10 000 person-times)	494.02	35.93	317.86	140.23
举办实用技术培训(次)	Practical Technical Training (time)	2 732	48	1 828	856
实用技术培训参加人数(万人次)	Trainees of Practical Technical Training (10 000 person-times)	37.87	0.17	30.17	7.53
举办青少年科技竞赛(次)	Youth Science Competition (time)	867	4	789	74
青少年科技竞赛参加人数(万人次)	Competitors of Youth Science Competition (10 000 person-times)	117.74	35.20	47.43	35.11
青少年科技竞赛获奖人数(人次)	Winners of Youth Science Competition(person-time)	30 579	5 000	23 068	2 511
青少年参加国际及港澳台科技交流活动(次)	International and Hong Kong, Macao and Taiwan Technology Exchange Activities (time)	41	10	27	4
青少年参加国际及港澳台科技交流活动人数(人次)	Participants in International and Hong Kong, Macao and Taiwan Technology Exchange Activities(person-time)	1 436	500	804	132
举办青少年科学营(次)	Youth Science Camp (time)	157	3	123	31
青少年科学营参加人数(人次)	Participants in Youth Science Camp(person-time)	81 737	1 235	77 776	2 726
举办青少年科技教育培训(次)	Youth Science and Technology Education and Training (time)	2 118	390	1 477	251
青少年科技教育培训参加人数(万人次)	Trainees of Youth Science and Technology Education and Training (10 000 person-times)	44.64	9.01	34.56	1.06

表 19.21 各级科协机构和人员（2012）
INSTITUTIONS AND PERSONNEL OF SCIENCE AND TECHNOLOGY ASSOCIATIONS AT VARIOUS LEVELS

指 标	Indicators	市级科协 Municipal Level Associations	区级科协 District Level Associations	县级科协 County Level Associations
机构数（个）	Institutions(unit)	1	16	1
人 员(人)	Personnel(person)	69	223	6
各级学会在册个数（个）	All Levels Societies Registered(unit)	185	427	28

表 19.21 续表 continued

指 标	Indicators	机构数(个) Quantity of Institutions (unit)	个人会员(万人) Individual Members (10 000 persons)	团体会员数(个) Organization Members (unit)	所属分科学会(个) Attached Associations (unit)
市级学会	Prefectural Societies	185	21.62	14 686	992

表 19.22 科协系统学术交流情况（2012）
ACADEMIC EXCHANGES OF SCIENCE AND TECHNOLOGY ASSOCIATIONS

指 标	Indicators	合 计 Total	其中 of which #市级科协 Municipal Level Associations	#市级学会 Municipal Level Academies
国内学术会议	**Domestic Academic Conferences**			
举办次数（次数）	Times(time)	2 801	8	2 181
参加人数（人次）	Participants (person-times)	296 376	28 060	218 654
交流论文（篇）	Papers Exchanged (piece)	38 687	1 691	34 900
境内国际学术会议	**International Academic Conferences**			
举办次数（次数）	Times(time)	201	1	175
参加人数（人次）	Participants (person-times)	44 724	126	40 349
交流论文（篇）	Papers Exchanged (piece)	6 821	73	6 354
港澳台地区学术会议	**Quantity of Academic Meeting Related with Hong Kong, Macao and Taiwan**			
举办次数（次数）	Times(time)	27	1	26
参加人数（人次）	Participants (person-times)	2 742	260	2 482
交流论文（篇）	Papers Exchanged (piece)	736	125	611
参加国外科技活动人数（人次）	**Participants in Foreign Scientific and Technological Activities (person-time)**	**504**	**15**	**453**
参加港澳台地区科技活动人数（人次）	**Participants in Hong Kong, Macao and Taiwan Scientific and Technological Activities (person-time)**	**563**	**22**	**521**
接待国外专家学者（人次）	**Reception of Foreign Experts and Scholars (person-time)**	**1 119**	**108**	**946**
接待港澳台地区专家学者（人次）	**Reception of Hong Kong, Macao and Taiwan Experts and Scholars (person-time)**	**319**	**20**	**258**

表 19.23　主要年份民营科技企业状况
SCIENTIFIC AND TECHNOLOGICAL RESEARCH INSTITUTIONS RUN BY LOCAL PEOPLE IN MAIN YEARS

指　标	Indicators	2000	2010	2011	2012
机构数（个）	**Number of Institutions (unit)**	**12 316**	**18 008**	**21 117**	**24 226**
从业人员（万人）	**Employment (10 000 persons)**	**26.33**	**94.25**	**123.79**	**131.66**
#从事科技活动人员	Scientific & Technological Personnel	12.95	21.69	29.62	31.40
#高中级技术职称人员	Personnel with Medium and Senior Titles	8.90	12.12	14.61	14.74
资产总额(亿元)	Total Assets(100 million yuan)	1 064.07	9 070.91	14 970.39	15 851.28
总收入(亿元)	Revenue(100 million yuan)	811.35	8 462.57	14 567.37	12 307.78
企业内部用于科技活动的经费支出(亿元)	Inner Expenditure on Scientific and Technological Activities (100 million yuan)		473.32	587.29	608.44
当年形成用于科技活动的固定资产(亿元)	Annual Fixed Assets Formation on Scientific and Technological Activities (100 million yuan)		78.17	103.30	104.44
使用来自政府部门的科技活动资金(亿元)	Government Funds on Scientific and Technological Activities (100 million yuan)		69.80	80.35	49.55
委托外单位开展科技活动的经费支出(亿元)	External Expenditure on Scientific and Technological Activities (100 million yuan)		14.52	30.98	27.50
工业总产值(亿元)	Gross Output Value(100 million yuan)	311.22	5 687.91	7 670.93	7 536.24
利润总额(亿元)	Total Pre-tax Profits(100 million yuan)	47.58	601.59	1 099.65	878.65
税金总额(亿元)	Total Tax and Duties(100 million yuan)	28.64	417.57	653.34	660.04
出口创汇(亿美元)	Foreign Exchange Income(100 million USD)	2.83	647.36	452.87	319.04
专利申请量(件)	Patent Applications(piece)	452	31 997	23 936	31 192
#发明专利	Inventions		11 259	13 446	14 111
专利授权量(件)	Patent Certified(piece)	1 169	15 052	18 805	21 858
#发明专利	Inventions		3 912	5 203	5 967

注：本表统计范围是指经上海市科委确认的独立核算国有、集体、私营以及国有与集体联营等科技型中小企业。

Note: Private Scientific and Technological Enterprises in the table refers to the small and medium enterprises with independent accounting systems such as state-owned, collective-owned, individual, private and state-collective joint units certified by Shanghai Municipal Science and Technology Commission.

表 19.24 主要年份规模以上工业企业研究与试验发展(R&D)活动情况
BASIC STATISTICS OF SCIENTIFIC AND TECHNOLOGICAL ACTIVITIES IN MAIN YEARS

指 标	Indicators	2000	2010	2011	2012
有 R&D 活动单位数(个)	**Quantity of Science and Technology Institutions (unit)**	**327**	**1 193**	**1 480**	**1 562**
R&D 人员投入情况	**Personnel Investment on R&D**				
R&D 人员(人)	R&D Personnel(person)	26 253	82 095	100 298	108 347
R&D 人员全时当量(人年)	Full-time Equivalent of R&D Personnel(person-year)	20 576	69 077	79 147	82 355
#基础研究	Basic Research			11	
应用研究	Applied Research	764	244	1 085	409
试验发展	Experimental Development	19 812	68 833	78 066	81 946
R&D 经费投入情况	**Expenditure on R&D**				
R&D 经费内部支出(亿元)	Intramural Expenditure on R&D (100 million yuan)	31.15	274.05	343.76	371.51
#基础研究	Basic Research			0.01	
应用研究	Applied Research	1.33	2.00	12.40	3.24
试验发展	Experimental Development	29.82	272.05	331.36	368.27
#政府资金	Government Funds	31.15	16.77	18.21	27.38
企业资金	Self-raised Funds by Enterprises	0.37	253.75	321.42	339.85
境外资金	Offshore Funds	20.19	2.37	2.15	3.29
R&D 项目(课题)情况	**R&D project**				
R&D 项目(课题)数(项)	Quantity of Projects (10 000 item)	2 412	9 240	12 378	12 833
R&D 项目(课题)人员全时当量(人年)	Personnell Engaged in Projects (person-year)		60 232	70 209	74 667
R&D 项目(课题)经费内部支出(亿元)	Inner Expenditure on Projects (100 million yuan)	28.14	247.29	293.21	303.37
科技产出及成果情况	**Output of Science and Technic Activities**				
新产品产值(亿元)	Output Value of New Products(100 millon yuan)	1 355.19	5 870.20	7 142.05	6 652.92
新产品销售收入(亿元)	Sales Revenue of New Products(100 millon yuan)	1 351.69	6 543.07	7 772.20	7 399.91
发表科技论文数(篇)	Quantity of Science and Technic Papers Published (case)		2 846	3 061	3 212
形成国家或行业标准数(项)	Becoming The formation of National or Industry Standards (item)		630	840	690
专利申请受理数(件)	Number of Patents Applications Accepted(piece)	1 455	14 967	19 365	24 873
#发明专利	Inventions	221	6 474	8 176	9 901
有效发明专利数(件)	Effective Invention Patents(piece)	468	9 822	12 530	16 805

注：本表 2000 年数据统计范围为大中型工业企业。
Note: Statistics range of data of 2000 is large and medium-sized industrial enterprises.

表 19.25 规模以上工业企业科技活动人员情况（2012）
PERSONNEL FOR SCIENCE AND TECHNIC ACTIVITY IN INDUSTRIAL ENTERPRISES ABOVE THE SET SCALE

单位：万人（10 000 persons）

类 别	Types	从事科技活动人员数 Technological Development Personnel	其中 of which: # R&D 人员 R&D personnel	# 高中级技术职称人员 Personnel with High and Medium Technic Titles
总 计	**Total**	**19.79**	**10.83**	**5.23**
按隶属关系分	**By Subordination**			
中央单位	Central Units	3.04	1.50	1.31
地方单位	Local Units	16.76	9.34	3.93
按登记注册类型分	**By Registration Categories**			
内 资	Domestic Funded	10.02	5.46	2.97
# 国 有	State-owned	1.05	0.44	0.49
有限责任公司	Companies with Limited Liabilities	3.45	1.93	1.09
股份有限公司	Share-holding Companies with Limited Liabilities	1.87	1.12	0.66
港澳台商投资	Hong Kong, Macao and Taiwan Funded	1.92	1.19	0.41
外商投资	Foreign Funded	7.86	4.18	1.85
按企业规模分	**By Size**			
# 大型企业	Large	9.33	5.03	2.80
中型企业	Medium	5.91	3.34	1.32
小型企业	Small	4.53	2.45	1.11
按行业分	**By Sectors**			
# 高技术产业	**High Technology Industry**	**5.36**	**2.74**	**1.49**
信息化学品制造	Information Chemical Product Manufacturing	0.03	0.03	
医药制造业	Medicine Manufacturing	0.77	0.49	0.22
航空航天器制造	Aviation and Aircraft Manufacturing	0.33	0.25	0.09
电子及通信设备制造业	Electronic and Communicantion Equipment Manufacturing	2.94	1.42	0.65
电子计算机及办公设备制造业	Electronic Computer and Office Equipment Manufacturing	0.48	0.11	0.30
医疗设备及仪器仪表制造业	Medical Machinery amd Measuring Instrument Manufacturing	0.81	0.44	0.22
按登记注册类型分	**By Registration Categories**			
# 六个重点发展工业行业	**Six Key Industries**	**14.67**	**8.21**	**3.89**
电子信息产品制造业	Electronic Information Product Manufacturing	4.39	2.03	1.12
汽车制造业	Automobile Manufacturing	2.94	1.70	0.58
石油化工及精细化工制造业	Petrochemical and Fine Chemical Products Manufacturing	1.04	0.61	0.31
精品钢材制造业	Fine Steel Manufacturing	0.53	0.37	0.28
成套设备制造业	Equipment Complex Manufacturing	4.59	2.80	1.27
生物医药制造业	Bio-medicine Manufacturing	1.18	0.70	0.33

表 19.26 规模以上工业企业科技项目数与科技经费支出情况（2012）
SCIENCE AND TECHNICAL PROJECTS AND EXPENDITURES OF INDUSTRIAL ENTERPRISES ABOVE THE SET SCALE

类　别	Types	科技项目数（项）Quantity of Science and Tehnic Project (item)	科技活动经费内部支出（亿元）Inner Expenditures on Science and Technic Activity (100 million yuan)	其中 of which #新产品开发经费支出 on New Products Development
总　计	**Total**	**21 176**	**579.98**	**484.00**
按隶属关系分	**By Subordination**			
中央单位	Central Units	3 027	138.12	117.37
地方单位	Local Units	18 149	441.86	366.63
按登记注册类型分	**By Registration Categories**			
内　资	Domestic Funded	11 646	288.44	237.07
#国　有	State-owned	973	25.54	17.35
有限责任公司	Companies with Limited Liabilities	4 126	124.33	102.18
股份有限公司	Share-holding Companies with Limited Liabilities	2 016	78.38	72.54
港澳台商投资	Hong Kong, Macao and Taiwan Funded	1 950	48.40	43.98
外商投资	Foreign Funded	7 580	243.14	202.96
按企业规模分	**By Size**			
#大型企业	Large	7 152	354.16	305.99
中型企业	Medium	6 942	130.20	103.16
小型企业	Small	6 905	94.68	74.03
按行业分	**By Sectors**			
#高技术产业	**High Technology Industry**	**4 201**	**148.06**	**129.58**
信息化学品制造	Information Chemical Product Manufacturing	36	0.95	0.95
医药制造业	Medicine Manufacturing	1 178	21.31	17.61
航空航天器制造	Aviation and Aircraft Manufacturing	116	22.91	22.32
电子及通信设备制造业	Electronic and Communicantion Equipment Manufacturing	1 762	77.94	72.11
电子计算机及办公设备制造业	Electronic Computer and Office Equipment Manufacturing	136	9.45	3.92
医疗设备及仪器仪表制造业	Medical Machinery amd Measuring Instrument Manufacturing	973	15.48	12.68
#六个重点发展工业行业	**Six Key Industries**	**14 464**	**473.91**	**406.78**
电子信息产品制造业	Electronic Information Product Manufacturing	3 190	108.61	93.70
汽车制造业	Automobile Manufacturing	2 893	117.89	105.69
石油化工及精细化工制造业	Petrochemical and Fine Chemical Products Manufacturing	1 389	32.27	24.39
精品钢材制造业	Fine Steel Manufacturing	1 110	52.92	45.03
成套设备制造业	Equipment Complex Manufacturing	4 282	133.28	114.53
生物医药制造业	Bio-medicine Manufacturing	1 600	28.93	23.44

表 19.27 规模以上工业企业 R&D 经费内部支出来源构成（2012）
STRUCTURE OF R&D INNER EXPENDITURE SOURCE IN INDUSTRIAL ENTERPRISES ABOVE THE SET SCALE

单位：亿元（100 million yuan）

类 别	Types	R&D 经费内部支出合计 Total of R&D Inner Expenditure	其中 of which #政府资金 Government Funds	#企业资金 Enterprise Funds	#境外资金 Foreign Funds
总 计	**Total**	**371.51**	**27.38**	**339.85**	**3.29**
按隶属关系分	**By Subordination**				
中央单位	Central Units	91.94	18.35	73.55	
地方单位	Local Units	279.57	9.04	266.30	3.29
按登记注册类型分	**By Registration Categories**				
内 资	Domestic Funded	186.64	22.24	163.50	0.23
#国 有	State-owned	13.52	0.87	12.63	
有限责任公司	Companies with Limited Liabilities	77.36	17.32	59.70	0.01
股份有限公司	Share-holding Companies with Limited Liabilities	58.82	2.63	56.08	0.11
港澳台商投资	Hong Kong, Macao and Taiwan Funded	32.07	2.53	28.96	0.46
外商投资	Foreign Funded	152.80	2.61	147.39	2.60
按企业规模分	**By Size**				
#大型企业	Large	233.68	22.51	209.55	1.58
中型企业	Medium	83.80	2.84	79.65	0.99
小型企业	mall	53.64	1.97	50.32	0.72
按行业分	**By Sectors**				
#高技术产业	**High Technology Industry**	**88.65**	**21.46**	**65.27**	**1.84**
信息化学品制造	Information Chemical Product Manufacturing	0.79		0.78	
医药制造业	Medicine Manufacturing	15.45	1.03	14.30	0.10
航空航天器制造	Aviation and Aircraft Manufacturing	22.12	15.31	6.81	
电子及通信设备制造业	Electronic and Communicantion Equipment Manufacturing	39.95	4.57	34.17	1.16
电子计算机及办公设备制造业	Electronic Computer and Office Equipment Manufacturing	2.43	0.04	2.34	0.04
医疗设备及仪器仪表制造业	Medical Machinery amd Measuring Instrument Manufacturing	7.91	0.49	6.86	0.54
#六个重点发展工业行业	**Six Key Industries**	**306.95**	**26.25**	**277.10**	**2.89**
电子信息产品制造业	Electronic Information Product Manufacturing	54.06	4.99	47.24	1.73
汽车制造业	Automobile Manufacturing	85.09	0.33	84.38	0.12
石油化工及精细化工制造业	Petrochemical and Fine Chemical Products Manufacturing	17.60	0.38	16.79	0.37
精品钢材制造业	Fine Steel Manufacturing	44.54	1.65	42.89	
成套设备制造业	Equipment Complex Manufacturing	86.61	17.65	68.26	0.42
生物医药制造业	Bio-medicine Manufacturing	19.06	1.25	17.54	0.25

表 19.23 规模以上工业企业办科技机构情况(2012)
SCIENCE AND TECHNIC RESEARCH INSTITUTIONS FUNDED BY INDUSTRIAL ENTERPRISES ABOVE THE SET SCALE

类别	Types	科技机构数(个) Technological Development Institutions (unit)	机构人员数(万人) Quantity of Personnel (10 000 persons)	机构经费支出(亿元) Expenditure of Institutions (100 million yuan)	机构仪器设备原价(亿元) Original Value of Equipment (100 million yuan)
总计	**Total**	**1 179**	**9.26**	**302.23**	**250.99**
按隶属关系分	**By Subordination**				
中央单位	Central Units	51	1.31	52.43	53.76
地方单位	Local Units	1 128	7.95	249.80	197.23
按登记注册类型分	**By Registration Categories**				
内资	Domestic Funded	679	4.30	116.79	98.88
#国有	State-owned	27	0.30	10.91	7.58
有限责任公司	Companies with Limited Liabilities	211	1.68	42.75	47.11
股份有限公司	Share-holding Companies with Limited Liabilities	101	1.02	41.07	23.96
港澳台商投资	Hong Kong, Macao and Taiwan Funded	124	0.88	25.05	15.25
外商投资	Foreign Funded	376	4.08	160.39	136.86
按企业规模分	**By Size**				
#大型企业	Large	228	5.18	212.11	176.20
中型企业	Medium	541	2.95	64.46	59.77
小型企业	Small	408	1.13	25.49	14.87
按行业分	**By Sectors**				
#高技术产业	**High Technology Industry**	**259**	**2.75**	**76.77**	**65.29**
信息化学品制造	Information Chemical Product Manufacturing	1	0.01	0.36	0.24
医药制造业	Medicine Manufacturing	77	0.41	12.32	6.95
航空航天器制造	Aviation and Aircraft Manufacturing	4	0.11	2.21	4.03
电子及通信设备制造业	Electronic and Communicantion Equipment Manufacturing	124	1.72	50.58	49.68
电子计算机及办公设备制造业	Electronic Computer and Office Equipment Manufacturing	10	0.12	2.11	2.84
医疗设备及仪器仪表制造业	Medical Machinery amd Measuring Instrument Manufacturing	43	0.38	9.19	1.55
#六个重点发展工业行业	**Six Key Industries**	**818**	**7.45**	**258.42**	**209.30**
电子信息产品制造业	Electronic Information Product Manufacturing	195	2.21	62.82	55.97
汽车制造业	Automobile Manufacturing	118	1.84	90.68	61.65
石油化工及精细化工制造业	Petrochemical and Fine Chemical Products Manufacturing	113	0.44	16.66	9.21
精品钢材制造业	Fine Steel Manufacturing	6	0.08	11.59	15.07
成套设备制造业	Equipment Complex Manufacturing	284	2.26	59.54	59.14
生物医药制造业	Bio-medicine Manufacturing	102	0.62	17.13	8.26

表 19.29 规模以上工业企业其他技术活动费用支出情况(2012) SPECIAL TECHNICAL PROJECT FUNDS OF INDUSTRIAL ENTERPRISES ABOVE THE SET SCALE

单位:亿元 (100 million yuan)

类 别	Types	技术改造经费支出 Expenditures of Technical Transformation	技术引进经费支出 Expenditures of Technical Introduction	购买国内技术支出 Expenditures of Buying Domestic Technology
总 计	**Total**	**129.84**	**58.31**	**28.29**
按隶属关系分	**By Subordination**			
中央单位	Central Units	58.79	13.17	25.05
地方单位	Local Units	71.06	45.14	3.25
按登记注册类型分	**By Registration Categories**			
内 资	**Domestic Funded**	**86.15**	**19.09**	**26.49**
#国 有	State-owned	2.01	0.03	0.56
有限责任公司	Companies with Limited Liabilities	43.07	5.80	6.35
股份有限公司	Share-holding Companies with Limited Liabilities	36.77	12.97	19.54
港澳台商投资	Hong Kong, Macao and Taiwan Funded	4.52	2.88	0.11
外商投资	Foreign Funded	39.18	36.35	1.70
按企业规模分	**By Size**			
#大型企业	Large	101.63	51.04	27.64
中型企业	Medium	19.92	5.24	0.36
小型企业	Small	8.28	2.03	0.29
按行业分	**By Sectors**			
#高技术产业	**High Technology Industry**	**12.62**	**7.01**	**0.65**
信息化学品制造	Information Chemical Product Manufacturing			
医药制造业	Medicine Manufacturing	7.82	0.81	0.13
航空航天器制造	Aviation and Aircraft Manufacturing			
电子及通信设备制造业	Electronic and Communicantion Equipment Manufacturing	4.18	4.37	0.52
电子计算机及办公设备制造业	Electronic Computer and Office Equipment Manufacturing	0.03	0.34	
医疗设备及仪器仪表制造业	Medical Machinery amd Measuring Instrument Manufacturing	0.59	1.50	
#六个重点发展工业行业	**Six Key Industries**	**94.72**	**53.87**	**26.23**
电子信息产品制造业	Electronic Information Product Manufacturing	5.83	5.51	0.52
汽车制造业	Automobile Manufacturing	31.11	29.83	2.19
石油化工及精细化工制造业	Petrochemical and Fine Chemical Products Manufacturing	8.61	0.51	0.38
精品钢材制造业	Fine Steel Manufacturing	27.83	9.60	20.80
成套设备制造业	Equipment Complex Manufacturing	12.53	7.45	2.21
生物医药制造业	Bio-medicine Manufacturing	8.81	0.96	0.13

表 19.30 规模以上工业企业新产品产出情况（2012）
OUTPUT OF NEW PRODUCTS OF INDUSTRIAL ENTERPRISES ABOVE THE SET SCALE

单位：亿元（100 million yuan）

类别	Types	新产品产值 Output Value of New Products	新产品销售收入 Sales Revenue of New Products	其中 of which #新产品出口 Exports of New Products
总计	**Total**	**6 652.92**	**7 399.91**	**1 054.40**
按隶属关系分	**By Subordination**			
中央单位	Central Units	1 374.32	1 284.27	384.94
地方单位	Local Units	5 278.60	6 115.63	669.46
按登记注册类型分	**By Registration Categories**			
内资	Domestic Funded	2 416.46	2 400.52	397.10
#国有	State-owned	214.99	255.74	12.79
有限责任公司	Companies with Limited Liabilities	1 314.10	1 251.27	267.93
股份有限公司	Share-holding Companies with Limited Liabilities	460.02	462.22	75.71
港澳台商投资	Hong Kong, Macao and Taiwan Funded	436.11	449.49	183.21
外商投资	Foreign Funded	3 800.35	4 549.90	474.09
按企业规模分	**By Size**			
#大型企业	Large	5 060.10	5 734.84	831.90
中型企业	Medium	1 039.34	1 074.86	170.80
小型企业	Small	553.02	589.76	51.55
按行业分	**By Sectors**			
#高技术产业	**High Technology Industry**	**777.88**	**781.37**	**309.28**
信息化学品制造	Information Chemical Product Manufacturing	3.40	3.40	3.34
医药制造业	Medicine Manufacturing	148.52	158.75	5.17
航空航天器制造	Aviation and Aircraft Manufacturing	9.49	11.74	0.38
电子及通信设备制造业	Electronic and Communicantion Equipment Manufacturing	538.39	530.01	267.86
电子计算机及办公设备制造业	Electronic Computer and Office Equipment Manufacturing	29.19	28.28	21.65
医疗设备及仪器仪表制造业	Medical Machinery amd Measuring Instrument Manufacturing	48.89	49.18	10.88
#六个重点发展工业行业	**Six Key Industries**	**5 373.93**	**6 126.98**	**812.67**
电子信息产品制造业	Electronic Information Product Manufacturing	779.64	777.80	319.88
汽车制造业	Automobile Manufacturing	2 449.70	3 245.52	59.34
石油化工及精细化工制造业	Petrochemical and Fine Chemical Products Manufacturing	335.27	338.78	23.65
精品钢材制造业	Fine Steel Manufacturing	267.40	267.50	39.26
成套设备制造业	Equipment Complex Manufacturing	1 369.82	1 314.67	362.80
生物医药制造业	Bio-medicine Manufacturing	172.11	182.70	7.72

注：新产品既包括经政府有关部门认定并在有效期内的新产品，也包括企业自行研制开发，未经政府有关部门认定，从投产之日起一年之内的新产品。
Note: New Products include new products certified by relevant government agencies within the period of certification, as well as new products designed and produced by enterprises within a year without certification by government agencies.

表 19.31 主要年份大中型工业企业科技活动情况
SCIENCE AND TECHNIC ACTIVITIES OF LARGE AND MEDIUM INDUSTRIAL ENTERPRISES IN MAIN YEARS

指标	Indicators	2000	2010	2011	2012
企业办科技机构数（个）	**Science and Technic Institutions Funded by Enterprises (unit)**	**264**	**638**	**644**	**769**
从事科技活动人员数（万人）	**Personnel Engaged in Science and Technic Activities (10 000 persons)**	**7.48**	**11.96**	**14.72**	**15.24**
#R&D 人员	R&D Personnel	2.63	6.64	7.88	8.37
#高中级技术职称人员	Personnel with High and Medium Technic Titles	3.10	3.17	4.06	4.12
科技活动经费支出情况(亿元)	**Expenditures on Science and Technic Activities(100 million yuan)**				
内部经费支出	Inner Expenditures	91.63	356.24	453.31	484.36
#R&D 经费支出	R&D Expenditures	30.98	237.75	292.44	317.48
#新产品开发经费支出	Expenditures on New Products Development	47.56	302.45	379.58	409.16
外部经费支出	External Expenditures	9.15	33.12	36.37	50.01
其他技术活动费用支出(亿元)	**Other Expenditures on Technic Activities (100 million yuan)**	**117.47**	**235.63**	**237.81**	**232.48**
技术改造经费支出	Expenditures on Technological Transformation	75.31	123.21	125.75	121.55
技术引进经费支出	Expenditures on Technological Introduction	39.00	61.09	63.00	56.28
用于消化吸收的经费	Expenditures on Technological Digesting and Absorbing	2.41	28.68	27.33	26.65
购买国内技术支出	Expenditures on Buying Domestic Technology	0.75	22.65	21.73	28.00
科技项目情况	**Science and Technic Project**				
项目数（项）	Quantity of Projects (item)	5 140	11 384	13 631	14 094
项目人员（人）	Personnel of Project Groups (person)	45 254	94 165	119 693	126 674
项目经费内部支出(亿元)	Intramural Expenditure on Projects (100 million yuan)	63.72	309.75	382.02	396.51
科技活动产出情况	**Output of Science and Technic Activities**				
新产品产值(亿元)	Taxes of New Products (100 million yuan)	1 355.19	5 504.38	5 566.66	6 099.44
新产品销售收入(亿元)	Prime Operating Revenue (100 million yuan)	1 351.69	6 180.81	7 183.45	6 809.70
#新产品出口	New Products Exported	197.41	1 023.11	988.52	1 002.70

上 / 海 / 统 / 计 / 年 / 鉴

主要统计指标解释

■ 科技活动

指在自然科学、农业科学、医药科学、工程与技术科学、人文与社会科学领域(简称科学技术领域)中,与科技知识的产生、发展、传播和应用密切相关的有组织的活动。可分为研究与试验发展(R&D)、研究与试验发展成果应用及相关的科技服务三类活动。

■ R&D

R&D 是"科学研究与试验发展"的英文缩写。指在科学技术领域,为增加知识总量,以及运用这些知识去创造新的应用进行的系统的创造性的活动。R&D 包括基础研究、应用研究、试验发展三类活动。

■ 基础研究

指为了获得关于现象和可观察事实的基本原理的新知识(揭示客观事物的本质、运动规律,获得新发现、新学说)而进行的实验性或理论性研究,它不以任何专门或特定的应用或使用为目的。其成果以科学论文和科学著作为主要形式。用来反映知识的原始创新能力。

■ 应用研究

指为获得新知识而进行的创造性研究,主要针对某一特定的目的或目标。应用研究是为了确定基础研究成果可能的用途,或是为达到预定的目标探索应采取的新方法(原理性)或新途径。其成果形式以科学论文、专著、原理性模型或发明专利为主。

■ 试验发展

指利用从基础研究、应用研究和实际经验所获得的现有知识,为产生新的产品、材料和装置,建立新的工艺、系统和服务,以及对已产生和建立的上述各项作实质性的改进而进行的系统性工作。其成果形式主要是专利、专有技术、具有新产品基本特征的产品原型或具有新装置基本特征的原始样机等。在社会科学领域,试验发展是指把通过基础研究、应用研究获得的知识转变成可以实施的计划 (包括为进行检验和评估实施示范项目) 的过程。人文科学领域没有对应的试验发展活动。

■ 科技活动人员

指直接从事科技活动、以及专门从事科技活动管理和为科技活动提供直接服务,累计从事科技活动的时间占全年制度工作时间 10%及以上的人员。(1)直接从事科技活动的人员,包括:在独立核算的科学研究与技术开发机构、高等学校、各类企业及其他事业单位内设的研究室、实验室、技术开发中心及中试车间(基地)等机构中从事科技活动的研究人员、工程技术人员、技术工人及其它人员;虽不在上述机构工作,但编入科技活动项目(课题)组的人员;科技信息与文献机构中的专业技术人员;从事论文设计的研究生等。(2)专门从事科技活动管理和为科技活动提供直接服务的人员包括:独立核算的科学研究与技术开发机构、科技信息与文献机构、高等学校、各类企业及其他事业单位主管科技工作的负责人,专门从事科技活动的计划、行政、人事、财务、物资供应、设备维护、图书资料管理等工作的各类人员,但不包括保卫、医疗保健人员、司机、食堂人员、茶炉工、水暖工、清洁工等为科技活动提供间接服务的人员。

■ R&D 人员

R&D 人员一般用折合全时当量来表示。即参加 R&D 项目人员的全时当量及应分摊在 R&D 项目的管理和直接服务人员的全时当量两部分相加计算。一个折合全时当量是一人年。例如,一个人在 R&D 活动上花费了 30%的正常工作时间而 70%的时间用于其他工作,则其折合全时当量为 0.3。

■ 科技活动经费支出

指企事业单位实际支出的全部科技活动费用,包括来自科研渠道的经费、教育事业费、基本建设投资、技术改造投资等实际用于科技活动支出的费用。科技活动经费支出分为内部支出和外部支出。

■ R&D 经费内部支出

指企事业单位用于内部开展 R&D 活动(包括基础研究、应用研究、试验发展)的实际支出。包括用于 R&D 项目(课题)活动的直接支出,以及间接用于 R&D 活动的管理费、服务费、与有关的基本建设支出以及外协加工费等。不包括生产性活动支出、归还贷款支出以

主要统计指标解释

及与外单位合作或委托外单位进行 R&D 活动而转拨给对方的经费支出。

■ 专 利

是专利权的简称，是对发明人的发明创造经审查合格后，由专利局依据专利法授予发明人和设计人对该项发明创造享有的专有权。专利包括发明、实用新型和外观设计三种类型。

■ 发 明

指对产品、方法或者其改进所提出的新的技术方案。是国际通行的反映拥有自主知识产权技术的核心指标。

■ 实用新型

指对产品的形状、构造或者其结合所提出的适于实用的新的技术方案。反映具有一定技术含量的技术成果情况。

■ 外观设计

指对产品的形状、图案、色彩或者其结合所作出的富有美感并适于工业上应用的新设计。反映拥有自主知识产权的外观设计成果情况。

■ 新产品

指采用新技术原理、新设计构思研制、生产的全新产品，或在结构、材质、工艺等某一方面比原有产品有明显改进，从而显著提高了产品性能或扩大了使用功能的产品。新产品既包括政府有关部门认定并在有效期内的新产品，也包括企业自行研制开发，未经政府有关部门认定，从投产之日起一年之内的新产品。

■ 独立研究与开发机构

指有明确的任务和研究方向，有一定学术水平的业务骨干和一定数量的研究人员，具有研究、开发、开展学术工作的基本条件，主要进行科学研究与技术开发活动，并且在行政上有独立的组织形式，财务上独立核算盈亏，有权与其他单位签订合同，在银行有单独户头的单位。

SHANGHAI STATISTICAL YEARBOOK

EXPLANATORY NOTES TO MAJOR STATISTICAL INDICATORS

□ Scientific and Technological Activities (S&T Activities)

Scientific and Technological Activities (S&T Activities) refer to organized activities which are closely related with the creation, development, dissemination and application of the scientific and technical knowledge in the fields of natural sciences, agricultural sciences, medical sciences, engineering and technological sciences, humanities and social sciences (referred to as scientific and technological fields). S&T activities can be classified into 3 categories: research and development (R&D) activities, application of R&D results, and related S&T services.

□ R&D

R&D is an abbreviation which stands for 'Science Research and Experimental Development', which means systematic and creative endeavors aimed at expanding the overall volume of knowledge and applying the knowledge in systematic creation. R&D includes basic studies, application research and experimental development.

□ Basic Research

Basic Research refers to empirical or theoretical research aiming at obtaining new knowledge on the fundamental principles of phenomena of observable facts to reveal the nature and law of movement of objects and to acquire new discoveries or new theories. Basic research takes no specific or designated application as the aim of the research. Results of basic research are mainly released or disseminated in the form of scientific papers or monographs. This indicator reflects the original innovation capacity of knowledge.

□ Applied Research

Applied Research refers to creative research aiming at obtaining new knowledge on a specific objective or target. Purpose of the applied research is to identify the possible use of results from basic research, or to explore new (fundamental) methods or new approaches. Results of applied research are expressed in the form of scientific papers, monographs, fundamental models or invention patents.

□ Experimental Development

Experimental Development refer to systematic activities aiming at using the knowledge from basic and applied researches or from practical experience to develop new products, materials and equipment, to establish new production process, systems and services, or to make substantial improvement on the existing products, process or services. Results of experiment and development activities are embodied in patents, exclusive technology, and monotype of new products or equipment. In social sciences, experiment and development activities refer to the process of converting the knowledge from basic or applied researches into feasible programmes (including conduct of demonstration projects for assessment and evaluation). There are no experiment and development activities in the science of humanities.

□ Personnel Engaged in S&T Activities

Personnel Engaged in S&T Activities refer to personnel directly engaged in S&T activities, in the management of S&T activities, and in providing direct service to S&T activities, who spend over 10% of the total working hours in a year in S&T activities. (1) Personnel directly engaged in S&T activities include researchers, engineers, technicians and other related personnel engaged in S&T activities in independent-accounting R&D institutions, institutions of higher learning, and in research institutes, laboratories, technology development centers and central experiment workshops under enterprises and institutions. Also included are people working in S&T information archiving institutes, and graduate students working on the design of their thesis. (2) Personnel engaged in the management of S&T activities and in providing direct service to S&T activities include senior management people responsible for S&T activities in independent-accounting R&D institutions, S&T information archiving institutes, institutions of higher learning, and in enterprises and institutions where S&T activities are undertaken. Also included are people responsible for the planning, administration, personnel management, financial management, logistics supply, equipment maintenance, information and library management that are related with S&T activities. People providing indirect services are excluded, such as security, medical service, drivers, plumbers, cleaners and those providing catering and related service.

EXPLANATORY NOTES TO MAJOR STATISTICAL INDICATORS

□ R&D Personnel

R&D Personnel generally amount to the full-time equivalent. It equals the full-time equivalent of personnel engaged in the R&D projects plus the full-time equivalent of personnel directly manage and service the allocated R&D projects. A full-time equivalent refers to a person year. For example, a person spent thirty percents of common working time on R&D activities and seventy percents on other jobs, then the full-time equivalent is 0.3.

□ Expenditures on Science and Technical Activities

Expenditures on Science and Technical Activities refers to the total expenditures that the enterprises actually spent on science and technical activities. It includes expenditures on scientific research, education expenses, basic construction investment, investment on technical transformation. It is divided into internal expenditure and external expenditure.

□ Internal Expenditure on R&D

Internal Expenditure on R&D refers to the actually expense on R&D activities inside enterprises. It includes the direct expense on R&D projects, and indirect expense, such as management fees, service fees, basic construction investment and processing fees, on R&D activities. But it does not include the expenditures for productive activities, expenditures on repay the loans and the expenditures pay for the R&D activities entrusted to other enterprises.

□ Patent

Patent is an abbreviation for the patent right and refers to the exclusive right of ownership by the inventors or designers for the creation or inventions, given from the patent offices after due process of assessment and approval in accordance with the Patent Law. Patents are granted for inventions, utility models and designs.

□ Invention

Inventions refer to the new technical proposals to the products or methods or their modifications. This is universal core indicator reflecting the technologies with independent intellectual property.

□ Utility Models

Utility Models refer to the practical and new technical proposals on the shape and structure of the product or the combination of both. This indicator reflects the condition of technological results with certain technical content.

□ Exterior Design

Designs refer to the aesthetics and industrially applicable new designs for the shape, pattern and color of the product, or their combinations. This indicator reflects the appearance design achievements with independent intellectual property.

□ New Products

New Products refer to new products produced with new technology and new design, or products that represent noticeable improvement in terms of structure, material, or production process so as to improve significantly the character or function of the older versions. They include new products certified by relevant government agencies within the period of certification, as well as new products that are not certified by relevant government agencies and are designed and produced by enterprises within one year since they are put into production.

□ Independent Research and Development Institutions

Independent Research and Development Institutions refer to the state-owned institutions which have direct mission and research purpose, a certain research level and quantities of personnel, favorable conditions for R&D and engaging in scientific research and technological development. The institutions also have their own independent organization, accounting system authority to sign contract with other units, and their own accounts in banks.

第二十篇

CHAPTER 20

教　育

EDUCATION

简要说明

一、本章资料的主要内容

教育统计资料包括公办教育和民办教育、学历教育和非学历教育。具体有高等教育(研究生教育、普通高等教育和成人高等教育)、中等教育(高中阶段教育、初中阶段教育和成人中等教育)、初等教育(小学)、学前教育(幼儿园)、特殊教育(特殊教育学校和工读学校等)和留学生教育等资料。主要指标包括学校数主要指标包括学校数、在校学生数、招生数、毕业生数、教职工数和专任教师数等。

二、本篇资料的来源

教育统计资料由上海市教育委员会提供。

BRIEF INTRODUCTION

I. Main Contents

Data on education cover the situations on education funded by government and non-government agencies, and the education with and without academic credentials including higher education (education of postgraduates, general higher education and adult education), secondary education (senior and junior high schools), elementary education (primary schools), preschool education, special education (schools for the blind, deaf-mutes and mentally retarded) and overseas education. The main indicators include the number of schools, the number of students enrolled, the number of new students enrolled, the number of graduates, the number of staff and workers, the number of full-time teachers.

II. Sources of Data

Data on education are provided by Shanghai Municipal Education Commission.

表 20.1　主要年份教育事业基本情况
BASIC STATISTICS OF EDUCATION IN MAIN YEARS

指标	Indicators	2000	2010	2011	2012
学校数（所）	**Quantity of Schools (unit)**	**2 225**	**1 730**	**1 728**	**1 728**
普通高等学校	Regular Institutions of Higher Education	37	66	66	67
普通中等学校	Secondary Schools	1 133	869	869	871
中等专业学校	Specialized Secondary Schools	84	65	64	61
职业中学	Vocational Secondary Schools	60	26	28	28
技工学校	Technical Worker Schools	115	10	10	9
普通中学	Regular Secondary Schools	861	755	754	760
工读学校	Reformatory	13	13	13	13
普通小学	Primary Schools	1 021	766	764	761
特殊教育学校	Special Education Schools	34	29	29	29
教职工数（万人）	**Quantity of Teachers and Staff (10 000 persons)**	**22.73**	**21.42**	**21.41**	**21.38**
普通高等学校	Regular Institutions of Higher Education	6.01	7.42	7.41	7.33
普通中等学校	Secondary Schools	10.43	8.26	9.02	8.99
中等专业学校	Specialized Secondary Schools	1.27	0.91	0.89	0.85
职业中学	Vocational Secondary Schools	0.66	0.43	0.42	0.40
技工学校	Technical Worker Schools	0.77	0.13	0.13	0.11
普通中学	Regular Secondary Schools	7.66	6.73	7.53	7.58
工读学校	Reformatory	0.07	0.06	0.05	0.05
普通小学	Primary Schools	6.13	5.58	4.82	4.90
特殊教育学校	Special Education Schools	0.16	0.16	0.16	0.16
专任教师（万人）	**Quantity of Full-time Teachers (10 000 persons)**	**12.83**	**14.52**	**14.71**	**14.99**
普通高等学校	Regular Institutions of Higher Education	2.05	3.92	3.96	4.01
普通中等学校	Secondary Schools	6.26	5.97	6.00	6.05
中等专业学校	Specialized Secondary Schools	0.53	0.50	0.50	0.48
职业中学	Vocational Secondary Schools	0.39	0.29	0.29	0.28
技工学校	Technical Worker Schools	0.30	0.07	0.06	0.07
普通中学	Regular Secondary Schools	5.01	5.07	5.11	5.18
高中	Senior Secondary Schools	1.42	1.67	1.66	3.52
初中	Junior Secondary Schools	3.59	3.40	3.45	1.66
工读学校	Reformatory	0.03	0.04	0.04	0.04
普通小学	Primary Schools	4.43	4.52	4.63	4.81
特殊教育学校	Special Education Schools	0.09	0.11	0.12	0.12

注：普通中学学校数中，完全中学 94 所，高级中学 134 所，初级中学 358 所，九年一贯制学校 149 所，十二年一贯制学校 19 所。

Note: In regular secondary schools, there are 94 whole secondary schools, 134 senior high schools, 358 junior high schools, 149 system schools of 9 years and 19 system schools of 12 years.

表 20.1 续表 continued

指 标	Indicators	2000	2010	2011	2012
毕业生数(万人)	**Graduates (10 000 persons)**	**55.67**	**46.77**	**47.33**	**46.12**
普通高等学校	Regular Institutions of Higher Education	4.09	13.37	13.90	13.99
普通中等学校	Secondary Schools	32.76	22.63	20.25	19.09
中等专业学校	Specialized Secondary Schools	3.86	3.34	3.14	2.77
职业中学	Vocational Secondary Schools	3.99	1.38	1.24	1.04
技工学校	Technical Worker Schools	1.86	0.31	0.32	0.30
普通中学	Regular Secondary Schools	22.92	16.13	15.48	14.91
高 中	Senior Secondary Schools	7.18	6.24	5.85	5.44
初 中	Junior Secondary Schools	15.74	9.89	9.63	9.47
工读学校	Reformatory	0.13	0.08	0.07	0.07
普通小学	Primary Schools	18.73	12.44	13.09	12.95
特殊教育学校	Special Education Schools	0.09	0.09	0.09	0.09
招生数(万人)	**New Student Enrollment (10 000 persons)**	**52.23**	**50.66**	**52.44**	**52.33**
普通高等学校	Regular Institutions of Higher Education	8.13	14.46	14.11	13.67
普通中等学校	Secondary Schools	33.71	21.07	21.32	21.35
中等专业学校	Specialized Secondary Schools	3.00	2.99	2.78	2.76
职业中学	Vocational Secondary Schools	2.44	1.23	1.24	1.23
技工学校	Technical Worker Schools	1.68	0.42	0.38	0.30
普通中学	Regular Secondary Schools	26.46	16.33	16.84	17.00
高 中	Senior Secondary Schools	7.84	5.39	5.22	5.25
初 中	Junior Secondary Schools	18.62	10.94	11.62	11.75
工读学校	Reformatory	0.13	0.10	0.08	0.06
普通小学	Primary Schools	10.28	15.05	16.94	17.23
特殊教育学校	Special Education Schools	0.11	0.08	0.07	0.08
在校学生(万人)	**Student Enrollment (10 000 persons)**	**207.61**	**197.70**	**198.87**	**200.80**
普通高等学校	Regular Institutions of Higher Education	22.68	51.57	51.13	50.66
普通中等学校	Secondary Schools	105.53	75.47	74.14	73.61
中等专业学校	Specialized Secondary Schools	11.89	10.91	10.22	9.88
职业中学	Vocational Secondary Schools	8.48	3.77	3.52	3.55
技工学校	Technical Worker Schools	5.37	1.08	1.05	0.98
普通中学	Regular Secondary Schools	79.54	59.44	59.17	59.04
高 中	Senior Secondary Schools	23.94	16.89	16.11	15.77
初 中	Junior Secondary Schools	55.60	42.55	43.06	43.27
工读学校	Reformatory	0.25	0.27	0.18	0.16
普通小学	Primary Schools	78.86	70.16	73.11	76.04
特殊教育学校	Special Education Schools	0.54	0.50	0.49	0.49

表 20.2　每万人口在校学生数、每个教师负担学生数(1978～2012)
STUDENTS ENROLLMENT PER 10 000 PERSONS AND STUDENTS TAUGHT BY EACH TEACHER

单位:人(person)

年　分 Year	平均每万人口在校学生数 Students Enrollment per 10 000 Persons				平均每个教师负担学生数 Students Taught by Each Teacher		
	大学生 College and University	中专生 Speciallized Secondary School	中学生 Secondary School	小学生 Primary School	普通高等学校 Institution of Higher Education	普通中等学校 Regular Secondary School	普通小学 Primary School
1978	46	14	908	789	3	17	18
1979	60	21	719	774	4	16	19
1980	67	24	544	742	4	13	18
1981	78	25	427	713	5	11	17
1982	71	28	451	665	4	12	16
1983	66	30	433	665	4	10	16
1984	74	37	404	686	4	11	17
1985	88	48	391	683	4	12	17
1986	94	55	387	693	5	11	17
1987	97	55	381	706	5	11	17
1988	100	51	355	764	5	11	18
1989	96	49	351	809	5	11	19
1990	90	46	362	826	5	11	19
1991	87	45	379	825	5	12	19
1992	88	47	401	830	5	13	22
1993	95	54	417	845	6	14	21
1994	100	66	468	815	6	15	21
1995	101	76	512	776	7	16	20
1996	102	68	525	734	7	16	20
1997	103	75	500	688	8	16	20
1998	108	81	483	630	8	17	19
1999	119	83	489	556	9	17	19
2000	141	74	494	490	11	17	18
2001	168	73	481	433	13	16	17
2002	194	74	461	393	14	17	17
2003	214	78	427	367	16	16	17
2004	227	77	451	293	15	17	14
2005	234	72	407	283	14	16	14
2006	237	70	362	272	14	15	14
2007	235	62	318	258	14	14	14
2008	235	56	289	276	14	13	14
2009	232	52	273	304	13	13	15
2010	224	47	258	305	13	13	16
2011	218	44	252	311	13	12	16
2012	213	42	248	319	13	12	16

表 20.3　各级各类学校在校学生数(1978～2012)
STUDENTS ENROLLMENT BY VARIOUS SCHOOLS

单位:万人 (10 000 persons)

年　份 Year	普通高等学校 Institutions of Higher Education	普通中等学校 Secondary School	其中 of which 中等专业学校 Specialized Secondary School	普通中学 Regular Secondary School	职业学校 Secondary Vocational School	技工学校 Technical Worker School	普通小学 Primary School	特殊教育学校 Special Education School
1978	5.06	101.81	1.55	100.26			87.06	0.18
1979	6.74	90.80	2.42	81.72		6.66	88.00	0.18
1980	7.67	71.68	2.81	62.71	0.29	5.87	85.47	0.18
1981	9.11	58.82	2.94	49.93	0.45	5.50	83.22	0.16
1982	8.39	61.69	3.30	53.53	0.85	4.01	78.88	0.16
1983	7.87	60.53	3.61	52.04	1.71	3.17	79.82	0.23
1984	8.99	61.01	4.48	49.18	3.07	4.28	83.47	0.21
1985	10.79	63.50	5.92	48.23	4.69	4.66	84.18	0.23
1986	11.77	64.82	6.86	48.31	4.71	4.94	86.56	0.25
1987	12.25	64.50	7.03	48.21	4.08	5.18	89.35	0.28
1988	12.82	61.20	6.52	45.68	3.69	5.31	98.39	0.30
1989	12.61	61.01	6.45	46.10	3.54	4.92	106.02	0.32
1990	12.13	62.59	6.17	48.31	3.66	4.45	110.19	0.33
1991	11.69	65.92	6.01	51.24	3.97	4.70	111.38	0.35
1992	11.95	70.84	6.41	54.77	4.90	4.76	113.37	0.38
1993	13.10	76.54	7.58	57.69	6.39	4.88	116.70	0.44
1994	14.04	87.23	9.23	65.56	7.54	4.90	113.98	0.52
1995	14.41	96.38	10.85	72.40	8.64	4.49	109.78	0.57
1996	14.79	99.97	9.95	76.23	9.12	4.67	106.46	0.62
1997	15.38	100.81	11.10	74.43	10.29	4.99	102.44	0.63
1998	16.51	102.53	12.38	73.85	10.72	5.58	96.14	0.52
1999	18.63	105.66	13.06	76.69	10.21	5.70	87.16	0.53
2000	22.68	105.28	11.89	79.54	8.48	5.37	78.86	0.54
2001	28.00	104.37	12.12	80.23	7.48	4.54	72.28	0.48
2002	33.16	103.59	12.66	78.97	7.56	4.40	67.24	0.55
2003	37.85	100.71	13.69	75.47	7.04	4.51	64.83	0.55
2004	41.57	106.94	14.05	82.78	6.43	3.68	53.74	0.54
2005	44.26	99.24	13.67	77.02	5.76	2.79	53.50	0.52
2006	46.63	92.25	13.70	71.17	5.33	2.05	53.37	0.50
2007	48.49	85.17	12.81	65.60	5.20	1.56	53.33	0.50
2008	50.29	79.97	12.08	61.77	4.80	1.32	59.06	0.51
2009	51.28	77.07	11.50	60.37	4.14	1.06	67.12	0.50
2010	51.57	75.20	10.91	59.44	3.77	1.08	70.16	0.50
2011	51.13	73.96	10.22	59.17	3.52	1.05	73.11	0.49
2012	50.66	73.45	9.88	59.04	3.55	0.98	76.04	0.49

注：本表中普通中等学校在校学生数中不包括工读学校在校学生。
Note: Quantity of students enrollment of secondary school in this table doesn't include those of reformatory schools.

表20.4 主要年份各阶段教育实施情况
BASIC STATISTICS OF VARIOUS PHASES EDUCATION IN MAIN YEARS

单位:%

指 标	Indicators	2000	2010	2011	2012
小 学	**Primary School**				
小学学龄儿童净入学率	Enrollment Rate of Schoolage Children	99.9	99.9	99.9	99.9
初 中	**Junior School**				
初中学生净入学率	Enrollment Rate of Students in Junior Secondary School Phase	99.9	99.9	99.9	99.9
高 中	**Senior School**				
高中阶段新生入学率	Enrollment Rate of Students in Senior Secondary School Phase	97.0	96.5	96.0	96.0
普通高中招生比例	Recruit Students Rate of Regular Senior Secondary Schools	51	51	52	55
高 校	**Institutions of Higher Education**				
普通高等学校录取率	Admission Rate of Students in Regular Institution of Higher Education	67.4	85.1	87.8	88.3

表20.5 主要年份各级民办学校基本情况
BASIC STATISTICS OF CIVIL SCHOOLS IN MAIN YEARS

类 别	Types	2000	2010	2011	2012
民办高等学校	**Civil Institutions of Higher Education**				
学校数(所)	Schools (unit)	3	20	20	20
在校学生(万人)	Students Enrollment(10 000 persons)	0.67	9.37	9.04	8.78
专任教师(人)	Full-time Teachers(persons)	304	3 906	3 922	3 968
民办中等专业学校	**Civil Specialized Secondary Schools**				
学校数(所)	Schools (unit)		3	3	3
在校学生(万人)	Students Enrollment(10 000 persons)		0.14	0.15	0.15
专任教师(人)	Full-time Teachers(person)		98	81	47
民办职业高中学校	**Civil Vocational Schools**				
学校数(所)	Schools (unit)	1	2	2	2
在校学生(万人)	Students Enrollment(10 000 persons)	0.08	0.11	0.12	0.10
专任教师(人)	Full-time Teachers(person)	30	25	23	23
民办中学	**Civil Secondary Schools**				
学校数(所)	Schools (unit)	155	109	106	107
班级数(个)	Class(unit)	1 842	2 103	2 048	2 024
在校学生(万人)	Students Enrollment(10 000 persons)	8.48	7.87	7.66	7.48
高 中	Senior	4.54	1.68	1.45	1.39
初 中	Junior	3.94	6.19	6.21	6.09
专任教师(人)	Full-time Teachers(person)	2 400	4 583	4 625	5 078
民办小学	**Civil Primary Schools**				
学校数(所)	Schools (unit)	35	184	181	180
班级数(个)	Class(unit)	987	3 747	3 776	3 830
在校学生(万人)	Students Enrollment(10 000 persons)	3.95	16.42	16.67	16.98
专任教师(人)	Full-time Teachers(person)	831	7 181	7 368	7 869
民办幼儿园	**Civil Kindergarten**				
学校数(所)	Schools (unit)	92	396	459	500
班级数(个)	Class(unit)	636	3 584	4 204	4 655
在校学生(万人)	Students Enrollment(10 000 persons)	1.77	9.91	12.05	13.64
专任教师(人)	Full-time Teachers(person)	1 056	7 161	8 073	8 785

表 20.6 民办学校(园)基本情况(2012)
BASIC STATISTICS OF CIVIL SCHOOLS

单位:人(person)

指 标	Indicators	学校数(所) School (unit)	毕业生数 Graduate	招生数 Students Recruited	在校生数 Students Enrollment	专任教师数 Full-time Teacher
普通高等学校	Institutions of Higher Education	20	26 905	25 852	87 805	3 968
普通中等专业学校	Specialized Secondary School	3	495	448	1 458	47
职业高中学校	Secondary Vocational School	2	229	358	985	23
普通中学	Regular Secondary School	107	20 248	20 084	74 781	5 078
高 中	Senior School	–	5 274	4 470	13 869	1 264
初 中	Junior School	–	14 974	15 614	60 912	3 814
普通小学	Primary School	180	27 658	37 643	169 791	7 869
幼儿园	Kindergarten	500	36 358	48 229	136 356	8 785

注：根据《民办教育促进法》的新规定，民办中、小学统计口径中扣除了公立转制学校。
Note: According to new provision of Civil Education Advance Law, the scope of civil secondary and primary school excluded public schools transformed School excluded public schools transformed.

表 20.7 主要年份外国留学生情况
STATISTICS OF FOREIGN STUDENT IN MAIN YEARS

指 标	Indicators	2005	2010	2011	2012
外国留学生人数(人)	**Quantity of Foreign Students(person)**	**13 691**	**17 340**	**18 531**	**19 367**
按费用来源分	By Tuition Resource				
#中国政府资助	Chinese Government Sustentation	934	2 585	2 859	3 424
本国政府资助	Homeland Government Sustentation	15	347	338	286
国际组织资助	International Organization Sustentation				5
学校间交换	Inter-school Communion	463	1 570	1 754	2 227
自 费	Commoners	12 279	12 838	13 580	13 425
按地区来源分	By District				
亚 洲	Aisa	10 490	11 689	12 182	12 079
非 洲	Africa	289	969	1 233	1 366
欧 洲	Europe	1 927	3 023	3 257	4 201
北美洲	North America	766	983	1 239	1 138
南美洲	South America	129	477	403	389
大洋洲	Oceania	90	199	217	194

表 20.8 主要年份研究生人数
QUANTITY OF GRADUATE STUDENTS IN MAIN YEARS

单位：人(person)

年份 Year	获博士学位人数 Quantity of Doctor's Degrees Obtained	获硕士学位人数 Quantity of Master's Degrees Obtained	研究生 Postgraduates					
			毕业生数 Graduates		招生数 New Students Enrollment		在读人数 Students Enrollment	
			普通高等学校 Institutions of Higher Education	研究所(院) Research Institutions (Academies)	普通高等学校 Institutions of Higher Education	研究所(院) Research Institutions (Academies)	普通高等学校 Institutions of Higher Education	研究所(院) Research Institutions (Academies)
1978			9		1 072		1 253	
1980			6		410		2 696	
1985	57	1 371	1 543	37	4 264	83	8 163	170
1990	300	2 746	2 953	369	2 803	324	8 533	1 035
1991	342	2 739	2 936	320	2 717	302	8 020	949
1992	343	2 124	2 262	264	3 323	345	8 858	997
1993	368	2 489	2 569	315	3 919	363	10 037	1 008
1994	442	2 363	2 608	251	4 665	465	11 905	1 185
1995	606	2 742	3 038	317	4 776	525	13 378	1 335
1996	627	3 233	3 537	323	5 915	592	15 307	1 528
1997	890	3 585	4 117	358	6 163	562	16 841	1 619
1998	1 090	3 552	4 253	389	7 281	593	19 499	1 663
1999	1 323	4 288	5 196	415	8 758	655	22 656	1 764
2000	1 307	4 546	5 435	433	11 796	856	28 582	2 032
2001	1 487	5 330	6 380	437	14 751	1 075	36 528	2 515
2002	1 655	6 067	7 481	445	17 848	1 363	45 713	3 183
2003	1 994	7 683	9 501	578	20 767	1 757	55 092	3 998
2004	2 678	10 580	12 788	681	23 545	1 789	64 747	4 690
2005	3 119	13 245	15 857	884	25 845	1 847	73 557	5 171
2006	3 772	15 957	18 833	1 098	28 250	1 849	81 487	5 419
2007	4 355	19 250	22 691	1 235	28 748	1 862	86 177	5 586
2008	4 483	20 734	24 431	1 322	30 195	1 947	89 778	5 720
2009	4 661	23 622	26 949	1 342	35 418	2 007	97 639	5 853
2010	4 749	23 458	26 843	1 364	36 619	2 024	105 711	6 006
2011	4 610	25 568	29 431	1 385	37 971	2 109	112 902	6 115
2012	4 913	29 270	33 189	1 417	41 899	2 330	120 503	6 511

注：2001 年前的获博士学位和获硕士学位的人数为当年毕业生人数。
Note: Quantity of Doctor's and Master's Degrees obtained refer to quantity of graduates in this year before 2001.

表20.9 普通高等学校基本情况（2012）
BASIC STATISTICS OF INSTITUTIONS OF HIGHER EDUCATION

类别 Types		学校(所) Institutions (unit)	毕业生数(人) Graduates (person)	招生数(人) New Students Enrollment (person)	在校学生人数(人) Students Enrollment (person)	教职员工(人) Staff and Workers (person)	其中 of which #专任教师 Full-time Teacher	其中 of which #正、副高级 Senior and Associate Title
总计	**Total**	**67**	**136 697**	**139 841**	**506 596**	**73 348**	**40 118**	**19 391**
#综合大学	Comprehensive Universities	3	14 387	13 838	56 788	19 175	8 094	5 040
理工院校	Science and Engineering	26	57 067	58 405	213 590	27 049	15 264	7 081
农林院校	Agriculture and Forestry	2	4 700	4 443	16 372	1 523	1 087	449
医药院校	Medical	3	2 600	3 818	11 430	2 050	1 245	443
师范院校	Teacher Training	2	8 838	9 487	37 426	6 841	3 803	2 183
语文院校	Linguistics and Literacy	3	5 336	5 156	17 387	1 968	1 235	445
财经院校	Economics and Finance	18	31 537	32 808	112 508	9 189	5 967	2 463
政法院校	Politics and Law	3	7 371	6 765	23 313	2 399	1 645	570
体育院校	Physical Culture	2	1 068	1 153	4 491	1 227	620	332
艺术院校	Art Schools	5	3 793	3 968	13 291	1 927	1 158	385

注：学生数中未包括在读研究生人数，在分类院校学生数中未包括成人高等学校中的普通本专科学生。
Note: Post-graduates are not included in the students enrollment. Undergraduates and junior college students in adult education schools are not included in the students.

表20.10 普通高等学校分科专任教师数(2012)
FULL-TIME TEACHERS IN INSTITUTIONS OF HIGHER EDUCATION BY SUBJECTS

单位：人 (person)

类别 Types		专任教师数 Full-time Teachers	其中 of which 正高级 Senior Title	副高级 Associate Title	中级 Junior Title	初级 Primary Title	无职称 Non-Title
总计	**Total**	**40 118**	**6 781**	**12 610**	**16 498**	**2 877**	**1 352**
哲学	Philosophy	1 010	171	315	394	88	42
经济	Economics	2 423	405	871	968	114	65
法学	Law	2 542	377	719	1 125	222	99
教育学	Education	3 862	317	824	1 917	568	236
文学	Literature	8 889	993	2 314	4 366	852	364
历史学	History	435	135	127	150	17	6
理学	Science	4 031	1 102	1 456	1 288	75	110
工学	Engineering	11 285	2 322	4 198	4 055	466	244
农学	Agriculture	423	86	155	142	27	13
医学	Medical	2 235	391	598	950	253	43
管理学	Administrotion	2 983	482	1 033	1 143	195	130

表 20.11 普通高等学校本科分科学生数(2012)
UNDERGRADUATE STUDENTS IN INSTITUTIONS OF HIGHER EDUCATION BY SUBJECTS

单位:人 (person)

类 别	Types	毕业生人数 Graduates	招生人数 New Students Enrollment	在校学生人数 Students Enrollment
总 计	**Total**	**85 714**	**92 594**	**359 007**
哲 学	Philosophy	120	181	635
经济学	Economics	8 372	8 153	32 020
法 学	Law	6 038	5 464	22 029
教育学	Education	1 712	2 399	8 716
文 学	Literature	14 697	16 010	61 431
历史学	History	247	177	848
理 学	Science	6 528	7 245	27 996
工 学	Engineering	28 104	31 438	122 803
农 学	Agriculture	529	476	1 902
医 学	Medical	1 965	2 358	9 982
管理学	Administrotion	17 402	18 693	70 645

表 20.12 中等专业学校基本情况(2012)
BASIC STATISTICS OF SPECIALIZED SECONDARY SCHOOLS

单位:人 (person)

类 别	Types	毕业生数 Graduates	招生数 New Students Enrollment	在校学生 Students Enrollment	专业课专任教师 Full-time Teachers in Professional Course	其中 of which: #正副高级 Senior and Associate Title	#中 级 Junior Title
总 计	**Total**	**27 670**	**27 637**	**98 815**	**4 797**	**1 154**	**2 385**
#土木水利工程	Construction and Water Conservancy Engineering	1 366	1 959	6 102	132	38	64
加工制造	Machining and Manufacture	4 734	4 415	15 785	323	105	142
交通运输	Transport	2 990	2 954	9 386	184	40	97
信息技术	Information Technology	2 388	3 738	11 092	362	75	207
医药卫生	Health	3 150	2 639	11 080	269	82	145
财经商贸	Trade and Tour	8 013	6 804	26 687	507	110	258
旅游服务	Finance and Economics	550	900	2 073	31	6	16
文化艺术与体育	Arts and Physical Culture	1 243	1 579	5 999	511	126	256
公共管理与服务	Society Commonality Business	542	240	1 149	14	3	6

表 20.13 各区、县普通中学基本情况(2012)
BASIC STATISTICS OF REGULAR SECONDARY SCHOOLS BY DISTRICTS AND COUNTIES

地 区	District	学校(所) Schools (unit)	毕业生数(人) Graduates (person)	招生数(人) New Students Enrollment (person)	在校学生(人) Students Enrollment (person)	教职员工(人) Staff and Workers (person)	其中 of which #专任教师 Full-time Teachers
总 计	**Total**	**760**	**149 061**	**169 986**	**590 395**	**75 758**	**51 790**
浦东新区	Pudong New Area	149	34 535	40 958	139 828	15 165	11 329
黄 浦 区	Huangpu	36	6 789	6 974	24 822	3 576	2 453
徐 汇 区	Xuhui	38	9 887	10 352	36 677	4 382	3 401
长 宁 区	Changning	27	5 085	5 420	19 264	2 866	1 831
静 安 区	Jing'an	15	3 240	3 386	12 335	1 717	1 121
普 陀 区	Putuo	49	7 402	8 034	28 487	4 537	2 740
闸 北 区	Zhabei	36	6 792	6 720	24 568	3 235	2 203
虹 口 区	Hongkou	41	6 985	6 690	24 698	3 327	2 515
杨 浦 区	Yangpu	53	9 174	9 068	33 502	4 352	3 185
闵 行 区	Minhang	63	10 265	13 903	45 219	6 513	4 141
宝 山 区	Baoshan	56	9 679	12 202	41 504	4 993	3 485
嘉 定 区	Jiading	36	5 587	8 184	26 041	3 124	2 140
金 山 区	Jinshan	29	6 431	6 825	23 490	2 939	2 144
松 江 区	Songjiang	33	7 630	8 855	32 529	4 542	2 448
青 浦 区	Qingpu	24	6 033	7 191	25 635	3 043	2 120
奉 贤 区	Fengxian	38	6 782	9 911	31 128	4 085	2 255
崇 明 县	Chongming	37	6 765	5 313	20 668	3 362	2 279

表 20.14 各区、县普通中学初、高中学生基本情况(2012)
BASIC STATISTICS OF REGULAR JUNIOR AND SENIOR SCHOOLS' STUDENTS BY DISTRICTS AND COUNTIES

单位:人 (person)

地 区 District		毕业生数 Graduates		招生数 New Students Enrollment		在校学生 Students Enrollment	
		初 中 Junior	高 中 Senior	初 中 Junior	高 中 Senior	初 中 Junior	高 中 Senior
总 计	**Total**	**94 645**	**54 416**	**117 489**	**52 497**	**432 686**	**157 709**
浦东新区	Pudong New Area	23 084	11 451	29 616	11 342	105 718	34 110
黄 浦 区	Huangpu	3 741	3 048	3 800	3 174	15 243	9 579
徐 汇 区	Xuhui	6 006	3 881	6 418	3 934	25 018	11 659
长 宁 区	Changning	3 276	1 809	3 520	1 900	13 789	5 475
静 安 区	Jing'an	1 967	1 273	2 023	1 363	8 280	4 055
普 陀 区	Putuo	4 607	2 795	5 292	2 742	20 417	8 070
闸 北 区	Zhabei	4 155	2 637	4 364	2 356	17 559	7 009
虹 口 区	Hongkou	4 081	2 904	4 139	2 551	16 717	7 981
杨 浦 区	Yangpu	5 218	3 956	5 343	3 725	22 222	11 280
闵 行 区	Minhang	6 634	3 631	10 244	3 659	34 693	10 526
宝 山 区	Baoshan	6 511	3 168	8 794	3 408	31 506	9 998
嘉 定 区	Jiading	3 652	1 935	6 183	2 001	20 160	5 881
金 山 区	Jinshan	4 069	2 362	4 861	1 964	17 194	6 296
松 江 区	Songjiang	5 308	2 322	6 503	2 352	25 553	6 976
青 浦 区	Qingpu	3 916	2 117	5 257	1 934	19 644	5 991
奉 贤 区	Fengxian	4 655	2 127	7 843	2 068	24 943	6 185
崇 明 县	Chongming	3 765	3 000	3 289	2 024	14 030	6 638

表 20.15 各区、县普通小学基本情况(2012)
BASIC STATISTICS OF REGULAR PRIMARY SCHOOLS BY DISTRICTS AND COUNTIES

地区	District	学校(所) Schools (unit)	毕业生数(人) Graduates (person)	招生数(人) New Students Enrollment (person)	在校学生(人) Students Enrollment (person)	教职员工(人) Staff and Workers (person)	其中 of which #专任教师 Full-time Teachers
总　计	**Total**	**761**	**129 542**	**172 297**	**760 377**	**48 936**	**48 066**
浦东新区	Pudong New Area	165	31 230	42 718	183 060	10 502	10 755
黄浦区	Huangpu	30	3 523	3 979	17 897	2 057	1 664
徐汇区	Xuhui	43	6 081	6 958	31 490	2 581	2 232
长宁区	Changning	24	3 546	4 090	18 668	1 652	1 456
静安区	Jing'an	12	1 809	1 955	9 067	986	717
普陀区	Putuo	26	5 589	6 663	29 068	1 589	2 093
闸北区	Zhabei	34	4 083	4 778	21 520	1 939	1 547
虹口区	Hongkou	34	3 984	4 656	21 293	1 852	1 806
杨浦区	Yangpu	44	5 359	5 899	27 176	2 372	2 265
闵行区	Minhang	62	13 021	19 019	81 309	4 567	4 562
宝山区	Baoshan	73	11 196	14 661	63 313	3 912	4 124
嘉定区	Jiading	39	7 129	10 988	48 995	2 612	2 504
金山区	Jinshan	31	5 035	5 864	28 509	2 162	1 850
松江区	Songjiang	33	8 822	13 368	60 390	2 621	3 125
青浦区	Qingpu	45	7 017	11 166	48 952	3 094	2 888
奉贤区	Fengxian	34	8 508	11 102	50 529	2 077	2 544
崇明县	Chongming	32	3 610	4 433	19 141	2 361	1 934

表 20.16 主要年份实验性示范性中学基本情况
BASIC STATISTICS OF SECONDARY CAMPUS SCHOOL IN MAIN YEARS

指 标	Indicators	2000	2010	2011	2012
学校(所)	Schools (unit)	84	128	130	139
班级数(个)	Classes (unit)	2 584	4 063	4 037	4 246
在校学生(万人)	Students Enrollment(10 000 persons)	12.10	14.67	14.52	15.04
教职员工(万人)	Staff and Workers (10 000 persons)	1.40	1.88	1.90	1.98
#专任教师	Full-time Teachers	0.88	1.42	1.44	1.53

注：实验性示范性中学包括重点中学和寄宿制高级中学。
Note: Seconcary campus school includs important secondary school and boarding high school.

表 20.17 主要年份幼儿园基本情况
BASIC STATISTICS OF KINDERGARTENS IN MAIN YEARS

指 标	Indicators	2000	2010	2011	2012
幼儿园(所)	Kindergartens (unit)	958	1 252	1 337	1 401
幼儿数(万人)	Children Enrollment (10 000 persons)	24.12	40.03	44.42	48.06
教职员工(万人)	Staff and Workers(10 000 persons)	2.52	4.09	4.58	4.90
#教　师	Teachers	1.50	2.67	2.92	3.13

表 20.18 主要年份特殊教育基本情况
BASIC STATISTICS OF SPECIAL EDUCATION IN MAIN YEARS

指 标	Indicators	2000	2010	2011	2012
学校(所)	Schools (unit)	34	29	29	29
毕业生数(人)	Graduates(person)	868	918	907	806
招生数(人)	New Students Enrollment(person)	1 141	776	732	737
在校学生(人)	Students Enrollment(person)	5 407	5 036	4 927	4 723
教职员工(人)	Staff and Workers(person)	1 584	1 596	1 577	1 580
#专任教师	Full-time Teachers	943	1 143	1 158	1 177

表 20.19 网络教育本科学生情况(2012)
BASIC STATISTICS OF UNDERGRADUATE STUDENTS OF NETWORK EDUCATION BY SUBJECT

单位:人(person)

类别	Types	毕业生人数 Graduates	招生人数 New Students Enrollment	在校学生人数 Students Enrollment
总 计	**Total**	**19 065**	**14 804**	**32 080**
经济学	Economics	1 396	550	1 389
法 学	Law	382	292	605
教育学	Education	1 924	2 355	4 533
文 学	Literature	1 287	1 043	2 098
历史学	History	2		
理 学	Science	404	436	777
工 学	Engineering	2 737	1 994	4 427
医 学	Medical	1 304	1 570	2 959
管理学	Administration	9 629	6 564	15 292

表 20.20 各级各类成人学校基本情况(2012)
BASIC STATISTICS OF ADULT SCHOOLS AT VARIOUS LEVELS

类别	Types	学校数(所) Schools (unit)	毕业生人数(人) Graduates (person)	招生数(人) New Students Enrollment (person)	在校学生人数(人) Students Enrollment (person)	教职员工人数(人) Staff and Workers (person)	其中 of which #专任教师 Full-time Teachers
成人高等教育	**Adult Higher Education**	**16**	**56 598**	**58 542**	**183 650**	**1 733**	**933**
广播电视大学	Broadcasting and TV Universities	1				310	150
职工高等学校	Staff Higher Education Schools	11	4 478	3 715	9 038	1 067	640
管理干部学院	Institutes for Administrative Officials	4	1 010	342	1 187	356	143
普通高等学校办	Run by Regular High Education Institutions	63	51 110	54 485	173 425		
函 授	Correspondence Programs	9	3 805	3 236	10 113		
业 余	Spare Time	50	46 642	51 249	163 241		
脱 产	Full Time	4	663		71		
成人网络本、专科	**Adult Network Education**		**58 750**	**54 603**	**137 555**		
成人中等教育	**Adult Secondary Education**	**35**	**5 627**	**5 430**	**18 787**	**624**	**328**
成人中等专业学校	Specialized Secondary Schools	23	4 029	5 383	14 142	532	245
成人中学	Adult Spare-time Secondary Schools	12	1 598	47	4 645	92	83
成人职业技术学校	**Adult Technical Secondary Schools**	**799**	**222 033**		**271 424**	**17 407**	**7 289**

①"( )"指高等院校举办的各类成人教学点数据。成人中学学校在校学生数为在校注册学生数
②成人职业技术学校毕业生及在校学生数为培训半年以上人数。
❶The figures with"( )" refer to the number of the adult education places conducted by higher education institutions. Students enrollment of adult spare-time secondary schools refers to the number of students registered at school.
❷Graduates and Students Enrollment of adult technical secondary schools refers to accumulative total number of students registered at schools who has been trained more than half a year.

上／海／统／计／年／鉴

主要统计指标解释

学　校

指按国家规定的设置标准和审批程序批准设立的，招收适龄人口实施各级各类教育活动的教育机构。

普通高等学校

指按照国家规定的设置标准和审批程序批准举办的，通过全国普通高等学校统一招生考试，招收高中毕业生为主要培养对象，实施高等教育的全日制大学、独立设置的学院和高等专科学校、高等职业学校和其他机构。大学、独立设置的学院主要实施本科层次以上教育，高等专科学校、高等职业学校实施专科层次教育，其他机构是承担国家普通招生计划任务不计校数的机构。包括普通高等学校分校和批准筹建的普通高等学校等。

成人高等学校

指按国家规定的设置标准和审批程序举办的，通过全国成人高等教育统一招生考试，招收高中毕业或同等学历的人员为主要培养对象，利用函授、业余、脱产的多种形式对其实施高等学历教育的学校。包括：职工高等学校、农民高等学校、管理干部学院、教育学院、独立函授学院、广播电视大学、其他机构等。

中等专业学校

指经县或县以上教育行政部门批准设立，招收初中毕业生实施中等专业课程教育的教学机构。

职业中学（职业高中、职业初中）

指经县或县以上教育行政部门批准设立，招收小学或初中毕业生实施中等职业技术教育的教学机构。按学校性质类别可分为：独立设置的职业中学（包括：职业初中、职业高中、职业初高中合设学校）；附设有普通中学班的职业中学。

普通中学（普通高中、普通初中）

普通中学分为普通高级中学和普通初级中学两个阶段。普通初级中学是指独立设置的招收小学毕业的适龄人口进行初级中等基础教育的机构；普通高级中学是指独立设置的招收初中毕业的适龄人口进行高级中等基础教育的机构；完全中学是指普通初、高中合设的教育机构；一贯制学校是指在一所学校连续实施中小学教育的机构。其中包括实施九年义务教育的九年一贯制学校和实施高中教育的十二年一贯制学校。（说明：一贯制学校的办学条件如能划分为小学、初中、高中，则分开填报；如不能划分清楚，可按就高不就低的方法填入初中、高中报表中，不能重复填写。）

普通小学

指由区或区以上教育行政部门批准，招收学龄儿童实施初等教育的教学机构。

幼儿园

指招收三周岁以上（含三周岁）学龄前幼儿，对其进行保育和教育的单位。

特殊教育学校

指本市独立设置的招收盲聋哑和智残儿童，以及其他特殊需要的儿童、青少年进行普通或职业初、中等教育的教学机构。

小学学龄儿童净入学率

小学学龄人口中正在接受小学教育人数所占比重。

初中学生净入学率

是指初中阶段教育（接受普通初中教育和职业初中教育）在校学生总数占初中阶段教育学龄人口数的比重。

预算内教育经费

指中央、地方各级财政或上级主管部门在年度内安排，并计划拨到教育部门和其他部门主办的各级各类学校、教育事业单位，列入国家预算支出科目的教育经费，包括教育事业拨款、科研经费拨款、基建拨款和其他经费拨款。

SHANGHAI STATISTICAL YEARBOOK

EXPLANATORY NOTES TO MAJOR STATISTICAL INDICATORS

□ School Institutions

School Institutions refer to education establishment set up according to the government evaluation and approval procedures, enrolling population of the right age, providing various phase education activity.

□ Regular Institutions of Higher Education

Regular Institutions of Higher Learning refer to educational establishments set up according to the government evaluation and approval procedures, enrolling graduates from senior secondary schools and providing higher education courses and training for senior professionals. They include full-time universities, colleges, high professional schools, high professional vocational schools and others.

Universities and colleges are mainly providing undergraduate courses; those high professional schools and high professional vocational schools are mainly providing professional trainings; and others refer to educational establishments, which are responsible for enrolling students but not covered in the total number of schools, including: branch schools of universities and colleges, and universities and colleges that have been proved and prepared to construct.

□ Institutions of Higher Education for Adults

Institution of Higher Learning for Adults refer to educational establishments, set up in line with relevant rules approved by the government, enrolling personnel with senior secondary schools or equivalent education, and providing higher education courses in many forms of correspondence, spare time, or full time for adults. Institutions of higher schools for adults include schools of higher educations for staff and workers, schools of higher education for peasants, colleges for management cadres, pedagogical colleges, independent correspondence colleges, Radio and TV universities and other educational establishment, etc.

□ Specialized Secondary Schools

Specialized Secondary schools refer to educational establishment set up according to approval and permission by educational administration department of district and above government, enrolling graduates from junior secondary schools and providing secondary professional education courses.

□ Vocational Secondary Schools (senior secondary schools and junior secondary schools)

Vocational Secondary Schools (senior secondary schools and junior secondary schools) refer to educational establishment set up according to approval and permission by educational administration department of district and above government, enrolling graduates from primary schools and junior secondary schools and providing secondary vocational education courses.

□ Regular Secondary Schools (senior secondary schools and junior secondary schools)

Regular Secondary Schools (senior secondary schools and junior secondary schools) are classified as senior secondary schools and junior secondary schools. Junior Secondary Schools refer to educational establishment enrolling graduates from primary schools and providing junior secondary educational courses. Senior Secondary Schools refer to educational establishment enrolling graduates from junior secondary schools and providing higher secondary educational courses.

□ Regular Primary Schools

Regular Primary Schools refer to educational establishment set up according to approval and permission by educational administration department of district and above government, enrolling graduates from children of school age and providing primary educational courses.

□ Kindergartens

Kindergartens refer to nursery and education establishment, enrolling children in 3 years old and above.

□ Special Education Schools

Special Education Schools refer to educational establishments set up independently, enrolling blind, deaf, dumb, amentia or other special children, and educational establishment, providing regular or vocational junior and senior secondary education for hobbledehoy.

EXPLANATORY NOTES TO MAJOR STATISTICAL INDICATORS

□ Enrollment Rate of School-age Children

Enrollment Rate of School-age Children refers to the proportion of school age children enrolled at schools to the total number of school age children both in and outside schools.

□ Enrolment Rate of Students in Junior Secondary School Phase

It refers to the proportion of total quantity of student in junior secondary school to the population of junior school age.

□ Budgetary Fund for Education

Budgetary Fund for Education refers to education fund that is planned to allocate to various schools and education institutions by central and local financial departments at various levels within the reference year, which is within the state budgetary expenditure, including: appropriate funds for education, science and research, capital construction and others.

第二十一篇

CHAPTER 21

卫生、社会保障和社会福利业

HEALTH, SOCIAL SECURITY AND SOCIAL WELFARE

简要说明

一、本章资料的主要内容

本篇主要反映卫生、社会保障和社会福利的发展情况。

卫生部分主要包括卫生机构、卫生技术人员、卫生机构床位、医疗机构诊疗入院、疾病死亡原因、婴儿死亡原因、三大死亡率、防病工作、家庭病床、妇幼卫生工作、公民献血用血等情况。

社会保障部分主要包括城镇基本养老保险、城镇职工基本医疗保险、城镇居民基本医疗保险、城镇职工失业保险、城镇职工生育保险、城镇职工工伤保险、农村合作医疗、少儿住院基金等参保人数情况。

社会福利部分主要包括社会保障标准、社会福利事业机构、民间组织、养老服务、医疗服务和红十字会等情况。

二、本篇资料的来源

卫生部分资料由上海市卫生和计划生育委员会提供。社会保障资料由上海市人力资源和社会保障局提供。社会福利资料中，社会保障标准、社会福利事业机构、民间组织、养老服务资料由上海市民政局提供；医疗服务资料由上海市卫生和计划生育委员会提供；红十字会资料由上海市红十字会提供。

BRIEF INTRODUCTION

I. Main Contents

Data in this chapter mainly reflect the development of public health, social security, and social welfare.

Data on public health include mainly the number of medical and healthcare institutions, beds available at such institutions, medical personnel, in–patients medical treatment and death–causing diseases, infant death–causing diseases and composition, top three death–causing diseases, disease prevention, family sickbeds, work of gynecology and pediatrics, blood offered and used by citizens.

Data on social security include mainly the numbers of participants in urban basic pension insurance, urban employee basic medical care insurance, urban basic medical care insurance, unemployment insurance, maternity insurance, work injury insurance, rural social medical care insurance, and medical fund of children.

Data on social welfare include social security standards, social welfare institutions, civil organizations, services for aged people, medical services and basic statistics about the Red Cross Society of China Shanghai Municipal Branch

Data on social welfare include social security standards, social welfare institutions, civil organizations, services for aged people, medical services and basic statistics about the Red Cross Society of China Shanghai Municipal Branch

II. Sources of data

Data on public health are provided by Shanghai Municipal Health and Family Planning Commissio. Data on social security are provided by Shanghai Municipal Human Resources and Social Security Bureau. Of data on social welfare, data on social security standards, social welfare institutions, civil organizations, and services for aged people are provided by Shanghai Civil Affairs Bureau; data on medical services are provided by Shanghai Health and Family Planning Commission; data on Red Cross are provided by the Red Cross Society of China Shanghai Municipal Branch.

表21.1 卫生事业基本情况(1978~2012)
BASIC STATISTICS OF PUBLIC HEALTH

年份 Year	卫生机构数(个) Health Care Institutions (unit)	其中 of which #医院 Hospital	卫生技术人员(万人) Medical Professionals (10 000 persons)	其中 of which #医生 Doctors	卫生机构床位数(万张) Beds in Health Care Institutions (10 000 beds)	其中 of which #医院 Hospital	每万人口医生数(人) Doctors per 10 000 Persons (person)	每万人口医院床位数(张) Hospital Beds per 10 000 Persons (bed)
1978	4 823	388	8.50	3.35	5.47	4.68	30	42
1979	5 627	394	8.88	3.58	5.56	4.78	31	42
1980	6 067	399	9.41	3.92	5.80	4.94	34	43
1981	6 337	403	9.57	4.37	5.84	4.99	37	43
1982	6 445	408	9.88	4.72	5.93	5.11	40	43
1983	6 451	415	10.09	4.87	6.00	5.20	41	43
1984	6 318	420	10.24	4.84	6.16	5.34	40	44
1985	7 245	405	10.42	4.85	6.02	5.32	39	43
1986	7 306	419	10.71	4.91	6.22	5.47	39	44
1987	7 330	431	11.00	5.05	6.38	5.60	40	44
1988	7 471	444	11.46	5.40	6.79	5.89	42	46
1989	7 550	460	11.65	5.73	6.87	6.04	44	46
1990	7 690	462	11.84	5.82	6.96	6.21	44	47
1991	7 554	463	11.92	5.89	7.01	6.31	44	47
1992	7 363	454	11.82	5.88	7.07	6.42	43	47
1993	6 077	486	11.53	5.75	7.12	6.75	42	49
1994	5 606	497	11.20	5.52	7.20	6.81	39	49
1995	5 286	485	11.06	5.37	7.10	6.69	38	47
1996	5 200	477	10.95	5.24	7.00	6.73	36	46
1997	5 028	474	10.89	5.13	7.00	6.78	34	46
1998	4 637	473	10.84	5.03	7.02	6.83	33	45
1999	4 620	465	10.81	5.06	7.24	7.06	32	45
2000	4 400	459	10.71	4.99	7.53	7.31	31	45
2001	3 813	432	10.51	4.85	7.88	7.63	30	47
2002	2 422	436	10.16	4.38	8.15	8.13	27	50
2003	2 319	452	10.22	4.41	8.44	8.11	26	47
2004	2 577	489	10.17	4.38	8.64	8.50	25	49
2005	2 527	487	10.35	4.40	9.08	8.93	25	50
2006	2 519	505	10.90	4.55	9.44	9.28	25	51
2007	2 646	288	12.24	4.88	9.59	7.54	26	41
2008	2 809	301	12.77	5.12	9.78	7.78	27	41
2009	3 013	296	13.09	5.11	9.97	7.95	27	41
2010	3 270	306	13.54	5.13	10.51	8.48	22	37
2011	3 358	308	13.91	5.21	10.71	8.75	22	37
2012	3 465	317	14.61	5.42	10.96	9.00	23	38

①2002 年开始，卫生指标按照新的《中国卫生统计调查制度》统计。其中，医生为执业医师和执业助理医师；护师、护士为注册护士。
②2007 年开始，医院统计范围按照新的《2007 国家卫生统计调查制度》统计，不再包括社区卫生服务中心、妇幼保健院和专科防治院。
❶Since 2002, statistics of health care has been based on "China Health Care Statistical Investigation System". Of which, Doctors refer to certified physicians and certified assistant physicians, senior and junior nurses refer to registered nurses.
❷Since 2007, statistics of hospital has been based on "2007 National Health Care Statistical Investigation System", not including the community health care service center, maternity and child care hospital and special disease hospital.

表 21.2 各类卫生机构、床位及人员数(2012)
VARIOUS HEALTH CARE INSTITUTIONS, BEDS AND PERSONNEL

机构类别	Type of Institutions	机构数（个）Health Care Institutions (unit)	床位数（张）Beds (bed)	从业人员数（人）Personnel (person)
总　计	**Total**	**3 465**	**109 612**	**182 104**
# 医疗机构合计	Medical Institutions	3 369	109 612	173 407
# 医　院	Hospitals	317	89 971	122 417
综合医院	Comprehensive Hospitals	184	54 829	87 396
中医医院	Hospitals of Traditional Chinese	17	5 222	8 281
中西医结合医院	Hospitals of Combination of	7	2 657	3 822
专科医院	Special Diseases Hospitals	92	23 228	21 433
护理院	Nursing Home	17	4 035	1 485
基层医疗卫生机构	Basic Medical and Health Institutions	3 004	17 397	45 965
社区卫生服务中心(站)	Community Health Care Centers	1 002	17 286	31 898
门诊部	Policlinic	533	111	8 427
诊所、卫生所、医务室	Clinic, Health Center and Infirmary	1 469		5 640
专业公共卫生机构	Professional Medical and Health Institutions	99	1 482	11 458
疾病预防控制中心	Disease Prevention and Control Centers	20		3 093
专科疾病防治院(所、站)	Special Disease Hospitals and Institutions	19	160	1 318
健康教育所(站、中心)	Health Education Institutions	2		99
妇幼保健院(所、站)	Maternity and Child Care Hospital and Institutions	21	1 322	2 844
急救中心(站)	First-aid Centers	11		2 162
采供血机构	Blood Collection and Supply Institutions	8		637
卫生监督所(中心)	Health Supervision Centers	18		1 305
其他卫生机构	Other Health Care Institutions	45	762	2 264
疗养院	Sanatoriums	3	762	482
卫生监督检验(检测、监测)所(站)	Health Supervision and Inspection Institutions	2		32
医疗科学研究机构	Institutions of Medical Science	9		473
医学在职培训机构	Medical In-service Training Institutions	8		439
临床检验中心(所、站)	Clinical Test Centers	5		381
其　他	Others	18		457

表 21.2 续表 continued

机构类别	Type of Institutions	#卫生技术人员 Medical Professionals	其中 of which #医生 Doctors	#护师、护士 Senior and Junior Nurses
总　计	**Total**	**146 148**	**54 218**	**63 229**
#医疗机构	Medical Institutions	141 059	52 328	62 730
#医　院	Hospitals	100 061	32 901	48 591
综合医院	Comprehensive Hospitals	72 481	24 271	35 307
中医医院	Hospitals of Traditional Chinese	6 798	2 519	2 824
中西医结合医院	Hospitals of Combination of	3 143	1 117	1 411
专科医院	Special Diseases Hospitals	16 584	4 763	8 491
护理院	Nursing Home	1 055	231	558
基层医疗卫生机构	Basic Medical and Health Institutions	37 034	17 794	12 545
社区卫生服务中心(站)	Community Health Care Centers	26 077	11 624	8 995
门诊部	Policlinic	6 601	3 301	2 390
诊所、卫生所、医务室	Clinic, Health Center and Infirmary	4 356	2 869	1 160
专业公共卫生机构	Professional Medical and Health Institutions	7 920	3 226	1 822
疾病预防控制中心	Disease Prevention and Control Centers	2 173	1 300	46
专科疾病防治院(所、站)	Special Disease Hospitals and Institutions	1 047	526	317
健康教育所(站、中心)	Health Education Institutions	34	2	
妇幼保健院(所、站)	Maternity and Child Care Hospital and Institutions	2 443	962	1 159
急救中心(站)	First-aid Centers	723	405	95
采供血机构	Blood Collection and Supply Institutions	460	31	205
卫生监督所(中心)	Health Supervision Centers	1 040		
其他卫生机构	Other Health Care Institutions	1 133	297	271
疗养院	Sanatoriums	302	111	118
卫生监督检验(检测、监测)所(站)	Health Supervision and Inspection Institutions	26	1	
医疗科学研究机构	Institutions of Medical Science	263	82	6
医学在职培训机构	Medical In-service Training Institutions	87	16	40
临床检验中心(所、站)	Clinical Test Centers	172	34	
其　他	Others	283	53	107

表21.3 各区、县卫生机构基本情况(2012)
STATISTICS OF HEALTH CARE INSTITUTIONS BY DISTRICTS AND COUNTIES

地 区	District	机构数（个）Health Care Institutions(unit)	床位数（张）Hospital Beds (bed)	卫生技术人员(人) Medical Professionals (person)	其 中 of which	
					#医 生 Doctors	#护师、护士 Senior and Junior Nurses
总 计	**Total**	**3 465**	**109 612**	**146 148**	**54 218**	**63 229**
浦东新区	Pudong New Area	606	15 508	20 927	8 017	8 711
黄浦区	Huangpu	228	10 458	16 367	5 840	7 274
徐汇区	Xuhui	293	13 446	18 226	6 196	8 156
长宁区	Changning	231	4 914	8 332	3 077	3 611
静安区	Jing'an	129	5 886	8 883	3 163	3 957
普陀区	Putuo	155	5 440	6 878	2 612	2 943
闸北区	Zhabei	130	5 315	6 291	2 274	2 730
虹口区	Hongkou	155	6 655	8 220	3 129	3 556
杨浦区	Yangpu	167	7 453	8 755	3 138	4 090
闵行区	Minhang	284	6 993	8 934	3 466	3 806
宝山区	Baoshan	268	5 232	7 323	2 813	3 136
嘉定区	Jiading	221	3 545	5 379	2 175	2 252
金山区	Jinshan	111	4 001	4 542	1 628	2 032
松江区	Songjiang	164	4 230	5 380	2 216	2 144
青浦区	Qingpu	125	2 607	3 884	1 448	1 652
奉贤区	Fengxian	81	4 835	4 228	1 643	1 692
崇明县	Chongming	117	3 094	3 599	1 383	1 487

表21.4 医疗机构病床使用情况(2012)
STATISTICS OF HOSPITAL BED USAGE IN MEDICAL TREATMENT INSTITUTION

机构类别	Types	平均开放床位数(张) Average Beds Opened(bed)	病床周转次数(次) Turnover Times of Beds(time)	病床使用率(%) Usage Rate of Beds(%)	出院者平均住院日(日) Average Days to Inpatient in Hospital(day)
总 计	**Total**	**113 062**	**26.73**	**96.23**	**12.20**
卫生部门	Medical Institutions	91 246	28.33	99.23	11.87
#医 院	Hospital	94 133	28.91	98.00	11.41
#综合医院	Comprehensive Hospitals	45 726	37.62	102.81	9.91
中(西)医医院	Hospitals of Chinese (Western) Wedicine	7 798	29.57	94.83	11.75
护理院	Nursing Hospitals	515	1.63	104.20	112.38
社区卫生服务中心	Community Health Care Centers	16 746	6.09	89.02	46.47
其他部门	Other Departments	21 815	18.36	83.66	14.32

表21.5 医疗机构诊疗人次和入院人数(2012)
PATIENTS TREATED AND INPATIENTS IN MEDICAL TREATMENT INSTITUTION

机构类别	Types	诊疗人次(万人次) Total Patients Treated(10 000 person-times)	其中 of which #门、急诊 Outpatients and Emergency Patients	入院人数(万人) Inpatients (10 000 persons)	每百诊次的入院人数(人) Inpatients per 100 Patient-times (person)
总 计	**Total**	**21 402.13**	**21 114.29**	**298.80**	**1.40**
医 院	Hospitals	12 942.58	12 882.47	272.45	2.11
综合医院	Comprehensive Hospitals	9 534.38	9 481.96	204.63	2.15
中(西)医医院	Hospitals of Chinese(Western) Medicine	1 838.79	1 838.09	23.05	1.25
传染病医院	Infectious Diseases Hospitals	48.15	48.15	1.42	2.95
精神病医院	Mental Hospitals	126.72	125.15	1.18	0.93
结核病医院	Tuberculosis Hospitals	71.99	71.99	5.07	7.04
肿瘤医院	Tumor Hospitals	96.46	96.45	4.71	4.88
儿童医院	Children's Hospitals	488.76	488.76	8.23	1.68
其他专科医院	Other Specialized Hospitals	709.59	704.18	23.15	3.26
护理院	Nurse Hospitals	27.74	27.74	1.01	3.64
社区卫生服务中心	Community Health-care Service Centers	7 544.16	7 331.92	10.14	0.13
妇幼保健院(所、站)	Maternity and Child Care Hospital	253.02	242.68	8.35	3.30
其他医疗机构	Other Medical Facilities	662.37	657.22	7.86	1.19

表 21.6 前十位疾病死亡原因和构成(2012)
THE TOP 10 DEATH-CAUSING DISEASES AND COMPOSITION

死亡原因	Cause of Death	死亡专率(1/10 万) Death Rate(1/100 000)	占死亡总数(%) Percentage of Total Death(%)
循环系病	Circulation Diseases	304.46	37.02
肿　瘤	Tumor	252.25	30.67
呼吸系病	Respiratory System Diseases	86.21	10.48
内分泌营养代谢病	Endocrine-Immunity-Metabolic Diseases	38.39	4.67
损伤中毒	Damnification and Poisoning	37.33	4.54
消化系病	Digestive System Diseases	22.71	2.76
神经系病	Nervous System Disease	9.89	1.20
传染病及寄生虫病	Infectious & Parasitic Diseases	9.14	1.11
精神病	Mental System Diseases	7.71	0.94
泌尿生殖系病	Genitourinary Diseases	7.19	0.87

表 21.7 婴儿前五位疾病死亡原因和构成(2012)
THE TOP 5 INFANT DEATH-CAUSING DISEASES AND COMPOSITION

死亡原因	Cause of Death	死亡专率(1/10 万) Death Rate(1/100 000)	占死亡总数(%) Percentage of Total Death(%)
围生期疾病(新生儿病)	Neonatal Disease	122.96	45.00
先天异常	Congenital Anomaly	106.73	39.06
损伤中毒	Damnification and Poisoning	12.81	4.69
神经系病	Nerwns System Disease	11.10	4.06
肿　瘤	Tumor	5.12	1.88

表 21.8 婴儿死亡率、新生儿死亡率、孕产妇死亡率(2009～2012)
DEATH RATE OF INFANT,NEW BORN,PREGNANT AND LYING-IN WOMAN

指　标	Indicators	2009	2010	2011	2012
婴儿死亡率(‰)	Death Rate of Infant(‰)	2.89	5.97	5.70	5.04
新生儿死亡率(‰)	Death Rate of New Born(‰)	1.94	2.03	2.96	2.58
孕产妇死亡率(1/10 万)	Death Rate of Pregnant and Lying-in Woman(1/100 000)	7.08	9.61	7.36	7.10

表21.9 主要年份防病工作情况
BASIC STATISTICS OF DISEASE PREVENTION IN MAIN YEARS

指标	Indicators	2000	2010	2011	2012
传染病发病总例数(甲、乙)(万例)	**Cases of Contagious Diseases Reported (A,B)(10 000 cases)**	**3.58**	**2.22**	**2.30**	**2.14**
发病率(1/10万)	Disease Rate(1/100 000)	271.66	161.17	163.91	151.66
传染病死亡总人数(人)	Quantity of Deaths Caused by Contagious Diseases (person)	179	127	118	104
死亡率(1/10万)	Death Rate (1/100 000)	1.36	0.92	0.84	0.74
结核病登记病人数(千例)	T. B. Patients Registered (10 000 cases)	3.09	3.26	3.29	3.50
登记患病率(‰)	Registered Disease Rate(‰)	0.23	0.23	0.23	0.25
结核病新发病人数(千例)	Newly Reported T. B. Cases(10 000 cases)	5.18	3.76	3.85	3.77
登记新发病率(1/万)	Registered Newly Diseased Rate (1/10 000)	3.94	2.67	2.72	2.65
结核病死亡人数(人)	Quantity of Deaths Caused By T. B (person)	293	112	145	112
死亡率(1/10万)	Death Rate (1/100 000)	2.22	0.80	1.02	0.79
牙病受检人数(万人)	Quantity of People Undergoing Tooth Disease Check (10 000 persons)	51.89	54.85	52.28	53.02
龋牙患病率(%)	Rate of Caries Patients (%)	28.3	38.6	37.5	36.2
小学生视力不良率(%)	Nearsight in Primary School Rate(%)	26.0	36.1	29.0	32.1
初中生视力不良率(%)	Nearsight in Junior High School Rate(%)	55.0	70.0	67.1	67.9
高中生视力不良率(%)	Nearsight in Senior High School Rate(%)	78.5	85.7	85.4	85.1
免疫规划疫苗常规免疫接种率(%)	Conventional Vaccines of Vaccine Immunization Programmes Recipients Rate	99.7	99.8	99.9	99.8
乙肝疫苗全程接种率(%)	Hepatitis-B Inoculation Rate(%)	99.9	99.8	99.9	99.9

表21.10 家庭病床情况(2012)
FAMILY SICKBEDS

机构类别	Types	开展工作机构数(个) Running Institutions (unit)	上门诊疗总次数(次) Total Times of Family Call (time)	年底实有病床数(张) Year-end Sickbeds (bed)	年内开设总病床数(张) Sickbeds Set up in 2009 (bed)
总　计	**Total**	**214**	**1 550 053**	**21 964**	**48 224**
医　院	Hospitals	8	59 094	845	1 378
社区卫生服务中心	Community Health-care Centers	206	1 490 959	21 119	46 846

表21.11　主要年份妇幼卫生工作情况
BASIC STATISTICS OF GYNAECOLOGY AND PAEDIATRICS IN MAIN YEARS

指　标	Indicators	2000	2010	2011	2012
妇女病普查人数(万人)	**Quantity of People Surveyed for Female Diseases (10 000 persons)**	**40.27**	**86.54**	**76.04**	**84.45**
患病率(%)	Sufferers Rate(%)	35.0	33.3	32.6	31.7
治疗率(%)	Patients Treated Rate(%)	91.1	98.7	96.6	94.2
胎儿娩出顺产数(万人)	Quantity of Smooth Delivery (10 000 persons)	4.05	8.81	9.57	11.39
顺产率(%)	Smooth Delivery Rate(%)	47.5	45.1	47.6	48.2
出生低体重儿(人)	Quantity of Low-weight Newborns (person)	2 567	6 961	7 462	8 670
占活产总数(%)	Proportion in All Deliveries (%)	3.0	3.6	3.7	3.7
出生缺陷人数(人)	Quantity of Newborns with Innate Problems (person)	764	2 496	2 087	2 361
出生缺陷率(‰)	Disabled Among All Deliveries Rate (‰)	8.96	12.80	10.46	11.71
0~6岁儿童保健管理率(%)	Children, 0~6 Years Old under Health Programm Rate(%)	94.3	97.0	98.9	98.8
婚前检查人数(万人)	Quantity of People Undergoing Pre-marriage Checkup (10 000 persons)	17.36	8.53	8.67	8.05
婚检率(%)	Pre-marriage Checkup Recipients Rate(%)	98.4	35.4	31.7	30.9

表21.12　主要年份公民献血、用血情况
BASIC STATISTICS OF BLOOD DONATION AND USE IN MAIN YEARS

指　标	Indicators	2000	2010	2011	2012
无偿(义务)献血(万人份)	Volunteer or Compulsory Blood Offer (10 000 person unit)	35.19	46.27	46.10	46.00
临床用血量(万人份)	Clinic Blood Use Volum (10 000 person unit)	34.70	42.02	42.05	42.06

表21.13 主要年份社会保险参保人数
QUANTITY OF PARTICIPANTS IN SOCIAL INSURANCE IN MAIN YEARS

单位:万人(10 000 persons)

指标	Indicators	2000	2010	2011	2012
城镇基本养老保险	**Urban Basic Pension Insurance**				
城镇职工	Urban Staff and Workers	431.27	522.44	902.58	921.11
个体工商户和自由职业人员	Individual Businessman	9.82	20.43	24.35	26.87
领取养老金的离退休人员	Retired Veteran Cadres and Retired Staff and Workers with Pensions	234.23	352.02	363.95	378.40
城镇职工基本医疗保险	**Basic Medical Insurance for Urban Staff and Workers**				
城镇职工	Urban Staff and Workers	364.59	608.41	937.95	954.46
享受医保的离退休人员	Retired Veteran Cadres and Retired Staff and Workers with Medicare	202.14	391.33	404.11	421.52
城镇居民基本医疗保险	**Basic Medical Insurance for Urban Residents**		**259.17**	**249.75**	**262.59**
城镇职工失业保险	Unemployment Insurance of Urban Staff and Workers	434.86	556.20	604.22	617.35
城镇职工生育保险	Generational Insurance of Urban Staff and Workers		657.30	703.08	711.53
城镇职工工伤保险	Injured Insurance of Urban Staff and Workers		555.36	879.75	898.94
农村合作医疗	Cooperartion Medicare Insurance in Country		148.95	147.20	113.21
少儿住院基金	Medicare Fund of Children	212.47	197.19	204.69	208.65

注：根据《中华人民共和国保险法》，2011年对社会保险政策进行了调整。原参加"小城镇社会保险"和"来沪从业人员综合保险"的从业人员被纳入城镇职工保险范围内，并对养老、医疗、工伤、失业、生育保险的相关政策作出了调整。

Note: According to Insurance Law of the People's Republic of China, the social insurance policy has been adjusted since 2011. Employees, who have participated in Town Social Insurance and General Insurance of Employment of Migratory Population before, are now within the range of insurance for urban staff and workers. Relative policies of pension, medical, injured, unemployment and generational insurances have also been adjusted.

表21.14 主要年份社会保障标准
SOCIAL SECURITY STANDARD IN MAIN YEARS

单位:元/月(yuan/month)

指标	Indicators	2000	2010	2011	2012
职工工资最低标准	Minimum Standard of Wages of Staff and Workers	445	1 120	1 280	1 450
城镇基本养老金最低标准	Minimum Standard of Urban Basic Pension Insurance	460	460	460	460
城镇居民生活保障最低标准	Minimum Standard of Urban Living Security	280	450	505	570

表21.15 社会福利院、儿童福利院、社会福利医院和收养性老年福利机构情况(1980～2012)
INSTITUTIONS OF SOCIAL WELFARE, CHILDREN WELFARE, SOCIAL WELFARE HOSPITALS AND ADOPTIVE SENIORS WELFARE INSTITUTIONS

年 份 Year	社会福利院 Social Welfare Institutions			儿童福利院 Children Welfare Homes		
	单 位(个) Units (unit)	床位数(张) Beds (bed)	年末在院人数(人) Year-end Population Housed (person)	单 位(个) Units (unit)	床位数(张) Beds (bed)	年末在院人数(人) Year-end Population Housed (person)
1980	9	1 555	1 337	2	600	559
1981	9	1 621	1 313	2	650	634
1982	9	1 525	1 495	2	650	672
1983	9	1 644	1 491	2	600	676
1984	10	1 948	1 635	2	600	633
1985	10	1 727	1 630	2	580	625
1986	10	1 697	1 648	2	550	612
1987	10	1 991	1 770	2	378	449
1988	13	2 189	1 790	2	387	458
1989	14	2 418	2 012	2	538	481
1990	15	2 679	2 019	2	589	586
1991	14	2 687	2 138	2	611	592
1992	14	2 776	2 431	2	665	651
1993	14	2 874	2 554	2	708	690
1994	15	2 931	2 648	2	878	862
1995	15	3 006	2 722	2	988	919
1996	17	3 294	2 866	2	988	943
1997	21	4 012	3 441	2	988	946
1998	24	4 596	3 678	2	1 004	984
1999	20	4 215	3 498	2	981	958
2000	23	4 884	4 137	2	1 100	1 092
2001	26	5 570	4 410	2	1 221	1 221
2002	27	5 590	4 760	3	1 491	1 429
2003	26	5 818	4 779	2	1 087	1 512
2004	26	5 876	4 848	6	1 300	1 893
2005	23	5 999	4 809	6	2 016	1 986
2006	25	6 583	5 024	6	1 252	2 142
2007	24	6 499	5 068	6	1 252	2 341
2008	26	6 864	5 215	6	2 490	2 454
2009	26	7 686	5 351	6	2 584	2 552
2010	25	7 944	5 774	6	2 454	2 423
2011	29	8 297	6 013	6	2 427	2 336
2012	30	8 703	6 200	6	2 455	2 289

表21.15 续表 continued

年份 Year	社会福利医院 Social Welfare hospitals			收养性老年福利机构 Adoptive Seniors Welfare Institutions			
	单位（个） Units (unit)	床位数（张） Beds (bed)	年末在院人数（人） Year-end Population Housed (person)	机构（个） Institutions (unit)	床位数（张） Beds (bed)	年末在院人数（人） Year-end Population Housed (person)	其中 of which #老人 Elder
1980	3	1 475	1 424	42		630	
1981	3	1 460	1 430	53		762	
1982	3	1 490	1 422	58		1 022	
1983	3	1 490	1 432	90		1 402	
1984	3	1 460	1 380	135		2 328	
1985	3	1 480	1 360	199	3 870	3 038	2 786
1986	3	1 510	1 354	249	4 655	3 446	3 100
1987	3	1 497	1 342	277	5 520	4 262	3 893
1988	3	1 497	1 313	322	5 969	4 754	4 429
1989	3	1 433	1 324	349	6 281	5 129	4 835
1990	3	1 497	1 298	332	6 275	5 031	4 452
1991	3	1 391	1 285	341	6 731	5 763	5 642
1992	3	1 510	1 404	351	7 002	6 035	5 655
1993	3	1 510	1 394	331	7 143	6 365	5 934
1994	3	1 510	1 392	333	7 533	6 838	6 541
1995	3	1 510	1 409	330	8 576	7 405	6 633
1996	3	1 510	1 429	333	10 270	8 361	7 867
1997	3	1 500	1 452	323	11 253	9 295	8 647
1998	3	1 500	1 455	339	13 958	11 122	10 826
1999	3	1 710	1 703	331	16 526	12 698	12 013
2000	3	1 840	1 779	398	22 244	16 988	16 541
2001	3	1 894	1 894	378	23 627	17 363	16 923
2002	3	1 917	1 901	417	33 413	20 900	20 309
2003	3	1 680	1 881	422	36 791	23 451	22 682
2004	3	1 780	1 829	414	33 891	26 993	25 902
2005	3	1 811	1 811	450	43 131	31 301	30 181
2006	3	1 860	1 796	479	52 427	35 946	34 447
2007	3	1 852	1 806	536	64 115	42 665	40 731
2008	3	1 851	1 809	556	72 365	46 107	44 226
2009	3	1 842	1 808	589	84 714	51 974	49 789
2010	3	1 835	1 800	600	89 897	56 860	55 118
2011	3	1 821	1 776	602	93 599	58 660	57 597
2012	3	1 802	1 753	601	96 512	61 268	59 383

表21.16 主要年份社会福利事业机构数和职工人数
QUANTITY OF SOCIAL WELFARE INSTITUTIONS AND STAFF AND WORKERS IN MAIN YEARS

指标	Indicators	2000	2010	2011	2012
机构数(个)	**Total Institutions (unit)**				
收养性福利单位	Adopting Social Welfare Institutions	427	635	641	641
优抚类	Subsidy	1	1	1	1
福利类	Welfare	426	634	640	640
社会福利企业	Social Welfare Enterprises	3 352	1 375	1 315	1 223
优抚安置单位	Subsidy and Arrangement Institution	45	41	35	35
救助类单位	Salvation Institution	16	22	5	6
婚姻登记服务单位	Marriage Rigister Service Institutions		16	16	16
殡仪服务单位	Funeral and Interment Service Institution	68	79	78	78
福利彩票发行单位	Issue Institution of Welfare Lottery	16	19	18	17
职工人数(人)	**Staff and Workers (person)**				
收养性福利单位	Adopting Social Welfare Institutions	7 793	19 966	21 509	22 807
优抚类	Subsidy	35	47	42	42
福利类	Welfare	7 758	19 919	21 467	22 765
社会福利企业	Social Welfare Enterprises	177 260	92 351	102 083	95 886
优抚安置单位	Subsidy and Anargment Institution	745	714	705	680
救助类单位	Salvation Institution	472	403	55	65
婚姻登记服务单位	Marriage Rigister Service Institutions		110	129	134
殡仪服务单位	Funeral and Interment Service Institution	2 577	3 201	3 239	3 036
福利彩票发行单位	Issue Institution of Welfare Lottery	86	87	110	127

表21.17 主要年份民间组织情况
STATISTICS OF CIVIL ORGANIZATIONS AND CHARITY IN MAIN YEARS

指标	Indicators	2005	2010	2011	2012
民间组织数(个)	**Quantity of Civil Organization (unit)**	**7 556**	**10 104**	**10 385**	**10 730**
社会团体	Social Organizations	2 952	3 634	3 686	3 693
民办非企业	Civil Non-Enterprises	4 537	6 353	6 572	6 897
基金会	Fonndations	67	117	127	140

表21.18 主要年份养老服务
ENDOWMENT SERVICE IN MAIN YEARS

指 标	Indicators	2005	2010	2011	2012
机构养老服务	**Endowment Service of Institutions**				
机构数(家)	Quantity of Institutions (unit)	474	625	631	632
床位数(张)	Quantity of Beds (bed)	49 529	97 841	101 896	105 215
#新增养老床位	Newly Added Endowmet Beds	10 094	10 843	5 541	5 531
养老床位占60周岁及以上老年人口比例(%)	Ratio of Endowment Bed in Population above 60 (%)	1.9	3.1	3.0	3.0
居家养老服务	**Household Endowment Service**				
社区老年人日间服务机构机构数(家)	Community Service Institutions for Aged People Daytime Quantity of Institutions (unit)	83	303	326	313
日托老年人数(万人)	Population of Daytime Service Aged People (10 000 persons)	0.21	0.90	1.10	1.10
社区助老服务社(个)	Community Service Center for Assisting Aged People (unit)	233	233	233	231
社区居家养老服务月服务人数(万人)	Monthly Population of Community Household Endowment Service (10 000 persons)	5.48	25.20	26.20	27.20
获得政府补贴的老年人(万人)	Population of Aged People Gained Governmental Subsidy (10 000 persons)	3.94	13.00	13.30	12.60

表21.19 主要年份老年医疗服务
MEDICARE SERVICE FOR AGED PEOPLE IN MAIN YEARS

指 标	Indicators	2005	2010	2011	2012
老年护理院	**Nursing Home for Aged People**				
独立老年护理院	Independent Nursing Home for Aged People				
机构数(所)	Quantity of Institutions (unit)	13	14	15	17
建筑面积(平方米)	Structure Area (sq. m)	59 742	101 048	109 399	221 099
床位数(张)	Beds (bed)	2 353	3 285	3 505	4 03[illegible]
住院人次(人次)	Person-time in Hospital (person-time)	4 346	10 322	11 495	9 72[illegible]
老年医院	**Hospital for Aged People**				
机构数(所)	Quantity of Institutions (unit)	3	4	4	5
住院人次(人次)	Person-time in Hospital (person-time)	9 124	15 520	16 213	16 [illegible]43
家庭病床总数(张)	**Total Quantity of bed in home (bed)**	**40 745**	**43 880**	**44 296**	**45 565**

表21.20 主要年份红十字会基本情况
BASIC STATISICS ON RED CROSS SOCIETY OF CHINA SHANGHAI MUNICIPAL BRANCH IN MAIN YEARS

指标	Indicators	2005	2010	2011	2012
红十字会组织机构	**Institutions(unit)**				
红十字会各级组织机构(个)	Organizing Institutions(unit)	2 934	3 042	3 493	3 365
红十字会医疗机构(个)	Medical Institutions(unit)	67	72	74	65
志愿工作管理机构(个)	Administrative Institutions on Voluntary Work(unit)	20	20	20	20
红十字会会员人数(万人)	**Quantity of Member(10 000 persons)**	**61.62**	**86.52**	**98.00**	**94.07**
#青少年会员(万人)	Hobbledehoy Member(10 000 persons)	37.16	58.64	58.00	48.02
红十字会团体会员单位(个)	Team Member(unit)	970	969	1 181	1 500
社区公益服务站点(个)	**Community Commonweal Service Station (unit)**	**1 589**	**3 077**	**4 314**	**3 077**
组织各种宣传活动	**Times of Publicizing Activity(time)**				
在报刊登载宣传文章(篇)	Articles on Newspaper and Periodical (piece)	831	609	333	800
电视台播报宣传节目(条/次)	Programs on Television (piece/time)	459	200	85	211
参加艾滋病预防宣传教育活动人次数(万人次)	Person-time Attended AIDS Prevention Activities (10 000 person-times)	9.86	18.84	0.58	25.04
参加普及宣传无偿献血活动人次数(万人次)	Person-time Attended Publicizing Volunteer Blood Donation Activiies (10 000 person-times)		23.76		22.16
卫生救护工作	**Sanitation Rescue**				
救护普及培训(万人次)	Rescue Popularization Training (10 000 person-times)	24.72	37.35	69.79	45.83
造血干细胞捐献工作	**Contributing Trunk Cell**				
当年参加造血干细胞捐献志愿人数(万人)	Quantity of Subscribers (10 000 persons)	5.60	10.42	11.35	12.13
遗体捐献工作	**Contributing Reliquiae**				
遗体捐献登记站(个)	Register Center(unit)	27	25	24	25
遗体捐献接收站(个)	Accepting Center(unit)	8	7	7	8
全年接受捐献遗体登记(人)	Quantity of Contributing Reliquiae(Person)	1 284	1 170	1 514	1 793
全年接受角膜捐献登记(人)	Quantity of Contributing Cornea(Person)	133	73	184	694
社会救灾和社区救助工作	**Working on Social Relieving**				
救灾投入(万元)	Relieve Devotion (10 000 yuan)	10 635.36	19 267.76	3 344.99	977.82
社区救助款物投入(万元)	Community Salvation Devotion (10 000 yuan)	1 538.12	4 780.71	5 241.83	5 606.96
受益人次(万人次)	Quantity of Beneficiaries (10 000 person-times)	2.87	4.11	7.29	10.43

注：救灾受益人次不包含外省市受益人次。
Note: Persons benefited from disaster relief do not contain people from other provinces and cities.

表21.21 全市残疾人各残疾类别人数情况(2012)
THE NUMBER OF CASES OF EACH TYPE OF DISABILITY

单位:人(person)

地区	District	总计 Total	视力 Vision	听力 Hearing	言语 Speech	肢体 Limb	智力 Intelligence	精神 Spirit	多重 Multiple
全市	**Total**	**370 442**	**68 380**	**34 441**	**3 944**	**160 178**	**56 150**	**43 849**	**3 500**
浦东新区	Pudong New Area	69 985	13 332	7 904	760	27 158	12 052	8 288	491
黄浦	Huangpu	26 558	8 025	2 698	207	8 887	2 796	3 654	291
徐汇	Xuhui	17 888	4 199	1 373	149	6 476	2 517	2 923	251
长宁	Changning	14 030	2 507	1 090	164	6 564	1 410	1 945	350
静安	Jing'an	7 192	1 699	757	52	2 536	836	1 238	74
普陀	Putuo	21 896	3 655	1 807	203	10 218	2 647	2 812	554
闸北	Zhabei	21 045	4 611	2 122	172	9 356	2 094	2 523	167
虹口	Hongkou	16 418	3 597	1 595	103	6 377	2 068	2 519	159
杨浦	Yangpu	25 899	5 217	2 256	198	11 971	2 863	3 073	321
闵行	Minhang	21 432	3 759	2 046	157	9 221	3 459	2 615	175
宝山	Baoshan	19 751	3 520	1 588	210	8 311	3 419	2 623	8[illegible]
嘉定	Jiading	15 360	1 761	1 264	153	7 530	2 852	1 677	123
金山	Jinshan	15 135	1 938	711	681	6 700	3 336	1 709	60
松江	Songjiang	18 098	2 539	1 380	134	9 762	3 053	1 185	45
青浦	Qingpu	18 020	1 904	1 657	116	10 490	1 790	2 026	37
奉贤	Fengxian	15 193	1 336	1 194	333	7 212	3 590	1 464	64
崇明	Chongming	26 542	4 781	2 999	152	11 409	5 368	1 575	258

注：本表数据由市残疾人联合会提供。
Note: Date in this table are provided by Shanghai Disabled Persons' Federation.

上/海/统/计/年/鉴

主要统计指标解释

■ 卫生机构

是指从卫生行政部门取得《医疗机构执业许可证》，或从民政、工商行政、机构编制管理部门取得法人单位登记证书，为社会提供医疗保健、疾病控制、卫生监督服务或从事医学研究和医学在职培训等工作的单位。

■ 医疗机构

指从卫生行政部门取得《医疗机构执业许可证》的机构，包括医院、疗养院、社区卫生服务中心(站)、卫生院、门诊部、诊所(卫生所、医务室)、妇幼保健院(所、站)、专科疾病防治院(所、站)、急救中心(站)和临床检验中心，但不包括村卫生室(单纯统计)。

■ 医　院

包括综合医院、中医医院、中西医结合医院、民族医院、各类专科医院和护理院，不包括专科疾病防治院、妇幼保健院和疗养院

■ 卫生技术人员

包括执业医师、执业助理医师、注册护士、药师(士)、检验技师、影像技师(士)、卫生监督员和见习医(药、护、技)师(士)等卫生专业人员。不包括从事管理工作的卫生技术人员(如院长、副院长、党委书记等)。

■ 执业(助理)医师

一律按领取医师执业证书且实际从事临床工作的人数统计，不包括从事管理工作的医师。

■ 优抚对象

优抚指政府对革命烈士家庭、病故残疾工作人员以及参战负伤致残的民兵、民工的抚恤和人民群众对其的优待。优抚对象包括革命烈士家属、因公牺牲和病故军人家属、革命伤残人员、现役军属、退伍红军老战士、红军失散人员、复员军人、退伍军人、在职退役军人、在乡退役军人、带病回乡退伍军人、复员军人精神病员、孤老优抚对象等。

■ 社会福利事业单位

指集中收养社会孤老、残、幼的机构。包括由民政部门管理的社会福利院、儿童福利院、精神病人福利院和城镇集体办的福利院，以及农村集体办的敬老院。

■ 基本养老保险

1.(参保)职工人数：指报告期末按照国家法律、法规和有关政策规定参加基本养老保险并在社保经办机构已建立缴费记录档案的职工人数，包括中断缴费但未终止养老保险关系的职工人数，不包括只登记未建立缴费记录档案的人数。

2.(参保)离退休人员人数：指报告期末参加基本养老保险的离休、退休和退职人员的人数。

3.基本养老保险基金收入：指根据国家有关规定，由纳入基本养老保险范围的缴费单位和个人按国家规定的缴费基数和缴费比例缴纳的养老保险基金，以及通过其他方式取得的形成基金来源的收入。包括单位和职工个人缴纳的基本养老保险费、基本养老保险基金利息收入、上级补助收入、下级上解收入、转移收入、财政补贴和其他收入。

4.基本养老保险基金支出：指按照国家政策规定的开支范围和开支标准从养老保险基金中支付给参加基本养老保险的离休、退休、退职人员个人的养老金、丧葬抚恤补助，以及由于保险关系转移、上下级之间调剂资金等原因而发生的支出。包括离休金、退休金、退职金、各种补贴、医疗费、死亡丧葬补助费、抚恤救济费、社会保险经办机构管理费、补助下级支出、上解上级支出、转移支出、其他支出等。

5.基本养老保险基金累计结余：指截止报告期末基本养老保险基金收支相抵后的累计余额。

■ 基本医疗保险

1.参保人数：指报告期末按国家有关规定参加基本医疗保险的人数。包括参加保险的职工人数和退休人员人数。

2.基金收入：指根据国家有关规定，由纳入基本医疗保险范围的缴费单位和个人，按国家规定的缴费基数和缴费比例缴纳的基金，以及通过其他方式取得的形成基金来源的款项，包括：单位缴纳的社会统筹基金收入、个人缴纳的个人账户基金收入、财政补贴收入、利息收入、其他收入。

主要统计指标解释

3.基金支出：指按照国家政策规定的开支范围和开支标准从社会统筹基金中支付给参加基本医疗保险的职工和退休人员的医疗保险待遇支出，和从个人帐户基金中支付给参加基本医疗保险的职工和退休人员的医疗费用支出，以及其他支出。包括：住院医疗费用支出、门急诊医疗费用支出、个人账户基金支出、其他支出。

4.基金累计结余：指截止报告期末基本医疗保险的社会统筹和个人帐户基金累计结余金额。包括银行存款、财政专户、债券投资和其他。

■ 失业保险

1.参保人数：指报告期末按照国家法律、法规和有关政策规定参加了失业保险的城镇企业事业单位的职工及地方政府规定参加失业保险的其他人员的人数。

2.失业保险基金收入：指按照规定从企业、事业及其他单位筹集的失业保险费及其他并入失业保险基金收入的总额。包括单位和个人缴纳的失业保险费、失业保险基金利息收入、上级补助收入、下级上解收入、转移收入、财政补贴和其他收入。

3.失业保险基金支出：指报告期内为保障失业人员和下岗职工基本生活、促进其再就业等支出的基金总额。包括失业救济金、医疗费、死亡丧葬补助费、抚恤救济费、转业训练费支出、失业保险经办机构管理费、补助下级支出、上解上级支出、转移支出和其他支出。

4.基金累计结余：指截止报告期末失业保险基金收支相抵后的累计余额。

■ 工伤保险

1. 参加保险人数：指报告期末依据国家有关规定参加工伤保险的职工人数。

2.享受保险待遇人数：指劳动者因工负伤致残、死亡或因患职业病致残，根据有关规定享受工伤保险待遇职工或供养直系亲属人数。包括伤残人数、职业病人数、因工死亡人数、供养直系亲属人数。

3.基金收入：指根据国家有关规定，由参加工伤保险的单位按国家规定的缴费基数和缴费比例缴纳的工伤保险基金，以及通过其他形式取得的形成基金来源的款项。包括：单位缴纳的社会统筹基金收入、财政补贴收入、利息收入、其他收入。

4. 基金支出：指按照国家政策规定的开支范围和开支标准从工伤保险基金中支付给参加工伤保险的人员及供养直系亲属工伤保险待遇支出及其他支出。包括工伤医疗费、伤残补助金、工亡补助金、护理费、丧葬补助费、工伤预防费用、职业康复费用和其他支出。

5. 基金累计结余：指截止报告期末工伤保险基金累计结余金额。包括银行存款、财政专户、债券投资和其他。

■ 生育保险

1. 参保人数：指报告期末依据有关规定参加生育保险的职工人数。

2.基金收入：指根据国家有关规定，由参加生育保险的单位按照国家规定的缴费基数和缴费比例缴纳的生育保险基金，以及通过其他方式取得的形成基金来源的款项，包括：单位缴纳的基金收入、利息收入和其他收入。

3. 基金支出：指按照国家政策规定的开支范围和开支标准，从生育保险基金中支付给参加生育保险的职工，因妊娠、分娩和计划生育手术而享受的待遇及其他支出。包括：生育津贴、医疗费用支出及其他支出。

4. 基金累计结余：指截止报告期末生育保险基金累计结余金额。包括银行存款、财政专户、债券投资和其他。

SHANGHAI STATISTICAL YEARBOOK

EXPLANATORY NOTES TO MAJOR STATISTICAL INDICATORS

□ Health Care Institutions

Health Care Institutions refer to the unit which have been qualified the Certification of Health Care Institution by the administration of public health, or qualified the Certification of Corporate Unit by the civil affairs, administration for industry and commerce, commission office for public sector reform, and engaging in medical care, disease prevention and control, health supervision and inspection, medicine research and health professional education, etc.

□ Medical Organizations

Medical Organizations refer to the institutions which have been qualified the Certification of Health Care Institution by the administration of public health, including: hospitals, health centers, community health service centers (stations), health centers, clinics (health stations and infirmaries), women and children care agencies (centers and stations), special disease prevention and curing agencies (centers and stations), first-aid centers (stations) and clinic inspection centers, but excluding village health care rooms.

□ Hospitals

Hospitals includes comprehensive hospitals, traditional Chinese medicine hospital, traditional Chinese and western medicine hospital, ethnic minority medicine hospital, various special disease hospitals and nursing homes, but excludes special disease prevention and curing agencies, women and children care agencies and health centers.

□ Medical Technical Personnel

Medical Technical Personnel includes licensed doctors, licensed assistant doctors, pharmacist (assistant pharmacist), inspection technician, image technician (assistant image technician), health care inspector and practice doctor (pharmacist, nurse, and technician), excludes medical technical personnel engaging in administrative jobs.

□Licensed Doctors (Assistant Doctors)

It refers to the medical workers who have obtained the licenses of qualified doctors of assistant doctors and are employed by medical institutions, but excludes the doctors engaging in administrative jobs.

□ Special Care

Special Care is offered by the government to the family member of the martyrs, disabled or demobilized servicemen or laborers who were injured on duty. Entitled to the special care are family members of the revolutionary martyrs, family members of servicemen who dies on duty or died of an illness, disabled servicemen, family members of servicemen on active service, retired veteran Red Army soldiers, scattered Red Army soldiers, demobilized servicemen, ex-servicemen, servicemen who were demobilized while on duty, ex-servicemen back to their rural homes, ex-servicemen who were demobilized because of an illness and have gone back to their rural homes, ex-servicemen who suffer from mental illness and elderly persons with no family.

□ Social Welfare Institutions

Social Welfare Institutions refer to institutions taking care of old people without children, handicapped people and orphans. They include social welfare institutions run by civil affairs departments, children's welfare institutions, welfare institutions for mental patients, and collectively-run old people's homes in rural areas.

□ Basic Pension Insurance

1. Number of staff and workers covered refer to staff and workers participating in basic pension insurance programme in line with national laws, regulations and related policies by the end of reference period, who have already had payment records in social security management agencies, including those who interrupt payment without terminating the insurance programme. Those who have registered in the programme with no payment records are not included.

2. Number of retirees participating in basic pension insurance programme refer to number of retirees participating in basic pension insurance programme by the end of reference period.

3. Revenue of basic pension insurance refer to payments made by employers and individuals participating in pension insurance programs in accordance with the basis and proportion

EXPLANATORY NOTES TO MAJOR STATISTICAL INDICATORS

stipulated in state regulations, and income from other sources that become source of pension insurance fund, including the premium paid by employers and staff and works, interest income, subsidies from higher level agencies, income as transfer from subordinate agencies, transferred income, government financial subsidies and other income.

4. Expenses of basic pension insurance refer to payment made to those retired and resigned people covered in pension insurance program in terms of pension or compensation within the scope and standards of expenditure according to related national policies, and expenditure occurred due to shift of the insurance relationship or adjustment of funds among agencies, including pension for resigned people, pension for retired people, pension for people quitting jobs, various subsidies, medical fees, funeral subsidies, compensation pension, management fees for social security agencies, expenses on subsidies to lower subordinates, expenses as transfer to agencies at higher level, transferred expenditure and other expenditure.

5. Balance of basic pension insurance refers to the balance of basic pension insurance at the end of the reference period after deducting expenses from revenue

□ Basic Medical Care Insurance

1. Number of people participating in the insurance programme refers to people participating in the basic medical care insurance programme according to related regulations by the end of reference period, including number of staff and workers and retirees participating in this insurance programme.

2. Revenue of insurance programme refer to payments made by employers and individuals participating in medical care insurance programs in accordance with the basis and proportion stipulated in state regulations, and income from other sources that become source of medical insurance fund, including income of social comprehensive funds paid by employers, income from individual accounts, government financial subsidies, interest income and other income.

3. Expenses of insurance programme refer to payment made from social comprehensive funds to those retired and resigned people covered in basic medical care insurance within the scope and standards of expenditure according to related national policies, and medical care payment made from individual accounts to staff and workers and retirees, and other expenses, including medical expenses of hospital inpatients, medical expenses for outpatients and emergency patients, payment from individual accounts and other expenditure.

4. Balance of basic medical care insurance refer to the balance of medical care insurance of social comprehensive funds and individual accounts at the end of the reference period, including bank savings, special fiscal accounts, investment in bonds and others.

□ Unemployment Insurance

1. Number of people covered refers to staff and workers in urban enterprises or institutions who have participated in unemployment insurance programme in line relevant policies and regulations, and other people who have participated according to local government regulations, by the end of reference period.

2. Revenue of unemployment insurance refer to payments made by employers and individuals participating in unemployment insurance programme in accordance with relevant regulations and other income contributed to this programme, including unemployment insurance premium made by employers and individuals, interest income, subsidies from higher level agencies, income as transfer from subordinate agencies, transferred income, government financial subsidies and other income.

3. Expenses of unemployment insurance refer to total expenses during the reference period to guarantee the basic livelihood of unemployed people and laid-off staff and workers and to encourage their re-employment. Included are unemployment relief, medical fees, funeral subsidies, compensation pension, training expenses, management fees for unemployment insurance agencies, subsidies to lower level agencies, expenses as transfer to higher level agencies, transferred expenditure and other expenditure.

4. Balance of unemployment insurance refer to the balance of unemployment revenue deducting unemployment expenses at the end of the reference period.

□ Work Injury Insurance

1. Number of people covered refers to staff and workers who have participated in work injury insurance programme in line with relevant national regulations.

2. Number of beneficiaries refers to staff and workers and their direct dependents who can, in line with relevant regulations, benefit from work injury insurance, as a result of work injury leading to disability or death of the staff/worker, or occupational disease leading to disability. Included in this category are number of injured and disabled people, number of people with occupa-

EXPLANATORY NOTES TO MAJOR STATISTICAL INDICATORS

tional diseases, number of deaths at work places, and number of direct dependents.

3. Revenue of work injury insurance refer to payments made by employers participating in work injury insurance programs in accordance with the basis and proportion stipulated in state regulations, and income from other sources that become source of work injury insurance fund, including income of social comprehensive funds paid by employers, government financial subsidies, interest income and other income.

4. Expenses of work injury insurance refer to payments made from work injury insurance funds to those who participated in the work injury insurance programme and their direct dependents within the scope and standards of expenditure according to related national policies, and other expenditure, including medical fees for work injury, injury and disability subsidies, death subsidies, nursing fees, funeral subsidies, injury prevention fees, rehabilitation fees for occupational diseases and other expenditure.

5. Balance of work injury insurance refer to the balance of the work injury funds at the end of the reference period, including bank savings, special fiscal account, investment in bonds and others.

□ Maternity Insurance

1. Number of people covered refers to staff and workers who have participated in maternity insurance programme according to relevant regulation at the end of the reporting period.

2. Revenue of maternity insurance refers to payments made by employers participating in maternity insurance programs in accordance with the basis and proportion stipulated in state regulations, and income from other sources that become source of maternity insurance fund, including income of funds paid by employers, interest income and other income.

3. Expenses of maternity insurance refer to payments made from maternity insurance funds to staff and workers who participated in maternity insurance programme within the scope and standards of expenditure according to related national policies, expenses paid for pregnancy, child delivery or surgeries related to family planning, and other expenditure, including allowance for child bearing, medical fees and other expenditure.

4. Balance of the maternity insurance refers to the balance of the maternity insurance funds at the end of reference period, including bank savings, special fiscal account, investment in funds and others.

第二十二篇

CHAPTER 22

文化和体育

CULTURE AND SPORTS

简要说明

一、本章资料的主要内容

本篇主要反映文化、文物、广电、新闻出版、档案、体育事业发展情况。

内容包括全市艺术表演团体、艺术表演场馆、群众文化活动机构、文物机构、文化娱乐机构、公共图书馆、新闻出版机构、档案机构等单位的机构、人员、经费和业务活动情况；全市广播电视机构设施、制作播出节目时间情况；全市电影摄制、译制和发行反映情况；全市图书、期刊、报纸、音像电子出版数量情况；全市优秀运动员、教练员、体育系统职工、群众体育健身活动场所情况。

二、本篇资料的来源

文化、广电资料由上海市文化广播影视管理局提供；文物资料由上海市文物局提供；新闻出版资料由上海市新闻出版局提供；档案机构资料由上海市档案局提供；体育资料由上海市体育局提供。

BRIEF INTRODUCTION

I. Main Contents

Data mainly reflect the development of culture; cultural relics; radio broadcasting, films and television; news and publication; archives and sports undertakings.

Data mainly include: data on institutions and employed persons, funds and activities of art troupes, art venues, mass cultural institutions, heritage institutions, cultural entertainment institutions, public libraries, press and publications, archival institutions, etc; data and playing hours of television stations and broadcasting stations, data on production, dubbing and showing of films, data on books, periodicals, newspaper, electronic audio and video products published, data on excellent athletes, coaches, staff and workers in sports sectors, mass physical activities.

II. Sources of data

Data on culture, television and broadcasting are from Shanghai Municipal Administration of Culture Radio Film& TV; data on historical relics are from Shanghai Municipal Administration of Cultural Heritage; data on news and publishing are from Shanghai Municipal Press and Publication Bureau; data on archive institutions are from Shanghai Municipal Archives; data on sports are from Shanghai Municipal Sports Bureau.

表 22.1 主要年份文化机构数
QUANTITY OF CULTURAL INSTITUTIONS IN MAIN YEARS

单位：个(unit)

年份 Year	图书馆 Libraries	群众文化活动机构 Mass Culture	艺术教育事业 Art Education	文艺科研机构 Research	文物机构 Agency of Historic Relics	档案机构 Archives Institutions
1978	23	364	3		7	
1980	21	367	2	2	8	
1985	46	369	3	2	9	
1986	49	403	3	2	11	
1987	50	407	3	2	13	127
1988	54	416	3	2	16	125
1989	52	405	3	2	19	134
1990	51	410	3	2	18	137
1991	31	397	3	2	18	671
1992	31	394	3	2	20	745
1993	31	376	3	2	21	720
1994	31	371	3	2	23	
1995	31	332	3	2	23	768
1996	32	348	4	2	24	674
1997	32	352	4	2	24	681
1998	32	355	4	2	23	643
1999	32	349	4	2	24	994
2000	31	340	4	2	24	792
2001	32	276	3	2	23	614
2002	32	270	1	2	26	652
2003	35	261	1	2	26	656
2004	28	251	1	2	99	513
2005	28	248	1	2	106	545
2006	28	250	1	2	106	439
2007	30	247	1	2	111	524
2008	29	245	1	2	111	524
2009	29	242	1	2	112	533
2010	28	240	1	2	115	707
2011	25	241	1	2	125	677
2012	25	240	1	2	115	734

注：自 2004 年起文物保护机构中包括系统外的机构数。
Note：Agency of Historic Relics Preservation refers to total quantity of Agency Bureau.

表 22.2　影剧院、艺术表演场所、艺术表演团体数(1978～2012)
QUANTITY OF CINEMAS, THEATRES AND ART PERFORMANCE TROUPES

单位:个(unit)

年　份 Year	电影放映单位 Film Projection Units	其　中　of which #影、剧院 Cinemas and Theatres	艺术表演场馆 Art Performance Places	其　中　of which #剧　院 Theatres	#书　场 Storytelling Places	艺术表演团体 Art Performance Troupes
1978	803	109	31	26	4	17
1979	799	115	46	32	5	45
1980	770	119	47	43	6	48
1981	804	127	60	56	6	49
1982	815	134	31	48	6	46
1983	822	140	54	49	8	46
1984	815	146	54	48	8	44
1985	847	156	52	47	8	44
1986	859	169	53	49	9	42
1987	890	199	51	48	8	42
1988	734	215	53	50	8	40
1989	579	213	52	49	8	37
1990	577	211	49	46	8	38
1991	548	229	51	47	9	38
1992	530	249	51	47	9	37
1993	462	254	49	40	9	34
1994	462	254	47	39	8	35
1995	452	249	43	35	7	31
1996	488	280	45	38	7	31
1997	466	263	45	38	7	31
1998	445	242	44	39	5	29
1999	445	242	44	41	4	29
2000	445	242	44	39	5	29
2001	370	273	41	35	3	28
2002	370	273	37	31		28
2003	328	238	180	174	4	72
2004	311	225	177	163	7	75
2005	236	193	160	150	5	85
2006	245	186	148	137	2	97
2007	233	175	150	140	6	103
2008	235	172	139	134	5	10[illegible]
2009	226	169	104	100		[illegible]7
2010	152	136	97	86	2	[illegible]9
2011	161	146	103	90	4	102
2012	153	140	111	99	3	138

注：自 2003 年起文化统计范围扩大到全行业。
Note: The scope of statistics to culture expands to total sectors in 2003.

表22.3 主要年份主要文化机构从业人员数
QUANTITY OF EMPLOYEES IN MAJOR CULTURAL INSTITUTIONSS IN MAIN YAERS

单位:人(person)

	机构类别 Category of Institution	2000	2010	2011	2012
总　计	**Total**	**217 572**	**274 267**	**293 629**	**298 841**
艺术机构	Art	4 759	9 482	10 467	11 368
图书馆	Libraries	2 513	2 180	2 264	2 089
档案机构	Archives Institution	2 330	3 822	3 765	4 125
群众文化活动机构	Mass Culture	3 874	4 702	4 856	4 775
文物机构	History Relic	1 136	2 558	2 736	3 292
文化市场经营机构	Cultural Market Operation Institutions	63 297	60 358	61 966	67 616
新闻出版机构	Institutions Engaged in News and Publishing	138 492	185 620	199 890	202 037
其他文化机构	Other Cultural Institutions	1 171	5 545	7 685	3 774

表22.4 主要文化机构和人员数(2012)
MAJOR CULTURAL INSTITUTIONS AND PERSONNEL

	机构类别 Category of Institution	机构数(个) Institutions(unit)	从业人数(人) Employees(person)
艺术机构	**Art**	**253**	**11 368**
艺术表演团体	Art Performance Troupes	138	8 524
艺术表演场馆	Art Centers	111	2 751
艺术创作机构	Art Inditing	1	9
艺术教育机构	Art Education	1	37
文艺科研机构	Literaturde and Art Research	2	47
图书馆	**Libraries**	**25**	**2 089**
#少儿图书馆	Libraries for Children	5	157
档案机构	**Archives Institution**	**734**	**4 125**
群众文化活动机构	**Mass Culture**	**240**	**4 775**
群众艺术馆	Mass Art Centers	1	60
文化馆	Cultural Centers	26	991
文化站	Cultural Stations	213	3 724
文物机构	**Historical Relic**	**115**	**3 292**
文物保护管理机构	Heritage management agencies	5	73
博物馆	Museums	109	3 150
文物商店	Cultural Relic Shop	1	69
文化市场经营机构	**Cultural Market Operation Institutions**	**4 492**	**67 616**
新闻出版机构	**Institutions Engaged in News and Publishing**	**13 137**	**202 037**
其他文化机构	**Other Cultural Institutions**	**129**	**3 774**

表 22.5 群众艺术馆和文化馆(站)情况（2012）
MASS ART AND CULTURAL CENTERS

指 标	Indicators	合 计 Total	群众艺术馆 Mass Art Centers	文化馆 Cultural Centers	文化站 Cultural Stations
单位数（个）	Quantity of Units（unit）	240	1	26	213
从业人员（人）	Employees（person）	4 775	60	991	3 724
组织活动	Organizing Activity				
文艺活动（次）	Literary Activity（time）	32 342	50	3 412	28 880
理论研讨和讲座（次）	Theoretics Conference and Chair（time）	390	32	358	
举办训练班	Conducting Training Courses				
班 次（次）	Quantity of Classes（time）	31 682	172	7 858	23 652
结业人次（万人次）	Persons Completing the Courses（10 000 person-times）	173.23	5.25	19.39	148.59
举办展览个数（个）	Exhibitions Conducted（unit）	2 754	32	378	2 344

表 22.6 艺术表演团体情况（2012）
BASIC STATISTICS OF ART TROUPES

类 别	Types	剧团数（个） Troupes（unit）	从业人员（人） Employees（person）	国内演出场次（场） Times of Domestic Performance（time）	观众人数（万人次） Spectators（10 000 person-times）
总 计	**Total**	**138**	**8 524**	**27 977**	**1 247**
按隶属关系分	**By Administrative Relationship**				
市 级	Perfectural level	18	3 043	9 344	374
区 级	District level	118	5 447	18 464	869
县 级	County level	2	34	169	4
按剧种分	**By Type of Drama**				
话剧、儿童剧、滑稽剧团	Drama, Children's Play & Comedy Troupes	31	1 867	8 553	231
歌剧、舞剧、歌舞剧团	Opera and Dance Troupes	7	628	917	122
乐团、歌舞团、轻音乐团	Philharmonic, Song & Dance, Light Music Troupes	35	3 560	4 923	197
戏曲剧团	Local Opera Troupes	25	1 461	8 705	241
曲艺、杂技、木偶、皮影团、马戏	Recitation & Ballad, Acrobatics & Cirus, Puppet Show, Shadow Puttet,Circus	11	491	2 769	255
综合性艺术表演团体	Comprehensive Art Troupe	29	517	3 110	201

表22.7 艺术表演场所基本情况(2012)
ART PERFORMANCE PLACES

类别	Types	机构数(个) Institutions (unit)	从业人员(人) Employees (person)	座席数(个) Seats (unit)	演(映)出场次(场) Quantity of Art Projections & Performances (time)	其中 of which #艺术演出场次 Quantity of Art Performances	观众人次(万人次) Spectators (10 000 person-times)	其中 of which #艺术演出场次 Quantity of Art Performances
总　计	**Total**	**111**	**2 751**	**123 611**	**81 879**	**11 401**	**979.45**	**618.57**
市　级	Municipal Level	13	709	44 342	3 309	3 141	246.22	237.71
艺海剧院	Yihai Theater	1	24	1 377	461	461	0.04	0.04
上海人民大舞台	Shanghai People's Big Stage	1	5	1 002	153	146	8.39	7.20
上海长江剧场	Shanghai Changjiang Theater	1	7					
上海兰心大戏院	Shanghai Lyceum Theater	1	29	681	299	236	17.08	14.48
上海美琪大戏院	Shanghai Meiqi Theater	1	26	1 328				
上海音乐厅	Shanghai Concert Hall	1	50	1 243	462	409	23.20	20.38
上海上戏艺术发展有限公司	Shanghai Theatre Academy Art Development Co., LTD	1	30	910	265	223	18.50	16.60
上海马戏城	Shanghai Circus World	1	56	2 182	588	588	51.48	51.48
奔驰文化中心	Benz Cultural Center	1	80	18 000	47	47	34.70	34.70
上海大剧院演艺中心	Shanghai Grand Theater	1	131	2 451	691	691	42.00	42.00
上海文化广场剧院管理有限公司	Shanghai Culture Square Theater Management Co., LTD	1	105	1 949	170	170	21.85	21.85
上海宛平剧院	Shanghai Wanping Theater	1	35	1 003	136	136	10.88	10.88
上海大舞台	Shanghai Stadium	1	131	12 216	37	34	18.10	18.10
区　级	District Level	97	2 031	78 225	77 290	8 219	721.80	377.52
县　级	County Level	1	11	1 044	1 280	41	11.43	3.34

表22.8　博物馆、纪念馆情况(2012)
STATISTICS OF MUSEUMS AND MEMORIALS

类　别 Types		机构数 (个) Quantity of Institution (unit)	馆内藏品实际数量 Real Quantity of Collections (万件) (10 000 pieces)	#一至三级藏品 Collections of Class One to Three	展览活动 (个) Exhibit Activity (unit)	参观人次 (万人次) Visiting Person-times (10 000 person-times)
总　计	**Total**	**109**	**314.49**	**26.44**	**326**	**1 521.32**
综合性	Comprehensive	14	10.36	3.57	82	394.51
历史类	Historical	20	17.85	3.41	63	247.67
艺术类	**Art**	**8**	**103.59**	**14.27**	**24**	**205.13**
科学类	Scientific	2	28.11	0.45	8	344.59
人物类	Character	17	8.88	2.33	39	64.56
行业类	Industrial	22	134.11	0.77	64	173.20
高校类	University	10	6.23		22	19.42
其　他	Others	16	5.38	1.62	24	72.24

表22.9　主要年份文物保护维修情况
PRESERVATION AND MAINTAIN OF HISTORICAL RELICS IN MAIN YEARS

指　标	Indicators	2005	2010	2011	2012
保护维修项目数(个)	Items of Preservation and Maintaining (item)	44	45	19	38
#国家级	National	4	10	2	7
市　级	Municipal	18	6	6	17
维修面积(万平方米)	Areas of Maintaining (10 000 sq. m.)	2.30	13.51	5.10	4.74
项目总预算(万元)	**Aggregate Budget of Items (10 000 yuan)**	**19 650**	**20 555**	**7 905**	**11 538**
#专项补助	Special Assistance	934	8 463	769	1 439
已拨入专项补助(万元)	Special Assiatance Appropriated(10 000 yuan)	1 209	8 463	769	1 169
当年保护维修支出(万元)	Expend on Preservation and Maintaining (10 000 yuan)	19 571	20 554	3 029	5 606

表22.10 主要年份广播电台、电视台情况
TELEVISION STATIONS AND BROADCASTING STATIONS IN MAIN YEARS

类 别	Types	2005	2010	2011	2012
广播电台	**Broadcasting Stations**				
中、短波发射台(座)	Relaying Stations of Medium and Short Wave Broadcast (uint)	4	4	4	4
发射功率(千瓦)	Transmited Power (kw)	390	240	240	240
公共广播节目套数(套)	Public Radio Program (set)	21	21	21	21
付费广播节目套数(套)	Pay Radio Program(set)	1	1	1	1
日均播音时间(小时)	Broadcasting Time a day (hour)	347	360	378	378
全年制作节目时间(小时)	Length of Programs Produced (hours)	83 665	85 262	72 344	83 309
电视台	**Television Stations**				
发射台(座)	Realying Stations (uint)	11	11	11	11
发射功率(千瓦)	Transmitted Power (kw)	170	172	172	172
公共电视节目套数(套)	Public TV Programs (set)	25	25	25	25
付费电视节目套数(套)	Pay TV Programs (set)	15	16	16	16
周均播放时间(小时)	Broadcast Time a week (hour)	2 871	3 361	3 399	3 455
全年制作节目时间(小时)	Length of Programs Produced (hours)	62 819	49 507	42 695	53 274
广播电视卫星地球站(座)	Satellite Earth Station of Radio and TV Programs(uint)	1	1	1	1

表22.11 电视和广播公共节目播出时间(2012)
PLAYING HOURS OF TELEVISION AND BROADCASTING PUBLIC PROGRAMS

单位:小时(hour)

类 别	Types	电视台 Television Stations			广播电台 Broadcasting Stations		
		合 计 Total	市 级 Municipal Level	区县级 District Level	合 计 Total	市 级 Municipal Level	区县级 District Level
总 计	**Total**	**180 644**	**129 321**	**51 323**	**138 385**	**81 821**	**56 564**
新闻资讯类节目	News Program	30 825	23 309	7 516	36 564	19 425	17 139
专题服务类节目	Subject Service Program	36 993	27 295	9 698	32 680	23 914	8 766
综艺类节目	Recreational and Artistic Program	12 898	11 403	1 495	45 486	27 550	17 936
影视剧类节目	Film and TV Program	65 054	42 273	22 781			
广播剧类节目	Broadcasting Drama Program				6 277	753	5 524
广告类节目	Advertising Program	17 702	9 892	7 810	15 053	9 839	5 214
其他类节目	Others	17 172	15 149	2 023	2 325	340	1 985

表22.12 主要年份有线电视基本情况
BASIC STATISTICS ON CABLE TELEVISION IN MAIN YEARS

指 标	Indicators	2000	2010	2011	2012
有线电视总用户数(万户)	Quantity of Cable TV Users(10 000 households)	303.0	573.0	627.0	648.0
#数字电视用户	Digital TV Users		235.6	285.6	409.0
有线电视入户率(%)	Popularity of Cable TV (%)	64.50	112.36	120.78	124.13
有线广播电视传输网络干线总长(公里)	Lines Total Length (kilometer)	604	36 211	37 475	39 805

表 22.13 电影摄制、译制和放映情况(1978～2012)
PRODUCTION, DUBBING AND SHOWING OF FILMS

年 份 Year	摄制和译制电影片 Production and Dubbing 故事片(部) Feature Films (film)	动画电影(本) Animated Film(reel)	科学教育片(本) Popular Science Films(reel)	译制片(本/部) Dubbed Films (reel/set)	电影放映 Film Showing 放映场次(万场) Showing (10 000 times)	其中 of which #影、剧院 Cinemas and Theatres	观众人次(万人次) Spectators (10 000 person-times)	其中 of which #影、剧院 Cinemas and Theatres
1978	10	24	84	275	35	17	27 405	15 291
1979	14	25	95	315	40	20	32 763	29 743
1980	**17**	**30**	**105**	**382**	**39**	**20**	**29 304**	**18 039**
1981	17	32	109	289	38	19	26 823	16 203
1982	19	35	112	604	38	20	25 828	15 586
1983	19	34	116	666	37	20	25 204	15 124
1984	19	40	117	633	36	21	24 149	15 539
1985	15	43	140	426	34	21	21 885	14 748
1986	19	38	150	450	36	24	23 220	16 720
1987	17	38	151	378	37	28	21 985	17 067
1988	13	29	156	501	38	30	20 461	16 742
1989	17	29	140	398	37	32	20 776	18 216
1990	**16**	**47**	**142**	**340**	**38**	**33**	**19 351**	**17 021**
1991	17	37	146	272	36	31	15 766	13 615
1992	17	42	146	325	29	25	9 145	8 089
1993	16	35	91	251	16	14	3 862	3 332
1994	14	13	69	162	22	20	4 001	3 617
1995	17	37	22	266	23	20	4 419	3 913
1996	10	58	6	283	27	25	4 420	3 783
1997	11	17	8	312	25	23	3 670	3 023
1998	4	16	6	271	23	21	2 924	2 451
1999	17	10	14	372	20	19	2 055	1 678
2000	**10**	**20**	**12**	**438**	**18**	**17**	**1 794**	**1 452**
2001	12	2	8	237	18	17	1 553	1 315
2002	10	2	11	204	20	17	1 198	921
2003	9	10	2	216	20	19	971	870
2004	12	1		248	24	23	1 364	1 183
2005	13			183	28	26	1 509	1 323
2006	9			312	27	26	1 254	1 173
2007	9			211	33	32	1 385	1 277
2008	17	8		248	35	34	1 456	1 381
2009	11			284	44	43	1 938	1 844
2010	**19**	**2**		**151**	**55**	**54**	**2 289**	**2 174**
2011	25			358	76	75	2 792	2 668
2012	22	6		24	96	95	3 154	3 074

注：2012 年起，译制片的统计口径发生变化，单位由过去的"本"改为"部"。
Note: Since 2012, the statistical calibre of dubbed films has been changed from reel to set.

表 22.14 主要年份电影发行放映情况
BASIC STATISTICS OF FILM DISTRIBUTION AND PROJECTION IN MAIN YEARS

指标	Indicators	2005	2010	2011	2012
放映场次(万场)	**Projection Times (10 000 times)**	**27.60**	**54.63**	**75.98**	**95.90**
#电影院	Cinema	22.20	51.72	72.56	91.85
影剧院	Theater	3.90	2.19	2.58	2.83
开放礼堂、俱乐部	Open Auditorium and Clubs	1.16	0.68	0.77	1.13
观众人次数(万人次)	**Quantity of Audience (10 000 person-times)**	**1 509.31**	**2 287.84**	**2 792.18**	**3 153.51**
#电影院	Cinema	893.92	2 052.62	2 553.20	2 969.64
影剧院	Theater	428.63	121.33	115.16	104.81
开放礼堂、俱乐部	Open Auditorium and Clubs	36.24	55.99	96.63	51.52
放映收入(万元)	**Projection Revenue (10 000 yuan)**	**27 192.03**	**93 875.11**	**109 115.31**	**131 950.71**
#电影院	Cinema	23 591.47	89 302.91	104 670.94	127 389.72
影剧院	Theater	2 389.52	2 697.84	2 895.44	3 051.69
开放礼堂、俱乐部	Open Auditorium and Clubs	1 009.58	1 807.88	1 515.71	1 462.31
平均每一放映场次	**Average on per Projection Time**				
观众人数(人)	Quantity of Audience (Person)	54.69	41.88	36.75	32.88
放映收入(元)	Returns (yuan)	985.22	1 718.38	1 436.11	1 375.92
日均放映场次(场)	**Projection Time a Day (time)**	**756.16**	**1 496.71**	**2 081.64**	**2 620.22**
日均观众人次(万人次)	**Average Audience a Day (person)**	**4.14**	**6.27**	**7.65**	**8.62**

表 22.15 电影公益场放映情况(2009～2012)
FILM PROJECTION FOR PUBLIC GOOD

指标	Indicators	2009	2010	2011	2012
放映影片(部)	Film Projected (reel)	2 748	821	991	1 313
放映场次(万场次)	Projection Times (10 000 times)	8.72	9.20	10.33	8.97
观众人次(万人次)	Quantity of Audience (10 000 person-times)	897.88	959.90	789.89	731.64
放映费用(万元)	Cost of Projection (10 000 yuan)	1 212.68	1 849.92	1 204.18	905.39
#政府补贴	Government Subsidies	814.99	1 378.60	789.79	509.57

表 22.16 文化娱乐机构基本情况(2012)
BASIC STATISTICS OF CULTURE AND ENTERTAINMENT INSTITUTIONS

类 别	Types	从业人员(人) Employees (person)	主营业务收入(万元) Major Business Revenue (10 000 yuan)	主营业务利润(万元) Major Business Profits (10 000 yuan)	房屋建筑面积(万平方米) Floor Space of Buildings (10 000 sq. m)
总 计	**Total**	**64 644**	**2 112 155.8**	**615 814.6**	**283.6**
歌舞娱乐场所	Singing & Dancing Rooms	30 456	269 240.5	33 098.5	108.0
游戏电子游艺经营场所	Gaming Rooms	6 171	67 097.6	21 263.0	90.6
其他娱乐场所	Other Places	6 073	82 015.3	15 989.5	20.4
网 吧	Internet Bar	7 601	53 364.8	15 576.7	45.6
经营性互联网文化单位	Internet-Culturel Business Unit	14 343	1 640 437.6	529 886.8	19.0

表 22.17 公共图书馆情况(2012)
PUBLIC LIBRARIES

指 标	Indicators	合 计 Total	市 级 Municipal Level	区、县级 District and County Level
机构数(个)	Institutions (unit)	25	2	23
从业人员(人)	Employees (person)	2 089	777	1 312
总藏量(万册、件)	Collection (10 000 copies)	7 202.43	5 446.60	1 755.83
#图 书	Books	2 815.88	1 361.97	1 453.91
报 刊	Newspaper and Magzines	353.68	325.76	27.92
本年新购藏量(万册、件)	Publications Newly Bought (10 000 copies)	305.17	56.27	248.90
建筑面积(万平方米)	Floor Space of Buildings (10 000 sq. m)	38.67	12.32	26.35
#书 库	Stack Room	8.18	5.29	2.89
阅览室	Reading Room	9.46	1.32	8.14
阅览座位(个)	Seats in Reading Room (unit)	21 594	2 318	19 276
书刊文献外借情况	Books Lending			
人 次(万人次)	Readers (10 000 person-times)	580.01	57.59	522.42
册 数(万册次)	Books (10 000 copy-times)	1 972.56	330.35	1 642.21
信息化装备	Information Equipment			
计算机(台)	**Computer(unit)**	**5 885**	**1 986**	**3 899**
#电子阅览室终端数	E-reeding Romm Terminals	1 816	325	1 49[illegible]
为读者举办各种活动	Activities Held for Readers			
组织各类讲座次数(次)	All Kinds of Lectures (time)	1 795	213	1 582
参加人次(万人次)	Participants (10 000 person-times)	25.97	6.24	19.73

表22.18 图书出版数量(1978～2012)
BOOKS PUBLISHED

年 份 Year	种 数 (种) Quantity of Publications (type)	其 中 of which #新出版 Newly Published	总印数 (亿册) Total Printed (100 million copies)	总印张数 (亿印张) Total Ptrinted Signatures (100 million signatures)
1978	1 666	1 332	3.92	12.19
1979	2 040	1 563	4.58	15.54
1980	2 338	1 804	5.62	17.73
1981	2 801	1 949	6.01	22.89
1982	3 395	2 057	6.07	21.76
1983	3 653	2 254	4.65	21.31
1984	3 848	2 328	5.37	25.58
1985	4 176	2 634	4.96	23.95
1986	4 531	3 045	3.66	17.81
1987	5 103	3 151	4.26	19.84
1988	5 538	3 658	4.33	19.04
1989	6 765	4 960	3.28	14.52
1990	7 767	4 887	2.98	14.66
1991	8 141	4 756	3.11	17.30
1992	8 095	4 179	2.75	17.19
1993	7 721	4 272	2.26	15.34
1994	7 812	4 382	2.35	17.01
1995	8 338	4 185	2.44	17.92
1996	9 234	4 445	2.79	20.10
1997	9 928	4 844	2.70	18.00
1998	10 718	5 083	2.83	18.69
1999	11 381	5 880	2.68	18.69
2000	12 682	6 936	2.54	19.05
2001	14 000	7 947	2.68	21.24
2002	14 537	8 156	2.59	21.38
2003	15 636	8 726	2.74	23.27
2004	16 449	9 391	2.67	23.54
2005	15 504	9 286	2.59	23.65
2006	17 283	9 338	2.54	24.86
2007	15 958	9 085	2.40	24.05
2008	17 780	9 945	2.64	24.97
2009	18 873	10 615	2.74	25.46
2010	19 519	11 241	2.89	26.34
2011	22 056	12 542	2.89	27.37
2012	23 792	13 142	3.35	31.35

表 22.19 期刊出版数量(1978 ~2012)
PERIODICALS PUBLISHED

年 份 Years	种 数 (种) Quantity of Publications (type)	每期平均印数 (万册、份) Average Publications Issued (10 000 copies)	总印数 (亿册) Total Printed (100 million copies)	总印张数 (亿印张) Total Printed Signatures (100 million signatures)
1978	42	459	0.47	1.12
1979	90	721	0.73	2.08
1980	126	1 061	1.22	3.37
1981	266	1 873	2.03	5.95
1982	308	2 203	2.31	6.37
1983	349	2 572	2.51	7.07
1984	402	3 502	3.1	8.56
1985	491	3 424	3.45	9.21
1986	541	3 073	3.03	8.17
1987	546	3 058	3.13	8.05
1988	535	2 624	2.66	6.63
1989	527	1 793	1.86	4.58
1990	522	1 735	1.73	4.24
1991	504	1 749	1.79	4.44
1992	527	1 794	1.84	4.59
1993	535	1 668	1.82	4.95
1994	556	1 569	1.72	4.87
1995	565	1 583	1.78	5.30
1996	582	1 530	1.66	5.14
1997	587	1 513	1.66	5.35
1998	591	1 503	1.65	5.81
1999	606	1 493	1.78	6.87
2000	613	1 489	1.85	7.38
2001	616	1 413	1.85	7.58
2002	621	1 332	1.80	7.77
2003	626	1 335	1.83	8.51
2004	612	1 184	1.93	8.94
2005	612	1 130	1.90	8.96
2006	616	1 125	1.83	8.76
2007	624	1 117	1.83	8.75
2008	623	1 105	1.90	9.27
2009	621	1 039	1.79	9.02
2010	632	1 019	1.78	9.04
2011	632	1 023	1.82	9.42
2012	626	938	1.76	9.67

表22.20 报纸出版数量(1978～2012)
NEWSPAPER PUBLISHED

年份 Years	种数 (种) Quantity of Publications (type)	每期平均印数 (万份) Average Publication Issued (10 000 copies)	总印数 (亿份) Total Printed (100 million copies)	总印张数 (亿印张) Total Printed Signatures (100 million signatures)
1978	5	257	6.41	6.20
1979	8	349	7.32	7.08
1980	12	464	8.55	8.20
1981	15	640	10.28	9.77
1982	31	936	14.93	13.13
1983	34	1 185	18.13	15.49
1984	41	1 429	19.63	16.57
1985	89	1 656	19.54	17.07
1986	93	1 750	19.94	18.37
1987	90	2 003	22.45	20.49
1988	83	1 958	21.38	22.07
1989	81	1 477	15.85	16.25
1990	81	1 510	16.16	16.76
1991	75	1 506	18.48	19.16
1992	77	1 506	24.76	24.76
1993	81	1 506	32.27	32.27
1994	87	1 369	30.43	30.43
1995	86	1 358	19.04	34.00
1996	87	1 357	18.93	36.96
1997	87	1 397	19.34	43.19
1998	80	1 441	19.73	49.84
1999	75	1 311	18.42	46.26
2000	103	1 135	16.77	44.57
2001	101	1 060	16.98	47.67
2002	101	983	16.46	51.42
2003	101	886	17.05	66.13
2004	103	939	19.71	83.66
2005	102	903	19.06	89.94
2006	101	850	17.89	87.33
2007	101	815	17.04	86.75
2008	100	787	17.24	88.29
2009	100	741	16.33	77.94
2010	100	752	15.90	78.65
2011	00	734	15.61	79.38
2012	100	686	14.54	68.03

表 22.21 主要年份新闻出版机构和人员数
NUMBER OF INSTITUTIONS AND EMPLOYEES ENGAGED IN NEWS AND PUBLISHING IN MAIN YEARS

指　标	Indicators	2000	2010	2011	2012
图书出版机构	**Publishing Houses**				
机构数（个）	Institutions（unit）	37	40	40	40
从业人员（人）	Employee（person）	3 666	3 949	3 999	3 829
书刊印刷机构	**Printing Houses**				
机构数（个）	Institutions（unit）	4 543	4 606	4 630	4 571
从业人员（万人）	Employee（10 000 persons）	11.54	16.02	16.51	16.79
发行机构	**Issuing Houses**				
机构数（个）	Institutions（unit）	6 743	9 327	8 982	8 526
从业人员（万人）	Employee（10 000 persons）	1.94	2.14	3.08	3.03

注：发行机构数中包括发行网点数。
Note：Issuing Houses include quantity of net places.

表 22.22 图书出版数量(2012)
BOOKS PUBLISHED

类　别	types	种　数（种）Number of Publications（type）	其中 of which #新出版 Newly Published	总印数（万册）Total Printed（10 000 copies）	总印张数（万印张）Total Printed Signatures（10 000 signatures）
总　计	**Total**	**23 792**	**13 142**	**33 479.24**	**313 483.57**
书　籍	**Books**	**18 788**	**11 692**	**18 498.87**	**190 888.44**
哲学、社会科学	Philosophy and Social Science	3 708	2 766	2 445.61	31 824.30
文化教育	Culture and Education	6 656	3 730	6 710.06	70 483.32
文学艺术	Literature and Art	4 770	2 899	3 714.57	53 288.66
自然科学技术	Natural Science and Technology	2 043	1 464	1 764.33	18 222.49
少年儿童读物	Children's Reading Materials	1 611	833	3 864.31	17 069.67
课　本	**Textbooks**	**4 992**	**1 438**	**14 979.20**	**122 357.[illegible]**
大专及以上课本	University and College	2 841	920	3 235.24	50 908.56
中专技校教材	Specialized Secondary and Technical Worker School	150	33	116.81	1 269.29
中学课本	Secondary School	663	92	6 219.48	43 428.53
小学课本	Primary School	385	42	4 889.66	19 49[illegible].55
业余教育课本	Spare-time Education	307	211	371.30	5 3[illegible].43
教学用书	Teaching References	646	140	146.71	1 8[illegible]5.73
图　片	**Pictures**	**12**	**12**	**1.17**	**238.03**

表 22.23 期刊出版数量(2012)
PERIODICALS PUBLISHED

类别	Types	种数(种) Quantity of Publications (type)	出版期数(期) Quantity of Issue (issue)	总印数(万册) Total Printed (10 000 copies)	总印张数(万印张) Total Printed Signatures (10 000 signatures)
总计	**Total**	**626**	**6 303**	**17 631.68**	**96 733.21**
综合	Comprehensive	14	147	1 329.71	6 584.72
哲学、社会科学	Philosophy and Social Science	126	1 466	4 557.13	29 295.58
自然科学技术	Natural Science and Technology	357	3 029	2 835.34	25 024.98
文化教育	Culture and Education	75	844	1 529.40	9 597.41
文学艺术	Literature and Art	32	382	5 741.87	20 519.60
少年儿童读物	Children's Reading Materials	21	423	1 628.95	5 668.05
画刊	Pictorial	1	12	9.28	42.87

表 22.24 报纸出版数量(2012)
NEWSPAPER PUBLISHED

类别	Types	种数(种) Quantity of Publications (type)	期数(期) Issue (issue)	每期平均印数(万份) Average Publication Per Issue (10 000 copies)	总印数(万份) Total Printed (10 000 copies)	总印张数(万印张) Total Printed Signatures (10 000 signatures)
总计	**Total**	**100**	**11 362**	**685.51**	**145 390.17**	**680 278.63**
综合报	Comprehensive	12	3 485	252.33	84 517.61	499 019.93
专业报	Specialized	88	7 877	433.18	60 872.56	181 258.70

表 22.25 音像电子出版数量(2012)
AUDIO, VIDEO AND ELECTRON PUBLISHED

类别	Types	种数(种) Quantity of Publications (type)	出版数量(万张、万盒) Quantity of Publications (10 000 piece box)	发行数量(万张、万盒) Quantity of Issued (10 000 piece box)	发行总金额(万元) Total Values (10 000 yuan)
总计	**Total**	**3 077**	**4 443.24**	**5 060.99**	**35 369.87**
电子出版物	Electronic Publication	632	1 557.32	2 627.62	20 348.81
数码激光视盘	DVD	104	93.60	81.97	314.21
高密度激光视盘	EVD	391	459.29	255.51	3 517.96
激光唱盘	CD	1 079	749.57	666.79	3 435.91
录音带	Tape	476	1 241.64	1 168.19	5 418.89
其他	Others	395	341.82	260.91	2 334.09

表22.26 档案机构基本情况(2012)
BASIC STATISTICS OF ARCHIVE INSTITUTIONS

指　标	Indicators	合　计 Total	档案行政管理部门 Archival Administrative Department	档案馆 Archives Library	档案室(处、科) Archives
机构数(个)	**Quantity of Institutions(unit)**	**734**	**18**	**37**	**679**
从业人员(人)	**Employees(person)**	**4 125**	**315**	**662**	**3 148**
专　职	Full-time	2 053	314	662	1 077
兼　职	Part-time	2 072	1		2 071
馆藏档案	**Archives Collected**				
全　宗(个)	Overall Rolls(unit)	7 298		5 754	1 544
案卷(万卷)	Rolls(10 000 rolls)	2 770.23		1 217.00	1 553.23
以件为保管单位档案(万件)	Archives(10 000 pieces)	573.22		180.32	392.90
录音、录像、影片档案(万盘)	Recprd, Video and Film(10 000 disks)	11.48		3.04	8.44
照片档案(万张)	Photo Records(10 000 pieces)	204.07		117.96	86.11
底图(万张)	Base Maps(10 000 pieces)	1 718.64		17.11	1 701.53
数字档案(GB)	Electronic Records(10 000 disks)				
归档电子文件	Filing of Electronic Files	277 770 943		31 671	277 739 272
数字化档案	Digital Archives	73 897 859		91 636	73 806 223
微缩胶片	Microfilm				
平片(万张)	Flat Film(10 000 pieces)	9.22		7.77	1.45
开窗卡(万张)	Open Window Card(10 000 pieces)	66.55		22.82	43.73
档案利用	**Records Utilized**				
已开放档案	Records Opened				
案　卷(万卷)	Rolls(10 000 rolls)	180.46		180.46	
案　件(万件)	Cases(10 000 cases)	1.86		1.86	
开放档案目录(万条)	Catalog of Records Opened(10 000 pieces)				
案卷级	Roll Grade	143.00		143.00	
文件级	Document Grade	499.00		499.00	
本年利用档案	Records Utilized in 2008				
卷　次(万卷次)	Roll-times(10 000 roll-times)	270.47		45.96	224.51
件　次(万件次)	Piece-times(10 000 piece-times)	64.85		40.68	24.17
人　次(万人次)	Person-times(10 000 person-times)	47.19		26.69	20.50

表22.27　主要年份优秀运动员、教练员情况
BASIC STATISTICS ON EXCELLENT ATHLETES AND COACHES IN MAIN YEARS

单位：人（person）

指　标	Indicators	2000	2010	2011	2012
等级裁判员	Certified Referees	880	559	751	796
优秀运动员	Excellent Athletes	899	771	949	967
#女运动员	Women	402	371	468	432
优秀运动队专职教练员	Full-time Coaches	196	73	124	170
#女专职教练员	Women	30	22	43	47

表22.28　体育系统职工人数（2012）
STAFF AND WORKERS IN SPORTS SECTORS

单位：人（person）

指　标	Indicators	总　计 Total	其中 of which: #优秀运动队 Excellent Sports Teams	#体育运动学校 Physical Education and Sports Schools	#普通业余体校 Popular Sparetime Sports School	#公共体育场（馆） Public Stadiums and Gymnasiums
总　计	**Total**	**6 134**	**1 933**	**355**	**1 170**	**1 942**
#专职教练员	Full-time Coaches	1 119	170	79	673	90
运动员	Athletes	1 073	967	17	50	9
管理干部	Administraive Staff	1 427	201	76	191	595
专职教师	Full time Teachers	307	215	45	46	
科技人员	Scientific and Technical Personnel	79	7	2	14	
医务人员	Medical Personnel	70	49	10	4	7

表22.29　群众体育健身活动场所情况（2009～2012）
MASS PHYSICAL ACTIVITIES IN MAIN YEARS

指　标	Indicators	2009	2010	2011	2012
社区体育健身设施数（个）	Quantity of Community Fitness Facilities (unit)	4 845	4 845	6 309	6 429
#健身点	Fitness Centers	4 586	4 586	4 586	4 586
社区健身场地面积（万平方米）	Area of Community Fitness Space (10 000 sq. m)	301	301	416.9	426.9
社区公共运动场（个）	Quantity of Community Public Playground (unit)	261	316	324	324
社区公共运动场面积（万平方米）	Area of Community Public Playground (10 000 sq. m)	239	246.7	45.5	46.7

上 / 海 / 统 / 计 / 年 / 鉴

主要统计指标解释

■ 文化机构

是指专门从事文化工作具有法人资格，独立核算的事业，企业单位，以及单独核算，附属于事业单位的经营性专业文化活动单位。包括从事艺术、图书馆、档案馆、群众文化、文物保护、艺术教育、艺术研究、文化娱乐、新闻出版等机构，以及其他文化机构。

■ 电影放映单位

指具有放映机器设备、固定或不固定的放映场所与专职或兼职的放映技术人员，经有关部门登记批准，经常为一定的观众对象放映电影的机构。包括电影院、影剧院、开放礼堂、俱乐部、放映队、对内礼堂俱乐部。

■ 艺术表演团体

指从事戏曲、音乐、舞蹈、杂技等专业艺术表演，有独立账户的单位，不包括半工半艺、半农半艺和民间职业剧团。该指标主要反映上海专业艺术表演团体发展规模水平。

■ 艺术表演观众人次

指售票、包场演出或民族地区免费演出的艺术表演观众人次数，不包括彩排审查和内部观摩演出的观看人次数。该指标主要反映上海观看专业艺术表演团体演出的效益规模。

■ 等级运动员人数

指经考核正式批准授予等级运动员称号的人数。运动员等级分为国际级运动健将、运动健将、一级运动员、二级运动员、三级运动员、少年级运动员。该指标主要反映运动员队伍的技术质量水平。

■ 等级裁判员人数

指经考核正式批准授予等级裁判员称号的人数。裁判员等级分为国际裁判、国家级裁判、一级裁判、二级裁判、三级裁判。该指标主要反映裁判员队伍的技术质量水平。

SHANGHAI STATISTICAL YEARBOOK

EXPLANATORY NOTES TO MAJOR STATISTICAL INDICATORS

□ Cultural Institutions

Cultural Institution refers to undertaking and business institutions which specialize in cultural work and have legal personality and independent accounting system, and those professional cultural institutions attached to undertaking institutions and have independent accounting system. It includes institutions specialize in art, library, archives, mass culture, historical relic protection, art education, art research, entertainment, news and publication and other cultural institutions.

□ Film Projection Units

Film Projection Units refer to units with film projection equipments, full -or part-time projectionists, permanent or non-permanent places, approved by related administrative departments to show films regularly for certain groups of audience, including cinemas, theaters, public auditoriums, clubs, film projection teams, and interior auditorium clubs.

□ Art Troupe

Art Troupe refers to the troupe which is engaged in drama, opera, music, dance, acrobatics or other art performance, opens independent accounts with banks and has self-supporting accounting system; excluding the troupes which are engaged partly in industrial or agricultural activities, partly in art performance and the professional troupes organized by the people. This indicator reflects the development of Shanghai's professional art troupes.

□ Quantity of Spectators at Art Performance

Number of Spectators at Art Performance refers to the number of attendants at commercial shows, completely booked shows or free shows given in minority national areas, and does not include the number of spectators at rehearsals for examination and internal shows for study. This indicator reflects beneficial results of spectators at Professional Art Performance.

□ Quantity of Athletes in Grades

Number of Athletes in Grades refers to the number of athletes who have been given titles through examination. The titles of athletes include international masters of sports, masters of sports, first-grade, second-grade and third-grade sportsmen and young athletes. This indicator reflects skill of the athletes.

□ Quantity of Referees in Grades

Number of Referees in Grades refers to the number of referees who have been given titles after examination. They are classified as international referees, national referees and referees of the first, second and third grades. This indicator reflects the skill of referees.

第二十三篇

CHAPTER 23

法律、公证和其他

LAWS, NOTARY AND OTHERS

简要说明

一、本章资料的主要内容

本篇主要包括公检法司的情况。

内容主要包括律师机构、公证机构、人民调解委员会的机构、人员、主要业务活动情况；公安机立案的刑事案件及查处的治安案件情况；交通事故和火灾事故的次数、伤亡人数和损失折款情况；检察院直接立案侦查案件、民事行政案件办理、申诉案件处理情况；法院各类案件办理、执行案件和各类案件结案情况。

二、本篇资料的来源

律师、公证和人民调解等资料由上海市司法局提供；刑事案件、治安案件、交通火灾事故等资料由上海市公安局提供；检察院相关案件资料由上海市检察院提供；法院相关案件资料由上海市高级人民法院提供。

BRIEF INTRODUCTION

I. Main Contents

Data in this chapter reflect statistics on public security,procuratorial,legal and judicial affairs.

Data include mainly general information, personnel, and main activities of law firms, notarizations and meditations; criminal cases registered and offense cases handled by the public security agencies; casualties, and losses in traffic or fire accidents, cases under direct investigation by procurator's office, civil cases, administrative cases and appeals handled by procurator's offices; cases handled, executed, and closed by courts.

II. Sources of Data

Data on law firms, notarizations, and meditations are provided by Shanghai Municipal Bureau of Justice; data on criminal cases, offense cases, and traffic and fire accidents are provided by Shanghai Municipal Public Security Bureau; Data on procurators are provided by Shanghai Municipal People's Procurator's Offices; data on courts are provided by Shanghai Municipal Senior People's Court.

表23.1 主要年份律师、公证及调解工作基本情况
BASIC STATISTICS OF LAWYERS, NOTARIZATIONS AND MEDIATIONS IN MAIN YEARS

指标	Indicators	2000	2010	2011	2012
律师工作	**Lawyers**				
法律律师事务所（个）	Law Offices (unit)	415	1 064	1 110	1 163
律师人数（人）	Lawyers (person)	4 642	13 027	13 540	14 868
#专职律师	Full-time Lawyers	3 522	11 749	12 960	14 245
兼职律师	Part-time Lawyers	731	549	580	623
全年办理	**Total Transacted**				
民事案件诉讼代理（万件）	Civil Lawsuit(10 000 cases)	7.05	7.69	8.07	8.30
刑事诉讼辩护及代理（万件）	Criminal Lawsuit and Vindication(10 000 cases)	1.13	1.49	1.46	1.39
非诉讼法律事务（万件）	Non-litigation Action(10 000 cases)	2.65	3.32	3.22	3.60
解答法律询问(万人次)	Legal Advisory Services (10 000 person-times)	10.36	13.09	13.08	14.28
代写法律事务文书（万件）	Legal Documents Written on Behalf of Clients(10 000 cases)	1.92	2.67	2.47	2.38
公证工作	**Notarizations**				
公证处（个）	Notarial Offices (unit)	22	22	21	21
公证人员（人）	Notarial Personnel (person)	366	821	909	923
#公证员	Notaries	243	359	407	413
办理公证文书（万件）	Documents Notarized (10 000 cases)	47.72	40.76	40.69	51.79
#国内经济合同公证	Domestic Economic Contracts Notarized	18.73	8.17	8.05	10.37
在办理公证文书中	Documents Notarizing				
涉外公证（万件）	Foreign (10 000 cases)	19.93	20.98	21.53	26.30
国内公证（万件）	Domestic (10 000 cases)	27.79	18.54	18.23	24.06
公证费收入（亿元）	Revenue of Notarial Fees (100 million yuan)	1.13	4.7	4.94	4.86
人民调解工作	**People's Mediation**				
专职司法助理员（人）	Full-time Judicial Assistants (person)	416	734	741	807
人民调解委员会（万个）	People's Mediation Committees(10 000 units)	0.89	0.63	0.64	0.65
调解人员（万人）	Mediators (10 000 persons)	3.55	3.41	3.44	3.34
调解民间纠纷（万件）	Civil Disputes Mediated (10 000 cases)	6.37	23.24	23.58	26.47
#婚姻家庭	Family Disputes	1.97	3.63	3.67	3.48
邻　里	Neighbor Disputes	2.51	5.12	5.24	5.83
赔　偿	Compensation	0.25	3.02	4.76	5.53
房屋宅基地	Housing and Housing Sites	1.04	1.29	1.51	1.86

注：办理公证文件中包括涉及港、澳、台公证文件。
Note: The number of notarized documents handled included Hong Kong, Macao, and Taiwan's.

表 23.2 主要年份国内和涉外公证文书分类情况
DOMESTIC AND FOREIGN NOTARIAL DOCUMENTS BY TYPE IN MAIN YEARS

单位：件(case)

指 标	Indicators	2000	2010	2011	2012
国内公证	**Domestic Notarized**	**277 949**	**185 425**	**182 251**	**240 555**
经济公证	Business Notarized	187 304	81 662	80 511	103 655
#贷款合同	Loans Contracts	80 980	24 100	25 839	29 785
招标、投标	Bidding	55	82	58	86
劳务合同	Labour Contracts	4 982	9	8	8
财产租赁	Property Leases	22	711	578	391
法人资格	Legal Person Identification	109	116	64	90
法人委托书	Legal Person Certificate of Entrustment	227	3 643	3 402	4 521
民事公证	Civil Legal Relations Notarized	90 645	103 763	101 740	136 900
#继承权	Rights of Inheritance	5 217	17 482	16 227	22 940
遗 嘱	Testaments	1 709	4 468	5 041	7 111
委托书	Certificate of Entrustment	4 520	48 788	43 566	54 563
赠与书	Presentation Documents	5 196	1 062	1 930	2 508
声明书	Declarations	10 424	5 404	6 330	5 477
其他民事协议	Other Civil Agreements	15 552	1 563	2 447	2 981
涉外公证	**Foreign Notarized**	**199 323**	**209 813**	**215 331**	**262 951**
#出 生	Births	28 535	28 627	30 500	35 847
学 历	Schooling	21 644	2 107	1 544	1 204
亲属关系	Kinship	22 488	19 286	17 929	23 716
婚姻状况	Marriages	20 274	7 246	6 550	6 299
受、未受刑事处分	Criminal Records & Uncriminal Records	20 669	22 550	21 548	26 585
文本相符	Confirmation of Copies and Photo-offset Copies to Originals	23 645	58 999	79 280	84 676

表23.3 主要年份公安机关立案的刑事案件情况
CRIMINAL CASES REGISTERED IN PUBLIC SECURITY ORGANS IN MAIN YEARS

单位:起(time)

类 别	Types	2000	2010	2011	2012
总 计	**Total**	**104 946**	**119 691**	**126 976**	**135 682**
杀 人	Homicide	252	174	146	163
伤 害	Injury	1 553	2 545	2 711	2 740
抢 劫	Robbery	3 033	1 558	1 330	1 110
强 奸	Rape	396	448	436	462
诈 骗	Fraud	8 425	16 598	16 383	17 885
盗 窃	Larceny	77 912	78 322	86 699	79 245
其 他	Others	13 375	20 046	19 271	34 077

表23.4 主要年份公安机关查处治安案件情况
OFFENSE CASES AGAINST PUBLIC ORDER HANDLED BY PUBLIC SECURITY ORGANS IN MAIN YEARS

单位:起(time)

类 别	Types	2000	2010	2011	2012
总 计	**Total**	**194 141**	**566 607**	**515 163**	**726 395**
#扰乱工作、公共秩序	Disturbing Work and Public Order	23 568	25 787	23 850	36 704
结伙斗殴、寻衅滋事	Gang Fighting or Picking Quarrels and Making Trouble	3 373	3 315	3 190	3 631
阻碍国家工作人员执行职务	Obstructing the Goverment Workers to Perform Their Duty	1 029	658	815	949
殴打他人	Beating Other Body	16 973	59 876	42 201	57 764
骗取、抢夺、敲诈勒索财物	Defrauding, Snatching or Extoring and Racketeering Valuables	2 936	24 510	32 582	59 169
伪造倒卖票券、证件	Forging and Fraudulently Selling Bills or Certificates	5 551	524	249	126
卖淫、嫖娼	Prostitution or Going Whoring	4 631	7 281	7 118	9 771
赌 博	Gambling	17 464	21 760	35 722	51 331

表 23.5 交通事故和火灾情况 (1980 ~2012)
BASIC STATISTICS OF TRAFFIC ACCIDENTS AND FIRES

年 份 Year	交通事故 Traffic Accidents 次 数(万次) Times(10 000 times)	死亡人数(人) Death(person)	受伤人数(万人) Injuries(10 000 persons)	损失折款(万元) Losses Converted -into Cash(10 000 yuan)	火 灾 Fires 次 数(万次) Times(10 000 times)	死亡人数(人) Death(person)	受伤人数(人) Injuries(person)	损失折款(万元) Losses Converted -into Cash(10 000 yuan)
1980	1.10	445	1.01	96	0.08	17	126	457
1981	1.18	507	1.06	119	0.09	33	81	202
1982	0.83	434	0.77	98	0.07	33	76	255
1983	0.73	443	0.70	99	0.06	24	67	533
1984	0.83	503	0.75	123	0.05	21	71	177
1985	0.71	687	0.57	318	0.05	30	74	374
1986	0.84	678	0.62	576	0.06	25	54	790
1987	1.01	811	0.67	959	0.06	51	56	575
1988	0.84	707	0.56	1 117	0.06	58	53	460
1989	0.75	652	0.49	1 137	0.03	30	30	394
1990	0.76	608	0.47	1 345	0.21	45	137	1 868
1991	0.75	594	0.45	1 530	0.17	38	112	937
1992	0.45	591	0.18	2 029	0.17	40	57	2 742
1993	0.81	699	0.29	4 652	0.14	73	128	2 252
1994	1.26	722	0.33	8 337	0.11	51	95	2 378
1995	1.67	788	0.38	12 077	0.11	47	86	2 100
1996	2.01	783	0.44	13 462	0.09	87	96	2 206
1997	2.16	780	0.58	13 682	0.74	51	138	2 639
1998	2.40	781	0.65	15 186	0.72	42	114	2 205
1999	2.61	726	0.78	15 924	0.66	43	90	1 487
2000	4.13	1 492	1.61	20 391	0.52	40	57	1 919
2001	4.21	1 503	1.57	23 883	0.32	31	65	966
2002	4.71	1 400	1.57	30 052	0.60	39	58	1 313
2003	5.42	1 406	1.12	39 721	0.58	47	85	1 724
2004	2.71	1 543	1.13	19 149	0.51	30	47	1 681
2005	0.92	1 393	0.88	7 961	0.43	54	84	1 731
2006	0.66	1 231	0.67	3 292	0.45	45	54	2 292
2007	0.40	1 171	0.38	1 943	0.42	50	45	2 650
2008	0.27	1 100	0.26	1 469	0.35	50	57	14 523
2009	0.28	1 042	0.27	1 226	0.61	63	41	3 990
2010	0.22	1 011	0.19	967	0.57	101	125	22 949
2011	0.21	944	0.18	1 349	0.58	43	46	11 010
2012	0.23	916	0.21	1 488	0.45	39	45	6 524

表23.6 交通事故情况(2012)
BASIC STATISTICS OF TRAFFIC ACCIDENTS

类别	Types	发生数（起） Number (case)	死亡人数（人） Death (person)	受伤人数（人） Injuries (person)	损失折款（万元） Losses Converted -into Cash (10 000 yuan)
总计	**Total**	**2 256**	**916**	**2 053**	**1 488.04**
#死亡事故	Death Accident	881	916	333	809.53
伤人事故	Injury Accident	1 346		1 720	655.36
#机动车	Motor-driven Vehicles	1 713	753	1 599	1 272.01
#汽车	Automobiles	1 480	647	1 397	1 182.32
摩托车	Motorcycles	209	88	186	79.53
非机动车	Non-motor-driven Vehicles	411	105	370	132.22
#自行车	Bicycles	68	18	53	22.44
行人乘车人	Pedestrians and Passengers	127	55	83	83.78
其他	Other	5	3	1	0.03

表23.7 火灾事故情况(2012)
BASIC STATISTICS OF FIRES

指标	Indicators	合计 Total	按事故发生程度分 By Serious Degree of Fires 较大 Serious	一般 Ordinary
次数（起）	Number (case)	4 469	1	4 468
死亡人数(人)	Deaths (person)	39	3	36
受伤人数(人)	Injuries (person)	45		45
损失折款(万元)	Losses Converted into Cash (10 000 yuan)	6 924	11.10	6 912.90
平均每起事故损失(万元)	Average Loss per Fire (10 000 yuan)	1.50	11.10	1.55

表 23.8 检察院直接立案侦查案件情况(2012)
CASES UNDER DIRECT INVESTIGATION BY PROCURATOR'S OFFICES

类 别	Types	受 案(件) Cases Accepted (case)	立案件数(件) Quantity of Cases Registered (case)	立案人数(人) Person of Cases Registered (person)	侦查终结件数(件) Quantity of Cases Settled (case)	侦查终结人数(人) Person of Cases Settled (person)
总 计	**Total**	**1 327**	**372**	**443**	**403**	**479**
贪污贿赂案件	**Quamitity of Cases on Corruption and Bribery**	**1 161**	**334**	**400**	**371**	**441**
贪 污	Corruption	459	91	127	99	136
贿 赂	Bribery	630	217	243	241	268
挪用公款	Misappropriation of Public Funds	35	22	24	25	27
集体私分	Collective Illegal Possession of Publice Funds	15	2	3	3	5
巨额财产来源不明	Huge Amount of Property From Unidentified Sources	22	2	2	1	1
其 他	Others			1	2	4
渎职侵权案件	**Quamitity of Cases on Abuse and Dereliction of Duty**	**166**	**38**	**43**	**32**	**38**
滥用职权	Abuse of Power	89	18	22	14	17
玩忽职守	Dereliction of Duty	29	12	12	10	10
徇私舞弊	Fraudulent Practice	27	3	3	3	4
侵犯公民权利	Infringement of Civl Right	20	4	5	4	5
其 他	Others	1	1	1	1	2

表 23.9 检察院民事、行政案件办理情况(2012)
CIVIL CASES AND ADMINISTRATIVE CASES HANDLED BY PROCURATOR'S OFFICES

单位:件(case)

类 别	Types	受 案 Cases Accepted	审查处理 Cases Investigated	其中 of which: 立 案 Cases Registered	结案处理 Cases Settled	其中 of which: 抗 诉 Appeals Rejected
总 计	**Total**	**2 101**	**3 275**	**686**	**678**	**121**
民事案	**Civil Cases**	**1 927**	**2 950**	**671**	**664**	**121**
合同纠纷案	Contract Disputes	755	1 179	314	331	76
权益纠纷案	Rights and Interests Disputes	487	822	143	140	22
劳动争议	Labour Disputes	169	304	47	49	6
婚姻家庭	Marriages	91	132	25	22	5
继承纠纷	Inheritance Disputes	63	105	13	18	5
其 他	Others	362	408	129	104	7
行政案	**Administrative Cases**	**174**	**325**	**15**	**14**	

表 23.10 检察院申诉案件处理情况(2012)
APPEALS HANDLED BY PROCURATOR'S OFFICES

单位:件(case)

类 别	Types	受 案 Cases Accepted	审查处理 Cases Investigated	其中 of which: 分送本院其他部门 Dilivering to Other Department of Such Procurator's Offices
总 计	**Total**	**12 393**	**12 389**	**3 535**
首次申诉	**Appeals First Time**	**5 706**	**5 703**	**2 646**
#不服不起诉	Appeals Against Non-prosecution	10	10	2
不服不立案	Appeals Against Rejection of the Case	226	226	198
不服逮捕	Appeals Against Arrest	2	2	
不服刑事判决	Appeals Against Judgment of Criminal Case	196	196	17
不服民事行政裁决	Appeals Against Aadminnistration Arbitrament of Civil Case	2 582	2 582	2 077
重复申诉	**Appeals Repeated**	**6 687**	**6 686**	**889**

表 23.10 续表 continued

单位:件(case)

类 别	Types	其中 of which: 移送其他检察院 Removing to Other Procurator's Offices	移送公安机关 Removing to Public Security Organs	移送其他机关 Removing to Other Organs	直接答复 Direct Reply
总 计	**Total**	**2 666**	**721**	**4 089**	**595**
首次申诉	**Appeals First Time**	**942**	**308**	**1 080**	**402**
#不服不起诉	Appeals Against Non-prosecution	3			
不服不立案	Appeals Against Rejection of the Case	21	3		3
不服刑事判决	Appeals Against Judgment of Criminal Case	34		13	19
不服民事行政裁决	Appeals Against Aadminnistration Arbitrament of Civil Case	382		66	49
重复申诉	**Appeals Repeated**	**1 724**	**413**	**3 009**	**193**

表 23.11 法院各类案件办理情况(2012)
CASES HANDLED BY COURTS

单位:件(case)

类别	Types	收案 Cases Accepted	结案 Cases Settled	其中 of which 判决 Judgement	裁定 Arbitration	调解 Mediation
一审刑事案件	**First Trial Criminal Cases**	**29 036**	**28 790**	**28 677**	**110**	**3**
#侵犯公民人身权利、民主权利罪	Offences Against Citizens' Personal and Democratic Rights	2 602	2 621	2 573	45	3
侵犯财产罪	Offences Against Properties	9 657	9 614	9 601	13	
妨碍社会管理秩序罪	Offences Against Social Management of Order	6 810	6 780	6 770	10	
一审民事案件	**First Trial Civil Cases**	**272 985**	**273 332**	**81 522**	**114 901**	**76 909**
婚姻家庭、继承案件	Marriages and Inheritance Cases	29 759	30 006	8 984	7 181	13 841
婚姻家庭案件	Marriages and Fimily Cases	24 499	24 760	8 020	6 412	10 328
继承案件	Inheritance Cases	5 260	5 246	964	769	3 513
合同纠纷案件	Contract Disputes Cases	170 238	169 839	46 366	89 882	33 591
#买卖合同纠纷	Trade Contracts	15 992	16 196	6 431	5 654	4 111
房地产开发经营合同纠纷	Real Estate Development Contracts	3 496	3 596	1 697	1 113	786
借款合同纠纷	Loan Contracts	27 355	26 391	10 091	11 210	5 090
租赁合同纠纷	Lease Contract	9 207	9 293	3 388	3 525	2 380
劳动争议	Labor Disputes	13 413	13 396	6 097	3 341	3 958
劳务合同	Labor Contracts	1 117	1 158	420	348	390
权属、侵犯纠纷及其他民事案件	Disputes of Right Infringement of Right and Other Civil Affaires	72 988	73 487	26 172	17 838	29 477
#所有权及与所有权相关权力纠纷	Ownership and Related Rights	10 807	10 929	4 361	3 676	2 892
人身权纠纷	Personal Rights	49 578	49 962	17 113	7 527	25 322
一审行政案件	**First Trial Administrative Cases**	**2 190**	**2 128**	**1 182**	**945**	

表23.12 法院执行案件情况(2012)
CASES EXECUTED BY COURTS

单位:件(case)

类别	Types	收案 Cases Accepted	结案 Cases Settled	其中 of which 自动履行 Automatic Performance	和解 Mediation	强制执行 Compellent Execution
总计	**Total**	**105 311**	**105 602**	**47 138**	**13 890**	**33 934**
刑事	Criminal Cases	1 825	1 823	987	69	390
民事	Civil Cases	90 162	90 386	40 904	12 373	28 474
行政	Administrative Cases	286	351	109	29	186
行政非诉审查与执行	Non-litigious Investigation and Execution of Administration	1 975	2 059	786	281	342
仲裁	Arbitration	10 425	10 384	4 272	1 026	4 297
公证债权文书	Notary Creditor's Rights	552	507	78	110	243
其他	Others	86	92	2	2	2

表23.13 主要年份法院各类案件结案情况
CASES ENDED BY COURTS IN MAIN YEARS

单位:起(time)

类别	Types	2005	2010	2011	2012
总计	**Total**	**283 230**	**406 582**	**412 923**	**438 781**
刑事案件	Criminal Cases	17 353	22 137	23 045	31 212
婚姻家庭、继承案件	Marriages and Inheritance Cases	28 563	31 114	31 660	31 626
合同纠纷案件	Contract Disputes Cases	128 118	180 459	177 839	184 532
权属、侵犯纠纷及其他民事案件	Disputes of Right Infringement of Right and Other Civil Affairs	31 153	64 395	75 120	79 147
行政案件	Administrative Cases	3 016	2 135	2 657	3 230
申诉、申请再审	Second Trial on Appeals and Requisition	4 023	4 120	3 891	3 403
司法赔偿	Justice Compensation	6	1	12	29
执行案件	Executed Cases	70 998	102 221	98 699	105 602

上/海/统/计/年/鉴

主要统计指标解释

■ 律　师

指依法取得律师执业证书，担任法律顾问，民事(刑事、行政)案件代理人、刑事案件辩护人、办理非诉讼业务，解答法律询问，代写法律事务文书等，为社会提供法律服务的人员。

■ 公证人员

指在国家机关依法办理公证事务的司法人员。包括公证员、助理公证员和在公证处工作的其他人员。

■ 公证文书

指公证处根据当事人申请，依照事实和法律，按照法定程序制作的，具有法律效力的司法证明文书。根据公证书用途和使用地，公证书分为国内公证书、国内经济公证书、涉外民事公证书、涉外经济公证书四类。

■ 调解民间纠纷

指调解委员会按照法律规定，根据自愿原则，用说服教育的方法调解民间发生的有关民事权利和义务争执的件数，包括调解成功数和调解未成功数。该指标主要反映人民调解委员会的工作量。

■ 立　案

指人民检察院对受理的报案、控告、举报或自首及自行发现的犯罪线索、犯罪嫌疑人进行初步调查后，认为存在职务犯罪事实和应追究刑事责任，并决定作为刑事案件进行侦查的诉讼活动，是追究犯罪的开始。该指标主要反映人民检察院依法将职务犯罪线索作为刑事案件进行侦查的诉讼活动。

■ 申　诉

指经检察机关信访部门审查处理后，移送到检察机关申诉部门的申诉案件，包括不服检察机关处理决定和不服法院刑事判决和裁定的申诉的案件。

SHANGHAI STATISTICAL YEARBOOK

EXPLANATORY NOTES TO MAJOR STATISTICAL INDICATORS

□ Lawyers

Lawyers are certified legal workers according to law, and who are employed by legal counseling firms to act as legal advisers, agents in criminal or civil lawsuits, or defenders in criminal lawsuits, or to handle non-litigious legal affairs, to advise on matters of law or to write legal papers for others, and provide service to the public.

□ Notary Personnel

Notary Personnel are judicial workers of the state notary organs handling notarization work according to law. They include notaries, assistant notaries, and other people working in notary firms.

□ Notary Documents

Notary Documents refer to the judicatory notary documents drawn up by the request of the party and are in accordance with facts and laws and following certain legal proceedings. According to usage and locality, the notary documents are divided into following 4 types: domestic notary documents, domestic economic notary documents, foreign-related civil notary documents and foreign-related economic notary documents.

□ Mediation of Civil Disputes

Mediation of Civil Disputes refers to number of cases made by mediation committees in mediating in civil disputes concerning civil rights and duties through persuasion and education in accordance with the provisions of law on a voluntary basis, so as to solve disputes by helping the parties involved come to an agreement and understanding, including those unsuccessful ones. This indicator reflects the workload of the mediation committees.

□ Acceptance of Case

Acceptance of Case refers to the decision made by the people's procuratorate office on reported cases, prosecution, impeachment, surrender, self-found criminal clues or suspects after initial investigation to confirm the act of crime and to start legal proceedings of the case as criminal case.

□ Appeals

Appeals refer to cases transferred to the appeal departments of procurator's offices after initial review by departments dealing with complaint letters and calls of the public. Included are appeals against decisions made by procurator's offices and appeals against court rules and verdicts.

第二十四篇

CHAPTER 24

企业景气指数与消费者信心指数

PROSPERITY INDEX ON ENTERPRISES AND CONSUMER CONFIDENCE INDEX

简要说明

一、本章资料的主要内容

本章资料包括企业景气调查和消费者信心指数。

二、企业家景气调查的资料来源和调查方法

1. 主要内容：

一是企业基本情况，包括单位详细名称、组织机构代码、单位负责人、联系电话、详细地址、单位规模、行业代码、营业收入等。

二是企业家对本行业景气状况的判断及对本企业生产经营状况的判断等。

2. 调查方法：

企业景气调查由上海市统计局服务业调查中心组织实施，被抽样选中企业按照上海市统计局统一制定的《企业景气调查制度》上报资料，上海市服务业调查中心审核后汇总计算。

2013年上海企业景气调查样本量为860家。其中，建筑业企业100家，批发和零售业企业250家，交通运输、仓储和邮政业企业70家，住宿和餐饮业企业110家，信息传输、软件和信息技术服务业企业90家，金融业企业50家，房地产业企业100家，社会服务业企业90家。

调查样本的抽取办法为根据《统计上大中小微型企业划分办法》(国统字〔2011〕75号)对企业规模重新的认定，将所有大类前30家企业和上市公司作为必选样本，其他企业按照与样本规模成比例的概率进行抽样(PPS)，并且在保证调查连续性和可比性的基础上，每年对中、小型企业样本进行轮换。

三、消费者信心指数的资料来源和调查方法

消费者信心指数采用计算机辅助电话和拦截相结合的方式调查，调查对象为上海市区范围20-70岁的常住城市市民。由国家统计局上海调查总队提供。

BRIEF INTRODUCTION

I. Main Contents

Data in this chapter include business sentiment survey and consumer confidence index

II. Data sources and survey methodology of business sentiment survey

(1)Main contents

(a)basic conditions of businesses, including detailed name of businesses, organization code, person in charge, contact phone number, detailed address, business scale, industry code, and revenue.

(b)business owner's judgment on industry sentiment, and on the enterprise's production and operation conditions.

(2)Survey methods

Business Sentiment Survey is organized and carried out by Shanghai Service Sectors Survey Center of Shanghai Municipal Statistics Bureau. Enterprises sampled report data according to Survey System on Business Sentiment made by Shanghai Municipal Statistics Bureau. Shanghai Service Sectors Survey Center compiles and calculates the results after verifying the data.

The number of samples included in 2013 Shanghai Business Sentiment Survey was 860. Among them, 100 are enterprises in the construction sector, 250 are enterprises in wholesale and retail trades, 70 are enterprises in transportation, warehousing and postal services sectors, 110 are enterprises in accommodation and catering services sectors, 90 are enterprises in telecommunication, software and information technology services sectors, 50 are financial institutions, 100 are property developers, and 90 are enterprises in social service sectors.

Survey samples are extracted according to re–classification of enterprise sizes according to 2011's Standards of Enterprises by Size. Thirty largest enterprises in each sector and all listed companies are required samples, and other sample enterprises are chosen based on using Probability Proportional to Size (PPS) sampling technique. Samples of medium and small–sized enterprises are rotated each year on the basis of ensuring continuity and comparability.

III. Data sources and survey methodology of Consumer Confidence Index

Consumer Confidence Index uses a combination of computer–assisted telephone and intercept surveys. Survey samples are permanent urban residents in Shanghai aging between 20 and 70 years old. Data are provided by Survey Office of the National Bureau of Statistics in Shanghai.

表 24.1　消费者信心指数(2012)
CONSUMER CONFIDENCE INDEX

项　目	Item	一季度 First Quarter	二季度 Second Quarter	三季度 Third Quarter	四季度 Fourth Quarter
消费者信心指数	**Consumer Confidence Index**	**108.7**	**108.1**	**108.5**	**111.6**
整体经济信心指数	Index of Confidence of Macroeconomy	113.1	111.7	110.3	119.1
就业形势信心指数	Index of Confidence of Employment Status	105.3	106.6	106.6	108.7
家庭收入信心指数	Index of Confidence of Household Income Status	116.4	111.9	112.3	112.0
生活质量信心指数	Index of Confidence of Quality of Life	111.5	110.3	111.6	114.2
耐用商品购买时机信心指数	Index of Confidence of the timing of Purchase of Durable Goods	97.3	100.2	101.6	104.1
消费者现状指数	**Consumer Status Quo Index**	**106.9**	**107.2**	**108.5**	**109.7**
整体经济现状指数	Index of Status Quo of Macroeconomy	116.4	113.6	115.0	118.6
就业形势现状指数	Index of Status Quo of Employment Status	103.4	106.4	108.8	105.3
家庭收入现状指数	Index of Status Quo of Household Income Status	114.1	110.3	110.7	109.9
生活质量现状指数	Index of Status Quo of Quality of Life	107.1	106.8	108.2	111.4
耐用商品购买时机现状指数	Index of Status Quo of the timing of Purchase of Durable Goods	93.5	98.7	100.0	103.5
消费者预期指数	**Consumer Expectation Index**	**110.5**	**109.1**	**108.5**	**113.5**
整体经济预期指数	Index of Expectation for Macroeconomy	109.7	109.7	105.7	119.5
就业形势预期指数	Index of Expectation for Employment Status	107.3	106.9	104.4	112.0
家庭收入预期指数	Index of Expectation for Household Income Status	118.6	113.5	114.0	114.2
生活质量预期指数	Index of Expectation for Quality of Life	115.9	113.7	115.1	117.0
耐用商品购买时机预期指数	Index of Expectation for the timing of Purchase of Durable Goods	101.0	101.7	103.2	104.8

表 24.2　企业景气指数、企业家信心指数(1999 ~ 2012)
PROSPERITY INDEX ON ENTERPRISES AND INDEXS OF CONFIDENCE ON MACRO ECONOMY BY ENTERPRISERS

年　份 Year	企业景气指数 Prosperity Index on Enterprises				企业家信心指数 Confidence on Macro Economy by Enterprises			
	一季度 First Quarter	二季度 Second Quarter	三季度 Third Quarter	四季度 Fourth Quarter	一季度 First Quarter	二季度 Second Quarter	三季度 Third Quarter	四季度 Fourth Quarter
1999	115.1	112.7	97.8	116.6	100.3	88.4	82.7	96.8
2000	125.2	121.5	133.2	131.0	105.0	107.6	121.8	118.6
2001	129.4	134.9	122.8	126.3	117.0	125.3	120.7	109.1
2002	123.4	138.7	139.4	144.3	118.4	122.9	130.4	138.6
2003	147.5	126.9	140.1	151.1	141.8	115.5	136.5	140.1
2004	145.4	142.2	141.7	137.8	145.5	138.9	135.9	133.6
2005	134.7	136.4	136.0	133.4	135.0	117.8	118.1	117.5
2006	130.1	134.8	127.1	138.5	125.3	124.4	122.1	133.9
2007	135.9	148.9	143.8	144.8	138.1	141.2	142.6	136.7
2008	146.8	148.6	132.4	100.5	147.7	141.2	127.7	85.2
2009	101.3	110.5	120.9	126.8	78.8	101.6	115.4	125.2
2010	136.2	136.7	137.3	135.7	134.5	130.7	128.8	132.8
2011	133.5	133.1	128.9	125.6	131.3	127.8	121.2	115.4
2012	120.9	122.4	117.5	121.9	113.0	114.5	110.4	115.9

注：2012 年企业景气调查和企业家信心调查采用新方案，调查结果与往年存在不可比因素，不能作简单比较。

Note: In 2012, the survey of prosperty of enterprises and the survey of confidence on macro economy by enterprisers adopted new programs, and therefore, the result of the surverys couldnt be comparable with the former years.

表24.3 企业景气指数(2012)
PROSPERITY INDEX ON ENTERPRISES

项 目	Item	一季度 First Quarter	二季度 Second Quarter	三季度 Third Quarter	四季度 Fourth Quarter
企业景气指数	**Prosperity Index on Enterprises**	**120.9**	**122.4**	**117.5**	**121.9**
按登记注册类型分	**Grouped by Registration Status**				
国有企业	State-owned Enterprises	125.7	126.1	122.3	125.6
集体企业	Collective-owned Enterprises	136.8	117.0	130.9	132.7
股份合作企业	Cooperative Enterprises	123.5	130.7	116.0	125.3
有限责任公司	Limited-Liability Corporations	114.9	114.7	108.0	112.0
股份有限公司	Share Holding Corporations Ltd.	129.4	131.3	128.0	128.3
私营企业	Private Enterprises	119.6	119.9	115.7	121.0
港、澳、台投资企业	Enterprises with Funds from Hogkong, Macao and Taiwan	121.5	127.9	118.5	122.6
外商投资企业	Foreign Funded Enterprises	131.6	127.0	124.8	126.5
按行业分	Grouped by Sector				
工 业	Industry	126.1	128.0	122.2	125.4
建筑业	Construction	124.6	129.0	122.9	121.0
交通运输、仓储和邮政业	Transport, Storage, Posts	109.4	107.1	98.5	97.9
批发和零售业	Wholesale and Retail Trade	119.2	115.2	111.5	119.9
房地产业	Real Estate	106.7	112.5	108.1	123.2
社会服务业	Social Services	138.6	126.8	122.4	123.6
信息传输、计算机服务和软件业	Information Transmission, Computer Services and Software	133.1	132.8	126.7	126.5
住宿和餐饮业	Hotels and Restaurants	118.5	115.4	119.8	112.8
按企业规模分	**Grouped by Size of Enterprises**				
大 型	Large-sized	140.7	133.2	128.3	131.9
中 型	Medium-sized	122.7	123.5	118.4	122.6
小 型	Small-sized	116.2	112.2	112.8	110.0

注：社会服务业包括租赁业，商务服务业，专业技术服务业，生态保护和环境治理业，公共设施管理业，居民服务业，其他服务业，广播、电视、电影和影视录音制作业，文化艺术业和娱乐业(下表同)。

Note: Social services include leasing industry, business service industry, professional and technical services, ecological protection and environment treatment industry, public facilities management industry, resident services, other services, broadcast, television, movie and video recording industry, culture and art industry, entertainment(the same as the next table).

表 24.4 企业家信心指数(2012)
INDEX OF CONFIDENCE ON MACRO ECONOMY BY ENTERPRISERS

项目	Item	一季度 First Quarter	二季度 Second Quarter	三季度 Third Quarter	四季度 Fourth Quarter
企业家信心指数	**Index of Confidence by Enterprisers**	**113.0**	**114.5**	**110.4**	**115.9**
按登记注册类型分	**Grouped by Registration Status**				
国有企业	State-owned Enterprises	116.6	113.4	115.1	119.7
集体企业	Collective-owned Enterprises	120.5	117.6	129.7	126.1
股份合作企业	Cooperative Enterprises	121.2	122.7	113.3	113.3
有限责任公司	Limited-Liability Corporations	107.7	110.6	100.1	105.3
股份有限公司	Share Holding Corporations Ltd.	114.6	115.8	117.6	121.5
私营企业	Private Enterprises	117.3	117.4	111.8	114.2
港、澳、台投资企业	Enterprises with Funds from Hogkong, Macao and Taiwan	123.0	123.2	118.1	121.4
外商投资企业	Foreign Funded Enterprises	131.4	125.0	121.2	122.8
按行业分	**Grouped by Sector**				
工业	Industry	124.6	122.3	118.1	121.3
建筑业	Construction	112.9	119.4	114.5	122.0
交通运输、仓储和邮政业	Transport, Storage, Posts	101.3	100.0	87.1	88.4
批发和零售业	Wholesale and Retail Trade	110.5	107.9	105.5	110.1
房地产业	Real Estate	73.3	90.3	87.1	108.3
社会服务业	Social Services	137.5	128.0	118.4	112.9
信息传输、计算机服务和软件业	Information Transmission, Computer Services and Software	144.8	134.7	126.3	128.8
住宿和餐饮业	Hotels and Restaurants	121.7	120.9	126.5	113.0
按企业规模分	**Grouped by Size of Enterprise**				
大型	Large-sized	131.7	124.7	123.1	123.3
中型	Medium-sized	118.9	117.2	111.9	117.0
小型	Small-sized	112.3	110.3	108.8	107.2

上 / 海 / 统 / 计 / 年 / 鉴

主要统计指标解释

消费者信心指数

是综合反映并量化消费者对当前经济形势评价和对经济前景、收入水平、收入预期以及消费心理状态的主观感受，是预测经济走势和消费趋向的一个先行指标，是监测经济周期变化不可缺少的依据。消费者信心指数由消费者满意指数和消费者预期指数构成。其中消费者满意指数反映了消费者对当前经济生活的评价；消费者预期指数反映了消费者对未来一段时期经济前景发展变化的期望。

企业景气指数

是根据企业决策者对本企业当前生产经营状况的判断及未来企业生产经营状况的预期（选择“良好”、“一般”、“不佳”）而编制的指数，是企业决策者对企业生产经营现状及未来景气动向的一种综合评价和判断。

企业家信心指数

是根据企业决策者对本行业发展状况的判断及其未来走势的预期（选择“乐观”、“一般”、“不乐观”）而编制的指数，反映企业决策者对国家宏观经济发展的信心和预期，是企业决策者对当前宏观经济状况及未来走势的一种感受、体验和期望。

SHANGHAI STATISTICAL YEARBOOK

EXPLANATORY NOTES TO MAJOR STATISTICAL INDICATORS

□ Consumer Confidence Index

Consumer Confidence Index is an indicator reflecting and quantifying the consumers' evaluation on current economic situation, and their personal feeling about the economic prospect, income level, income expectation, and psychological state of consumption. It serves as a leading indicator predicting the trend of economy tendency of consumption, and an essential basis for monitoring the changes in economic cycle. and other conditions as well as expectation on the economic prospect in a future period of time. Consumer Confidence Index consists of consumer satisfaction index and consumer expectation index. Of which, consumer satisfaction index reflects consumers' evaluation on current economic life; consumer expectation index reflects consumers' expectation on the development and changes in the economic prospect in a future period of time.

□ Prosperity Index on Enterprises

Prosperity Index on Enterprises , which is indexed according to estimations and expectations of enterprise decision makers' opinions and expectation on the enterprise's current and future production and operation status (choice of "good", "moderate" and "bad"). It represents the enterprise decision makers' comprehensive evaluation and judgment on the current situation and future trend of the enterprise production and operation.

□ Index of Confidence by Enterprisers

Index of Confidence by Enterprisers , which is indexed according to the enterprise decision makers' opinions and expectations (with choices of "optimistic", "moderate" and "non-optimistic") on the development status of the sector and its future trend. It reflects the enterprise decision makers' confidence about and expectation on the national macroeconomic development. It serves as the enterprise decision makers' feeling, experience and expectation about current macroeconomic status and its trend.

图书在版编目(CIP)数据

上海统计年鉴. 2013 : 汉英对照 / 上海市统计局，国家统计局上海调查总队编
——北京：中国统计出版社, 2013.7
ISBN 978-7-5037-6849-1

Ⅰ. ① 上…
Ⅱ. ① 上… ② 国…
Ⅲ. ① 统计资料—上海市—2013—年鉴—汉、英
Ⅳ. ① C832.51-54

中国版本图书馆CIP数据核字(2013)第152194号

上海统计年鉴—2013

作　　者 / 上海市统计局　国家统计局上海调查总队
责任编辑 / 余竞雄　刘金成
装帧设计 / 蔡旭洲
出版发行 / 中国统计出版社
通信地址 / 北京市丰台区西三环南路甲6号
邮　　编 / 100073
电　　话 / 邮购 (010) 63376909　书店 (010) 68783171
网　　址 / http://csp.stats.gov.cn
印　　刷 / 上海万卷印刷有限公司
经　　销 / 新华书店
开　　本 / 890 × 1240 毫米　1/16
字　　数 / 139.36 万字
印　　张 / 33.5
版　　别 / 2013年7月第1版
版　　次 / 2013年7月第1次印刷
定　　价 / 480.00元

本书附同版本CD-ROM一张，光盘内容以书面文字为准。
如有印装错误，由本社发行部调换。